JACKETS OF GREEN

By the same author and published by Collins

The Story of England
MAKERS OF THE REALM B.C.-1272
THE AGE OF CHIVALRY 1272-1381

KING CHARLES II 1630-1685

RESTORATION ENGLAND 1660-1702

Samuel Pepys
THE MAN IN THE MAKING 1633-1669
THE YEARS OF PERIL 1670-1683
THE SAVIOUR OF THE NAVY 1683-1689

The Napoleonic Wars
THE YEARS OF ENDURANCE 1793-1802
YEARS OF VICTORY 1802-1812
THE AGE OF ELEGANCE 1812-1822
NELSON
THE GREAT DUKE

ENGLISH SAGA 1840-1940

The Alanbrooke Diaries
THE TURN OF THE TIDE 1939-1943
TRIUMPH IN THE WEST 1943-1946

English Social History
THE MEDIEVAL FOUNDATION
PROTESTANT ISLAND
THE FIRE AND THE ROSE

THE LION & THE UNICORN

JIMMY

Jackets of Green

A Study of the History,
Philosophy, and Character of the
Rifle Brigade

ARTHUR BRYANT, C.H.

COLLINS
St James's Place, London

William Collins Sons & Co Ltd
London · Glasgow · Sydney · Auckland
Toronto · Johannesburg

First published December 1972
Reprinted December 1972

© Arthur Bryant 1972

ISBN 0 00 211723 1

Set in Monotype Fontana
Made and printed in Great Britain by
William Collins Sons & Co Ltd Glasgow

I write for Riflemen, at the desire of Riflemen and to preserve the memory of the deeds of Riflemen . . . Nothing will be considered trivial, nothing out of place in a history of the Regiment which records the valour, the acts, the sufferings or preserves an anecdote of any (of whatever rank) of the members of that brotherhood.

SIR WILLIAM COPE
The History of the Rifle Brigade

"Now, Salter, we'll drink to the 'Victory of the Alma' and 'Success to the Rifles!' "
    I held the cup to his lips and, as he drank, he muttered,
    "And many more of 'em . . . And many like 'em!"

Conversation between Colonel Willoughby Verner and a dying Crimean veteran, Rifleman Salter, in the Infirmary of the Royal Hospital, Chelsea, July 1908

CONTENTS

Foreword: A Corps of Riflemen   11

I. "THESE HEROES OF ANTIQUITY" 1800-1814

1. A Beacon for the General   21
2. The Bloody Fighting Ninety-Fifth   41

II. "DOMINION OVER PALM AND PINE" 1815-1914

3. The Figure of Fame   89
4. Over the Hills and Far Away   125
5. Fighting All over the World   148
6. The Perfectionists   181

III. "IN THE TIME OF THE BREAKING OF NATIONS" 1914-1945

7. Stand to Your Front   225
8. Starting All Over Again   297
9. "A Hawk Upon His Wrist"   335

A Postscript to History: "Success to the Rifles!"   431
Appendices   447
Abbreviations   457
Index   459

ILLUSTRATIONS

The plates listed below are reproduced by permission of the Trustees of the Rifle Brigade Museum Trust and of the Royal Green Jackets with the exception of the portrait "Sergeant Edwards of The Rifle Brigade" which is the copyright of the Trustees of the E. H. Kennington Estate and reproduced with their kind permission.

The line drawings which appear at intervals throughout the book are reproduced with the kind permission of the artist Pamela Street and represent an officer in the Rifle Corps 1800; a private Rifleman of the 95th about 1806; a bugle horn 1804; an early pouch plate; a Baker rifle and sword; the Stewart sword and a Regimental badge.

Officer and Rifleman	*between pages* 56-7
The Rear Guard	56-7
Major General Robert Craufurd	56-7
The Duke of Wellington	104-5
The Morning of Waterloo	104-5
Bugle Horn	104-5
Lt.-General Sir Harry Smith	136-7
Fording the Alma	136-7
Major The Hon. H. H. Clifford, V.C.	136-7
Bandmaster W. Miller	152-3
Rifle Brigade in Action, Indian Mutiny	152-3
H.R.H. Field Marshal The Duke of Connaught	152-3
Bergendal	*opposite page* 240
Field Marshal Sir Henry Wilson	240
Brigadier General Sir John Gough, V.C.	241
"Sergeant Edwards of the Rifle Brigade"	256
Sgt. W. Gregg, V.C., and Rfn. W. Beesley, V.C.	257
Sidi Saleh or Beda Fomm, February 1941— The surrender of the 10th Italian Army—after the oil painting by Terence Cuneo	*Front Endpaper*
The Snipe or Kidney Ridge action, October 1942 —after the oil painting by Terence Cuneo	*Back Endpaper*

A CORPS OF RIFLEMEN

This book is a history and study of the spirit, philosophy and character of a Regiment of the British Army, the Rifle Brigade—today part of the Royal Green Jackets—during the 165 years of its separate existence. "It is curious how almost unknown the regimental history of the British Army is to the ordinary Englishman," I once wrote. "Our highbrows have never heard of it; our learned historians ignore it. With a few exceptions the annals of the Regiment have been compiled at the end of each campaign by some pious but unlettered veteran whose sense of reverence for his dead comrades and pride in his corps has done gallant but halting duty for experience in research and skill in writing. Yet the theme of any of our Regiments is worthy of the Muse of a Trevelyan or Macaulay. Where in so little is so much of human achievement and virtue as in the annals of a British Regiment of the Line? Here is triumph over toil, monotony, discomfort, hardship and adversity; here is constancy and loyalty, true to the sun of its faith in the darkest hour; here is love and companionship without reward; here is heroism and self-sacrifice and devotion. And when a great Regiment salutes its Colours it is expressing this truth. Its members are commemorating their predecessors who suffered, endured and died in its service, and are dedicating themselves to do likewise."*

I have always wanted to write such a history. The Regiment I have chosen had no Colours; it had only a silver badge worn by all its members, bearing the names of almost every famous victory in more than a century and a half of British history. In the hour of crisis its Riflemen could not rally, like others, round a Colour, for they fought in extended order, every man depending for courage on the invisible colours carried in his heart—

> "*the black and the green,*
> *the finest colours ever seen.*"

* *The Lion and The Unicorn*, 315-16.

It had not even, like other Regiments, a number giving it precedence in the Army List, for, after Waterloo, on the recommendation of the Duke of Wellington, in recognition of its signal services there and in the Peninsula, it was taken out of the Line and constituted, like the Household Troops of the Sovereign, as a separate Brigade called after the weapon its men had handled in outpost and battle with such superlative skill. No similar honour had ever been paid a Regiment of British Infantry.

It must always seem invidious to praise one Regiment when every Regiment can claim, with pride and some justification, to be peerless. To do so is also, to some extent, to falsify history. For, except on rare occasions, a Regiment fights its battles and campaigns in association with others, and to concentrate exclusively, or even mainly, on its doings—as a regimental historian must—is to be unjust to other Regiments which shared its victories and hardships. Yet if, in one sense, a regimental history falsifies the story of a war or battle, in another it illuminates it. For, by concentrating on the individual fighting man's experience within the limits of the corporate unit through which alone he normally experiences it, it shows how matters went at the sharp end; and that is where every war or battle is decided. As Field Marshal Wavell said in his Lectures on Generalship, in the last resort the end of all military training and the deciding factor in battle is that, sooner or later, Private So-and-So will have, of his own free will, to advance to his front in face of the enemy. All the immense preparation, expenditure, training and equipment of war are designed for, and dependent on, what happens at that moment. If the soldier fails the test all will have been in vain.

This is the meaning and significance for a soldier of the word "morale". Douglas Wimberley, who commanded the Highland Division at Alamein, in a lecture when he was Director of Infantry drew attention to the fact that, while a sailor has his ship, a gunner his gun, a cavalryman his horse or tank, the infantryman has nothing to keep him to the sticking-point in battle but his morale, which he derives solely from his Regiment. It is this, and this alone, which enables him to go forward and risk death and wounds when no other eye is on him and where he has nothing but his own manhood and sense of honour to sustain him. A good Regiment is a school of manhood, honour and selfless co-operation, and, in nine cases out of ten, a soldier is a good soldier to the extent that his Regiment or unit has made him so.

No Regiment has ever depended more on morale than the Rifle Brigade because, by reason of its role and tactics, its members have so often had to operate and fight in isolation. It was originally Britain's military answer to a challenge which occurred at the turn of the 18th and 19th century, when the French, fired by their Revolution, drove Britain's Army from Europe and turned all her former allies against her. To survive, she had to arouse the Continent against its conquerors before they could consolidate their domination. To do this her Army had to learn to defeat a new technique of war. In the summer of 1800 Colonel Coote Manningham raised and trained the first purely British corps of Riflemen as a counter-measure to the shock tactics—which had overthrown every Continental army—of dense columns of conscript levies preceded by clouds of picked sharpshooters. He armed it with a new weapon of precision with far greater range and accuracy than the old smoothbore musket, clothed its men in bottle-green uniforms to give protective cover, and taught them to move and attack in open order to the sound of bugle-horns. Its revolutionary training gave the Regiment an impress which it never lost—of "the fighting, thinking soldier": a corps, not of automata acting *en masse*—the ideal of Frederick the Great and, to a lesser extent, of Napoleon—but of alert, intelligent, adventurous individual marksmen, trained to act in separation to a common purpose. Every man was expected to kill with every shot, to be master both of his weapon and of the means of bringing it to bear on the enemy at the place and time where it would hurt most. Mobility, concealment and killing power, and an elastic yet unbreakable drill and discipline to co-ordinate these qualities, have distinguished the Regiment ever after.

The story of the Rifle Brigade in peace and war, as seen through the eyes of its officers and men, is in microcosm the history of all those who made, garrisoned and defended the British Empire during the century and a half when it was the principal factor in shaping the fate of the world. In doing so—sustained by the Navy's absolute command of the seas, and with the aid of the Indian Army which it had fashioned in its own image—the British Regular Army, small though its numbers and material resources, played a major part. "Nobody in particular noticed that between 1878 and 1902 the

British Army added to the Empire an area of territory equal to the United States, but the British soldier naturally noticed it because he did it. In the mountains that girdle the North-West Frontier, amidst the rocks of Afghanistan, through the swamps and forests of Burma and Africa, on the Veldt, in Egypt and in the deserts of the Sudan, an Empire was being carved out by the old Army in a quiet, unostentatious but methodical sort of way, . . . overcoming inconceivable difficulties with small means. The path of Empire was paved with the bones of the fallen of the old Army, but enough good men remained to assist . . . in creating 'the perfect thing apart',"* which is how the German General Staff described Britain's professional Army after it had encountered it in battle.

In that work, both of extending, maintaining and garrisoning the Empire, and of training for battle, no Regiment played a greater part than the Rifle Brigade. When war came, in 1914 and 1939, to a Britain in other ways tragically ill-prepared and ill-equipped for it, this famous corps, with its passion for perfection, was in the highest state of preparedness, and, though the arms given it by neglectful and parsimonious rulers may have been inadequate, no one can deny that they were used with superlative professional competence and with a moral devotion to duty and selfless sacrifice beyond price. The story of what it endured, suffered and achieved in the First World War, and of the tens of thousands of volunteer Riflemen who filled its depleted ranks and so proudly and worthily bore its stamp and image, is told in these pages and, by the very plenitude of the sacrifice, speaks for itself. In the last War, given, with its novel assignment as motorised infantry, a role comparable to that of its Peninsular days—"the first in the field and the last out of it, the bloody, fighting Ninety-fifth!"—it fought and died at Calais, played a leading part in the destruction and capture of the Italian "Army of Egypt" in the Western Desert, made a decisive contribution to the victory of Alamein, helped to capture Tunis, battled its way up the Apennines from one end of Italy to the other, and with the armour led the three famous breakouts across Northern France and Belgium, the North German plain, and Lombardy and Venetia, finishing with half its victorious battalions on the shores of the Baltic and North Sea and half in Austria and on the eastern Adriatic littoral. Then, as always, it proved itself to be what it had been under Moore, Craufurd and

* Col. C. à Court-Repington, "Death and Resurrection", *The Times*, 31st October 1916.

Wellington, a shining exemplar of all the fighting soldier's virtues.

In all its wars the spirit of the Rifle Brigade has never changed. "Please God, I'll keep the bridge," were the last words of Daniel Cadoux to his brother officers as he left them for his impossible, heroic assignment at the Bridge of Vera in 1813. "Keep on firing! Keep on firing!" were those of Vic Turner as, with his torn scalp, he continued to inspire his men in the Snipe action which helped to decide the issue at Alamein and won him the Victoria Cross. Yet the Regiment never allowed its tradition to deaden its sense of the present. Its vision was always forward, never backwards. In every age the spirit of the Rifle Brigade was the spirit of adventure: its greatest pride, as at its start, a new weapon and a new role.

Second to none in discipline, the Regiment from the beginning made comradeship between all ranks the foundation of its achievements. To be cheerful, good-humoured and gay, particularly in adversity, has been in every age the hallmark of a good Rifleman. It was that gallant officer, Johnny Kincaid, who during an agonising wait behind a very thin tree in a hail of bullets, enunciated the dictum that the best method of teaching a recruit to stand at attention was to place him behind a tree and fire balls at him. That is the spirit of the Rifle Brigade: the spirit of jest and good-natured chaff between brave men who respect one another.

As Harry Smith wrote in the days of Wellington, Riflemen have always tended to be "proper, saucy fellows." Wherever they were gathered together there was sure to be a joke in circulation and some form of sport. This remains true today of the Royal Green Jackets, in whom the inextinguishable tradition of the Rifle Brigade lives on. It is more than a century and a half since Anne Barnard wrote to her husband of "the grace and intrepidity and lightness of step and flippancy of a young Colonel with a rill of grasshoppers at his heels in their green coats." Times have changed, and so have uniforms and weapons, but the spirit, alert forward-looking outlook and gallantry of the Rifleman remain the same. It is to define that character that this book has been written.

*   *   *

Wherever possible I have allowed Riflemen to tell their own story. Indeed when, more than two years ago, I promised my old friend, that devoted Rifleman the late Danny Meighar-Lovett, that I would write something about his Regiment, it was as a Rifle Brigade anthology contributed mainly by Riflemen that I planned it. Though, because of the nature and fascination of the subject, my book, especially in its later chapters, has grown into something far more ambitious, it is lavishly illustrated from the letters, diaries and memoirs of both officers and men of the Regiment. Of these it has an astonishing wealth, for throughout its history its members have shown exceptional gifts of self-expression. Most of the best personal accounts of the Peninsular War, as Sir John Fortescue pointed out, were those of Riflemen: Sir Harry Smith's neglected Autobiography with its enchanting saga of married love, Johnny Kincaid's two delightful books of racy reminiscence, Yorkshire George Simmons's diary and letters published nearly a century after they were written—valiant, simple, uncomplaining George Simmons who, with his giant frame, so cheerfully and manfully endured hardships unending to support, out of a subaltern's pittance, his ne'er-do-well parents and family of growing brother and sisters, and remained through it all indomitably cheerful, happy in the respect and companionship of his fellow Riflemen. It is surprising that in half a dozen years one Regiment should have given posterity so much. Nor, in an age of staggering social inequality, was the gift of literary expression confined to the commissioned ranks of the Regiment. Dorset shepherd-boy Harris's account of the retreat to Corunna, with its unforgettable portrait of "Black Bob" Craufurd steeling the hearts of his men while dire disaster closed in on them; Bugler Green's comparable narrative; Sergeant Costello's account of the vicissitudes of an adventurous life which he so appropriately ended, like that of Gilbert's Sergeant Meryll, as a Yeoman Warder of the Tower of London, are all classic self-portraits of humble and so-called "uneducated" Britons who learnt the business of living and perfected their manhood in the hard, but comradely, school of the Rifle Brigade.

The power of literary expression given to Riflemen did not end with the Peninsula. Henry Clifford's letters from the Crimea, first published only a few years ago, is perhaps the best first-hand account of the battles and hardships of that terrible campaign—unequalled for stark horror even in the annals of the British Army's long history of hardship and neglect manfully endured. Nor has anything in the great wealth of literature about the First World War more vividly portrayed what men of our race suffered and overcame in the trenches than Rifleman McCarthy's account of his experiences in "A" Company of the 1st Battalion of the Rifle Brigade during the Second Battle of Ypres—homeric in its stoic understatement and descriptive power.

Even more than to the published works of individual Riflemen, I am indebted to the annual volumes of the Rifle Brigade Chronicle which Colonel Willoughby Verner founded in 1890 and edited until his death in 1922 and which his successors, Major H. G. Parkyn—"Parkyno" to the Regiment—Colonel W. P. S. Curtis and Lt.-Col. Ulick Verney continued to edit until 1965 when its place was taken by the Royal Green Jackets Chronicle. For nearly half the Regiment's existence, its professional doings in peace and war, its sports, pastimes and shooting-competitions, the work of its Territorial and Associated Regiments and of its Regimental Association, and the biographies and obituaries of its members were recorded in this incomparable Chronicle, including annual Letters from the Officers', Sergeants' and Corporals' Messes of all its four Battalions and the Depot. In each of these seventy-six volumes there are also anything up to a dozen articles or reminiscences, contributed by Riflemen, about the Regiment's past. Many are of high literary quality, all are of historical interest and value. My debt to their authors is unbounded, as it is to those, all of them historians and one—Willoughby Verner—a great historian, who collected and edited them.

I am as much indebted to the Regiment's first historian, Sir William Cope; to Willoughby Verner's two noble volumes of his unfinished *History and Campaigns of the Rifle Brigade*; to Captain Reginald Berkeley and Brigadier William Seymour for their full and authoritative history of the Regiment in the First World War, and, nearer our own time, to Colonel R. H. W. S. Hastings for his equally valuable history of the Regiment in the Second World War, and for his and Major A. T. M. Durand's war history of the London Rifle Brigade—all works of exceptional scholarship and distinction. Nor can I sufficiently express my debt and that of the Regiment to Brigadier C. E. Lucas Phillips and Messrs. Heinemann for their great generosity in allowing us to use the former's superb account of the Snipe action at Alamein, taken from his definitive book on that battle, one of the classics of British military history.

J.G.   B

Limitations of space alone prevent me from mentioning by name all the many members of the Regiment who have generously contributed information about its past. It only remains for me to thank those without whose tireless work this book could never have been written—in particular, my secretary Pamela Street and my constant coadjutant and mentor Lt.-General Sir Richard Fyffe. He and his fellow members of the Rifle Brigade Historical Sub-Committee, Brigadier David Pontifex, Lt.-Colonel Ulick Verney and the late Lt.-Colonel Vic Turner, V.C.—who, alas, died before the book could be published—gave me generous help at every stage of its writing, as over the correction of the proofs did my wife, General Fyffe and Mrs. Geoffrey Bardsley, and Mrs. Susan With over the preparation of the text and Index.

Part I

"THESE HEROES OF ANTIQUITY"
1800-1814

Chapter One

A BEACON FOR THE GENERAL

Oh! Colonel Coote Manningham, he was the man,
For he invented a capital plan,
He raised a Corps of Riflemen
To fight for England's Glory!

He dressed them all in jackets of green
And placed them where they could not be seen
And sent them in front, an invisible screen,
To fight for England's Glory!

OLD REGIMENTAL SONG

A REGIMENT has two purposes. It is an administrative unit which, under the Law, trains, disciplines and marshals men in arms for the preservation of a nation's peace and security. Because in the last resort its duty, in Virgil's words, is "to impose the way of peace, to spare the humble and to war down the proud", it has also to evoke from its members an habitual self-mastery and capacity for comradely selflessness and obedience which will enable them willingly to sacrifice their bodies and lives in the course of duty. Since by nature men are impelled by strong instincts of self-interest and self-preservation the second of these ends is the more difficult of the two. That is what Napoleon meant when he said that in war morale is to material as three is to one.

The Rifle Brigade began its existence when the country was at war with a new phenomenon—a revolutionary State with three times Britain's population, controlled by ruthless men accustomed to brook no opposition, who were seeking by force, for both ideological and material ends and in disregard of international treaties, to make their neighbours conform to their will. In doing so France, a nation in arms, had evolved a new technique of war which enabled her to use the superior number of fighting men called into being by a national *levée en masse* to overwhelm the smaller and more elaborately trained professional armies of the Continent. Attacking in dense columns, marshalled by drum, and preceded by intensive artillery bombardments and clouds of picked marksmen, her new conscript armies had overrun the greater part of Europe, turning its fleets and armies against the island State which, protected from invasion by command of the sea, had alone consistently resisted her. To save herself and restore the liberties of Europe, Britain was seeking a soldier's answer to a military formula which had proved too much for all her former allies.

The Rifle Brigade was part of that answer. In response to proposals made after the disastrous Helder campaign of 1799 by two military reformers, Colonel Coote Manningham and Lt.-Col. the Hon. William Stewart, an Experimental Corps of Riflemen was assembled at Horsham in the spring of 1800 to provide a skirmishing force and reconnaissance screen of expert marksmen to head the advance, cover the movements and guard the retreat of British troops in the field. Dressed in uniforms of bottle-green to give protective covering, its men—drawn from the pick of fifteen regiments—were armed with a new weapon of precision, the grooved Baker rifle which, unlike the old smooth-bore musket with an effective range of less than 100 yards, was capable of great accuracy up to 300 and, in the hands of a master, even 500 yards. Trained that summer in Windsor Forest and operating in isolated groups in close country inaccessible to cavalry, they were taught to judge distance and use cover and varied ground, to fire always to kill and never to waste a shot.

Before the Experimental Corps could be formally embodied in the Army List three of its Companies were called upon to take part in a hastily improvised amphibious expedition of 13,000 men against the great naval base of Ferrol in north-west Spain. Here, on August 25th 1800, they covered the landing and, after the place was found to be impregnable, subsequent re-embarkation. The anniversary was always afterwards kept as the Regimental birthday. Meanwhile in England, brought up to strength with volunteers, including contingents from the Highlands and from Irish Fencible Regiments, the Corps was officially gazetted and stationed at Blatchington Camp in Sussex. To ensure its development on the lines he and Colonel Coote Manningham had envisaged, the Second-in-Command, Lt.-Colonel Stewart—while recovering from wounds received at Ferrol—prepared detailed Standing Orders which, under the title of *Regulations for the Rifle Corps formed at Blatchinton Barracks under the Command of*

Colonel Manningham, August 15th 1800, were published in the following year. These prescribed the future Regiment's system of
discipline, chain of command and interior economy.

Their overall object was to establish, in place of a rigid system of
unthinking subordination, a rational two-way trust and respect
between all ranks—that of a happy family under discipline. Its
officers and men—down to the smallest sub-unit and even to the individual Rifleman—were to be trained and habituated to act when
necessary on their own. "Every inferior, whether officer or soldier,"
it was laid down, "shall receive the lawful commands of his superior
with deference and respect, and shall execute them to the best of his
power. Every superior in his turn, whether he be an Officer or a
Non-commissioned Officer, shall give his orders in the language of
moderation and of regard to the feelings of the individual under his
command; abuse, bad language or blows being positively forbid in
the Regiment."*

Personal responsibility and initiative within a framework of
elastic but clearly defined structure of command were to be the
distinguishing mark of the Rifles.

> "Every Officer and Non-commissioned Officer will observe that
> it is an invariable rule and principle in discipline that, in the
> absence of a superior, the whole of the duty or charge which was
> entrusted to that superior devolves upon the next in rank, so that a
> blank or chasm is never to exist in the various responsible situa-
> tions of the corps . . . In a Regiment of Riflemen each Company
> must be formed upon the principle of being separate from and
> totally independent of another. All the lieutenants are to be there-
> fore equally divided and are never to be exchanged from Company
> to Company; and, if the necessity of the service may occasionally
> require a subaltern officer doing duty with another, he is always to
> return to his original company on the earliest opportunity . . .†
>
> "This attention to retaining the same men and officers together
> is on account of Riflemen being liable to act very independently of
> each other and in numerous small detachments in the field when
> they will feel the comfort and utility of having their own Officer,
> Non-commissioned Officer and Comrades with them. The service

* *Rifle Brigade Chronicle*, 1897, 44.
† *Idem*, 45-6.

will be benefitted by the tie of friendship, which will more naturally subsist between them.

"In every half-platoon one soldier of merit will be selected, and upon him the charge of a squad devolves in the absence of both the Non-commissioned Officers of it. As from among these four *Chosen Men* (as they are to be called) all Corporals are to be appointed; the best men are alone to be selected for this distinction.

"The gradation of rank and responsibility from the Colonel of the Regiment to the *Chosen Men* of a squad . . . is in no instance to be varied by whatever Officer may command the corps. It is the groundwork of all other regulations of either discipline or interior economy, and the *principle* of it need on no occasion be necessarily lost sight of, however various the situations in which the Regiment may hereafter find itself and however inadequate the means at Headquarters of fully carrying into execution every minute part of it . . ."*

For this reason every Company was to be divided into two equal, and these again into two smaller equal, parts, with a corresponding proportion of Officers and Non-commissioned Officers for each.

"The Captain, . . . having formed his company thus equally, will arrange comrades. Every Corporal, Private and Bugler will select a comrade of the rank differing from his own, i.e. front and rear rank, and is never to change him without permission of his Captain. Comrades are always to have the same berth in quarters; and, that they may be as little separated as possible in either barracks or the field, will form the same file on parade and go on the same duties with arms . . . The Corporal's comrade should either be the *Chosen man* or some steady man of the squad or who can occasionally help him in his duty; and the Bugler's comrades the odd men of any two squads when there are any.

"After this arrangement is made the Captain will then establish his messes, which are to be invariably by squads. Ten is the best number for a mess to consist of; from that number to 18 the squad will still consist of but one mess. But whenever it amounts to that number it will be divided into two messes, at the head of the one will be the Corporal, and of the other the acting Corporal or the Chosen man . . .

* *Idem*, 47-8.

"All messing is regarded by the Colonel as bearing a very important place in the good order and economy of a Regiment. Comfort and unanimity at meals, whether it be among officers or soldiers, is the source of friendship and good understanding. He therefore directs that in the first place all officers shall belong to one mess, which, being calculated upon economical terms, he must consider any officer withdrawing himself from it as indicating a wish not to corps with his brother officers, in which case the sooner he leaves the Regiment the better. The officer who commands the Regiment will make it his study to render every assistance in his power consistent with the duty of the Service, to make the officers' mess comfortable and upon the most just terms of economy.

"In the next place the Colonel directs that all Sergeants shall mess together, and on no occasion whatever with the Rank and File and Buglers. The rules of their mess are to be also submitted to him for approbation . . . Every assistance will be also given by the Commanding Officer to render the Sergeants' mess comfortable and as economical as possible . . .

"Respect to Superiors is the very essence of discipline. It is therefore an order from the Colonel that not only all Inferiors shall show . . . respect to their Superiors in their several ranks, but that all Superiors, whether they be Commissioned or Noncommissioned Officers, shall insist upon the same, never permitting without reprimand the smallest *marked* inattention or want of respect from those who are subordinates. No recruit is therefore ever to be dismissed from drill until he is master of all salutes. He, on the other hand, directs that neither negligence or indifference is to prevent the salute or exterior mark of respect being returned to the Officer or Soldier who makes it with becoming politeness . . .

"It is the Colonel's particular wish that duty should be done with cheerfulness and inclination, and not from mere command and the necessity of obeying . . . It is not enough for an Officer or Noncommissioned Officer of his Regiment merely to do his duty. He must do more than is always required. He must volunteer his services on many occasions, because a Corps of Riflemen is expected to be one where intelligence is to distinguish every individual, and where both Officers and men are occasionally liable to act very independently and separately from each other . . . The rules for discipline may be what they will and the system for the good order, appearance and conduct of a Regiment may be laid down by the Colonel with what precision he thinks just, yet the whole will never attain the wished-for perfection unless a general anxiety that it should do so lies in every man's breast, . . . and unless his Officers in particular are animated with an equal desire of their Regiment's doing honour to the Army they are in. To aid their endeavours in doing well a system and a rule of conduct is here given them . . . The officer must, however, remember that example is the most powerful of all preceptors, and he will find that what he does not himself observe with regard to conduct will not be attended to . . . by those whom he commands . . . From the Officers of the Regiment the Colonel expects every example of what is good and great in a Soldier's and Gentleman's character."

The Regulations also prescribed the uniform of the Corps. "In the soldier's dressing well and with smartness the principal object is first cleanliness (and cleanliness is at all times health) and afterwards a certain degree of self-pride which being well-dressed gives every Soldier, and which self-pride should be encouraged, for it will in the end make him a better man." Officers' full dress was optional and only to be worn at Court—long green coat, white breeches and black top-boots, a cocked hat with a sweeping green feather, a black polished leather high-necked stock bound with velvet, with about six inches of shirt-frill appearing under it, and a sash worn over the sword-belt, gloves and cane. His everyday parade or service dress was to consist of a slung green jacket, a silver-buttoned waistcoat hooked at the top, dark-green cloth pantaloons, a black leather and velvet stock and cuffs, silver-embroidered epaulettes, half-boots piqued and bound with black cord and a tassel, and a hussar helmet, sash and sabre. For both Officers and Sergeants the distinguishing mark of authority was a pistol-pouch with a silver whistle attached and a cross-belt. The Riflemen were to wear dark-green jackets and pantaloons with silver buttons, black leather belts and equipment, instead of the customary white pipe-clay of the scarlet-coated Line, and forage caps with a short green horsehair tuft in front.* And "to enable the Regiment to exercise at all pastimes of activity as well as

* Hence the old Rifle Brigade toast, "Green Tufts and Short Barrels!", the Baker rifle being shorter than the "Brown Bess" musket of the Line.

to preserve the regimental dress in the highest order for duty and parades" there was to be an undress—for officers a white duffel jacket edged with green, white waistcoat and loose white dimity trousers, and for men a flannel jacket, green cape and white duck trousers.

Every Rifleman on parade or in the field was to carry, strapped to his back, a small black leather box or portmantua, a pouch for cartridges, and cow-horn containing fifty or sixty charges of powder, suspended from a green cord slung over the shoulder. The rifle—his most precious possession—was to be carried on a long sling, in which a Rifleman, lying on his back for a distant shot, could rest his foot to steady his aim. Worn at the side was a $27\frac{1}{2}$ inch flat-bladed sword with a handle which, when fixed to the rifle, gave it the same length and reach as the longer muskets and bayonets of the infantry of the Line. Movements in extended order were to be directed by the officers' and sergeants' whistles and by cow-horns carried by the buglers attached to every Company and platoon. Being formed to work in isolated groups and extended order, the Regiment carried no Colours round which to rally like other Regiments. Their place was to be taken by individual morale and the deadly marksmanship of its Riflemen. To perfect the latter every Company Commander was empowered to offer premiums for first-class shots styled "marksmen", who were to be distinguished by a green cockade. All Riflemen were to be classified as first, second or third-class shots, while the best shooting Company of the year was always to take the place of honour on parade.

Coote Manningham and Stewart did not only endow their men with a distinctive uniform to give them pride, self-respect and panache and ensure them the maximum chance of survival in their honourable but dangerous role. They sought to educate and foster in them every generous impulse. At a time when there was no national education for the poor, they established a regimental library and a school of reading, writing, arithmetic and geometry "for the instruction of those who wish to fit themselves for the situation of Noncommissioned Officers". They also instituted—one of the first ever to do so—regimental awards and medals for Good Conduct, Long Service and Special Merit. These last—of silver—were to be given both for deeds of outstanding courage and for "voluntary acts of generosity towards either an enemy or those who are in an enemy's country". "The nature of the Rifle Corps' services", it was pointed out, "will in general call it to the outposts and detach it probably over a considerable extent of country. The smallest inhumanity, therefore, towards an enemy who in action may surrender himself or towards an innocent peasantry, by either plundering their possessions or injuring their persons, will be most severaly punished. It is by conduct the very opposite to this that medals of honour are to be won."

The Regulations sought also to foster "Exercises of Activity" or organised games, which were considered to be "particularly characteristic of a light corps", "both of use in the field and tending to the health of Officers and Soldiers in quarters and in camp". These could "never be too much encouraged."

"The Captains and other Officers of the Corps, are requested to show every encouragement to their men to amuse themselves at the game of cricket, hand or football, leap-frog, quoits, vaulting, running, foot races, etc. etc. and in short at all manly and healthy exercises. Money is never to come in question as a prize, but any other descriptions of premium which may be thought of. Dancing is a most excellent way of passing long evenings. It keeps up good humour and health, and, what is of infinitely more consequence, prevents the men from passing their idle hours in the canteens and alehouses . . .

"All those who serve in a light corps should swim. The passage of rivers, and with British troops the frequent embarkations and landings which they are liable to, call for this exercise. Bathing is always recommended when place and opportunity suit.

"The undress of the Corps is established very much with the view of encouraging, by its convenience, the active exercises of all descriptions, and the Colonel does not hesitate to avow his intentions of rendering all duties as pleasantly light as possible, provided he perceives a general inclination to good conduct, good humour and activity, which will ultimately lead both Officers and Men with more mutual attachment into the field than the perpetual adherence to duty, and even to official forms, would do."*

*   *   *

* *Idem*, 47-87.

The qualities of the new Regiment were quick to attract the notice of Britain's then two greatest commanders, the one a sailor, the other a soldier. A few months after it was embodied, Nelson—who two years earlier had given a check to Revolutionary France's drive to world dominion by annihilating her Mediterranean fleet at the battle of the Nile—was sent on an expedition to the Baltic to forestall a hostile coalition of the Northern Maritime Powers. His orders were to immobilise the Danish Navy under the guns of Copenhagen. Before sailing he asked that the young Lt.-Colonel of the newly-formed Rifle Corps, William Stewart, with a contingent of his trained marksmen, should be attached to his command and take part in the attack on the Danish line-of-battle, as it lay moored under protection of the shore and floating batteries.

It thus came about that on April 2nd 1801, the Regiment won the earliest of its battle honours when Nelson's ships, in a hard-fought engagement, broke the Danes' will to resistance. Its Adjutant had his head cut off by a cannon-ball while helping to serve the guns of the *Isis*, while its Commanding Officer spent the day on the flagship's quarterdeck by Nelson's side. "Hard pounding," the latter remarked to him, "but, mark you, I would not be anywhere else for a thousand pounds!" "The Hon. Colonel Stewart," he wrote in his Despatches, "did me the honour to be on board the *Elephant*, and himself, with every officer and soldier under his orders, shared with pleasure the toils and dangers of the day." To Stewart we owe the account of how Nelson, at the height of the engagement, after disregarding his anxious chief's signal to break off the fight, despatched an emissary to his hard-pressed foes, calling on them, as "the brave brothers in arms of Englishmen", to surrender:

"I was with Lord Nelson when he wrote the note to the Crown Prince of Denmark, proposing terms of arrangement. A cannon-ball struck the head of the boy who was crossing the cabin with the light to seal it. 'Bring another candle', said his lordship. I observed that I thought it might very well be sent as it was, for it would not be expected that the usual forms could be observed at such a moment. 'This is the very thing I should wish to avoid, Colonel', replied he, 'for if the least appearance of precipitation were perceptible in the manner of sending this note it might spoil all'."

Surviving letters testify to the regard and affection which Nelson felt for the man who commanded British Riflemen in their two earliest actions*—that "excellent and indefatigable young man and the rising hope of our Army," as he described him to his fellow admiral, Lord St. Vincent. "I should rejoice, my dear Colonel," he wrote to Stewart soon after the battle "that we could be employed on some joint expeditions. And that time must come, for the Commanding Officers of the two Services, to make the service easy and pleasant, should have most perfect confidence in each other." During the Peace of Amiens—when the British Government tried to reach an agreement with a military dictator who, set on world dominion, would not brook contradiction or be bound by treaty—Nelson expressed his view of such attempts in characteristic fashion:

" *My dear Stewart,*
Your letters are like yourself always kind, affectionate and friendly . . .
We have had two good opportunities of knowing each other—sailing
together and fighting together . . . I dislike all these childish rejoicings
for peace. It is a good thing I hope, but I would burst before I would let
a damned rascal of a Frenchman know that either peace or war affected
me with either joy or sorrow.
" I hope the Government will increase your Rifle Corps. Although it is
peace we must always be on our guard against Corsican treachery in-
grafted upon French infamy. Damn them all! is the constant prayer of,
my dear Stewart,
" Your most obliged and affectionate Friend,

NELSON AND BRONTE."

A later letter from Nelson to Stewart reached him when the great admiral was waiting with the Combined Fleet off Cadiz for his final encounter with the French and Spanish fleet at Trafalgar.

"Victory,
8th October, 1805

" *My dear Stewart,*
You will, I hope, forgive me, as many, many of my friends have been

* The only other Rifle Regiment in the Army at that time was the 60th Royal Americans —afterwards the King's Royal Rifle Corps. Though raised earlier in 1755 to counter the marksmanship of the French-Canadian backwoodsmen of the North American forests, until the reign of George IV it was composed mainly of foreign, and chiefly German, mercenaries.

kind enough to do, my not answering your kind letter when I was in England; but it was impossible if I had been blessed with six hands, and the days as long again. But I know you will forgive me. I was surprised to find you from the sea-coast; but the promotion of Brigadiers has made great changes in the destination of officers for commands; and, in the various expeditions going forward, I can venture to believe you will not be suffered to remain. But the making of our militia and volunteer soldiers was a wise plan; and we were very near having occasion to use them. Some day or other it certainly will happen that Buonaparte, if he lives, will attempt the invasion and conquest of Great Britain. At least it will do no harm for the country always to think so, even in a fancied peace.

" I have 36 sail of the line looking me in the face. Unfortunately there is a strip of land between us; but it is believed they will come to sea in a very few days. The sooner the better. I don't like to have these things on my mind. And if I see my way through the fiery ordeal I shall go home and rest for the winter, and shall rejoice to take you by the hand. Good Captain Hardy is still with me, and Rev. Dr. Scott, who both desire their kind remembrances; and believe me ever, my dear Stewart, your most sincere and faithful Friend,

NELSON AND BRONTE."

When this letter reached him, Stewart, having been promoted, was no longer commanding the Rifles. For the past two years it had been serving with two other Regiments of Foot—the 43rd and the 52nd—under the man who, more than any other, was the Army's counterpart to Nelson. Major-General Sir John Moore probably first encountered Riflemen trained in Stewart's and Coote Manningham's tactics after the evacuation from Ferrol, when a number of them took part in the expedition to Egypt which, in 1801, compelled the surrender of the French invaders of that country. When war broke out again in 1803 and Napoleon assembled his *Grande Armée* on the Channel shore for the invasion of England, Moore was appointed to guard the sector of the Kentish coast immediately threatened by a landing. Here, in the camp at Shorncliffe, while waiting to repel an invasion which never came, he directed and trained a brigade of Riflemen and Light Infantrymen who were to become the nucleus of the famous Light Division, the finest fighting formation in Europe. The pacemaker and original exemplar of this force were the Rifles, who, on the renewal of hostilities in 1803, had been gazetted in the Army List as the 95th (Rifle) Regiment and set to watch the coastline from Shorncliffe to Rye.

Moore's training, like that of Stewart and Coote Manningham, was based on treating soldiers, not as the rigid drill automata of the 18th century Army, but as human beings capable of individual initiative and self-improvement. His goal, as theirs, was "the thinking fighting man". Officers were encouraged to get to know their men as individuals, to study their particular aptitudes, to bring out the best of which each was capable, and teach them to think for themselves. Wherever possible, they were to be shown the why and wherefore of things; to be "put in the picture"; to understand their orders instead of merely obeying them blindly out of fear or mechanical routine. Punishment, particularly of the "curse, hang and flog" kind that robbed a man of dignity, was discouraged. Its place was taken by a discipline of example and encouragement, whose object was the prevention rather than the punishment of crime. As in the Rifle Corps, medals and distinguishing badges were instituted for merit and good behaviour; self-respect, pride, comradeship, the desire to shine were enlisted to fit men for their duties. In an Army notorious for inability to fend for itself in the field, every man of Moore's Light Brigade—taking a leaf from the book of the self-reliant French—was taught to cook and tailor and take pride in living sparely against the day when he would have to depend solely on himself. Troops were trained for war under war conditions; when they marched they bivouacked by the roadside instead of in a town or village. The formal brass, feather and pipeclay review so dear to military pedants was abandoned for the field-day—an exercise in which war conditions were reproduced as closely as possible. Everything was made to serve the great end of reality, the defeat of Napoleon's invincibles.

In all this Moore worked with nature instead of against it. In the quick march which he and his assistants, following the Rifles' example, devised for light infantrymen, the constrained and rigid movements of the Prussian march were abandoned for a free and natural rhythm whose object was the maximum of speed with the minimum of fatigue. "To bring down the feet easily without shaking the upper part of the body," ran the Regulations of the Rifle Corps, "is the grand principle of marching." By being taught to move quickly men learnt to think quickly. In the same way the art of fire was taught, not as an automatic contribution to blind mechanical volleys, but as a highly individualised application of the qualities of observation, vision, judgment and skill. Men were trained not as machines but as fighting craftsmen, the consciousness of whose martial expertise—the best guarantee for their survival on the battle-field—gave them courage and self-confidence.

Above all, Moore's men were schooled in that art which, though repeatedly forgotten under the shock of successive inventions and weapons, is in all ages the ultimate arbiter of war: the practised combination of fire-power and movement. The essence of the work of light troops was movement, whether in search of information or in protecting the army of which they were part. And fire was taught as the concomitant of movement, so that, at all times and in all places, movement, with its obvious dangers, should be covered by accurate, well-timed and economical fire. A Rifleman or Light Infantryman in battle was the instrument of an orchestra in which every change of position, whether of individual or unit, was to be protected by co-ordinated fire, directed at the precise spot from which interference with that movement might come. The Light Brigade's system of field drill was directed to this end. Taught to the recruit by word of mouth in close order on the parade ground, it was sub-sequently carried out in extended order by bugle-horn and whistle. It aimed at combining the action of highly individualised and rapidly-moving men and units, working together to destroy or outwit the enemy.

At the back of every Rifleman's mind Moore instilled the principle that the enemy was always at hand ready to strike. Whether on reconnaissance or protective duty, he was taught to be wary and on guard: to explore country, gather information, watch and question travellers and inhabitants, investigate and map out roads, paths, fords and bridges. It was the pride of the Rifles and their brother Regiments of the Light Brigade never to be caught napping or to have an outpost or piquet surprised. When attacked the latter were to fall back without giving away the position of their main body; rules carefully devised, but always elastic and capable of infinite adjustment, were laid down for setting and relieving sentry posts and patrols by day and night, for defending approaches to villages, bridges and road junctions, for utilising hedges, woods and orchards and every inclination of the ground for cover and fire. The British

Army of the future was to be encompassed at all times and places by an invisible screen of marksmen, watching the enemy from behind bushes and stones, each one an alert and intelligent individual acting in close but invisible concert with his comrades.

At the outset of Moore's great and germinative work of creating a new model for the Army, Colonel Coote Manningham delivered in the spring of 1803 to the officers of his Regiment, four lectures on the duties of Riflemen which were to serve as a blueprint both for the operations of the Light Brigade and Division in the Peninsular War and, despite all the tactical and mechanical changes of the next hundred and sixty years, for the corps he had founded throughout its history. "Light troops," it began, "are, as it were, a light or beacon for the General, which should constantly inform him of the situation, the movements and nature of the enemy's designs. It is upon the exactness and intelligence of what they report that he is enabled to regulate the time and manner of executing his own enterprises. The Officer who is deprived of this support, being ignorant of what his enemy is preparing to execute, his views on every occasion anticipated, and arriving constantly too late to prevent some mischief, will experience daily losses, checks without end and such disheartening circumstances as may lead eventually to a general defeat. The safety of an army, the justness of those measures which have so direct an influence upon success, depend frequently on the vigilance, the expertness and the superiority of the light troops compared with those of the enemy.

"Every officer of light troops should know how to occupy a post, how to keep it, how to support it, or to retire from it when requisite. He should be well acquainted with the means and precautions necessary to secure himself upon all marches, how to penetrate the enemy's chain of sentries, to reconnoitre his position, his force and his movements, the circumstances which favour an attack upon those places he may occupy, as well as such as are unfavourable to himself when attacking."*

These lectures covered every aspect of a Rifleman's functions in the

* Military Lectures delivered to the Officers of the 95th (Rifle) Regiment at Shorncliffe Barracks, Kent, during the spring of 1803 by Coote Manningham (Colonel of the 95th (Rifle) Regiment). Printed for T. Egerton, Military Library near Whitehall, 1803. (Reprinted by Willoughby Verner, Lt.-Colonel, late Rifle Brigade, Royal Military College, February 1897.)

field. They set out how the environs of an advanced post were to be
reconnoitred and cleared of everything that could prevent an
approaching foe from being seen; how sentries of an outpost chain
should be stationed so that they could both see one another and stop
any bottom, hollow road or ravine between them from being used
without their knowledge; how sentries near hostile forces should
always be doubled so that one man could give warning to the supporting body of their approach while the other continued to observe
their movements. They gave detailed instructions to an officer in
charge of a reconnaissance party how to obtain from the country
every piece of information likely to be of value.

"During the day as soon as an officer has taken possession of an
advanced post and has reconnoitred the environs, and made such
dispositions as the first appearance of the ground and the rules of
the service require, if he is not acquainted with the country where
he is posted he must procure an inhabitant from the nearest houses.
He must next take his map of the country, which he should never
be without, and interrogate the man who has been brought to him
respecting the names of the villages, the farms and the houses in
the neighbourhood. He will observe the roads and paths which
lead to it, whether adapted for large or small carriages, from
whence too he may judge if they are practicable for heavy artillery;
whether the roads are crossed by rivers or rivulets, if bridges be of
stone or of wood, if there be any ponds, morasses, dykes, ditches or
other obstructions, if woods in the neighbourhood, and whether
timber woods or copses. If he should find that these sort of difficulties exist, he must correct his first dispositions according to the
further knowledge he may have acquired. He will reconnoitre in
person every spot immediately near his post, will sound the fords
and morasses, examine the passages, their depth and the state of
the bridges, and he will post his sentries at the approaches, that
the enemy may not make use of them to surprise him . . .

"The commanding officer will carefully examine all persons
coming towards his post, whether peasants or travellers. He will
learn from them whither they are going, or what their business
may be in camp or elsewhere. He will endeavour to find out
whether they can give any intelligence of the enemy, or of the
places or positions he occupies, and according to the instrnctions

he may have received upon this head he will either suffer them to pass, or cause them to be conducted to the general or staff officer. He will observe the same rule towards the people who bring provisions into the camp, and if he is ordered not to let them pass he will send them back with mildness and good humour, and without suffering the smallest injury to be offered them. In conducting himself in this manner an officer frequently learns from the people of the country, who pass and repass, many circumstances of which advantage may be taken. But it must likewise be recollected that the enemy send people to the camp also for the purpose of gaining intelligence . . .

"The officer commanding will visit his sentries, will instruct and interrogate them upon what they have to do, and to observe and learn whether they have received the countersign or watchword. Towards evening he will explain to the officers and non-commissioned officers the manner in which they are to go their rounds, and send out their patrols during the night, and he will take care if possible to distribute them on such parts of the ground, as each of them shall have visited during the day . . ."

In his second lecture Colonel Manningham dealt with the work of advanced troops in the hours of darkness.

"During the night the sentries leave the heights and take post on the reverse of, and some way down the slopes, the summit of which serves them as a horizon, because it is easier to see from a low situation a high one during the night than a low one from a height, and the person so observing is more concealed. The advanced sentries of course should be doubled at these times, and posted at such a distance from each other, that nothing should be able to pass between them without being heard . . .

"The grand guards of the army usually retire to their posts appointed for the night at sunset, but the advanced guards, that must always be near the enemy, should endeavour to conceal the knowledge of their position for the night from him, and should not retire until nightfall when their motions can be no longer observed.

"The post for the night will be fixed according to circumstances at 400, 500 or 600 paces in the rear of the day-posts; and when the advanced guard is placed very near the enemy, one must not go from post to post in a direct line, but by making a detour, which may deceive the enemy who might observe any movement of the other kind . . .

"An officer charged either to occupy or reconnoitre ground during the night should be extremely exact, and should well consider the danger to which his negligence might expose the army. If he is attacked in this situation, and so hard pressed as to be obliged to retire, he should recollect that it is his duty to retreat as slowly as possible, that the army may have time to receive the enemy in good order. One may judge at night whether troops enter or depart from the enemy's camp, or even if the whole army is put in motion, by the clashing of arms on the march, by the noise of the carriages, and conductors of artillery, the cracking of whips, and neighing of horses. Should the noise continue but diminishing it is a sign that troops are going away or the army retiring. If the sound appears fixed, and fresh fires are lighted, it is a sign that more troops are arrived; if one hears the driving of pickets, it is a sign that there is cavalry amongst them; when fires go out by degrees it is a further proof that the enemy has left his camp. But these circumstances are not always to be regarded as positive proofs, because the enemy frequently leaves his light troops to keep up the fires though the enemy should have decamped . . .

"When an officer is sent during the night with a detachment to get intelligence of the enemy he must form an advanced guard in proportion to the strength of it, taking care to detach it or keep it closer to him according as the night is more or less obscure. And the same rule is to be observed with respect to the men he detaches on his flanks. The detachment will make frequent halts in order to listen if anything is stirring. By applying the ear to the ground distant sounds may also be discovered . . . The greatest silence must be observed on these occasions; no horse liable to cough nor dog must be taken; the men must not be allowed to smoke. Noise obviously prevents one from hearing afar off, and the least spark of fire is sufficient to discover a party to the enemy, especially on the march. If it is necessary for the officer to have recourse to his watch or compass he must strike a light under his cloak and extinguish it as soon as possible.

"If a number of dogs are heard to bark it is to be presumed that people are in motion near them, in which case a trusty man or non-commissioned officer must be sent forward to ascertain this by endeavouring to glide towards the spot from which the noise proceeds. Should it come from a village and nothing is to be seen outside, a man or two must endeavour to pass through the hedges and gardens, and if he sees a light in a window of any of the houses, after having fully ascertained that the enemy are not there, he will endeavour to gain admittance and will try to find out from the owner whether there are any troops in the village or in the environs, and, having ascertained this point, he will return and give information to the commanding officer of the party . . ."

Among the duties of Riflemen were those of covering both the advance of an army and its retreat. "The safety of a whole army," Colonel Manningham pointed out, "frequently depends upon the activity and intelligence of an officer commanding an advanced guard or a detachment sent either by day or night to reconnoitre an enemy."

"An officer stationed at any advanced post should take every precaution to ensure his retreat and, if he is placed in a wood he should secure an entrance and a sortie by means of intersected ground, a succession of hedges, of houses or of orchards. He may also make use of a river or rivulet to protect his movements, and, in order to ensure his retreat from being cut off, he should keep one or more small supports or parties upon his flanks that he may have timely notice of anything approaching his rear. But should a retreat not be able to be effected without crossing the open country, the commanding officer must consult with the officer of the nearest cavalry post and must retire under his protection . . .

"When time is to be gained, whether it be for the arrival of troops destined to support the advanced guard, to warn the army of the march and approach of the enemy or to prevent a surprise, it is the duty of the advanced guard neither to suffer its retreat to be cut off nor its flanks turned, but to retire slowly, and in succession if possible, yielding but little ground at a time, but keeping up a constant fire and skirmishing, in order by this method to apprise the army of the enemy's movements . . .

" . . . When a retreat is absolutely necessary it should be conducted with all possible steadiness, every advantage being taken to defend any pass or bridge so as to check the enemy and so oblige him eventually to discontinue the pursuit. When time admits of it a road may be blocked up or a bridge destroyed.

"An officer should take every possible precaution to prevent any of his people from falling into the enemy's hands. Steady and well instructed riflemen are of great value."

The Colonel concluded his last lecture with some general observations. "That a Corps of Riflemen or Light Infantry should at all times be in the completest order with respect to their arms, ammunition and appointments is sufficiently obvious. The stock of necessaries to be carried in the field must not be too great, and no possible want of ammunition should occur; though at the same time from their being frequently so far detached, and from the difficulty attending the constant supply of that article to an advanced corps, the greatest caution must be observed that the men neither lose their ammunition nor throw away their shots idly. The baggage that can be allowed to a Rifle Corps will be small, the nature of their service making it impossible to carry it with them, and it is scarcely worthwhile to take it into the field merely to throw it away."

Above all, Riflemen must know how to protect landing operations, cover retreats and immobilise hostile artillery by infiltration and high-precision marksmanship. They "may be employed", the Colonel pointed out, "with great success against field artillery"—the Napoleonic weapon *par excellence*—"if the country is wooded or intersected taking up their ground accordingly, or, if in the open, forming, as it were, a semicircle at 350 or 400 yards from it, when, by keeping up a steady fire, the enemy's guns, if unsupported, will soon be obliged to withdraw." It was by doing this that the Riflemen of the 1st Battalion, holding the sunken lane on the ridge at Waterloo, were able to prevent Napoleon's gunners, at the crisis of the battle, from blasting a decisive hole through Wellington's crumbling centre.

It was this practised perfection of co-ordinated movement with precise and economical marksmanship, taught with such imagination and foresight as to be instantaneously applicable to any situation that could conceivably arise, which made the Rifles such a formidable band of soldiers. "Six years could not detect a flaw in their system," William Napier was to write of that wonderful amalgam of the 95th and its two supporting Regiments, the 43rd and the 52nd, in his

History of the Peninsular War, "nor were they ever matched in courage or skill. Those three Regiments were avowedly the best that England ever had in arms. This is no idle boast. War was better known, the art more advanced under Napoleon than in any age of the world before, and the French veterans—those victors of a thousand battles —never could stand an instant before our gallant men."

Chapter Two

THE BLOODY FIGHTING
NINETY-FIFTH

Hurrah for the first in the field and the last out of it, the bloody
fighting Ninety-fifth!

OLD PENINSULAR TOAST
(quoted by Sir John Kincaid)

We Light Division gentlemen were proper saucy fellows.

GEN. SIR HARRY SMITH, Autobiography

SIX years after he had written his *Regulations for the Rifle Corps*,
Brigadier William Stewart published a pamphlet entitled *Outlines
for A Plan for the General Reform of the British Land Forces.* "We have
an enemy to contend with," he wrote, "who aims at nothing less
than the subjugation of the whole civilised world, and among the
number of whose victims, though probably the last, we may expect
to fall unless energies similar to his own be adopted on our part." At
that time, having in 1806 overwhelmed in turn the Austrians,
Russians and Prussians, Napoleon controlled almost the entire
continent of Europe. Only the command of the oceans stood between
Britain and submission to the all-conquering genius whose aim was
the mastery of mankind.

"Without a radical change in our present military system,"
Stewart held, "Britain will certainly not long continue to be either
formidable or secure."

"To the superiority of regular and well disciplined armies, the
greatest revolutions in the affair of mankind may be ascribed.
Reliance on forces imperfectly disciplined has ever led to destruction, and, on the other hand, in proportion as they have been
effective, they have uniformly proved sources of internal strength,
as well as of extensive dominion. It is not so much on mechanical
dexterity as on the acquirement of peculiar moral habitudes that
the superiority of regular troops depends; discipline is rendered
most perfect when authority is softened by the feelings of honour

and affection. It has invariably been the object of great commanders to mingle authority with lenity, to inspire their troops with confidence in their own capacity, to call forth their enthusiasm, and to create one common feeling between the officer and the soldier . . . Effective and well-disciplined forces are the best, and ultimately the least expensive to every State, and without the agency of regular armies Great Britain can never be secure at home, command dominion abroad, and far less effect that revolution in the political world which may restore Europe to any degree of equilibrium . . .

"Our enemy, who is grasping at universal empire, gives us no time to lose, and scarcely a choice unless between defeat and victory."

The means to transform the British Army which Stewart envisaged already existed in the pioneer Regiment which he and Coote Manningham had founded—the encouragement of excellence in the ranks by honours, privileges and rewards, the discouragement, except for major military crimes, of excessive corporal punishment —"which tends . . . to debase the minds and destroy the high spirits of soldiers"—channels of promotion from the ranks, regimental schools and depots, above all, the training of "marksmen and vedettes adapted for the most arduous services in the field."

On Stewart's promotion he had been succeeded as Lt.-Colonel in command of the Regiment by another superlative trainer and leader of men, his friend and protégé, the 32-year-old Thomas Sydney Beckwith, who had served with him by Nelson's side at Copenhagen. In the year of Trafalgar a 2nd Battalion was raised at Canterbury. There was no difficulty in recruiting for it, for the prestige, panache and distinctive uniform of the Rifles made a strong appeal to the adventurous young. "Young gentleman, would you like to be an officer?" Harry Smith remembered Brigadier Stewart saying to him when he and his Yeomanry Corps were inspected by him in the spring of 1805. "Of all things," replied he. "Well, I will make you a Rifleman, a Green Jacket and very smart." Another future Peninsular veteran and chronicler of the Regiment's doings, Jonathan Leach, exchanged into it in the following year, having ardently wished to wear its uniform ever since he had served alongside it at Shorncliffe Camp three years before.

So, too, William Green of Lutterworth—Bugler Green as he became—having at the age of 19 "a disposition to ramble," transferred
with 150 of his comrades from the Leicester Militia, then stationed
at Canterbury, into the newly formed 2nd Battalion. Another country
lad, Benjamin Harris, a Dorset shepherd's son who had been ballotted
for the Army of Reserve, while serving in Dublin saw a detachment
of the 95th Rifles "and fell so in love with their smart, dashing,
appearance that nothing", he recalled,

"would serve me till I was a Rifleman myself. So, on arriving at
Cashel one day and falling in with a recruiting-party of that
regiment, I volunteered into the 2nd Battalion. This recruiting-
party were all Irishmen and had been sent over from England to
collect . . . men from the Irish Militia and were just about to
return to England. I think they were as reckless and devil-may-
care a set of men as ever I beheld, either before or since. .

"Being joined by a Sergeant of the 92nd Highlanders and a
Highland piper of the same regiment—also a pair of real rollicking
blades—I thought we should all have gone mad together. We
started on our journey one beautiful morning in tip-top spirits,
from the *Royal Oak*, at Cashel; the whole lot of us, early as it was,
being three sheets in the wind. When we paraded before the door
of the *Royal Oak*, the landlord and landlady of the inn, who were
quite as lively, came reeling forth with two decanters of whiskey
which they thrust into the fists of the sergeants, making them a
present of decanters and all, to carry along with them and refresh
themselves on the march. The piper then struck up, the sergeants
flourished their decanters, and the whole route commenced a
terrific yell. We then all began to dance, and danced through the
town, every now and then stopping for another pull at the whiskey
decanters. Thus we kept it up till we had danced, drank, shouted
and piped thirteen Irish miles, from Cashel to Clonmel. Such a
day, I think, I never spent as I enjoyed with these fellows; and, on
arriving at Clonmel, we were as glorious as any soldiers in all
Christendom need wish to be."*

For the first six years after their early baptism of fire at Ferrol and
Copenhagen the Rifles, learning their skirmishers' and marksmen's
craft in the backwoods of the Kentish and Sussex Weald, were

* *Rifleman Harris*, 6-8.

without an opportunity of practising their expertise against a real foe. Yet for all Napoleon's seemingly unchallengeable dominance of the continent the time was approaching when their country's command of the sea would give them a chance to show what they could do. It first came in the winter of 1806-7 when three companies of the 2nd Battalion served on an expedition against the Spanish colonies in South America, taking part in the storm and capture of Monte Video. On this occasion the little contingent, which lost an officer and ten men killed and 21 others wounded, were specially thanked in General Orders, eleven of its sergeants being awarded the Regiment's silver medal for valour. Later in the summer of 1807, reinforced by five Companies of the 1st Battalion, it played a gallant, though unsuccessful, part in an assault on Buenos Aires, suffering 300 casualties in street fighting and, like the rest of the army, witnessing with indignation an unnecessary withdrawal and evacuation due to a failure of will by the General Officer commanding.

Meanwhile, nearer home, the rest of the Regiment was employed for the second time in a successful operation against Copenhagen in August 1807 to prevent the Danish fleet falling into the hands of the French. Covering the landing, it served under the command of Sir Arthur Wellesley, the future Duke of Wellington, helping him to win his first victory on European soil at Kiöge. In July of the following year four Companies of the 2nd Battalion sailed under the same commander—now the Army's youngest Lt.-General—for another European destination, this time in the Iberian peninsula, whose peoples had risen against the French armies which had taken over their countries and driven their ruling houses into exile. After covering the landing at Mondego Bay with their fellow Riflemen of the 60th Royal Americans, they led the little expeditionary force in its southward dash on Lisbon, serving as the advanced-guard on August 15th and 17th in the first skirmishes of the Peninsular War—Obidos and Roliça—the Regiment's third battle honour.*

Four days later they were engaged in a more important engagement, when the main French army under Junot attacked Wellesley's force at Vimiero. Rifleman Harris left a vivid description of the scene.

"Our lines glittering with bright arms; the stern features of the

* In which it is erroneously spelt Roleia.

men, as they stood with their eyes fixed unalterably upon the enemy, the proud colours of England floating over the heads of the different battalions, and the dark cannon on the rising ground, and all in readiness to commence the awful work of death . . . Altogether, the sight had a singular and terrible effect upon the feelings of a youth who, a few short months before, had been a solitary shepherd upon the Downs of Dorsetshire, and had never contemplated any other sort of life than the peaceful occupation of watching the innocent sheep as they fed upon the grassy turf . . .

"I myself was very soon so hotly engaged, loading and firing away, enveloped in the smoke I created and the cloud which hung about me from the continued fire of my comrades, that I could see nothing for a few minutes but the red flash of my own piece amongst the white vapour clinging to my very clothes. This has often seemed to me the greatest drawback upon our present system of fighting; for . . . on a calm day, until some friendly breeze of wind clears the space around, a soldier knows no more of his position and what is about to happen in his front, or what *has* happened, even amongst his own companions, than the very dead lying around.

"The Rifles, as usual, were pretty busy in this battle. The French, in great numbers, came steadily down upon us, and we pelted away upon them like a shower of leaden hail. Under any cover we could find we lay, firing one moment, jumping up and running for it the next; and, when we could see before us, we observed the cannon-balls making a lane through the enemy's columns as they advanced, huzzaing and shouting like madmen.

"Such is my remembrance of the commencement of the battle of Vimiero. The battle began on a fine bright day, and the sun played on the arms of the enemy's battalions, as they came on, as if they had been tipped with gold. The battle soon became general; the smoke thickened around, and often I was obliged to stop firing and dash it aside from my face and try in vain to get a sight of what was going on, whilst groans and shouts and a noise of cannon and musketry appeared almost to shake the very ground. It seemed hell upon earth."*

Two years later the wife of a Lisbon merchant told George

* *Rifleman Harris*, 38-40.

Simmons of the 95th how, after the battle, a dying French officer who had been billeted on her spoke of the British soldiers and, above all, the Riflemen, who had so unexpectedly defeated him and his supposedly invincible countrymen. "My dear lady," he said, "the fine fellows that daily paraded before your windows for so many weeks are now lifeless and inanimate clay, and will trouble you no more. Would to God it had been my fate also! . . . I was sent out to skirmish against some of those in green—grasshoppers I call them—you call them Rifle Men. They were behind every bush and stone, and soon made sad havoc amongst my men, killing all the officers of my company and wounding myself without being able to do them any injury."*

*   *   *

Later that year, under Sir John Moore, both the 1st and 2nd Battalions who had subsequently joined the force which had liberated Portugal, entered Spain at the very moment when Napoleon, infuriated by Spanish resistance, invaded the Peninsula in person to bring the war there to a conclusion. But for the British he would have done so. For after he had routed the Spanish armies and captured Madrid, Moore, to save Portugal and southern Spain, struck at his communications, compelling the infuriated Emperor to recross the Guadarramas in pursuit. Narrowly evading encirclement Moore had to make a hasty retreat in mid-winter over the Galician mountains towards the sea and his transports. In its course both the commissariat and the morale of the army broke down.

Yet the scenes of shame and degradation on the line of march were redeemed by the fortitude and discipline with which the Rifles and Light Infantry covered the retreat. While the former's 1st Battalion acted as a rearguard to the main force falling back on Corunna, the 2nd Battalion, with the rest of the Light Brigade under the command of Major-General Robert Craufurd, withdrew under equally grim climatic conditions to Vigo. Rifleman Harris's account of the retreat and its hardships is among the classics of military history.

"The shoes and boots of our party were now mostly either de-

* *A British Rifleman*, 102.

stroyed or useless to us from foul roads and long miles, and many of the men were entirely barefooted . . . The officers were also, for the most part, in as miserable a plight. They were pallid, way-worn, their feet bleeding, and their faces overgrown with beards of many days' growth . . . Many of the poor fellows, now near sinking with fatigue, reeled as if in a state of drunkenness, and . . . we looked the ghosts of our former selves. Still we held on reso-lutely. Our officers behaved nobly, and Craufurd was not to be daunted by long miles, fatigue, or weather. Many a man in that retreat caught courage from his stern eye and gallant bearing. Indeed, I do not think the world ever saw a more perfect soldier than General Craufurd . . . He mingled amongst the men as we stood leaning upon our rifles, gazing earnestly in our faces as he passed, in order to judge of our plight by our countenances. He himself appeared anxious, but full of fire and spirit, occasionally giving directions to the different officers, and then speaking words of encouragement to the men. It is my pride now to remember that General Craufurd seldom omitted a word in passing to my-self. On this occasion, he stopped in the midst, and addressed a few words to me, and glancing down at my feet, observed:

" 'What! no shoes, Harris, I see, eh?'

" 'None, sir,' I replied; 'they have been gone many days back.' He smiled and, passing on, spoke to another man, and so on through the whole body.

"Craufurd was terribly severe, during this retreat, if he caught anything like pilfering amongst the men. As we stood, however, during this short halt, a very tempting turnip-field was close on the side of us, and several of the men were so ravenous that, although he was in our very ranks, they stepped into the field and helped themselves to the turnips, devouring them like famishing wolves. He either did not or would not observe the delinquency this time, and soon afterwards gave the word, and we moved on once more . . . I do not think I ever admired any man who wore the British uniform more than I did General Craufurd.

"I could fill a book with descriptions of him, for I frequently had my eye upon him in the hurry of action . . . The Rifles liked him, but they also feared him; for he could be terrible when in-subordination showed itself in the ranks. 'You think, because you are Riflemen, you may do whatever you think proper,' said

he one day to the miserable and savage-looking crew around
him . . .; 'but I'll teach you the difference before I have done with
you.' I remember one evening, during the retreat, he detected two
men straying away from the main body: it was in the early stage
of that disastrous flight, and Craufurd knew well that he must do
his utmost to keep the division together. He halted the brigade
with a voice of thunder, ordered a drum-head court-martial on the
instant, and they were sentenced to a hundred a-piece. Whilst this
hasty trial was taking place, Craufurd dismounting from his
horse, stood in the midst, looking stern and angry as a worried
bull-dog. He did not like retreating at all, that man . . .

"He marched all that night on foot; and when the morning
dawned, I remember that, like the rest of us, his hair, beard, and
eye-brows were covered with the frost, as if he had grown white
with age. We were, indeed, all of us in the same condition. Scarcely
had I time to notice the appearance of morning before the general
once more called a halt—we were then on the hills. Ordering a
square to be formed, he spoke to the brigade, as well as I can
remember, in these words, after having ordered three . . . men of
the 95th to be brought into the square:—

" 'Although,' said he, 'I should obtain the good-will neither of
the officers nor the men of the brigade here by so doing, I am
resolved to punish these three men, according to the sentence
awarded, even though the French are at our heels. Begin with
Daniel Howans.'

"This was indeed no time to be lax in discipline, and the general
knew it. The men, as I said, were, some of them, becoming careless and ruffianly in their demeanour; whilst others, again, I saw
with the tears falling down their cheeks from the agony of
their bleeding feet, and many were ill with dysentery from the
effects of the bad food they had got hold of and devoured on the
road . . .

"A hundred was the sentence; but when the bugler had counted
seventy-five, the general granted him a further indulgence and
ordered him to be taken down, and to join his company. The
general calling for his horse, now mounted for the first time for
many hours; for he had not ridden all night, not, indeed, since the
drum-head court-martial had taken place. Before he put the

brigade in motion again, he gave us another short specimen of his eloquence, pretty much, I remember, after this style:—

" 'I give you all notice,' said he, 'that I will halt the brigade again the very first moment I perceive any man disobeying my orders, and try him by court-martial on the spot.' He then gave us the word, and we resumed our march.

"Many who read this . . . may suppose this was a cruel and unnecessary severity under the dreadful and harassing circumstances of that retreat. But I, who was there, and was, besides, a common soldier of the very regiment to which these men belonged, say *it was quite necessary*. No man but one formed of stuff like General Craufurd could have saved the brigade from perishing altogether; and, if he flogged two, he saved hundreds from death by his management . . .

"It was perhaps a couple of days after this had taken place that we came to a river. It was tolerably wide, but not very deep, which was just as well for us; for, had it been deep as the dark regions, we must have somehow or other got through. The avenger was behind us, and Craufurd was along with us, and the two together kept us moving, whatever was in the road. Accordingly, into the stream went the light brigade, and Craufurd, as busy as a shepherd with his flock, riding in and out of the water to keep his wearied band from being drowned as they crossed over. Presently he spied an officer who, to save himself from being wet through, I suppose, and wearing a damp pair of breeches for the remainder of the day, had mounted on the back of one of his men. The sight of such a piece of effeminacy was enough to raise the choler of the general, and in a very short time he was plunging and splashing through the water after them both.

" 'Put him down, sir! put him down! I desire you to put that officer down instantly!' And the soldier in an instant, I dare say nothing loth, dropping his burden like a hot potatoe into the stream, continued his progress through. 'Return back, sir,' said Craufurd to the officer, 'and go through the water like the others. I will not allow my officers to ride upon the men's backs through the rivers: all must take their share alike here.' . . .

"General Craufurd was, indeed, one of the few men who was apparently created for command during such dreadful scenes as we were familiar with in this retreat. He seemed an iron man;

nothing daunted him—nothing turned him from his purpose. War was his very element, and toil and danger seemed to call forth only an increasing determination to surmount them . . . The Rifles being always at his heels, he seemed to think them his familiars. If he stopped his horse, and halted to deliver one of his stern reprimands, you would see half-a-dozen lean, unshaven, shoeless and savage Riflemen, standing for the moment leaning upon their weapons, and scowling up in his face as he scolded; and when he dashed the spurs into his reeking horse, they would throw up their rifles upon their shoulders, and hobble after him again."*

While the 2nd Battalion of the 95th, with its sister regiments of the Light Brigade, the 43rd and 52nd, covered the retreat to Vigo, the 1st Battalion covered that of the main army to Corunna. Here also, in this Regiment so rich in literary talent, the best account of the hardships of the retreat comes from the pen of 24-year-old Bugler Green.

"The French cavalry, forming their advanced guard, were close up to our rear and teasing us from morning to night. Their cavalry had a rifleman mounted behind each dragoon and, when any good position or bushes by the road side gave them any advantage to give our men a few shots, those riflemen would dismount and get under cover of the bushes, so that we were obliged to do the same. Their dragoons at the same time, dismounting and laying their carbines on their saddles, with their horse standing in front of them for a sort of defence, would give us a few shots as well. In this way we were obliged to make a stand and drive them back. We used to laugh to see the riflemen run to the road, put their feet into the stirrups, and mount behind the dragoons, and gallop back. We served many of these fellows off; and then we had to run to get up to the regiment . . .

"A long march about 250 English miles, before we could arrive at Corunna. We had no tents; a blanket had to be served out to each man. We marched from daylight to dark; the bullocks were driven before us and slaughtered as they were needed; they had little or no fat on them . . . We had no shelter but the canopy of heaven, and we seldom halted more than two hours. And, having

* *Rifleman Harris*, 126-40.

wood and water to seek to cook our victuals, before we could do so the order would be given to get under arms and get on the march. We had some artillery with us, six pounders; and we had to muffle the gun-wheels with grass, or anything we could find, to prevent the enemy from hearing us move; and we made up large fires, and moved on the road as still as possible.

"This was the game we had to play many nights, as the French advanced-guard would seldom be more than half a mile from us when we halted . . . At daylight the enemy would be close on our rear; they had seen our fires burn out; and then the day proved as the day before, a continual harassing. Many days we had no commissary with our bread; our spirits so low with hunger and fatigue, that we often said we would as soon die as live! . . .

"We then had enough to carry; fifty round of ball cartridge, thirty loose balls in our waist belts, and a flask and a horn of powder, and rifle and sword, the two weighing 14 pounds. These were plenty for us to carry with empty bellies, and the enemy close at our heels . . . We had seven or eight women belonging to the regiment. There were no baggage wagons on which they could ride; and some of them fell into the hands of the enemy; and after using them as they pleased, they gave them some food and sent them to us! When we had marched two or three hours on a night, our colonel would give the word to halt, for the purpose that the men might do what they wanted; and I have seen many who did not want to drop out of the ranks for that purpose, drop down nine or ten on each other, some with big coats on, some with blankets; and they would be fast asleep on the snow, huddled together, in the space of a minute; and when the word was given to 'fall in', the sergeants would have to kick them very hard to awaken them.

"On the 15th (January) we received orders to be ready to embark . . . We passed the afternoon pretty quiet; yet a little skirmishing between the armies was carried on. We made our fires at night; the French did the same; we lay down with our great coats on; and near me lay our brave Colonel Beckwith, and our Adjutant Stewart; they both wrapped themselves up in their boat cloaks; and some of the men feathered some straw, and covered them from the cold. At daylight, on the 16th, Sunday, the Adjutant rose from his bed, and rubbing the straw off his trousers, saw, and caught a large louse . . . The Colonel rose, put his spy-glass to his eye, looked towards the French camp, and said 'Though we are under orders for embarkation, mark my word for it, we shall have something to do in another shape; for I see Soult is preparing for another attack!' And so it turned out; for as we were attending with our camp kettles for our daily wine, a cannon ball was fired at us from the French. Our bugles sounded the advance; away went the kettles; the word was given 'Rifles in front extend by files in chain order!' The enemy's sharp shooters were double and triple our numbers. We soon got within range of their rifles, and began to pick them off. We held them in check till our light division formed in line, and then the carnage commenced. The roar of cannon and the roll of musketry was so loud, that without great attention the word of command could scarcely be given, and the sound of the bugle hardly heard.

"... Our loss in the regiment was not so great as might have been expected after four hours' fighting. We then made our fires for the night, and remained on the battle-field until five o'clock in the morning, when an order came for us to move on into Corunna. Ours was the last regiment that left the battle-field ... We marched through the streets into the harbour; the boats of the men of war and transport ships pushed to the shore to take us on board; but what confusion was there! many of the Hussars' horses were galloping on the beach like mad things. There was not time to embark them. Several were shot or we should have been rode over, or trodden to death.

"By this time Soult had got six pieces of cannon playing on the ships and boats. The vessels were at anchor. We got into any ship or boat we could. The sailors from the shore rowed to the ship. The grape shot from the French guns came plentifully through the rigging of the ships, as well as amongst the soldiers of the boat. But presently an English line-of-battle ship weighed her anchor, and sailed within range of the French guns, and crippled four of them out of the six. I think the ship was called the *Bellerophon*. A signal was then made for the master of transports to cut their cables, leave the anchors aground, and get out of the harbour to see poor old England."*

Captain Harry Smith, then 21, who was assisting Colonel Beck-

* *R.B.C. 1947*, 154-63.

with in procuring rations for his hungry men, gave his own sum-
mary of the retreat and evacuation: "Never did corps so distinguish
itself during the whole of this retreat as my dear old Rifles. From the
severe attack on our rear-guard at Calcavellos until the battle of
Coruña, we were daily engaged with a most vigorous and pushing
enemy, making most terrific long marches (one day 37 miles). The
fire of the Riflemen ever prevented the column being molested by
the enemy. But the scenes of drunkenness, riot, and disorder we
Reserve Division witnessed on the part of the rest of the army are
not to be described; it was truly awful and heartrending to see that
army which had been so brilliant at Salamanca so totally dis-
organised, with the exception of the reserve under the revered Paget
and the Brigade of Guards . . . For three weeks we had no clothes but
those on our backs; we were literally covered and almost eaten up
with vermin, most of us suffering from ague and dysentery, every
man a living, still active, skeleton. On embarkation many fell asleep
in their ships and never awoke for three days and nights, until in a
gale we reached Portsmouth (21 Jan.). I was so reduced that Colonel
Beckwith, with a warmth of heart equalling the thunder of his voice,
on meeting me in the George Inn, roared out, 'Who the devil's ghost
are you? Pack up your kit—which is soon done, the devil a thing
have you got—take a place in the coach, and set off home to your
father's. I shall soon want again such fellows as you, and I will
arrange your leave of absence!' I soon took the hint, and naked and
slothful and covered with vermin I reached my dear native home,
where the kindest of fathers and most affectionate of mothers soon
restored me to health."[*]

* * *

The miracle of Corunna[†]—for the army's escape from Napoleon's
jaws after it had forced him to turn back from Madrid, leaving
Portugal and southern Spain unconquered, was something of a
miracle—enabled Britain to retain her precarious foothold on
Napoleon's conquered continent and for the Peninsular War to

[*] *Harry Smith, I,* 16-17.
[†] Among those who paid the price for it was the founder and Colonel of the Regiment,
Major-General Coote Manningham, who died that summer as a result of the hardships of
the Retreat in which he had served in command of a Brigade.

continue. In the next five years it offered continuous occupation for the 95th Rifles. Four months after the retreat to Corunna, though both its Battalions were at that time still recuperating in England, a Company of the Regiment, formed from riflemen who had served in Sir Arthur Wellesley's campaign of the previous summer, headed that officer's advance on Oporto which he captured, after a daring passage of the Douro, on May 12th, 1809. Shortly afterwards the 1st Battalion sailed again for Portugal with the rest of the Light Brigade to reinforce Sir Arthur. Though too late to take part in the battle of Talavera on July 28th, the Brigade under Maj.-Gen. Craufurd made one of the most famous forced marches in British military history, covering 42 miles in 22 hours under a blazing sun.

Though, owing to the failure of his Spanish allies, Lord Wellington, as Sir Arthur Wellesley now became, was forced to withdraw to the Portuguese frontier, he successfully contained greatly superior French forces there for nearly a year. He was able to do so largely because of the way in which the 95th Rifles, with its two fellow Light Infantry Regiments, provided a protective reconnaissance screen. Forty miles in advance of the main army, the Rifles and Light Infantry whom Moore had trained—now reconstituted as the Light Division under Maj.-Gen. Robert Craufurd, and consisting of the 1st Battalions of the 43rd, 52nd and 95th, a troop of Horse Artillery, a Regiment of Hanoverian Hussars and two Battalions of Portuguese Caçadores or Light Infantry, about 4000 men in all—kept watch on the Spanish plain beyond the Agueda River. Their instructions were to screen the army, maintain communications with the Spanish frontier fortress of Ciudad Rodrigo and keep Wellington punctually supplied with intelligence of every enemy movement.

"Never was reconnaissance more brilliantly carried out. Since the retreat from Corunna and his return to Spain Craufurd had been improving on Moore's rules in the light of experience. To the original handiwork of his master he had added a wonderful polish. Impulsive and hot-tempered in action, 'Black Bob' was under ordinary circumstances a man of immense method. He once insisted on a commissary keeping a journal like a log-book so that he might see how and where he spent every moment of his time. Wherever he went himself he carried a pocket-book and, whenever he encountered anything worthy of remark, down it went. From this he elaborated his divisional Code of Standing Orders which governed all movements on the march, in camp and on outpost duty. It was designed to ensure an automatic response to every order and to give his entire force the precision of a single section on the parade ground. 'All sounds preparatory to turning out and marching,' it began, 'will commence at the quarters of the Assistant Adjutant-General and be immediately repeated by the orderly bugles attending on the officers commanding regiments. As soon as possible after the first sound all the bugles are to assemble at the quarters of the commanding officers of regiments from whence all the other sounds will be repeated.'

"From this start everything went with a steady, unhalting, unhurrying swing which only an earthquake could have interrupted. Officers and camp-colourmen went ahead to the night's quarters, the baggage was packed and loaded, and, an hour after the first, a second bugle call sounded for the companies to fall in. Thereafter bugle horns in carefully-timed succession brought the companies together and set the regiments marching to the accompaniment of music. Step and perfect dressing were observed until the word was given to march at ease. During the march guides, who had already gone over the ground, directed the head of the column, and every officer and N.C.O. kept his appointed place. Straggling was forbidden: no man was to leave the ranks save with his company commander's permission and only after a signed ticket had been issued. Any one straying or stopped by the camp-guard without a ticket was to be arrested, tried by drumhead court-martial and flogged. In crossing streams and other obstacles, no regiment, company or section was to defile or break rank unless the preceding unit had done so:* any man who disobeyed was to be given a dozen lashes on the spot. Where defiling was necessary, it was to be carried out with precision by the proper words of command. Hurrying or exceeding the regulation step were forbidden; half an hour after the start and at hourly intervals—to be governed by the proximity of water—the division was to halt for five minutes, during which time, and at no other, the men were to fill their water-canteens.

* Kincaid, *Random Shots*, 46. "Sit down in it, Sir, sit down in it," Craufurd himself would cry if he saw a soldier avoiding a puddle.—*Seaton*, 173.

"The reason for all this—mercilessly enforced and, at first, much disliked—was made clear to all. Every battalion defiling on the march caused a delay of ten minutes or, in a brigade of three battalions, of half an hour. In a country like Portugal, with innumberable water-courses, many hours could be lost in this way. The tail of the division might arrive at its destination hours late, perhaps drenched to the skin, and be confronted at the day's end with all the confusion and discomfort of bivouacking in a strange place in the dark. Experience demonstrated the wisdom of Craufurd's rules: punishment, at first frequent, became almost negligible. 'The system once established,' wrote an officer, 'went on like clockwork, and the soldiers became devotedly attached to him; for while he extracted from all the most rigid obedience, he was, on his part, keenly alive to everything they had a right to expect from him in return.'

"By sterner methods engendered by the realities of war, Craufurd systematised Moore's training of common sense and humanism. His rules made it second nature for men to do the right thing. By obeying them all grew accustomed to looking after themselves in all circumstances. The troops of the Light Division did not give way to fatigue after a long march and drop asleep when they halted, later to awake in the dark, cold, supperless and miserable. Instead, the moment the bugle sounded for them to dismiss, they bustled about securing whatever the neighbourhood could contribute to their night's comfort. Swords, hatchets and bill-hooks were soon busy hacking at trees and bushes, huts were reared with roofs and walls of broom, pine branches or straw, fires lit and camp kettles set boiling; and presently, when the regulation pound of beef had been fried, tired but happy souls, their feet toasting round the cheerful blaze, would fall on their meal with a will, taking care, however, like good soldiers, not to consume anything that belonged to the morrow's ration. And, before they slept, wrapped in sedge mat or cloak and leather cap and with sod or stone for pillow, every man carefully arranged his accoutrements ready for nocturnal emergencies.

"The value of all this became plain in the presence of the enemy. Seven minutes sufficed to get the whole division under arms in the middle of the night and fifteen to bring it in order of

Statues flanking the Rifle Brigade War Memorial—John Tweed
An officer in the uniform of 1800 and a Rifleman in that of 1806

The Rear Guard—J. P. Beadle
Covering the retreat 1808-9

Major General Robert Craufurd

battle to its alarm posts, with the baggage loaded and assembled under escort in the rear. And this, as Johnny Kincaid wrote, not upon a concerted signal or at a trial, but at all times and certain. The moment the Division or any of its units halted, guards and piquets were posted automatically, while every road was examined, cleared, and reported upon so that the troops could move off again at once in any direction. Unless otherwise ordered, one company of every battalion served as outlying piquet, placed sentinels at all approaches and stood to arms from an hour before sunrise until a a grey horse could be seen a mile away.

"With less than 3000 British infantry so trained and their Portuguese and Hanoverian auxiliaries, Craufurd for six months guarded a river line of more than forty miles between the Serra de Estrella and the Douro, broken by at least fifteen fords and with an open plain in front. His men were never less than an hour's march off 6000 French cavalry with 60,000 infantry in support. Yet they never suffered their lines to be penetrated or allowed the slightest intelligence of Wellington's strength and movements to reach the enemy. 'The whole web of communication,' as Sir Charles Oman has written, 'quivered at the slightest touch.'

"On one occasion, on the night of March 19th, 1810, a greatly superior force of Voltigeurs attempted to surprise a detachment of the 95th Rifles at the bridge of Barba del Puerco. A French general had been informed by a Spanish traitor that the British officers were in the habit of getting drunk every night. He accordingly assembled six hundred picked troops at midnight under the rocks at the east end of the bridge. Creeping across in the shadows cast by the rising moon, with every sound drowned by the roar of the mountain torrent below, they succeeded in surprising and bayoneting the two sentries at the other end before they could open fire. But a sergeant's party higher up the rocks saw them and gave the alarm to the piquet company. Within a few minutes the rest of the Regiment, with hastily donned belts and cartridge-boxes slung over flapping shirts, led by Colonel Beckwith in dressing-gown, night-cap and slippers, was tumbling them down the rocks and across the bridge whence they had come. The French casualties in the affair were forty-seven, the British thirteen.

"It was through this screen and its patrols of Riflemen and Hussars, ranging far beyond the enemy's lines into Spain, that

Wellington obtained his knowledge of French movements. It was work which required, as Kincaid said, a clear head, a bold heart and a quick pair of heels, all three being liable to be needed at any hour of the day or night. Founded on the training, habits and virtues of a few hundred humble British soldiers, its effect on the course of the European war was incalculable. For, in conjunction with the work of the Spanish guerillas, it deprived the enemy of all knowledge of Wellington's strength and dispositions. While the British Commander knew from day to day what was happening on the other side of the lines and saw his enemy silhouetted, as it were, against the eastern sky, the French faced only darkness. This out-weighed all their superiority in numbers. For it meant that, when the time came to strike, Goliath with his mighty sword lunged blindly. David with his pebble and sling had no such handi-cap."*

When, jealous of his independent command and operating in the presence of forces beyond his strength to contain, Craufurd on July 24th 1810 allowed himself to be attacked with the Coa river behind him, the situation—and the Light Division with it—was saved by the training and morale of the 95th Rifles and its two companion Regiments. What happened was described by Lieutenant George Simmons, a young former apprentice surgeon from Yorkshire, who had joined the Regiment from the Lincolnshire Militia to help support his parents and brothers and sisters.

"A little after daybreak the enemy advanced against our piquets and drove them in. The Division was put into position, the left upon Almeida and the right in rugged ground upon the Coa, which river was running furiously in its course. Several com-panies of Rifle Men and the 43rd Light Infantry were placed be-hind stone walls. The enemy now advanced in vast bodies; the whole plain in our front was covered with horse and foot advan-cing towards us. The enemy's infantry formed line and, with an innumerable multitude of skirmishers, attacked us fiercely. We repulsed them; they came on again, yelling, with drums beating, frequently the drummers leading, often in front of the line, French officers like mountebanks running forward and placing their hats upon their swords and capering about like madmen, saying, as

* *Years of Victory*, 363-7.

they turned to their men, 'Come on, children of our country. The first that advances, Napoleon will recompense him' . . .

"We kept up a very brisk fire. Several guns began to play upon us, and as the force kept increasing every moment in our front, and columns of infantry were also moving upon our right flank, we were ordered to retire half the company. Captain O'Hare's retired, and the remainder, under Lieutenant Johnston, still remained fighting for a few moments longer. I was with this party. We moved from the field into the road, our men falling all round us, when a body of Hussars in bearskin caps and light-coloured pelisses got amongst the few remaining Riflemen and began to sabre them. Several attempted to cut me down, but I avoided their kind intentions by stepping on one side. I had a large cloak rolled up and strapped across my body; my haversack was filled with little necessary articles for immediate use; thus I got clear off.

"A volley was now fired by a party of the 43rd under Captain Wells, which brought several of the Hussars to the ground. In the scuffle I took to my heels and ran to the 43rd, Wells calling out 'Mind the Rifleman! Do not hit him, for heaven's sake.' As I was compelled to run into their fire to escape, he seized me by the hand and was delighted beyond measure at my escape.

"The road to a small bridge across the Coa, which the Division would have to retire over, was very bad and rocky. Our gallant fellows disputed manfully every inch of ground and retired towards the river. Every place we left was covered with the enemy's Light Infantry in ten times our number. As we got near the river the enemy made several attempts to cut us off. General Craufurd ordered a number of Riflemen who had occupied a place that prevented the French from stopping our retreat over the bridge to evacuate it before half the 52nd, who were on the right, had filed over. The enemy directly brought up their infantry to this hill, which commanded the bridge, and kept up a terrible fire. Colonel Beckwith, a most gallant and clever soldier, saw this frightful mistake and ordered us to retake the wall and hill instantly, which we did in good style, but suffered severely in men and officers. Lieutenant Harry Smith, Lieutenant Thomas Smith, and Lieutenant Pratt were wounded, and I was shot through the thigh close to the wall, which caused me to fall with great force.

"Being wounded in this way was quite a new thing to me. For a few moments I could not collect my ideas, and was feeling about my arms and body for a wound, until my eye caught the stream of blood rushing through the hole in my trousers, and my leg and thigh appeared so heavy that I could not move it. Captain Napier took off his neckerchief and gave it to a sergeant, who put it round my thigh and twisted it tight with a ramrod, to stop the bleeding. The firing was so severe that the sergeant, on finishing the job for me, fell with a shot through the head. Captain Napier was also about the same time wounded in the side . . . The ground was very rugged and rocky close to the bridge, so that Riflemen were placed behind every stone, and two companies of the 43rd hid themselves and were ready to support our men. . .

"A number of French officers and some drummers headed the storming party. Our fellows allowed them to come close to the bridge. Some officers got over before they fell, but few went back to tell the tale, either men or officers. They attempted to force the bridge several times before the evening, and finding it impossible to effect their purpose, they made a signal to cease firing. An officer came forward waving a white handkerchief and requested to be allowed to remove their wounded, as the bridge and its vicinity were covered with their killed and wounded. This request was granted. The officer said he had heard of the English fighting well, but he could not have supposed men would have fought against such fearful odds. He complimented our men much upon their gallantry, and observed what a pity it was we were enemies."*

There is an account in the autobiography of Simmons's brother Rifleman, Harry Smith, of his and and his wounded companions' agonising journey in bullock carts across the mountains to the Mondego and Lisbon.

"The wounded were ordered to the rear, so as to embark on the Mondego at Pinhel. In collecting transport for the wounded, a sedan chair between two mules was brought, . . . and, fortunately for me, I was the only person who could ride in it, and by laying my leg on the one seat and sitting on the other, I rode comparatively easy to the poor fellows in the wretched bullock-carts, who suffered excruciating agony, poor brother Tom, who was very

* *A British Rifleman*, 76-80.

severely wounded above the knee, among the rest. This little story will show what wild fellows we were in those days. George Simmons' bullocks at one stage had run away. As I was the spokesman, the surgeon in charge came to me in great distress. I sent for the village magistrate, and actually fixed a rope in my room to hang him if he did not get a pair of bullocks (if the Duke of W. had known he would have hung *me*). However, the bullocks were got, and off we started. The bullocks were not broken, and they ran away with poor George and nearly jolted him to death, for he was awfully wounded through the thick of the thigh. However, we all got down to Pinhel (31 July), and thence descended the Mondego by boats, landing every night. At one house a landlord was most insolent to us, and Lieut. Pratt of the Rifles, shot through the neck, got very angry. The carotid artery must have been wounded, for it burst out in a torrent of blood, and he was dead in a few seconds, to our horror, for he was a most excellent fellow . . . On our reaching the mouth of the Mondego, we were put on board a transport.''*

How the young officers of the 95th Rifles faced up to wounds and the dreadful surgery of the day is also described by Harry Smith:

"My ball was lodged on my ankle-joint, having partially divided the *tendo Achillis*. However, we heard of the army having retired into the celebrated Lines of Torres Vedras, and nothing would serve us but *join the Regiment*. So our medical heroes very unwillingly sent us off to Belem, the convalescent department under Colonel Tucker, 29th Regiment, a sharp fellow enough. When I, George Simmons, and Charlie Eeles, 3rd Battalion, just arrived sick from Cadiz, waited on him to express our desire to join, he said, 'Oh, certainly; but you must be posted to do duty with convalescents going up the country.' I was lame and could not walk, George Simmons cantered on crutches, and Charlie Eeles was very sick. However, *go or no go*, and so we were posted to 600 villains of every Regiment in the Army under a long Major Ironmonger of the 88th . . . On the first day's march he pretended to faint. George Simmons, educated a surgeon, *literally* threw a bucket of water over him. He recovered the faint, but not the desire to return; and the devil would have it, the command devolved on me, a subaltern,

* *Harry Smith, I*, 32-3.

for whom the soldiers of other corps have no great respect, and such a task I never had as to keep these six hundred rascals together. However, I had a capital English horse, good at riding over an insubordinate fellow, and a voice like thunder. The first bivouac I came to was the Guards (these men were very orderly). The commanding officer had a cottage. I reported myself. It was raining like the devil. He put his head out of the window, and I said, 'Sir, I have 150 men of your Regiment convalescent from Belem.' 'Oh, send for the Sergeant-major,' he very quietly said;— no 'Walk in out of the rain.' So I roared out, 'We Light Division men don't do duty with Sergeant-majors, nor are we told to wait. There are your men, every one—the only well-conducted men in 600 under my charge—and these are their accounts!' throwing down a bundle of papers, and off I galloped, to the Household man's astonishment. That day I delivered over, or sent by officers under me, all the vagabonds I had left. Some of my own men and I reached our corps that night at Arruda, when old Sydney Beckwith, dear Colonel, said, 'You are a mad fool of a boy coming here with a ball in your leg. Can you dance?' 'No,' says I; 'I can hardly walk but with my toe turned out.' 'Can you be my A.D.C.?' 'Yes; I can ride and eat,' I said, at which he laughed, and was kind as a brother; as was my dear friend Stewart or Rutu, as we called him, his Brigade Major."

Two months later, after the French had been driven back to Santarem and there was a lull in the fighting while they essayed the impossible feat of surviving in the starveling wilderness in which Wellington had marooned them, this indomitable young officer, still with the ball in his leg, returned to hospital to have it removed.

"Colonel Beckwith going to Lisbon, and I being his A.D.C., it was voted a capital opportunity for me to go to have the ball cut out from under the tendon Achillis, in the very joint. I was very lame, and the pain often excruciating, so off I cut.

"Soon after we reached Lisbon . . . a Board was held consisting of the celebrated Staff Surgeon Morell, who had attended me before, Higgins, and Brownrigg. They examined my leg. I was all for the operation. Morell and Higgins recommended me to remain with a stiff leg of my own as better than a wooden one, for the wounds in Lisbon of late had sloughed so, they were dubious of the result. Brownrigg said, 'If it were my leg, out should come the ball.' On which I roared out, 'Hurrah, Brownrigg, you are the doctor for me.' So Morell says, 'Very well, if you are desirous, we will do it *directly*.' My pluck was somewhat cooled, but I cocked up my leg, and said, 'There it is; slash away.' It was five minutes, most painful indeed, before it was extracted. The ball was jagged, and the tendonous fibres had so grown into it, it was half dissected and half torn out, with most excruciating torture for a moment, the forceps breaking which had hold of the ball. George Simmons was present, whose wound had broken out and obliged him to go to Lisbon. The surgeon wanted some linen during the operation, so I said, 'George, tear a shirt,' which my servant gave him. He turned it about, said, 'No, it is a pity; it is a good shirt;' at which I did not —— him a few, for my leg was aching and smoking from a wound four or five inches long. Thank God Almighty and a light heart, no sloughing occurred, and before the wound was healed I was with the regiment. Colonel Beckwith's ague was cured, and he had joined his Brigade before I could move, so when I returned to Vallé he was delighted to see his A.D.C. . . .

"I found the army in hourly expectation to move, and the Captain of my Company—Leach—was gone sick to the rear, so I said to my Colonel, 'I must be no longer A.D.C., sir. However grateful I am, my Company wants me.' 'Ah, now you can walk a little, you leave me! Go and be d——d to you; but I love you for the desire.' Off I started, and the very next day we marched [6 Mar. 1811], Massena retreating out of Portugal, and many is the skirmish we had. My leg was so painful, the wound open, and I was so lame."*

While Colonel Beckwith's 1st Battalion had been serving under Wellington on the Coa, and in the retreat to the Lines of Torres Vedras—during which it shared in the victory of Busaco—and the subsequent advance to the Portuguese-Spanish frontier in pursuit of Massena's starving army, the 2nd Battalion had been suffering terribly from the agues and fever contracted during the ill-fated Walcheren expedition. This attempt to capture Antwerp in the late summer of 1809, while Napoleon was engaged in a new—and, as it turned out, victorious—campaign against Austria, only resulted in

* *Harry Smith*, *I*, 33-5, 39-41.

the crippling of the flower of Britain's home army. It was on this expedition, during the siege of Flushing, that, having dug a hole for himself with his sword, a Rifleman named Jackman neutralised the fortress's guns by picking off every French gunner who showed himself at the embrasures. With a third of its men wiped out by disease and hardships for the second time in a year, it was not till the spring and summer of 1810 that units of the 2nd Battalion, operating in the Regiment's tradition as independent Companies, began to filter back to the Peninsula, some for service at Tarifa in the extreme south, where Anglo-Spanish forces were holding out against Marshal Soult, the French Viceroy of Andalusia, and others joining Wellington's main force in Portugal where they served alongside the 1st Battalion. Meanwhile, such was the prestige which the Regiment had already acquired, that a 3rd Battalion was raised in 1809, over 1100 men being recruited in three days from the Militia. In the following year, under its young Lt.-Colonel, Andrew Barnard, it reinforced the Anglo-Spanish garrison of Cadiz, then besieged by Marshal Victor. Here, on the 5th March, 1811, with two companies of the 2nd Battalion under Lt.-Colonel Amos Norcott, it took part in the victory of Barrosa which relieved Cadiz from danger and, with Wellington's operations in the north, began the liberation of southern Spain.

During the summer of 1811 the 1st Battalion and part of the 2nd, serving with Craufurd's Light Division, helped to turn the tide at Fuentes d'Onoro in what Napier described as the most dangerous hour of the war. By now the Light Division had become the most famous fighting force in Europe—only equalled, but not surpassed, by Napoleon's supposedly invincible Imperial Guard. "There perhaps never was nor never will be again," wrote Johnny Kincaid, who joined the 2nd Battalion before the Walcheren expedition and arrived in Portugal in time to share in the repulse and expulsion from that country of Massena's army, "such a war brigade as that which was composed of the 43rd, 52nd and the Rifles." "It did one's very heart good," he wrote, "to look at our Battalion, ... seeing each Company standing a hundred strong, and the intelligence of several campaigns stamped on each daring bronzed countenance, which looked you boldly in the face, in the fulness of vigour and confidence as if it cared neither for man nor devil ... We were the light Regiment of the Light Division and fired the first and last shot in almost every battle, siege and skirmish in which the Army was engaged during the war . . . Our old and gallant associates, the 43rd and 52nd, as a part of ourselves, bore their share in everything . . . Wherever *we* were, *they* were, and . . . although the nature of our arm generally gave us more employment in the way of skirmishing, yet whenever it came to a pinch, independent of a suitable mixture of them among us, we had only to look behind to see a line in which we might place a degree of confidence almost equal to our hopes in heaven, nor were we ever disappointed. There never was a corps of Riflemen in the hands of such supporters."*

Nor were others unsparing of such tributes. Before the storm of Ciudad Rodrigo, the colonel of the great Irish fighting regiment, the 88th, called out to his men, "Come on, my noble Connaught Rangers, the 95th, the glory of your country, is in your front."† Of the Rifles' performance at Sabugal in April 1811, Wellington wrote in his Despatches, "Nothing could be more daring and more characteristic of British courage than the way Beckwith with a handful of men withstood and thrice repulsed and then pursued a whole *Corps d'Armée* placed in a strong position. I consider the action fought by Colonel Beckwith to be one of the most glorious the British troops were ever engaged in." Throughout the fight, wherever the danger was greatest, the calm-sounding voice of that officer—Harry Smith's adored colonel—could be heard: "Now my lads, we'll just go back a little if you please. No, no," as some of the men began to run, "I don't mean that—we are in no hurry—we'll just walk quietly back and you can give them a shot as you go along." All the while he continued riding in their midst, the blood streaming down his face from a head wound, until he judged the moment was ripe and faced about, crying, "Now, my men, this will do—let us show our teeth again."‡ For Beckwith's manner of command on such occasions, as Kincaid recalled, "was nothing more than a familiar sort of conversation with the soldier." So on another occasion, Colonel Norcott of the 2nd Battalion, when attacked by a column of the Young Guard with his men in extended order, calmly told the centre to walk backwards firing and the flanks to walk inwards, so confusing the assailants by this familiar and personal system of command and by

---

* Kincaid, *Adventures in the Rifle Brigade*, 11-12, 144, 148.
† *R.B.C. 1926*, 259. Testimony of Sergeant John Lowe.
‡ Kincaid, *Random Shots*, 166-9.

the green-jacketed marksmen's instinctive response to it, so that they broke and fled. For the beauty of the Rifles' system of discipline, as Kincaid said, lay in their "doing everything that was necessary and nothing that was not, so that every man's duty was a pleasure to him and the *esprit de corps* was unrivalled." Their most marked characteristics, Colonel Henderson wrote of them in his *Science of War*, "were that when they were left alone they almost invariably did the right thing; that they had no hesitation in assuming responsibility; that they could handle their regiment and companies, if necessary, as independent units, and that they constantly applied the great principle of mutual support."

There is an account in Kincaid's *Adventures in the Rifle Brigade*, of the Regiment bivouacking for the night preparatory to attacking the retreating French in the morning:

"When a regiment arrives at its ground for the night, it is formed in columns of companies, at full, half, or quarter distance, according to the space which circumstances will permit it to occupy. The officer commanding each company then receives his orders; and, after communicating whatever may be necessary to the men, he desires them to 'pile arms, and make themselves comfortable for the night . . .' The soldiers of each company have an hereditary claim to the ground next to their arms, as have their officers to a wider range on the same line, limited to the end of a bugle sound, . . . for the nearer a man is to his enemy, the nearer he likes to be to his friends . . . In a ploughed or a stubble field there is scarcely a choice of quarters, but whenever there is a sprinkling of trees, it is always an object to secure a good one, as it affords shelter from the sun by day and the dews by night, besides being a sort of home or sign-post for a group of officers, as denoting the best place of entertainment; for they hang their spare clothing and accoutrements among the branches, barricade themselves on each side with their saddles, canteens, and portmanteaus, and, with a blazing fire in their front, they indulge, according to their various humours, in a complete state of gipsyfication.

"There are several degrees of comfort to be reckoned in a bivouac . . . The first, and worst, is to arrive at the end of a cold wet day, too dark to see your ground, and too near the enemy to be permitted to unpack the knapsacks or to take off accoutrements;

where, unencumbered with baggage or eatables of any kind, you have the consolation of knowing that things are now at their worst, and that any change must be for the better. . .

"The next, and most common one, is, when you are not required to look quite so sharp, and when the light baggage and provisions come in at the heel of the regiment. If it is early in the day, the first thing to be done is to make some tea, the most sovereign restorative for jaded spirits. We then proceed to our various duties. The officers of each company form a mess of themselves. One remains in camp to attend to the duties of the regiment; a second . . . goes to the regimental butcher, and bespeaks a portion of the only purchaseable commodities,—hearts, livers, and kidneys; and also to see whether he cannot do the commissary out of a few extra biscuit, or a canteen of brandy; and the remainder are gentlemen at large for the day. But while they go hunting among the neighbouring regiments for news, and the neighbouring houses for curiosity, they have always an eye to their mess, and omit no opportunity of adding to the general stock.

"Dinner hour, for fear of accidents, is always the hour when dinner can be got ready; . . . every good officer parading himself round the camp-kettle at the time fixed, with his haversack in his hand. A haversack on service is a sort of dumb waiter. The mess have a good many things in common, but the contents of the haversack are exclusively the property of its owner; and a well regulated one ought never to be without the following furniture . . . viz a couple of biscuits, a sausage, a little tea and sugar, a knife, fork, and spoon, a tin cup, (which answers to the names of *tea-cup*, *soup-plate*, *wine-glass*, and *tumbler*) a pair of socks, a piece of soap, a tooth brush, towel, and comb, and half-a-dozen cigars.

"After doing justice to the dinner, if we feel in a humour for additional society, we transfer ourselves to some neighbouring mess, taking our cups, and whatever we mean to drink, along with us; for in those times there is nothing to be expected from our friends beyond the pleasure of their conversation: and finally we retire to rest. To avoid inconvenience by the tossing off of the bedclothes, each officer has a blanket sewed up at the sides, like a sack into which he scrambles, and with a green sod or a smooth stone for a pillow, composes himself to sleep . . . Habit gives endurance, and fatigue is the best night-cap; no matter that the veteran's countenance is alternately stormed with torrents of rain, heavy dews, and hoar-frosts; no matter that his ears are assailed by a million mouths of chattering locusts, and by some villanous donkey, who every half hour pitches a *bray* note, which, as a congregation of Presbyterians follow their clerk, is instantly taken up by every mule and donkey in the army, and sent echoing from regiment to regiment, over hill and valley, until it dies away in the distance. . . .

"All are unheeded, until . . . the first note of the melodious bugle places the soldier on his legs like lightning; when, muttering a few curses at the unseasonableness of the hour, he plants himself on his alarm post, without knowing or caring about the cause.

"Such is a bivouac . .

"March 12th.—We stood to our arms before daylight. Finding that the enemy had quitted the position in our front, we proceeded to follow them; and had not gone far before we heard the usual morning's salutation, of a couple of shots, between their rear and our advanced guard. On driving in their outposts, we found their whole army drawn out on the plain, near Redinha . . .

"I was one of a crowd of skirmishers who were enabling the French ones to carry the news of their own defeat through a thick wood, at an infantry canter, when I found myself all at once within a few yards of one of their regiments in line, which opened such a fire, that had I not, rifleman-like, taken instant advantage of the cover of a good fir tree, my name would have unquestionably been transmitted to postcrity by the night's gazette. And, however opposed to it may be the usual system of drill, I will maintain from that day's experience that the cleverest method of teaching a recruit to stand at attention, is to place him behind a tree and fire balls at him . . .

"This was a last and a desperate stand made by their rear-guard, for their own safety, immediately above the town, as their sole chance of escape depended upon their being able to hold the post until the only bridge across the river was clear of the other fugitives. But they could not hold it long enough; for while we were undergoing a temporary sort of purgatory in their front, our comrades went working round their flanks, which quickly

sent them flying, with us intermixed, at full cry, down the
streets . . ."*

*　　*　　*

In the opening months of 1812, in bitter weather, the Rifles took
part in the capture of the Spanish frontier fortresses of Ciudad
Rodrigo and Badajoz whose possession was the first indispensable
step to the expulsion of the French from the Peninsula. Because
Wellington lacked an adequate siege-train and sufficient sappers,
both fortresses had to be carried by storm. That of Ciudad Rodrigo
took place on the night of January 19th when four Companies of the
Rifles under Colonel Cameron, advanced to the crest of the glacis to
give covering fire to a storming-party consisting of three officers
and a hundred volunteers from each Regiment of the Light Division.
A Forlorn Hope of an officer and twenty-five volunteers was assigned
to leap into the ditch and swarm up the breached walls or mount the
fausse-braye with scaling ladders. Kincaid, who was in the storming
party, described what happened—

"At a given signal the different columns advanced to the
assault. The night was tolerably clear, and the enemy evidently
expected us; for, as soon as we turned the corner of the convent
wall, the space between us and the breach became one blaze of light
with their fire-balls . . . The whole glacis was in consequence swept
by a well-directed fire of grape and musketry, . . . but our gallant
fellows walked through it, to the point of attack, with the most
determined steadiness . . . We had some difficulty at first in finding
the breach, as we had entered the ditch opposite to a ravelin, which
we mistook for a bastion. I tried first one side of it and then the
other, and seeing one corner of it a good deal battered, with a
ladder placed against it, I concluded that it must be the breach,
and, calling to the soldiers near me to follow, I mounted with the
most ferocious intent, carrying a sword in one hand and a pistol
in the other. But, when I got up, I found nobody to fight with,
except two of our own men who were already laid over dead
across the top of the ladder. I saw, in a moment, that I had got into
the wrong box, and was about to descend again, when I heard a
shout from the opposite side that the breach was there; and, mov-

* Kincaid, *Adventures in the Rifle Brigade*, 42-52.

ing in that direction, I dropped myself from the ravelin and landed in the ditch opposite to the foot of the breach, where I found the head of the storming party just beginning to fight their way into it. The combat was of short duration; and, in less than half an hour from the commencement of the attack, the place was in our possession . . .

"There is nothing in this life half so enviable as the feelings of a soldier after a victory. Previous to a battle, there is a certain sort of something that pervades the mind, which is not easily defined; it is neither akin to joy nor fear, and, probably, anxiety may be nearer to it than any other word in the dictionary. But, when the battle is over, and crowned with victory, he finds himself elevated for awhile into the regions of absolute bliss. It had ever been the summit of my ambition to attain a post at the head of a storming party:—my wish had now been accomplished, and gloriously ended; and . . . after all was over, and our men laid asleep on the ramparts, I strutted about as important a personage, in my own opinion, as ever trod the face of the earth; and had the ghost of the renowned Jack-the-Giant-killer itself passed that way at the time, I'll venture to say that I would have given it a kick in the breech without the smallest ceremony. But, as the sun began to rise, I began to fall from the heroics; and, when he showed his face, I took a look at my own, and found that I was too unclean a spirit to worship, for I was covered with mud and dirt, with the greater part of my dress torn to rags."*

Less than three months later, the Light Division was again used as a living battering-ram against the breaches of a still more formidable fortress, Badajoz. "The scene that ensued," wrote Kincaid, who this time was acting as Adjutant to the four Companies of the Rifles who lined the crest of the glacis to give covering support to the storming parties, "furnished as respectable a representation of hell itself as fire, sword and human sacrifices could make it." His friend, Harry Smith, Brigade Major to one of the two Light Division brigades who, under Sir Andrew Barnard, led the attack, went through five hours of that hell and afterwards described it.

"We flew down the ladders and rushed at the breach, but we were

* Kincaid, *Adventures in the Rifle Brigade*, 109-18.

broken, and carried no weight with us, although every soldier was a hero. The breach was covered by a breastwork from behind, and ably defended on the top by *chevaux-de-frises* of sword-blades, sharp as razors, chained to the ground; while the ascent to the top of the breach was covered with planks with sharp nails in them. However, devil a one did I feel at this moment. One of the officers of the Forlorn Hope, . . . was hanging on my arm—a mode we adopted to help each other up, for the ascent was most difficult and steep. A Rifleman stood among the sword-blades on the top of one of the *chevaux-de-frises*. We made a glorious rush to follow, but alas! in vain. He was knocked over. My old captain, O'Hare, who commanded the storming party, was killed. All were awfully wounded except, I do believe, myself and little Freer of the 43rd. I had been some seconds at the *revêtement* of the bastion near the breach, and my pockets were literally filled with chips of stones splintered by musket-balls. Those not knocked down were driven back by this hail of mortality to the ladders. At the foot of them I saw poor Colonel Macleod with his hands on his breast . . . He said, 'Oh, Smith, I am mortally wounded. Help me up the ladder.' I said, 'Oh no, dear fellow!' 'I am,' he said; 'be quick!' I did so, and came back again. Little Freer and I said, 'Let us throw down the ladders; the fellows shan't go out.' Some soldiers behind said, 'D—— your eyes, if you do we will bayonet you!' and we were literally forced up with the crowd. My sash had got loose, and one end of it was fast in the ladder, and the bayonet was very nearly applied, but the sash by pulling became loose. So soon as we got on the glacis up came a fresh Brigade of the Portuguese of the 4th Division. I never saw any soldiers behave with more pluck. Down into the ditch we all went again, but the more we tried to get up the more we were destroyed. The 4th Division followed us in, marching up to the breach.

"Both Divisions were fairly beaten back; we never carried either breach . . . After the attacks upon the breaches, some time before daylight Lord Fitzroy Somerset came to our Division. I think I was almost the first officer who spoke to him. He said, 'Where is Barnard?' I didn't know, but I assured his Lordship he was neither killed nor wounded. A few minutes after his Lordship said that the Duke desired the Light and 4th Divisions to storm again. 'The devil!' says I. 'Why, we have had enough; we are all knocked to pieces.' Lord Fitzroy says, 'I dare say, but you must try again.' I smiled and said, 'If we could not succeed with two whole fresh and unscathed Divisions, we are likely to make a poor show of it now. But we will try again with all our might.' Scarcely had this conversation occurred when a bugle sounded within the breach, indicating what had occurred at the citadel and Puerto de Olivença; and here ended all the fighting. Our fellows would have gone at it again when collected and put into shape, but we were just as well pleased that our attempt had so attracted the attention of the enemy as greatly to facilitate that success which assured the prize contended for.

"There is no battle, day or night I would not willingly react except this. The murder of our gallant officers and soldiers is not to be believed. Next day I and Charlie Beckwith . . . went over the scene. It was *appalling*. Heaps on heaps of slain,—in one spot lay nine officers. Whilst we were there, Colonel Allen of the Guards came up and beckoned me to him. I saw that, in place of congratulating me, he looked very dull. 'What's the matter?' I said. 'Do you not know my brother in the Rifles was killed last night?' 'God help him and you! no, for I and we all loved him.' In a flood of tears, he looked round and pointed to a body. 'There he lies.' He had a pair of scissors with him. 'Go and cut off a lock of his hair for my mother. I came for the purpose, but I am not equal to doing it.' . . .

"Now comes a scene of horror I would willingly bury in oblivion. The atrocities committed by our soldiers on the poor innocent and defenceless inhabitants of the city, no words suffice to depict. Civilized man, when let loose and the bonds of morality relaxed, is a far greater beast than the savage, more refined in his cruelty, more fiend-like in every act; and oh, too truly did our heretofore noble soldiers disgrace themselves, though the officers exerted themselves to the utmost to repress it, many who had escaped the enemy being wounded in their merciful attempts! Yet this scene of debauchery, however cruel to many, to me has been the solace and the whole happiness of my life for thirty-three years. A poor defenceless maiden of thirteen years was thrown upon my generous nature through her sister, as described so ably in Johnny Kincaid's book, of which this is an extract—

" *I was conversing with a friend the day after, at the door of his tent, when he observed two ladies coming from the city, who made directly towards us; they seemed both young, and when they came near, the elder of the two threw back her mantilla to address us, showing a remarkably handsome figure, with fine features; but her sallow, sun-burnt, and care-worn, though still youthful, countenance showed that in her 'the time for tender thoughts and soft endearments had fled away and gone.' She at once addressed us in that confident heroic manner so characteristic of the high-bred Spanish maiden, told us who they were—the last of an ancient and honourable house—and referred to an officer high in rank in our army, who had been quartered there in the days of her prosperity, for the truth of her tale. Her husband, she said, was a Spanish officer in a distant part of the kingdom; he might, or he might not, still be living. But yesterday she and this, her young sister, were able to live in affluence and in a handsome house; to-day they knew not where to lay their heads, where to get a change of raiment or a morsel of bread. Her house, she said, was a wreck; and, to show the indignities to which they had been subjected, she pointed to where the blood was still trickling down their necks, caused by the wrenching of their ear-rings through the flesh by the hands of worse than savages who would not take the trouble to unclasp them! For herself, she said, she cared not; but for the agitated and almost unconscious maiden by her side, whom she had but lately received over from the hands of her conventual instructresses, she was in despair, and knew not what to do; and that, in the rapine and ruin which was at that moment desolating the city, she saw no security for her but the seemingly indelicate one she had adopted—of coming to the camp and throwing themselves upon the protection of any British officer who would afford it; and so great, she said, was her faith in our national character that she knew the appeal would not be made in vain, nor the confidence abused. Nor was it made in vain! Nor could it be abused, for she stood by the side of an angel! A being more transcendingly lovely I had never before seen—one more amiable I have never yet known.*

" *Fourteen summers had not yet passed over her youthful countenance, which was of a delicate freshness—more English than Spanish; her face, though not perhaps rigidly beautiful, was nevertheless so remarkably handsome, and so irresistibly attractive, surmounting a figure cast in nature's fairest mould, that to look at her was to love her; and I did love her, but I never told my love, and in the mean time another and a more impudent fellow stepped in and won her! But yet I was happy, for in him*

she found such a one as her loveliness and her misfortunes claimed—a man
*of honour, and a husband in every way worthy of her!"**

"I confess myself", commented Harry Smith, "to be the 'more
impudent fellow,' and if any reward is due to a soldier, never was
one so honoured and distinguished as I have been by the possession
of this dear child (for she was little more than a child at this
moment), one with a sense of honour no knight ever exceeded in
the most romantic days of chivalry, an understanding superior to
her years, a masculine mind with a force of character no consideration could turn from her own just sense of rectitude, and all
encased in a frame of nature's fairest and most delicate moulding,
the figure of an angel, with an eye of light and an expression which
then inspired me with a maddening love which, from that period
to this (now thirty-three years), has never abated under many and
the most trying circumstances . . . From that day to this she has
been my guardian angel. She has shared with me the dangers and
privations, the hardships and fatigues, of a restless life of war in
every quarter of the globe. No murmur has ever escaped her."†

That summer, as soon as there was forage for the horses and pack-
animals, the Army took the offensive and advanced into Spain,
"diving a little deeper into that land of romance than we had
yet done." Harry Smith and his bride went with it. "My wife," he
wrote,

"could not ride in the least at first. . . However, I had one of my
saddles turned into a side-saddle, . . . and at first made her ride a

* Kincaid, *Random Shots by A Rifleman*, 292-6. "Thrown upon each other's acquaintance
in a manner so interesting, it is not to be wondered at that she and I conceived a friendship
for each other, which has proved as lasting as our lives—a friendship which was cemented
by after-circumstances so singularly romantic that imagination may scarcely picture them!
The friendship of man is one thing—the friendship of woman another; and those only who
have been on the theatre of fierce warfare, and knowing that such a being was on the spot,
watching with earnest and increasing solicitude over his safety alike with those most dear
to her, can fully appreciate the additional value which it gives to one's existence. About a
year after we became acquainted, I remember that our Battalion was one day moving down
to battle, and had occasion to pass by the lone country-house in which she had been lodged.
The situation was so near to the outposts, and a battle certain, I concluded that she must
ere then have been removed to a place of greater security, and, big with the thought of
coming events, I scarcely even looked at it as we rolled along, but just as I had passed the
door, I found my hand suddenly grasped in hers. She gave it a gentle pressure, and, without
uttering a word had rushed back into the house again, almost before I could see to whom I
was indebted for a kindness so unexpected and gratifying."

† *Harry Smith, I*, 64-72.

great brute of a Portuguese horse I had. But she so rapidly improved, took such pains, had so much practice and naturally good nerves, that she soon got ashamed of her Portuguese horse and wanted to ride my Spanish little fellow, who had so nobly carried me at Redinha and in many other fights. I always said, 'When you can ride as well as you can dance and sing, you shall,' for in those accomplishments she was perfect. In crossing the Tormes [21 July], the very night before the battle of Salamanca (there are quicksands in the river), her Portuguese horse was so cowardly he alarmed me, and hardly had we crossed the river when a clap of thunder, louder than anything that can be described, burst over our heads. The Portuguese horse was in such a funk, she abjured *all Portuguese*, and insisted hereafter on riding her own gallant countryman, as gallant as any Arab . . . The next day she mounted her Tiny, and rode him ever afterwards over many an eventful field, until the end of the war at Toulouse. She had him afterwards at my father's house. The affection between them was of the character of that between spaniel and master. The dear, gallant horse lived to twenty-nine years of age, and died a happy pensioner on my brother Charles's estate.

"It is difficult to say who was the proudest on the morning of the battle [22 July], horse, wife, or Enrique, as I was always called. She caracoled him about among the soldiers, to their delight, for he was broken in like a Mameluke, though very difficult to ride. The soldiers of the whole Division loved her with enthusiasm from the events so peculiar in her history, and she would laugh and talk with all, which a soldier loves. Blackguards as many of the poor gallant fellows were, there was not a man who would not have laid down his life to defend her, and among the officers she was adored, and consulted on all occasions of baggage-guard, etc. Her attendant, who also had a led horse in case of accident, with a little tent and a funny little pair of lanterns, my dear, trusty old groom West, as the battle began, took her to the rear, much to her annoyance, and in the thunder of cannon, the pride of equestrianism was buried in anxiety for him on whom her all depended. She and West slept on the field of battle, he having made a bed for her with the green wheat he had cut just in full ear. She had to hold her horse all night, and he ate all her bed of green wheat, to her juvenile amusement; for a creature so gay and vivacious, with all her sound sense, the earth never produced."*

The weeks of triumph which followed the victory of Salamanca and the liberation by Wellington's troops of the Spanish capital did not last. By the autumn, faced by a concentration of the still greatly superior French forces in Spain, the British Army was forced to retreat again to the Portuguese frontier. As always, it was the Light Division which acted as rearguard. The Rifles, Harry Smith and his Juana with them, were among the last troops to leave.

> "This retreat was a very severe one as to weather, and although the enemy did not actually press us, as he did the column from Burgos, we made long marches and were very broad awake, and lost some of our baggage and stores, which the wearied bullocks obliged us to abandon . . . It rained in torrents, and the roads rose above the soldiers' ankles. Our supplies were nil, and the sufferings of the soldiers were considerable . . . We had nothing to eat that night, . . . and there was this young and delicate creature, in the month of November in the north of Spain, wet as a drowned rat, with nothing to eat and no cover from the falling deluge. Not a murmur escaped her but once. I had had no sleep for three nights, our rear being in a very ticklish position. In sitting by the fire I had fallen asleep, and fell between the fire and her. She had previously been roasted on one side, a cold mud on the other. This change of temperature awoke her, and for the only time in her life did she cry and say I might have avoided it. She had just woke out of her sleep, and when cold and shivery our feelings are acute. In a moment she exclaimed, 'How foolish! you must have been nice and warm, and to know that is enough for me.' "†

Though a third of the Army was on the sick-list after the retreat, the Rifles were little affected. It was an essential part of their system to fend for themselves, keep fit and subsist somehow under the most adverse conditions, even when, as rarely happened, Wellington's commissariat failed. "The soldiers," wrote Kincaid, "had become so inured to toil and danger that they seemed to have set disease, the elements and the enemy alike at defiance. Headaches and heartaches were unknown amongst them, and whether they slept under a roof, a tent or the open sky, or whether they amused themselves with a

* *Harry Smith, I,* 75-7.   † *Harry Smith, I,* 83-6.

refreshing bath in a stream or amused the enemy with a shot was all a matter of indifference."* Above all, they prided themselves, in Harry Smith's words, "upon destroying the enemy and preserving themselves." "Do you see those men on the plain," Major O'Hare barked to the latest batch of recruits from England as, surrounded by the tattered cheery veterans who were to be their comrades, they looked down from their rocky fastness on the frontier. " 'Es, zur." "Well then, those are the French and our enemies. You must learn to do as these old birds do and get cover where you can. Recollect, recruits, you come here to kill and not to be killed. Bear this in mind; if you don't kill the French, they'll kill you!"†

The great object of every "Johnny Newcome" when he joined his battle-scarred comrades in the field was to be worthy of them. "The 3rd Battalion Company behaved like Riflemen," wrote George Simmons after their first engagement, "and were complimented." He himself wrote of his own initiation, "Thank God, I have succeeded far above my expectation in everything; I mean I have established my name as a man worthy to rank with the veterans of my regiment and am esteemed and respected by every brother officer."‡ The Ninety-fifth was drawn from every part of the British Isles, from, to quote Kincaid—"the grave-looking but merry-hearted Englishman, the canny, cautious and calculating Scotchman, and the devil-may-care nonchalance of the Irish." But the system of the Regiment made them one. Kincaid mentions that in the summer of 1812, when after Salamanca the Army occupied Madrid, he brought up his battalion's numbers by recruiting Spanish peasants from the neighbouring villages, distributing them ten to each company. "Those we got," he wrote, "were a very inferior sample of the Spaniard and we therefore expected little from them, but to their credit . . . they turned out admirably well. They were orderly and well-behaved in quarters and thoroughly good in the field, and they never went into action that they had not their full portion of casualties."§

"This is the regiment to make the soldiers," George Simmons recorded proudly. "Some deserters that came from the enemy stated that the French did not like those *green fellows* at all; we made sad

---

* Kincaid, *Random Shots*, 226.   † *Costello*, 70.   ‡ *A British Rifleman*, 104.
    § Kincaid, *Random Shots*, 268-9. "There were fifty of them originally, and at the close of the war, I think there were about seventeen remaining; and there had not been a single desertion from among them."

havoc amongst them, particularly their officers. Numbers of our men are most capital shots. It would astonish you to see how coolly they go on and take the same aim as at a bird. I feel great pleasure to be with such fighting fellows and hardy soldiers. The men are so seasoned, that rain or any other kind of weather makes no impression ... We have been in want of tents for months together, sleeping on the ground without any other covering than the canopy of heaven. I never slept better." "Having been marching and fighting without tasting anything since two o'clock that morning," he wrote on another occasion, "I fried some ham upon the point of my sword, drank a good dose of *Johnny's* wine, and fell fast asleep upon the spot, forgetting even my blankets, and was lost to the cares of the world until daylight. The men standing to their arms awoke me, when I found myself wet through with the dew of the night. What strange vicissitudes of life the soldier meets with! Campaigning is the life for me. I have never felt such happiness since I became a soldier. I often think that to be living in England after this wild, romantic existence would not give me half so much satisfaction."*

"Equal to turn the tide of victory any day," and with such a firmly-founded confidence in themselves that they were at all times ready for anything and would, as one of them put it, have attempted to carry the moon had Wellington told them to do so, the Rifles were, with it all, the gayest fellows. "Ours," wrote Johnny Kincaid, "was an *esprit de corps*, a buoyancy of feeling animating all which nothing could quell. We were alike ready for the field or the frolic, and, when not engaged in the one, went headlong into the other ... In every interval between our active service, we indulged in all manner of childish trick and amusement with an avidity and delight of which it is impossible to convey an adequate idea. We lived united, as men always are who are daily staring death in the face on the same side and who, caring little about it, look upon each new day added to their lives as one more to rejoice in."

Coursing, fox-hunting, the chase of wolf and wild boar with a score of ragged, cheering riflemen acting as beaters, greyhound matches and boxing contests, football and donkey races with "every Jack sitting with his face to the tail and a smart fellow running in front with a bunch of carrots," were for this sporting corps the

---

* *A British Rifleman*, 108, 307.

characteristic prelude to the venture which in 1813 was to drive the French out of Spain. Straight across country and no flinching was the rule in their contests; a favourite sport was for two officers to wager that each would reach a distant church-tower by a given time, whereupon off they would go with the entire Mess at their heels, stopping for nothing on the way—swamp, wall or ravine. At night there were theatricals in barns or gay, unconventional balls with the local senoritas and village girls joining uproariously in bolero, fandango and waltz to an improvised band of flute and guitar, and a supper of roast chestnuts, cakes and lemonade to follow. If sometimes the more squeamish of the ladies left early, no one minded so long as the rest remained. "Charlie Gore gave a ball," Harry Smith recalled, "where there was as much happiness as if we were at Almack's, and some as handsome women, the loves of girls of Sanguessa." "I knew no happier times," wrote Kincaid, "and they were their own reward."

It was a long road that the gay, good-humoured Riflemen and their comrades of the 43rd and 52nd had travelled since they marched behind their band of thirty bugle-horns to take boat at Dover in 1809. Their jackets were patched and faded, their trousers indiscriminately black, blue and grey, and even parti-coloured, their shakos dented, for Wellington did not mind what his men looked like so long as they were well-appointed for battle and carried their sixty rounds of ammunition. But the silver-mounted bugle-horns still sounded their merry invocation of "Over the Hills and Far Away", and, for all their rags and tanned, weather-beaten faces, "the grace and intrepidity and lightness of step and flippancy of a young colonel with a rill of grasshoppers at his heels in their green coats" had lost none of its power to bring "the dear little dark creatures with their sweeping eyebrows," running with fluttering handkerchiefs and clapping hands to the windows and roadside.

*   *   *

"The morrow promised to be a bloody one, but we cared not for the morrow, . . . the song and the jest went merrily round." In the early summer of 1813 the Rifles led the Army in the great march which carried it, 80,000 strong, in six weeks from northern Portugal to the Douro, culminating in the rout of King Joseph's forces at Vittoria and the expulsion of the French from Spain. Harry Smith, as always, was in the thick of the fight.

"At the Battle of Vittoria (21 June) my Brigade, in the middle of the action, was sent to support the 7th Division, which was very hotly engaged. I was sent forward to report myself to Lord Dalhousie, who commanded. I found his lordship and his Q.M.G., Drake, an old Rifle comrade, in deep conversation. I reported pretty quick, and asked for orders (the head of my Brigade was just getting under fire). I repeated the question, 'What orders, my Lord?' Drake became somewhat animated, and I heard His Lord-ship say, 'Better to take the village,' which the French held with twelve guns . . . and seemed to be inclined to keep it. I roared out, 'Certainly, my Lord,' and off I galloped, both calling to me to come back, but, as none are so deaf as those who won't hear, I told General Vandeleur we were immediately to take the village. There was no time to lose, and the 52nd Regiment deployed into line as if at Shorncliffe, while our Riflemen were sent out in every direc-tion, five or six deep, keeping up a fire nothing could resist. I galloped to the officer commanding a Battalion in the 7th Division . . . 'Lord Dalhousie desires you closely to follow this Brigade of the Light Division.' 'Who are you, sir?' 'Never mind that; disobey my Lord's order at your peril.' My Brigade, the 52nd in line and the swarms of Riflemen, rushed at the village, and although the ground was intersected in its front by gardens and ditches, nothing ever checked us until we reached the rear of the village, where we halted to reform—the twelve guns, tumbrils, horses, etc., standing in our possession. There never was a more impetuous onset— nothing could withstand such a burst of determination. Before we were ready to pursue the enemy—for we Light Division ever reformed and got into order before a second attack, thanks to poor General Bob Craufurd's most excellent tuition—up came Lord Dalhousie with his Q.M.G., Drake, to old Vandeleur, exclaiming, 'Most brilliantly achieved indeed! Where is the officer you sent to me for orders?' 'Here I am, my lord.' . . . 'Upon my word, sir, you receive and carry orders quicker than any officer I ever saw.' 'You said "Take the village." My lord, there it is,' I said, 'guns and all.' He smiled, and old Drake burst into one of his grins, 'Well done, Harry!'

"We were hotly engaged all the afternoon pursuing the French over very broad ditches. Until we neared Vittoria to our left, there was a plain free from ditches. The confusion of baggage, etc., was indescribable. Our Brigade was moving rapidly on, when such a swarm of French Cavalry rushed out from among the baggage into our skirmishers, opposite a Company of the 2nd Battalion Rifle Brigade, commanded by Lieutenant Tom Cochrane, we thought they must have been swept off. Fortunately for Tom, a little rough ground and a bank enabled him to command his Company to lie down, and such a reception they gave the horsemen, while some of our Company were flying to their support, that the French fled with a severe loss. Our Riflemen were beautiful shots, and as undaunted as bulldogs."*

Though one or more of the three battalions of the Regiment were engaged in every battle of the remaining nine months of the war—all of them victories—there were three occasions in which it particularly distinguished itself. The first centred round the heroism of a single Company and its commander who were needlessly sacrificed at the Bridge of Vera to the stupidity and obstinacy of a general temporarily in command of a Brigade of the Light Division. Harry Smith, who was his Brigade Major, tells the story.

"My new General, I soon discovered, was by nature a gallant Grenadier, (and no Light Troop officer, which requires the eye of a hawk and the power of anticipating the enemy's intention) and was always to be found off his horse, standing in the most exposed spot under the enemy's fire while our Riflemen were well concealed, as stupidly composed for himself as inactive for the welfare of his command. When the enemy put back our piquets in the morning, it was evidently their intention to possess themselves of the bridge . . .

". . . We did not occupy Vera, but withdrew on our own side of it, and I saw the enemy preparing to carry the houses near the bridge in the occupation of the 2nd Battalion Rifles. I said, 'General Skerrett, unless we send down the 52nd Regiment in support, the enemy will drive back the Riflemen. They cannot hold those houses against the numbers prepared to attack. Our men will fight like devils, expecting to be supported, and their loss, when driven out,

* *Harry Smith, I,* 97-9.
J.G.   F

will be very severe.' He laughed (we were standing under a heavy fire exposed) and said, 'Oh, is that your opinion?' I said—most impertinently, I admit,—'And it will be yours in five minutes,' for I was by no means prepared to see the faith in support, which so many fights had established, destroyed, and our gallant fellows knocked over by a stupidity heretofore not exemplified.

"We had scarcely time to discuss the matter when down came a thundering French column with swarms of sharpshooters, and, as I predicted, drove our people out of the houses with one fell swoop, while my General would move nothing on their flank or rear to aid them. We lost many men and some officers, and the enemy possessed the houses, and consequently, for the moment, ... the passage of the bridge. From its situation, however, it was impossible they could maintain it, unless they put us farther back by a renewed attack on our elevated position. So I said, 'You see now what you have permitted, General, and we must retake these houses, which we ought never to have lost.' He quietly said, 'I believe you are right.' I could stand this no longer, and I galloped up to Colonel Colborne, in command of that beautiful 52nd Regiment, ... who was as angry as he soon saw I was. 'Oh, sir, it is melancholy to see this. General Skerrett will do nothing; we must retake those houses. I told him what would happen.' 'I am glad of it, for I was angry with you.' In two seconds we retook the houses, for the enemy, seeing our determination to hold them, was aware the nature of the ground would not enable him to do so ...

"The evening came on very wet. We knew that the enemy had crossed the Bidassoa (31 Aug.), and that his retreat would be impossible from the swollen state of the river. We knew pretty well the Duke would shove him into the river if he could; this very bridge, therefore, was of the utmost importance, and no exertion should have been spared on our part so to occupy it after dark as to prevent the passage being seized. The rain was falling in torrents. I proposed that the whole of the 2nd Battalion Rifles should be posted in the houses, the bridge should be barricaded, and the 52nd Regiment should be close at hand in support. Skerrett positively laughed outright, ordered the whole Battalion into our position, but said, 'You may leave a piquet of one officer and thirty men at the bridge.' ... I had a little memorandum-book in my pocket; I took it out for the first time in my life to note my

General's orders. I read what he said, asking if that was his order. He said, 'Yes, I have already told you so.' I said most wickedly, 'We shall repent this before daylight.'. . .

"I galloped down to the houses, ordered the Battalion to retire, and told my brother Tom, the Adjutant, to call to me a piquet of an officer and thirty men for the bridge. Every officer and soldier thought I was mad. Tom said, 'Cadoux's Company is for piquet.' Up rode poor Cadoux, a noble soldier, who could scarcely believe what I said, but began to abuse me for not supporting them in the morning. I said, 'Scold away, all true; but no fault of mine. But come, no time for jaw, the piquet!' Cadoux, noble fellow, says, 'My company is so reduced this morning, I will stay with it if I may. There are about fifty men.' I gladly consented, for I had great faith in Cadoux's ability and watchfulness, and I told him he might rest assured he would be attacked an hour or two before daylight. He said, 'Most certainly I shall, and I will now strengthen myself, and block up the bridge as well as I can, and I will, if possible, hold the bridge until supported; so, when the attack commences, instantly send the whole Battalion to me, and, please God, I will keep the bridge.'

"It was then dark, and I rode as fast as I could to tell Colborne, in whom we had all complete faith and confidence. He was astonished, and read my memorandum. We agreed that, so soon as the attack commenced, his Battalion should move down the heights on the flank of the 2nd Battalion Rifles, which would rush to support Cadoux, and thus we parted, I as sulky as my hot nature would admit, knowing some disaster would befall . . .

"In the course of the night, as we were lying before the fire, I far from asleep, General Skerrett received a communication from General Alten to the purport 'that the enemy were retiring over the swollen river; it was, therefore, to be apprehended he would before daylight endeavour to possess himself of the bridge; that every precaution must be taken to prevent him.' I, now being reinforced in opinion, said, 'Now, General, let me do so.' As he was still as obstinate as ever, we were discussing the matter (I fear as far as I am concerned, very hotly) when the 'En avant, en avant! L'Empereur récompensera le premier qu'avancera,' was screeched into our very ears, and Cadoux's fire was hot as ever fifty men's was on earth . . . My only hope was that Cadoux could keep the bridge as he anticipated. The fire of the enemy was very severe, and the rushes of his columns most determined; still Cadoux's fire was from his post. Three successive times, with half his gallant band, did he charge and drive back the enemy over the bridge, the other half remaining in the houses as support. His hope and confidence in support and the importance of his position sustained him until a melancholy shot pierced his head, and he fell lifeless from his horse. A more gallant soul never left its mortal abode. His company at this critical moment were driven back; the French column and rear-guard crossed, and, by keeping near the bed of the river, succeeded in escaping. . .

"I was soon at the bridge. Such a scene of mortal strife from the fire of fifty men was never witnessed. The bridge was almost choked with the dead; the enemy's loss was enormous, and many of his men were drowned, and all his guns were left in the river a mile or two below the bridge . . . The Duke was awfully annoyed, as well he might be, but, as was his rule, never said anything when disaster could not be amended . . . Poor Cadoux! I really believe, had he survived, he would have held the bridge, . . . I wept over his gallant remains with a bursting heart, as, with his Company who adored him, I consigned to the grave the last external appearance of Daniel Cadoux. His fame can never die."*

The other two occasions enshrined in the permanent annals of the Regiment took place, the one in November 1813 when Wellington's army stormed the heights of the Nivelle on the French frontier and broke into the Gascony plain, the other at Tarbes on the road to Toulouse in the last month of the war. Harry Smith's is the best account of the former when the Light Division carried the heights of the Petite Rhune, breaking through the redoubts of Soult's fortified lines like a screen of reeds. "Nor did we ever meet a check," he wrote, "but carried the enemy's works . . . by one fell swoop of irresistible victory."† At Tarbes, on March 19th, 1814—a purely Rifle affair in which all three Battalions were engaged—an officer of another regiment described their astonishing prowess.

"Nothing could exceed the manner in which the 95th set about this business. Certainly I never saw such skirmishers. They could do the work much better and with infinitely less loss than any other

---

* *Harry Smith*, I, 118-25.　　† *Harry Smith*, I, 145-6.

of our best Light Troops. They possessed an individual boldness, a mutual understanding and a quickness of eye which I never saw equalled. They were as much superior to the French Voltigeurs as the latter were to our skirmishers in general. As our regiment was often employed in supporting them I think I am fairly qualified to speak of their merits."*

Three weeks later it was all over. "My old 1st Battalion," wrote Harry Smith, "had embarked at Dover just before Talavera, 1050 rank and file. During the war only 100 men joined us. We were now reduced to about 500. There was scarcely a man who had not been wounded. There was scarcely one whose knowledge of his duty as an outpost soldier was not brought to a state of perfection, and, when they were told they must not drink, a drunken man was a rare occurrence indeed, as rare as a sober one when we dared give a little latitude. My old Brigade was equal to turn the tide of victory any day."†

The final word on the Rifles's Peninsular epic comes from Johnny Kincaid. "At the close of the war, when we returned to England, if our battalion did not show symptoms of its being a well-shot corps, it is very odd . . . Beckwith with a cork leg—Pemberton and Manners with a shot each in the knee, making them as stiff as the other's tree one—Loftus Gray with a gash in the lip and minus a portion of one heel which made him march to the tune of dot and go one—Smith with a shot in the ankle—Eeles minus a thumb—Johnston, in addition to other shot-holes, a stiff elbow, which deprived him of the power of disturbing his friends as a scratcher of Scotch reels upon the violin—Percival with a shot through his lungs—Hope with a grapeshot lacerated leg—and George Simmons with his riddled body held together by a pair of stays, for his was no holiday waist, which naturally required such an appendage lest the burst of a sigh should snap it asunder, but one that appertained to a figure framed in nature's fittest mould to 'brave the battle and the breeze!' "‡

---

* *Twelve Years Military Adventures.*　　† *Harry Smith, I, 185.*
‡ Kincaid, *Random Shots*, 290-1.

Part II

"DOMINION OVER PALM AND PINE"
1815-1914

Chapter Three

THE FIGURE OF FAME

The true test of real excellence is not immediate success but durable fame.

SIR HARRY SMITH

AFTER Napoleon's abdication the 1st and 2nd Battalions of the Rifles returned to England, while the 3rd, after a brief stay at Plymouth, crossed the Atlantic on one of those vaguely conceived amphibious enterprises so dear to Britain's parliamentary statesmen —the capture of New Orleans as a means of forcing the Americans, with whom since 1812 she had been at war, to make peace. Four Companies of the Regiment—one from the 1st Battalion, one from the 2nd and two from the 3rd—remained for the present on the Continent as part of the garrison of Belgium which—once part of the Spanish and more recently of the Austrian Netherlands—had been incorporated since 1793 in Revolutionary and Napoleonic France. Now, little to the liking of its Catholic inhabitants, it had been allotted by the victorious peacemakers at Vienna to the new Kingdom of the Netherlands under the Protestant and Dutch royal House of Orange.

These four Companies of the 95th, under the command of Lt.-Col. Alexander Cameron—one of the founder officers of the Experimental Rifle Corps—had originally formed part of an expedition hastily despatched during the last winter of the war in an abortive attempt to capture Bergen-op-Zoom and Antwerp. Here they had greatly distinguished themselves under extremely adverse climatic conditions. An officer of another Regiment who was present described how well, at the battle of Merxem in February 1814, the young Riflemen behaved.* Under the walls of Bergen-op-Zoom he watched a trial of skill between a crack marksman of the 95th and a French

---

* General Sir Thomas Graham in his Despatches wrote that "Lieut.-Col. Cameron and all Officers and Men of the 95th Rifle Regiment greatly distinguished themselves and nobly supported the high character of that distinguished Corps . . . No veterans ever behaved better than these men who met the enemy for the first time." *R.B.C. 1926*, 243-8.

tirailleur, each firing at the other from behind a tree at a hundred yards' range. The Rifleman won by sticking a loaf of bread crowned by his cap on the point of his sword-bayonet, waiting for it to be hit and then plunging about on the ground as though he was mortally wounded, until his adversary—eager to plunder his corpse—emerged from his cover and was promptly shot dead by him.*

When, therefore, in the spring of 1815 Napoleon escaped from Elba, these four Rifle Companies were still in Belgium. Here, where a polyglot international army was hastily assembled under the Duke of Wellington, they were joined by five Companies of the 2nd Battalion and six of the 1st, the remaining five Companies of the 3rd Battalion being still on the far side of the Atlantic after the ill-planned expedition of which they were part had been bogged down by the defenders of New Orleans. Though, like every other unit of Wellington's army, brought up to strength by a strong infusion of new recruits, with their old Light Division comrades of John Colborne's 52nd they brought to the Waterloo campaign a higher proportion of experienced soldiers than any other Regiment.

When on June 15th Napoleon crossed the frontier and struck at the Prussians, the 1st Battalion, then quartered at Brussels, was the first to engage the French. Marching at dawn on the 16th at the head of Picton's Division it reached Quatre Bras, twenty miles to the south, in blistering heat, at three o'clock that afternoon. Here, under the command of Colonel Sir Andrew Barnard and the personal super-vision of the Duke himself, it at once went into action. By driving and holding back, until reinforcements arrived, vastly superior French forces who were attempting to cut off Wellington's army from its Prussian allies before turning on the latter, it played a vital part in preventing Ney's corps from falling on the flank of Blücher's army, which, a few miles to the east at Ligny, was engaged in a life and death struggle against Napoleon.

Two days later on the ridge at Waterloo, where, in order to remain in touch with the defeated and retreating Prussians, the British had withdrawn on the day after their victory at Quatre Bras, the 2nd Battalion under Lt.-Col. Norcott, together with two Companies of the 3rd, were posted on the extreme right of Wellington's defensive line as part of his tactical reserve. The 1st Battalion, which had suffered heavily at Quatre Bras, was stationed in the centre along a

* *Old Stickleg*, cit., *R.B.C. 1926*, 243-8.

sunken lane which crossed the main Charleroi-Brussels highway at
the top of the ridge the British-Netherlander Army had to defend.
Three of its Companies occupied a small knoll and sand-pit opposite
the farm of La Haye Sainte, a hundred yards down the slope up
which the French were expected to advance on Brussels. Shortly
before the battle, Wellington and his staff, visiting the outposts,
stopped there to refresh themselves from a camp-kettle of hot sweet
tea which Captain Kincaid, the Adjutant—like the good Rifleman he
was—had had brewed up to revive his men after the torrential down-
pour of the previous night. It was while they were bivouacked during
it in the cornfields of the Waterloo plain that that veteran officer of
the Battalion, Lieutenant George Simmons—"a universal favourite
with men and officers" for his inexhaustible good humour and
resource*—had greatly impressed a young greenhorn subaltern by
advising him to pick up a dirty discarded blanket which, daubed
with mud and clay, kept them both dry as they lay on the rain-soaked
ground, enabling them to sleep in peace and rise "fresh as larks and
dry as bones".

It was Captain Kincaid in his advanced post with his sharpshooters
in the La Haye Sainte gravel-pit, who left posterity the best account
of how the battle went in the centre.

"From the moment we took possession of the knoll, we had busied
ourselves in collecting branches of trees and other things for the
purpose of making an abatis to block up the road between that and
the farm-house . . . It was put to the proof sooner than we expected
by a troop of our own Light Dragoons, who, having occasion to
gallop through, astonished us not a little by clearing away every
stick of it. We had just time to replace the scattered branches when
the whole of the enemy's artillery opened, and their countless
columns began to advance under cover of it.

"The scene at that moment was grand and imposing. . . The

* From a letter in possession of Colonel Sir James Neville, Bt. M.C., printed in the *Rifle
Brigade Chronicle 1930*, 255-8. "If there were any eatables within the possibility of reach,
George Simmons was sure to come in for them . . . In Spain the Major was unanimously
voted caterer. He kept the best and most economical Mess in the Army and rarely failed in
his supply. He had a deer-skin sack . . . which held 120 bottles of wine with a regular lock
and key." At Quatre Bras this valiant and resourceful Yorkshireman, then still, as many
years later, a subaltern, had performed an action which in a later age would almost certainly have earned him a Victoria Cross, volunteering to recover a dangerously wounded
man lying within a few feet of the French lines.

column, destined as our particular friends, first attracted our notice, and seemed to consist of about ten thousand infantry. A smaller body of infantry and one of cavalry moved on their right; and, on their left, another huge column of infantry and a formidable body of cuirassiers, while beyond them it seemed one moving mass. We saw Bonaparte himself take post on the side of the road immediately in our front, surrounded by a numerous staff; and each regiment, as they passed him, rent the air with shouts of 'Vive l'Empereur!' Nor did they cease after they had passed; but, backed by the thunder of their artillery and carrying with them the rub-a-dub of drums and the tantarara of trumpets in addition to their increasing shouts, it looked at first as if they had some hopes of scaring us off the ground. It was a singular contrast to the stern silence reigning on our side, where nothing, as yet, but the voices of our great guns told that we had mouths to open when we chose to use them. Our rifles were, however, in a very few seconds required to play their parts and opened such a fire on the advancing skirmishers as quickly brought them to a standstill. But their columns advanced steadily through them, although our incessant tiraillade was telling in their centre with fearful exactness, and our post was quickly turned in both flanks, which compelled us to fall back and join our comrades behind the hedge, though not before some of our officers and theirs had been engaged in personal combat.

" When the heads of their columns showed over the knoll which we had just quitted they received such a fire from our first line that they wavered and hung behind it a little. But, cheered and encouraged by the gallantry of their officers, who were dancing and flourishing their swords in front, they at last boldly advanced to the opposite side of our hedge and began to deploy. Our first line, in the meantime, was getting so thinned that Picton found it necessary to bring up his second, but fell in the act of doing it. The command of the division at that critical moment devolved upon Sir James Kempt, who was galloping along the line, animating the men to steadiness. He called to me by name, where I happened to be standing on the right of our battalion, and desired 'that I would never quit that spot.' I told him that he might depend upon it: and in another instant I found myself in a fair way of keeping my promise more religiously than I intended. For, glancing my eye to the right, I saw the next field covered with the cuirassiers, some of whom were making directly for the gap in the hedge where I was standing. I had not hitherto drawn my sword, as it was generally to be had at a moment's warning; but, from its having been exposed to the last night's rain, it had now got rusted in the scabbard and refused to come forth! I was in a precious scrape! . . . I confess that I felt considerable doubts as to the propriety of standing there to be sacrificed without the means of making a scramble for it. My mind, however, was happily relieved from such an embarrassing consideration before my decision was required. For the next moment the cuirassiers were charged by our Household Brigade; and the infantry in our front giving way at the same time under our terrific shower of musketry, the flying cuirassiers tumbled in among the routed infantry, followed by the Life Guards, who were cutting away in all directions. Hundreds of the infantry threw themselves down and pretended to be dead, while the cavalry galloped over them, and then got up and ran away. I never saw such a scene in all my life.

"Lord Wellington had given orders that the troops were, on no account, to leave the position to follow up any temporary advantage. So we now resumed our post, as we stood at the commencement of the battle, and with three Companies again advanced on the knoll. . . Our division got considerably reduced in numbers during the last attack; but Lord Wellington's fostering hand sent Sir John Lambert to our support with the Sixth Division; and we now stood prepared for another and a more desperate struggle.

"Our Battalion had already lost three officers killed, and six or seven wounded; among the latter were Sir Andrew Barnard and Colonel Cameron. Someone asking me what had become of my horse's ear was the first intimation I had of his being wounded; and I now found that, independent of one ear having been shaved close to his head, (I suppose by a cannon shot,) a musket ball had grazed across his forehead, and another gone through one of his legs; but he did not seem much the worse for either of them.

"Between two or three o'clock we were tolerably quiet, except from a thundering cannonade; and the enemy had, by that time, got the range of our position so accurately that every shot brought a ticket for somebody's head. An occasional gun, beyond the plain, far to our left, marked the approach of the Prussians; but their progress was too slow to afford a hope of their arriving in time to take any share in the battle. On our right, the roar of cannon and musketry had been incessant from the time of its commencement; but the higher ground near us prevented our seeing anything of what was going on.

"Between three and four o'clock the storm gathered again in our front. Our three Companies on the knoll were soon involved in a furious fire. The Germans occupying La Haye Sainte expended all their ammunition and fled from the post. The French took possession of it; and, as it flanked our knoll, we were obliged to abandon it also, and fall back again behind the hedge. The loss of La Haye Sainte was of the most serious consequence, as it afforded the enemy an establishment within our position. They immediately brought up two guns on our side of it and began serving out some grape to us. But they were so very near that we destroyed their artillerymen before they could give us a second round.

"The silencing of these guns was succeeded by a very extraordinary scene . . . A strong regiment of Hanoverians advanced in line to charge the enemy out of La Haye Sainte. But they were themselves charged by a Brigade of Cuirassiers, and, excepting one officer on a little black horse who went off to the rear like a shot out of a shovel, I do believe that every man of them was put to death in about five seconds. A Brigade of British Light Dragoons advanced to their relief, and a few on each side began exchanging thrusts. It seemed likely to be a drawn battle between them, without much harm being done, when our men brought it to a crisis sooner than either side anticipated. For they previously had their rifles eagerly pointed at the cuirassiers, with a view of saving the perishing Hanoverians; but the fear of killing their friends withheld them until the others were utterly overwhelmed, when they instantly opened a terrific fire on the whole concern, sending both sides to flight. So that on the small space of ground, within a hundred yards of us, where five thousand men had been fighting the instant before, there was not now a living soul to be seen . . .

"The same field continued to be a wild one the whole of the afternoon. It was a sort of duelling-post between the two armies, every half hour showing a meeting of some kind upon it . . . For the two or three succeeding hours there was no variety with us, but one continued blaze of musketry. The smoke hung so thick about that, although not more than eighty yards asunder, we could only distinguish each other by the flashes of the pieces . . . A good many of our guns had been disabled, and a great many more rendered un-

serviceable in consequence of the unprecedented close fighting; for
. . . where they had been posted but a very few yards in front of the
line, it was impossible to work them.

"I shall never forget the scene which the field of battle presented
about seven in the evening. I felt weary and worn out, less from
fatigue than anxiety. Our Division, which had stood upwards of
five thousand men at the commencement of the battle, had
gradually dwindled down into a solitary line of skirmishers. The
Twenty-Seventh Regiment were lying literally dead, in square, a
few yards behind us. My horse had received another shot through
the leg, and one through the flap of the saddle, which lodged in his
body, sending him a step beyond the pension list. The smoke still
hung so thick about us that we could see nothing. I walked a little
way to each flank to endeavour to get a glimpse of what was going
on. But nothing met my eye except the mangled remains of men
and horses, and I was obliged to return to my post as wise as I
went.

"I had never yet heard of a battle in which everybody was
killed; but this seemed likely to be an exception, as all were going
by turns. We . . . burned with desire to have a last thrust at our . . .
vis-à-vis; for, however, desperate our affairs were, we had still the
satisfaction of seeing that theirs were worse. Sir John Lambert
continued to stand as our support at the head of three good old
Regiments, one dead (the Twenty-Seventh) and two living ones;
and we took the liberty of soliciting him to aid our views. But the
Duke's orders on that head were so very particular that the gallant
general had no choice."*

It was a private Rifleman in one of the 1st Battalion's dwindling
squares on the shot-ridden ridge who saw the Duke emerge from the
smoke-charged air as he went calmly about his business of restoring
the morale of his all-but broken centre in the penultimate crisis of
the battle. Riding up to the square, which had lost all its officers, he
himself gave the command—characteristically using the correct
Rifleman's order—"95th, unfix your swords, left face and extend
yourselves once more; we shall soon have them over the hill!" Then,
the Rifleman recalled, "he rode away on our right, and how he
escaped being shot, God only knows, for all that time the shot was
flying like hailstones."†

* Kincaid, *Adventures in the Rifle Brigade* 341-52.   † Booth, *Waterloo II*, 275.

The battle was resolved by the action on the far right of the British line of the other Battalion of the Regiment—the 2nd, with the two skirmishing Companies of the 3rd—and its two companion veteran Regiments of Adam's Brigade, the 52nd and 71st Light Infantry, which Wellington had expressly kept in reserve for this moment. They had suffered heavy casualties during the prolonged French artillery bombardment, and when, an hour or two before the hour of final decision, the Duke moved them into the front line, according to Captain Joseph Logan of the 2nd Battalion they were

"cruelly mauled with shot and shell. About five minutes after we went into action I succeeded to the command of the Battalion in consequence of our three Field Officers being severely wounded. We were now attacked in square by Lancers and Cuirassiers supported by 18 guns which played onto our square at one hundred yards distance. We repelled this attack but suffered severely; one shot knocked down nine men. We were attacked again four different times, but my little Battalion maintained their ground . . . Soon after Napoleon advanced with his Imperial Guard and commenced a heavy attack. Lord Wellington rode up to me and ordered I should attack them immediately. I moved on with the 52nd and 71st Regiments on my right and such a carnage never beheld. The roaring of guns was so great that the man next to me could not hear my orders."*

It was Colonel Colborne of the 52nd on the right of Adam's Brigade—with the two skirmishing Companies of the 3rd Rifles protecting its own right from the French cavalry—who had first taken the initiative of moving out of the line and throwing his Regiment—closely followed by the 2nd Battalion of the Rifles and the 71st—against the flank of the Imperial Guard. According to another account, "the attacking column of the Imperial Guard, having Maitland's Brigade of Guards in its front, were evidently staggered by finding Adam's Brigade on its flank. It halted and, wheeling up its left sections, began to fire. Colborne also halted the 52nd and fired into the column and the 2nd Battalion 95th, coming up at that instant on the left, poured a deadly fire into the Guard. Then Colborne checked the fire and calling out 'Charge! Charge!', led his men against the column. The 2nd Battalion joined vigorously in this

* *R.B.C. 1950*, 178-9.

charge which . . . was remarkable for the order, the steadiness, the resoluteness and the daring by which it was characterised. The Imperial Guard wavered, reeled and then, breaking up, fled in inextricable confusion . . . The Brigade, continuing its triumphal march across the field and bringing its left shoulder, the 2nd Battalion, rather forward, halted near the Charleroi road with the left of the 2nd Battalion close to the orchard of La Haye Sainte."* According to Captain Logan, Wellington himself rode beside the Riflemen, several times calling out, "Move on, my brave fellows!" as they and their Light Infantry comrades advanced eastwards across the battlefield, rolling up the discomfited French.

"Presently," wrote Kincaid, still with the remnants of the 1st Battalion in the battered centre of the hard-pressed line,

"a cheer which we knew to be British commenced far to the right and made every one prick up his ears. It was Lord Wellington's long wished-for orders to advance. It gradually approached, growing louder as it grew near; we took it up by instinct, charged through the hedge down upon the old knoll, sending our adversaries flying at the point of the bayonet. Lord Wellington galloped up to us at the instant and our men began to cheer him. But he called out, 'No cheering, my lads, but forward, and complete your victory!'

"This movement had carried us clear of the smoke, and to people who had been for so many hours enveloped in darkness, in the midst of destruction and naturally anxious about the result of the day, the scene which now met the eye conveyed a feeling of more exquisite gratification than can be conceived. It was a fine summer's evening, just before sunset. The French were flying in one confused mass. British lines were seen in close pursuit and in admirable order, as far as the eye could reach to the right, while the plain to the left was filled with Prussians. The enemy made one last attempt at a stand on the rising ground to our right of La Belle Alliance. But a charge from General Adam's Brigade again threw them into a state of confusion, which was now inextricable, and their ruin was complete. Artillery, baggage and everything belonging to them fell into our hands. After pursuing them until dark we halted about two miles beyond the field of battle, leaving the Prussians to follow up the victory.

*Cope, 206.

"This was the last, the greatest, and the most uncomfortable heap of glory that I ever had a hand in."*

By the time the victory was won, close on a third of the Green Jackets who had stood to arms on the fateful morning of June 18th 1815, had been killed or wounded. So outstanding had been their services that when, three weeks later, the British entered Paris, it was, on Wellington's orders, the 2nd Battalion, led by its adjutant, Thomas Smith—one of Harry Smith's two Riflemen brothers,—which headed the march into the French capital. On the Duke's recommendation the Regiment was also granted the right to bear the word "Waterloo" on its appointments, and, in February 1816, the London Gazette announced that the Prince Regent had been pleased to direct that the three Battalions of the 95th should henceforward be styled the Rifle Brigade and be promoted out of the numbered Line— an honour never before conferred on any Regiment. When four years later its Colonel-in-Chief, General Sir David Dundas, died, it was the Duke of Wellington who succeeded him, remaining Colonel-in-Chief of the Regiment until his death 32 years later. It was on his recommendation that, in recognition of its distinguished services under his command, it was granted as Battle Honours, in addition to Waterloo, the victories of Roliça and Vimiero, Busaco, Barrosa, Fuentes d'Honor, Ciudad Rodrigo, Badajoz, Salamanca, Vittoria, Nivelle, Nive, Orthes and Toulouse. To these were added, though won under other commanders, Copenhagen, Monte Video and Corunna. As a Rifle Regiment carried no Colours, they were borne on a silver badge on the Officers' pouch-belt and on the head-dress of Other Ranks, consisting of the Cross of the Order of the Bath—an honour awarded to each of the Regiment's three Battalion Commanders after Water-loo—encircled by a laurel wreath above the inscription "Waterloo" and surmounted by a winged figure of Victory, known, until it was replaced in 1821 by a Crown, as the "Figure of Fame".

*   *   *

While at the end of 1815 the 3rd Battalion was posted to the regimental depot at Shorncliffe, and, in the following year, to Ireland, the 1st and 2nd Battalions remained in France as part of the Army of Occupation until the autumn of 1818. Then, with the

* Kincaid, *Adventures in the Rifle Brigade*, 353-4.

return to a peacetime economy, the sad business of demobilisation began, the 3rd Battalion being disbanded in January 1819 and the other two, reduced in size, being relegated to garrison duty at home. Even that battle-scarred veteran of thirty-one, Harry Smith, after seven years on the Staff as Brigade Major with the rank, since Waterloo, of a Brevet Lt.-Colonel, reverted on his Battalion's return to England to the regimental rank of captain. "I was given," he wrote, "an entirely new Company, that is one composed of recruits. I interceded with Colonel Norcott, however, to give me a few of my dear old comrades into each squad, and, with their help and example, I soon inspired the rest with the feelings of soldiers."

Among those whom he inspired and taught was a young subaltern named Henry Havelock, who forty years later was to relieve Lucknow and become one of the heroes of Victorian England. The latter loved to recall how in his youth, his captain, Harry Smith, was one of the few who ever took the trouble to teach him anything, encouraging him to study military history and the art of war, and how, while everyone else made him feel that soldiering consisted mainly in blackening and whitening belts with patent varnish and pipe-clay, his captain pointed his mind to "the nobler parts" of his "glorious profession".*

"My battalion," Harry Smith wrote of that first Christmas in England,

"was ordered to Gosport, and soon after at Shorncliffe, which had been the depot of the Regiment during the whole war, not a Rifleman was left. I marched . . . , in command of the Headquarters Division, all our old soldiers. Neither they nor I could help remarking the country as a difficult one to make war in. You would hear the men, 'I say, Bill, look at that wood on the hill there and those hedgerows before it. I think we could keep that ourselves against half Soult's Army. Ah, I had rather keep it than attack it! But, Lord, the war's all over now! . . .' During this march, when the men were billeted in the inns and scattered over the country, I could not divest myself of the feeling of insecurity I had acquired after so many years' precautionary habits; and although I repeated to myself a hundred times daily, 'You are in England,' the thought would arise, 'You are in the power of your enemy.' Before dismiss-

* D.N.B.; Marsham, *Memoirs of Sir Henry Havelock* (1867), 66, 165.

ing the men I always told them the hour I should march in the morning, and men who were billeted either ahead or on the sides of the road were to join their Companies as I arrived. During the whole march I never had a man absent or irregular. Such a band of practised and educated soldiers may never again traverse England . . .

"While we were here" (at Gosport) "300 of our oldest and best soldiers were discharged. Every one came to say farewell to my wife; and there was a touching parting between officers and soldiers, now about to be dispersed through Great Britain after so many years association under such eventful circumstances. There was not one who could not relate some act of mutual kindness and reciprocity of feeling in connection with the many memorable events in which they had taken part. I and many of the officers marched several miles on the road with these noble fellows. In the Barrack Square they had prayed me to give them the word of command to march off. 'Sure,' says an Irishman, 'it's the last after the thousand your honour has given us.' I did so; but when the moment arrived to part every man's tears were chasing each other down his bronzed and veteran cheeks. They grasped their officers' hands,—'God bless your honour!' then such a shout and cheer. Such feelings in time of peace are not, cannot be, acquired. My faithful old West was of the party; but he parted from me and his mistress in our house. Poor faithful noble fellow, as gallant as a lion, he had been with me from Vimiero and Corunna until 1819."*

Those who remained with the Regiment did not forget the comradeship forged in the furnace of war. "The 18th of June," wrote Harry Smith of Waterloo Day 1819, " was such a day throughout the Regiment with dinners for the soldiers, non-commissioned officers, wives and children. Among the officers there was such a jubilee of mirth, mingled with grief for our lost comrades, as must be conceived, for never was there a Regiment in which harmony and unanimity were more perfect." At the earliest regimental dinner, held in the autumn of 1813 in the Pyrenees, with the officers sitting with their legs in a trench dug round a table of greensward, such had been the storm of cheering which followed every toast that the alarmed French stood to arms.† A second dinner to celebrate the

* *Harry Smith, I,* 319-22.   † *Cope,* 147.

Regiment's birthday had been held at St. Germain-en-Laye on August 25th 1815 when all three Battalions were still quartered around Paris. But though regimental dinners did not become regular annual events until the 'seventies, more informal gatherings of old Peninsula comrades often took place. "Nearly fifty of the gallant fellows whom I had the honour once to have under my command," wrote Sir Andrew Barnard to his wife on August 24th 1821, "gave me a dinner on Wednesday last. Few circumstances could afford me so great a gratification as such a mark of esteem and affection and friendship from men whom I regarded as companions as much as I admired them as soldiers and with whom I had passed . . . the happiest and most interesting moments of my career in this world."*

It was not only between officers, but between officers and men that this spirit of comradeship found expression. When in 1826 Harry Smith was appointed to the Staff in Jamaica, his Company came in a body to ask him to allow them to give him a dinner. " 'We don't expect your honour to sit down with us,' they said, 'but we will have a dinner and you will drink with us a parting glass.' I readily consented . . . Old Johnny Kincaid, who succeeded me as Captain, and my subalterns were present, and the parting glass was drunk with that mutual feeling of strong affection which exists between officers and soldiers."†

Those relegated to civil life were less fortunate. The officers were placed on half-pay, which for a lieutenant or captain was a mere pittance. Among them was William Humbley, who had joined the Regiment in the spring of 1807, had fought at Kiöge, Roliça, Vimiero, Calcavellas, Corunna, Walcheren, Barrosa, Salamanca, Vittoria, the Bridge and Heights of Vera, the Bidassoa, Nivelle, Nive, Orthes, Tarbes, Toulouse, Quatre Bras and Waterloo, and had been five times severely wounded, the last time at Waterloo with a musket-ball in each shoulder, one of which stayed there to his dying day. Placed on half-pay when the 3rd Battalion was disbanded on Christmas Day 1818, he remained without employment for more than thirty-five years until 1854, at the age of 62, he was recalled to the Service on the outbreak of the Crimean War.

As for the rank and file, thrown out on a stony laissez-faire world,‡

---

* *Barnard Letters*, 298.   † *Harry Smith*, I, 341.
‡ In 1853 Rifleman Harris, then making shoes in George Street, Golden Square, London, was still without the pension of 6d a day he had been granted on being invalided out of the

how such treatment affected one discarded Rifleman—a man of dauntless spirit—is described in Edward Costello's book, *Adventures of A Soldier*. Sergeant Costello, who in later years became an officer in the British Volunteer Legion in the Carlist civil wars in Spain and died at the age of 84 as a Yeoman Warder of the Tower of London, while apprenticed as a lad to a Dublin cabinet maker was fired by ambition to be a soldier and joined the Rifles in the year after Trafalgar. He fought in almost every battle of the Peninsular War, volunteered for and took part in the Forlorn Hope at both Ciudad Rodrigo and Badajoz and was repeatedly wounded. Wounded again at Quatre Bras, where he lost the trigger finger of his right hand, while serving with the 1st Battalion in the Army of Occupation he secretly married, against the wishes of her well-to-do peasant parents, a French girl called Augustine, from whom he was forcibly parted when the Regiment returned to England in 1818. His book tells the story of what happened.

"Disembarking at Dover, our regiment marched to Shorncliffe Barracks, where we had not long been quartered when an order arrived from the Horse Guards for two sergeants and two corporals of each company of the Rifles to be discharged. Men who had been wounded were to be first, and old men next. I was accordingly, although only about thirty-one years of age, invalided by our doctor on account of my wounds, and immediately departed for Chatham to await an order from Chelsea to proceed to London to pass the Board. Here, to my astonishment, one day Augustine presented herself before me. Her appearance almost electrified me. 'Edouard—mon cher Edouard,' she exclaimed, 'je te suivrai partout.' I then learned that, having arrived at Shorncliffe Barracks, and inquired for me, Colonel Leach had kindly paid her passage by coach to Chatham, directing her where to find me. Here she gave birth to a child. Shortly afterwards I received orders to appear before the Chelsea Board, and we proceeded to London with others. On our arrival, our circumstances being very needy, we took a single room in Red Lion Street, Chelsea, where we resolved to live as sparingly as possible. I passed the Board, but soon found the pittance allowed me insufficient to maintain us,

Service with Walcheren Fever but had forfeited in 1815 through his inability to rejoin before Waterloo.

being only sixpence per day. I had yet hopes, however, that my case was not understood, and I therefore applied to my Colonel, Sir Andrew Barnard, and explained it to him. Sir Andrew instantly gave me a note (which I now hold in my possession)* for Sir David Dundas, the then Governor of Chelsea. Thus provided, and equipped in my uniform, I set out for Sir David's residence, and found him walking about the grounds in front of his house at Chelsea College. I handed my paper to him in person, and retired aside while he perused it. But Sir David† having scanned it without turning his head, tossing aside his pigtail with his forefinger, coolly handed the note over his shoulders to me, remarking at the same moment that he dared say the Lords Commissioners of Chelsea had given me what they thought I deserved. The old gentleman, I suppose, possessed too much of the Spartan blood to notice me more than he did; and like the two survivors of Thermopylae, he thought my return to England highly inglorious and unbefitting a soldier, since it had made me a sixpenny burthen on the country I had served.

"Day after day we struggled with our necessities, and I confess I saw nothing but starvation staring me in the face . . . My faithful Augustine deliberated with me in our misfortune with great patience, and we agreed that it would be most desirable for her to return to her uncle and endeavour to move the family of her father to a reconciliation with us both. Her infant, she thought, could not fail to excite commiseration; but how were we to defray the expenses of so long a journey? However, having received several wounds in the service, I was entitled to what is commonly termed 'blood money.' A certificate to that effect, and signed by my commanding officer and the adjutant of my regiment, I now had by me. This was to be presented to the parson of the parish in which I was resident one month after my discharge. The Honourable Dr. Wellesley, brother to the Duke of Wellington, being rector of

---

* "28 Berkeley Square, March 2nd, 1819. I strongly recommend to your notice, and to the attention of the Board of Chelsea, the bearer, Edward Costello, late sergeant in the first battalion Rifle Brigade, for an increase of pension for his gallant services, he having been discharged in consequence of wounds received in action."

† General Sir David Dundas—known to the Army as "Old Pivot" from his martinet's addiction to the drill-book—though appointed to the Colonelcy-in-Chief of the Regiment on Coote Manningham's death in 1809, had never been a Rifleman and stood for almost everything which the Regiment opposed.

Chelsea, I appealed to him, and he referred me to a Mr. Walsford, Secretary of the Patriotic Fund, No. 80, Cornhill. But this gentleman was even more Spartan than the Lords Commissioners, for after two or three struts up and down his office, he suddenly stopped, and staring me very stupidly in the face, said, 'Damn it, Sir! did you expect to fight with puddings or Norfolk dumplings? If men go to battle, what else can they expect but wounds! I am now busy, and cannot be troubled with you.' I returned to Chelsea —represented my situation to Mr. Wellesley, and through him, succeeded in obtaining a small sum—five pounds—for the wound at Waterloo, but none for the others which I received in the Peninsula. With this scanty supply we proceeded to Dover, thence to Calais, and from thence to St. Omer, where, taking leave of my beloved Augustine and her infant (for the last time), we parted . . .

" Without a farthing in my pocket, for I had given the last sou to her and was determined to forage my own way home the best way I could, I again set off for Calais, where I arrived in much distress. Here fortune was favourable to me. A brother mason kindly befriended me and gave me a free passage to Dover. Had it not been for this kind assistance, I know not how I should have crossed the Straits. At Dover nothing could exceed my wretchedness; I had struggled with difficulties in a foreign country, but I was now returned to my own as if I had been an outcast upon earth without a friend or farthing in the world . . . For a day and a night I walked the streets of Dover and scarcely tasted food."

Here Costello encountered by chance an old Peninsular comrade who advised him to lay his Chelsea discharge before the Military Commandant of Dover, Colonel Ford, and solicit from him sufficient means to carry him to London.

"This was to beg—a task contrary to my nature. I asked him what I was to say? how act? for I had been a soldier since I was sixteen years of age, and was unacquainted with the forms of civil life. He gave me such advice as occurred to him, accompanied me on the road, and showed me the house at which the Colonel resided . . .

" With an unwilling hand I rung the bell. The door was immediately opened. 'Is the Colonel at home?' said I. 'Do you wish to see him?' answered the footman, surveying my person. 'I do,' was my reply, 'tell him that a sergeant of the Rifles wishes to speak to

Arthur Wellesley, 1st Duke of Wellington—Briggs

The Morning of Waterloo—J. D. Aylward
The Duke of Wellington stops for a cup of tea with the 95th

Bugle Horn of 95th (Rifle) Regiment, 1804

him.' The servant then, stepping across the hall, went into the
room, and while the door was ajar, I heard the Colonel ask, 'Is he
in uniform or in coloured clothes?' 'In coloured clothes,' was the
answer. 'Tell him to come in.' I entered the room slowly, and
believe me, I went with more spirits on the Forlorn-hope at
Badajoz than I now did into the presence of this officer. He was
standing with his back to the fireplace. 'Well, friend,' said he,
'what do you want?' In a doubtful tone, I answered, 'I want to
know, Sir, if you will lend me a little money, to carry me to London, and I will pay you when I get my pension.' While thus de-
livering myself, which I did in a very confused manner, the
Colonel stooped, and staring me full in the face, as if he thought
me mad, with a stentorian voice, he exclaimed, 'God damn you,
Sir! who are you, what are you, what do you want?' The Colonel's
uncouth manner suddenly overwhelmed my already sinking heart;
but the whole spirit of the 'man' rebounding from the shock,
instantaneously brought me about again, for recovering myself,
in a firm, earnest, yet determined manner, I replied, 'Sir, I am a
man brought to the last pitch of distress, without friend or
money. If you will assist me, pray do so, but do not insult my
feelings.' Then laying my papers on the table, I added 'There,
Sir, are my papers; keep them until I refund the money. I am a
Sergeant of the Rifle Brigade, who has seen service.' Taking my
Chelsea discharge, and reading over attentively the wounds I had
received, he looked at me with altogether an altered expression,
and said, 'You must have been a gallant fellow, or you would not
have got so many scars in the service; which Battalion did you
belong to?' I told him the First. He then asked me what money I
wanted to take me to London. I answered it was only seventy-one
miles, and two shillings would be sufficient, as I could walk more
than thirty-five miles a day, I had no knapsack to carry, and a
shilling per day would do for me.

"There my feelings overpowered me, and he, seeing my emotion,
turned himself round to the fire-place, evidently affected; then,
facing me again, said, 'Tut, tut! a brave soldier should not mind a
little poverty;' for at this time I could not answer him. Then,
ringing the bell, the footman who was in attendance came into
the room, 'Tell the cook,' said he, 'to get a good dinner ready for a
gallant soldier.' Then, putting a chair towards me, in a friendly

manner he told me to sit down and began conversing familiarly. He asked a number of questions concerning the Peninsular war; but we were shortly interrupted by the servant, informing him dinner was ready. 'Go, now,' said he, 'and take some refreshment.' But, alas! my appetite was gone; I could have eaten a donkey before, but now I could not break bread. The servants, observing me so discomposed, went and informed the Colonel of it, when he came to me himself, tapping me on the shoulder, saying, 'Come, come, make a good dinner,' then, turning to the servant, ordered him to bring a bottle of wine. After my repast he again returned, accompanied by a lady, perhaps his wife or daughter, to whom he had probably been speaking of me and who may have felt curious to see the rough soldier who had gone through so memorable a campaign. He now slipped some twelve half-crowns into my hand, and desired me on no account to walk but to take coach to London; at the same time he presented me my papers. I thanked him, but requested he would keep them until I could return the money. 'No, no;' he replied, 'I make you a present of it.' He then, in a very kind manner said, 'Your old Colonel, Colonel Barnard, is made a General and a Knight. He is now Major-General Sir Andrew Barnard; and, if you wish it, I will write to him about you.' Again I thanked him and said, 'The Colonel is well acquainted with me.' I left the house with feelings of gratitude which I could not give utterance to; and never, although many years have passed, shall I forget the kindness of Colonel Ford.

"On my return to London I wrote to Augustine, but received no answer. I waited with anxiety, and then came the mournful intelligence of her death; most likely owing to her father, as he remained inexorable to the last. Poor Augustine! Peace be to thy memory!"*

*   *   *

For nearly forty years after Waterloo, except for troops serving in the East India Company's dominions, the British Army, and the Rifle Brigade with it, were strangers to war. The latter's two battalions were employed on peacetime and ceremonial garrison duties and were without experience of active service. For a short time after their return from France both were used in support

* Edward Costello, *Adventures of a Soldier*, 207-13.

of the civil arm, the 1st Battalion in the distressed manufacturing districts of Glasgow where peace had brought widespread unemployment and social unrest; and the 2nd in Ireland where disturbance was endemic and where at the end of 1820 the 1st Battalion joined it. Here it remained until 1825 when it was sent to Canada. Harry Smith, who was quick to make the best of any situation, described his Battalion's duty during what was known as "the radical war" in Glasgow—"a most melancholy dirty smoky city"—as being

"very laborious and irksome. We had neither enemy nor friends: a sort of *Bellum in Pace* which we old campaigners did not understand. But, although constantly insulted by the mob in the streets, either individually or in a body, our deportment was so mild that we soon gained rather the respect than otherwise of the misguided and half-starved weavers. They had many old soldiers amongst them and had organised themselves into sixteen Battalions. Many of these old soldiers I knew; one was a Rifleman—an old comrade who had lost his arm at New Orleans—and from him I ascertained their perfect organization . . . The regiments were formed by streets . . .

"One day my Company was sent out, . . . just before daylight, to arrest a party of delegates. We had magistrates etc. with us and succeeded in arresting every man. I saw a violent storm of mob assembling. I put the prisoners in the centre of my Company under the command of my subaltern, Henry Havelock, . . . a clever, sharp fellow . . . Brickbats, stones etc. were flying among us half as bad as grapeshot. The magistrates were horribly timid and frightened lest I should order the troops to fire."*

The ordered restraint shown by the Rifles was proof against every provocation. At the end of their thirteen months' service in the city they received the thanks of the Provost and magistrates for their "admirable discipline and propriety of conduct under very trying and harassing circumstances." When five years later the 2nd Battalion, after seven years in Ireland, sailed from Cork for Malta it, too, was congratulated by the civil authorities on "the gentlemanlike demeanour of the officers and steady, soldier-like conduct of the non-commissioned officers and privates."†

* *Harry Smith, I*, 325-7.
† *Cope*, 228. This was the more commendable in that during the troubles in south-

From 1825 until 1835 the Service Companies of the 1st Battalion were in Canada, mainly in Nova Scotia, and from 1826 to 1837 those of the 2nd Battalion in Malta and the Ionian Islands, the Depot Companies of both remaining in Ireland and England. Almost the most important piece of regimental history in those quiet years was the substitution in 1832 of double-breasted for single-breasted uniforms and of black horn-buttons for silver and white-metal ones. At the time of Queen Victoria's coronation in 1838 both Battalions were in England and lined Piccadilly in extended order from Apsley House to St. James's Place. Later that summer, after taking part in a review in Hyde Park, they were inspected by their Colonel-in-Chief, the Duke of Wellington, and his—and their—old adversary, Marshal Soult.

During the Chartist agitation in the Midlands and the riots in South Wales in the early 'forties, both Battalions were employed again in helping to preserve public order, the 1st in Birmingham, where it was once pelted with stones in the Bull-ring, and the 2nd in Newport, Swansea and Merthyr Tydfil. As before, both won golden opinions for what the Mayor of Newport called the "peaceable, orderly and soldierlike manner in which the men had conducted themselves". "For a considerable period," ran the *Address* of the Birmingham authorities *to the Officers, Non-commissioned Officers and Privates of Her Majesty's Rifle Brigade*, "during which we were indebted to you for aid and protection, we had frequent occasions to admire the order, courage and humanity which marked your performance of some of the most painful duties which it falls to the lot of a British soldier to fulfil. Nor can we forget that alike by officers and men these duties, often dangerous and always irksome, were discharged with uniform cheerfulness and alacrity."*

Then in 1841 the six Service Companies of the 1st Battalion were posted to Malta and, two years later, to Corfu and the Ionian Isles. In 1842 the 2nd Battalion, increased to twelve Companies, sailed for Canada, its six Service Companies serving during the next ten years at Halifax, Montreal, Toronto and Kingston and its Depot Companies at Quebec. But though those in the Regiment who had seen

---

western Ireland in 1822 a gang of brutal "patriots" calling themselves "Captain Rock's men" waylaid a party of soldiers' wives travelling in three jaunting cars and subjected them to mass rape as a deliberate affront to the Regiment, sending one poor woman permanently out of her wits. *Cope*, 223.

* *Cope*, 237-8, 240.

active service were by now growing very few, one of its members at least continued to add to his already considerable experience in the art of war. Harry Smith, who had been born in 1787 at Whittlesea the son of a horse-loving provincial surgeon, had risen in ten years during the War to the rank of Brevet Lt.-Colonel, serving with brilliant distinction in the Peninsula as Brigade Major, in the war against America as Assistant Adjutant-General and Military Secretary to the Commander-in-Chief. In the Waterloo campaign he had been Assistant Quartermaster-General to the 6th Division, and was made, at the age of 28, a Companion of the Bath. But with peace and the return of the Army to England, where promotion was governed almost entirely by purchase or slow seniority, he had to wait another ten years before his great military talents won him a regimental majority, and ten more before, in his fiftieth year, he became a full Colonel. Yet, unlike the ordinary officer without private means or aristocratic connections, he held through sheer ability a succession of staff appointments, and, in 1826, was appointed Second-in-Command and Deputy Quartermaster-General of the Forces in Jamaica and, two years later, at the Cape of Good Hope. Something of the quality of the man—his ardour, unconventionality and strong, shrewd sense—is shown in a letter which he wrote from the Cape to a former comrade in arms, Major Thomas Powell, who had been with him in the storm of Ciudad Rodrigo:

" *As all letters must be more or less egotistical, I must tell you something about myself. After a prity tolerable sojourn at Glasgow I joined my dear old Corps at Down Patrick where two troops were with me heavy heavy and could not shoot. I was told the Rifles wd not carry more than 200 yards correctly. So I swore and worked until I made the range of 200 yards as a matter of course and increased my range to real good shooting at 350 yards, after which I again called them Riflemen, went out to Halifax, had the command of the Bn. some time and knocked them about a bit on sham-fights etc. was then A.D.C. to Sir J. Knight, then D.Q.M.G. at Jamaica where I kicked the yellow fever in the A—— . . .*
" *As in Jamaica second In Command so I was appointed Commandant of Cape Castle, Senior Member of Council, D.Q.M.G., all which blushing honours I sustained on 19s. a day and forage in kind for three horses, so that my treasury is, like that of our dear country, tolerably empty. Never having been good at finance I know better what it is to receive a bill than*

the bearer does to have it paid. Curse my former folly, laugh, swear, ride, hunting and coursing six days in the week, go to Church on Sundays with my Garrison, am very uxurious, reputed a sharp officer by some, a d——d bore by others.

" I care not a twopence what anyone but my dear old friends think, and, having a beautiful turn-out of two superb Regiments in due season, I slap them about . . . totum humbug according to this new system, march into Bivouacks, Piquets, sham fights, at arm and escalades as nearly as possible like the old system, target practice with six-pounders and my garrison in manoeuvres to the great astonishment of modern pretty-spoken delicate humbugs and very much to my own gratification.

" This history of Ego brings me to the present day, the place is not bad, very healthy, the people slow but civil. We, my wife (no daughters) great cronies at Government House, have aided much to abolish a d——d old custom here of abusing your neighbour, and if ever I report anyone I tell him I intend to do so, which makes all fair and above board. So I go to bed, the evil of the day being sufficient thereof.

" Sigh for the past glorious days in wᶜʰ you and I were in our own opinions rosy, bless Bill Napier for his superb Military History but d—— him for his too gross occasional abuse and more particularly of the poor Spaniards. But Bill has immortalised himself his . . . . . . a masterpiece of military language and glaring truth, his death of Sir J. Moore elegant, pathetic and like what a soldier ought to expect. He carries you so through the thread of his history, he at once places you in every Bivouack, shows you every division and induces you to roar Hurra now forward my boys at it, the very chattering of the Musquets were around one. His dedication to dear old Chin* most classical, most soldier-like, most noble. God bless Bill Napier but I wish the fiery beast could ride in a curb . . .

" My dear dear old Colonel and Brigadier, Because how much I am indebted to dear old Sydney I cannot with my democratical heart use fine autocratical expressions, but that I love him with a greatful heart I will avow as I can utter Rifleman.

" O dear old Powell the heaviest day of my life was the farewell dinner the dear old Corps gave me and my old . . . God knows the pluck it cost me to stand up like a man and speak out, but I did so and sat down . . . the happy relief of a flood of tears and, amongst so many dear old com-rades, mine were not the only wet eyes.

* Wellington.

" We may have another campaigning army, but never such one as fought the battle of Toulouse. The pipe-clay sticks to the present age so infernally. However by shouting at them the real work of look, march and shoot in which is comprised every requisite of a soldier may be obtained, but not immediately. The cut of the coat will neither make a Vidette or a Piquet Officer, but sound the trump of war and let us try again.

" Now my dear old friend and gallant soldier, God bless and preserve you and believe you have not a stauncher friend than your old comrade.

HARRY SMITH."*

When at the end of 1834 savage Kaffir hordes crossed the Great Fish River, the eastern frontier of Cape Colony, and burst like a flood on the defenceless farming homesteads around Grahamstown, destroying everyone and everything in their path and carrying off a quarter of a million cattle and sheep, Harry Smith was ordered by the Governor to proceed immediately to Grahamstown to take command of the minute armed forces in the town and rally its panic-stricken inhabitants. Rather than delay by going by sea, he at once set off on horseback with a single African attendant to cover the 600 miles of rough, almost roadless mountain country between Cape Town and Grahamstown. In his autobiography he described his six days' ride—today one of the sagas of South African history.

"I started with a single Hottentot for a ride of 90 miles the first day (1 January 1835), the heat raging like a furnace. My orders, warrants, etc. were sewn in my jacket by my own dear wife . . . I was off before daylight with a tremendous ride before me, over mountains, etc., etc. About half-way I met the mail from Grahamstown . . . Not till I had opened the last bag did I find the packet of letters I wanted from the Commandant and the Civil Commissioner, Grahamstown. Their descriptions of disaster, murders, and devastations were awful; the Commandant talked of the troops being obliged to evacuate Grahamstown. I made comments on all these letters and resolved to reach Grahamstown in two days. The heat to-day and the exertion of opening the letter-bags were fatiguing. On my arrival at my stage I . . . sent on expresses all night to have the horses ready a day before they were ordered, being determined to reach Uitenhage the next night, . . . the fifth from Cape Town,—500 miles . . .

* R.B.C. 1927, 272-6.

"... Off again next morning for Grahamstown. If the previous day's work had been excessive, it was short of what I this day encountered from the wretched brutes of knocked-up horses laid for me. About half way I found the country in the wildest state of alarm, herds, flocks, families, etc., fleeing like the Israelites. Everything that moved near a bush was a Kaffir. I was forced to have an escort of burghers on tired horses, and oh, such a day's work, until I got within ten miles of Grahamstown! There I found awaiting me a neat clipping little hack of Colonel Somerset's . . . and an escort of six Cape Mounted Rifles. I shall never forget the luxury of getting on this little horse, a positive redemption from an abject state of misery and labour. In ten minutes I was perfectly revived, and in forty minutes was close to the barrier of Grahamstown, fresh enough to have fought a general action, after a ride of 600 miles in six days over mountains and execrable roads, on Dutch horses living in the fields without a grain of corn. I performed each day's work at the rate of fourteen miles an hour, and I had not the slightest scratch even on my skin . . .

"... On reaching the barricaded streets I had the greatest difficulty to ride in . . . Consternation was depicted on every countenance I met, on some despair, every man carrying a gun, some pistols and swords too. It would have been ludicrous in any other situation than mine, but people desponding would not have been prepossessed in my favour by my laughing at them, so I refrained, although much disposed to do so. I just took a look at the mode adopted to defend Grahamstown. There were all sorts of works, barricades, etc., some three deep, and, such was the consternation, an alarm, in the dark especially, would have set one half of the people shooting the other. I at once observed that this defensive system would never restore the lost confidence, and I resolved, after I had received reports and assumed the command, to proclaim martial law. . .

"I rode to Somerset's, where I was treated *en prince*. I sent for the Civil Commissioner, Captain Campbell, and from him learned the exact state of the country—that despondency did exist to a fearful extent, originating from the sight of the horrors perpetrated by the remorseless enemy, but any vigorous steps and arbitrary authority boldly exerted would still ensure a rallying-point for all. I said, 'Very well; I clearly see my way. At as early an hour as possible to-morrow morning I shall declare martial law, and woe betide the man who is not as obedient as a soldier. Be so good as to prepare the necessary document and copies to be printed for my signature. I will be with you soon after daylight in your office, where I shall take up my abode.' I was there according to my appointment, and found everything ready upon this and every other occasion when I required the services of this able public officer . . .

"I received a report that a body of 200 burghers of the Graaf Reinet district, under their Civil Commissioner Ryneveld, was approaching. I knew the front of the 72nd Regiment in wagons would reach me in a day or two. I resolved, therefore, as soon as possible to make an inroad into the heart of the enemy's country in one direction, reoccupy Fort Willshire, and thence march to rescue the missionaries who were assembled in one house, 'Lonsdale,' in Kaffirland, and whose safety could not be calculated on for one moment. I then directed the population of Grahamstown, so soon as martial law was proclaimed, to be formed into a Corps of Volunteers, and I would issue them arms. The church in the square in Grahamstown being occupied as a military post and a council chamber, I desired the principal gentlemen to assemble, to name their own officers, etc., and to submit them for my approval, and told them that they and the organization of the corps should be instantly gazetted.

"This was in progress, when there were so many speakers and so few actors, the Civil Commissioner recommended me to go to the meeting. I deemed this a good opportunity to display my authority, which I was resolved on doing most arbitrarily on such a momentous occasion. When I went in, there was a considerable assembly of very respectable-looking men. I asked what was the cause of delay in executing my demands? One gentleman, a leader in what was called the Committee of Safety, which I very soon complimentarily dissolved, stood up and began to enter into argument and discussion. I exclaimed in a voice of thunder, 'I am not sent here to argue, but to command. You are now under martial law, and the first gentleman, I care not who he may be, who does not promptly and implicitly obey my command, he shall not even dare to give an opinion; I will try him by a court martial and punish him in five minutes.'

"This sally most completely established my authority, and I never met with any opposition afterwards; on the contrary, a desire on the part of all to meet my wishes. The corps were formed, officers gazetted . . . My attention was next turned to the defence of Grahamstown. I found that the officer in command of the 75th Regiment had taken great care of the barracks, distant half a mile or more, but that he was averse to detaching troops to the defence of Grahamstown. This I soon settled, opened all the barricades, established fresh alarm posts and at once showed the alarmed inhabitants that defence should consist in military resources and military vigilance, and not in being cooped up behind doors, windows and barricades three deep, from which they would shoot each other. That evening, the first after I assumed the command, the aspect of affairs had changed. Men moved like men and felt that their safety consisted in energetic obedience."*

Harry Smith's arrival made as electric an impact on the war as on the panic-stricken inhabitants of Grahamstown. Though the force at his disposal consisted only of 700 regulars and 850 volunteers—a mere fraction of the savage hordes around him and little better armed than they—he at once took the offensive. Sending the Boer burghers to guard his communications with the sea at Algoa Bay, he despatched a flying column of 300 men under a former Rifleman, Major William Cox—whom he described as "a soldier by experience, nature and courage"—to attack the kraal of the nearest Kaffir chief. This bold move across the frontier had exactly the effect he intended; "from that moment," he wrote, "all the invading Kaffirs rapidly withdrew from the Colony." He followed it up by ordering Cox to continue into the heart of Kaffir-land to rescue the seven beleaguered missionaries who were expecting every moment to have their throats cut.†

Then, with units of the 72nd Regiment arriving by sea from Cape Town, he set out with 3000 men to clear the country between the great Fish and the Keiskamma rivers. Before doing so he raised two corps of Hottentots to reinforce his 1100 Britons and Boers, "consisting," he wrote, "of every loose vagabond I could lay hand on,

* *Harry Smith*, *II*, 12-20.

† "This rescue of the missionaries was the best thing I ever did during the war, but one which these holy gentlemen and their Societies never acknowledged as they ought, though always ready to *censure*." *Harry Smith*, *II*, 22.

called the 1st and 2nd Battalion Hottentot Infantry . . . It is scarcely
to be credited how rapidly these men trained as soldiers . . . Their
presence in the army greatly dismayed the Kaffirs who never believed
they would fight against them." Marching 218 miles in seven days
over a rugged and mountainous country intersected by deep rivers
at the bottom of precipitous ravines, Smith defeated the enemy in two
sharp engagements, recaptured 4000 plundered cattle and brought
back to safety with them more than a thousand members of the
friendly Fingo tribe who would otherwise have been massacred.
Later, not receiving any response to his pacific overtures, he invaded
the territory of an aggressive Kaffir chieftain, Hintza, and compelled
him to release thousands of cattle plundered from the colonists.
When Hintza, who surrendered himself as a hostage, tried to escape,
Smith pursued him and, evading his assegai, rode him down single-
handed, forcing him to take refuge in the bush where he was subsequently shot. At one moment on the return march, he and his little
rearguard were surrounded by a vast multitude of warriors. "In all
my previous service," he recalled in his autobiography, "I was never
placed in a position requiring more cool determination and skill,
and, as one viewed the handful of my people compared with the
thousands of brawny savages all round us, screeching their war-cry,
calling to their cattle and indicating by gesticulations the pleasure
they would have in cutting our throats, the scene was animating to
a degree."*

It was characteristic of this remarkable Rifleman that, having
expelled the invaders and halted the tide of massacre and arson, he
should have tried to convert them to civilisation and peaceful habits.
"I told them," he wrote, "that they should soon see the difference in
me between a friend and an enemy; that, as I had waged vigorous
war on them, so would I teach them by every kindness to become men
and shake off their barbarism." Appointed to administer the country
between the great Fish and Kei rivers, which had been taken over by
a Commission to give better future security to the colony, in his own
words he "joyfully and enthusiastically entered upon the task of
rescuing from barbarism thousands of our fellow creatures endowed
by nature with excellent understanding and powers of reasoning as
regards the *present*," though "there was only one man of them—
Umhala, the chief of the T'slambie tribe—who had an idea of the

* *Harry Smith, II,* 57.

result of measures or futurity.* I saw that innovations must be introduced as to render them agreeable, not obnoxious, and that anything acquired by conciliatory and palatable means was an important point gained . . . I had upwards of 100,000 barbarians to reclaim who had no knowledge of right or wrong beyond arbitrary power, desire and self-will. To attach the people to the new order of things was of vast importance; to lessen the power of the chiefs equally so; but this had to be gradual, for if I removed the hereditary restraint of the chiefs I should open the gates to an anarchy which I might not be able to quell."†

Being, like the people he was sent to govern, a simple-hearted man, Harry Smith soon won their trust and affection. Having made himself familiar with their laws, he ruled them with the same firm, direct and humane hand with which he had led his Riflemen in the Peninsula. There was a natural sympathy between them; "the world," he wrote, "does not produce a more beautiful race of blacks than these Kaffirs, both men and women; their figures and eyes are beautiful beyond conception and they have the gait of princes." "If I can extend the blessings of civilisation and Christianity in a distant land," he said in after years on returning to South Africa as Governor of the Cape, "it will be a gratification to me beyond expression." Unfortunately the rulers of distant Britain had other views and, reversing his policy, "caused," as he put it, "the allegiance the Kaffirs had sworn to be shaken off and the full plenitude of their barbarity to be restored." The result was not only a return to the tyranny and cruelty of bloodthirsty chiefs and witch-doctors, but a renewal, with the loss of the security he had won for them, of the racist fears of the European settlers. "Such," he recalled afterwards, "was the disgust of hundreds of valuable members of the Dutch population . . . that they emigrated in masses and seized the country of the Zulus and became a thorn in the government of the Cape. Had my system been persisted in, and the order of things so firmly planted and rapidly growing into maturity been allowed to continue, not a Boer would have migrated." The whole history of South Africa might have been different had Harry Smith's bold and generous

* "The poor savage always buries the past in oblivion and regards the present only. He has not the most distant idea of right or wrong as regards his line of conduct. Self-interest is his controlling impulse, and desire stands for law and rectitude." *Harry Smith, II*, 35.

† *Harry Smith, II*, 72-7.

conception of Christian man's duty towards those emerging from
barbarism into civilisation been applied and extended.

* * *

His administrative work undone, as a soldier's work so often is, by
a blind and remote authority, Smith returned to his duties at the
Cape. Four years later he was appointed Adjutant-General to the
Queen's Forces in India. Here, in December 1843, at Maharajpur, in
action under Sir Hugh Gough against the Mahrattas—the brave,
hereditary fighting men who had first taught his old Commander-
in-Chief, Wellington, the business of war—he won the distinction
and golden opinions he never failed to gain in every action in which
he took part, being made a Knight Commander of the Bath for his
services. Subsequently he wrote in confidence to his old Peninsular
and Waterloo commander, Sir James Kempt, a letter which pin-
pointed the defects after a long period of peace of the British Forces
both in India and, as events in the Crimea were to show, at home. In
it he reverted to those unchanging rules of warfare taught to his old
Regiment forty years before by Coote Manningham, William Stewart
and John Moore and proved so repeatedly on the battlefields of
Portugal and Spain.

"In the late conflict *no one* gave our foe credit for half his daring
or ability; hence our attack was not quite so scientifically powerful
by a combination of the different arms as it might have been, and
the defects of the unwieldy machine called the British Indian
Army rendered most glaring:—its appalling quantity of baggage,
its lack of organization and equipment of the soldiers, its want of
experience in Generals and in officers, the extreme willingness
but total inexpertness and inaptitude of the soldier in the arts of
war, in the conflict, on piquet, on every duty which a protracted
campaign alone can teach effectually. In this country almost every
war has been terminated in one or two pitched battles fought so
soon as the one army comes in sight of the other, and accordingly
all the science attaching to advance and retreat, the posting of
piquets, reconnaissance of the enemy, the daily contemplating his
movements, both when he is before you and on the march, are lost,
and war is reduced at once to 'There are people drawn up who will

shoot at you, so fire away at them.' You blindly and ineptly rush upon them, drive them from the field with considerable loss, take all their guns, and never see the vestige of them after. Thus we must judiciously and with foresight organize ourselves for a campaign in the Punjab—a very probable event. For the armies of India are not now the rabble they were in Clive's time, but organized and disciplined by European officers of experience (many French), and the art of war has progressed rapidly among our enemies, whose troops are invariably far more numerous than those we oppose to them. Thus by superior ability we could alone calculate on their defeat. As it is, we calculate alone on the bulldog courage of Her Majesty's soldiers, and our loss becomes what we lately witnessed.

"To obviate these deficiencies, apparent even to the most inexperienced eye, we must in the first place reduce our baggage, next give our Sepoys canteens and haversacks (a Regiment told me they were exhausted for want of water, the water-carriers having run away). We must then, every cold season, have divisions of the army assembled, and post the one half opposite the other, with outlying piquets, etc., and daily alarms, skirmishes, etc., then general actions with blank cartridges. Without this the British Indian Army will remain as it now is—a great unwieldy machine of ignorant officers and soldiers. The drill of the Sepoy is good enough, and that of his officer, and never will attain greater perfection. But unless the officers in their separate commands know how, as I call it, to feed the fight, to bring up or into action successively in their places their command, when the attack is ordered, I defy any general to defeat his enemy but by stupid bull-dog courage. It may be conceit in Harry Smith, but if 10,000 men were given him in one cold season, if by sham fights, etc., he did not make them practical soldiers, he would resign in disgust, for the material is excellent and willing, but now, like a dictionary, it contains all the words, but cannot write a letter."*

Two years later, in war against the most formidable of all Britain's adversaries in India, the Sikhs of the Punjab, Harry Smith's perception and foresight were borne out. At the hard-fought battles of Mudki, Firozshah and Sobraon it was he rather than his gallant Commander-in-Chief, Lord Gough, who was the architect of victory.

* *Harry Smith*, *II*, 136-7.

In the one engagement in which he was in sole command, Aliwal, he won, in the face of immense odds, a triumph so complete that every one of the enemy's fifty guns remained in his hands at the end of the day. Speaking in the House of Lords the Duke of Wellington declared that he had never read the account of any battle in which more ability, energy, and experience were displayed. "I know," he said, "of no one in which an officer ever showed himself more capable . . . in commanding troops in the field. He brought every description of troops to bear, with all arms in the position in which they were most capable of rendering service; the nicest manoeuvres were performed under the fire of the enemy with the utmost precision, and at the same time with an energy and gallantry on the part of the troops never surpassed on any occasion whatever in any part of the world."*

Aliwal made Harry Smith a national hero. When in April 1847, at the age of 59, he returned to England after an almost continuous absence of 22 years, he received the thanks of both Houses of Parliament, was created a baronet and given the Grand Cross of the Bath, an Honorary Degree at Cambridge and the Freedom of the Cities of London and Glasgow. Yet probably the recognition which pleased him most were the congratulations of the Peninsular veterans of his old Regiment. Johnny Kincaid wrote that he had nobly vindicated the opinion entertained of him by everyone who had had the opportunity of judging his rare professional qualities, describing him as "one of Nature's generals", who, when previous battles had been won by the bull-dog courage of the soldier with a consequent unnecessary sacrifice of human life, had gained a great victory over superior numbers with comparatively little loss—"the judicious proceedings throughout stamping it as a general's and not a soldier's victory.'†
This endorsed Harry Smith's own two dicta—the guiding-stars of his military life, expressed at a dinner given him by the survivors of the old Light Division, where he said, "He is the best officer who does the most with the least loss of life . . . The tone of courage is taken from the officers; whatever the conduct of officers is, such will be the soldiers'."‡

Among the letters he received after Aliwal was one from his old Rifle Brigade comrade, Major George Simmons, now after his many wounds and forty years of ill-requited service, living in retirement

* *Harry Smith, I*, 201.   † *Harry Smith, II*, 197.   ‡ *Harry Smith, II*, 222.

in Jersey. To him Sir Harry replied in his characteristic vein of audacity, comradely sentiment and shrewd good sense.

"My dear old Comrade, George Simmons,

. . .Nothing can make me a vain ass, but when I tell you I have received since the battle of Aliwal upwards of 150 letters of heart-felt gratification conveying to me theirs and your participation in every feeling of success which Almighty God has so guided me to, then, George, my heart expresses its fulness through the eyes by tears of gratitude and reciprocal affection. From every old friend—I have several still left to us—from every old comrade of the Light and 4th Division, have I received every expression of their approbation, their happiness in my having realised their often-expressed anticipations . . . Then, George, comes the *econium* of THE DUKE. Dear old master! if I have done that which meets *your* approbation, then is the cup of glory full indeed, for it is to your example I have desired to apply any share of the ability bestowed upon me.

"I have had too from him the kindest of messages, and to his old friend Juanita, as he still calls her. George, my fight of Aliwal was really beautiful, and now I cannot say I wish on that day I had done this or that. But what I give myself any credit for was on the 21st January, when the enemy, with his army of 24,000 men and 50 guns, so ably, energetically and secretly anticipated my move to effect a junction with the corps at Loodiana, and nothing but pluck, Light Division experience, and inflexible adherence to purpose, brought me to the desired field of Aliwal. I lost some of my baggage, but should not have done that if my orders had been obeyed, but *Finis coronat opus* . . . Dear George, we little thought at Belem, when hopping about there, I should become master of that art we were both 'gurning' under, or a swimming master, with pupils at Sutlej!

"I certainly hurried the rogues over the river a little unceremoniously, and the credit you all give me is not thrown away, I do assure you. I am appointed to a Divisional command, and must leave these hills at rather a bad season of the year, viz. the rainy. Between the alternations of a fiery sun and torrents of rain, some 600 miles, Juana will go, through not staying here as I advised her. I begin to long to get once more to my native land. Mine has been an awful banishment. I do so long to seize by the hand all those old friends who have so adhered to me notwithstanding my absence, and who thus so kindly feel *my* success and honour *their own*. If anything could make a man an ass *this* ought."*

In a further letter to George Simmons written from Calcutta just before his return to England, Harry Smith wrote:

"Your letter of the 27th of December, which I yesterday got arouses recollections, which altho' subdued for the moment can never be effaced or forgotten. After my return from Buenos Ayres, we became acquainted at Hythe, that acquaintance soon ripened into a friendship as durable as ever existed between two comrades whom fate, career, hardship, privations, honours, and glory were so blended throughout the whole of the glorious Peninsular War from Barba del Puerco, Almeida, to Waterloo. We have been wounded in the same Fields, have shared the same couch—the same biscuit, and the same (often) nothing whatever. You in wounds have been unlucky, and never did man, hero and soldier, bear intense suffering as you did; after Waterloo your own presence of mind saved you by making a Brussels surgeon bleed you. There are moments when the moral courage of man becomes so conspicuous, when excruciating pain and distress so torture him, far more than with all glorious battlefields where honour, our country, our soldiers excite us and lead us to the one, while we lead on the other, whenever we can get a head of them, for such is their valour it is difficult. In all these situations I have seen you my gallant comrade. Do you remember the night of the Storm of Ciudad Rodrigo, being sent for the ladders, some delay occurred, and how you exerted yourself to overcome all obstacles, and successfully too. Were I to record events and circumstances in which we have been mutually associated one hundred letters would not suffice. I must wind up therefore by assuring you of the interest I take in the welfare of my dear old comrade, and his family, and may the gallantry and intrepidity of the father descend upon the son; his honour, integrity, his filial affection, his piety and his love for his neighbour. Then will he be as bright an ornament to his Queen and Country, to his profession and his faith, as the high-minded man and gallant, most gallant, soldier my friend, comrade, and

* *A British Rifleman*, 381-3.

brother Rifleman, George Simmons, is the prayer, hope and the confidence of

HARRY SMITH."*

Perhaps of all the letters he received the one which may have moved Harry Smith most was one from Turin where his erstwhile fellow-Rifleman, Charles Beckwith—who, after a brilliant Peninsular career only equalled in a young officer by that of Harry Smith himself, had lost a leg at Waterloo—was devoting the last thirty-five years of his life to missionary and educational work among the poverty-stricken Waldenses of the Piedmontese mountain valleys.

" *My dear Harry,*

The noise of the guns at Aliwal and Sobraon having died away in the echoes of the Himalaya, and the eclat and movement of those brilliant days having melted into the calmer atmosphere of ordinary life, I have good hopes that the handwriting of one who has never faltered for one moment in the deep feeling of respect and affection which he will cherish to his dying day for all his old companions in arms, will not be unwelcome.

" *From the hour in which I saw your name associated with the army of the Sutlej, you may imagine how carefully I followed all your movements, how I rejoiced in your success, how anxious I felt in the usual intervals of doubt and trial.*

" *I laughed heartily when you lost your baggage, I knew fully well the hearty damns that you sent after Sikhs, coolies, syces, and the whole rabble rout; saw your keen face as you galloped on the sand, and admired the cool close order of your movements in the teeth of an enemy who held-in his very breath in anxious doubt and dread whether he should dare to touch you; saw the noble array of your clear decided movement of Aliwal, and went along with you pell-mell as you drove your enemy headlong into the waters of the Sutlej; triumphed in the crowning efforts of a long soldier's life, formed in the school of true science, common sense and right-hearted action, and felt a secret pride that I had been formed in the same school and was able to estimate such men as Hardinge and Harry Smith. But what did Juana do in all this row? Was she on horseback abaxo de los canonacos? Give my kind love to her and kiss her for me.*

" *Many years have now gone by, and our outward frames are but the shadows of what they were, but my mind continues of the same sort. Character never loses its indelible stamp. Thin and black, my hair is not*

* *R.B.C. 1932, 295-7.*

yet grey, and you would yet be able to recognise the Charley Beckwith of the Light Division . . . The last enemy has done his worst on very many of our Peninsular companions. Sir Andrew and some Riflemen still remain to dine together sometimes in Albermale Street. Charley Rowan is letter A. No. 1. Old Duffy regulates the Club, Johnny Bell cultivates dahlias at Staines, Will Napier misgoverns the Guernseymen, Johnny Kincaid regulates the secrets of a prison-house, Jonathan Leach writes histories; thus each labours in his vocation, and has still a conceit left him in his misery. The chronicle of the out-pensioners of Chelsea is more spirit-stirring in its former than its latter day . . . Adieu Harry, and believe me that you may always depend on the affection of your old friend,

CHARLES BECKWITH"*

Harry Smith did not remain long in England after his triumphant return in the spring of 1847, for in the autumn of the same year he sailed once more for South Africa as Governor of the Cape, where, as a result of the disregard of his healing work of twelve years before, another Kaffir war had broken out. Here, after being separated from it for twenty-one years, he found himself, as Commander-in-Chief, in contact again with his old Regiment, of whose 2nd Battalion, still in Canada, he had been appointed Colonel-Commandant earlier that year and whose 1st Battalion, hastily despatched from Corfu, had been campaigning in Kaffir-land under conditions of great hardship and privation since the previous Christmas. On December 22nd at Williamstown Sir Harry was able to congratulate it in person on its bravery and endurance. A few months later, when the Boers, deprived of the protection he had formerly given them and increasingly disaffected with their British rulers, broke out in open rebellion, he assembled a flying column—consisting of two Companies of the 1st Rifle Brigade, two of the 45th and two of the 91st, with four squadrons of the Cape Mounted Rifles and a couple of six-pounder guns. Acting with his usual vigour and speed, he marched it across three hundred miles of veldt to attack a force of 3000 burgher marksmen encamped in a strong hill position overlooking the Boemplaats plain beyond the Orange river. Addressing before action his fellow Riflemen—and being "answered by such a cheer", according to the earliest historian of the Rifle Brigade "as Riflemen can give to an old Rifleman who leads them into the fight"—he launched

* *Harry Smith, II, 210-11.*

them in extended order, when, they "drove the enemy at the point of the sword from the first and through the second range of heights and kept up a galling fire on them as they retreated to the third and highest crest. Here the Boers rallied their whole force and delivered a telling fire under which men and officers fell fast. But nothing could stand the dash of the Riflemen; this last position was carried, and at the end of two hours' hard fighting the Boers fled."*

It was Harry Smith's last engagement, and his Regiment's first against Europeans since Waterloo. Eighteen months later, after a ten years' tour abroad, the 1st Battalion was ordered home, leaving behind 165 of its N.C.O.s and men as settlers. From Canterbury, where it rejoined its Depot Companies, it marched on the last day of 1850 to Dover. Here in September 1851 it was reviewed for the last time by its Colonel-in-Chief, the Duke of Wellington, before being recalled at the beginning of 1852 for a further two years' spell of duty and active service in South Africa, where a third Kaffir colonial war had by then broken out.

The Depot Companies, however, remained in England, being stationed at Walmer where Wellington, as Lord Warden of the Cinque Ports, was in residence when he died on September 14th 1852. While 6000 miles away on the Kei river, the men of the 1st Battalion, in patched and many-coloured garments, campaigned among burnt-out and devastated farms and homesteads, maintaining the honour and traditions of the Regiment in the field, the Depot Companies, in immaculate uniforms and order, mounted guard every day for two months over the coffin of their dead Colonel-in-Chief. On the night of November 10th, when it was taken to London for burial, the entire Depot escorted it by torchlight to the railway station at Deal. A week later on the 18th, the 2nd Battalion, which had returned earlier in the year from Canada, headed the stately funeral cortège through London as, to the strains of the Dead March in Saul, it slowly processed from the Horse Guards to St. Paul's. So it accompanied the great Duke on his last journey on earth, just as, 37 years before, it had marched beside him, to the thunder of the guns, across the stricken field of Waterloo with Napoleon's Imperial Guard dissolving in defeat before it.

---

* Cope, 258-9.

Chapter Four

OVER THE HILLS AND
FAR AWAY

And what more can be said of you Riflemen than that wherever
there has been fighting there you have been employed, and
wherever you have been employed, you have distinguished
yourselves.

DUKE OF CLARENCE
afterwards King William IV

NINE days after his death, even before the 2nd Battalion, in full
ceremonial dress with draped shakos, escorted him on his final
journey to St. Paul's, the Duke of Wellington was succeeded as
Colonel-in-Chief of the Rifle Brigade by H. R. H. Albert the Prince
Consort. About the same time, in far-away Queen Adelaide's land on
the frontiers of Cape Colony, amid houses in ruins, devastated
gardens and marks of Kaffir incursions everywhere, four Companies of the 1st Battalion returned to Fort Beaufort after six
months' campaigning on the Kei river—weary, ragged and unshaven—while the band led them into camp to the music of the new
quick-step march, "Ninety-five", which Bandmaster Miller had set
from a popular comic song. Unlike its fellow Battalion, which had
not seen active service since Waterloo, the men of the Regiment's
senior Battalion had twice in three years known what it was to go
hungry in a desert, to be outnumbered and surrounded by savage
hordes, and to triumph over their country's enemies by the military
virtues of fortitude, discipline in action and tactical skill and resource acquired from experience in the harsh school of war. In the
Battle of Berea on 20th December, 1852, Rifleman John Fisher, after
marching 500 miles, took part with his Company under Lieutenants
Leicester Curzon and H. G. Lindsay in the storming of Mount
Berea and, with the rest of the force—about 600 strong, including
Sir George Cathcart, Governor and Commander-in-Chief of the
Cape—was surrounded by 7000 mounted and well-armed Basutos.

"They yelled like so many devils, and closed upon us to within fifty yards. Colonel Eyre said to us, 'Men, you are on this ground, and this ground you must keep. You and I, and even His Excellency, must die on this spot rather than leave it.' We were in a small space, and could all hear him. We all thought it very probable that none of us would get away, so we fought on. We could see nothing except the flash of our own guns and the fire of the enemy. We Riflemen now found the use of the ten smooth balls which we carried; we could load rapidly with them, whereas the belted bullet which we generally used had to be put carefully into the rifle, or else it would jamb. Finally, at about 8 p.m., the enemy retired, but it was not until we had nearly reached the end of our ammunition."*

When at the end of the Basuto campaign, the Battalion left South Africa in November 1853 on its two months' voyage home, it was, compared with the rest of the British Army outside India, a corps of veterans.

It landed at Portsmouth in January 1854 to find England on the verge of war. A few weeks later its untried sister Battalion received immediate orders to proceed to Turkey, whose territorial integrity, threatened by Russia, had been guaranteed by France and Britain. Before it sailed, a hundred volunteers were hastily transferred to it from the 1st Battalion whose ranks were brought up to strength by drafts of young soldiers. Stopping en route at Malta and Gallipoli, the Battalion reached Varna on the Black Sea at the end of May where during the summer, it suffered, like the rest of the Anglo-French-Turkish army, from cholera. The 1st Battalion, under Lt.-Colonel Sidney Beckwith—nephew of the great Sir Thomas Beckwith who had commanded it in the Peninsula—left England again in July and, travelling by way of Malta, Constantinople and Scutari, where a number of its men went down with cholera, reached Varna early in September.

As by now the Russians had abandoned their invasion of Turkey, it was decided to strike at their command of the Black Sea by destroying the great naval port of Sebastopol in the Crimea. On September 13th and 14th, both Battalions of the Rifle Brigade landed in Kalamita Bay, sixty miles north of the town, the 1st as part of the 4th Division

* United Service Magazine, 1898, cit. R.B.C. 1934, 239.

commanded by Sir George Cathcart—under whom it had served in South Africa—and the 2nd with the Light Division under a 64-year-old Peninsular veteran, Lt.-General Sir George Brown, a martinet with, according to *The Times*'s Special Correspondent, a penchant for "pipe-claying, close-shaving and tight-stocking". As part of the mismanagement which characterised the expedition, and of the nation's unpreparedness for war after four decades of peace, the men were landed without knapsacks, tents or any change of clothing. The 1st Battalion were a little better off than the 2nd owing to the fact that General Cathcart presented each man with a piece of oil-cloth with which to keep his blanket dry. "We were all pleased to see our old General," wrote Colour-Sergeant Fisher, "it was only ten months since we had left him in South Africa. We cheered him heartily, and he was all the more welcome when we found that he had a present for each of us in the shape of a waterproof ground sheet which proved invaluable as long as they lasted. No such thing had ever been known in the Army before and no other Regiment was so well off."*

The landing was described in the journal of Major William Norcott—son of Sir Amos Norcott who had commanded the 2nd Battalion at Waterloo. Norcott was a man of great character, universally known for his dry wit; on one occasion, when a testy general snapped at him, "You damned Riflemen think yourselves better than other people!" he replied, "No, sir, we don't, *but the Army does*." He was accustomed to speak of his Crimean services, which were distinguished throughout by great gallantry and efficiency, as "carrying on the business of the old 95th with punctuality and despatch."†
His account of the start of the campaign bears this out:

"Our gallant allies were the first on shore and stuck their tricolour in the soil as a necessary preliminary! . . . On the preconcerted signal, boats came off to the different ships, and without standing on the order of our going, everybody pushed ashore . . . The men carried a greatcoat, a blanket, a pair of boots and their mess-tins, together with the cumbrous water canteen. From the yielding nature of the blanket and coat (the knapsacks were ordered to be left on board), the load was anything but compact, sat badly

* *R.B.C. 1953*, 71-81. (Diary of Colour-Sergeant J. Fisher.)
† *R.B.C. 1965*, 109.

and was heavy. Officers were desired to take only such things as they could carry on their persons . . .

" . . . The Division swept on at the rate of a hunt, halting after a march of about six miles . . . I was sent then to a village about a mile off from the extreme left and had orders to barricade and make myself secure. It began to rain about this hour, six o'clock, and the Army had a wet night of it. By ten o'clock, I was regularly barricaded, having pressed arabeas, gates, stones, casks, an old wheel, etc., etc., and it was well I did. While the main body of the Army lay out on the bare ground (they had no tents), my lads screwed themselves into haystacks or got on the lee side of them. I and the rest of the officers took up our abode in the headman's house, i.e. five of us, and threw ourselves down in a little room twelve feet square and kicked out the night.

"It was a sight to see the inhabitants come out of the village as we swept down like falcons. Each bore a pumpkin or fowl and made signs of submission and welcome. This night a Cossack cantered right down on the village; his object evidently to find out if it was occupied. The advanced sentries did their best to give him tangible proof, but they had not re-capped after the heavy rain, and he gained his information at a cheap rate.

"*15-18 September* At Kamishly. Harassed by attacks of Cossacks by night and the immense dispositions I was forced to make to keep the French as well as English from plundering the village . . . I took much on myself which Sir G. Brown confirmed and approved and had the satisfaction of hearing that Lord Raglan was much pleased at my protection of the village. Everything was paid for and the people brought forth much grain . . . I had, however, terrible work, and had sometimes two hundred men on sentry round the village and the rest ready to back up. I caught some Highlanders literally endeavouring to carry away the crossbeams of the bridge by which alone I could be communicated with by the Army or get to them. Many a time have I required my best French and perseverance to determinedly bow back some two or three French officers backed by a hundred Zouaves or others, who just wanted to get a drink of water or *morceau du tabac*! As if my Kamishly had a shop! . . ."*

* *R.B.C. 1931, 207-10.*

Kinglake, the historian of the Crimean War, who had landed with the Army, remembered the impression the Riflemen made on the village folk among whom they were quartered, and how they "made up for the want of a common tongue by acts of kindness. They helped the women with their household work, and the women, pleased and proud, made signs to the stately Rifles to do this and to do that, exulting in the obedience which they were able to win from men so grand and comely. When the interpreter came and was asked to construe what the women were saying so fast and so eagerly . . . the Rifles were made out to be heroes more strong than lions, more gentle than young lambs."*

By September 19th the Army was ready to advance towards the Alma river, on the heights above which the Russians under Prince Menshikoff were barring the way to Sebastapol. As it had done in the Peninsula, the Rifle Brigade, operating with the Light Cavalry, provided an advanced-guard and protective screen. The 1st Battalion, whose Commanding Officer, Lt.-Colonel Beckwith, had succumbed to cholera,† was employed in defending the attackers' exposed landward flank against Cossack attack, while the 2nd Battalion, in skirmishing order, led the way. The "red" army—Guards and Line Regiments—followed it in close column, shoulder to shoulder. The Green Jackets were still wearing the long-tailed coatees of their Peninsular past, with crossbelt, waistbelt with ball-pouch, sword with brass handle, and rifle with butt-trap for holding grease.‡ Norcott's account continued,

"Marched from Kamishly, joining the Army on the Sebastopol road about four miles from where I started. Saw Lord Cardigan and told him about Cresswell . . . After a time, the whole Army advanced, my wing leading and covering the front of the Light Division and the Duke of Cambridge's, consisting of the Guards and Highland Brigade. Passed the Bulganak, a small swampy muddy stream with a small bridge and post-house. Whilst en-

---

* Kinglake, *Invasion of the Crimea*, II, 187, cit. *Cope*, 304.

† Major Norcott while at Kamishly recorded a similar case of cholera. "Captain Creswell, 11th Hussars, was sent to put himself under my orders and strengthen the front. He brought with him twenty-five men, coming on the 17th. On the night of the 18th he was attacked by cholera. Poor fellow. Death was in his face as I took his hand before moving off on the 19th. I left my Assistant Surgeon with him. He died an hour after. His poor wife in the bay, doubtless seeing her husband in every second horseman!"

‡ *R.B.C. 1930*, 199-200. (Major H. Hone, *My Young Days with the Rifle Brigade*.)

deavouring to get a drop of water that the cavalry (who ought to have been held in hand till the infantry had drunk), had not turned into mud, the alarm that the enemy's cavalry were in sight was passed. Our guns, with fifty Riflemen to each battery, and cavalry went instantly to the front, and the infantry, resuming its order of march, backed up . . . The enemy show in Cossacks, and our cavalry extend and skirmish with them. At length a squadron in close order draws up across the road. In a second, the flash of a gun. The shot plunged right into our fellows, who stood as steady as rocks, though the shell . . . literally burst *in* the horse. Five horses down and three or four men came to the rear, wounded.

"All this time, the shot came dancing through our skirmishers and trundling up to the columns in rear. Our guns unlimbered, began firing, and in a few minutes some five hundred Cossacks broke from their close order and covered the plain below, about a mile off. A few shells soon sent them off. The whole then fell back. This was the first encounter with the enemy. I occupied myself whilst the pickets were getting ready to relieve us, in collecting dromedary's dung in my Albert shako; a use it seems admirably fitted for, and so catered for my bivouac fire!

"*20 September*. Up, and in my place. The Alma was to be passed to-day and everybody looked for and longed to find the enemy there. I had prophesied we should fire the first shot at the Bulganak and fight for the water of the Alma. Our supply of water depended wholly on our being able to drink at these rivers. Lawrence covered the front this day and I the flank. We had Cossacks hovering all round us and regular cavalry was seen on our flank. We kept the Sebastopol road, walking over vast and undulating plains; the men suffering much from thirst, for we had been under arms since seven o'clock and, as our bivouac of the previous night was some two miles from the Bulganak, few had obtained the requisite supply of water.

"We walked on, however, and after about six miles, saw the line of the Alma. The river is nothing more or less than a gully or gorge running down to the sea, with precipitous banks, difficult of ascent, here and there. This valley, or gorge, may be from 200 to 300 yards or more in breadth. The river varying from 40 to 50 yards wide; here deep, there shallow, runs serpentining down the middle, having vineyards and gardens on either side, though

principally on the north side on which the enemy awaited us . . .
The holes round the vine roots formed natural *trous des loups*,
whilst the embankments of the gardens had been heightened,
leaving a small ditch. Every house, and there were three or four
fell to my share, had been made defensible, and altogether the
enemy had made as clear a way for us to be seen and got at, and as
secure a position for himself, as can well be imagined.

"As we approached the river we could see the distant hills
covered with lines of troops and the intermediate ones with
masses. Certain dark streaks on the crests of the nearer hills told
of guns, but we could not calculate their number or calibre. The
Army halted for ten minutes, as if for breath. We then advanced
about 300 yards and again halted. Again advanced about 50 yards
and again halted. And then, like some great animal that has got
itself well together, the whole moved on. There was no further
halt, unless for those who fell, until all was over.

"As the Army descended . . . the columns, which had only
partially deployed, now wholly formed line. The artillery and
cavalry taking ground to the left under cover of my Riflemen, who,
as each successive Regiment came into line, came up in its front.
The whole Battalion was now in extended order in front of the
Army, with supports of Companies. Our skirmishers might have
been 300 yards in front. I rode with them. As we descended the
'downs,' we suddenly saw smoke and flame burst out from the
other side of what turned out to be a sunken road, but which,
having a fall of some 6 or 7 feet into it, had been hidden from our
view, and so hindered us from seeing the cause of this fire and
smoke . . . All became clear in a minute. Simultaneous with the
outburst of smoke and flame, there came such a singing, such a
continuous stream of balls, as to make one's horse quite uneasy
and the men astonished. There came a volume of white wool from
a distant hill, then another, then six, seven, eight, then fifty.
Eventually a hundred guns belched forth their iron load and the
earth was torn and rent with their violence.

"We neared the road, not firing a shot. How could we? We saw
nobody! The village now showed through the smoke and flame.
We neared it and the walls of the vineyards. The men more than
once asked me should they push on to the wall, and at a sham
fight, I should have done so long before. I feared, however, any

undue idea of danger, and saying, 'All right, all right; let us be cool; a few yards more,' walked on till within 40 yards of the wall which we then gained by a rush, lying under and looking over it, endeavouring through the thick smoke, to catch sight of the hornets that filled the air with rifle balls.

"Not a man of mine had been hit. How I escaped on this road, shot and grape tearing up the earth within 6 feet of my horse's feet, I know not. I got my supports well jammed up, but many were the hairbreadth escapes. At length the line came up and, without a moment's pause, I threw Fyers' and Erroll's Companies over the walls into the vineyards. Pushed my supports . . . down by a road that led through these to a farmhouse, and, pressing on under a murderous fire from rifles whose whereabouts it was impossible to conjecture, we crossed the river, gained the farm and, swarming the high ridge on the other side, first saw the enemy infantry! The enemy had so many guns that they favoured everybody without robbing anyone! My movement, however, had been so rapid, that this and my extended order saved me greatly. I did not gain the ridge, however, without having Erroll severely wounded in the hand and thirty-four men killed and wounded.

"The burning villages had completely stopped the rest of the Army, who were compelled to make great detours. When, then, I turned round expecting to see the line advised by my position that all was clear behind me, to my surprise I found myself perfectly isolated and, somewhat to the disturbance of my mind, saw some sixty or seventy Cossacks coming down a road on my left, followed by a column of infantry. My position was critical and I felt I should be turned and cut off from the Army. I was afraid to retire lest I should create a bad impression. I then thought of edging away to my right, in the hopes of finding somebody to 'happen on.' But not a soul could I see save a column of enemy walking down the plateau on my left.

"I resolved to retire from the ridge and get into the next that I had driven the enemy out of. Putting two Companies in, thick about the walls of the farmhouse, I threw Forman's into some vineyards and placing my fourth Company, Colville's, on the road down which my friends were coming, determined to have it out and trust to those behind coming to my support. It was an anxious moment. I had anticipated such a move on the enemy's part, for

on first crossing the river I cantered 'Inkyboy' from where Colville
was placed, past the embankment I put Forman on. I dared not
go far. All I have written in the last thirty lines, was the sight,
thought and action of ten seconds.

"I cantered again to the ridge to watch the enemy's approach
and direct action, when lo! I saw they were retiring. I looked
behind me and saw our line coming on! In the meantime, or at
the same time, I perceived the 1st Brigade crossing to my right,
under a fire we were all treated to. Two columns of the enemy
were moving right down from the Battery of 24- and 32-pounders,
which was playing the devil with everybody. I determined to
edge away towards this Brigade which was passing the river in
great confusion, and did so, keeping nothing but our heads above
the ridge, and blazing away as best we could, obliquely into the
enemy's columns. I gained the flank front of the Battery, threw my
men down and galloped some 50 yards to the Brigade, which having passed the river in lines of Regiments, from which 30 file a
Company would pause to drink or fill their canteens (the gaps so
made, closing in, to the utter exclusion of these men), begged all
hands for Heaven's sake, to get into two deep. One is bold in
action and says what one thinks. To General Codrington, to
Colonel Blake, to Chester Saunders, it was all the same thing: 'By
Heavens, they are only 150 yards from you. You will annihilate
them. Only get into two deep.'

"It was impossible. The men, dead beat, sat down. Some to
drink water, others literally pulling out bread and meat and beginning to eat! At length the enemy columns came within 100
yards of the bank or steep under which the Brigade lay, and three
or four skirmishers literally came to the brink and fired down on
the hat caps of those below. Then the mass of men, twenty deep,
rose up and ascending the steep bank, yet not so high as to catch
the plateau on which the columns were, began firing at the
Battery! On however they went, mobbed as they were, gallantly
and desperately, but halting and firing all the time.

"The enemy's columns retired before their onward move. I, in
the meantime, who had offered General Codrington to take them
into action, brought up the left of my whole line of skirmishers,
throwing in a flanking fire and advancing at the same time
rapidly. The enemy guns, seeing their columns in full retreat and

the 2nd Brigade . . . moving towards the rear of their right, were off; but not until the 32-pounder—there was no mistaking the demon shriek of this gun—had been discharged when I was within 30 yards of its muzzle. It made the earth shake and one's flesh quiver.

"The enemy columns, however, showed again at the Redoubt. It was touch and go. Sir George Brown was riding fearlessly at the head of the Brigade urging them on. My right-hand skirmisher, Hughie Hannan, was close to him. 'Allow us to storm, sir,' said I. 'Certainly, Norcott; storm,' said Sir George. I drew my sword, more to make my encouragement conspicuous to the men, and galloping forward, called, 'Come on, my hearties,' rode right up to within five yards of the Battery. The enemy had just turned to retire, and General Codrington, cantering up and pressing on, went into the Redoubt to show no one was there. Young Campbell of ours, his A.D.C., and I went in. But I do record it here, that the first man up to the embrasures of the Battery was a Green Jacket."*

Owing to the general confusion and incompetence which, in contrast to the British army's gallantry, characterised its higher command, the Great Redoubt was lost to a Russian counter-attack soon after the Rifles had gained it. Norcott recounted the sequel.

"The loss at this moment was frightful. Manfully did the mass stand up; such as were in front, firing. Here Chester fell and the better part of his officers and men. It was too much, and the mass, like a partially loosened cliff, began to slide down and down; now slowly, now more rapidly. The enemy pushed on, regained the Redoubt and lined it.

"At this time the Guards were formed on the plateau below. They were perfectly formed as at St. James's, and should have advanced and assisted the 1st Brigade of the Light Division and not waited for it to fall back. As it was, they stood waiting for the mass to pass them. It did so in great confusion. Previous to this, on seeing Codrington's Brigade giving way, I galloped down to the Guards (I left my Lincoln Greens, knowing they could take care of themselves), for it was a time for men to rally each other, and passed the three Battalions, calling out, 'Steady, gentlemen,

* R.B.C. 1931, 211-18.

and for God's sake preserve your two deep; they are not half your numbers.'

"The Guards now opened fire, but were met with a severe one, and the centre Battalion for a moment, after firing about two rounds, went to the right about. However, it quickly recovered itself, wheeled, turned as on one heel, and the whole three mounted the slope. The teeth of the Battery had been knocked out by the Light Division, but though there were no guns to receive them, they were well plied by riflemen. The Brigade of Highlanders coming up at the same moment completed the advance.

"I was wild at the loss of the Battery and got my fellows together in rear of the Guards, their packs off, all ready to lead in again. At this moment an A.D.C. came galloping down. I thought he was coming to tell me to back up the Guards, and sang out in anticipation: 'All right, sir; you'll see us in before them yet,' when he said: 'The Brigadier desires you will instantly form a reserve and act as support.' At this identical moment, up comes Lawrence with the right wing. Where they came from I know not. Bradford and Colville with his Company found their way somehow or other down to where I was when my left was threatened. They ought to have been in front of Codrington's Brigade. They missed the road, however, whilst I, away half a mile to the left, from a combination of circumstances, and acting on my own hook, found and so gained the opportunity Lord Raglan so kindly and flatteringly speaks of . . .

"The Redoubt was regained. The two wings of Rifles fell into battalion under Lawrence and sloping arms walked on. The day was over. The Guards and Highlanders had done their work well and a gun or two (at length!) had helped us. The dead and dying lay thick. Struck in eleven places; in three clean through the body, in the chest with grape shot and in the off fore leg with a round shot, my noble horse 'Inkyboy', his service over, stood still, unable to proceed the 100 yards to where the column halted."[*]

The Commander-in-Chief, Lord Raglan, stated in his Despatches that the capture of the Great Redoubt "was materially aided by the advance of four Companies of the Rifle Brigade under Major Nor-

[*] *R.B.C. 1931*, 219-20. "This is not intended as an account of the Battle of the Alma, but, careless of the charge of egotism, an exact account and detail of what I saw, said and did."

cott". The commander of the Light Division, Sir George Brown, went further and, when the Victoria Cross was instituted, recommended him for it:

"Colonel (then Major) Norcott had command of four Companies of the 2nd Rifle Brigade attached to the 2nd Brigade of the Light Division at Alma and was the first to cross the stream. He stole up the steep ground in front of that Brigade, and availed himself so judiciously of the form and irregularities of the ground in posting his Riflemen, as to take the enemy's principal Battery in flank and completely enfiladed it, at the same time that it was assailed in front by the 23rd and 19th Regiments. Major Norcott's conduct on that occasion was not only conspicuous to the whole Division, but attracted the notice of the enemy, for the officer in command of the Russian Battery, and who was subsequently made prisoner, informed Lord Raglan that he had laid a gun specially for the daring officer in the dark uniform on the black horse. The black horse was killed before the day was over."*

Another chronicler of the scene that day was Colour-Sergeant J. Fisher of the 1st Battalion, whose men, in skirmishing order, were keeping off a large body of enemy cavalry threatening the advancing Army's left flank. "In all my life," he wrote, "I have never seen a field-day as clearly as I saw the battle of the Alma, for . . . the whole battlefield was under our view . . . After about three hours hard fighting, the Russians hastily retired, leaving the ground covered with killed and wounded. As soon as the heights were carried, the 4th Division and Cavalry crossed the river, the latter moving by the road while we took a straight cut through gardens, vineyards and whatever came our way. After crossing the Alma we went straight up the hill, marching over the ground which was covered with dead and wounded . . . Lord Raglan and his staff came riding along the line, and the whole army cheered him. I can see the scene now."† Fifty-four years later, in the Infirmary of the Royal Hospital, Chelsea, another Rifleman, William Salter, who had taken part in the attack on the Great Redoubt, as he lay dying, recalled to the Regiment's historian, Colonel Willoughby Verner, his memories of the Alma; of "old Billy Norcott", as he called him, telling his men on the eve of the battle that they would have to fight for a drink of

* R.B.C. 1930, 245-6.   † R.B.C. 1953, 71-81. Diary of Colour-Sergeant J. Fisher.

Lieutenant General Sir Harry Smith—Henry Moseley

Fording the Alma, September 1854 – Louis Johns

Major the Hon. H. H. Clifford V.C.—Francescio Podesti

water on the morrow; of Sir George Brown rating them as thieves and plunderers for picking the grapes from the vineyards as they advanced; of the round-shot bounding through their ranks; of "red soldiers" being sent back next day to pick up their shakos from the battlefield while the Greenjackets, who detested them, contemptuously left theirs behind.* "I told Salter," wrote Verner, who had filled an egg-cup of rum to revive him—for the old soldier was sinking fast—"that I had recently visited the lodge at Bramshill—where Salter had lived after his retirement as gatekeeper to another Rifle Brigade officer and historian, Sir William Cope—and that it was looking beautiful. On which he said, 'Ah! It *was* a beautiful morning, that was.' " Imagining he referred to some day at Bramshill, Verner asked which? " 'The Alma, of course,' said the old man. 'Such a beautiful morning, it wor, as we marched down to the river.' His thoughts were far away. I recalled General Earle's description of how the British lines advanced, the brilliant sunshine playing on the bright uniforms and sparkling bayonets whilst the drums beat, the bands played and the Colours were borne aloft—the last of the old order never to return—and I feel sure old Salter saw it all, just as it happened on that bright morning in September fifty-four years ago. After a time I rose to go and, filling up the egg-cup, said, 'Now Salter, we'll drink to the "Victory of the Alma" and "Success to the Rifles".' I held the cup to his lips and as he drank he muttered 'And many more of 'em . . . And many like 'em'. These were his last words to me."†

Norcott—the hero of the day—never got the V.C. for which he was recommended, but the command he was given of the 1st Battalion after Beckwith's death, and a letter from the doyen of his corps, Sir Harry Smith—then commanding the Northern Military District in England—may have pleased him more: "My dear Bill Norcott," it read:

"*Was not I delighted to see your name in the Despatches, and also that you have got rank and command, and that the dear old Rifles have not alone* maintained *their previous character, but have added fresh and imperishable laurels to their many old ones.*

"*You see, Bill, how Riflemen, if they know their work, fight with comparatively little loss.*

* Colour-Sergeant Fisher later found these unwanted adornments very useful, when filled with clay, for building shelters against the Crimean winter.

† *R.B.C. 1908*, 133-8. "These were his last words to me."

" *We are all at home most anxious to see what is to come next. Sebastopol once in our hands— forts and all—then we could lick the Russian Army in the Field, but the being between two fires is hot work.*

"*Make our Rifles* pride *themselves on* fighting *hard with* little loss; *it is to be done, as indeed both Battalions have again shown on these occasions. How delighted your dear old father would have been could he have lived to see you in his shoes. Tell every Green Jacket how proud I am of* their *glory, and if I could be put back in age 20 years I would have shared and cheerfully endured all your hardships. Lady Smith sends her love.*

Ever your old friend,

HARRY SMITH."*

Sebastapol was taken, in the end, after a year's siege, but Harry Smith's hope of his beloved Rifles being able to show how to take it with little loss was not realised. The opportunity of following up the Alma by an early capture of Sebastapol before its landward fortifications had been strengthened was thrown away by the dilatoriness and lack of imagination of the Allied commanders, and, in the grim stalemate trench-warfare siege that followed, the kind of individual initiative and skill which the founders of the Regiment had prescribed was at a discount. In the first of the two battles, Balaclava and Inkerman, fought to prevent the enemy from raising the siege before the Russian winter, the Rifles' part was minimal, but in the second both Battalions were engaged. "On the morning of November 5th 1854," wrote Colour-Sergeant Fisher of the 1st Battalion, "we fell in before daybreak as usual, and we were now wearing greatcoats, the weather having become so cold. While falling in we heard an alarm that an attack was taking place on our right . . . We hurried off immediately; . . . we could not see much as there was a thick fog and drizzling rain . . . We soon found ourselves hotly engaged. The struggle went on for hours, and no intelligible story of the fight can possibly be written . . . We advanced and attacked a dense column which we drove before us; we then saw fresh masses of infantry marching on us; these again we drove back, and again other bodies of fresh troops advanced. All the time, and this was for many hours, the Russian artillery poured a crushing fire into us and must, I believe, have killed many of their own men. I think most of

* *R.B.C. 1892,* 82

our killed fell before this artillery-fire, for the dense columns did not fire when advancing, only their skirmishers fired. After we had broken them up and they were retiring, they fired heavily; and in retreat their conduct was most gallant—on many occasions they turned and fired in our very faces. Incessantly we rallied and formed some sort of line; several times we were driven back by sheer weight of numbers, almost to our guns, which all the time were firing over our heads. Indeed, at one time we were actually driven among our artillery, and then we, one and all, set our teeth and said we would go back not a step further. We then made our last rally, and whether we could have made another is a question . . . In the part of the field where I was we were nearly annihilated when the French troops came to our rescue."*

There is another account of the battle by a member of the Regiment, Captain the Hon. Henry Clifford, A.D.C. to Brigadier George Buller who had led the 1st Battalion Companies at Boemplaats and was now commanding one of the two brigades of the Light Division. Though on the staff, Clifford, like Harry Smith in the Peninsula,† was always in the thick of the fighting, taking on himself the direction of operations when other control was lost and engaging in personal combat like the humblest front-line soldier. "On reaching the left brow of the hill," he wrote in a letter home next day, "I saw the enemy in great numbers in our front about 15 yards from us; it was a moment or two before I could make General Buller believe that they were Russians. 'In God's name,' I said, 'fix bayonets and charge.' He gave the order and in another moment we were hand to hand with them . . . 'Come on,' I said, 'my lads,' and the brave fellows dashed in amongst the astonished Russians, bayoneting them in every direction. One of the bullets in my revolver had partly come out and prevented it revolving, and I could not get it off. The Russians fired their pieces off within a few yards of my head, but none touched me. I drew my sword and cut off one man's arm who was in the act of bayoneting me, and a second, seeing it turned round and was in the act of running out of my way when I hit him over the back of the neck and laid him dead at my feet.‡ . . . Out of

* R.B.C. 1957, 91-2.
† And young Major "Billy" Congreve, V.C., D.S.O., M.C., in World War I. *The Congreves*, *passim*.
‡ *Clifford*, 88-9. "The excitement certainly was tremendous while it lasted, and it is well

the small party with me—twelve—six men were killed and three wounded, so my escape was wonderful . . . The Russians, who kept up a tremendous fire upon us with heavy guns from 6 in the morning till 5 in the evening, kept sending up fresh columns of infantry to try and take our position, but they were always repulsed with very great slaughter . . . I rode over the field of battle after it was over and the sight was truly heart-rending. The Russians lay in such heaps it was quite impossible to form any idea of their numbers . . . But they never drove us one inch from our position—not a Russian with arms in his hands saw over the hill on which we first took up our stand and on which, had we taken common precautions by throwing up works, many a brave officer and man would not have fallen on our side."*

For his part in the battle Henry Clifford received the Victoria Cross. To his pen we owe the best contemporary description of the earlier battle of Balaclava and the Charge of the Light Brigade, of which he was an appalled witness. He also described vividly the sufferings of his ill-equipped comrades in the terrible Russian winter that followed when, unlike the well-supplied French, the British, through want of shelter, transport and effective commissariat were reduced by cold, exposure, under-nourishment, sickness and cholera to a phantom army of scarecrows, scarcely at one point, Clifford reckoned, 12,000 strong. "The poor men are suffering," he wrote, "more than human nature can stand. They are dying off fast every day . . . If the weather, with its consequent hardships is to continue till the end of March, what will become of us?"† "Major-General Buller," he added, "is no longer a Rifleman;

---

perhaps it is so, for I am sure in cold blood I never could strike a man as I did then and, if I had not, in all probability those with me would not have charged and we should have lost our lives. This morning, as I passed the Russian prisoners and wounded, a man amongst them ran up and called out to me and pointed to his shoulder bound up. It was the poor fellow whose arm I had cut off yesterday; he laughed and said, 'Bono Johnny'. I took his hand and shook it heartily and the tears came in my eyes. I had not a shilling in my pocket; had I a bag of gold he should have had it. I enquired if he had been cared for, and the doctor told me he had and was doing well." *Idem*, 91.

  * *Clifford*, 88-93.

  † "For the next three months we were on the verge of starvation and suffered frightfully from the cold. No one can imagine what it was like but those who went through it. Only the strongest men lived. We had no firewood but the roots of the little oak trees which we grubbed out of the ground after we had found them under the snow. The grubbing had to be done with pickaxes without handles; the handles, being wood, were soon burnt." Diary of Colour-Sergeant J. Fisher. *R.B.C. 1957*, 91-8.

his rank does not stop his grumbling, and with the best natural spirits in the world it is very hard to keep cheerful with him."

Yet, though his ailing chief was invalided to England, Clifford's own spirit—and the philosophy of cheerfulness in extremity which he derived from his Regiment and his Roman Catholic Faith—never failed him. "They may overpower us," he wrote of the Russians said to be moving south in great numbers to relieve the beleaguered fortress, "but it will cost them very dear; not a man out here but would be glad to hear we were to be attacked, and few would care for loss of life such as theirs. Some have been so bold as to breathe the word, 'Peace!' I am not one of them, and, strange though it may sound, I who have so many ties to make me love life and home, would turn my back with regret on Sebastapol not taken." His spirit was reflected in the behaviour of his fellow Riflemen in the trenches, who despite their emaciated bodies and scarecrow rags, remained, as their deeds showed—unlike poor General Buller—Riflemen. Towards the end of November 200 men of the 1st Battalion, under Lieutenant Henry Tryon, carried out a brilliant operation by rushing, under cover of darkness, some strongly defended rifle-pits known as the Ovens, from which heavy casualties were being inflicted on French and British working-parties. Tryon, who led the first charge, was killed in the moment of triumph, and others fell, but the survivors beat off every attempt of the Russians to recapture the position. "We kept them off by our fire," wrote Colour-Sergeant Fisher, "we were hard at it all night and shouted constantly to make it appear we were stronger than we really were. At one time only myself and one man, Beaky Fearn, were left alive or unwounded at one of the pits."* Both the surviving officers received the Victoria Cross† at the end of the war, as did three Riflemen of the 2nd Battalion—Joseph Bradshaw, Roderick MacGregor and R. Humpston—who, in the spring of 1855, to revenge a dead comrade, carried out a similar operation on their own. So did Rifleman Francis Wheatley of the 1st Battalion who picked up a live shell when it fell in a crowded trench and threw it to safety, and Lieutenant John Knox—a former sergeant in the Scots Guards rewarded for his gallantry at the Alma by a commission in the Rifle Brigade—

---

* *R.B.C. 1957*, 91-8.

† Lieutenant, later Colonel Claude T. Bourchier and Lieutenant, later Major, Sir William Cunningham, Bart. *Cope*, 323.

who led the ladder party in the Waterloo Day attack on the Redan
in which both Battalions took part. At the first presentation of the
Victoria Cross by the Queen in Hyde Park, when Knox, his breast
blazing with decorations, marshalled his fellow recipients, eight of
the forty-seven crosses won by the Army in the Crimea went to the
Rifle Brigade, five more than the number won by the next most
honoured regiment, the Royal Artillery.

How high—despite the infusion of large drafts of half-trained
recruits from England—was the *esprit de corps* of the Regiment is
shown by a story told by Field Marshal Lord Wolseley of a young
soldier of the 2nd Battalion, beside which he himself had served as a
subaltern in the Crimea.

"The left of our third parallel, indeed of all the parallels in the
right attack, rested upon the Woronzoff Road ravine. This young
soldier was the left-hand sentry of the Company posted there, and
was told to keep a good look-out for the enemy to his front and
left flank. In a sortie the Russians took possession of a long stretch
of the third parallel, driving our trench guards from it . . . After
some delay, our supports coming forward sent the Russians flying
back to their own works. The third parallel was re-occupied and
fresh sentries were posted beyond it. During this process the
officer sent to the extreme left to post a sentry there, found to his
astonishment that there was one there already. It was the young
Rifleman who had been posted there early in the evening. He was
coolly looking over the parapet as if there had been no fighting in
his neighbourhood, no charges and countercharges, or no trenches
taken and re-taken close beside him. Asked what he was doing
there, he said he was a sentry. 'But how came it you are here alone;
what took place when the Russians jumped into the parallel and
drove our men out?' Answering very calmly, and in a matter-of-
fact fashion, he said: 'I stayed because, when I was posted here, the
officer told me to remain until I should be relieved. I saw the
Russians come in, but none came at me, and I obeyed my orders.'
I am sorry to say I cannot say who he was, for I would fain record
the name of so good, so brave a soldier."*

In his farewell to the 1st Battalion Rifle Brigade at the end of the
war the Officer Commanding the 4th Division referred to "their

* *United Service Magazine*, November 1854, cit. *R.B.C. 1895*, 73.

magnificent *esprit de corps* which descended from their predecessors, the old 95th." A correspondent of a London journal at the front was more explicit.

> "The Rifles are always the foremost in battle and the last in retreat. They perform their duties under every disadvantage; in fact they are trained not only to contend with the enemy but with every hardship to which a soldier can be exposed . . . Availing themselves of every fragment of shelter, they fire from behind trees; . . . at other times they approach the enemy lines on their hands and knees and fire prone on the ground extended. But of all their services in the Crimea those in the trenches have been the most severe, constant and glorious. Night and day they have had to do battle with the Russians; at all hours and in all kinds of weather—one day up to their hips in water, the next half blinded by sleet and hail—they had to keep up their deadly fire of Minié balls or those of the old regulation rifles.* But whatever sort of weapon they used their aim was unerring; and . . . the French sharpshooters—so celebrated for their almost mathematic certainty of fire—have gallantly acknowledged that the British riflemen were their equals in every respect. So celebrated a corps could scarcely fail to be distinguished whenever the opportunity served."†

But the highest tribute of all came from the great Russian general and engineer, Todleben, whose genius for so long made Sebastapol impregnable. It was the Rifles, he said, who caused most trouble to the defenders.‡

*   *   *

One result of the Crimean War, which cost the Rifle Brigade the lives of eleven officers and 931 men—or roughly half the number who had sailed for the Black Sea in 1854—was the restoration to the

---

* In 1837, as a result of the recommendations of a Board of which Colonel Eeles, then commanding the 1st Battalion, was a member, the Baker rifle had been superseded by the heavier Brunswick rifle. On embarking for the Crimea both Battalions were armed with the Minié rifle—similar to those carried by Line regiments—and, later, with the Enfield rifle.
† *The London Journal*, cit. *R.B.C. 1954*, 70.
‡ Walter Wood, *The Rifle Brigade*, *1901*, 128.

Army List, in April 1855, of the 3rd Battalion which had been disbanded thirty-seven years before on the return of Wellington's Army of Occupation from France. Though it was not raised in time to fight the Russians, who, in the spring of 1856, following their withdrawal from Sebastopol in the previous September, sued for peace, its services were soon needed. For in the summer of 1857 alarming news reached England frcm India where, following the mutiny of the bulk of the Bengal Sepoy army in May, and the massacre of British officers, women and children which accompanied it, every regular soldier who could be spared was packed into transports for the long, crowded voyage to the Ganges, where a handful of troops were struggling against immense odds to save British rule in the East India Company's dominions. While the 2nd and 3rd Battalions were on their way, a 4th Battalion of the Regiment was formed on September 22nd 1857 at Winchester under Lt.-Colonel F. R. Elrington, one of the heroes of Inkerman who, in command of a Company of the 2nd Battalion on that fateful day, had been largely responsible for preventing the Russians from breaking through the British outpost line and reaching the sea.*

Sailing in small transports, each carrying up to 350 officers and men, the 2nd and 3rd Battalions reached Calcutta at different times in November 1857 in six separate divisions, each commanded by a Lt.-Colonel. All were rushed, as soon as they landed, by steamer, railroad, boat and bullock-cart and, after Allahabad and Futtehpore, on foot, to the decisive theatre of war five hundred miles away, where desperate fighting was in progress round the besieged city of Lucknow and Cawnpore—scene of the treacherous massacre at Nana Sahib's orders of two hundred British women and children. The 2nd Battalion was first to arrive, its advanced division under Brevet Lt.-Colonel Woodford—who was soon afterwards killed—going into action on the morning of November 26th at Cawnpore, where less than 4000 loyal troops were facing 30,000 mutineers. Here, fighting in extended order, it was joined next day in the nick of time by the second contingent under Lt.-Colonel William Fyers, whose march, clad in thick European uniforms, of 49 miles in 26 hours in intense heat, surpassed even the 1st Battalion's famous Peninsular

---

* He was recommended for the V.C., but never received it. He rose to be a full General and died in 1904 in his 85th year, the oldest living "wearer of the green jacket". *R.B.C. 1904*, 227-32.

march to Talavera. Weary and footsore though they were, the men went straight into battle.

On the same day the first contingent of the 3rd Battalion, under Captain Atherley—which had landed at Calcutta on November 8th—joined in the ding-dong struggle before Cawnpore where, with their fine marksmanship, the assembled Riflemen helped to neutralise the enemy's enormous artillery superiority by picking off the gunners. Their timely arrival helped, too, to cover the evacuation from Lucknow of its long besieged garrison and 400 women and children. They also succeeded in rescuing several abandoned eighteen-pounder and naval guns by dragging them under fire to safety with the slings taken off their rifles. Most of the time, and during their forced marches, exposed to intense heat by day and bitter cold at night they lived off tea, rum and a little dry biscuit, such exiguous rations sometimes only affording them a single meal a day.

Before the long battle of Cawnpore ended in final victory on December 6th, the remainder of the 3rd Battalion, delayed at sea by hurricanes, arrived on the scene, a detachment under Lt.-Colonel Julius Glyn covering the last 75 miles between the evening of the 3rd and the morning of the 5th, marching for the whole of two nights and a day without sleep.* The four Companies of the Headquarters division of the Battalion under Colonel Horsford also reached the front between December 3rd and 5th, the men lurching from side to side as they battled with sleep during the last thirty-six hours of their march. On the 6th both Battalions went into action together, deployed in line and fixing swords as they advanced, later extending to clear the woods and houses between the canal and the town of Cawnpore. Colonel Horsford was wounded but continued to lead his Battalion as the extended line of Riflemen drove the rebel army back in final rout.

Throughout 1858 the 2nd and 3rd Battalions served under the Commander-in-Chief, General Sir Colin Campbell—raised to the peerage that summer as Lord Clyde—as they helped to disperse and finally destroy the still numerous rebel forces. On March 6th they led Sir Colin's army in skirmishing order, the Line regiments follow-

---

* "Considering that this detachment consisted mostly of young soldiers, the Battalion having only been formed two years before; that these men had disembarked hardly three weeks, after being cooped up on board ship during a four months' voyage; that they had already made long and fatiguing marches up the country; this march ... is perhaps hardly paralleled in military history." *Cope*, 358.

ing in quarter-column distance, at the start of the final battle of
Lucknow, which resulted, after a fortnight's fierce fighting, in the
capture of the city—the capital of Oudh—and in the winning of a
new and much valued battle honour for the Regiment. In its course
an officer and two men of the 2nd Battalion gained the Victoria
Cross, Corporal W. Nash and Rifleman David Hawkes carrying a
wounded comrade to safety under heavy fire while their retreat from
an apparently hopeless cul-de-sac was covered, single-handed, by
their Company Commander, Captain Henry Wilmot. Another V.C.
was gained for the Regiment later that year by Corporal Samuel
Shaw of the 3rd Battalion who, though wounded in the head, coolly
took on in single combat, and killed, a giant fanatic Ghazee.

During the summer of 1858, with the thermometer often standing
at 110 and sometimes even higher, the Regiment exchanged its green
cloth jackets for a campaign-uniform of dust-coloured linen—or
khaki as it became called—with black facings. For neither Battalion,
engaged in ceaselessly pursuing the scattered columns of the enemy,
was there much rest. On their long marches the men suffered much
from heat-stroke, some fatally; on one terrible march that June the
2nd Battalion lost nearly a hundred men. Working in close co-
operation with the 7th Hussars—among whose troopers it was a
standing joke "that they could not get rid of these little fellows"*
who kept up with their horses so gamely—the Battalion spent the
autumn in routing out rebel forces in Rohilkhand. *The Times*
correspondent, William Howard Russell, sent home a description of
it at the end of the year when for nearly a fortnight it had made a
series of marches of up to twenty miles with hardly a casualty:

> "The Rifle Brigade, who are with us, are as hard as nails; faces
> tanned brown and muscles hardened into whipcord; and to see
> them step over the ground with their officers marching beside
> them is a very fine sight for those who have an eye for real first-
> class soldiers. Lord Clyde is greatly pleased with the officers be-
> cause they do not ride on ponies as many officers of other regi-
> ments are accustomed to do."†

Meanwhile the 3rd Battalion was similarly engaged, often operating in thick jungle where large parties of the rebels had taken refuge.
On one occasion a detachment of a hundred Riflemen advancing in

* *Cope*, 408.   † Sir William Howard Russell, *My Diary in India*, *II*, 370.

extended order under a young officer, Lieutenant Andrew Green, lost touch with three of their number who were attacked by a large band of Sepoys. Hearing firing, Green, who was on horseback, went to their aid but was himself set on by six assailants. Shooting two with his revolver, he was cut down while dismounting and hacked at repeatedly as he lay on the ground. But, despite his wounds, he managed to rise and fell two more of his adversaries—now joined by three others—with the butt of his revolver and to shoot a third before they finally left him senseless and apparently dead with fourteen sabre cuts as well as a gunshot wound. Notwithstanding loss of blood, extreme fatigue—for he and his men had been under arms from four in the morning till three that afternoon—and the amputation of his left arm and right thumb, he recovered. Subsequently he rose to the rank of colonel, being universally known throughout the service as "Jolly" Green on account of his unfailing good-humour. He died in 1902 at the Royal Hospital, Chelsea, where for the last thirty-two years of his life he was Captain of Invalids.*

Not till the summer of 1859 were all the mutineers hunted down and the campaign at an end. During it the 2nd Battalion alone marched 1745 miles in 161 marches, keeping the field for twenty months without once going into quarters. Nearly a quarter of its officers and more than a fifth of its men had been killed, wounded or invalided. It remained in India as part of the British garrison until 1867, when it returned to England after an absence of ten years. The 3rd Battalion, which took part in 1863 in a punitive expedition against the Mohmund tribe on the North-west Frontier, did not leave India until the end of 1870, concluding its thirteen years' tour of overseas service with a year at Aden before landing at Portsmouth on New Year's Day, 1872.

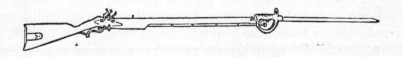

* Cope, 398-9. R.B.C. 1902, 171-3.

Chapter Five

FIGHTING ALL OVER
THE WORLD

We Riflemen obey orders and do not start difficulties.
GEN. SIR HARRY SMITH

IN the four decades which followed the Crimea and Mutiny, Great
Britain engaged in no major war. Nor was she in any European one
for nearly half a century—a longer peace even than that which
divided Waterloo from the Alma. Yet during this period the Rifle
Brigade was serving—and, at times, fighting—all over the world.
In 1861 the 1st Battalion, after a short spell in Ireland, was sent post-
haste to Canada to defend that country against a possible invasion
from the U.S.A., one of whose warships had forcibly taken off a
British packet-boat in mid-Atlantic two diplomats from its seceding
Southern States. No invasion took place, but during the American
Civil War repeated efforts were made by Federal agents to induce
British soldiers in Canada to desert and enlist in the North's armies.
As a private soldier's pay, after deduction for supplementary food,
washing, soap and cleaning materials, was only about 6d a day, it
was not surprising that some succumbed to such bribery. The only
Regiment which never lost a man to it was the Rifle Brigade.

While the 1st Battalion was quartered at Quebec a Rifleman named
Timothy O'Hea won the V.C. by boarding a run-away railway-van
loaded with ammunition and extinguishing a fire which threatened
to blow up the entire neighbourhood. Another, William Berry, was
recommended for the same decoration for rescuing a child under
circumstances of extreme gallantry in the great Quebec fire of 1866.
The Rifle Brigade at this time enjoyed immense social prestige. On
the death of its Colonel-in-Chief, Prince Albert, the Queen had conferred on it the title of the Prince Consort's Own. When, in 1868, its
Colonelcy-in-Chief again became vacant, it was given to the Prince
of Wales. A year later, the Sovereign's soldier son, the 19-year-old
Prince Arthur and future Duke of Connaught, joined the 1st Bat-

talion at Montreal, seeing service with it during the 1870 Fenian raid. Its Commanding Officer was Lord Alexander Russell, a son of the Duke of Bedford and brother to the then Prime Minister. He had a lordly way of dealing with administrative superiors, writing to them on blotting-paper until they complied with his request for a free issue of official stationery.*

A writer in the Rifle Brigade Chronicle has reconstructed the scene when this tremendous swell and his fellow officers arrived at Hamilton in February 1861—"the Dundreary whiskers and the smart Astrakhan roll collars of the officers' greatcoats, . . . the pouter pigeon chests set off by the black cross belts on which gleamed the large silver badge of the Rifles. The sartorial splendour of the unit was matched by its great fighting record. Emblazoned on the drums was the long roll of Peninsular battle-honours, each name displayed on a scroll. The honour, Waterloo, had pride of place; . . . Alma, Inkerman and Sebastopol proclaimed desperate actions in the late war with Russia. A high proportion of soldiers in the ranks wore the medal for the Crimea. Here and there a white and red ribbon marked a man who had marched to the relief of Lucknow. It was a veteran battalion."† So tough was it that when it landed at St. John's, New Brunswick, in January, 1862, this crack English Regiment travelled 300 miles by sleigh in the depth of the Canadian winter, its men clad in greatcoats, fur caps and mocassins, with blankets as ponchos with holes cut for their heads. Except for one or two cases of frost-bite, they did not lose a man.

For all the harsh life of the rank and file and the immense divisions of class of the time, the distinguishing feature of the Regiment was the spirit of respect and comradeship between officers and men. A gentleman ranker, known in the 1st Battalion as "Long" Thompson, who enlisted at Quebec in 1866 after being set on by a crowd of Irish Fenians in New York, recalled that he had never met anywhere officers or men to equal in good fellowship those of the Battalion. In his book, *Life is a Jest: the Testimony of a Wanderer*, he wrote:

* R.B.C. 1965, 107. He had taken over the Battalion at the end of the war in the Crimea during the illness of its then C.O., Lt.-Col. Edward Somerset, winning great eclat at a regimental banquet, according to a young Edinburgh volunteer surgeon attached to the Regiment, by singing "For they are jolly good Fellows" and substituting the words "For they led the way to the Alma." R.B.C. 1897, 61.

† Frank Jones, "Hamilton's Last British Army Garrison: Rifle Brigade Quelled U.S. Threat." R.B.C. 1958, 59-60.

"All my life I have pondered over the remarkable feature of the Rifle Brigade. The Battalion being on foreign service, there were about thirty officers with whom we were brought in contact and, with only two exceptions, they were regarded by us as being honourable, considerate, soldierly *gentlemen*. Many possessed the real affection—there is no other name for it—of the men of their respective companies. One of them, who had been given the barrack-room sobriquet, 'Played-Out', was especially idolized by us all; we would not have followed him into a hail of bullets, we would have got in front to shelter him—at least, that's how we youngsters felt about it. There seemed to be a feeling in the ranks that the officers, too, looked on us more or less as comrades-in-arms . . . In the Standing Orders of the Battalion the following was one of the items: 'The salute is a mark of goodwill and respect between two members of the same honourable profession; it shall be offered first by the junior in rank and returned by the senior'."

When, after two years' service, Prince Arthur* was temporarily posted away from the Regiment, he told the Orderly Room Sergeant —a friend of Thomson's—to let him know if he ever needed help. Some years later, when serving in India where the climate did not agree with him, this man, writing to the Duke of Connaught—as he then was—received by return a posting to the regimental depot at Winchester, where he was allowed to complete his twenty-one years' service and retire on a pension with a civil appointment in the Isle of Wight. "Is it any wonder," Thomson asked, "that we 'Boys of the old Brigade' held our officers in such high esteem?"†

*   *   *

It was the same in the other Battalions, including the newly formed 4th, which, under its Crimea War hero, Lt.-Colonel Frederick Elrington, after serving in Malta and Gibraltar, joined the 1st in Canada in 1865 and helped to repel a raid across the American border

---

* After the battle of Tel-el-Kebir in 1882 in Egypt, where the Duke of Connaught commanded an infantry brigade, the soldiers sang of him:

> "'E's ninepence a soldier an' threepence a Prince,
> 'E stood fire in Egypt and 'e didn't wince,
>   Not Arthur!"

R.B.C. *1929*, 44.
† R.B.C. *1925*, 221-2, 226, 236-7, 256-7.

by the so-called Irish Republican Army. It was in the sixties that R. E. Crompton—the future pioneer of electric lighting—then serving as a subaltern with the 3rd Battalion in India, "learnt," as he put it, "that the word Rifleman is synonymous with 'true unselfish gentleman.' I have a specially pleasant recollection of not only my brother officers but of the men . . . I owe much to the splendid comaraderie and the way in which the senior officers encouraged the young fellows to become real 'Riflemen'." Serving in the Battalion with him was another subaltern, Algernon Drummond, who, while stationed at Bombay in 1865, composed the music of the Eton Boating Song,* whose lilt and gaiety so perfectly expresses the spirit of the Rifle Brigade.

For it was still, as in Peninsular days, an incorrigibly gay regiment as well as a fighting one. "We are a happy, light-hearted lot," Major H. A. N. Fyers recalled of his subaltern days in the 'eighties, "and looked forward to an adventurous life in the Regiment."† Its officers were always jollying and ragging one another and finding amusement and entertainment under all the circumstances of their changing and often—because of the demands of their parsimonious, unmilitary but expansionist country—uncomfortable and hazardous existence. In the Nowshera earthquake of 1865, with the temperature standing at 106 in the shade, as the plaster of the bungalow ceiling started to fall on his head, Algernon Drummond heard a fellow subaltern giving a rendering, with supporting chorus, of the music-hall song, "So let the world shake about as it will, we'll all be free and easy still!" When, after long service abroad, the 2nd Battalion returned to Dover—a dull, uneventful station—the officer who contributed the annual Battalion letter to the Regimental Chronicle mentioned that a brother officer, whose hobby was collecting birds' eggs had given him a plover's egg as a great treat and that he had eaten it for breakfast and that it was "corked". To which the editor —a distinguished ornithologist—added a footnote: "We are informed that the egg our correspondent complains of was not a plover's but a carrion crow's (*corvus corone*). They *are* sometimes rather strong. (Ed.)"‡

As—even in a period when, with the expansion of Britain's worldwide Empire, her little, over-stretched professional Army was expected to keep order over a quarter of the habitable globe—garrison

* *R.B.C. 1933*, 155, 168; *1932*, 244-53.   † *R.B.C. 1932*, 196-200.   ‡ *R.B.C. 1890*, 108-9.

duty occupied more of a soldier's time than active service, sport afforded an outlet for the energies of a corps which had always encouraged its members to live at a stretch and exercise their faculties to the full. During the Peninsular War, Jonathan Leach had seized every opportunity of "wanders with his gun," and on several occasions during the Mutiny a skirmishing Rifleman, "unable to resist his sporting propensities," fired at a hare instead of the enemy. In the 'sixties, when both the 2nd and 3rd Battalions were garrisoning India, there was ample opportunity for those who sought it, for sport of every kind. Victorian India swarmed with game and was still a game-shooter's virgin paradise.* "Our stay in Delhi," wrote Surgeon Bradshaw of the 2nd Battalion,† "afforded ample scope for indulgence of sporting instincts, as jheels and jungles were not far away. H. Dugdale, an excellent shot, told me that the total of his bag of wild duck amounted to about one thousand; in one of his Himalayan expeditions he killed twenty-one bears. Game was made over to the Company messes so abundantly that eventually it ceased to be a welcome addition to the ordinary rations."‡

Not only big game shooting but every type of sport flourished in India, where each of the Regiment's four Battalions served repeatedly between the Mutiny and the outbreak of the First World War. Its officers played a part in introducing the British Army to polo—the traditional sport of the Indian native cavalry; as early as 1862 George Lloyd-Verney of the 2nd Battalion was reported as playing "hockey on horseback". In 1875, 1881, 1882 and 1883 the Rifle Brigade were runners-up in the Inter-Regimental Indian Polo Tournament, and in the last year of the century the 3rd Battalion won the all-India cup—the only infantry Regiment ever to do so except the Durham Light Infantry. Between 1884 and 1938, the last date on which the Regiment provided part of the garrison of British India, it won the Infantry Inter-Regimental Polo cup—founded in the former year—no less than seven times.§

Hunting, coursing, horse and pony racing, pig-sticking, cricket and football for all ranks, golf, rackets, walking and bicycling races

---

* "It was after the Mutiny in the 'sixties' and 'seventies' that the palmy days of sport in the Regiment began . . . It was full of keen sportsmen; sport was cheap and soldiering unexacting." Viscount Bridgeman, "Famous Sporting Regiments: The Rifle Brigade," *The Field*, 21st August, 1937.

† Later Surgeon Major-General Sir A. F. Bradshaw.

‡ *R.B.C. 1922*, 176.   § *R.B.C. 1894*, 150-1; *1937*, 242-51.

Bandmaster W. Miller

The Rifle Brigade in Action, Indian Mutiny 1857—Orlando Norrie

H.R.H. Field Marshal The Duke of Connaught

in the 'nineties, all figure continually in accounts of the Regiment's activities in whatever part of the world its Battalions were quartered. Fox-hunting, at its more classic, flourished notably in Ireland; in India it took a more elastic form and sometimes included jackals; "during the cold weather," ran one report, "Wood, Railston and Dimsdale ran a Bobbery Pack which provided us with many pleasant afternoon's amusement. The going was generally hard and in some places blind, but, though there were several tosses, no one was seriously damaged except Crosbie who had a very stiff shoulder for some time."* A subaltern quartered with the 1st Battalion at Belgaum—a remote station in southern Mahrattaland, 150 miles from the nearest railway—recalled in old age what life was like there in the 'eighties. "At this quiet little station we were rather thrown on our own resources. We chased jackal over the Maidan with two or three Rampore hounds. There were gymkhanas, cricket matches and polo of sorts. The latter was not very high-class, and there was an institution known as 'The Week'—a race-meeting, a cricket match and polo matches. At night there were dances at the Club . . . There used to be rather good shooting in the neighbourhood; jungle fowl was the principal game, besides snipe and quail, but there was a good deal of jungle some fifteen miles away, and at very rare intervals someone got a tiger."†

"Soldier cricket," a Rifleman wrote, "is really the jolliest cricket that can be found anywhere." Played at every time of the year in an empire on which the sun never set, it reached its apotheosis for the Rifle Brigade in the Greenjackets' Week at Winchester where every year from 1884 onwards it met in friendly rivalry on the lovely ground at St. Cross its fellow Rifle Regiment, the 60th or King's Royal Rifle Corps, whose heroism on the Ridge at Delhi—rewarded by no less than seven Victoria Crosses—had put it on a pinnacle of national fame and prestige. But the game was just as enthusiastically played and enjoyed in the most unlikely places. At Muree, R. E. Crompton recalled, "we used to train retriever dogs as extra fieldsmen, so that when the ball was hit over the *khud* or precipice at the edges of the ground, the dogs retrieved the balls for us and were very efficient at it." Once at Dinapore he and Joe Constable Maxwell of the 3rd Battalion made a stand of five hundred not out, while in

* R.B.C., *1909*, 105.
† R.B.C. *1932*, 196-8.

another match Rifleman Jordan, who played the big drum, hit a "niner" and ran it out.

As in other regiments, cricket-weeks and theatricals often went together. The Rifle Brigade was famous for its stage entertainments. "We had among us officers extraordinarily gifted with histrionic and musical powers," Crompton recalled of the 3rd Battalion in its post-Mutiny days. "Algernon Drummond . . . was a fine musician and a good actor. Mitchell-Innes was one of the best amateur actors I have known and was able to make up as an extraordinarily beautiful woman. Everywhere we went we were called upon to fit up theatres in barrack-rooms of many of the stations and we always had crowded audiences." It was from this love of theatrical entertainments—a tradition reaching back to the Peninsula—that the Regiment's famous quick march, "Ninety-five", originated. In 1842, while quartered at Malta, Rifleman Goodall of the 1st Battalion, dressed as an old woman, used to sing in the regimental theatre a comic song which so delighted his audiences that Bandmaster Miller turned it into a march.*

> "*I'm ninety-five, I'm ninety-five,*
> *And to keep single I'll contrive;*
> *It's needles and pins, it's needles and pins,*
> *And when a man marries his trouble begins.*"

"No one," Miller wrote, "took notice of it more than any other march, but when we got to the Cape in 1846 there were long marches and sore feet, and I now made use of 'Ninety-five' to help the men into camp. The first day the Battalion marched into it there was not a limping man amongst the lot." Played at Aldershot after the Crimean War before the Queen—who afterwards asked for a copy of it—it superseded the former regimental quick-march, the Huntsmen's Chorus from Weber's *Der Freischütz*, and became the sound to which, above all others, members of the Rifle Brigade throughout the world responded.

In the Victorian era a large proportion of a soldier's time was devoted to drill, and, though formed to counter the excessive formalism of the parade ground, the Rifle Brigade was no exception. The composer of the Eton Boating Song remembered an old musketry instructor who always maintained that the reason the Israelites

* *R.B.C. 1931*, 248-56; *1933*, 168.

had conquered their enemies was "their for-r-r-ty years dr-r-illing in the wilderness." "The Battalion when I joined," wrote an officer commissioned in the 1st Battalion in 1879 and later transferred to the 4th, "was nine hundred strong and exceedingly smart and efficient and their drill both steady and, in extended order, something to marvel at, while their turn-out was the acme of smartness. The drill was very complicated compared with what it is now, but the men prided themselves, and with reason, that they could not be caught out or clubbed . . . In the spring the Battalion went through spring drills which lasted about six weeks; all who could be spared had to be on parade, and the entire drill-book was gone through from standing at ease by numbers to the end of the book. The subalterns formed a squad for this purpose, and . . . we were at it all day."

"There was a great deal of formality connected with soldiering in those days. For instance, on a battalion parade, after the captains had inspected their Companies, they took post on the left of their respective Companies with swords drawn, state in hand. The Adjutant placed himself facing the left flank of the Battalion with his sword drawn. The C.O. then called the Battalion to attention and gave the order to 'Collect Reports', the band struck up '95', the Adjutant saluted the C.O. and called out 'Battalion all present Sir', or the number of absentees. In the 4th Battalion the Adjutant used to trot down the Battalion on his horse, the band playing 'Monymusk'. In the 1st Battalion there was a countersign each day, and in turning out the guard at night, the officer was halted and told, 'Advance one and give the countersign'; thereupon a corporal and one file doubled out from the Guard, rifles at the charge, the countersign was given, and the corporal and escort doubled back to the Guard in time to fall in when the officer arrived."*

The military skill on which the Regiment prided itself above all others was marksmanship. In this, with the 60th, it formed a model to the whole Army, and, in the eighteen-sixties, to the nation. After Napoleon III became Emperor of the French, and again in the years after the Indian Mutiny, there was an invasion scare and a revival of

* Captain the Hon. A. Somerset, "Old Days in the 1st Battalion." *R.B.C. 1937*, 162-6.

the Volunteer movement.* Volunteer Rifle Battalions, dressed in green or grey uniforms with rifle pouch-belts and based on the Rifle Brigade or on the King's Royal Rifles, sprang up all over the country, and a National Rifle Association was formed under the patronage of the Prince Consort to encourage marksmanship and the use of the rifle. By the 'seventies there were seventeen volunteer Battalions affiliated to the Rifle Brigade, including the London Scottish, the Inns of Court Rifles, the London Irish Rifles, the Artists' Rifles, the City of London Volunteer Rifle Corps and the two Battalions of the Tower Hamlets Rifles. In 1860 the first annual meeting of the National Rifle Association was held on Wimbledon Common and the Queen's Medal instituted as the supreme annual award for marksmanship for the Empire. It was won three times in its early years by a member of the Rifle Brigade, and, when in 1890 an annual competition for Young Soldiers was added, the Regiment won it five times in the first seven years and obtained second place four times. In the same year Major Montagu Curzon, who later commanded the 1st Battalion, presented the Regiment with thirty-six gold and silver shooting medals, "to be worn by the best shots of each Battalion and of each Company during the year".†

A by-product of the Rifleman's desire to excel, and of the Regiment's philosophy that whatever was worth doing was worth doing as well as it allowed, was the distinction gained by its members in activities far removed from regimental duty and even soldiering. In the last half of the 19th century the Army tended to be a somewhat closed and self-centred community, cut off from the main channels of contemporary life. Yet this was never true of the Rifle Brigade. R. E. Crompton, when stationed in India in the early 'seventies, pioneered a revolution in army transport by designing a steam-engine with rubber tyres capable of moving goods and men along the Indian trunk roads, and even persuaded the Viceroy and Government of India to institute an experimental "Government

* Marked by a poem in *The Times* on May 9th, 1859, by Tennyson:
> "*Let your Reforms for a moment go,*
> *Look to your butts and take good aims.*
> *Better a rotten borough or so*
> *Than a rotten fleet or a city in flames!*
> *Form! Form! Riflemen form!*
> *Ready, be ready to meet the storm!*
> *Riflemen, riflemen, riflemen form!*"

† *R.B.C. 1891*, 89; *1932*, 154-5. Lord Cottesloe, *The Englishman and the Rifle*, 54-60.

Steam Train" with himself as Superintendent. It was because he was a Rifleman with a Rifleman's outlook, he maintained, that he was able to do so. "The success of the first Indian experiment in road transport," he wrote, "was undoubtedly due to the splendid training that I had in the direction and management of men during my period of actual service with the Battalion . . . I recall with extreme pleasure the encouragement I received from a large proportion of my brother officers who helped me in many ways and encouraged me to carry on with the work." When the authorities in England failed through lack of imagination to use his ideas, he turned his inventive, adventuring mind to the study of electricity and played a major part in introducing electric lighting into Britain, becoming President of the Institute of Electrical Engineers and founder of the firm of Crompton, Parkinson & Co. Once he had the unique distinction of being slapped by Queen Victoria. For when in 1880 he was commanded to Buckingham Palace to demonstrate his new electric lamp, "Her Majesty," he recalled, "did not like it. She even told me to take it away. I suggested she should wait and see, and she slapped my face because I had the cheek to have my own way."*

Another Rifleman who gained distinction outside the Army was the great explorer and cartographer, Sir Thomas Mitchell, who was given a commission in the 95th by Wellington in 1813 and was used by him to make maps of the Peninsular battlefields. After his retirement from the Army he emigrated to Australia where his work as Surveyor-General of New South Wales played an important part in the development of eastern Australia. A later and parallel case was that of the Hon. E. Noel, who joined the Regiment in 1872 and served in the march to Coomassie and the Burma Campaign of 1885-8. Master of seven languages and a mathematician of distinction, he wrote a book on *The Science of Metrology or Natural Weights and Measures* which challenged the metric system. Despite an apparently fragile frame, he also climbed the Matterhorn and Mount Blanc and won fame as an oriental traveller.

This interest in activities outside the narrow bounds of conventional soldiering brought the Regiment into contact with the civil population of many distant places. "All of us who were sportsmen," wrote Crompton of the years after the Mutiny, "got into

* *R.B.C. 1965*, 105; *1933*, 166. "I am sure I am the only man whose face has been slapped by Queen Victoria—and I am proud of it."

extremely friendly relations with the Zemindars or native land-
owners, for whenever we went into camp near their villages we
tried to cultivate their friendships and to learn something about the
history of that part of India . . . When I revisited India to obtain the
Indian Electric Lighting Act in 1896 twenty years after . . . I found
that we Riflemen were still remembered by the native population
we had known in those early days . . . I feel that I ought to put on
record my recollections of the extraordinary affection shown to all
of us Riflemen, both officers and men, by everyone we met in India,
chiefly the leading officials of the Civil Service, the officers and men
of the Native Regiments with whom we served on duty or met at
shooting parties or social gatherings. When any of us were stricken
with the malaria which followed on our attacks of Peshawar fever,
we were nursed and cared for by the ladies of the Punjab hill station
at Murree, and later on, when we marched down-country, as if we
were members of one beloved family. I felt this personally and I
know that most of the officers of the Battalion shared my feelings.
At the same time I must admit that with the exception of the
Highland Regiments, the Line Regiments as a rule looked on us as
those stand-off swanky Riflemen; but they really had no cause for
this feeling, other than that they thought they were not so popular
in general Society as we were. During those early years I formed
many life-long friendships, and the children, and even grand-
children, of those early friends often tell me of the affection their
forbears had for us Riflemen."* At Peshawar in the 'nineties the
native regiments quartered with the 3rd Battalion called it "Jat
Pultan", the Regiment of Gentlemen—the only regiment, incidentally, whom the local Pathan rifle-stealers did not think worth
while to approach.

Though a little apart by its peculiar character from the rest of
the Army, the Rifle Brigade was a very human Regiment. It was,
above everything else, a family which prided itself on being one
and on the "separateness" which bound its members so closely. It
had its family peculiarities of custom, organisation and drill—of
not carrying Colours, of never using slang or the words of command "Attention" or "Slope Arms", of marching at the trail instead of the slope, of its junior officers not addressing senior officers
in the Mess as "Sir", of having family nicknames for everyone,

* R.B.C. 1933, 166-8.

of peculiar bugle calls called "horns" for marking the occasions and hours of military life, many of which the rest of the Army subsequently adopted. Its famous quick-step and double-march past the saluting base in close column were apt to cause confusion to other units at general parades; "when we struck up Ninety-five . . . at Brigade and Divisional inspections," recalled Bugle-Major Hone, "we set the 'red army' dancing."*

It was a Regiment, too, intensely conscious of its history and for that reason closer to the Regiments which had fought by its side in the old Light Division of Peninsular days than even to its fine fellow Rifle Regiments—the 60th, the Scottish Rifles or Cameronians, and the Royal Irish Rifles. Towards the "light Bobs" of the 43rd and 52nd —amalgamated after the Cardwell reforms in a single Regiment, the Oxfordshire and Buckinghamshire Light Infantry—the 11th Hussars and the Chestnut Troop of the Royal Horse Artillery, Riflemen reacted with touching warmth. Whenever their occasions brought them together they were referred to in the regimental Chronicle as "our old comrades-in-arms" or "our old Friends of the Light Division." Once in the 'seventies, when the 43rd and 52nd were brigaded with a Rifle Brigade Battalion at Aldershot and, during a disturbance in the garrison theatre, two Riflemen were hustled, there was a cry of "Stand by, the Light Division", and every representative of the three Regiments went to their aid. The War Office, with its bureaucratic passion for uniformity, was always attempting to whittle away the distinctions which gave the Rifle Brigade its historical identity, but without success. When in the 'eighties what one of its officers called "a very common and horrible helmet" with a spike at the top was given it in place of the busby—which after the Crimea had replaced the Albert shako— every officer of the Regiment with any influence, from the Duke of Connaught downwards, waged unrelenting war against it until higher authority relented and authorised the issue of more Riflemanlike headgear. "There were great rejoicings," wrote a happy Greenjacket when the good news came.

"After dinner a solemn procession was formed consisting of the subalterns' band in front; then the 'Corpse' (consisting of the Commanding Officer's old helmet) followed by the whole of the

* R.B.C. *1923*, 139: *1906*, 74.

officers of the battalion. The band played Lamb's symphony in
'B' flat which was very impressive. The procession having arrived
at the crematorium, the corpse was consigned to the flames; the
mourners then joined hands and danced round the funeral pyre
to the tune of '95' whilst it was being consumed, amidst ringing
cheers. The procession then re-formed, and the band playing that
well-known tune, 'It will never come back no more, boys', returned to the Mess-hut and drank the health of the new Hat,
coupled with the names of all those who have worked so hard to
get it back for us."*

For in some matters the Rifle Brigade was a law unto itself. When
an inspecting general had made some critical remarks, the 3rd
Battalion's Commanding Officer, who considered them unjustified,
dismissed the parade with the words, " My men, the General does not
appear to be very pleased with us; but what does it matter so long as
we are pleased with ourselves." " It was a very happy Battalion,"
Colonel C. H. B. Norcott commented, "that marched back to
Barracks to the tune of *Little Johnny Whopplestraw* on the bugles."†

Owing to the Regiment's tradition of tactical independence and
initiative, every Battalion and even sometimes Company, accustomed to operating on its own, had its own horn-calls, its own
cherished minor variations and distinctions of dress,‡ drill and
ceremonial, and commanded a partisan loyalty from its members.
When Major H. Hone, who had enlisted as a boy bugler in the 4th
Battalion on its formation in 1857, heard of its disbandment in 1922,
he wrote that it was like the loss of a ship to a sailor. "Now that it
has gone, my thoughts must follow the 2nd Battalion in which my
father served 21 years and in which I was born when the Battalion
was stationed in Nova Scotia in November 1843."§

Yet all Riflemen shared a common brotherhood. The annual
Battalion Letters, which became such a feature of the Regimental
Chronicle, always ended—with variations—"Wishing all brother
Riflemen the best of good luck." The highest praise one Rifleman

---

* *R.B.C. 1930*, 267.   † *R.B.C. 1924*, 169-70.
‡ *R.B.C. 1937*, 162-6; When George Cockburn, joining the 2nd Battalion at Gibraltar in
1877, entered the Mess for the first time conscious that he was correctly dressed in all particulars, he was greeted by an old Etonian contemporary with a chilling, "We don't wear
chinstraps!" *R.B.C. 1924*, 150-1.
§ *R.B.C. 1923*, 128.

could pay another was to say that he was "a good Rifleman". The Chronicle, founded in 1890 and continued till 1965, when a Royal Green Jackets one took its place, is full of tributes to past members who had no other claim to fame but this. "He loved the Regiment with his whole heart," it was written of Major Sir Bartle Frere, "and never failed to do the utmost in his power for those who had served in it." When Colonel A. H. S. Montgomery—"old Mac" who had been Adjutant of the 1st Battalion in the 'seventies—died at the age of 78, his headstone was given the simple inscription,

> *" A Good Rifleman.*
> *Erected by some of his old Comrades."**

Such modest and unseeking sons of the Regiment received as much affection and respect from their brother officers as those who rose to their highest summits of military rank and ambition. "He was a most painstaking, conscientious officer," it was written of Lt.-Colonel the Hon. Wenman Coke—"Wenny" to the Regiment—"and was much liked by all ranks. There was never any fuss or heat in the way in which he dealt with his men, and this engendered a confidence and trust which in military matters makes for discipline and order."† Even such a humble member of the Regiment as Walter Sydney Campbell, who was gazetted to it in 1864 and never rose beyond the rank of Lieutenant, received his meed of affection and remembrance. "He was greatly liked by all ranks and was popularly known as the Dormouse."

It was the greatest pride of a Rifleman to be "born in the green jacket". There were families both of officers and men who sent their sons into the Regiment generation after generation. None was more remarkable than that of the Norcott family, one of whom, Major-General Sir Amos Norcott, commanded the 2nd Battalion at Waterloo, another of whom—his son, Major-General Sir William or "Billy" Norcott—commanded it in the Crimea, while the latter's son, Colonel C. H. B. Norcott, who joined the 1st Battalion in 1867, commanded it in the South African War. His son, Lt.-Colonel H. B.

---

* *R.B.C. 1933*, 285-90; *1919*, 281.

† *R.B.C. 1895*, 226; *1931*, 362-9. Coke, a reserved and shy man to strangers, who served with the 4th Battalion in the Afghan campaign of 1878-9 and took part in the famous cholera march through the Khyber, contributed many items to the Rifle Brigade case at the Royal United Service Institution—the nucleus of the future Regimental Museum at Winchester.

Norcott, of the fourth generation, served with the Regiment in the First World War. Of C. H. B. Norcott it was written when he died at the age of 81, "the Regiment was to him, save only his family—for he was a most devoted husband and father—the one thing in this world which he worshipped. He was born and brought up in it and it was part of his being . . . Norcott was endowed with one of the sweetest and kindest of natures. I do not believe he was ever heard to say an unkind word of anyone nor to be ruffled or annoyed at anything that occurred, nor can I imagine his ever having had an enemy . . . His beautiful character never showed itself to greater advantage than in his last and lingering illness which he bore with exemplary patience."*

Nor was hereditary family devotion to the Regiment confined to the ranks of the commissioned. Fifteen-year-old William Peachey enlisted in the 1st Battalion two years before Waterloo, his son David at the age of thirteen in 1838, the latter's son at twelve in 1864 and a great grandson of the first William at fifteen in 1892, four generations of Peacheys thus contributing 101 years of service between 1813 and 1914.† It was a Regiment which evoked such dedication. When Captain Frederick Eyre Lawrence—son of General Sir Arthur Lawrence, who commanded the 2nd Battalion in the Crimea—was killed at the age of thirty-four on a punitive expedition in East Africa, he left the reversion of his entire estate, proved at £77,267, in trust to the Rifle Brigade for the welfare of all its members and the encouragement of "manly sports."‡ To such as he, as to Colonel C. G. Fortescue when, after thirty-one years' service, he relinquished his command of the 1st Battalion, it was "that glorious and beloved regiment," so dear that when at his final church parade the latter attempted to say good-bye to his command, he found himself unable to speak.§

---

* R.B.C. 1932, 338-9.

† Communicated by Mr. D. Marks, Country Life, 2nd March, 1972.

‡ "A more capable, unselfish and high-minded Rifleman and keener soldier never breathed. Ever foremost alike in improving the professional capabilities of his men and studying their welfare his whole life was devoted to the good of the Regiment." R.B.C. 1905, 44-6.

§ "Having sent my kit down to the railway station, I walked out of the barracks past the guard for the last time; the sentry presented arms (wrongly!) and I made my way on foot to Colchester railway station, feeling more unhappy than words can express at having ceased to belong to that glorious and beloved Regiment, the Rifle Brigade." Brig.-Gen. The Hon. C. G. Fortescue, Thirty-one Years Service in The Rifle Brigade. R.B.C. 1949, 117.

Perhaps the most remarkable example of dedication to the Regiment was the life of Colonel Willoughby Verner, the historian of its Peninsular campaigns, and the founder and editor of the Regimental Chronicle from its inception in 1890 until his death in 1922. Joining the Regiment in 1874 he passed first both in and out of the Staff College, and was one of the little group of those who served under Lord Wolseley in his prime and for whose genius he had unbounded admiration. In his early thirties he was D.A.A.G. in the Nile Expedition of 1884-5, serving with the future Lord Kitchener. Present at Abu Klea and El Gubat, he guided the famous "Fighting Square" on its march to the Nile. For seven years he was D.A.A.G. at Shorncliffe and, later, Professor of Military Topography at Sandhurst. At the age of 47 his brilliant military career—which might well have culminated in high command in 1914—was cut short by a near-fatal fall from his horse at the battle of Graspan, necessitating his retirement. But his country's loss was his Regiment's gain, for he devoted the rest of his life to its service, editing its annual Chronicle which he brought to a high pitch of perfection, and making it a link both between the Rifle Brigade's widely scattered Battalions and all Riflemen past and present. In 1890, following in the footsteps of its first historian, Sir William Cope—to whose "extraordinary research and hard work, great knowledge and marvellous memory," he paid generous tribute—he published his first historical book, *The British Rifle Corps* in 1890, and, after several other historical works, the two massive and immensely learned volumes of his *magnum opus*, *The History and Campaigns of the Rifle Brigade*. Inventor of the Magnetic and Prismatic Compasses and of the Cavalry Sketching Case and Plane Tables, a brilliant draughtsman and cartographer and lifelong ornithologist—his *My Life among the Wild Birds of Spain* is a classic—Willoughby Verner was perhaps the most versatile of all the many versatile men who have served the Rifle Brigade. Still at work on his unfinished third volume when death came in 1922, it was true of him as another great Rifleman, Field Marshal Sir Henry Wilson, said at his memorial service, that "he lived for the Regiment and died for the Regiment."*

An instance of dedication of a rather different kind was that of the Bandmaster William Miller. "Billy the Bugler" or "Bill Blowhard", as he was first known in the Regiment, began his forty-one

* *R.B.C. 1922*, 50-64; *R.B.C. 1965*, 100-1.

years' service at twelve when, 4 ft. 4 in. high, he was transferred
from the 84th whose band he had joined three years earlier. But his
apprenticeship to "the Black and the Green" had begun even earlier,
at the age of five, when his father had re-enlisted in the Rifle Brigade.
Having mastered every instrument in the band, he was appointed
Band-Sergeant of the 1st Battalion at Malta in 1842, subsequently
accompanying it to South Africa and the Crimea. As Bandmaster
he became one of the most famous figures of the Victorian Army,
receiving many marks of favour from the Queen, herself a lover of
music. One of Willoughby Verner's earliest recollections of the
Regiment was of this remarkable man's rendering of the post-horn
Gallop at a dance given by the 1st Battalion in 1873. "Mr Miller conducting the band on such an occasion was a sight never to be forgotten. Grasping his beloved keyed-bugle he would extract from it
marvellous notes. When it came to the post-horn call itself he would
raise himself on tip-toe (he was a very short and stout little man)
and, swinging his bugle upwards, would sound a melodious call
which, together with its refrain, must surely ring in the ears of all
who heard it, as it does in mine, to this day." There is another picture
of him two years earlier, at the first annual Regimental Dinner,
over which the Prince of Wales presided. "Some of us may still
recollect that little dapper figure, crowned with wig and spectacles,
beating time with his feet as well as with his conductor's baton,
and with his long post-horn at his lips or under his arm." In 1880,
the last year in which he played at the Regimental Dinner, Miller
claimed to have had the longest service of any Rifleman then living,
officer or man.*

From the Prince of Wales who, commanded in 1880 to hand over
his Colonelcy-in-Chief of the Regiment to his brother, the Duke of
Connaught, insisted on retaining the right to wear its black bugle-
horn buttons, to nineteen-year-old Henry Blishen, No. 3343 of the
2nd Battalion—afterwards killed in the Crimea—who proudly told
his parents, "Let me inform you that the Regiment is termed the
Advanced Guard of old England, the first in the field and the last
out," it was common ground to Riflemen of all ranks and ages that
there was no other Regiment like it. Old Oliver of Stonesfield who,
when serving with the 3rd Battalion, had seen Napoleon on his white

* R.B.C., 1891, 103-9; 1911, 115; 1915, 70-5. There is a touching letter from Miller written
in extreme old age to Lord Alexander Russell in the R.B.C. 1897, 174-5.

horse at Waterloo, though nearly blind and living on a pension of 1s 6d a day, used to sing out when shown a piece of regimental ribbon,

> " *The Black and the Green,*
> *The finest colours ever seen.*"

"No Rifleman would exchange with a red soldier, sir," a newcomer to the Regiment was told by one of his men whose brother had been offered a chance of better pay in the Guards. "Though I only served a little over four years in the Rifle Brigade," declared 'the fighting clerk', G. W. Mabin, who took part in the defence of Rorke's Drift— "I have never forgotten that 'once a Rifleman always a Rifleman', and I attribute my success in the Army to the training I received in that glorious Corps."*

Even animals sometimes seemed to share this corporate devotion. In the 'forties there was a raven known as Doctor Dakins who attached himself to the 2nd Battalion, knew all the bugle calls— especially those relating to rations—never missed a parade and was presented to Prince Albert who paid a special visit to the Regiment to meet him.† A decade later the same Battalion brought back a small black ram from the Crimea called Billy who took to its officers and would have nothing to do with any of the other Regiments at Shorncliffe. "It never allowed anyone to handle or to lead it," wrote Colonel Sir Herbert St. John Mildmay, "but, when the Regiment was drilling, Billy always placed himself about fifty yards in front, changing his place as the battalion changed. Sometimes he would suddenly turn round and charge the line, when a file quickly got out of his way, and he then trotted back to the front. I, with others, used to go across country jumping hedges, gates, etc. Billy was always with us and would fly a five-barred gate like a deer. Woe betide anyone who fell, for Billy charged him at once—only meant in play, but a butt from Billy was a serious matter! I used to bring three or four lumps of sugar with me from breakfast; when Billy would put his forefeet on my chest I would give him the sugar. When I had given him the last lump I had to throw Billy off and run, for he would at once try to butt me. The Battalion was sent up to London for the grand parade in Hyde Park where Queen Victoria

---

* *R.B.C. 1950*, 174; *1928*, 234.
† His story, as told by Major General W. H. Bradford, is printed in the Appendix.

gave away the first Victoria Crosses. Billy marched in front of the Battalion through the crowded streets and, when the Regiment was drawn up in line in the Park, Billy placed himself as usual and stood solemn and unperturbed till the ceremony was over. When the Battalion was ordered to Malta"—en route for India and the relief of Lucknow—" the Colonel decided not to take Billy and he was sent to Scotland to an estate of one of the officers. He became so savage, probably from being separated from those he knew and loved, that he had to be shot."*

* * *

Comradeship between men who had learnt to know and respect one another, as, with all good Regiments, was the cement which kept the Rifle Brigade so cohesive a force. The touchstone of such comradeship was unselfishness. It existed between Officer and Officer, and Rifleman and Rifleman, transforming the discipline of authority and fear into that stronger discipline whose sanction is the wish to obey. It continued after the bonds of discipline and daily contact were relaxed when the Rifleman retired or was discharged. In 1870 an association between past and present commissioned members of the Regiment was formed called the Rifle Brigade Club under the Presidency of the Prince of Wales, who, like his younger brother, Prince Arthur, the future Duke of Connaught—then a lieutenant serving with the 1st Battalion—continued a loyal member till the day of his death. It was during his reign that a Rifle Brigade Veterans' Association was founded—later to become the Rifle Brigade Association—open to Riflemen of all ranks, at whose first annual dinner in April 1908 the Crimean veteran, Rifleman Salter,† electrified the company by singing a song, "The Russians shall not drink Old England dry", which he and his comrades had sung on the heights above Sebastopol more than half a century before.

At the core of the comradeship which bound the Regiment, past, present and future, were the fighting philosophy and precepts which its founders had laid down. They were to be ever alert and active, to look always to the bow wave, not the stern, to do the work at hand with the utmost of endeavour of mind and body, to face difficulty and danger with optimism and gaiety. The worse the

* R.B.C. 1937, 305-6.   † See 137.

situation, the more incumbent it was on everyone to make light of it; joking to keep up the spirits of oneself and one's comrades became at such times a military and moral necessity. The Rifleman's guiding light in darkness was to press forward—cheerfully and briskly— and never to despair. The very speed at which he was taught to march, move and think, helped him here, for it made him both forward-looking and ready to respond quickly to the need of the moment and, by acting quickly, to forestall its menace. A Regiment whose tactics depended on units and men acting on their own and often in isolation, while co-ordinated to a common purpose and discipline, could afford no other philosophy.

It was teaching and instilling this spirit that officers and N.C.O.s of the Regiment felt to be their prime duty. They had to be teachers of men and to lead by teaching. The first rule in such teaching was example; it was this which evoked the desire of those they led to follow and emulate. Officers, born into a national society deeply founded on class distinction and differentiation of function, inevitably enjoyed social privileges unknown to their men. Yet, when it came to the essentials of war and fortitude in hardship, the officers' part was not merely to share the toils and dangers of their men but to embrace even more than their share. The prime function of an officer, the new-joined subaltern was taught by his seniors, was to look after his men and their well-being; the next to do, and be able to do, whatever they were ordered to do as well and better than they. When the future Major-General G. M. Lindsay—himself the son of an old Rifleman who had fought in the Kaffir wars and the Crimea— joined the 4th Battalion in Portobello Barracks, Dublin, in the last year of the century, the Second-in-Command took him up to his room to tell him certain things which he considered essential for an officer of the Regiment. "The first and most important duty," he said, "is the care and welfare of the men under his command. We expect that as soon as you have had time to get to know your men, they will look upon you as the person they will always go to for help and advice as regards any trouble they may be in, either in the Battalion or in their private lives. There are many officers in the Regiment who can hunt, shoot, play polo, etc., but, if you cannot afford these expensive amusements, you can be of more use by taking part in the games and pastimes of the men and helping to foster them in every way that you can. We always want as many officers as possible to do that." It was the same attitude to his men that Lindsay's father had expressed in his letters home from the Crimea, asking for warm articles of clothing and food to be sent to supplement their thread-bare uniforms and inadequate rations. "I spend what I can," he had written, "on buying them any little comforts, and they have upon all occasions behaved so admirably in spite of their great hardships that it is our greatest trial not to be able to do as much as we could wish for them."*

In the Victorian era the rank and file of the Regiment were recruited mainly from London. It had a much smaller infusion of Irish than most of the Line Regiments and was, by and large, Cockney. This accorded with its humorous, slightly quizzical outlook on life; at the end of a highly successful inaugural concert of the 4th Battalion's branch of the Army Temperance Association, the correspondent of the Rifle Brigade Chronicle reported that "when, after the first batch of heroes had taken the pledge, Hone was asked to sing the last verse of his song—

" *Mix me three whiskies and sodas*
And lay them all down in a row"—

it brought the first Temperance meeting to a highly appropriate conclusion." The men were mostly small in stature but broad in chest, for, while the Regiment took recruits one inch below the Line standard for height, it insisted on an extra inch in the chest measurements. This resulted, as one of its officers recalled, in "a very level type of small, stocky, powerful men, which we considered to be typical Riflemen", giving a Rifle Brigade Battalion on parade a neat, uniform appearance.†

Victorian Riflemen needed to be tough and sturdy. When Quartermaster W. Morrish enlisted in 1876 and was sent, after three weeks' drill at the depot, in a packed and water-logged transport, to join the 1st Battalion in Ireland, his starting breakfast consisted of a quarter of a pound of bread and "a basin of coloured liquor called—by the cook only—coffee."‡ His next meal, twelve hours later, before he was prostrated by sea-sickness, was some "nasty stringy stuff" out of a

---

* R.B.C. *1955*, 131-2. It was an old Rifle Brigade tradition. During the retreat to Corunna, Lieutenant W. Clarke—whose silver snuff-box, Rifle jacket, sash and cocked hat are in the Regimental Museum at Winchester—spent every penny he had in buying boots for his men." R.B.C. *1931*, 328-9.

† R.B.C. *1894*, 224; *1913*, 82-3; *1929*, 315-16.   ‡ R.B.C. *1937*, 162-6.

tin "called by the British soldier 'Harriet Lane' after the woman who was cut in pieces by the notorious murderer Henry Wainwright". In the Army cookhouses of the 'sixties everything was boiled; the regulation fare was soup, boiled meat, bread and potatoes, with vegetables and puddings only at Christmas and on special regimental occasions, and everything else, even what was called "teabread"—the sole official food served after the mid-day meal—had to be bought out of the soldier's exiguous pay. "Oh Mother, I'm growing so thin," the men of the 2nd Battalion used to sing,

> " For dinner they gives me a bone,
> I'm always in debt
> And I can't raise a wet,
> So send me some rooty from 'ome."

The Army at that time was recruited almost entirely from the poorest of the poor, so the standard of its food did not differ much from what the new entry was accustomed to. Before Forster's Education Act creating National School Boards, in every Company there were an average of up to ten men who could not read or write.*

Their quarters matched their rations. At Quebec in the 'sixties they were "dark, uncomfortable and insanitary" casements built under the ramparts, each housing a half Company, with little ventilation save a row of loopholes for musketry fire. "Imagine," wrote a Rifleman who experienced it, "a hundred feet of Metropolitan Underground Railway with one end of it bricked up and with a door and two windows at the other end; this gives a fair idea of our quarters."† Even as late as 1895, at Kowloon Barracks, Hong Kong, not only the men but the officers slept in thatched mat-sheds, with walls of dried palm leaves, so thin that they kept out neither the heat in summer nor the cold in winter, and roofs infested with enormous mosquitoes. "Oh! for those who refused us punkahs to do a night amongst these cheery little insects!" was the heartfelt wish of the author of the 1st Battalion Letter in the Chronicle of that year. "The Hong Kong Regiment are having new brick barracks built for them, but mat-shed accommodation is considered good enough for European troops out here—it is so cheap, you see."‡

* Captain the Hon. A. Somerset, "Old Days in the 1st Battalion," *R.B.C. 1937,* 162-6; *1913,* 80-3; *1929,* 315-16.

† *R.B.C. 1925,* 229-32.   ‡ *Idem 1895,* 215-16.

With the general improvement in social conditions during the last quarter of the 19th century there was a corresponding improvement in that of the Army, particularly in rations, health and hygiene. In that improvement the Rifle Brigade helped to lead the way. In 1890 an officer of the Regiment produced a 2d pamphlet of 24 pages " to place clearly before those who may wish to enter Her Majesty's Service the advantages to which they will become entitled by so doing and more especially should they enlist in the Rifle Brigade." It set out how Riflemen were now fed and cared for, and explained how they could improve their position, and how well-conducted men could, in addition to promotion, obtain suitable employment on passing into the Reserve. " Although it is only a plain statement of facts," a reviewer in the *Globe* wrote, " it brings strikingly into relief the advantages enjoyed by the Riflemen, one of which is the loyal spirit of union prevalent among all ranks. The officers of the Brigade have settled down to make the best of the material at their disposal. They may really be called *Soldiers' Friends*! . . . If further evidence were to be wanted it is to be found in the unvarying good conduct of this distinguished Regiment."*

In those days of long enlisted service—never less than twelve and usually twenty-one years—officers and men, despite the difference of their peacetime social life, came to know each other very well. " Having been pretty well brought up in my young days by the Rank and File," Colonel Norcott recalled, " I got much inside knowledge that was of value to me when I donned the green jacket, and, though I knew much, it was my earnest endeavour not to abuse the confidence placed in me. I have many happy recollections of my association with the men, and it was a great treat to me to be invited to tea in one of the Company Rooms. Not much milk and sugar, but my hosts' welcome more than made up for every deficiency, and we had many a happy evening together."†

It was a respect and affection reciprocated. One day when young Norcott's father, the Crimean veteran, then an old man, was walking along the parade at St. Leonard's-on-Sea, seeing a young Corporal in the familiar uniform he called him up and said how pleased he was to see how smartly and well he was turned out. "My compliments to your Colonel," he added, "and you can tell him Sir

---

* *R.B.C. 1891*, 90-1.
† *Idem 1925*, 287-9. Colonel C. H. B. Norcott, "Stories of the Regiment."

William Norcott said so." The young man drew himself up and saluting, asked, "Beg pardon, Sir, but are you the gentleman they used to call B —— y Bill?" "I have the honour to be that humble individual," the old soldier replied.* On another occasion, an officer paying off a London hansom, was greeted by the driver with a "Battalion all right, sir?" Asked how he was faring the driver answered, "I am getting on all right but I do miss the old Regiment. You see, sir, all the officers are gentlemen, and for the matter of that I'm d——d if the men aren't too."†

One thing that made the men respect their officers was that, true to the Regiment's tradition in the field, they shared their hardships. "Company officers deemed it a point of honour," wrote Surgeon Bradshaw, "to march always with their men; no one would ever mount his pony unless absolutely obliged to. Seeing this so heartened the men that they showed marked unwillingness to fall out, even when blistering of feet became quite painful. Arrived at the camping-ground no officer would go to his own tent before he had seen his men sheltered and cared for."‡ It was part, too, of the Rifle Brigade's code that an officer on the march should relieve an over-tired Rifleman of his pack or rifle; a fellow officer told the daughter of Sir William Cope how he remembered seeing her father on a march once hung with no less than seven men's rifles.

Sport was a great, and, as competitive games became more popular, growing solvent of the social gulf between officers and men. So were exhibitions of craftsmanship, theatricals and, still more, shooting-matches—an activity which the Regiment pursued with what seemed to others an almost fanatic enthusiasm. Once a year, when Lt.-Colonel C. G. Fortescue was commanding the Battalion, the officers gave a dinner to all Riflemen who had brought distinction to it, whether in shooting, cricket, football, hockey or any other sport, or had done some specially good work in the course of their duties. Nearly two hundred of all ranks usually attended, the Commanding Officer making a speech on the year's achievements after the dinner. The cost to each of the officers was a day's pay, and

* *R.B.C. 1924*, 173-4. Col. H. C. B. Norcott, "Reminiscences of the Regiment."
† *Idem*, 174.
‡ *R.B.C. 1938*, 152-3; *1922*, 170. Surgeon Major-General Sir A. F. Bradshaw, "Some Recollections of the 2nd Battalion in the Sixties."

it provided, as Fortescue recalled, one more means of strengthening
the bonds of comradeship between ranks.*

Another occasion which brought officers and men together was the
Regimental Birthday. Every 25th of August—the anniversary of the
engagement at Ferrol—all four Battalions, wherever they happened
to be, celebrated the great day with sports, supper and a concert, in
which all ranks joined. Thus in 1895, the 1st Battalion, then in
Hong Kong, made the usual holiday of the occasion, holding inter-
Company races and sports in the Happy Valley and a tug-of-war
between the officers and sergeants in which "the former", it was
noted, "came off second best". Afterwards there was a regimental
supper and a concert in the theatre organised—with the help of the
Bandmaster and Battalion string-band—by the Senior Company
Commander, Major A. R. Pemberton, who presented a handsome
silver cup to the Sergeant's Mess to be shot for annually at 200, 500
and 600 yards. "Colour-Sergeant Waight, Acting-Corporal Matthews and Acting-Corporal Meddemen," the Regimental Chronicle
reported, "were wildly encored. Ferguson gave us some Scotch and
Irish melodies on the pipes, and Mr. Spriggs a couple of first-rate
songs with good choruses on the banjo. The step-dancing of Private
Pincing would do credit to the Alhambra. Mr. Grayson, R.A., was
thrice encored, his "Appy 'Amstead' bringing down the house. . .
It was a first-rate show all round."†

Far from resenting the discipline of their superiors, so long as it
was justly and considerately administered the men saw it as an essential framework and, in the hour of trial, support of their rough,
adventurous lives. "His tongue was like a rasp and his methods
rough," wrote Quartermaster Morrish of Colour-Sergeant Gilbert
of the 1st Battalion, "but he made men of us, and we knew and liked
him for it."‡ Of Colonel Elrington, the first Commanding Officer of
the 4th Battalion, Francis Howard, who joined it as a subaltern in
Canada, recalled that he was "as kind and yet as strict as you make
them and many years ahead of the times with regard to military
training" and was "worshipped by every officer and man, including

* *R.B.C. 1949,* 115-16.   † *R.B.C. 1895,* 216-17.

‡ *R.B.C. 1913,* 82. Another famous trainer of men was Sergeant Major Bull of the 2nd
Battalion who, when training sentries to turn out the guard, would space them round the
square and then come roaring round, shouting as he approached each sentry, "I'm coming.
I'm coming. I'm the Duke of Connaught" or "I'm the Corpse" or "I'm the Sergeant
Major", and woe betide the sentry who turned out the guard to the latter. *R.B.C. 1965,* 106.

all the blackguards in the Battalion."* Of Howard himself, who commanded the 2nd Battalion in the 'nineties, it was said that he was "a born leader of men, a stern disciplinarian with an unfailing sense of humour who always took it for granted that his men would live up to the high standard of duty that he placed before them. And they, knowing he would never ask of them anything he was unwilling to do himself, never failed him. His courage and justice won their trust, and his achievements in the boxing ring and his big-game hunting expeditions held their admiration . . . Nor had any man a greater share of physical courage." During the march from Afghanistan to India in 1879, when cholera swept through and decimated the ranks, the devoted care and nursing he gave to the men of his Company were always remembered with gratitude.† Another Commanding Officer of the time who aroused a comparable devotion in his men was Lord Edward Clinton, whom a Rifleman recalled as being "loved by all ranks, a thorough disciplinarian and a terror to a slacker; praise from him always made us feel that we could do twice as much as we had done."

As in any good Regiment, much of its discipline and cohesion was due to its N.C.O.s and Warrant Officers. "I can never be forgetful," wrote Surgeon Major-General A. F. Bradshaw of the 2nd Battalion in its post-Mutiny days, "of the old non-commissioned officers and men of the Rifle Brigade. A truly splendid body of soldiers, victors in warfare, disciplined, brave and gallantly unmindful of hardships and dangers."‡ Their pride in the Regiment was unbounded; when Colour-Sergeant Mark Hampton lay on his death-bed, he said to his daughter, "Stand me up, so that I can die like a soldier!" Few members of the Officers' Mess were more honoured than those who had risen from the ranks. Such a one was Major W. Wadham, who enlisted in the Regiment in 1873 and rose to be Sergeant-Major of the 3rd Battalion and then Quartermaster, and who after his retirement became Quartermaster of the Corps of Commissionaires. "Loved and respected by all ranks," it was written of him, "he was a real credit to the Rifle Brigade, for which he had an intense devotion."§ Even better known and universally respected was Major Hone who had enlisted as a boy-bugler in the 4th Battalion at the

---

* *R.B.C. 1930*, 281. Later Maj.-Gen. Sir Francis Howard, K.C.B., K.C.M.G., Colonel Commandant 2nd Rifle Brigade, 1913-21.

† *R.B.C. 1930*, 279-87.　　‡ *R.B.C. 1922*, 168-9.　　§ *R.B.C. 1928*, 274.

time of its formation and, after rising to the rank of Bugle-Major, had left the band in 1870 to become, in turn, Colour-Sergeant, Quartermaster-Sergeant and ultimately Quartermaster. When in 1898, laden with gifts from his fellow officers, he retired after forty-one years' service, he felt that he had worn, as he sadly put it, "the old green jacket for the last time." Yet next year saw him back again in Portobello Barracks with the 15th Provisional Battalion for the South African War, and, when it was over, in a billet as Quartermaster of the 1st Essex Volunteer Battalion who wore the same uniform. "So," he wrote, "I was able to don the old green jacket again. They were afterwards turned into red, but I never changed a button . . . In 1909 I had to retire again owing to age, as I was now sixty-seven . . . As I sit at home I often look back and think of the happy days I spent with the Rifle Brigade. Once a year I make a point of attending the annual dinner where I meet old friends and talk of old times. Fifty years is a long time to have served one's country, and although now in my eightieth year, I sometimes feel that I would like to go through it all again."*

*   *   *

It was in their colonial campaigns and when stationed abroad in the tropical and malarial conditions of Britain's vast global empire, at a time when medical care and science were still, by modern standards, almost primitive, that Riflemen of all ranks were put to the test of their devotion to their corps and of their gay, Spartan, enduring philosophy. In 1863, one battalion on the Indian station alone had 200 of its 800 men sick with Delhi sores and another 200 unfit from other causes. In the Ashanti campaign of 1873-4, under Sir Garnet Wolseley, the 2nd Battalion before landing spent three weeks cooped up in an overcrowded transport off the Gold Coast under a tropical sun because no arrangements had been made for them to land. Though only thirty-five casualties occurred in battle against the Ashanti braves,† the march in that deadly climate across foetid

* R.B.C. *1923*, 156-7. Major H. Hone, "Recollections of over Fifty Years with the Rifle Brigade."

† *Cope*, 480. There was one characteristic episode when Sergeant T. Armstrong, who four years later won the Queen's Medal as the best shot in the Army, while escorting a section of unarmed native carriers, single-handed beat off a band of Ashanti braves, shooting one at arm's length range, cutting down a second with his sword and shooting a third. R.B.C. *1926*, 185.

swamp and malarial jungle to King Kofi Kari-Kari's capital cost the Regiment thirteen times as many through sickness. "It was a terrible country in those days," recalled ex-Colour-Sergeant Williams, a Crimean and Mutiny veteran who contracted dysentery on the expedition.* Only sixteen officers and 277 other ranks were fit for duty when the returning troopship steamed into Portsmouth, with the crews of all the men-of-war in the harbour manning the yards and cheering, and every ship's band playing "Ninety-five".

Five years later the 4th Battalion—which had seen active service for the first time in 1877 against the Jowakis on the North-West Frontier and in the following year was present at the capture of Ali Musjid in Afghanistan—suffered a terrible experience. For the Afghan war having apparently ended, the Battalion was ordered to withdraw to India through the Khyber Pass where cholera had recently broken out. "We tried to keep the news dark," wrote Major Hone, then serving as Quartermaster-Sergeant, "but it was of no use. Other men were soon struck down, and so from camp to camp the fatal disease took its toll and we left men at every stage of the march, many never to return . . . On one occasion . . . we discovered to our dismay that our camping-ground had recently been the site for a Regiment teeming with cholera." "I well remember when after marching through the night," one of the Company Commanders recalled, "we came to the rest camp where on the ground were lying a number of tents. On these our men threw themselves down to sleep. Too late we learnt these were cholera tents spread out to disinfect in the sun; nor had we long to wait to pay the penalty . . . The next victims were some forty young fellows, the whole of a draft which had just joined the Battalion from England. Poor Lord Ossulston's death I remember particularly; we had marched during the night in drenching rain and, on arriving at the camping ground in the early morning, a tot of rum was ordered to be issued to the men. I detailed Ossulston to superintend this and was standing talking to him whilst the issue was being made. Suddenly he said, 'I don't feel very well. Do you mind seeing to this for a few minutes? I shall be back directly.' But he never came back and in less than six hours was dead." "That terrible march back into India in the middle

---

* He and his men were supplied with small filters and bamboo tots through which he had to measure out their daily drink. "You needed it in that country too," he said. *R.B.C. 1931*, 311-12.

of the hot weather," wrote a subaltern, the future Lt.-General Sir
H. F. M. Wilson, "with men dying of cholera and heat apo-
plexy nearly every day was an experience one will never forget. It
was too hot to march by day"—at Peshawar the thermometer in the
hospital tents went up to 127°—"so we marched at night and stumbled along half asleep, being worn out from want of sleep, the heat
in the tents in the day being so great that one couldn't sleep."*

A year later the 4th Battalion was again in the field on the North-
West frontier, this time against the Waziris. By then it had been
joined in India by the 1st Battalion which had been rushed out from
England at a few days' notice after the disaster to a British column
at Maiwand in Afghanistan, though too late to take part in General
Roberts's subsequent victorious march to Kandahar. But both Battalions fought in Burma, the 1st in the Third Burmese War of
1885-7 which ended in the conquest of that country, and the 4th in
the Karen Expedition of 1888-9. A song written by No. 6526 Rifleman
D. May of the 1st Battalion, who served with a detachment of
Mounted Infantry in hunting down Dacoits in the Burmese jungles,
which the men used to sing round the camp fires at night, conveys
something of the spirit of that now remote war.

> " *All mounted upon Burman tats to the jungles off we go,*
> *Some sturdy steeds are found too fast and others far too slow.*
> *The friendly villagers depart and quickly run with fear*
> *When they see us ride and, by our side, bandook and bandolier.*
>
> " *The fierce dacoit is a creature strange, his life is doubtless gay,*
> *He does no work and spends his time in boozing and in play.*
> *When 'the Mounted' scour his jungle haunts he flees away in fear,*
> *When the bullet flies and the look-out spies bandook and bandolier.*"†

While the 1st and 4th Battalions were fighting in Burma, volunteer
detachments from the 2nd and 3rd Battalions served in the Rifle
Company of the daring, but tragically belated, expedition which,
striking across the Bayuda desert, vainly tried to save General
Gordon in beleaguered Khartoum. In 1895-6 a picked detachment of
the 2nd Battalion took part in another Ashanti campaign which
culminated in a second march to Coomassie, a final end to the

---

* *R.B.C. 1932, 218-43.*   † *R.B.C. 1891, 157-8.*

Ashanti's savage regime of slave-raiding and sacrificial massacres,* and the subsequent opening of the country to British trade and mining. During the march to King Prempeh's capital, one of the Riflemen came across, in the bush, a tree with cut deeply into the bark:

No. 1261 T.A.
2nd Bn.   B.R.B.
1874

The initials, it was found, belonged to Sergeant-Cook T. Armstrong who had won the Distinguished Conduct Medal for his gallantry in the Ashanti campaign of twenty-one years before.†

During these years, while the Regiment was playing its part in keeping and enforcing peace in Britain's ever-expanding empire, all its four Battalions were at times serving overseas simultaneously. Much of the time they were on the move. In five years between 1884 and 1889 the 3rd Battalion travelled 20,000 miles, being quartered in three continents and seven different stations—Aldershot, Gibraltar, Warley, the Tower of London (when it lined the west end of Piccadilly for Queen Victoria's Golden Jubilee procession), Cairo, Wynberg in South Africa and Jullundur in India without taking into account the service of its detachment in the Sudan. Then for a period longer than that recorded of any other Regiment of the British Army during the 19th century, it remained stationed in India. In 1897 during the widespread North-West frontier risings of that year, not having, much to the chagrin of its officers and men, seen action since the Mohmund campaign of 1863, it was suddenly called upon to make a forced march of several hundred miles at midsummer through the Derejat and the Tochi valley, one of the hottest districts in the world. The whole experience, wrote an officer, was a perfect nightmare: "the start just before sundown"—

* "In the Palace grounds there is a small grove in which almost daily human sacrifices were held. At the top of this part of the town is the great Fetish Tree and sacred grove . . . The grove was paved with human skulls and remains. No man's life was safe, but as a rule the slaves were the sufferers, as many as four hundred being tortured to death at a time . . . They were dragged to a large bowl and their heads were cut off into it, their blood being allowed to cover the king's stool and four other stools which stood around; part of the intestines were then drawn out and smeared over the stools. I saw three of these stools bathed in blood and the seats covered with the entrails." *R.B.C. 1895*, 268-9. Captain Arthur Hood, "The Ashantee Expedition."

† See 174. *R.B.C. 1895*, 273.

for it was too hot to march by day—" the constant call for water when none was available, the mug of tea half-way (sometimes so sweet as to make one thirstier than ever and sometimes not enough of it to go all round), the false hopes raised by lights seen in the distance which might mean the longed-for camp, . . . the dust, and, above all, the heat . . . And then the long weary days under the tents, in stifling heat, with horrible water, flies in plenty and, as often as not, a rainless dust-storm in the afternoon, so that rest became hopeless and sleep almost an impossibility . . . No wonder that amongst the men were some whose strength was unequal to the strain, though their hearts were stout and true enough. It is not a pleasant sight to see men fall unconscious on the road from exhaustion; . . . towards the end of a night's march, it was a common enough sight to see most of one's men, as soon as a halt was ordered, drop at once on their hands and knees in the middle of the road from sheer inability to stand up until the word was given to fall out . . . But under all these trials and discomforts the men behaved splendidly, singing and whistling on the march to lighten the burden of the weary road and of the unaccustomed hundred rounds of ammunition; never a grumble heard, and they marched with a pluck beyond all praise."*

Later in the campaign, which in the end fizzled out without the Battalion seeing action at all, its men had to endure tempests, floods, dust-storms and plagues of flies which settled in swarms on their unappetising food, vile smells and ever-mounting scourges of enteric and dysentery. "Deaths began to get more frequent and it was a common sight to see a hundred men marching to hospital when the sick-horn sounded." When in October the return march through the Tochi valley began, "instead of the strong, fit and hopeful Battalion which did the march up in such splendid style," wrote the recorder of that doleful campaign, "we had now only a mere handful of sound men with us; the others pale, feeble and worn out were either hospital patients or too weak to get along without assistance and had to be carried in bullock-carts." Of the twenty officers and 802 rank and file who had left for the front four and a half months before, only twelve officers and 540 rank and file returned to Umballa. "The enormous number of comrades we have lost," the Battalion Letter concluded, "the terrible spectacle of many others broken down through sickness and privation and the absence of any

* R.B.C. 1897, 116-18.

excitement in the way of fighting, have made the expedition an experience which none of us would willingly repeat. But the heroic manner in which the men underwent the hardships which they were exposed to, and the quiet pluck with which so many faced sickness and death, will ever remain a proud memory to all who were with them."*

*   *   *

Up to the time of the Mutiny in their wars against oriental mercenaries and even tribal savages, British soldiers had usually been pitted against enemies as well armed as themselves, and were forced to rely on superior discipline and morale to offset inferiority in numbers. But during the colonial wars of the second half of Victoria's reign, owing to the rapid development of British and European industry and invention their weapons were steadily improving.† In 1867 the Rifle Brigade's Enfield muzzle-loader, which had replaced the Minié rifle during the Crimean War, was superseded by the far more efficient Snider-Enfield breach-loader. This, in its turn, was replaced in 1874 by the Martini-Henry breach-loader, and in 1890 by the fast-firing Lee-Metford magazine rifle. During the last decade of the century the Maxim machine-gun gave the numerically small British overseas forces an overwhelming tactical superiority over non-Europeans, however numerous or brave. This became fully apparent in 1898 when the 2nd Battalion of the Rifle Brigade under Colonel Francis Howard took part in the victorious expedition which, thirteen years after Gordon's death, regained the Sudan from the Mahdi. At Omdurman, where it was stationed on the left of the brigade which under another Rifleman, Major-General Neville Lyttelton, protected the Army's left flank, more than 40,000 attacking Dervishes were routed, despite their fanatic bravery, by an Anglo-Egyptian force of 22,000. A young officer of the Bat-

* R.B.C. *1897*, 113-35. "I cannot bear too high testimony," wrote Major-General Bird, who commanded the Expedition, in his Despatch, "to the discipline which cheerfully endured and the pluck which combatted the scourge during a long and trying season." Major H. G. Parkyn, *A Short History of the Rifle Brigade*, 38.

† As late as March 1885, however, Rifleman J. Marsh, writing to a friend after the unsuccessful attempt to relieve Gordon, mentioned that the Mahdi's army had Krupp guns and Remington rifles, which, he wrote, "is a better rifle than ours out here, as the action of ours gets stopped by the sand and the extractors won't extract the empty cartridges." R.B.C. *1892*, 121.

talion, Lieutenant the Hon. E. G. Boyle, who died later of enteric fever, described what happened in a letter home.

" *All that night*" [*that of September 1st-2nd*] "*we lay under arms . . . At 6.30 we saw an immense long line advancing along the flat ground, with flags and banners, and making a vicious humming noise. At 6.45 a huge force began to appear over the saddle between the ridge and hill. At this moment the guns . . . opened shell-fire on the force on the flat ground and then on the other lot who were making straight for our Regiment. The carnage caused by the guns on this lot was something horrible, so, unfortunately for us, they swerved off to our right . . . We then doubled across the zareba; one man in my Company, about six inches off me, was hit on the head with a bullet, another in the Company ahead badly wounded in the groin. The fight . . . lasted two hours, and then the Dervishes fell back having suffered terribly; they lost in front of the zareba about 4000 killed and as many more wounded. In our Battalion we had one killed and eight wounded, no officers touched, though we all had narrow shaves . . . The pluck of these Dervishes is beyond belief. I saw one with his hand blown off and his scalp half torn off, sitting down and eating a biscuit quite calmly . . . All I had to eat from 3.30 on the morning of the fight till 5 next morning was two ration biscuits, and all I had to drink was two cupfuls of hot water! . . . The men behaved awfully well . . . They never had a chance of doing anything but were simply lying under fire waiting . . . Only one fellow gave in at all, and I carried his rifle and half carried him the last five miles.*"*

Boyle himself had been down with fever a few days earlier, and the march after the battle was made in the hottest time of the day.

Such was the battle of Omdurman. The Rifle Brigade had now to face the challenge of the 20th century.

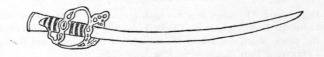

* R.B.C. 1953, 50-2.

Chapter Six

THE PERFECTIONISTS

Let us admit it fairly, as a business people should,
We have had no end of a lesson: it will do us no end of good.
KIPLING

IN the year of Omdurman—1898—there appeared in *Vanity Fair* an anonymous letter attacking the Rifle Brigade and King's Royal Rifle Corps for their alleged diversionism and their tiresome "fads", such as their quick step and open order tactics, and their reluctance to conform to the uniform drill and tactics prescribed by the War Office and the Aldershot High Command. This elicited a reply from a correspondent who signed himself "Red Light Bob". "*The Rifle Regiments,*" he wrote,

" have traditions which they try still to live up to, notwithstanding the amount of red tape which tries to trip them up and strangle them at every turn. It is ridiculous to decry their quick step—it's pure jealousy; they do march and they can march, if only allowed to. Yet instead of other regiments being brought up to their standard of celerity, every effort is made to bring them down to the 'grabby' standard; but, notwithstanding the retrograde motion and every attempt to quench the flame, it has never succeeded. The flame may be subdued for the time being, only to break out with renewed fierceness when opportunity arises. There is a certain amount of exclusiveness about the Rifle Battalions which is perhaps a little irritating, but we are not discussing Rifle Battalions from a narrow-minded or a social point of view, but for soldier-like qualities . . . It is mere folly, or jealousy, to scoff at the Rifle Battalions. Their standard of training is far higher than . . . in the ordinary Infantry Regiments.

" The 'standard' of the Army is far too low, and it will always remain so, so long as Regiments which through sheer hard work, combined with an excellent system of training, are brought down to the level of the cumbrous and slow-moving Regiments. We shall be taught a lesson, and a severe one, before long (perhaps sooner than may be anticipated). I was present only a few days ago at the field firing of a brigade. From the D.I.

*of M. to the Colonel Commanding was the universal cry, 'Why don't they get on?' Why? The answer is in a nutshell. They wanted a Light Infantry Regiment to lead them. It was merely a funeral procession, where every man was attending his own demise. In these days of Maxims, repeating or magazine rifles, this brigade would have been annihilated. It was suicide and murder. The brigade wouldn't 'get on.' Why? They were all 'grabby', from their helmet spikes to the soles of their feet. We cannot hope for years to come to rejuvenate the Army at large, but if only some credit were given to the Rifle Battalions and other Battalions who can do away with such unnecessary words of command (which the correspondent I am answering complains of) as 'attention', and several other rigmaroles, before attaining their object, let them do so. It is not the 'eye wash'; it is business. Why should any Battalion have to remain behind to listen to unnecessary words of command given by Battalion Commanders? 'Audax' from the British Army we all rely on, but for Celer? NO! save in the Rifle Battalions and a few—a very few—others.**

What the writer predicted—that the British Army would be taught a lesson and a severe one—came to pass much sooner than he could have foreseen. In the autumn of 1899, a long-smouldering dispute between Great Britain and the Transvaal Republic and Orange Free State came to a head with an ultimatum from President Kruger and a lightning invasion by armed Boers of British Natal and Cape Colony. During the next few months unlooked-for defeat after defeat was administered by a few thousand mobile and well-armed farmers on the Regular Forces of the Imperial Crown and on a military Establishment committed to outdated parade-ground formalism and an unrealistic reliance on the mass formation tactics which had triumphed in the Franco-Prussian War of 1870, before the development of automatic weapons.

For the Boer War, as was pointed out afterwards by a soldier who fought through it as a subaltern in the Rifle Brigade's 2nd Battalion, was "exactly like every other war in that it was unlike any other war". That is, it was not in the least like the war expected by Whitehall and Aldershot martinets who based their notions of the future merely on their experience of the past. "On the Boer side," he wrote, "the chief characteristics were their mobility, individualism, hunter's

---

* *Vanity Fair, cit., R.B.C. 1899,* 107-10.

lore, marksmanship and zeal. They lacked discipline and any really ordered cohesion. Each Boer was a dogged, tough, stout-hearted, intelligent, self-reliant, experienced hunter and marksman. He had a slouch-hat, a suit of plain clothes, a bandolier and probably a beard. He possessed a hardy pony which carried him, his blanket and his food . . .—biltong, a particularly unappetising, tough, dried meat that took up no room and could nourish a Boer for a long time. It was supplemented from the country which their lack of discipline allowed them to exploit to the full for food and for rest. They came and went more or less at will. They were free from the encumbrance of baggage. They thus possessed a marvellous mobility. But they provided a varying and most unreliable number of effectives at any place or time. They had very little artillery . . . They had no bayonets. This was most important. It meant they were incapable of making a final assault except at night and with complete surprise. They could not withstand an assault.

"The British Army was made up of the same excellent material as ever. It was not, of course, prepared for war. Its training, good in many respects, was, as usual, hardly suitable . . . The infantry was trained to form square and echelon and to manœuvre in line or in solid formations . . . Extended order movements were in their infancy. The special role of the rifleman and light infantryman had lapsed . . . At this time he was just an infantryman . . . While the Boer had mobility and individuality, we had solidity. While we had artillery and the bayonet, they had the stalker's skill and marksmanship. They could subsist on the country. We had to carry everything with us."*

At the start of the war the British Army was, therefore, punished in casualties, as well as in reputation, for false tactical assumptions, which proved utterly unrealistic in respect of the enemy it was fighting and of the terrain, coverless veldt and rocky kopje, over which it had to fight. Between October 1899 and February 1900, when superior discipline, growing numbers and new and more imaginative leadership reversed the tide of defeat, a series of humiliating disasters in Cape Colony and Natal attended every attempt to advance frontally in massed formation against a cunningly concealed and mobile enemy fighting on ground of his own choosing. Belmont, Graspan,

---

* *R.B.C. 1943*, 156-8. Col. W. E. Davies, C.M.G., C.B.E., D.S.O., "The 2nd Battalion in South Africa."

Modder River, Magersfontein and Stormberg in the south pointed the same lesson as Talana Hill, Elandsgate, Rietfontein, Colenso and Spion Kop in the east, where a British force of 12,000 under Sir George White had been cut off and besieged in Ladysmith and where, despite repeated attempts, the largest army Britain had put into the field since the Alma proved unable to relieve it. " Under the storm and stress of Maxim machine-gun and magazine-rifle fire," wrote a contributor to the Rifle Brigade Chronicle of 1899, "all preconceived notions of 'attack formations' had to be hastily abandoned. The terrible losses of the Naval Brigade at Graspan, amounting to over fifty per cent, were directly due to our sailors and Marines endeavouring in all good faith to conform to these pernicious formations for so long persisted in in our Army. One recalls the weary hours spent by officers and men . . . during the last twenty-five years trying slavishly to copy German theories and to learn, and as quickly unlearn, the successively invented 'New Forms of Attack . . . ' Even as far back as 1876 our men nick-named a certain 'Form of Attack', then specially in favour, as the 'God-help-us-Form of Attack'! . . . A Cape colonist, imbued with more candour of speech than respect for our military authorities, remarked recently: 'When will your Aldershot generals stop practising your fellows in those *antiquated* theatricals?' "

Once more, as in the days of the Peninsula, the test of war vindicated what the same writer called " the for-many-years severely repressed skirmishing-line of the Rifle and Light Infantry Regiments as the only possible formation for troops advancing to the attack."* Both the 1st and 2nd Battalions of the Regiment were involved in these initial disasters. The 2nd Battalion, hurriedly shipped from Crete to Durban and thence rushed northwards to join the fighting at Ladysmith, found themselves, only four days after landing, besieged in the little town named after the Spanish heroine wife of the greatest of all Riflemen, Harry Smith. The 1st Battalion at full war-strength, with 42 officers and warrant officers and 1428 other ranks including reservists, sailed from Southampton on October 28th—two days before its sister Battalion went into action at Ladysmith. It reached Durban on November 25th and joined Sir Redvers Buller's relieving army at the beginning of December, where, brigaded under a former officer of the Regiment, Major-General the

* *R.B.C. 1899*, 107-10.

Hon. Neville Lyttelton, it went into action on the Tugela River on the 15th. In the disastrous battle of Colenso that day, when Buller's forces were again repulsed, another Rifle Brigade officer, Captain Walter Congreve, serving on the Staff, won the Victoria Cross by taking up a limber team under fire to bring back guns from an exposed position and then, though wounded, returning under the same deadly fire to rescue a badly wounded fellow officer.*

Four days earlier, on the night of December 10th, five Companies of the besieged 2nd Battalion under Lt.-Colonel Metcalfe carried out a brilliant sortie from Ladysmith against a strongly held height called Surprise Hill, in the heart of the Boers' encircling lines, in order to destroy a heavy howitzer with which they were bombarding the town. A letter written by one of the Company commanders, Major G. H. Thesiger,† described the action:

" When we had gone about 1000 yards we had to halt for an hour
and a half on account of the brightness of the moon . . . We then
advanced very slowly in column of sections until reaching the
bottom of the hill when Gough's company deployed into line . . .
The men went up the hill magnificently, arriving at the top in an
excellent line. It wasn't till we got within about ten yards of the
top that we were discovered. We then fixed swords and charged . . .
The Boers ran and we carried on about 70 yards beyond the gun
and then lay down and fired volleys while the sappers took the
gun in hand . . . Unfortunately the first fuse went out and this
caused a delay of a most precious ten minutes or so. Altogether we
were at the top about half an hour. At last the gun blew up and
the Colonel gave the order to retire. We realized we were in a
pretty tight place as the Boers had worked round us . . . and were
between us and our comrades at the bottom of the hill . . . The men
behaved splendidly and we rolled down the hill somehow, and they

* The fellow officer, who died of his wounds, was Lieutenant Freddie Roberts, only son of
Lord Roberts, the Commander-in-Chief. Of his own wounds Captain Congreve wrote, "I
have never seen, even at field firing, bullets fly thicker. All one could see was little tufts of
dust all over the ground, and one heard a whistling noise and a phut where they hit and an
unceasing rattle of musketry somewhere in front. My first bullet went through my left
sleeve and just made the point of my elbow bleed; next a clod of earth caught me no end of
a smack on the other arm; then my horse got one; then my right leg one; my horse another
and that settled us, for he plunged and I fell off about a hundred yards short of the gun we
were going to." L. H. Thornton and Pamela Fraser, *The Congreves*, 29.

† Later Major-General Thesiger who was killed in action in France in September 1915.

pulled themselves together at the bottom and got into line. Each lot had to cut their way through independently and we managed to stick several of them. We lost pretty heavily, but I fancy there are very few Battalions who would have got out of it without disaster . . . It was a fine thing for the Battalion and has bucked the men up tremendously."*

A sergeant—W. E. Danton—in a letter to his wife described the melée as the Riflemen, their mission accomplished, fought their way back to safety through a force of 2000 Boers:

"There was not time for thought but to act at once and fight our way through at the point of the sword; bullets were flying like hailstorms . . . My captain was shot . . . in three places . . . He shouted for me to form up my men and get the wounded inside which we did; during that time men were shot on each side of me. After forming up we charged the Boers and cut our way through . . . I carried a poor fellow . . . for a time on my back. He was shot through the breast and leg, but he begged me to let him stop and die where he was. After this we made for our entrenchments at which, thank God, we arrived safely after five hours hard fighting."†

Sir George White in his despatch put down the successful extrication to "the good Company system that obtains in the Battalion, to the able way Company Commanders exercise their Commands and to the bravery with which the Riflemen closed with the enemy."

A few weeks later on January 6th, when the Boers made an all-out attack on Ladysmith, temporarily capturing two of its outlying defences, Wagon Hill and Caesar's Camp, the Rifles, now part of the garrison's mobile reserve, again distinguished themselves. Sent to regain Caesar's Camp, from which the Manchesters had been partially driven, they hung on grimly all day to the advanced positions they had gained and, with scarcely any cover from intense rifle fire and under a blazing sun, finally drove the Boers at evening from their dominating position. The same observer who was to define the character of the South African War, 2nd Lieutenant W. E. Davies, jotted down at the time his impressions of the day's events,

"We were in one line, in the open. There were very few rocks or

* R.B.C. 1935, 286-94.   † R.B.C. 1958, 63-5.

shrubs. The only cover we had was longish grass. It gave cover
from view but stopped our own view. I found a small cactus
rather larger than a pineapple . . . The ground here was fairly flat.
There was a jumbled sprinkling of rounded boulders and stones
which peered up over longish, rough dried grass. You could not
see what might be hiding amongst them. Above them there poked
up a number of scattered cactus bushes and scrubby shrubs and
trees. You could not see at all beyond, say, fifty yards.

"About forty yards in front of where I was, there was a small
stone wall sangar. Lying behind it, there were three khaki figures.
They were evidently casualties and unable to take any part in the
fight.

"The first thing to do was to try and find out more about the
flanks. The right seemed to be all right and was even able to edge
up a bit. The left was very uncomfortable. The Boers seemed to
be getting round that flank by stalking, in pairs . . .

"One thing was quite certain; there would be an ammunition
crisis . . . The Rifleman, firing very slowly, can easily get rid of all
the rounds he can carry in less than twenty minutes. So we ceased
fire—unless a target should be offered—collected from the casualties, tried to send for more and waited to be shot at. There was a
terrific fire; . . . on the next day I counted twenty bullet-holes
through my cactus, just above the level of my head.

"The first man to go for ammunition, Rifleman May, was
promptly shot dead. Rifleman Hughes volunteered and went at a
crawl . . . An effort . . . to signal with a flag only drew a hail of
bullets and was most unpopular, as well as unsuccessful. A handkerchief waved behind a cactus attracted no one's attention, except that of the Boers . . .

"The time was passed in trying, without success, to get in
touch with someone to the right, left or rear; in trying to avoid
being hit; and in trying to frighten the Boers. At 11 a.m. I wrote a
message. I have a copy of it, in my *The Officers' Notebook*. It runs:
'*From* 2nd Lieut. Davies. *To* O.C. Supports.
Place Firing Line
Time 11.00
Captain Mills is shot,
Our Right flank is all right
Our Left is threatened.'

"The Student of War may criticise it. To my mind it is a master-piece of clarity and brevity! It does not squeal for reinforcements. It is legible . . .

"I moved forward, myself just a little way, to a small rounded stone about a foot high and looked over it through my glasses. There was an awful blast and I dropped, shot, as I thought, through the forehead. I knew that I must be dead—or very near it. I thought I would die clean and so wiped away the blood. I found there was none, nor a hole. I took off my helmet and examined it. No hole. Then on the top of the stone I saw the mark of the bullet. It must have splashed just clear of my head. So I moved. And I waited. And I watched. Before long I saw a Boer rise slowly beside a tallish cactus. I up with my carbine which had a foresight and two protecting wings like young crowbars. I aimed one of these at his head. I shut my eyes and jerked the trigger. It went off. When I looked up he was gone. I had scared him, anyway. I met him, one Viljoen, a year and a half later. He had become one of our scouts. I had a long chat with him whilst waiting to pass him out of our lines. He gave me a description of the same battle, and of this incident. He had made the same mistake as I did. He thought he had got me. My bullet grazed the top of his head, so he withdrew for the day.

"The day wore on. We could hear the Boers talking and shouting orders, much as we were doing, only in Dutch . . . The time passed slowly. There was nothing to eat. The sun was scorching. The wounded had a wretched time. They did not act at all as is often suggested in emotional narratives. They did not writhe or shriek. They didn't even groan. They lay very still and quiet, but they did want water. I tried to get my water bottle to one. It broke . . .

"Still the time dragged on. There did not appear to be any change in the situation till about 4 p.m., when there came down a real good thunderstorm. It lasted twenty minutes or more. This somewhat altered our outlook, besides wetting us. We got drinks from the drips from our helmets. The firing in front of us was definitely less . . .

"The time seemed to have come to advance and have done with our unpleasant situation. Here the Student of War should note the difficulty of imparting an impetus to a prone mass after a period of protracted inertia. I learnt, for future use, either to avoid

losing initial momentum or else to rekindle it, by means of a fresh
mass, starting from cover of sorts.

"Our charge was ragged. Those who could see or hear and could
move came on at once. The Boers fired a few scattered shots and
fled. I was glad. I found I had only brought my walking stick!
The remnants of the Company, 46 in all (we had lost one-third of
our strength in casualties, as well as the few sent back for ammunition), occupied the crest, and blazed away till dark . . . We
saw dark objects carried down the stream, which we hoped and
believed were Boers. We used ammunition which had not been
removed from the Manchesters' piquets. The men had all been
killed except four wounded who had shammed dead. They gave
us vivid accounts of the hundreds of Boers on the hill till just
before we advanced.

"The experiences of the other Companies were much the same
as ours. The Battalion losses were about 12 per cent, but the
casualties amongst the officers with the Companies was about
50 per cent."*

The Boers made no further major attack on the seemingly doomed
town; they relied instead on famine and the ability of their covering
army to hold off all Buller's attempts to relieve it. The garrison's
main assailants during the four months' siege were hunger, weakness and disease and the temptation to despair. Against these they
fought manfully. "Nearly the whole time," the writer of the
Battalion N.C.O.'s Letter to the Chronicle reported, "was occupied
in wall building, trench digging and outpost duty, but through it
all that great characteristic of the Rifleman, cheerfulness of spirit,
was always to the front, especially upon wet days which were
numerous."† "My dearest wife and all at home," wrote Sergeant
Danton, "I thought of you all on Christmas Day. Tell Mother and
Dad I drank their health with water that you would not wash

* R.B.C. 1944, 147-53. "In the meantime, on this same day, 6th January, 1900, at a time
unspecified, occurred another event. The Battalion terrier, Nell, was delivered of twins,
They were christened Shot and Shell. Later on they were to prove expensive in sponges and
tooth-brushes. The Battalion had started from Crete with several dogs, a badger and two
ibexes, who had been left behind in Durban when it went up to Ladysmith. "The baggage
was built into fortifications to try to keep the Boers out and the pets in. They failed in the
latter capacity. One ibex alone survived to the end and became an integral part of the
Battalion for some years to come." R.B.C. 1943, 151; 1905, 102-4.

† "The spirit of cheerfulness and good fellowship, which has ever been characteristic
of the dear old Regiment, always dominated all ranks." R.B.C. 1901, 105-9.

clothes in; our food was beef and water, bread for pudding . . . We are waiting for General Buller to fight his way through to relieve us. There is a lot of sickness, enteric, men dying daily, worst luck. I am in rattling health, thank God. Now, my Darling, keep up your spirits as before and all will come right in the end. Give my love to Mother, Dad, our Tom, Jess, Flo, Albert Henry, the old Lady and all enquiring . . . I can't tell when this will reach you, but I trust in God that I shall be spared to write again and, in a few months, take you and the boy in my arms and never separate no more."*

The garrison only survived by turning the cavalry's maize mealies into biscuits and slaughtering the horses as they wasted away on such starveling fodder as the rough grass of the town's outskirts afforded. By the middle of January rations were down to a nominal pound of trek-ox or horse, nearly all bone and gristle, and half a pound of meal in the form of a medium sized dog-biscuit which had to last a man all day. There were no vegetables, butter, cheese, milk, jam, tobacco or extras of any sort. As a treat sometimes the biscuits were fried in wagon-grease. Lack of water, either to drink or to wash or shave in, was the worst privation of all— half a cupful for all purposes was the normal daily allowance. The men manning the trenches became so debilitated that even to walk a few hundred yards was almost beyond their strength. In the course of the siege two thirds of the garrison passed through the hospitals, many dying of typhoid and enteric. Day after day hope was deferred while they waited for renewed movement and gunfire on the hills to the south—"anxiously looking forward," as one Rifleman put it, "to Buller's arrival, and even more to that of the next meal."†

It came at last, and when no one was expecting it. The last day of February started misty, dull and cold. "Then as it cleared," recalled Lieutenant Davies, "watching from the look-out post it appeared as if the Boers were trekking. A cloud of dust in one place—then some more appearing from behind a hill in another place—then the first one had lengthened out—it looked like a string of horsemen moving fast north—so did the others—then another appeared nearer to us only 10 miles or so away—they were ox-wagons—they were indeed moving fast— they were gallumphing along not walking—there was something most unusual up."‡ "On February 28th," the writer

* R.B.C. 1958, 63-5.   † R.B.C. 1900, 209-13.   ‡ R.B.C. 1944, 171.

of that year's Battalion letter to the Rifle Brigade Chronicle recalled, "we saw the Boers trekking. It is *not* correct to say that an ox can go only at two miles an hour; they certainly lowered all records that day. . . . That evening we heard the cheering which announced the arrival of Gough's* brother with some of the cavalry and we knew that we had been relieved at last. Next day General Lyttelton and several of the 1st Battalion came up and saw us, full of congratulations, and what I daresay some perhaps liked even better, brought up a bottle of whisky and a tin of milk."

*   *   *

"I expect this war will revive the advantages of good skirmishing and independent firing," Major Thesiger had written during the early days of the siege. Six months after it ended, on August 27th, 1900, and two days after the hundredth anniversary of the Regiment's first action, the 2nd Battalion, restored to health and fighting trim, took part in a brilliant affair—the last major battle of the War—in which it showed what Riflemen could do when given the freedom of their own traditional tactics. By then Pretoria, the enemy's capital, had fallen and General Buller, advancing from Natal, and the victorious Commander-in-Chief, Lord Roberts, had joined forces near Belfast in the eastern Transvaal, where the Boers under Louis Botha had taken up an almost impregnable position. The key to it was Bergendal, a natural fortress affording perfect cover for the defenders and only approachable across an open glacis of between two or three thousand yards. It was carried by the 2nd Battalion Rifle Brigade, supported by the 1st Battalion Inniskillings. In the course of the fighting the Boer commandant was captured, and a Rifleman, A. E. Durrant, won the V.C. for carrying a wounded comrade to safety under intense fire. The day's doings were described, as he saw them, by a former London stockbroker, E. T. Aspinall, known to his brother officers as "City Man", who had been transferred to the Regiment from the Militia and was serving as a subaltern in the company commanded by Captain Reginald Stephens†—the "Stiff'un", as he was affectionately called by all.

---

* Afterwards General Sir Hubert Gough, brother of one of the 2nd Battalion's Company commanders, Captain John Gough, a future V.C. and general. *R.B.C. 1900*, 213.

† Later General Sir Reginald Stephens, K.C.B., C.M.G.

"It was winter on the High Veldt, we were over 6000 feet above sea-level, and as the sun went down the icy wind that sprang up and blew all night was something to remember . . . About 4 a.m. we rolled up the few blankets we had and were told to return them to our transport . . . We longed for a mug of nice hot tea to warm up our stone-cold insides, but this of course we could not get. We had, however, not long to wait, for orders arrived that 'A' and 'B' Companies were to push out on the left flank, which we promptly did, moving forward up rising ground for some distance, and found ourselves eventually on the top of a high ridge from which we looked across a broken and rock-strewn country.

"It was getting light, and in the grey cold dawn everything looked very bleak . . . Stephens told me to push on over the crest and go down the slope for about 100 yards or so before halting. It was very open, so as soon as we lay down I got the men started on trying to make a little head cover with the small entrenching tools they carried. These tiny spades and picks were, however, of little use in the sort of ground we were on . . . Rather below us and to our right front were some long low terrace-like kopjes of rock with flat tops. Behind these were a good number of the enemy; we could see them moving about. I drew Stephens's attention to them, as he had now joined us, and soon after this they opened fire. You could see where the bullets kicked up the dust, and, their shooting was not too good and mostly very short, and, except that it is unpleasant to be shot at, there really wasn't much to complain about. We were guessing the range at about 1,700 yards and we seemed to be making better practice than the Boers, who were now showing themselves very little.

"After a time I noticed several of the enemy come out from the right of their position well clear of the rocks; they were carrying something which looked very much like a small gun on a tripod. Sure enough in a few minutes we were being bombarded by what looked very like one of our own screw guns we lost outside Ladysmith when the mountain battery was captured . . . It is a curious sensation to lie out in the open, watching your enemies preparing for your annihilation, and having to wait for it. I admit I was relieved to find what poor shots they were, for there was no protection at all.

"Stephens sent me back to the half-company which he had left on the crest of the ridge; they were lining a low bank which would be useful if the Boers managed to make it too hot for our advanced portion of the company.

"In the distance, on our direct front, I had observed what appeared to be a farm-house and to the left of it was a long low kopje. What had attracted my attention was the number of men who seemed to be working feverishly to put it in a state of defence. It was a good way off, but through my field-glasses I could see very distinctly what they were doing . . .

"Generals Buller and Lyttelton rode up and, leaving their horses, came on foot up to the low bank our half-company were holding and began to examine the whole position very closely. After a while Lyttelton called me to go over to them and I went and lay beside them. Both he and Buller questioned me as to what I had seen since daylight. I gave them an account of what had taken place and I pointed out this low kopje to our front. Both generals had a good look at it through their glasses and I gathered from the remarks they made that it was in their opinion the key of the Boer position. Buller showed it to me on his map and pointed out the ground to its front, which we could not see from where we were. He had already studied it from where he could see the front. Lyttelton told me that our Battalion was now getting into position to attack this particular spot and that our two Companies would shortly be relieved by the Manchester Regiment, who would take over from us and advance from here when the time came. 'A' and 'B' Companies when relieved were to rejoin the Battalion, which was only waiting for us before commencing to open the attack . . .

"Stiff'un told me to get on with my half company and that he would catch me up. I got clear and then waited for him and we then marched away to our left, which brought us round to the front of the Boers' position, where we knew the Battalion was waiting for us. We hurried along and were more or less sheltered by a high bank that bordered the rough track from the rifle fire. On this bank we passed several batteries in action. Suddenly, there was a tremendous burst of fire, and we guessed the Battalion had just gone into action; but whether it was our fire or the Boers we were not near enough to judge. So we carried on until we came to Ronnie Maclachlan and our maxim-gun in action on the top of the bank. Just clear of them we halted, and Stephens and I climbed up the bank to get some idea of what was actually happening and to find out exactly where we were.

"We were opposite the right of the kopje we had seen the enemy so busy on all morning. As far as we could judge, it was about 2,000 yards away and the ground was as open as a tennis court and had absolutely no cover. To the left of the kopje was a long low ridge of rising ground stretching towards the railway. We could see our Battalion to our left front in open order advancing in short rushes under a very heavy fire, and on our right there appeared to be a similar movement in progress by some Companies of another Battalion. It was difficult to make out things very clearly except that our Battalion had obtained a good long start and that through no fault of ours we had fairly missed the boat.

"What was uppermost in Stephens's mind was how he could best help the Battalion in the fight. To chase after the supporting Companies did not appeal to him in the least; and after studying the position of things for a few seconds he turned to me and said, 'We will take half the Company and make straight for the kopje and see if we cannot find a gap on their right to work into.' This seemed a reasonable solution, if a dangerous one, as it would shorten the distance and enable us to overtake them. So I slid down the bank and began to extend our right half-company before they started to climb out into the open, and we left the remainder for the time being under cover. We made rapid progress by short rushes, not bothering to open fire on an enemy we could not see. We ran on until we were blown and then lay down until we got our wind back; there was no cover to make for, so one spot was as good as another. We reached a rough track that ran parallel with the kopje and here we made a longer pause and had a look round. It was, I should say, about half-way and we could now get a better idea of what was happening in the attack. Our Battalion on the left was advancing in the same manner but opening fire each time they flung themselves down, which made their advance distinctly slower than ours had been. They were keeping a very straight front and their advance was a model of steadiness, considering the heavy fire they were exposed to. On our right was part of another Battalion; they had made a start from near where some batteries were in action and were advancing on a line that would take them just clear of the kopje.

"Although our guns were shelling the enemy's position hard the rifle fire was intense and we already had several men hit in our half-company. I saw three go down together in the last rush . . . Our old liver-and-white springer spaniel had advanced with us. He was well in front with his tail in the air and his nose on the ground. He seemed excited and puzzled; this kind of a shoot was new to him, the little puffs of dust the bullets kicked up as they struck the ground around interested him enormously, and he kept running up to first one and then another, but he could not make them out. When we paused for breath in our rushes he ran up and down our line while we lay close to the ground, and before long he stopped a bullet just behind his left shoulder. We thought the old dog was done for, but after the first shock he recovered a bit and managed to drag himself after us and finally rejoined the company after the position was won.

"The Stiff'un was in a most cheerful mood and kept saying to me, 'This is a good show, City Man.' I dare say it was, but I was quite sure that I was not enjoying it in the least. We were much too exposed, and I hated those vicious little spurts of dust all round us and the singing of the bullets in the air, or the phut they made as they passed close to your ear.

"There was now no doubt that there would be a gap between our own Battalion and the one on our right into which we could fit ourselves, so I said to Stephens, 'What about our other half-company, we shall want them.' 'Oh, I expect they will follow us all right,' he replied, and I felt sure that they would do nothing of the kind. So I pointed out to him that we had left them with no orders and that both of us had gone forward leaving no one to give them a lead. 'We were not sure where we should get to our-selves when we started, so how can we expect them to know where we have got to.' 'Well, City Man,' said my skipper, 'if you feel so sure about them not coming on, you had better go back and fetch them, meanwhile I will push on with what we have to that patch of rocks, pointing to our right front, and you can support me there.'

"When we got up to go forward I turned and ran back, wasting no time over it either. I felt as if every Boer in the position was doing his best to stop me, and, if fear lends you wings, I had them all right on that journey, for I fairly skimmed over the ground. As I raced up the bank I was collared by two men. 'Let me go, you fools,' I panted. 'Oh! beg pardon, sir,' replied our two company stretcher-bearers, 'we thought seeing you come back that you must have been hit and returned for a dressing.'

"I found our left half-company still reposing where we had left them; and no bad judges either, I could not help thinking. They had no orders and by hanging on where they were we did at least know where to find them. 'String yourselves out into single rank at about two paces interval before we go over that bank'; and while they were shaking themselves out I turned to speak to Ronnie, who on seeing me return had come to ask for news. 'What is it like out there, City Man?' said he, pointing to our front. 'Anything like a panic on the Stock Exchange?' 'No, you idiot,' I replied; 'in a panic the worst that can happen is you lose your money.'

"It was anything but a joy to go out again into that bullet-swept zone, but I had to get back to the Stiff'un with as little delay as possible. It was slightly up-hill all the way, and I took them along at such a pace that I soon had them well pumped and had to lie down. Many of the Company were section 'D' and could not be expected to last at a much faster pace than a steady double. It took me three or four good long rushes before I got them where I wanted them.

"With the Battalion closing the gap to the left and the Stiff'un and the rest of the Company almost on our direct front, it was too risky for us to open fire, so we just had to lie there and be shot at. This seemed very trying and an endless wait, but in reality it could only have been a few minutes. Keeping an eye on our advanced half-company, in case they moved forward suddenly, I thought that they appeared quite numerous and I realized that they must have part of a Company of the Battalion on our right sharing the only bit of shelter there was and that was no great shakes, as the cross-fire was very bad, especially from the high ground towards the railway. There must have been a numerous enemy there having an undisturbed shoot, as most of our guns were shelling the kopje in front of us. There was also a galling fire from the right, and though it was not doing us much harm it no

doubt was most unpleasant to the Battalion on our right. The Boer
pom-pom was very active on the kopje. It was in front of us, and
the gunners seemed to be trying to reach our field batteries as the
shells were all going over us.

"Kennard, who was attached to the Brigade Staff that day, was
sent out with instructions to us to push on as fast as we could.
Well, we were as close as was possible for a single company to be,
and Stephens told him that he was only waiting for the Battalion
to stop shooting into the farm before we went ahead; shortly
afterwards our staff captain ran out with the same order. He was
not a favourite with us, and the Stiff'un was fast losing his temper. 'Do you think I am afraid?' said he, turning on him with his
tail well up. 'How can I advance any farther until the guns,
machine-guns, and the rest of the Battalion stop firing into the
farm? It's your job to co-ordinate the attack, and I will rush the
farm directly our firing stops.' The staff captain was so astonished
with the Stiff'un's frank criticism, and what he saw of the situation for himself, that without another word he faded away.

"Where we in support lay, there was not cover for a mouse, and
my British-warm was rolled and strapped to my belt at the back
and I felt that I must present a target to the enemy about the size
of a camel, and every now and then we got things that seemed to
explode like young shells. The men kept saying explosive bullets
and I began to wonder if there really were such things after all. I
knew, of course, about expanding ones. One of these noisy things
happened to land close to someone who picked it up when cool
enough and passed it round. I recognized the old Martini-Henry
big lead bullet. A few of the Boers, then, were using this old rifle,
and the all-lead bullet striking anything hard sounded just like a
small explosion.

"Sergeant Robins recalled my straying attention to the fact that
the Captain was going forward, and the next second we were away
too. It was very exciting now we were on the rush once more, and
one forgot all about bullets and danger and everything else as the
line swept on. As we passed the patch of rocks, we found the men
who had joined us were some Inniskillings; most of them had gone
forward with our fellows, but a few of the sticky ones still clung
to the rocks, and their young officer, a hefty lad of the name of
Brooke of the Connaught Rangers, was beating them up with his

walking-stick, shouting, 'Get on, yer divils.' What cracks he gave them, and we could not help laughing as they raced after us to get away from that terrible stick.

"The pace was now getting very hot and I found only the young soldiers could keep it up, so, leaving those who had passed their first youth to join when they could, we kept on. The leading line had almost reached the sloping ground that ran down from the rocks and we guessed the next would be the final assault. As the line rose for the last time they gave a savage yell (I read a month afterwards in a newspaper report that the 'Rifles' rose with a ringing cheer), and the language—Corporal Porter, a good judge, said he never heard worse—as they all raced up the slope and over the kopje.* Being on the right of the line I could see it very well, and it struck me as a wonderful effort, everyone together and the line marvellously straight, considering.

"We of 'B' Company passed over the very extreme right of the kopje and found the pom-pom gun and its attendant wagon deserted, so we pushed on to the open space behind the position. On our right stood the farm-house and from behind it dashed a few mounted Boers; they had to ride through a heavy fire, but as we had been running hard it was rather shaky and it did not stop many of them. Lying in front of the house was a desperately wounded Boer . . . We could do nothing for him, so we returned to the rear of the kopje; here I came across Stephens, and we greeted each other. He said, 'You are the only subaltern I have ever been able to keep on active service. Why, you are not even wounded.'

"The men had all been very worked up at the finish and would cheerfully have killed anybody, but a reaction had set in and they were now binding up several wounded Boers we found at the back of the kopje; one, a lad of about fourteen, with a severe wound in his shoulder, was the object of much pity among them and some were almost in tears about him, yet a few minutes before they would probably have put a bayonet in him.

"To the right of the kopje, between it and the farm, was a stone

---

* "The order was received with cheers by the men who had been so patiently waiting for it, and, as we rose, the fire was terrific and men fell on all sides, yet in perfect order the advance was . . . carried out." Private A. W. Parker, *From Liverpool to Lydenburg*, cit., *R.B.C. 1901*, 173.

cattle kraal. We did not stop to examine it in our swift advance as
it appeared to be empty. Now as we turned back towards the
position we were rather surprised to see some dozen Boers emerge
from it with their hands up. From their point of view it was as
well they had hidden themselves away out of sight until the
clouds rolled by, because our men were in a thoroughly bad
temper. By now, however, they had begun to recover their equilibrium. The leader of the Boers, who wished to surrender, was a
youngish man with a fair close-cropped beard; he wore riding
breeches and long boots, he had no coat and his shirt was a white
one . . . He was so much smarter looking than the average Dutchman. He came up to Stephens and said, 'Mr. Officer, we surrender,'
and he told us his name. He was the Commandant of the Zarps
(Johannesburg Police) and they had been the mainstay of the
resistance, having been detailed to hold the kopje.

"The sight of the prisoners in our midst produced immense
excitement among the Inniskillings, who promptly commenced
to open fire on them, quite oblivious to the fact that we were all
standing round. Our warning shouts of remonstrance were, however, sufficient to check this outrage with one exception. This man,
having knelt down and fired at the Boer Commandant and providentially missed him and Stephens, proceeded to reload and have
another try. Before he could fire again I reached him and, grabbing
his rifle, I sent him flying. Picking himself up, he came for me
shrieking, 'Man, can't you see he's a Boer,' and tried to get possession of his rifle. Seeing I had a madman to deal with, I hit him
such a crack with the butt that he took no further interest in the
proceedings for quite a while and we had no further trouble.

"A solitary mounted Boer appeared from behind the farm and,
making a dash for the gate, turned left and rode across our front.
Everyone had a shot at him and everyone missed except Sergeant
Ellis, who knelt down and took a steady aim and brought down
the horse; it looked a wonderful shot and possibly it was a lucky
one. The rider was knocked out with his sudden fall and was easily
added to the bag of prisoners.

"The first of the Staff to reach us was Colonel MacGregor (Pig)
our Divisional Chief of the Staff. He came up with the Gordons,
who now passed through us and took up the pursuit. I was the first
officer of the Battalion he encountered and he thumped me on the

back in his excitement and kept on saying, 'Well done, the Green-jackets.' "

Subsequently Generals Lyttelton, Redvers Buller and Lord Roberts all arrived on the scene to add their congratulations. "Lord Roberts said some very nice things and even Buller was complimentary, which was saying a lot. We all felt very pleased and proud of the Regiment; at the same time we were equally depressed at our losses . . . Lysley was dead, Bogey Steward mortally wounded, Campbell very seriously hurt. The Colonel, Alexander, Maitland and Basset, all more or less badly wounded, made a terrible gap in our domestic circle. Then there were all those good fellows among our non-commissioned officers and men. Seven officers and seventy-seven non-commissioned officers and men was the total for about fifteen minutes work."*

*   *   *

For the rest of the war which dragged on in a guerrilla form for nearly two more years, it was a case, particularly for the 1st Battalion, of "foot-slog-slog-slog-slogging over Africa", as the Rifles trailed after elusive commandos, guarded the railways and blockhouses and rounded up irreconcilable Boers and their families from the farms which sheltered them. "Wash me in the water they wash the dixies in", sang the Riflemen as they marched,

> "and I shall be whiter than the snow;
> I shall be whiter than the snow-ow-ow, I shall be whiter than the snow."†

It was scarcely a congenial assignment but, as was its wont, the Regiment made the best—and, wherever possible—a jest of it. "We had a series of night marches which were sufficiently disliked to be called 'jollies'," recorded the 2nd Battalion's Letter to the Chronicle for 1901. "They always resulted in the capture of tents, wagons, food, etc. and accounted for a certain number of Boers. The second of these . . . was the only occasion on which we lost a *bona fide* prisoner. This man, having been on convoy escort all the previous day and

---

* R.B.C. *1934*, 163-201.
† R.B.C. *1946*, 147. "When it came on to rain or for any other cause conditions were particularly unpleasant," recalled Colonel Davies, "the Rifleman, as ever broke into song."

marching all the previous night, had unfortunately fallen asleep in some out of the way place when we returned to Lydenburg We do not, however, make a practice of going to sleep under fire!"*

A political policy of burning farms and laying waste the country-side was too alien to the philosophy of the Rifles to be pursued whole-heartedly. They obeyed the letter of their orders but hardly the spirit. Humanity kept breaking in. "Many incidents occurred round Lydenburg concerning the Boers and ourselves," recalled Major Aspinall, "which often had nothing to do with the fighting."

"Flags of truce were by no means uncommon. The enemy were constantly asking for something. David Schoeman, whose commando had its laager in a pass of the Steenkampsburg Mountains some ten miles distant east of the town, was a very regular correspondent with General Headquarters. His white-flag parties usually appeared soon after breakfast on a low ridge to our front . . . This outwork, held by half the Battalion, was commanded by Reggie Alexander, one of our two remaining captains . . . Anyone not busy at the moment would ride out to the ridge and collect the letter, often not remembering to take an answering white flag with him.

"The Boers sometimes would stay for a while and talk. This depended upon how much English they knew rather than any wish to be abrupt or surly. The answers to these communications were prompt and carried out to the enemy lines by an officer of the Battalion . . . It happened to be Alexander's turn. The note he was taking required an answer, the instructions being, 'Bring back the reply if possible'. Accompanied by a mounted military police-man to carry the flag, an early start was made . . . Alexander had to ride up the pass to within a short distance of the Boer camp before he ran into a small party. This patrol was doubtful about an answer to the letter that day, explaining that their Commandant had gone to a meeting held at a distant commando's headquarters, and the time of his return was uncertain. As the matter appeared urgent, they offered to send a messenger with this letter to their leader and proposed that Alexander accompanied them back to the laager to await the answer . . .

"It appeared to be a day off in this Commando. They were

* R.B.C. 1901, 82.

sitting about in the shade, others in dirty old tents and wagons; all were quite friendly, also curious, asking many questions that were easy to reply to. Alexander you would describe as a good mixer; at home in any company, he possessed an infectious laugh, bubbled with good humour, and, given a crowd of good listeners, a rare old buckstick, so one can be sure his audience would be both interested and amused. They sat under the peach trees, a bottle of Hollands (Square Face) appeared; he was handed a generous peg—by no means a bad tipple, Reggie told us later: a trifle fiery for some tastes, but grateful and comforting, and so unexpected . . . These Boers in the North-East Transvaal were a truly rural type, living remote from large towns, so not much concerned with high politics, at the same time shrewd observers of anything that came their way. An elderly burgher gave it as his opinion that the discovery of gold in the Transvaal was the root of all their troubles. 'This is a millionaire's war', he kept driving home. 'If gold had not been found, who would have wanted our country?' Reggie could not help thinking that this Dutchman's argument was very near the truth in many aspects. They told him they bore no ill-feeling towards the British soldiers: the Army was only doing what it was paid for and they had no anxiety about their women and children left alone on their farms, because the troops treated those they came in contact with with consideration . . . Alexander had them smiling when he asked what had become of all their good shots. Their reply was that they often asked themselves the same question without arriving at a satisfactory conclusion, admitting readily that they were not the marksmen of twenty years ago, though there were still some crack shots among them. Game was not so plentiful as formerly; also many of the population, owing to the mining industry, had been absorbed, so had not handled a rifle for years. With sly humour they pointed out that the English soldiers no longer fought in a red coat and white helmet; in khaki he presented a very inconspicuous target.

    ". . . Late in the afternoon Schoeman returned; apologizing to Alexander for keeping him waiting, he commenced his reply to the General, in the middle of which he asked his advice. In the camp was a very sick man. At first they thought he was shamming to get off patrol; now they realized that he was very ill and in great pain. No one knew what the complaint was and they had no doctor. Should he mention the matter in his letter on the chance that the General would take a liberal view and allow a doctor to come out and advise them how to treat the case? Alexander told him to go ahead with the suggestion; the General was a very kindly man and would probably consent. Meanwhile, the Boers saddled his pony and a small patrol was ready to see him safely through their lines. No one suggested that he should be blind-folded and everyone insisted on shaking hands.

"Our G.O.C. raised no objection to a doctor visiting the laager, provided that he volunteered. McDermot, our own regimental doctor, was keen to go, and started off after sick parade. The Boers were glad to see him. Mac quickly diagnosed the trouble—strangulated hernia—which should have been operated on ten days ago. Now the patient was so far gone that there was very little hope that he would have the strength to survive; anyhow, it could not be done there: he must be taken to hospital. He sent back the white-flag bearer with a report to our senior medical officer with a request for a doolie and spare bearers. Late that evening the sick Boer was admitted to hospital and immediately operated on, with the result McDermot had feared; the man had no strength to recover and gradually sank from exhaustion. We gave him a military funeral; having no flag of the Transvaal Republic, a Union Jack covered the corpse. This impressed the Boers a good deal: Schoeman sent in a letter of grateful thanks for a very friendly act.

"It was not long before Schoeman's people were in trouble again. This time it was a girl of fourteen who had been accident-ally shot in the leg while in the laager. The bone was badly splintered and quite beyond their limited skill to cope with. As she was a child and a non-combatant would the General help them? Our popular P.M.O. Major Jones, went out himself, taking a doolie, spare bearers and an ambulance. On inspection he found the case by no means over-estimated. If the child's leg was to be saved, the only chance was hospital. Very alarmed at being borne off by her enemies, Jones made it easier by putting her in a room in the officers' hospital, which was run by a Dutch nurse, as the girl knew no English . . . This Boer child, with her leg in a cradle suspended from above, lay for many weeks, gradually recovering.

Eventually she was returned to her own people absolutely cured and speaking English well. She was sorry to go, for everyone had been kind to her, from the General downwards, taking her sweets and flowers, but she was most anxious to tell her fellow-countrymen how good the English had been to her all the time she was among them."*

Not long afterwards the 2nd Battalion was called upon to attack Schoeman's stronghold and after a sharp fight drove his commando from its laager. A few days afterwards a white flag appeared on the ridge, borne, instead of by the usual horsemen, by an elderly Boer in a cape-cart. Asked why he had come in a cart, he answered because he knew the contents of his Commandant's letter to the British General. It appeared that in the course of the capture of the laager someone had taken a portmanteau from the Commandant's tent containing his underclothes. "Now if your General agrees," he said, "that robbing a man of his spare vests and pants is not playing the game in civilized warfare, the necessary articles may be restored, and I cannot carry a portmanteau on horseback." The General did agree, and when, after some hours, the missing portmanteau had been traced and appeared, the old burgher, obviously pleased with the success of his mission, remarked to the escort as he left them, "You English fight fair!"†

"It took us less than a year to get from Durban to Lydenburg and over a year to get back only as far as Lydenburg," the 2nd Battalion letter for 1901 ended; "but we feel confident of addressing our next letter to you from some nice peace station where we shall be living in quiet, surrounded by beer and our wives and families, whom we have not seen for over three years, and all the luxuries of a soldier's civilization." When, in the summer of 1902, peace came at last, it found the Battalion holding a long section of railway at Middleburg in the Transvaal. A representative party under Captain Stephens was detailed to attend the Peace Thanksgiving Service at Pretoria.

"It was a fine show, but we were so badly done by the authorities, who camped us miles from our parade-ground and made us route-march all day that the men came back after three days of it, saying, 'If this is Peace, give us sanguinary War.' Our next employment

* *R.B.C. 1945*, 166-81.   † *R.B.C. 1945*, 172.

was rolling up the barbed wire we had put up at such expense and trouble along our section of the line . . . After peace was declared we got to work on the new Drill Book and learnt to stand at ease with our legs wide apart and various other accomplishments which will no doubt cause us to win the next great war."*

In September, just under three years after it landed at Durban in 1899 to join Sir George White's outnumbered force at Ladysmith, the Battalion sailed from Natal for Suez and its new station at Cairo. The 1st Battalion left Cape Town for Southampton ten days later, while the 4th Battalion, which had arrived from Ireland at the end of the previous year to relieve its two sister Battalions, remained for a few months longer at Bloemfontein.

*   *   *

During the next twelve years of peace—the lull before the storm— the Rifle Brigade's four Battalions continued to provide garrisons for a global Empire. The 1st, after a year at Portsmouth, was in Malta from 1904 to 1905, and from 1906 to 1910 in Ireland. The 2nd Battalion in 1904 went from Cairo to Khartoum and thence to India at the end of 1905 where it remained till 1914, while the 3rd, after more than twenty years in India, returned to England via Aden where it spent a year at the end of 1905. Its stay there was not entirely without incident. "The Arab is of a sporting character," the writer of the Battalion Letter reported, "and on the march from Aden to Dhala saluted the column with several rounds of ammunition. Rickman, however, would not believe it was merely a salute because, he said, two bullets passed exactly twelve inches above his left ear, so he returned it with interest. No damage was done on either side."†

The South African War had one important consequence. For the lessons learnt in the Transvaal were so taken to heart by those responsible for the Army's training that, during the twelve years which followed, it made greater advances in efficiency in almost every department of military skill and equipment than in any comparable period of its peacetime history. In doing so, it followed, unconsciously, the lessons which the Rifle Brigade had been taught by its first founders and to which, in spite of official discouragement,

* R.B.C. 1902, 79-83.   † R.B.C. 1904, 157-8.

it had remained so stubbornly faithful—accurate marksmanship, use of cover and concealment, the art of the skirmishing and piquet line, correlation of fire-power and movement, Company and platoon training, and self sufficiency and independent initiative down to the smallest sub-unit. It was astonishing how quickly that little long-service Army, building on its South African experiences, transformed itself into what, for its size, was to prove itself, in 1914, the finest professional military force in the world.

In that transformation officers of the Rifle Brigade played an important part. Almost the only general officer who went through the entire Boer War with an unblemished, and emerged with an enhanced, reputation was Sir Neville Lyttelton who had joined the 4th Battalion in 1885, served with the 3rd Battalion and commanded in turn both the 1st and 2nd Battalions—a Rifleman of Riflemen.* After commanding a Brigade at Omdurman and a Division in South Africa, he had taken over command of the British Forces in that country from Lord Kitchener in March 1902, doing during the next two years much to repair the past blunders of his political superiors and reconcile Boer with Briton. In 1904, following the reforms initiated by the Esher Committee, he became the first Chief of the new Imperial General Staff.

Lyttelton was only one of the Riflemen who, in the decade after the Boer War, endowed the Army with what was, virtually, a Green Jacket outlook. Another, though in a less exalted position, was Major-General Sir Francis Howard, who in 1903 was appointed Inspector-General of Recruiting and, later, G.O.C. Western Command. Throughout his career an impassioned advocate of Company training, which he held to be the key to military efficiency, he did much to make it the basis of infantry training.† Four years before the outbreak of the First World War, no less than four of the Army's principal training establishments were commanded by Riflemen— the Staff College by Brigadier-General Henry Wilson, who shortly afterwards became Director of Military Operations at the War

---

* Even when C.I.G.S. he loved to pay informal and unofficial visits to units of his old Regiment. "He came to dine on Tuesday evening, and after dinner sat on the fender seat in the ante-room till the small hours of Wednesday morning talking over the events of the South African campaign, interspersed with countless stories and anecdotes." *R.B.C. 1904*, 163 (4th Battalion Letter).

† Though retired on reaching the age of 61 in 1909, he returned to service during the First World War as Inspector of Infantry of the New Armies.

Office; the School of Musketry by the Colenso V.C., Colonel Walter Congreve—known to his contemporaries in the Regiment as "Squibbs" after the Congreve Rocket which an ancestor of his had sponsored; the Gymnasia at Aldershot by Colonel Vic Couper; and the School of Signalling by Major S. C. Long. In the same year Major-General John Cowans, formerly of the 4th Battalion, became Director General of the Territorial Army and, two years later, Quartermaster-General to the Forces. Another member of the Regiment, Colonel "Johnny" Gough, who in the year after the Boer War ended won a V.C. in Somaliland, was appointed in 1913 Chief of Staff to Sir Douglas Haig, Commander of the crack Aldershot Corps which was to spearhead the Expeditionary Force.

Gough had been one of three remarkable Company Commanders of the 2nd Battalion who had served through the siege of Ladysmith and led the assault on Bergendal and who all, bound in close friendship, rose to high command. As E. T. Aspinall, then a subaltern in the battalion, recalled, "Gough dominated us all. His was the strong will which combined a sound judgment with a quick decision and ... iron nerve." Had he not been killed in the first winter of the 1914-1918 War he would almost certainly have risen to the top of his profession.* His fellow Company commander, George Thesiger, who in 1909 was appointed Inspector-General of the King's African Rifles and rose to be a Divisional Commander, before being killed in action in France at the age of 46 was, Aspinall wrote, "a different type, methodical and thorough ... Everything he put his hand to he did well, for he had an infinite capacity for taking pains, and ... in his neat and tidy brain was stored much information ready for use when required." Stephens—"the Stiff'un"—the third of the trio, was, Aspinall thought, the best regimental soldier of the three. "His heart was in the Regiment and he was less ambitious to reach the Staff; in other words, he was more contented with his lot. Blessed with a bright and cheerful disposition and an even temper, he had few likes or dislikes, was everybody's friend and, as such, played an important role in the Battalion's 'family circle'. . . . Tough, wiry and in times of stress absolutely tireless, he was a fine example of the fighting soldier, for, with the prospects of a scrap ahead, he was

* He was paid the unique honour of being posthumously made a Knight Commander of the Bath, whose Companionate he had been awarded only two days before receiving the wound of which he died. R.B.C. 1915, 67-8.

as cheerful as a lark and, should the expected engagement mature, he instantly developed tremendous drive. There was something of the Nelson touch about him, for he was always for going forward; consequently it did not signify much where the fight commenced, his Company would soon be in the midst of it." He, too, after commanding both the 1st and 2nd Battalions rose, like his two friends, to general's rank in his forties and, unlike them, having survived the First World War, became a full General.*

To men like Stephens it was, above all, the well-being and life of the Regiment that mattered, and for them it was an all-absorbing passion. Willoughby Verner's editorship of the Chronicle—now completing its second decade—had helped to draw its four widely separated Battalions closer together and to give to the Rifle Brigade the same sense of family unity and brotherhood which it had enjoyed in its early days when all its components were serving together in the Light Division. The feeling of its history, which the Chronicle with its articles about the Regiment's past did so much to foster, was a strong contributory factor to that unity, and it affected not only officers. In 1904 Lt.-Colonel Paget of the Chestnut Troop—to whom and the Oxfordshire and Buckinghamshire Light Infantry, complimentary copies of the Chronicle were always sent—wrote to the Editor:

"I must tell you of an interesting coincidence which happened the other day. I went down to Gravesend to see some of my men at musketry and found parties of the Rifle Brigade and Oxfordshire Light Infantry—the old Light Division—on the range at the same time, and the men knew all about it and they have all fraternised. In these days of change, traditions like these are worth anything."†

In June 1908 there was a Light Division Centenary Dinner at the Hotel Cecil attended by members of all the Regiments concerned, at which a bugler of the 52nd sounded the 2nd Mess Horn—the old Light Division call—and an officer of that Regiment was present who had sat next to Sir Harry Smith at a similar dinner in 1847. King Edward VII—himself once Colonel-in-Chief of the Rifle Brigade—busied himself during his last sojourn in France, only a few weeks before his death, in visiting the Bridge of Vera and selecting the site

* R.B.C. 1937, 185-94.   † R.B.C. 1904, 120; 1908, 64-75.

for a memorial to commemorate that heroic episode in the Regiment's past.

Another unifying influence was the Depot at Winchester—since 1858 the regimental home and now shared with the 60th, whose brother Riflemen held the same ideals and standards and practised the same techniques. In 1893 the old royal palace of Charles II which, converted into barracks, housed the Depot was burned down, and for the next eleven years the latter was in temporary quarters at Gosport. But by 1904 the rebuilt barracks were ready for occupation, and on March 29th the Depot entrained for Winchester and, after forming up outside the station, marched through crowds of cheering people and flag-draped streets to the City Arch where the Mayor made a speech of welcome, and, in the words of the Chronicle, "the bugle sounded the Advance, and in a few moments we wheeled to the left and formed up on the well-known old Parade Square." At least once during the years of exile all Winchester had turned out to entertain a Battalion of the Regiment, as happened in 1895 when "the good people of Winchester, thrilled at seeing a Rifle Battalion once more marching through their streets and, anxious, apparently, to show how they missed the Rifle Depot . . . insisted on entertaining the Battalion in a truly magnificent and regal fashion," treating five hundred Riflemen in the Guildhall "to as good a feast as any epicure could wish for" with tobacco *ad lib* and a programme of music and song by a travelling company from London. A dinner for the officers was given in an adjoining hall, with the Mayor in the chair and the Lord-Lieutenant present.*

In addition to the annual dinner of the Rifle Brigade Club which, usually presided over by the Duke of Connaught, had by now become as unchanging a feature of the London year as the Derby, from 1908 onwards a dinner was held every year by the Rifle Brigade Veterans' Association, to which, for an annual subscription of 5s, all old Riflemen of whatever rank were eligible. At its first dinner the Chief of the Imperial General Staff, General Sir Neville Lyttelton,† presided and six other General officers and nine Colonels and Lt.-Colonels were present. A regimental charity, the Riflemen's

---

* *R.B.C. 1905*, 84-5; *1895*, 235-6.

† In 1920 and 1921, the Rifle Brigade Association Dinner was presided over by another Rifle Brigade Chief of the Imperial General Staff, Field Marshal Sir Henry Wilson.

Aid Association, to which every officer was expected to subscribe, also assisted old members of the Regiment to find employment and sought to relieve cases of hardship. Its guiding principle was that Riflemen should be entitled "to look to their brother Riflemen for help." In no Regiment was the social life and amusements of the rank and file more fostered and encouraged by its officers. The Colonel Commanding the 2nd Battalion in India in 1909, following a precept of the Regiment's founders, instituted a Battalion Dance Club. "When first proposed most of us gave the club a very short life; but we were wrong, and the club has now over 500 members who take the floor with the greatest regularity and enthusiasm two nights a week."*

The activity in which the Regiment continued most to excel was musketry and weapon-training. In this it still set, with the 60th, an example which, after the lessons of the Boer War,† was followed by the entire Army. In 1909 at the Aldershot Rifle Meeting, tutored and inspired by a young Musketry Officer of genius, Lieutenant Thomas Baring, the 3rd Battalion won the astonishing total of five Challenge Cups, six other Cups, a Medal and £179 10s 6d in Prize Money. In the following year it did better still, sweeping the board with all six Challenge Cups, nine other Cups, eight Medals and over £263 in Prize Money, compared with the £103 won by the next best Battalion. To an onlooker the serried mass of Green Jackets awaiting their prizes made the occasion look like a regimental rather than a national event, with a mere sprinkling from other corps of winners of open events. When, before its departure for Ireland, Sir Horace Smith-Dorrien, G.O.C., Aldershot—who had tried to join the Regiment thirty years before—addressed the Battalion, he said that it had set an example not only to Aldershot but to the Army in general. "You will now understand," he said, "how I regret the departure of the Rifle Brigade from the Command."‡

---

* "Colour-Sergeants Williams and Fitzgerald are the instructors and as the men complained that they could not get enough individual attention they have issued a drill-book on the Art of Dancing." *R.B.C. 1909*, 106.

† "In the days before the South African War very little interest appeared to be taken in musketry by many battalions of the 'Red Army' or by most cavalry regiments. The writer recollects on one occasion, when he was waiting with his company to fire on Ash ranges, hearing his squadron commander shout to his sergeant 'to get the —— rounds off!' " *R.B.C. 1932*, 154-5. Brigadier-General B. H. H. Cooke, "Marksmanship in the Rifle Brigade".

‡ *R.B.C. 1910*, 193.

The 3rd Battalion's success was paralleled by that of the 1st, which, in 1908, won nearly all the principal events in the All-Ireland Musketry and, in 1910, the Curragh Challenge Cup. The Young Soldiers' Cup, founded in 1890, was repeatedly won by the Regiment. In the 4th Battalion the Assistant Adjutant, John Savile, himself a crack shot, used to buy a small bottle of sal volatile at the chemist's before shooting competitions and "lie down beside a nervous youngster and soothe his nerves by giving him a dose and whispering in the lad's ear (or so we used to say, rightly or wrongly) tales of how proud his mother would be of him if he persevered. The shots would insensibly find their way on to the target and creep into the bull, and another member would be produced for the winning team of the Young Soldiers' Cup."[*]

To send into the field, should war occur, a force whose every infantryman was a practised master of accurate and rapid fire at moving targets, was the ideal which Walter Congreve preached during his germinative two years as Commandant of the School of Musketry at Hythe and which almost every musketry instructor in the Army was, as a result of the Boer War, trying to realise. Snap shooting at disappearing targets, the use of automatic weapons[†] and the art of indirect fire were the canons of the gospel he taught, in contrast to the reliance of the Continental conscript armies, and notably of the German Army, on mass volleying-firing. Side by side with musketry and weapon-training went that other transmitted Rifle Brigade recipe for success in the field—Company training, now at last being pursued from one end of Britain to the other by both Regulars and Territorials. More ambitious training-schemes included Battalion, Brigade and Divisional exercises, in which humble Company Commanders, little guessing how soon they would be called upon to do so on the battlefields of France and Flanders, found themselves directing the movements of imaginary tens of thousands of fighting men. "On August 8th," reported the 3rd Battalion's Letter for 1906, "we were off manœuvring again—this time to Salisbury Plain for Brigade and Divisional Training. Old and young, all who were fit to go were swept into the net . . . We all

---

* R.B.C. 1932, 155-8.

† Even before the 1914 War Congreve was a prophetic advocate of a strong machine-gun unit as an integral part of every infantry battalion. In this a parsimonious—where military equipment was concerned—Treasury and country were not prepared to support him. Lt.-Colonel L. H. Thornton and Pamela Fraser, The Congreves, 91-7.

look back with keen pleasure to those weeks under canvas . . . Congreve had fairly kept us on the move during Battalion Training, so all were fit and well and full of confidence that we could make rings round any other Battalion to be found on the Plain. We were a fine strong Battalion of over 700, with more than a stiffening of old soldiers . . . In spite of intricate General and Special Ideas (generally assuming that we were at war with the rest of Europe) the field-days, as a rule, resolved themselves into the old story of one brigade sitting on a hill and the other attacking it. George Thesiger, who a few weeks previously had been one of the most brilliant of the Staff and well used to dealing in Army Corps on this very ground, might be seen plodding along ahead of 'G' Company, keener and, let us hope, prouder of commanding Riflemen than of sitting on the most gilded office-stool. One of the best days was when Congreve commanded a skeleton force of several Divisions, and some of us were brigadiers in charge of some half-dozen red flags. We were out all day and bivouacked on the ground we had won."*

Still more ambitious were the annual Army manoeuvres. These, lacking the reality of war—made considerable demands, as the 1908 chronicler put it, on the participants' imaginative powers. "Salisbury Plain had become Bohemia, north had become south, rivers had changed round and were flowing in the opposite direction; day by day we marched across the Plain in the morning; sometimes we extended and advanced in open order, sometimes not even that, and then we marched wearily home again; and every day it blew and rained relentlessly and unpityingly. We never had any need to call on our imagination for that kind of weather."† The 3rd Battalion Letter for 1909, after retailing its shooting triumphs at Aldershot, supplied a spirited description of that autumn's manoeuvres.

"The 12th September saw us again on the war-path. We proceeded at an uncomfortably early hour by a slow train and circuitous route to Gloucester and encamped in an uncommonly damp field a few miles from the city on the Cheltenham road. There we spent one sodden dreary day. The next, we had a long, hard, enjoyable march over hilly country to Stow-on-the-Wold. The bivouac, on a breezy hill-top, on a chilly September night, was rather a cheerless affair . . .

* *R.B.C. 1906*, 117-19.   † *R.B.C. 1908*, 123.

" On the following day the opposing forces took the field for the decisive, and only, battle of the campaign. The 'General Idea' had allotted to the engagement a period of two days . . . One long day of hard fighting was, however, sufficient to establish the superiority of our side generally, and our consciousness of that quality particularly; and the battle gradually resolved itself into a debacle for the enemy. We cut their communications, captured most of their baggage, and only just missed leading their Headquarters captive. The war fizzled out in one of those farcical incidents without which the operations of peace would be incomplete.

"Kingham railway station was held by a detachment of the Guards Brigade, and the Battalion was launched to its capture. On the railway stood a train of laden coal wagons, affording good cover and inexhaustible stores of ammunition. In less time than we write it the men had taken possession of the coal train and were pelting the Guardsmen most unmercifully with its contents. The Guardsmen replied with great spirit and the same missiles, but victory, as is not uncommonly the case, was with the big battalion. If onlookers see most of the game, the clients of the Railway Company who were waiting for their train must have had a particularly good view of it. All the same they preferred to see it from a comfortable distance, and, leaving their baggage on the platform, bolted with unanimity, and made admirable use of available cover. The Guardsmen beat a sudden and hasty retreat . . . Across the field was a great quickset hedge, the interstices of which were too restricted to give easy thoroughfare to a Guardsman. Most braved the perils of the passage, but a small but gallant band being too bulky individually to get through, and scorning to surrender, made a last desperate stand. The odds, however, were against them. One by one they passed through the hedge on the butts of Riflemen's rifles appropriately applied. The kindly, obliterating mists of evening softly enwrapped the fleeting figures; and so they passed from mortal sight, one by one, and two by two, and even, sometimes, three by three. And that was the end of that war."*

While the 1st and 3rd Battalions prepared in England and Ireland for a European conflict which few believed would ever happen, the

* R.B.C. 1909, 113-15.

2nd and 4th Battalions bore their soldier's share of the White Man's Burden in Asia and Africa. At the end of 1913, it looked as though the 1st Battalion, then at Colchester, was about to join them; "we are all wondering," the Battalion Letter speculated, "what part of the world we shall be sent to." By 1914 the 2nd Battalion's tour of foreign service had almost rivalled in duration that of the 3rd Battalion's stay in the East from 1879 to 1905. Since it had embarked at Woolwich in the year of the Diamond Jubilee for Malta, it had covered nearly 40,000 miles, more than 3000 of them on foot, fought in the Sudan and South Africa, and served under, *inter alia*, seven Green Jacket generals including Field Marshal Lord Grenfell and General Sir Redvers Buller and three of its own regimental allegiance, Neville Lyttelton, John Cowans and Francis Howard. During that time, 121 officers and 4185 N.C.O.s and Riflemen passed through its ranks.

In the absence of colonial wars—except for the brief Somaliland punitive campaign of 1903 there was none in the decade before the First World War—Riflemen abroad sought activity and adventure in sport, exploration and travel. Before it left the Sudan for India in 1913 the officers of the 4th Battalion had ample opportunities for big game shooting in the generous leave-periods of those days.* The 1909 Chronicle contains narratives of shooting expeditions in the eastern Sudan, on the White Nile and in Rajputana, and a long account by Lieutenant the Hon. F. R. D. Prittie of the work of the Uganda-Congo Boundary Commission of 1907, of which, seconded from the Regiment, he had been a member. For in the peaceful years between 1903 and 1914 African exploration offered an outlet, in a half-virgin and underdeveloped continent, for the adventurous spirit which the Rifle Brigade both attracted and fostered. "The Semliki forest gave us a lot of trouble," Prittie reported. "It is exceedingly dense . . . We passed through it in wet weather and found it depressing in the extreme. It was terribly damp and infested with stinging ants and mosquitoes and midges. There is no bird life, nor are there any animals except elephants . . . The Semliki is a fine river from 60 to 100 yards in width. In the northern reaches are great numbers of crocodiles which, together with hippopotami, form a serious obstacle to navigation in small canoes. In Lake Albert we lost two Sudanese soldiers through a hippopotamus torpedoing their

* *R.B.C. 1913,* 145-6.

canoe . . . We had a certain amount of trouble with the Lendu who
are exceedingly treacherous and were always looking out for a chance
of cutting up small parties."*

In 1911, Prittie, now a Captain, served on another international
commission to re-define the frontiers of Uganda following the
Berlin Conference of 1910. In the Kagera plains, where the mountain
peaks were worshipped as gods and devils and where the three great
colonial empires of Britain, Germany and Belgium met, he came
across a purely pastoral people who did no work but were served by
the Bahutu who were virtually slaves. Among the Bakiga in Ruanda
he found whole villages mad with drink at seven or eight in the
morning; rising *en masse* they were in process of wiping out a large
part of a rival tribe of Bahutu, "equally bibulous and more unpleasant because under the influence of a particularly bloodthirsty
female witch-doctor."†

A still more famous work of exploration was the survey of the
waters between the Nile and the Niger carried out from 1904 to
1907 by two Rifle Brigade officers, Lieutenant Boyd Alexander and
Captain G. B. Gosling, in which the latter and Alexander's brother,
Claud, lost their lives. During it they passed through a country of
pagan cannibals. "The early state of their civilisation is shown,"
Boyd Alexander wrote, "by the fact that they have not yet evolved as
far as the village stage; each hamlet is against its neighbour; the
stronger prey upon the weaker, with the result that the former inhabitants have been driven right up to the peaks of the range where
they now live a most precarious existence. They are very hostile to
one another and are continually raiding their supplanters below to
get captives." Hidden in one of the boats of the Budumas, who swam
like otters under the waters of Lake Chad, the explorers found four
slave boys, in a shocking condition, whom they released—"victims
of a traffic between the Budumas and Tubus . . . The Yo districts were
in a most unsettled state; natives went about fully armed and only
travelled by night for fear of the Tubus who were on the warpath . . .
The effect of their poisoned arrows is very deadly and sudden. In a
few minutes the victim is thrown into convulsions." "The Dinkas,"

---

* *R.B.C. 1909*, 42-51. "The King of Toro volunteered to send us all his spearmen to assist
in exterminating this tribe, but unfortunately we were unable to take advantage of his
generosity!"

† *R.B.C. 1912*, 59-68. Prittie, like so many officers of the Regiment, was killed in the First
World War.

Alexander reported of another part of his journey, "on our first appearance ran away, but later, gaining confidence, flocked down to the river and lined the banks in hundreds. All naked and with their bodies painted a ghastly white, they shouted and danced and threw their spears into the air."*

The account of his travels and experiences, which he gave before the Royal Geographical Association on his return to civilisation in 1907, and which were subsequently published in two volumes dedicated to his lost companions, won him the Society's Gold Medal and international fame. Three years later he met his death in the French Congo at the hands of Arab fanatics while engaged on a further exploration of the surroundings of Lake Chad. "The news of Boyd Alexander's premature death," the Rifle Brigade Chronicle for 1910 recorded, "was received not only in England but throughout the whole civilised world—for he had made a world-wide reputation as a most daring and successful explorer—with profound regret. We Riflemen in addition had to mourn the loss of a good comrade of whom we were justly proud, while those of the old generation who had served with his father, Colonel B. F. Alexander, and who knew and esteemed him, most deeply sympathised with the parent who had thus lost another son, and this time his eldest, in the service of African Exploration . . . Thus in the very prime of life, having already at the early age of 37, covered himself with honour and glory, this splendid man was done to death . . . His supreme courage and absolute disregard for all perils and his confidence in his often-proved ability to deal with savage tribes led him to take the fatal step of pushing on into a dangerous zone whose inhabitants were bitterly hostile to white men, without allowing adequate time for his identity to become known."†

Less ambitious Rifle Brigade officers with a taste for exploration were able to combine it with the routine duties of their profession by devoting their leaves, while abroad, to travel—most of it highly uncomfortable—in little known lands. In doing so they kept, as befitted Riflemen, a sharp, shrewd eye on the world about them. The Chronicles contain many accounts of such journeys. "Hong Kong has one advantage, it is good place to get away from, and, with three months' leave before one, there is a wide field for choice," recalled Captain F. G. Talbot—who was to command a Battalion of

* R.B.C. 1907, 43-69.   † R.B.C. 1910, 43-56.

the Regiment in World War I—in describing a journey in Japan, Eastern Siberia and China which he and his fellow captain, Arthur Ferguson, "the Laird", another future commander of a Rifle Brigade Battalion in the 1914-18 War, took in 1896. He saw Japan in the course of its rapid transformation in little less than a decade from a closed medieval polity to modern industrial nationhood. "The Japanese," he wrote, "are utterly unreliable; they cannot be counted on to fulfil their part of a contract, and in business matters they have not yet learned that honesty is the best policy . . . Their conceit is boundless and the majority of the people are firmly convinced that they are capable of fighting the whole of Europe at a moment's notice. But whatever the people may be, their country is simply delightful. The climate, scenery and miniature houses, the people always bowing and laughing, are perfect, and one feels on landing as if one had stepped into a new planet . . . Yokohama is typical of the Japan of today; railways, overhead wires and electric light side by side with rickshaws, kimonos and Japanese lanterns. I once saw an electric tramcar stopped by a policeman because two men had met on the line and were bowing their shaven heads repeatedly to the earth, having first deposited their umbrellas on the ground between them. It is a curious blending of the East and West, and the same thought strikes one when, walking through a village, one finds all the ladies sitting in hip-baths in the middle of the road. They are not troubled with shyness, and an Englishman finds it embarrassing at first to be waited on by the ladies of the establishment when he is in his bath."

Korea and Siberia made a very different impression on the two Rifle Brigade travellers. Kensan, Captain Talbot wrote, is "one of the finest harbours in the world, thirteen miles long with only one narrow entrance . . . Any other race than the Koreans would long ago have made it an important trade-centre . . . A Korean who labours one day in five is considered hard working." At Vladivostock

"the hotel was a third-rate pot-house; food and sanitary arrangements indescribable. Vladivostock is simply a fortress; consuls are not allowed, and foreigners are not encouraged . . . We had to spend eight weary days in a railway carriage waiting for the line to be repaired. Happily there was a little shooting, so we made ourselves popular by providing our fellow-travellers with snipe."

Talbot was much struck by the difference between the Russians and the British in dealing with the Chinese. "An unfortunate Russian soldier had crossed the river and been murdered by the Chinese. The Governor of Habarovsk promptly sent four Companies to the place; thirteen Chinese were shot on the spot . . . As a Russian officer told us, 'Everybody was satisfied; they had an opportunity of testing their rifles and it saved a lot of correspondence.' "

"Cossacks do not come up to our idea of smartness. The officers wear long hair and ear-rings, . . . but there is no doubt they are hardy enough. Their military training is simple and effective. They are drawn up in a long skirmishing-line at fifty yards interval, given a point of compass to march on and ordered to go straight ahead for so many days or weeks. They kill everything they see, camp round a big fire at night and go on without stopping all day. They say they like it, as they get plenty of food. During the rest of the year they live on black bread and cabbages: no meat. There is no doubt that hordes of their troops would ravage a country, but it is doubtful whether they would help to win battles or give effective aid during a war.

"Russian food is as nasty as anything can well be; we lived on cabbage soup and chocolate most of the time. All Russians love grease; some moujiks, on the ship I came back in, broke into the purser's stores and devoured all the tallow candles they could lay their hands on."*

At Habarovsk the Governor-General

"was received with all honours. Every house was illuminated by order of the police, the streets lined with troops all dressed much the same in blouse, belt and long boots. As he walked down the line each company shouted, by word of command, 'God bless your Excellency'. There was a good deal of confusion in getting the troops away, as the crowd broke through and the officers fell out and drove home. The whole thing was much what one might see in a native state in India. With true Russian hospitality every-

---

* The same taste was shown by the Russian soldiers whom, a hundred years earlier, the Royal Navy transported from the Baltic for the Anglo-Russian Helder campaign of 1799, and who "lived on boiled grain and quas and even ate with relish the tallow which they scraped out of the ships' lanterns and washed down with train-oil." *Years of Endurance*, 287

thing was placed at our disposal; but as our kind friends were never for one moment sober, the whole time we were there we had great difficulty in getting anything to eat."

From Manchuria the two Rifle Brigade travellers passed to China. They found pre-Boxer Rising Peking "one large cesspool, which is scarcely surprising considering that it has been in existence some thousands of years and has always been innocent of drains except for the streets themselves . . . The walls are certainly wonderful: fifteen miles in circumference, fifty feet high, and it is possible to drive eight carriages abreast along the top. On one of the buttresses there are some astronomical instruments which were old in Marco Polo's day but of which the Chinese have long ago forgotten the use."

"The Examination hall is a curious place containing 1500 brick cells in which the candidates are shut up for a fortnight. In the middle there is a tower where the mandarin sits to prevent cribbing; but there is not much of this, as the culprit, when detected, is immediately beheaded."

Travelling through the countryside, where like all visitors to China he was deeply impressed by the Great Wall, Talbot was struck by the almost incredible ignorance of the coolies. "Had they heard of the Japanese?" "Yes, they gave trouble last year, but the Emperor had them all killed." "Had they heard of Russia or England?" "No, but they knew there were some islands on the coast of China where the Emperor allowed foreigners to live." The fact that they considered China to be the whole world accounted, Talbot thought, for "their entire lack of patriotism. An old man in Peking, who was asked if he remembered foreigners coming there and sacking the Summer Palace replied, "Oh yes, that was plenty good time, one dollar, one chicken."

"In the country the people are not offensive; children usually shout, 'Foreign devil' at one as one passes, but, when my companion dismounted and asked the parents what they meant by allowing their child to do so, they replied that he was too young to know better and he was made to kow-tow. There is no doubt that the mandarin and officials hate us with a deadly hatred, but the people merely look upon us with supreme contempt."

Shanghai, where the travellers spent the last week of their leave,

Talbot found far and away the finest town in the Far East . . .
"Guizot said that, if a Frenchman and an Englishman were put
down on a desert island, . . . at the end of the year the Frenchman
would have a wife and a family, while the Englishman would be
king of the island. This is very much what has happened in Shanghai,
and the difference as one crosses the narrow creek that divides the
English from the French Concession is very striking. Drink is the
curse of the place. It is the custom to drink champagne every morning before breakfast."*

In those years, before the older nations and communities of a still
widely diversified globe were drawn into the maelstrom of a universal European War, such Rifle Brigade travellers, using their leave
periods to widen their knowledge of a world they helped to police,
missed very little. Much that they saw and recorded in their Regiment's annual Chronicles could have considerably enlightened their
country's rulers and electors had the latter troubled to read their accounts. Naturally, being soldiers, they were interested most of all in
the fighting potentialities of the people they visited. "The Cypriot,"
wrote an officer of the 4th Battalion in 1909, when one of its detachments was quartered in that then peaceful island, "is not much of a
fighting man; his manners are mild and he settles any difference of
opinion with his neighbour by merely shooting him from behind a
tree in the dark, but a religious dispute brings him into the open and
he gives trouble." The Turks, on the other hand, though their troops
were dirty, ragged and ill-equipped, gave Captain R. E. Solly-Flood
—who saw something of them in the Yemen while he was serving
with a wing of the 3rd Battalion at Dhala in 1905, and who ten
years later was to fight against them in Gallipoli—the impression
that, if they were better looked after, their men were "as fine material
as one could wish for in soldiers."†

Of all the martial peoples Riflemen encountered, those who invariably impressed them most were the hill soldiers of Nepal. This
was the more natural for the Gurkha Regiments of the Indian Army
were trained and armed on the same lines as the two classic British
Rifle Regiments by whose side they fought against the Sepoys in the
Mutiny. At the Coronation Durbar at Delhi in 1903, of all the imperial pomps and glories of the occasion, what most thrilled the

---

* F. G. Talbot, *Three Months Leave to Siberia*, cit. *R.B.C. 1896*, 112-26.
† *R.B.C. 1909*, 127-9; *1905*, 81-3.

officers of the 3rd Battalion was "an impromptu parade in camp of all the old 2nd Gurkha veterans whom the Regiment had sportingly collected from their homes in Nepal—little pippin-faced warriors, wrinkled and shrunk, but escorted proudly about by their sons and grandsons still serving in the Regiment, all of them wearing war-medals won in the wars of half a century ago. These were the men who, with the 2/60th, so finely held Hindu Rao's House on the Ridge." Another of the Gurkha Rifle Regiments, the 4th, had formed a historic and lasting association with the 4th Rifle Brigade at Jellalabad in 1878/9 when they served and fought together in the Afghan War; the links between the two units remained particularly close throughout their joint existence. At a Grand Military Review in January 1907 of 30,000 troops before the Viceroy, the visiting Amir of Afghanistan and Lord Kitchener, the Commander-in-Chief, a complete Rifle Division took part, including the 2nd Rifle Brigade and eight Gurkha Battalions. " For the march past we first of all went by . . . in column of double Companies; this done, the Division formed up in quarter column of massed brigades in line, the Gurkha brigades in front. Then we all went by a second time to the good old band-and-bugle march, 'Marching through Georgia' played by the massed bands of the Division. From all accounts it was a very fine sight, and the onlookers were good enough to say that we all went by 'splendidly'."*

Eighteen months earlier a Frenchman had watched, and put down his impressions of the 2nd Battalion Rifle Brigade at another parade at Khartoum before the Duke and Duchess of Connaught. After the Egyptian and Sudanese troops had passed by, an English officer, who had been praising them, added "But look there!" "Between blue sky and yellow sand," wrote the Frenchman, "a line, almost invisible so like was it to the colour of the soil, advanced like a great snake, with a quickness, a swing and an energy almost incredible. These were the seven hundred men of the English Regiment stationed at Khartoum. There was about them such a strong, virile martial appearance that a great emotion seized me by the throat and I felt inclined to clap my hands and shout, 'Bravo', as when, at the finish of a review at Longchamps, the cavalry sweep down in a furious charge. What does it matter that these soldiers are young, what does it matter that their khaki uniforms fit badly, when the bodies

* R.B.C. 1907, 144; 1904, 74; 1923, 147.

that they cover are animated by unshaken will and energy, by intelligent courage, cool and calculating, against which the charges of the
Dervish fanatics, who knew no fear, broke like waves against a
rock? It was wonderful. Calm as statues, not an Englishman among
the spectators seemed to notice it."*

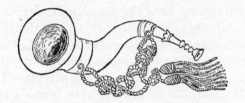

* A. B. De Guerville, *New Egypt*, cit. *R.B.C. 1905*, 107-8.

Part III

"IN TIME OF THE BREAKING OF NATIONS" 1914-1945

My heart's at the war with a good-natured Rifleman
Where he stands firing his foemen to slay;
While he was home with us, laughter and liveliness—
Night time or church time 'twas all holiday ...
Now that he's given himself up for a soldier,
All over the world his brave body to show,
How can you wonder that I in my anxiousness
Weep with my eyes on the willow-tree-bough.

CHARLES SCOTT-MONCRIEFF

Chapter Seven

STAND TO YOUR FRONT

Everywhere I go I hear nothing but praise of the Regiment . . .
It is a great heritage you old Riflemen have handed down to us.
GENERAL SIR W. CONGREVE, V.C.
It takes an awful lot to knock out a Rifleman.
RIFLEMAN F. J. MCCARTHY

DURING the Franco-Prussian War of 1870 the 4th Battalion Rifle
Brigade had been sent to Shorncliffe as part of a minute token-force
designed, in case either of the giant combatants should violate Belgian
neutrality, to cross the Channel and "turn them out".* In August
1914, in order to crush France quickly before striking down Russia,
the Germans, in pursuance of the Schlieffen strategic plan, poured
their armies into Belgium, whose neutrality Britain, like Germany,
had pledged herself to defend.

The 1st Battalion, stationed at Colchester, was the first Rifle
Brigade unit to cross to France. It did so on August 19th as part of
the 4th Division and, though not in time to take part in the Battle
of Mons, fought at Le Cateau on the 26th and helped to cover the
retreat of the army, marching more than 160 miles in ten days and
preserving the same state of discipline as its predecessor had done
on the road to Corunna. The 3rd Battalion, stationed at Cork when
war broke out, sailed from Southampton on September 8th for St.
Nazaire, going into action on the Aisne on the 23rd and, with the
1st Battalion, playing its part in the fighting which ended the war of
movement and contained the German attempt to overrun France.
Later, as the battle line extended northwards, both Battalions helped
to save the vital Channel ports. The 2nd and 4th Battalions under
Lt.-Colonels R. B. Stephens and R. B. Thesiger of Ladysmith and
Bergendal fame, were both in India. When, on the regimental birthday, the order of recall reached the 2nd Battalion at Rawalpindi "it
was a day," wrote the writer of the Battalion Letter, "none of us will
ever forget . . . For, at two in the morning the Colonel was woken

* *R.B.C. 1923*, 139-40.
J.G.   P

up by the telegram from Simla . . . In a few minutes all the officers
had collected in the Mess, and the mess-waiters had to be shown the
telegram before they could believe the news was true and that all the
officers had not suddenly gone mad." Landing at Liverpool on
October 23rd, after a fortnight at Hursley Camp, Winchester, the
Battalion crossed to France in early November. The 4th Battalion
remained at Dagshai till October when, to the general joy, Colonel
Thesiger, returning from Simla, told an officer on entering the Mess,
"You can sharpen your sword." "Till then," the Battalion chronicler wrote, "we had doubted whether we should ever be in time.
Captain Cole led the route to the armourer's shop where the grind-
stone turned apace and swords were sharpened . . . Five days later we
were marching to Kalka to entrain for Bombay." Sailing in convoy
for protection against commerce-raiders, the Battalion's enthusiasm
reached fever pitch as the troopship passed H.M.S. *Black Prince* in the
Suez Canal, a Rifleman in the prow performing "Rule Brittania" on
a cornet. "No finer body of men ever represented the British Army,"
recalled one of its officers, "the average service in the Battalion was
six years. The men were trained both physically and in their military
duties to the highest degree of perfection . . . Not a man was left
behind other than . . . one man who had broken his leg playing
football; there were no unfits."

The returning Riflemen needed all their hardihood. When after a
bad passage of the Bay they landed in November at Devonport and
proceeded to Magdalen Hill Camp near Winchester, the cold was
intense; for the first two days it froze, after which it rained continually for the three weeks they were there. "The camp became a
sea of mud, there were no floor-boards for the tents, . . . horses were
dying of pneumonia in the lines." Yet, though of the thirty reservists
who joined in England to bring the Battalion up to war-strength,
only two were able to stand up to the conditions and sail with it for
France on December 22nd, none of those from India, except one man
who died of pneumonia, had to be left behind. Thus by the end of the
year all four Regular Battalions were engaged with the enemy, one
of them, the 3rd, having already lost its Commanding Officer in
action.

By then there were more volunteers and re-enlisted men in the
Rifle Brigade than there were Regulars in the battle-line. Since
August a continuous stream of re-enlisted Riflemen had been pour-

ing through the Depot at Winchester to fill the ranks of the 5th and 6th Special Reserve Battalions—the successors of the old Militia Regiments affiliated to the Regiment—whose function it was to train and supply drafts for the Regular Battalions to make good the latter's growing casualties, already running into thousands. "Many old campaigners," wrote the writer of the Depot letter, "came forward, including some with Afghan ribbons ... Such a gathering and renewal of old acquaintanceship had never before been witnessed ... One striking feature was the uniformly cheerful manner in which the unavoidable discomforts were borne by all classes."

Far more of those who joined in those early months were civilians who responded, with such enthusiasm and in overwhelming numbers, to Lord Kitchener's appeal for volunteers to form a New Army. No less than eight Service Battalions of the Regiment were formed—the 7th, 8th, 9th, 10th, 11th, 12th, 13th and 16th, all but the last of which reached the battle line in France during the summer of 1915. At first there were no arms or uniforms for them, but their spirit was beyond praise, and the Regiment, with its pride, traditions and humane but binding discipline, did the rest. "The men who have enlisted for this Army," wrote one of their officers, "are a splendid lot; they are keen to learn, always cheery and take all the hard work they have to do with the greatest goodwill. We are a strong Battalion of over 1200, who are getting very fit and promise to make useful soldiers. To attain this object all hands are working to the best of their ability and we confidently hope that when the Battalion is put to the test it will fully maintain the tradition of the Regiment and in no way disgrace the badge it is privileged to wear."* And though, since the formation of the Territorial Army in 1908, the dozen or more Volunteer Corps which in Victorian times had been attached to the Rifle Brigade had been merged into the new composite London Territorial Regiment, the emotional links which bound them to the black and green remained unbroken. By 1916 seven of them—the Hackney, St. Pancras, Stepney, Post Office, Artists', Cyclists' and London Irish Rifles, four of whom had retained their Regular Rifle Brigade adjutants—were gazetted back to the Regiment.

To officer this great host and fill the terrible gaps, growing with every casualty list, in the commissioned ranks of its Regular Bat-

* *R.B.C. 1914*, 112, 12 Bn. Letter.

talions, the Regiment drew heavily on the University and public schools' Officer Training Corps. Ever since the beginning of the century the Rifle Brigade and the 60th had provided most of the Commandants and Adjutants for their annual Camps. Among the Rifle Brigade officers who served as Brigadiers at these were Henry Wilson, the future C.I.G.S., his namesake, H. M. F. Wilson, and R. B. Stephens—both future generals—and the two V.C.s, Walter Congreve and John Gough. With its insistence on initiative and alacrity, Rifle Brigade training made a natural appeal to boys; so did its idealism and encouragement of eagerness and activity. In his address on the last day of the 1907 Summer Camp at Aldershot, Colonel Gough had told the assembled cadets that "one day the Empire might require the services of them all, and that their present experience in the ranks would give them a wider sympathy with the hardships of their men if they were ever called upon to command soldiers in the field."*

With Rifle Brigade officers in command in 1914 of the Oxford O.T.C. and as Adjutants of both the Oxford and Cambridge, O.T.C.s, it was natural that large numbers of undergraduates should have applied for Special Reserve commissions in the Regiment. Not only was their number remarkable but their quality. Oxford provided 163, of whom 77 gave their lives, and Cambridge 217, of whom 97 were killed or died of wounds and 57 more wounded. Among those who joined the Special Reserve from Cambridge was a twenty-year-old Trinity undergraduate who in later life, as Percy Meighar-Lovett, was well known as a brilliant business man and Chairman of the Nuffield Nursing Home Trust. But to his dying day his abiding love was the Rifle Brigade, of whose Association's Executive Committee he was Chairman for more than a quarter of a century. "I had just returned from the Cambridge Training Corps Camp when war broke out," he recalled shortly before his death in 1970,

"when I received a typed memo offering me a commission in the Rifle Brigade and suggesting I should proceed to Winchester for an interview. With no military background, I am afraid I had very vague notions of what the Rifle Brigade really meant, except that both the Commanding Officer and the Adjutant of the Camp in

* R.B.C. 1907, 136; 1923, 158-70.

their beautiful green and silver mess kit appealed to me very strongly. After proceeding to Winchester and wangling my way through the medical (my eyesight was so bad that I had to use a certain amount of fiddling to get through the medical examination) I then proceeded to an unknown destination called the Isle of Sheppey. It was there that I started to learn something about my new family, and, as the weeks went by, so I started to understand what it was all about: what a really good Regiment meant—when we were all part of a large family who knew each others' weaknesses but would not let anybody else know. In due course I was drafted to the 3rd Battalion in France, almost more terrified of showing my fright than actually being frightened. To add to my embarrassment, when I joined the Battalion I had the most awful cold and, instead of being welcomed, as I could quite well have been, with very little enthusiasm, I was given a bottle of champagne and the cold was cured! I never got less frightened but we all knew that this was one of the things we kept to ourselves, and that a good Regiment was always kept cleaner, better shaved and had better trenches than anyone else. After being wounded and sent home I still did not feel that I could belong, as I had hardly been out with the Regiment long enough. Imagine my feelings, therefore, that when I eventually went back to France, I was welcomed by the Commanding Officer* (who had previously been my Company Commander) with 'How glad we are to see you *back*'. I was so elated because I now felt that I really belonged to this wonderful Regiment. Everyone seemed to feel the same family spirit, and so we grew in strength, affection and discipline (what I describe as the desire to obey). Ever since those days the doors of life have been thrown open to me at the mention of the Rifle Brigade. I have always felt that I only had to mention the magic words for me to become acceptable in any enterprise on which I was engaged."

In being posted, only seven months after the outbreak of war, to a

* Brigadier E. R. Kewley, who wrote of him, "During the time he was with the 3rd Battalion in France he proved himself not only an individual whom one could rely on under many and varied circumstances but one who showed leadership of the very highest standard." "The Regiment was his abiding joy," recalled Major-General Lord Bridgeman, whose 55 years of friendship with him began in the trenches at Armentières in 1915, "and I cannot imagine anyone, even the Peninsular heroes, who was more devoted to it and over half a century did more for it in so many ways."

Regular Battalion in the field, instead of, as most of his contemporaries, to a Service Battalion still in England, "Danny"—as he was always known to the Regiment—was most fortunate. At that time the 3rd Battalion, like its sister Battalions, was as near perfection, both as a fighting instrument and as a closely-knit brotherhood-in-arms, as any unit could be. The worth of its pre-war triumphs, and those of the 1st Battalion, on the musketry-ranges of Aldershot and Ireland became apparent when the British Expeditionary Force took its place on the flank of the French Army. For, despite the disastrous failure of the latter's High Command to anticipate the collapse of the Belgian frontier fortresses, and the strength and speed of the enemy's outflanking drive round the Allies' northern armies, the deadly rifle-fire of the British infantry gave a check to the invaders just long enough to rob them of the second Sedan they were seeking. Fifteen aimed shots to the minute was the British norm, contrasted with the mediocre marksmanship and volley firing which was that of the German conscript armies. Heavily armed with machine-guns as they were, the Germans found it almost impossible to believe that they were being held up only by rifle-fire. "So this," wrote Captain Bloem of the 12th Brandenburg Grenadiers, "was our first battle and this was the result. Our grand Regiment with all its pride and splendid discipline, its attack full of dash and courage, and now only a few fragments left! . . . They apparently did know something about war, those cursed English." A similar testimony was paid by an officer of the 3rd Jägers which, with two other Jäger battalions and a brigade of cavalry, was held up by three tired Companies of the 1st Battalion at Le Cateau on August 26th. "Over the open ground," he wrote, "we went almost as steadily as we did at home on the drill ground till we were 800 metres from the enemy position. It is not for nothing that our opponents are called the Rifle Brigade, the English *troupes d'élite*. They were well-trained veteran professional soldiers who have fought on every continent. They were a tenacious, experienced lot who loaded and fired, even when they were wounded, with the greatest *sang-froid* and who understood so well to take advantage of their favourable positions that it was difficult for even the sharpest-eyed Jäger to get a line on them."*

Yet the British stand at Le Cateau could win only the briefest

* *R.B.C. 1922,* 209; *1932,* 156.

breathing-space, and nothing could have saved the Expeditionary Force from encirclement but urgent and unplanned retreat. With its flanks exposed and the fog of war closing in on every side, it was the quickness of thought and action, the hour-by-hour grasp of what had to be done, and the cheerful resilience and calm under successive shocks of a Rifleman of genius which made the army's escape from the enemy's closing jaws possible. After seven years of responsibility at the Staff College and War Office, Henry Wilson in 1914 was just fifty and a junior major-general. Yet though he was only Sub-Chief of the Expeditionary Force's Staff and inferior in rank to its Chief of Staff, Quartermaster-General and Adjutant-General, as the former Director of Military Operations who had planned the Army's swift and successful passage to France he enjoyed the confidence of the Commander-in-Chief, Sir John French, and the trust of the French generals. As Sir John was now bemused by the unexpected turn of events and convinced that the French had betrayed him, and as Sir Archibald Murray, his Chief of Staff, collapsed under the strain, it was left to Wilson to retrieve a seemingly impossible situation. Though, since his early days with the 1st Battalion—when he had all but lost an eye and suffered permanent disfigurement in action against Burmese dacoits—his career had lain with the Staff rather than with the Regiment, few ever more faithfully observed the Rifleman's "golden rule of appearing cheerful under any and every circumstance" than this tall, quizzical Irishman in the hour when his own and his cherished Expeditionary Force's hopes were being so cruelly falsified. Alone in a migratory and bewildered Headquarters, with a weary, sleepless army staggering blindly southwards and a triumphant enemy at its heels, Henry Wilson kept his head and clarity of vision and for all practical purposes took charge and prevented the retreat from becoming a rout. Making a jest of disaster, he communicated cheerfulness and courage to all around him.* "His inimitable way," as bad news poured in, "of saying, on entering the Operations Room, 'Well, and where are we now?'," was, a sub-

---

* The Commander of the II Corps recalled how, after his brave decision to ignore Sir John French's orders and to fight at Le Cateau, Wilson spoke to him on the telephone and "asked what I thought of the chance of success, I replied that I was fully confident and hopeful of giving the enemy a smashing blow and slipping away before he could recover. He replied, 'Good luck to you. Yours is the first cheerful voice I have heard these three days!' With these pleasant words in my ears, which I shall never forget I returned to my headquarters." *Callwell*, I, 169. The humble Riflemen of "A" Company of the 1st Battalion who fought

ordinate recalled, like a tonic. So was his insistence that '*battre en retraite*' was "an operation of war familiar to all the great captains." When after ten days of retreat the Army reached safety behind the Marne, and the over-stretched Germans, as Wilson had anticipated, made a false move by crossing the British front, it was he who persuaded his disgruntled Commander-in-Chief to give fortune another chance and co-operate with the French in the decisive counter-attack which drove the invaders back to the Aisne and saved the Western alliance.*

The same indomitable courage and optimism, which animated Henry Wilson during those fateful days of late August and early September, animated the 1st Battalion of his Regiment as it covered the retreat of the 2nd Corps from Le Cateau. "We started fighting on the Regimental Birthday, August 25th," wrote a Rifleman to his former employer in England, "and for three days kept the enemy back on the retreat, and it was the best fight of the lot. We were outnumbered and we had the women and the fagged-out remains of the British and French armies to cover, so it was a fight worth having. We lost very heavily here but we hung on, as we were asked to until the order came along, 'Every man for himself!' And it was not until three days afterwards that the remains of the Battalion got together again, when we joined the Somersets in forming a rearguard for the 4th Division. For three weeks it was march and counter-march, the longest halt being for six hours; we had a skirmish here and there, but it was dreary work running away. On the advance we again did well, our best thing being the taking of Busy-de-Long. This we did on the top of a twenty-mile march, wet to the skin, with an hour's halt and then creeping in the dark for another five miles across the Aisne and a scramble up the heights. So well was it done that our artillery shelled us at daybreak, thinking the enemy still held the ridge."†

*   *   *

---

under General Smith-Dorrien also recalled Henry Wilson's gay and imperturbable courage as they detrained before the battle. "He had just come from the neighbourhood of Mons, but he looked as cheerful as ever and called out a greeting as the Company went by. After the gloom and apprehension in Le Cateau station such an encounter was a tonic to the men." *Berkeley*, 7.

* Major-General Sir C. E. Callwell, *Field-Marshal Sir Henry Wilson*, I, 166-75; Bernard Ash, *The Lost Dictator*, 154-61; Basil Collier, *Brasshat*, 176-89.   † *R.B.C. 1918*, 302-3.

Victory on the Marne was followed by stalemate on the Aisne. The Germans were still immensely strong and far superior in artillery,* and hopes of driving them back to the Meuse quickly faded. In October the battle moved northwards as both sides attempted to out-flank the other, the Allies seeking to save Antwerp and the Germans to reach the Channel ports. To defend the latter, the British Ex-peditionary Force was transferred to Artois and Flanders. It was still composed almost entirely of Regulars and its losses, particularly of officers, placed on it a strain which only a force with superlative discipline and morale could have borne. "The Germans seem quite determined to break through us at Neuve Chapelle and their efforts get more and more vicious," wrote 23-year-old Lieutenant Billy Congreve of the 3rd Battalion, the V.C. general's son, on October 27th while serving as a roving A.D.C. to the commander of the 6th Division. "The Battalions . . . who are holding these trenches are nearly done for, for this incessant shelling with these big shells is very terrible. They have hardly any officers left, and the men are few and rather nerve-broken. It's getting on for three weeks' hard and continuous fighting now, always under fire by day and driving off desperately hard-pushed attacks by night. Our men are really won-ders, but things begin to go ill now; trenches are lost and then retaken a few hours later, each time fewer men, and the devil is we have no fresh troops to shove in to help. However, I suppose all comes right in the end." At Ypres a fortnight later, where a thin dwindling line of strung-out exhausted regiments alone stood between the Germans and the Channel ports, he wrote again;

"A proper day this has been, beastly wet and cold, and the fiercest fighting we have yet had. The Guards Corps (Bill's Own) arrived to turn us out and get through to Calais. They haven't yet though. We have traced twelve Battalions of it so far: they were told that the infantry of the line could get no farther ahead, so they were being brought up 'to finish us off'. The result has been desperate fighting and the complete failure of the Germans up to date. Before

* Walter Congreve, V.C., now commanding the 18th Infantry Brigade, wrote from the Aisne on September 25th, "Black Maria's shells weigh 280 lbs and are thrown from miles back so that we cannot reach the guns, having nothing big enough up at present. The Ger-man gunners are A.I. and must have a most perfect system of observation by outlooks and spies." *The Congreves*, 112.

they attacked they gave our trenches and supports and guns the most terrific bombardment. I never have seen the like before . . . The shrapnel played up and down our lines exactly as one waters a line of flowers, backwards and forwards. Also there were heaps and heaps of crumpets, crumps and super-crumps—all over the place they were. This went on till 10 a.m., when a silence fell except for our guns, and the Germans came on. They told us . . . that they expected to see what was left of our men after the bombardment, but they were badly shocked, for they were met with bayonets and such musketry 'as they never dreamt could be possible'."*

"You must be very proud, Sir, having a son an officer in the old Regiment," the Rifleman of the 1st Battalion who had described the retreat from Le Cateau to his employer wrote to him, "and he has got the job of his life to live up to the reputation of the Rifle Brigade officers. They are the best out here; never have we waited for them to give the lead, and in the trenches they have shared and shared alike with us, with rations and with work; in fact some of them were better with the pick and shovel than we ourselves, and always have they set us the example of being cheerful both under fire and putting up with the hardships and miserable weather all through the winter."† Such, however, was their casualty rate that, by the end of the winter, of the officers who had come out with the original Expeditionary Force only a handful remained. "They are terribly changed since I left them," Billy Congreve wrote of the 3rd Battalion in February, "in November it was bad enough, now there are only a few I knew." Something of their spirit was expressed by a captain of the Battalion, who four years earlier had taken part in the last duel fought by a Regular serving officer.‡ A first cousin of the First Lord of the Admiralty, Winston Churchill, Norman Leslie wrote before his death in action that autumn:

"Try and not worry too much about the war. Units, individuals,

* *The Congreves*, 238, 250-1.

† *R.B.C. 1918*, 302. "Be with your men in dangerous times and uncomfortable times," General Sir Walter Congreve, V.C., had told the officers of a Corps School in 1918, "and in these especially be always cheery and optimistic. Stop all croaking and criticism, and do not offend in this way yourself. It means nothing and is a British failing, but it is harmful and must be stopped." *The Congreves*, 115.

‡ *Idem 1958*, 65-6. The rapier with which he did so is in the Rifle Brigade section of the Royal Green Jackets' Museum at Winchester.

cannot count. Remember we are writing a new page of history. Future generations cannot be allowed to read the decline of the British Empire and attribute it to us. We live our little lives and die. To some are given chances of proving themselves men, and to others no chance comes. Whatever our individual thoughts, virtues or qualities may be, it matters not, but when we are up against big things let us forget individuals and let us act as one great British unit, united and fearless. Some will live and many will die, but count the loss nought. It is better far to go out with honour than survive with shame."*

What conditions were like that winter, as the open fighting of the autumn changed to static trench warfare, is revealed in the diary which Billy Congreve kept as he moved, ceaselessly and cheerfully, from one danger-point to another while he fulfilled his mission of keeping contact between the Divisional Commander and his troops and helped wherever help was needed.†

"*November 20th* . . . It's awful cold, and the snow is thick on the ground . . . These last days it has steadily been getting colder and colder, and now there is an inch of snow and a hard frost as well. My word it *is* cold, and for the poor devils in the trenches it must be terrible. When we went to see them this morning they were all terribly stiff, and some were so numbed and rheumaticky that they could only just hobble, and some actually had to be lifted out of the trenches and carried back."

"*November 28th*. The great difficulty . . . is the mud and water. Some of the trenches are always flooded, and the ground is so spongy that drainage is nearly impossible. We are trying all sorts of dodges to get rid of the wet—brushwood, planks, sacks filled with straw, pumps and lastly barrels. The latter are really the best—beer barrels sawn in half with seats nailed across the top, and each man has one to stand on or sit in! It's a miserable type of existence, though, bad for morale and bad for health. . . ."

"*December 19th* . . . The Company was going up to do a relief, at

---

* *R.B.C. 1914*, 188.

† "The General lets me now do much as I like, . . . and I have a grip upon everything . . . I think a great maxim for Staff Officers is 'Help everybody whenever you can' . . . and that means one must always be doing something." *The Congreves*, 318.

night, of course, and on completing the relief the Company Commander found a man was missing. A short search was made without result, and it was concluded he had stopped one of the many stray bullets going about . . . Two days later this same Company was relieved, and, while moving back again in the dark, groans were heard and eventually traced to a disused water-logged communication trench where the missing man was found, up to his shoulders in mud and quite incapable of movement. He had got into the trench in the dark by mistake, went in up to his knees, floundered along a few yards when he went to his waist, and there he stuck and gradually sank. It took them four and a half hours to get him out, and then he died about ten hours later from exhaustion and exposure . . ."*

An officer of the 4th Battalion, Captain—later Lt.-Colonel—R. L. H. Collins, drew a picture in his reminiscences of what life was like in the trenches that winter.

"There was no respite from service in the line or digging in the rear and from the soul-destroying weather conditions. War with the enemy continued in some form or other day and night. The Bavarian Corps opposite the 27th Division was particularly active, especially in sapping and mining . . . During these early months the activity at night was a great contrast to the latter part of the war . . . Then the silence was broken by an occasional shot which would roar up for a moment into a veritable roar of musketry; now rifle fire was continuous and uninterrupted during the night, bombs exploded continually and the whole line was clearly defined by the light of flares . . . On frosty nights the rifle fire could be heard incessantly for many miles behind the line; away to the north from the Ypres salient came the rattle of the 75's."†

Yet the spirit of the Rifles remained unimpaired. "By day," Captain Collins recalled, "the snipers under R. C. Hargreaves hid themselves in a wood about six hundred yards from the German lines and harassed the Hun. Their marksmanship was good, and they varied their game with an occasional partridge." And when the night bombing of the Germans opposite became intolerable, making sleep

---

* *The Congreves*, 256, 258, 260.

† *R.B.C. 1926*, 217-24. Capt. R. L. H. Collins, "Some Reminiscences of a Regimental Transport Officer in 1914-15".

impossible, "a certain officer, having run out of bombs and being much annoyed by the persistent German bombing, rushed across the ten yards which separated the trenches and emptied a bucket over the offenders, who were so taken aback that he managed to get off scot-free."

*   *   *

During the early months of 1915 drafts of New Army troops from the training battalions in England began to reinforce the depleted ranks of the Regular Battalions. By the spring, with the arrival of the first Canadian and Territorial contingents, the British in France and Flanders were no longer outnumbered by the Germans who, having failed to win a quick victory in the West, had been forced to transfer divisions to the Russian front to defend East Prussia and Galicia. Under strong pressure from Sir Douglas Haig, Commander of the British First Army, Sir John French therefore decided to take the offensive in Artois as soon as the ground dried. But the British were still desperately short of artillery and machine-guns and, worse still, of shells. When, on March 10th, they attacked at Neuve Chapelle they were forced to send in the infantry without adequate preliminary bombardment against positions bristling with automatic weapons and supported by massive artillery. And a fortnight before the offensive Sir Douglas Haig's Chief of Staff, Brigadier John Gough, V.C.,—probably, after his fellow Rifleman, Henry Wilson, the most original-minded as well as one of the ablest, officers in the Army—was mortally wounded while making a reconnaissance of the Aubers Ridge from the trenches of his former Battalion, the 2nd Rifle Brigade. In the prevailing lack, not of military competence, but of imagination in the British High Command, and the too often unnecessary sacrifice of life that was to follow in the next three years, Gough's death at 43 was something of a national tragedy. It certainly proved so for his old Battalion, to whose "A" Company Mess he was brought in to die; for the absence of the kind of control he would otherwise have exercised over the attack was a contributory factor in its failure. The Battalion under his old comrade-in-arms, Reginald Stephens—the "Stiff'un" of Lady-smith and Bergendal days—carried all its first objectives and inflicted heavy casualties on the enemy. But, through conflicting orders from above and an inability on the part of the Staff to seize the opportunities it had won, it was left unsupported and was later forced to withdraw under a murderous fire from an impossible situation. The three days' battle cost the Battalion 16 officers and 362 N.C.O.s and Riflemen. It also won it two V.C.s—awarded to Company Sergeant Major H. Daniels and Acting Corporal C. R. Noble for cutting wire under intensive fire, the latter at the expense of his life.

A further example of the folly of attacking strongly held positions without adequate preliminary bombardment occurred a few days later, on the night of March 14/15th. After the Germans had driven the British from some overlooked and indefensible trenches near St. Eloi, and from the village of St. Eloi itself, the 4th Battalion under Colonel Thesiger was sent in to recapture the ground lost, including the village in which every house was now defended by two or more machine-guns. "The engagement," wrote Captain Collins, "left a good deal to be desired from the regimental officer's point of view. The retaking of the Rifle Brigade trench was a feasible proposition and was completed with success and some loss. The attack on the Mound would be more reasonably placed under the heading of the impossible. No information, no artillery support, no facility for covering-fire, confusion and obstruction by other units—a night attack up a street swept by machine-gun fire—it is remarkable that the goal was within an ace of being achieved. It was a tough proposition for those who had not years of discipline behind them. During the whole time the Battalion was in action Colonel Thesiger stood in the middle of the road, scorning to take cover, . . issued his orders and encouraged his men. He must have stood there an hour while bullets rattled on the ground like hail: this is no exaggeration —the miracle was that he was not hit. He was a man who inspired implicit confidence. Stopford-Sackville* with one rifleman worked his way through the houses on the left of the street till he arrived at the last one and from here could see the German machine-gunners at the top of the Mound; he emptied his revolver at them and thought he must have scored a bull, for one gun stopped; he also thought that he was a fool and would never get back, for bullets came through the plaster wall of the outhouse as if it were made of

* Lt. (later Major) Lionel Charles Stopford-Sackville, son of a former C.O. of the 4th Battalion. He was 21.

paper. King led the reserve company with his electric torch; Second Lieutenant Ritchie was last seen to fall into a trench at the foot of the Mound; he was followed by a Sergeant and one Rifleman. A few Riflemen remained in the houses next day, amongst them a Corporal Felgate, who was wounded sniping at the Germans. As Colonel Thesiger led the Battalion out of action he said to me: 'I don't mind being done down in a good show, but I do object to being done down in a rotten show like this. If I had had the original Battalion I should have done it.'* He issued an instruction that no one was to go out looking for wounded on the next night; he had already lost too many good men. In spite of this order, four of Hargreave's snipers went to St. Eloi on the night of the 14th and found him and brought him back to hospital."† Among the fallen was Major A. M. King— "Kingki" to the Regiment—General Congreve's brother-in-law and a famous long-range rifle shot. Of him Billy Congreve wrote in his diary: "I have just heard that poor old Kingki was killed at St. Eloi this morning. He must have been leading the counter-attack, so what better fate could one ask?"

Colonel Thesiger, promoted to a brigade after the battle, survived another six months, being killed in action at the end of September while commanding a division at Loos. Had he lived he might well, like Gough, have risen to the highest rank of all. His friend and erstwhile fellow Company commander, Colonel Reginald Stephens, who before the end of the war was to become a Corps Commander, was called upon to lead his beloved 2nd Battalion in an equally ill-planned and disastrous attack on the Aubers Ridge, only a month after its losses at Neuve Chapelle—since made good by fresh drafts from England. The British gunners had only enough shells for forty minutes' bombardment of the German trenches at Fromelles, and at 5.40 a.m., when the barrage ceased, the Battalion went in leading the assault. "The first line of attackers went right through the German first and second lines and over the crossroad beyond, but, with the

* "The marvel was that without artillery support of any kind the Riflemen had achieved so much. The barricades had been carried. The village was cleared of the enemy. Only the Mound remained in his possession. Such results might have satisfied all but the most exacting, but Colonel Thesiger was far from satisfied." Berkeley, 68.

† R.B.C. 1926, 223-37. Of Lieutenant Hargreaves, then 23, Billy Congreve had written a few weeks earlier, "I have seen . . . Reggie Hargreaves who is very happy and I hear a splendid fellow in every way. I hope he is all right but I hear disgustingly brave, so I suppose is certain to get hit sooner or later, as it's always the best who seem to be hit." The Congreves, 262-3.

enemy's wire almost wholly uncut, the Riflemen found themselves in the air and subject to a heavy fire from both flanks. Their officers were shot down one by one by German snipers, and there was nothing to be done but retire. All four Company Commanders were killed."* "The Battalion," Colonel Stephens wrote after the action, "was the only one which got into the enemy's trenches, with very heavy losses, of course. We hung on there for twenty-four hours, no one being able to help us, and were subjected the whole time to heavy shell-fire, rifle, machine-gun and bombing fire. In the end I withdrew, as our losses and the enemy's increasing numbers made it impossible to stay on. I could only collect one unwounded officer and 140 other ranks. We lost 640 N.C.O.s and men and 20 officers."†

There was a postscript to this further martyrdom of the 2nd Battalion—a letter found later on the body of a German Roman Catholic priest who had been serving as a volunteer in the ranks. "If the British Army is going to fight like this Rifle Brigade," he wrote, "Germany can never win the war."

"How these Englishmen had in twelve hours dug themselves in! The hundred fellows who were in our trenches had brought with them an enormous quantity of ammunition, a machine-gun and one they had captured from us. With the aid of the material lying about they had got everything ready and ship-shape for defence. Almost every single man of them had to be put out of action with hand-grenades. They were heroes all, brave and true to the end until death . . . They were all men of the active (sic) English Rifle-Brigade . . . Men who were only mercenaries could not behave like this."‡

Between the 4th Battalion's counter-attack at St. Eloi on March 15th, 1915, and the 2nd Battalion's immolation on the Aubers ridge on May 9th, the British forces in the Ypres salient were called upon to withstand the most intensive artillery bombardment they had experienced, accompanied by a new and terrible weapon, poison-gas,

---

* *R.B.C. 1925*, 174-7. Major W. H. Davies, "The Rifle Brigade War Memorial".

† *The Congreves*, 282. "If our lack of bombardment was due to shortage of ammunition," Billy Congreve commented, "then these thousands of casualties in the 8th Division were absolutely murdered, for time after time has the lesson been learnt by us and sent back to St. Omer" (G.H.Q.) "that, unless you *absolutely* smash up the enemy's trenches, it is murder to send in Infantry to attack."

‡ *R.B.C. 1926*, 177; *1918*, 60-1.

Bergendal, August 1900—J. P. Beadle

Field Marshal Sir Henry Wilson—Oswald Birley

Brigadier-General Sir John E. Gough V.C.

as part of a renewed German attempt to capture Ypres and threaten the Channel ports. In the middle of April there were rumours, though discounted, of an impending attack on the Ypres salient; a prisoner taken on the 14th reported that, as soon as the wind was favourable, the Germans intended using tubes filled with asphyxiating gas. "This prisoner had in his possession a small sack filled with a kind of gauze," Billy Congreve at 6th Division Headquarters reported in his diary, "dipped in some solution to counteract the effects of gas. The German morale is said to have much improved lately."*

No immediate attack followed, but on the 18th, the Germans began to bombard Ypres with heavy shells. Till then, except for its cathedral and medieval Cloth Hall, Ypres had shown little sign of damage. "It was possible to get an excellent meal at a restaurant in the Rue de Lille," wrote an officer of the 4th Battalion, which early in April had moved into the Salient; "the old ladies in their white bonnets still set out their stalls on the Place in front of the Cloth Hall." But on the third morning of the bombardment "there was a curious rushing sound like the arrival of a tube train, then a tremendous concussion. The first 220 mm had fallen in one of the houses in the Place . . . A horse, with its leg broken and swinging, hobbled past;... then came a funeral, shells began to fall faster at the Menin Gate, the driver of the hearse hesitated, half turned his horses and then, thinking better of it, started again. The mourners were not of the same mind and the whole cortège turned about and went back into the town. The scene on the Place was beyond description, bricks, beams, and debris of every kind littered the pavé. In spite of the bombardment of the day before, the old ladies had with unfailing commercial enterprise and great courage started business. Their stalls were overturned and several of them killed."†

These big shells—"16-in crumps, super-super crumps", as Billy Congreve called them—continued to arrive at regular intervals every twenty minutes until Ypres, an almost unharmed and lovely old place, was "burnt and broken and hopeless."‡ And on the afternoon of April 22nd, an officer standing in the courtyard of the farm which served as the 4th Battalion's Headquarters, noticed a peculiar

* *The Congreves*, 274. "This gas business must be pretty good nonsense. I can't think they will be quite such devils as that."

† *R.B.C. 1926*, 228-9. Captain R. L. H. Collins, "Some Reminiscences of a Regimental Transport Officer in 1914-15".

‡ *The Congreves*, 274-5.

sweet sickly smell. Almost immediately retreating French troops began to appear, half blinded and gasping for breath with news of the enemy advancing behind a cloud of poisonous mist. Simultaneously shrapnel started bursting along the line of the Yser canal a thousand yards away. The situation looked grim in the extreme, for, with the Germans now in possession of the Pilckem Ridge, there was nothing but one scattered British division between them and Poperinghe and the road to Calais.

The Battalion at once stood to arms and, in the absence of orders, moved into reserve to support the broken line.* That evening, for the first time since it arrived in France, all its officers dined under the same roof off champagne and plovers' eggs provided by a friend of their French interpreter, the Vicomte de la Metrie. When, before moving off after dark into Potijze Wood by the bridge known as Hell Fire Corner, "they left their excellent meal, many of them wondered whether they would live to enjoy such another and were comforted by the thought that . . . it had at least been a good one."

During the next day, while the Battalion lay in Potijze Wood under continuous shell-fire, losing many men and half its transport,† and later when it moved into the line to support the hard-pressed Canadians, who, though only recently arrived in France, had been thrown into the battle, two French Colonial divisions counter-attacked from behind the tenuous British line, repeatedly attempting to regain their lost positions on the northern face of the Salient. But on the afternoon of the 24th, when supported by a heavy preliminary barrage, the Zouaves and Turcos had again advanced in extended order across the British trenches, the enemy, helped by a change in the wind, once more let off their gas, "which," the Battalion reported, "rolled down the hill towards us like smoke. The French took alarm and bolted, rushing madly back over our lines. The Battalion stood fast and not one man joined in the rush, while the gas rolled over the trenches."‡ As the Riflemen manned the parapet of their

---

* A German reconnaissance pilot, later brought down by rifle fire from the Battalion, said he had been astounded to see how quickly the British had brought up their reserves on the day of the first gas attack. *R.B.C. 1926*, 231.

† "Corporal Ritchie was killed standing to his horses' heads, and we found his team of four, three horses killed, one standing listless with its head hanging dejectedly." *R.B.C. 1926*, 232, "Some Reminiscences of a Regimental Transport Officer".

‡ "For some minutes it made breathing very difficult." *R.B.C. 1918*, 96; *1922*, 118.

trenches they opened rapid fire on the gas-cloud, now drifting diagonally across their front, and on the invisible enemies behind it.

*   *   *

While, amid burning farms and a countryside lit by night by continuous flares and shell-fire, the 4th Battalion clung grimly to its positions, the 1st Battalion was rushed to the Salient from the south. Among the volunteer replacements from England, which since the beginning of the year had been reaching the Battalion, was a young Rifleman named F. J. McCarthy, who had enlisted in the Regiment on September 1st, 1914, and, after four months' training in the 6th Reserve Battalion at Queenborough, had been drafted to the 1st Battalion in January. Though later given a commission in the Royal Irish Rifles, he always looked back with intense pride to the spring of 1915 when he served as a Private Rifleman in the second battle of Ypres. "It would require the pen of a Napier," he wrote in a letter which appeared in the Rifle Brigade Chronicle for 1938, "to do full justice to the epic of what the Battalion endured during those long drawn-out days opposite Graventafel, St. Julien and Pilckem. In my memory those eight days from the 26th April until the night of the 3rd-4th May, when we withdrew to the new G.H.Q. Line nearer Ypres, stand out above all others as an example of the amazing capacity of British infantry to stand punishment which would quickly destroy the morale of any other infantry in the world." As a result of his letter, McCarthy was persuaded to write an account of his experiences in the battle which, published in the 1939 Chronicle, deserves a place among the classics of Rifle Brigade history.

"On, or about, the 12th April, 1915, the 1st Battalion The Rifle Brigade, which formed part of the 11th Infantry Brigade, 4th Division, was relieved in the St. Yves-Ploegsteert area, where it had been holding trenches throughout the previous winter, and was sent back for rest and to re-equip in the Steenwerck area. The Battalion was billeted in farms and cottages about two kilometres from the last-named village, and, the weather being glorious at the time, plunged into a round of field-training, games and sports, with enthusiasm. The previous six months had been spent in a dreary round of trench duty and billets, the latter being invariably in close proximity to the former, which were called trenches by courtesy only, and it was a tremendous relief to us all to be able to throw off the feeling of tension which always prevailed when men lived for long stretches at a time within range of rifle and machine-gun and never at any time out of the range of shell-fire.

"Drafts of reinforcements arrived, deficiencies in equipment were made good and inter-company rivalry at football and field sports was intense. Rumours as usual were rife. One, to which a certain amount of colour was lent by the type of training we were undergoing at the time, was to the effect that the Division was to form the spear-head of a big attack to be mounted in the Neuve Chapelle-Aubers area during the following month. This attack took place, but we had no part in it. Another, to which men clung with fervent hope, . . . had it that we were bound for Gallipoli. Visions of long sleepy days and nights on a ship bound through the Mediterranean coloured our talk a lot of the time.

"It was not to be, however, for on the 22nd or 23rd April . . . we heard whispers of a heavy German attack which had started up north, and Ypres was on everybody's tongue. On the evening of the 23rd rumours as to our move to 'Wipers' were confirmed as fact by the issue of an order to stand by in our billets, ready packed to move at an hour's notice . . . We stood by all that night. Men sat around conjecturing as to what the future had in store for us. A light-hearted gaiety and zest for life had changed all too suddenly into a feeling of tense expectancy . . .

"The Battalion marched out the following morning and swung along towards Steenwerck Station to the strains of an improvised band; a band of tin-whistles and tissue-papered combs, whose drums were the large tins in which the biscuit rations found their way up to us. How proud we were of our band that morning! How we had chaffed and gibed at them during the previous few days, when, full of enthusiasm, they hammered and blew on their 'instruments' at band-practice! It was due to them, however, that we were able to march into Steenwerck Station that morning to the strains of old 'Ninety-five', and the gaiety and pride with which our march was enlivened on that occasion was itself a fitting tribute to the enthusiasm of the worthy fellows who formed that band.

" . . . That evening, after a wearisome journey through Haze-brouck, where we changed trains, and Cassel, where the last of our Gallipoli wallahs woke up to realities, we detrained at Poperinghe, which, if I remember rightly, had at that time a gay little station with glass-roofed platforms and flower-beds. We were glad to stretch our legs and marched to a farm some distance out of the town, where we bivouacked for the night. It rained hard and I woke, or rather was violently awakened, by my mucking-in chum, Turner, to find myself in a cold wet pool . . . The following morning, the 25th April, we marched to the hutments outside Vlamert-inghe, where we rested all that afternoon, skylarking and gazing speculatively at the shell-bursts which cluttered up the sky over Ypres. Some ardent fellows joined the bombing squad and en-livened the waiting time by competitive feats with the long-handled Hales grenade . . .

" Ypres, or, to use the vernacular, 'Wipers', was catching it good and hard. The Boche artillery was playing a merry tune on the old city. None of their stuff came near us fortunately . . . Shortly after tea we got the order to dress in fighting order and fall in. Mr. K. S. Trotter, who commanded my platoon, No.3 of 'A' Company, then had a few words with us; . . . that we were going in at once, that things were serious and that he did not know whether we were going to take over trenches, dig new trenches, or just march on into the Boches. The line had broken and we were going up to give a hand in mending it. This news was . . . rather bewildering to most of us. We had been so used to lines that did not break . . . Personally, the only aspect of the matter which disturbed me, apart, of course, from the tension always felt when going into battle, was the thought of marching on until we bumped the Germans. It would be getting dark soon and I had, in the past, scoffed freely at bayonet fighting. I had regarded the sword as an un-Riflemanly weapon, and my heart began to jump about most disconcertingly in the neighbourhood of my solar plexus . . . After all, it had been impressed on me very thoroughly during training that the rifle was our true weapon, and now I was being told that I would probably have to use my sword in a . . . free-for-all in the dark some five or six kilometres beyond Ypres. To add to my misery I knew that the wretched sword did not fix at all securely on the boss and standard of my rifle . . . However, off we went down the road into Vlamertinghe to turn right-handed past the church, where we passed our new brigadier, General Hasler—who was soon to be killed—with the members of his brigade staff, in St. Jean . . . I consoled myself with the thought, 'Well, my lad, if the sun rises for you to-morrow and you know that you are alive, you will be alive.' . . .

"Darkness overtook us before reaching the outskirts of the city. We were halted short of the railway, and told to double when ordered forward, making as little noise as possible . . . So we doubled, rifles at the trail, spare hand on sword scabbard and entrenching-tool helve, over the railway into Ypres, making enough row with our equipment and paraphernalia—I remember, in particular, a white bag-full of rations tied to my water-bottle—to awaken all Boche guns for miles around . . .

"We passed through Ypres hurriedly and without mishap . . . The shelling was heavy at the time and when we were halted we were ordered into the ditch at the side of the road and told not to smoke or talk. But we talked, as the row was such, both from traffic passing along the road and from the shelling, as to effectively drown our voices. We were here for some time and some of us standing on the road were accosted by a Canadian driving a G.S. wagon who drawlingly and pungently told us that 'they sniped with whizz-bangs where we were going.' 'Them things,' pointing at our rifles, 'will be no good up there.' We told him who we were, but he did not seem in the least impressed, and he passed on into Ypres, rattling away behind his pair of horses . . .

"Our halt came to an end soon after and we pushed on in column of fours with intervals between platoons, 'I' Company being just ahead of us. We hurried through a village and were halted just beyond in order to receive whispered warnings to keep well closed up and in touch, to march on and keep ranks no matter what happened. We had been moving for a few minutes only when a shell smacked right into the middle of a platoon, marching just ahead of mine. It made a terrible mess, but did not throw the column into confusion at all. We hurried on past our unfortunate comrades with whispered enquiries as to who was hit and to the continued exhortation to 'close up', 'keep moving'. That shell was marked for us, we could tell that directly we heard it, and a shell bursting in the middle of a platoon of men marching on a hard pavé road has a devastating effect.

"Shortly after this incident we passed through another village and were halted for a very short time just beyond. It was at this halt that Turner and I were told to take charge of a box of Small Arms Ammunition—an awkward burden to carry when hurrying forward half-expecting to be blown up by a shell. The need must have been desperate and we fully realized this because we were hurried on even through patches of gas. Although we did not know it at the time, the Germans had used poison gas for the first time in warfare three days previously and patches of it hung about along our route. The first inkling we had of it was when passing through one of the villages. The peculiar smell, very like over-ripe fruit; our eyes began to water profusely. Then some Riflemen began to cough and choke. Two, or three, fell out and were violently sick. The rest of us, however, were exhorted not to stop, to keep moving, on and on, ever forward, keeping well closed up in fours. The agony suffered by our eyes . . . was intense; . . . nevertheless, on we went; we had to keep moving forward. We could hear heavy rifle fire ahead, and it seemed as if the very existence of everything depended on our being able to get to our destination as soon as possible. To add to my misery I was still helping to haul this heavy box of S.A.A., and, whenever we doubled, the infernal thing kept banging away at my legs. It was a nightmare of a march.*

" . . . At the time we were passing over a part of the road where an embankment was formed on the left-hand side. The fields came up unfenced to the road on the right. Soon after passing the commencement of the embankment we heard some shouting and were immediately subjected to terrific bursts of rifle fire which seemed to come from the top of the bank . . . There was a spontaneous dive for the cover of the embankment. At one second the road was full of quick-stepping Riflemen, the next it seemed to be empty except for figures flattening out on the pavé, seeking cover

---

* "25 April, 6 p.m. Marched just north of Ypres to St. Jean and halted while an attempt was made to discover where the 2nd Canadian Brigade was, from whom we had to take over. As no definite news was obtained, we marched on with 25 yards between platoons, 50 between Companies . . . along the Wieltje-Fortuin road, which was being fairly heavily shelled, lachrymatory shells being encountered for the first time. *R.B.C. 1918*, 18-19. "War Record of 1st Battalion."

behind its inequalities. I dived behind my box of S.A.A. which Turner shared with me. The situation was intolerable; we could do nothing, so we tried to pull the box, keeping it between our heads and the direction from which the bullets were coming, towards the open side of the road, where there was a ditch . . .

"This contretemps, though fierce, was short, and immediately the firing ceased orders came for us to move over into the fields on the right-hand side . . . Of course, Turner and I had left our precious box of S.A.A. behind in the confusion and were sent back to the road to retrieve the thing. In returning with it I fell into the ditch and got soused. As soon as we returned to the platoon we marched off in our original direction, that is towards what appeared to be, judging by the racket being made, the centre of trouble . . . We came finally to a hedge which cut across our route, were halted and ordered to extend to intervals and dig head cover for ourselves with our entrenching tools. It was from here that patrols were sent out. On their return we were ordered to cease digging and advance in extended order. This advance continued for some time until we finally halted at some old trenches which we were ordered to occupy, and get what rest we could.

"It was then that I slept. Slept on thoroughly exhausted until awakened for 'stand to' the following dawn . . . I did not know where we were; I did not care. All I knew was that we appeared to be in position, in trenches of some sort.* Thus ended the night of the 25th-26th April, 1915.

"The dawn of the 26th heralded another perfect day, in the weather sense . . . The early morning was quiet and we quickly set about the task of fitting into our position. The trenches in which we found ourselves were not so bad and could be easily defended. They were sited about three hundred yards from a road which ran parallel to our front, the intervening ground being fairly level and giving a good field of fire. On the further side of the road the ground was wooded in patches and sloped up to a ridge. A group of farm buildings stood immediately opposite our front, about half-way between the road and the crest of the ridge,

---

* "Eventually reached Hill 37, which had some large dug-outs constructed by the French on it. Sheltered in here just before daylight with two companies Somerset L.I. on our right and in touch with nothing on our left." *R.B.C. 1918*, 19. "War Record of 1st Bn."

with a lane running down from them to the road, which it joined at a small copse.

"The trench itself, though fairly deep and well traversed in the part known to me, was too wide and insufficiently provided with shelters to be of much protection from heavy shell-fire. Also it appeared to end a short distance to my right, so that No. 3 Platoon was separated from the rest of the Company. On our right front there appeared to be some breast-works or trenches occupied by British troops, but between them and our trenches was a huge gap in which German infantry were observed to be moving about; they did in fact come down to the road, but made no attempt to push forward against us. It seemed that the position we occupied was not in continuation of the line held by our troops, but that, to the right at any rate, our trench fell short of the line and over-lapped its break . . . We seemed to be 'en echelon' to the front line and overlapping a gap.

"We were not left long, however, in any doubt about our being in the centre of things, because the German artillery opened on us later in the morning. There had been a certain amount of move-ment in the open and Captain Railston, our company commander, had given emphatic orders for it to stop. It was at this time . . . that C.S.M. Kirwan was killed. He was hit by a shell shortly after passing the bay in which I was standing. For some time he had been moving over the open, warning men to get back into the trench and not to show themselves, when this happened. It seemed particularly unfortunate that one of our first casualties should have occurred in this fashion, but it was a salutary warn-ing to us all.

"The enemy very quickly got the range and it was not long before we were being treated to a rare dose of high explosive and shrapnel. One shell in particular did an enormous amount of damage to my platoon. It burst on the right-hand traverse of the bay in which I was on duty and killed, or wounded, everybody, with the exception of myself in the bay and one or two other Riflemen in the adjacent two bays. I was seated on the fire-step with my back to the parapet when suddenly someone shouted, 'Look out! Here's ours.' The scream of the shell and the crash of its bursting came to my ears almost simultaneously. The effect was disastrous; it was a very unlucky hit. Mr. Trotter and several

Riflemen were killed instantaneously, others received terrible wounds and died during the day. Two or three only were slightly wounded. A corporal sitting on my left was killed by concussion. He appeared to be forced rigidly upright, looking into the sky, and collapsed dead, without a mark on him. The Rifleman on my other side was gashed across the head. My nose bled fairly profusely, and although badly shaken I was not hurt at all. Turner, who was seated at the traverse, was very badly hurt, and, although I did what I could for him, died later in the day. Fortunately the shelling died down somewhat after this direct hit, and those of us who were unhurt were able to crawl to our unfortunate comrades and give them such help as we were able. We could do very little but apply the ordinary field-dressings, and they were not of much use. No one came near us, it appeared that no one could do so, and we spent the rest of that day crouching down near our wounded comrades, giving them such comfort as we were able until the long-drawn-out hours of daylight faded into darkness, when assistance came to us, and we were able to get them away and to bury our dead. We had been a very strong platoon that early morning, we went into action numbering over fifty; by the night of the 26th, shell-fire had reduced us to fourteen.

"We remained in this position, with slight variations in the Company fronts, throughout that night, and the following day 'A' Company did move. Late that night it was ordered to dig itself in on a line prolonging the Battalion's front obliquely to the road with a view, it seemed, to covering the flank of the gap. We were brought back the following night when the Battalion was assembled and moved forward to close the gap . . . Some Riflemen from other platoons had been transferred to No. 3, to make us respectably strong again. Among them I found a new 'mucking in' chum, a Rifleman named Canfor. After he and I had dug our bit of trench we scooped out a very small dugout for ourselves in the parapet at the level of the trench bottom. After breakfast, having nothing to do, we crept into this to sleep. We were awakened to find ourselves completely buried. Fortunately some of our comrades were aware of our predicament, for we heard them shouting for spades to dig us out. It was a hair-raising experience lying there flattened out, unable to breathe, with the earth, which had been blown in on top of us by the shell which did the damage, closing up our nostrils, eyes and mouths. We were unable to move hand or foot, asleep one second, awakened the next to find ourselves in a close-fitting tomb. We could hear our comrades outside clearing away the earth in order to pull us out. One of them gave me a fearful rap in the ribs with a spade whilst doing so, but I was in no position to protest. After that experience anything else that happened the rest of that day bore no significance for me. I was very glad that night to move away from that evil bit of trench.

"Sometime towards midnight on the night of the 27th-28th April, the Battalion was assembled and moved forward. We went in extended order, although my platoon actually went in fours, across the open to the road running across our front, and then advanced up the rising ground to the farm buildings mentioned in the earlier description of our position of the 26th April. We then wheeled left and dug ourselves in on a line roughly perpendicular to the one we had hitherto been holding. We did it with little or no opposition. It was a slow job, but the morning of the 28th found us under cover. 'A' Company was on the Battalion's right flank, then came 'B', 'C' and 'I', if I remember rightly, and in that order and in that position we stayed during the ensuing six days' fighting.

"Our position was weak. From a tactical point of view it was about as bad as it could be. 'A' Company's front was split by a stream. No. 3 Platoon was on the upper side, Company headquarters and the other platoons on the other side. To the right of our platoon's sector was a hedge bordering the grounds of a château, which, with the stream, gave the Boches two fine covered ways into our position. In the rear, some fifty yards, was the farm, and stretching away to a hedge about two hundred yards in our immediate front was a field of mustard crop standing about two feet high. Beyond the hedge, which ran parallel to our trench, was another ridge or hogsback, with a lot of dead ground intervening, which enabled them to mass in our front within assaulting range of our position . . . We had little or no artillery support, and their artillery did what it pleased with us. Our trenches very quickly became open ditches in which men stopped until they died. We were shelled continuously throughout the six days we held the position, from daybreak to nightfall, in front, enfilade and reverse. Of food and sleep we had very little. Rations did come up, when they could be brought up. The Boches did not permit us to get any rest by day, and the nights were spent in perpetual vigilance, expecting to be rushed by an enemy we knew to be in close proximity to our trenches, or in working hard to try to repair the havoc wrought by their guns during the hours of daylight. There was not even a wire entanglement to stop them; we had no wire. There was, it is true, a fence bordering the field of mustard crop, the usual type of three-strand wire fence used as a boundary to keep cattle from straying into crops.

"The general position at this, the top end of the Salient during this particular phase of the Second Ypres, known as the Battles of Gravenstafel and St. Julien, was very much like a hairpin in shape. The trenches held by the troops in our rear were not much more than four hundred yards away. The only line by which we could communicate with the outside was along a field track and the lane which led up to the farm in our rear. These ran parallel to our trenches some fifty-odd yards away.

"So there we stayed and fought it out. Fortunately we had a plentiful supply of S.A.A. Truly they did 'snipe us with whizz-bangs'. Their artillery tried literally to blast us out of our position. It would have been a great relief to have been able to have seen the hostile infantry more often; we did get our own back when their infantry did come forward, but they appeared to be very coy, or to be playing a secondary part to the artillery. The bulk of the time we simply had to stand and endure, to bow our heads to the storm and hold on. It seemed a miracle that we did hold on. We were beaten if ever troops were beaten, according to the rules of the game, but just did not know it, refused to recognize the fact . . .

"The dawn of the 28th broke fine, glorious sunshine, in fact so far as the weather conditions were concerned we had the best that were possible. It remained so throughout . . . The only other bit of luck we had was vouchsafed us by the Boches, whose sins of omission . . . enabled us to retrieve what was a very desperate situation.

"We soon got to work joining up the holes we had dug with those dug on our right and left. We were permitted to do this without molestation. All was quiet whilst this work was being carried out, so much so that Mr. Shaw-Stewart, one of our Com-

pany officers, passed over the open along the line exhorting us to
hurry up and get the job finished. On his return journey to Company headquarters he was wounded by a rifle bullet which, among
others, appeared to come from our rear! That seemed to put an end
to our peace, because, almost immediately after this incident, the
Boches opened fire, ranging shots at first, and then in earnest. At
first their gunnery was bad, or else they were concentrating on
the farm in our rear, which was soon in flames. A lot of S.A.A.
and trench material appears to have been stored in these buildings,
for we were treated to an interesting display of pyrotechnics as the
Verey flares and S.A.A. exploded. Our respite was of short duration,
however, for they soon began to bounce them down on us. Then
some batteries on our right flank chimed in with shrapnel which
burst in clusters of about thirty at a time up and down our
trenches. So it went on all that day . . . We could do little but keep
a sharp look out and crouch in the bottoms of our holes, which
we had not completed into a long continuous trench when this
business started, trying to get what shelter was available from
enemy shrapnel . . . They were able to 'crump' us at will, no retaliation of any sort was available to give us even some sort of
mental satisfaction . . .

"The next three days—the 29th-30th April and the 1st May—
were simply a repetition of the 28th. From dawn to dusk we just
had to endure everything in the way of shell-fire the Germans
were able to produce. Darkness brought us a considerable measure
of relief each day, though little rest, as, owing to our steadily
mounting casualty list, it was necessary for every man to be on
duty of some sort or other, generally on working parties making
good the damage done by the enemy artillery. We worked hurriedly, cleaning up the mess, strengthening our parapets, building
up traverses in order that we might get some cover from the en-
filading guns, and evacuating our wounded and dead. Our nights
were much more busy than our days, and it was with gratitude
that we welcomed the darkness, as, apart from the relief it brought
us from gun-fire we were able, under its friendly cloak, to make
things ship-shape and clear our trenches in readiness for the inevitable infantry attack which we knew was bound to come, and
to which many of us looked forward with a certain amount of
satisfaction.

"It would have been a bitter disappointment to most of us to have missed the opportunity of taking revenge out of the hides of their infantry. The idea of leaving the position, which by the night of the 1st-2nd May was almost untenable, never entered our heads. Their artillery was doing its best, or rather its worst, and we were feeling well able to stand up to anything they could inflict on us. It was the opposing infantry we wanted to see, and many of us prayed for their attack to start . . .

"Shortly after dawn broke on the 2nd May we were again crawling about and crouching on the bottom of our trench. The artillery fire, if anything, seemed fiercer and heavier than ever. So much so that Rifleman Byrne, a Section 'D' man in the platoon, was moved to assert that we were getting more shells in an hour than he saw throughout the Siege of Ladysmith. My pal Canfor was very quickly hit . . . After such breakfast as was available had been eaten, I suggested that we play a game of chess. He had a set of pocket chess-men and we had played some games during the past few days . . . On this occasion he refused; he did not feel up to chess so early in the morning, and stood up to take off his great-coat. At this instant a large shell burst some yards behind our parados without doing any damage. The nose-cap, however, came straight for us and I ducked down just before the thing hit with a loud 'phut' into the parapet just above my head. Canfor, who was standing up holding the coat stretched ready to slip off his shoulders, had the thing whizz through the right-hand pocket, missing his thigh by a matter of an inch or so. His look of amazement as he turned to me holding the pocket, or rather the place where the pocket had been, for inspection was comic. After some chaffing about the luck of those born to be hanged, he took off his great-coat and promptly started to scratch about in the parapet for the nose-cap. I protested and begged him to leave the thing alone. I thought such a souvenir would be unlucky. He thought otherwise and, having found the thing, put it in the other pocket of the great-coat and proceeded to bestow coat and souvenir where he could keep an eye on them. Hardly had he done so, however, when I heard 'ours' coming and yelled to him to get down. He hadn't time. I heard and felt the burst, was in fact temporarily blinded by it, and after it heard the groanings of poor Canfor, who had been badly hit in the groin and stomach. I gathered my wits together and, with the help of the two men holding the next bay, was able to get him to the sheltered side of a traverse where we made some sort of a job of dressing his wounds. Fortunately, the shell was a light one—'whizz-bang' variety—and the pieces which hit him were quite small. He stayed with me all that day, and being unable to get him away that night, he had to stay until nightfall the next.

"Soon after the above incident the German artillery fire became very heavy, and orders were passed along to man our parapets as it was thought that his infantry would be coming over. By this time we were so badly reduced in effectives that it was exceptional to see two Riflemen manning one bay. We spread out as best we could in order to give the impression of strength and got such lightly wounded men as were available to sit down with all the S.A.A. we could gather in clips around so that we could hand to them our rifles to reload. Every rifle was garnered, its magazine fully charged, and, with sword fixed, placed handy against the parapet. All spare equipment, and other impedimenta, was placed in the corners of the traverses out of the way, and the badly wounded men placed i n such shelter as was available, usually up against the reverse sides of the traverses to those which faced the direction from which we were being enfiladed. An elder Rifleman passing me very busy in my bay about this time remarked, 'Well, Sonny, won't you have a tale to tell if ever you get out of this pickle!' . . .

"That evening they started to come—the people we had been waiting for—over the ridge to our front. This ridge or hogsback ran roughly parallel to our trenches at a range it was impossible to ascertain owing to the amount of dead ground which lay between its lower slopes and the hedge, which was our nearest target on the far side of the mustard crop. The range to the hedge was about two hundred yards, but, as we had no range-finding instruments, we could not tell the range to the top of the ridge. The Boches came over the crest at the double in a continuous single line, and ran obliquely across our front to disappear into the aforementioned dead ground. Some of us opened on them, but with little or no result . . . as very few of them appeared to be hit. The firing, such as there was, was independent and by guesswork at this stage. I did not open fire; to do so seemed to me a waste of ammunition. We had absolutely no fire-control either on this day or the next. We had no officers or N.C.O.s. It appeared to be each man for himself, and, although we worked in pairs; generally speaking there was little or no concerted effort. It is amazing that we did keep them at bay. They came so very quickly that only a very heavy and sustained rapid fire could have had any appreciable effect. We were not able to produce such an amount of rapid fire at this or any other stage of this phase of the battle, so we had to content ourselves with such independent shooting as we could do and send out warnings to our right and left. It was the hedge in front which received our main attention, and we peered very long and very earnestly at this strip of, what appeared to be an ordinary quickset hedge for the first signs that the Boches had reached thus far. The German artillery continued to bestow their favours.

"It was during this part of the proceedings that something akin to a miracle happened. Suddenly a lonely 'bark', easily distinguishable from the rest of the racket, came from behind us, and we listened thunderstruck to a shell whining over our heads. It burst with a tiny puff of smoke over the continuous line of German infantry. High up in the air it cracked and, as the smoke lazily dispersed, bang again went the lonesome piece. The Riflemen in the bays nearest to me gaped in bewilderment at this phenomenon until one more quick in the uptake shouted at the top of his lungs, 'Gawd! We've got a —— gun!'

". . . Soon the people over the way began to appear at the hedge in front, some also at a few cottages about half left from our position. We opened on the hedge: just short bursts of rapid. We could see nothing tangible even at the hedge, just faint shadows flitting about at which we banged away heartily. Darkness, however, soon came and put a stop to the meagre efforts we were making to prevent the Boches getting into position for the morrow . . . They were still coming over the ridge when darkness fell. How many had arrived up to that time we did not know; there seemed to be an awful lot of them. We had our tails well up by this time. Our solitary gun and the fact that we were becoming active had worked wonders, and the situation was becoming familiar to us, was becoming one with which we felt fully able to cope

Sergeant Edwards of 3rd Battalion, 1915—Eric H. Kennington

Sgt. W. Gregg V.C. and Rfn. W. Beesley V.C. after being decorated
by King George V, 1918

"We received orders to 'stand to' all night. We were not to move from the trench under any circumstances, but were to maintain a constant 'look out'. That night was a terrible affair. The strain imposed on everybody was terrific. It seemed as if we had reached the limit of human endurance, and the drain on our resources, both individual and as a unit, had been enormous. The possibility of our holding our position if and when the Boches did advance to the attack appeared in the hours of darkness to be very dubious to most of us . . . It must have seemed, as it did to me, that the only thing left for us to do on the morrow, if they did not rush us that night, would be to hold them up to the very last and then to go for them and have it out with the sword. The thought of leaving never entered my head, at least, no one else mentioned the idea to me. However, I did wish that I could get Canfor away. He realized the hopelessness of our position as much as anybody, and although we gave him and the other badly wounded men to understand that the position was quite normal, he did ask me to promise not to leave him alone if the Boches got into our trench . . . However, we were each and all of us much too busy and occupied in one way or another to spend any time futilely dreaming as to what the morrow would bring forth. The platoons on the other side of the stream cutting into the Company front had suffered more heavily than we had. We had received some sort of reinforcements on the night of, I think, the 1st May, but they had done little more than slightly increase our strength of that morning. By this time most of them had become casualties.

"The dawn of the 3rd May arrived like the other dawns. First the sun, then the German artillery. Their fire was very accurate and simply drenched our line in a storm of high explosive and shrapnel.* A few walking wounded trickled past, the last until the end. We had the consolation at any rate of knowing that we would not suffer heavily in casualties from this outburst; we were too weak to incur many. They could not kill or maim all of us, though they did their level best to ensure a walk-over for their infantry. It takes an awful lot to knock out a Rifleman.

* "3 May, 4.30 a.m. A German field battery opened fire from the Gravenstafel ridge at a range of under 1000 yards from our right . . ." "By 8.30 a.m. 'A' Company which was on the right had been badly knocked about and most of their trenches were demolished . . . It was decided not to reinforce 'A' Company . . . as any men put into the trench would certainly be knocked out by shellfire." *R.B.C. 1918*, 20-1. "War Record of 1st Bn."

J.G.   R

"The German infantry attack when it started found us reduced to such a strength as made it impossible to man our bays in
pairs, and, bad as was our situation, that of the remainder of the
Company was even worse, for those platoons had been reduced to
an effective strength of four—Captain H. G. M. Railston, and
three Riflemen—and they were forced to adopt the expedient of
doubling up and down their trench from bay to bay, firing a
magazine or two of rapid from each, in order to create the illusion
of some strength. Fortunately, as was the case with us, a few
wounded Riflemen were available to assist in the good work by
keeping the magazines of as many rifles as were in use fully
charged. I think they were attacked by infantry earlier in the
morning than we. The people opposite our handful seemed to be
very coy, and it was not until we realized, by noting their continuous movement to our right flank, that they were going to use
the hedge, running from within a few yards of our trench to the
hedge behind which they were gathering, as a covered way for a
flank attack, that we fully understood the reason for their bash-
fulness. Fortunately they absolutely neglected the stream, use of
the bed of which would have provided them with an excellent
covered way into the heart of our position.

"Very early we received demands from the three or four Riflemen whose duty it was to cover the end of the hedge, and we
passed the word down for Mr. Gibbs and his bombers, who soon
passed through on their way to the seat of the trouble and quickly
restored the *status quo ante* by driving the Boches back. Mr. Gibbs
and his very small party constituted a sort of flying column
throughout the day, and proved an effective mobile support by
hurrying to acutely threatened spots to restore the situation.
They responded nobly to the call, spent an agonizing time crouching under cover, every now and then bobbing up for a quick earnest scanning of our front. The German infantry were quiet, or
appeared so. Our wounded suffered badly during this 'strafing'
and poor Canfor from behind his traverse appealed to me very
earnestly not to leave him behind if we had to go. I promised not
to do so, but . . . at the time I had no idea how to implement the
promise had it been necessary to start a withdrawal from our
position. Our walking wounded had in most cases got away, and
those remaining with us were mostly serious cases requiring

stretchers. Many of them were of material and willing assistance in aiding the defence, and contributed in no small measure to its success by their ability in keeping those of us who were on our feet well supplied with loaded rifles . . .

"When their artillery fire lifted, trouble soon broke out again at the hedge. Our post there had by now been reduced to two, and Mr. Gibbs, with his stout fellows, soon passed us on their way to put things right. The Boches proved a bit more obstinate this time, however, and it required the services of another Rifleman and myself to help in ejecting them. This we soon did, Mr. Gibbs leading the way with the greatest dash, and, if I remember rightly, getting a slight wound in doing so. Again I had a tremendous stroke of good fortune. One fellow turned back and took a standing shot at me at the distance of a few paces, so close in fact that I tasted the tang of his bullet in my mouth for some time afterwards. He missed, and I got him full in the chest.

"Having cleared them back, we returned to our original position, taking with us the two Riflemen and leaving Mr. Gibbs with his bombers to hold the post. We arrived back in time to be greeted by a furious fusillade from the mustard crop, several Germans having crept close up to our parapet. Bullets smacked round our heads at a great rate, but our opponents, apart from the fact that their shooting was very poor, appeared to have no heart in them for a 'mad minute' soon turned them and sent some of them scuttling back to the cover of the hedge. The people at the hedge made no attempt to support their friends in the mustard crop and the attack was not pushed home. The whole affair seemed to be very disjointed and of a half-hearted nature; their infantry did not appear to have the 'guts'; otherwise a well-driven-home attack would have been the end of us. Fortunately none of us was hurt during this affray; if three or four of us had been hit at this juncture the defence would have collapsed . . . We fully realized by this time that, in addition to keeping them out, it was of the utmost importance not to get hit ourselves . . . By this time it was sheer bluffing, just one gigantic piece of make-believe supported by our array of sword tips showing over the parapet and our rushing about firing 'rapid'. It was a bluff that was succeeding; nevertheless, because the afternoon was drawing to a close and, as we knew that we were going to evacuate the position that night, we bluffed with all our might in the hope that we could get clear away. We imposed on them very successfully. Curiously enough, though we fully realized the amazing game we were playing, I don't think any of us thought for an instant that the Germans would turn us out against our will. We had more than held our own and were very confident that we could hold them off to the bitter end. Our tails were well up, and, as time went on towards nightfall, we came to regard the Boches with contempt . . . The situation was, no doubt, one of tense drama, but to us who were playing the parts, the dramatic aspect was not obvious. I think that the knowledge that we were going after all may have contributed largely to our mood of exaltation, but I do know that, as that trying day drew to its close, we had quite made up our minds that the order of our going would be decided by ourselves and not by the Boches, whom we regarded as a very poor lot. . .

"Towards dusk we were left alone. Their artillery seemed to have given us up as hopeless . . . Their infantry were content to stay put; they had had all they wanted . . . We, of course, understanding to the full our precarious position, were not sorry to see the arrival of night. We remained, however, strictly on the alert, and kept scanning our front as long as we were able. We did, however, get a smoke. We had had no time for smoking before.

"As dusk fell a few Riflemen from one of the other Companies were doubled up to help us. We received orders that we were to stay in position until such time as another Battalion was moved up to support us in our retirement. We were obviously too weak to retire without support; besides, the Germans were very close to us in many places, and an unsupported withdrawal might have led to trouble. Arrangements were made to get our wounded away and we were put on to fatigue, those of us not helping with the wounded or on sentry, cleaning up the mess. We had, whilst maintaining strict vigilance, to tidy up our trenches, collect up all rifles and equipment for removal, and bury such stuff as we could not carry. The job of getting our wounded away was a pitiful business. It was really heart-rending. The poor fellows, some with terrible wounds, had uncomplainingly stuck it out under the more than trying conditions of the past forty-eight hours, but when we came to move them down to where the stretchers, etc., would be awaiting them, I am afraid that their pains and troubles

must have been intense. All the care and tenderness going—and a
very great deal of affectionate attention and care was expended
on these our unfortunate mates by our Riflemen that night—
did not prevent that journey from being a most painful affair for
them. I was returning from helping a Rifleman who had been
shot in the groin when I came across two lads carrying poor little
Foster, who had lost his legs, bandy-chair fashion. He must have
been in great pain, but, when I spoke to him, seemed quite bucked
at being got away. I kept Canfor in the trench, and kept near him
most of the time until our supports came up, when I was fortunate
enough to borrow a stretcher for him.

"The night was a very clear one, quite bright and light, so that
we were able to keep a good look-out. Patrols were not necessary
except that an occasional visit or rather passage of our front was
made by pairs of Riflemen. The Germans did not interfere, despite
their close proximity to us. Probably they were cowering down in
their cover, wondering what on earth we were up to. I am positive
that they did not know we were withdrawing. Not a shot was fired,
and we went calmly and collectedly about our jobs, making everything nice and tidy for them to take over whenever they cared to
do so.

"Supplies of the old cotton gauze type of gas respirator had been
rushed up to us on, I think, the previous day, and we wore them,
for some reason or other, that night. They made our people look
like a lot of muzzled wraiths and caused considerable amusement.
Our supports marched up behind our trenches, and, after I had
begged from them a stretcher for Canfor, preparations were made
for moving off. Five of us took care of Canfor and assured him that
all would be well. We carried him down to the road, the Battalion
headquarters, but found on arrival that everybody, with the
exception of the rear party, had moved off. So off we went, across
the road, in what we knew to be the general direction of Ypres,
near the ruins of which we hoped to get news of the Battalion, as
we had no very clear orders as to our destination.

"We marched with our burden across the fields towards the
great conflagration which was the city of Ypres. At that distance
it seemed as if the whole place were one great fire and stood like
some huge beacon glowing in the distance to guide us to safety and
rest. We could hear a great racket going on over to the north-west

Apparently some demonstration was being made with a view to assisting the withdrawal of the troops from the part of the Salient which was being abandoned. We had no intention of getting mixed up in that business, so on we trudged with our friend on our shoulders, using the burning city as a guide. We halted every now and then to rest, also to silence the continued apologies of Canfor, who appeared to be very concerned over the trouble which he thought he was giving us. We were fortunate enough to find our way on to a road which led in the general direction we were going, and, after trudging down it for some time, to meet a motor ambulance. We halted this vehicle by the simple expedient of lining across the road and bawling at the driver to stop. He told us that his orders were to get to St. Julien. We politely informed him that he was wasting time as St. Julien had been in German hands for over ten days, and that if he went much further along that road he would run into the arms of the Germans. Thus we persuaded him to about turn and take Canfor with him. We quickly pushed our brother Rifleman into the vehicle and, wishing him a happy time, sped him off on his way towards safety and hospital.

"Shortly afterwards we got lost. The Germans commenced to drop their heavy stuff on the road and we promptly shied off it into the fields. This annoyed us very much, but, as we had been for long enough the objects of this sort of random shooting at night, we preferred the uncertainty of finding our way across the field, to the certainty, mixed with these annoyances, of the road. By this time the reaction to the excitement of the past week was beginning to set in; not only that, but we were very tired and began to concentrate on the effort required to walk. Added to this, the general flare which we had seen earlier on became several flares as we approached Ypres, so that we soon became uncertain as to our correct direction. So down we sat to debate our situation. We were certain that we were not clear of potential trouble from the Boches, who we thought to be advancing behind us, but we were desperately uncertain as to our actual whereabouts. We had not been debating long, however, when we heard the tramp of marching feet to our left, and we promptly flattened out, peering in the direction of this rather disturbing sound. The column loomed up through the dark, and, after telling the others to get ready to bolt if these people turned out to be Germans, I jumped up and walked over to the road to meet them. Much to my relief, they turned out to be a Battalion of the Northumberland Fusiliers, and, after asking to be directed to Ypres, I rejoined my comrades considerably more at home with the lay of the land.

"Everything was plain sailing now and we soon came to a village in front of which men were working like beavers putting the finishing touches to trenches which we were given to understand were the new 'G.H.Q. Line'. We rejoined the main road to Ypres here and, on passing through the village, were stopped by an officer who demanded particulars as to our identity and our destination in a very commanding manner. I informed him in as loud a voice as his own that we were Riflemen of the 1st Battalion The Rifle Brigade, and that we were trying to find our Battalion, of whose whereabouts we were very uncertain. After receiving some advice and guidance, we turned to move off when a voice shouted out, 'Hi! 1st R.B., 1st R.B., who are you?' We approached a group of stretchers at the side of the road and found Beckett, also of 'A' Company, who was very concerned regarding the whereabouts and fate of young Peter Bennett. We were able to assure him that Peter was all right so far as we knew; I had seen him earlier that day, and up to then he had not been hit. I learned later, however, that Peter had been hit that evening . . .

"We left Beckett after wishing him the best of luck, and, pushing on, ascertained that the Battalion would probably be found in the vicinity of Elverdinghe. We crossed the Canal over the bridge on barges to the north of Ypres and walked, or rather crept, completely done up, into Boesinghe, where, somehow or other, I don't quite know why, we made up our minds to stop until daylight. So we flopped down where we stopped and fell fast asleep. The strain had lifted and we just caved in, too far gone to move another step. We made no attempt to get into shelter, because I was roughly shaken into wakefulness next day to find two officers, one of whom was Colonel Prowse, who had taken over the Brigade after the death of General Hasler, bending over me. I was lying in the roadway, the rain steadily coming down, and was for some time completely bemused. Colonel Prowse assured us that everything was all right; he thought that we had chosen an extraordinary place in which to sleep, but that we should now hurry on to find our Battalion, who were only a short distance away, bivouacked in a field on the left-hand side of the road. I apologized, and, after he had gone, on we pushed off as fast as we could to find the Battalion.

"Never were men more glad to get home than we that morning. We found the Battalion and were soon being helped by our comrades to as much stew as we could gorge. The Quartermaster and the cooks had produced this feed, great dishes of it, thick with vegetables and meat, piping hot, and I have never before or since enjoyed a meal so much. I ate and ate, simply wolfed it out of a dixie lid and washed it down with mugs full of scalding tea. We lived on the fat of the land that day.

"Some hours later we moved into some woods near a stream. Here we slept and rested all the afternoon; many of us busied ourselves with the task of getting clean. We cleaned our rifles, oiled the rounds of our ammunition, made up deficiencies in equipment, and made some attempt to rid ourselves of our 'next of skin'. We were most of us, of course, dreadfully lousy, and there was a great activity on the seams of shirts, vests, trousers, and underpants. Riflemen were to be seen, dotted about on the banks of the stream, solemnly engaged in hunting down and slaying these pests, bathing, shaving, washing and busily getting cleaned. A draft of reinforcements, a large one, marched in to join us whilst this was going on. They were soon told off to Companies and I picked up a new friend, a young lad named Gibbons, who was eager to learn all I had to tell of the doings of the Battalion, how things were done, and to pick up all of the many little tricks by which we made life comfortable. The survivors of the old Battalion paired off with these Riflemen who were to re-new the Battalion, and soon set to work showing them the ropes and the tricks of our trade. Thus ended the first phase of the Second Ypres.

*   *   *

"The second phase opened, for us, on the evening of the 8th May. In the interim we had enjoyed four days of perfect peace and rest. We had moved on the evening of the 4th from the vicinity of Elverdinghe to nearer Vlamertinghe, and had settled down in another wood. Our time was spent largely in writing letters and in laying about, just recuperating in mind and body. The Battalion shook down into its normal self very quickly, and very soon it was difficult, apart from certain small signs, to tell the veterans from the reinforcements.

"One incident, of an amusing nature, occurred to remind us that despite the peaceful aspect of our sylvan retreat, the War was ever present, and proved that our awareness of the fact impinged continually on our subconscious minds, try as hard as we may to forget. On the second day of our stay 'Granny' gave tongue, or rather bellowed, and sent the veterans scuttling for cover with an alacrity which amazed our new draft men. 'Granny' was a large gun. The largest, I think, on our side in the Ypres area at that time, and her emplacement, so expertly concealed that none of us was aware of her proximity, was situated at the edge of the wood close to where 'A' Company had taken up their abode. No warning, just a loud roar which rudely shattered our peace. Ever after, when she fired during our stay, our Riflemen took a deep interest in the proceedings, some standing close behind the gun to watch the large shell fly away on its mission of castigation. Others staying at home, wondering when the Boches would start searching for 'Granny'. Fortunately no retaliation took place, at any rate not during our stay, so though most of us hated to hear 'Granny's' hoarse bellow, we felt some small satisfaction from the fact that when she spoke her utterances probably meant trouble for some of our tormentors of the last few days.

"The evening of the 8th May saw us pack and move. Late that night we marched back to the Canal in front of Boesinghe, where we went to earth on the Canal bank near the bridge on the barges in the early morning of the 9th. We stayed in this position all that day, not troubled at all except by occasional shrapnel, until that evening, when we moved up through La Brique or Brijke, and took over some trenches covering the right front of the village and facing towards Pilckem.

"The 10th May was a fairly peaceful day, that is by comparison with those spent near St. Julien. We suffered a few casualties from shelling, but it was here that we made the acquaintance of a weapon—the trench mortar—which up to that date was unknown to us. One was in position on 'A' Company's front and gave us a very worrying time until we became used to its vagaries. The first bomb burst near our parapet absolutely unheralded and set us all to wondering what new mischief had come to plague our existence. We had heard no guns fired, all we had heard was a sudden fluttering sort of whirr, a loud plop and then a shattering roar. Fortunately one of the sentries in the trench saw the next one and was able to give us some idea of its performance. He, poor man, was new to the game and rather awestruck by what he had seen. His description, however, was accurate enough and sufficiently lurid to make us all put aside such mundane tasks as letter writing, or oiling ammunition, to devote our energies to watching for this new phenomenon. Everybody took to peering intently into the air and very soon our vigilance was rewarded by the appearance of a curious-looking missile, afterwards named a flying pig, which lazily climbed up into the sky from the Boche trench opposite, and, having reached the top of its trajectory, shot down in a completely unadvertised direction and most disconcerting manner, to burst with an awe-inspiring row. Most of us were soon able to locate the position from which this thing was being fired and also became aware of a warning sound, as we soon connected a loud click, which we kept hearing just before the arrival of the missile over the Boche parapet, with the engine that was firing the beastly things.

"When the novelty had worn off we resumed our various tasks, not with our previous sang-froid, however, because it was easy to see from the strained expression worn by all, and from the fact that our talk dropped down in tone to monosyllabic whispers, that everybody had their ears attuned listening for the 'click'. When the 'click' was heard, up we would jump, stare expectantly at the beastly thing until it turned, and then run like blazes in the opposite direction to that in which it was descending. Dodging these foul contrivances was not as easy as it looks on paper. It was absolutely necessary to stand closely watching the thing until it reached the top of its trajectory because the direction of its upward flight was no indication of the direction it would take when coming down. The pig had a most disconcerting habit of leaving the Boche trench opposite, shall we say, 'A', and heading in the direction of 'B' until reaching the turn, when it might double back and come down 'plop!' —'crash!'—at 'A', or even go on to 'C', some yards on the other side of 'B'. Added to this, the noise and the destruction wrought on bursting were terrific, and any fellow who was unfortunate enough, through not sticking very closely to the rules of the game, to run in the wrong direction, met a decidedly messy end . . .

"The trench taken over by No. 3 Platoon was a very poor affair. It was an isolated trench or, rather, open ditch, which later became an open grave for nearly every one of its defenders. As at Gravenstafel, a farmhouse was at our backs, the trench ran between this place and its attendant moat, . . . and had no shelter or traverse throughout its length, which was some twenty-five to thirty yards. Its depth was about waist high at the deepest point and it sloped upwards to ground level at either end. Its previous occupants belonged to the East Lancashire Regiment, who had either evacuated it or been driven from the trench, because a lot of their equipment and some of their dead were in it when we took over. I believe the Boches held the farmhouse, and their trench in front was only some one hundred yards away.

"Dawn of the 12th May found us in this miserable place and the reception accorded us at 'stand to' quickly convinced us that to 'stand' was the height of folly. We dared not, in fact could not, stand. To kneel even in most parts of our trench meant a bullet through the head instantly. However, we made the best of a very bad business, and despite our crowded and highly dangerous situation, kept such observation as we were able. We placed 'look-outs' at either end, and one hour on this job was a very long and very precarious time. Our trench periscope had been shattered immediately it was put up. So there was no alternative, the unfortunate Riflemen on 'look-out' duty had to keep putting their heads up. It was a horrible predicament; our people were being killed and wounded, mostly the former, with frightening regularity. To go on 'look-out' meant either certain death or a terrible wound, yet I never saw any hesitancy on the part of any Rifleman when detailed for the job. Our Riflemen were, with one or two exceptions, all new draft men and entirely fresh to such a business, and it speaks volumes for their courage and endurance that throughout the whole of that long, weary and exceptionally trying day, not one of them made the least attempt to shirk or broke down.

"We would do nothing in retaliation; the position came as a

complete surprise to us at dawn. I got hit early in the morning. I was asleep, in fact, when it happened. A shell, I think, burst on the parados and I was hit by two pieces, the smaller went through the right foot and the larger just below the right knee. Rifleman Gibbons, my new partner, was killed instantaneously, a piece going through his head. I tried to awaken him when I realized that I was hit, and, on turning him over, saw that he was dead. My first feeling on finding that I was hit was one of elation. I quickly ripped off my boot and ripped up my trousers-leg to dress the wounds, and whilst doing so came to the conclusion that my two 'Blighties' were not much use to me, as the possibility of ever getting out of that place alive was very remote. This conclusion was reinforced, for no sooner had my knee been dressed than I heard the sickening noise made by a bullet fired at very close range when hitting a man through the head. The 'look-out' down the trench had been killed.

"By this time I was the 'oldest soldier', and so the duties of taking charge devolved on me, and I decided to abandon the 'look-out' posts. By crawling down the trench to the moat I was able to get in touch with the platoon on our left. Their trench ended in a 'block' some thirty yards from the end of ours, but on higher ground, and it was possible to shout out messages to them through the racket. After explaining our position and situation I arranged that they should post a man at the 'block' to overlook our front, and in order to keep in touch with him I placed a man, under cover, with instructions to keep his eyes on their sentry. By this means we could dispense with our 'look-outs' and the arrangement was quite successful Then I had every rifle fully loaded and placed, with sword fixed, against the parapet, the sword-tips showing over the top. Having done this and got all the defenders to the trench, with the exception of the aforementioned man on duty at the lower end and one man I had placed at the upper end for emergencies, into the deepest part, we set about the task of clearing up the mess and moving our dead and wounded to the upper and lower ends of the trench. We settled down to await either the Boches or darkness, hoping that the latter would arrive first, as I had already been given orders that we were to evacuate the place that evening.

"About mid-afternoon, whilst sitting with my back to the

parapet gazing fixedly at the rear wall of the trench pondering our situation, my vision was disturbed by little 'falls' in the wall of earth which seemed vaguely familiar to me. For some time my mind failed to grasp the significance of these small disturbances. Bullets were smacking about with great frequency, and it was some time before I connected these phenomena with bullets. I could hear the continuous 'bump' of rounds into our parapet, and whenever one hit very close to where I was sitting the 'thump' of the bullet was followed by one of these little 'falls'. I then realised that the parapet was not bullet proof and that the 'falls' I saw were similar to those seen on the range when a bullet strikes the 'stop-butt'. I shouted at once for everyone to lie down immediately, and then crawled along to tell the few Riflemen what I had noticed. The rest of that day we spent on our stomachs or backs, flat on the floor of that wretched ditch. We were extremely fortunate that nobody was hit in this fashion. The Boches must have been shooting at the parapet, using the sword-tips as a guide, at least that is the conclusion I came to, as I had them all pulled down under cover.

"Night came at last, but, just as dusk was deepening into darkness the Germans put up a terrific fusillade with rifles and machine-guns on our parapet, so we had to stay until they ceased. It seemed a wicked thing to do to the sorely tried people who were waiting to clear out. They did not come over for us, neither did they interfere with us from the direction of the farm buildings. When our unwounded had got away a N.C.O. and a party of Riflemen came from the platoon on our left flank to cover our withdrawal, and we did so without molestation. One of this covering party, a very big fellow whose name I never knew, picked me up and carried me in his arms, despite all protests on my part, to the trench where I reported to Captain Railston and told him of our casualties.

"Then I left for the Battalion Aid Post in La Brique, which I reached at about 11.30 p.m. with the help of a Rifleman who had been hit through an arm. I had my wounds properly dressed and was given a great bowl of hot tea by the Medical Officer's orderly. The M.O. told me to await an ambulance, but, as I knew of only one route for ambulances, and as that lay through Ypres, I requested permission to push on to Vlamertinghe with my friend of the wounded arm, who kindly volunteered to see me through. This was granted, so off we went down the road to the bridge over the Canal, through Boesinghe, then over the fields to Vlamertinghe, which we reached before dawn. I was very very glad to reach that place and even more so, by dint of making light of my hurts, to be put straight into an ambulance for Poperinghe, where I boarded a hospital train. That day was Wednesday. On the following Friday afternoon I was bathed and put to bed in Colchester Military Hospital.

"So my narrative ends. It has been . . . an arduous task to keep to the sober facts and to make a reasoned telling of all that happened at the time, from memory, nearly a quarter of a century after the event. It is doubtful whether a pen dipped in such an inundated substance as ink could do full justice to what the Battalion endured and its Riflemen suffered . . . No epic could pay tribute to the wonderful sense of duty and *esprit de corps d'élite* which pulled the Battalion through one of the most trying ordeals of its long history. The Second Ypres will, I am confident, rank with Moore's Retreat, the march to Talavera, the storming of Badajos and Tarbes, as one of the high lights in the Battalion's history. If so, then I for one will be well satisfied that the memory of those many Riflemen, who died in those few yards of open ditches outside Ypres, will endure, as they did undoubtedly uphold the traditions laid down by their forbears who disputed the passage of the Coa."*

*   *   *

Though Rifleman McCarthy's ordeal at Second Ypres ended for him before dawn on May 13th, that of his Battalion continued for the rest of that day until it was finally relieved at nightfall. Two outlying platoons—or what remained of them—fought and died almost to the last man in their isolated position in Shell-trap Farm. "As there were no traverses or cover of any kind," the Battalion War Record noted laconically, "the garrison were probably all killed by the preliminary shell fire. A corporal, an acting corporal and a rifleman from B Company—all of whom received the D.C.M.—were cut off for nine hours, "during which," it was recorded, "they pre-

* *R.B.C. 1939*, 131-73.

vented the enemy with their fire from digging in behind a hedge 150 yards to our right front and finally drove them off."*

The 4th Battalion was not relieved till the following day. For the past week it had been without any proper water supply. Earlier, as reinforcements arrived to fill the gaps of the threatened northern face of the Salient, it had withdrawn to its former place with the 80th Brigade nearer the city and dug itself in. It had even had a day or two of comparative peace. "The south of the Salient," wrote Captain Collins, "was now quiet at night except for an occasional shot and the sound of harassing fire to the rear; the nightingale sang in Sanctuary Wood to the accompaniment of the distant roar of the transport and ammunition wagons passing over the cobbles in Ypres."† But on May 15th the Germans again subjected the Battalion to intense bombardment both with high explosives and gas, as well as with machine-gun fire at close range. Through lack of guns and ammunition, there was little retaliation, and the Battalion, though brought up to strength by substantial replacements, suffered another 342 casualties. During the barrage of May 10th—heavier than any yet experienced—which preceded a final German attempt to break the British line, the Battalion Transport Officer and Colour-Sergeant Pompa, in "the weary business of sitting out a bombardment, . . . found some interest in watching a robin which sat contentedly chirping on a rose bush." Throughout the day, Captain Collins recalled, "Riflemen Forbes and Coleman . . . did excellent work, the former carrying messages, the latter ammunition. Coleman's round face would appear at the most unexpected moments with a load which he would dump; he would crack a joke and then depart with the utmost unconcern. Rifleman Slaymaker, one of the original bandsmen, continued, as he had always done, carrying the wounded with complete disregard for his personal safety."

On the night of May 14th, having lost in all, during their three weeks of battle, 15 officers and 887 other ranks, "bearded and covered with dirt the Riflemen marched from the Salient where they had

---

* *R.B.C. 1918*, 24, "War Record of 1st Bn."

† Billy Congreve in his diary for May 1st noted a similar phenomenon during a musketry duel near St. Eloi. "Above all this noise out of the wood came the singing of a nightingale! It was really wonderful. The wood is shelled by the Germans every day and is only 400 yard from their trenches, and bullets are constantly knocking up against the trees, and yet there was Mr. Nightingale singing away to his lady-love as if there was nothing wrong with the world at all." *The Congreves*, 280.

been continually on duty since 22nd April. The moon was shining as they passed through Ypres; a gun-team lay cold and still in the middle of the square. They had left a beautiful city, they returned to a heap of ruins."*

*　　　*　　　*

For the first nine months of the war it had been the Regular Army— long-service, professional, officered by the gentry and recruited from the poor—which had borne the heat and dust of the day while an unprepared Britain made ready. For the remaining three and a half years the burden passed to the New Army which was the nation itself or, rather, that part of it which was of military age and had voluntarily offered itself for service. "The old Army died a glorious death," wrote Colonel Repington, *The Times* Military Correspondent and a former Rifle Brigade officer, "but its spirit survived in the first hundred thousand, and in the second, and in the third. Not once, but many times, were some of its units completely renewed . . . Every man of spirit joined up and every class, profession and trade supplied its best . . . In their hundreds of thousands they filled up the depleted ranks of the old Regiments and created the new from the ashes of the old. The old Army gave the note of intense regimental feeling which distinguished the new troops. It trained these troops after its own fashion, implanted in them the sense of discipline and set them an example on the field of battle . . . The old Army was a caste. The new Army is a nation."†

This new Army, enlisted in the autumn and winter of 1914 and growing all the time, was now ready to take the field. By the autumn of 1915, despite the all but annihilation of the original Expeditionary Force, it had brought Sir John French's command up to more than a million men, already grouped in three separate Armies, ten Army Corps and over forty Divisions. In it were seven of the Rifle Brigade's eight new Service Battalions, the remaining

---

* *R.B.C. 1926*, 238-40. "Reminiscences of A Transport Officer with the Fourth Battalion." The fine Canadian Regiment by whose side it fought, the Princess Patricia's Canadian Light Infantry—which after the War became affiliated to the Rifle Brigade—came out of the line with only 150 men left. *R.B.C. 1918*, 99-104.

† "What sum of toil, sacrifice and devotion the old Army has given in this way and what splendid returns it has obtained." *The Times*, 31st Oct. 1916, cit. *R.B.C. 1918*, 3-9.

one, the 16th, reaching France in the following spring. Even the four Regular Battalions—one of which, the 4th, was sent in November 1915 with an Anglo-French force to Salonica—were now mainly filled, and even officered, by war-time volunteers. Though these lacked the meticulous training of the long-term Regulars into whose shoes they so readily stepped, in their noble spirit, standard of intelligence and dedicated patriotism and resolve for victory, they constituted a fighting force never surpassed, perhaps never equalled, in the annals of arms.*

Lord Ailwyn, who as Lt.-Colonel Ronald Fellowes commanded the 1st Battalion from 1916 to 1918, later set down his recollection of those who served under him, and the affection, pride and admiration he felt for their courage in the face of danger and every kind of unpleasantness, and for their good comradeship and intense keenness and love of the Regiment. "Amongst them," he wrote, "were Regular and non-Regular officers, warrant officers and N.C.O.s, . . . but the majority of them were men who in times of peace had never dreamt of soldiering and had taken temporary commissions in the Regiment for the period of the war. Nearly every profession and branch of life was represented amongst these officers; there were ex-lawyers and barristers, ex-sailors and marines, ex-schoolmasters, clerks, commercial travellers, engineers and university dons, boys who had just left school and older men from Australia, South Africa, Fiji, Hong-Kong and the uttermost parts of the world. There can be nothing but praise for the part they all played. And as the officers were, so were the N.C.O.s and Private Riflemen. It is not easy to find words in which to honour their deeds in and out of battle, their behaviour at all times and the way they upheld the spirit and tradition of the Regiment . . . Officers and men together formed the best lot of fellows to work with, fight with and play with that ever a Battalion possessed."†

This amalgam and natural blending between the surviving officers and men of the old Army and those of the new, serving together in the same Battalions, was perfectly described by Rifleman

* General Sir Bernard Paget, was once asked by the writer which, in his view, was the finest Army this country had ever produced—the Peninsular Army which Wellington led over the Pyrenees, the little 1914 Regular Army in which Paget had served, or the Army which he trained between 1941 and 1943 for the invasion of Europe.—He replied, None of them, but the New Army which "went over the top" on July 1st, 1916.

† *R.B.C. 1927*, 205-7. Lord Ailwyn, "The 1st Battalion in France and Flanders."
J.G.   S

McCarthy, writing of the first winter of the war when the volunteer entry first began to take its place beside the old.

"The same light-heartedness, what could be called 'Rifleman's impudence', animated all ranks. I will always remember the look of sheer disgust on the face of our platoon sergeant ... when, one day in that first winter, he gathered us up just outside the wood near Ploegsteert whilst we were marching back for our usual three days' rest in the village school. He was a very spick and span fellow, very regimental, always ready for parade; we, his flock, looked a muddy, rag-and-bob-tailed crew. He stood staring at us as we filed off the 'corduroy' out on to the road, leaning on his rifle, not uttering one word, but looking his disgust of us in every feature; then, when we had lined up, just slung his rifle, turned, and ordered us forward with 'Come on, you ——— oafs,' to be followed by a great shout of laughter. But, despite our filthy and scarecrow appearance, every man in that platoon was a 'Rifleman' from the soles of his feet to the crown of his head, inasmuch as the most exacting inspection would not have found one speck of dirt on our rifles or the ammunition in our pouches. Our persons, our bodies, no doubt, were foul, but our rifles and ammunition received the same loving care and attention as the most devoted mother spends on a favourite child."*

It was the same in the new Service Battalions where the thousands who volunteered, officers and men, were taught their business by a sprinkling of Regular officers, warrant officers and N.C.O.s—many of whom had returned to the Regiment on the outbreak of war and who subsequently served with them in the field. Three of these new Battalions—the 7th, 8th and 9th, raised in August 1914—formed part of the 14th Light Division under a former Rifle Brigade officer, Major-General Vic Couper who had commanded the 4th Battalion in Malta. The 7th and 8th were brigaded with two Battalions of the King's Royal Rifle Corps in a purely Greenjacket Brigade, and the 9th in a mixed Greenjacket and Light Infantry one. In September a second Light Division, the 20th, was formed, with the 10th and 11th Battalions, in another composite Greenjacket Brigade under a fine old Rifle Brigade officer, Brigadier-General Cameron Shute,† and the

* R.B.C. 1938, 302.
† Afterwards General Sir Cameron Shute, Colonel Commandant of the First Battalion from 1929 to 1936.

12th in a mixed Greenjacket and Light Infantry Brigade. The 14th Division, with the 7th, 8th and 9th Battalions landed in France in May 1915; the 20th Division, with the 10th, 11th and 12th Battalions in July.* Billy Congreve, a good judge of such matters, who visited the Headquarters of the 8th Battalion in a farm on May 31st just before it went into the line, "much admired the general appearance of the good Riflemen; they may be new," he wrote, "but they look splendid and have such a fine lot of officers."

What happened to them when they went into the line was, in one sense, a Rifle Brigade tragedy. Trained, as Riflemen should be, for open warfare, they found themselves committed to a static troglodyte existence in flooded, rat and fly haunted trenches and dugouts in which machine-guns, hand-grenades, phosphorus bombs, knobkerries and gas vied with rifles as weapons and in which the only diversions, except intermittent and often continuous shelling, were working-parties, night-patrols and raids in No Man's Land, and, more occasionally, suicidal attacks and counter-attacks carried out in a murderous inferno of shells and automatic-fire from an invisible enemy entrenched in concrete trenches and pill-boxes behind sheets of barbed wire. A few weeks after the 8th Battalion went into the Salient, and only ten days before he himself was killed under circumstances of extreme gallantry, Sidney Woodroffe, a 19-year-old subaltern who less than a year before had been Head Prefect at Marlborough, wrote to a school-friend describing the conditions under which he and his comrades were living,

"All the water in this God-forsaken country is undrinkable, and every drop of water we consumed in the trenches was brought up by hand in petrol tins over a mile at night, so our daily ration was about a pint and a half. In one part we were in, all the streams had been poisoned with arsenic . . . You can occasionally find a Jack Johnson hole into which water has drained—probably via an impromptu cemetery and a few refuse pits—and this affords a doubtful wash. You never get your boots off the whole time you are in the trenches . . . One thing that particularly turns you inside out at first is the flies. Every kind of disgusting and bloated bluebottle and fly in various stages of torpor buzz about or sleep on

* The 13th Battalion (Lt.-Colonel C. F. Pretor-Pinney) was in the Line before September 1915; the 16th landed in France on March 8th, 1916. *Berkeley I*, 132, 145.

beams, and flop down your neck when you bang your head on them.

"The first day we were there they gassed us with (prussic acid) gas shells. My God, it is bestial! With those foul shells which possibly explode a few yards away from you, the stuff is on you and inside you before you have time to make a selection from your stock of respirators and helmets . . . It makes your eyes (and nose!) simply stream, you cough and retch and have a beastly sore throat and violent headache . . . The next day we were treated to a similar gassing, one of the shells knocking down the parapet about 5 yards away from me and covering me with earth. That night I had the most horrible time I have ever had, and ever hope to have. I was sent with a party of 100 men to clear up a trench which had never been touched or occupied since we had captured it from the Germans a fortnight before; since nicknamed 'Dead Man's Alley'. I had a look in the daylight first, though couldn't start work until dark as it was under fire, and the place nearly made me sick, although you get used to a good deal out there. There was I landed in the dead of night on my own entirely to make 100 none too willing men work in this perfectly godless place. Besides all the countless equipment, rifles, overcoats, etc. we collected, we buried 23 corpses (4 English), two heads, a dismembered hand and foot. As it was a pitch dark night what I had to do was wander about myself, and on smelling something that nearly knocked one over backwards, cautiously shine my torch until I saw a ghastly blackened face grinning up at me—and then tell off a small party to dispose of it! Every one of us had to wear our respirators the whole of the 3½ hours we were there . . .

"The next day we were gas-shelled again—properly this time. They got the range exactly and put them right on the parapet. The first smashed to pieces our one and only anti-gas sprayer; the second blew to blazes the stretcher-bearers' dug-out and buried a stretcher; the third blew the head clean off the captain of my Company, killed two corporals in my platoon and wounded a sergeant and another man in about 5 places, and so on. You can't imagine how bestial it was with the place in an absolute fog, and everyone coughing and choking in their helmets. I was wearing three myself so couldn't see or hear! In desperation, finally to get out of the blasted place, I got hold of a sergeant and we sweated off with one of the men on a stretcher. It was a pretty absurd thing to do as it meant haring down a road which can be seen and is invariably shelled if anyone shows his nose on it. One shell removed practically the entire road not more than 10 yards in front of us and nearly knocked us silly. The man we were carrying on the stretcher had been hit in the head and practically the whole of the inside of his head came out on the way down.

"That night they bombarded us and knocked the trenches about a lot; early the next morning a party of German bombers came and bagged the trench occupied by one of our platoons. I was shaken up in a very deshabillé and sleepy condition and told to take my platoon and help get it back. I had not the haziest idea what was happening and had never seen that particular trench before. Feeling extraordinarily frightened and trying not to look it, I collected a party of bombers and stalked up (unfortunately discovering on the way that the only kind of bomb we were carrying was the only kind I had never seen in my life before and not knowing how on earth to work them). Luckily, a platoon of another Regiment on our left came to the rescue and had helped to clear the devils out before I arrived. We slew about eight of them in all. The Germans then got sick and bombarded us until 4 in the afternoon, banging our trenches to pieces, knocking out a lot of men and preventing me from getting anything to eat until 5 p.m.

". . . Such is life here. Time drags in the trenches, nothing done to further the interests of our country as far as one can see, and the Battalion lost five officers and 100 men and the Brigade about 350 in all. This is war! The German supply of shells seems quite unlimited. If our guns fire we cheer, even when they lay out men by dropping them in our trenches (which has happened twice to us) we don't like to discourage them. As a matter of fact their gunners aren't a patch on ours, and it will make all the difference in the world when we get the ammunition."*

Sidney Woodroffe—one of whose brothers in the Regiment had already been killed and another of whom was to fall a year later after winning the Military Cross—never lived to see that day. On July 30th, only ten days after writing this letter and when his Battal-

* R.B.C. 1961, 46-51.

ion had taken over new trenches on the outskirts of Hooge, the Germans, realising that they had unseasoned troops to deal with, launched a sudden attack with a new and terrifying weapon, jets of liquid fire. In one advanced trench not a man escaped. Forced to give ground the young Battalion did so with splendid discipline, the men lying down, as one of its subalterns, G. V. Carey,* recalled, every few yards and firing at the oncoming enemy "with the coolness of an Aldershot field day." Surrounded with his platoon by the enemy Sidney Woodroffe himself held off all attacks until his bomb supply was exhausted and then, by superb leadership, extricated his men in good order. Later, when the 7th and 9th Battalions joined the remnants of the 8th in a counter-attack, he won the Victoria Cross at the cost of his life by attempting to cut a way through the enemy's barbed wire under a hail of machine-gun and rifle fire. Of that counter-attack the Brigade commander wrote, "The men showed no hesitation in following their officers, and the officers sacrificed themselves in a devotion to duty to which no words can adequately do justice." Nineteen officers and 469 men of the 8th Battalion fell, and sixteen officers and 300 men of the 7th. Another Victoria Cross was won a few months later by the 8th Battalion, when Corporal A. Drake, returning from a patrol in No Man's Land, insisted on remaining with a badly wounded officer under heavy fire and, by bandaging his wounds, saved his life at the expense of his own.†

Further losses were suffered by the Regiment that September in subsidiary operations accompanying an attempt to break the German line at Loos. In these, though not themselves engaged in the main battle—which saw the death in action while commanding his Division of that great Rifleman, Major-General G. H. Thesiger—the 2nd Battalion lost nine officers and 244 men, the 12th seven officers and 322 men, and the 9th the appalling total of twenty-five officers and 750 men.

*   *   *

Yet this was only a prelude to what was to come. At the end of 1915,

---

* Afterwards Lt.-Col. G. V. Carey, who later in 1917 temporarily commanded the Battalion and from 1929-38 was Headmaster of Eastbourne College.

† Berkeley I, 129, 140; R.B.C. 1916, 124-5.

Sir Douglas Haig succeeded Sir John French as Commander-in-Chief. This reserved Lowland Scottish cavalryman and dedicated professional soldier was sustained in his lonely task by two convictions; one that it was his duty, by constantly attacking, to relieve the dangerous pressures on his country's overstrained and flagging allies, France, Russia and Italy; the other that the war could only be won by a process of attrition, of so hammering and bleeding the enemy's troops by repeated bombardments and offensives, both great and small, that in the end, worn down in numbers and morale, they would break and collapse. He saw the war as Wellington had seen Waterloo: as a pounding match in which the test was who could pound the longest.

Unfortunately such attrition was a two-way process. As during the first two years of his command the British Army did most of the attacking and neither side had as yet found a way of "bridging the gap between the barrage and the bayonet", in the face of the immense killing-power of automatic weapons the heaviest casualties fell on the British. Here Haig, and his Army with him, were handicapped by the fact that he was a cavalryman in control of a war in which—unlike that in which he had won his spurs in South Africa—all the fighting had to be done on foot. And as part of the self-discipline he imposed on himself, he believed that a Commander-in-Chief should deliberately isolate himself from the sufferings and losses which had to be sustained by his troops lest his will for victory at all costs should be shaken. As a result, he and his immediate entourage at his remote and peaceful G.H.Q. in the chateau of Montreuil, never fully realised the appalling conditions in which his troops were called upon to live and fight. Nor was sufficient consideration given to the technical and tactical means by which those conditions might be ameliorated and overcome. From this followed two tragic consequences. One was that, though the leadership given at Company and Battalion, and, frequently at Brigade level by the officers of the old Regular Army was of the highest quality, in the higher echelons of command there was too often a failure of understanding, on the part both of Commanders and Staff, of what orders drafted in an Olympian calm far from the battlefield involved when put into practice in the muddy, blood-stained inferno of the trenches. Such failure was common to the Higher Commands of all the combatant armies, but it particularly affected one which had expanded so rapidly that men, who in 1914 were commanding only Battalions or Companies, found themselves dealing with Divisions, Army Corps and even Armies, without having had time to master the logistics of their wider responsibilities and the baffling techniques of the new mechanical warfare. The other was that while, by its sacrificial fortitude in a four years' duel of attrition, Britain won the war, she lost the peace and found herself, twenty years later, facing another war because most of the men who should have given her wise and effective leadership, had, under her voluntary system, selected themselves for almost certain death in the holocausts of France and Flanders.

The first of these occurred on the Somme in the summer of 1916. Originally planned as a joint Franco-British offensive in which France, with her conscript Army, would still play the senior role, it was to have been launched in mid-August as soon as Britain's belated armament was ready. But owing to the fact that in February, Germany, intent on breaking the French by a similar process of attrition, had staged a massive offensive against Verdun which, by the summer, had all but bled France white, the Somme offensive was brought forward six weeks and conducted mainly by British arms. On July 1st, the opening day of the battle, the Expeditionary Force—brought up by the continuing flow of new drafts from Britain and the Empire to more than a million and a quarter men— suffered sixty thousand casualties. On that day the 1st Battalion Rifle Brigade lost seventeen officers, including its commander, and 457 men. "At first," ran the Battalion Report, "the advance behind the barrage appeared to go quite well, but when the first wave was within a few yards of the enemy's front line, a hail of rifle and machine-gun fire opened . . . So heavy was this fire that only a few of our men succeeded in reaching the enemy's wire." Those who got through to the German second and third lines, though they clung on all day, found themselves committed to a trench mêlée with knob-kerry and bomb and were gradually overcome and forced back by superior numbers.

A few days after the 1st Battalion's martyrdom on the wire of No Man's Land, the 13th Battalion, though carrying all its first objectives, lost its Commanding Officer, Adjutant, all its Company commanders, 14 other officers and 300 men. Later in the month, serving in the XII Corps under that fine Rifleman, Lt.-General Walter

Congreve, V.C.,* the 3rd Battalion went "over the top" with each of its Companies advancing in perfect formation on a hundred yards' front immediately behind the creeping barrage, to capture, after two of them had lost 75 per cent of their personnel, Guillemont Station. One young officer, Lieutenant L. G. Butler, while lying wounded and paralysed in a shell-hole, kept encouraging his men to hang on. "Two Riflemen tried to get him back but he would not let them touch him, saying that they would only get shot themselves. Later on they went to him again, but still he would not let them touch him, although he was dying fast. On being ordered to withdraw after dark these two Riflemen again went to get him back but could find no trace of him. There is little doubt that he was blown to pieces by a shell."† Between August 18th when it went into battle and September 6th when it was relieved, the Battalion lost twenty officers and 472 men.

Among those who fell in the early part of the Somme offensive was General Congreve's son, Billy. A Brigade Major and a D.S.O. and M.C. at twenty-five, his death in action on July 20th won him the Victoria Cross which his father had gained before him at Colenso. "The very embodiment of noble youth," as Sir Martin Conway called him, his brilliant professional qualities and selfless goodness had made him universally loved, not only in the Regiment but throughout the Army. "I have lost many youngsters whom I liked to look on as my friends," the Commander of the Second Army, the future Field Marshal Lord Plumer wrote, "but I looked on Billy as something more than that." Another Field Marshal, Sir Henry Wilson, considered his record "the finest of the War".‡

Neither casualties nor the weather, which presently turned to almost continuous rain, eroded the British Commander-in-Chief's iron resolve. By this time, pulverised by the massed artillery of two

---

* "He was to us in the 3rd Battalion more like a well-loved father than our Divisional Commander. He was continually visiting us in the trenches, . . . and, even now, after so many years, I can see his lone figure, always by himself, coming up over the open from behind, and this always seemed to be when the shelling was hottest." Communicated by Brig.-Gen. Sir Robert Pigot, Bt., D.S.O., M.C., to Field Marshal Sir Francis Festing, G.C.B., K.B.E., D.S.O.

† *R.B.C. 1919*, 137-8, "War Record of the Third Battalion".

‡ *The Congreves*, 199-210, 224. "Forgetfulness of self, and thought for others and an absolute faith in God gave him courage unsurpassed. All men loved him and spoke well of him; only he ever forgot to speak well of himself." *Idem*, 210.

great armies, the state of the Somme trenches beggared description. On the night of August 25/26th, after the battle had been raging for eight weeks, the 10th Battalion, put into the line near Guillemont, found the whole area "a shambles of human remains littered over a barren waste of mud and shell holes . . . Not merely was the front line impossible to be held"—for, under the combined effect of flooding and shelling, the walls repeatedly fell in and buried their occupants—"it could only be approached by men of the most iron fortitude . . . What horrified the senses and shocked the imagination was not what might come from outside the trenches but what was in them. From end to end they were choked with British dead, on their backs, on their faces, hideously doubled up, distorted with pain, blackened and bloated by the sun, the prey of myriad upon myriad of carrion flies, odiously green with corruption."*

All through the autumn the slaughter continued. When early in September, under the orders—"a model of lucidity"—of their Brigade commander and fellow Rifleman, Brigadier-General Shute, the 10th and 11th Battalions captured Guillemont village, the 10th lost both its Commanding Officer and Adjutant, and the 11th every officer but three, one of whom was its acting colonel, A. E. Cotton, who only two years before had enlisted as a private Rifleman. A little later in the month the 8th Battalion lost all its officers except one. Before the battle was called off at the end of November, by which time the Army's casualties had risen to over 400,000 men, the 7th Battalion was reduced to six officers, four sergeants and 150 men, and the 8th Battalion to 160 men, while the 9th Battalion had lost its Commanding Officer and Second-in-command—both mortally wounded—and the 12th Battalion eight officers and 223 other ranks.

When after a period of recuperation in the Ypres salient, the 1st Battalion returned to the Somme in the middle of October, the mud over the whole waterlogged battle area was anything from eight inches to two feet deep. "The men," wrote Colonel Fellowes, "were soaked to the skin, chilled to the bone and a mass of slimy mud from head to foot." Yet when they attacked in the small hours of the 18th and, after carrying its immediate objectives, one Company got lost, it spent the rest of the night wandering about behind the enemy lines, and, wherever it met, as it repeatedly did, Germans and their machine-guns, it "went for them tooth and nail, killed a lot and

* *Berkeley*, 178.

destroyed several machine-guns. Eventually," Colonel Fellowes reported, "some fifty of them scrambled back home after the whole Company had been given up for lost."* Eight officers and 259 men was the price paid for the 1st Battalion's second Somme offensive. A few days later, in another attack, it lost five more officers and 117 men. Its sister Battalion, the 2nd, lost eight officers and 230 men. About the same time, in another part of the battlefield, the 16th Battalion lost a fifth of its personnel, in what was called a demonstration, while in November, in a new attack on the Ancre, the 13th Battalion under Lt.-Colonel Prideaux-Brune suffered another 324 casualties, twelve of them officers.

In no case, the historian of the Regiment in World War I recorded, did any of the eleven Rifle Brigade Battalions engaged on the Somme "fail to win the warmest commendation of the Commanders under whom they served and to prove by the harvest of decorations their dash and stubbornness as fighters. The officers, whose utter disregard of danger was revealed by the severity of their losses and the high proportion of killed to wounded were in every way worthy of men who only asked to be led to achieve conspicuous success and who, at a pinch, as they proved on numerous occasions, were capable, when their officers and N.C.O.s were killed, of providing excellent leadership from their own ranks."† There were brilliant individual achievements like the storming of Rainbow Trench by the 12th Battalion and the attacks by the 3rd, 10th and 11th Battalions at Guillemont. Yet though the five months' battle was acclaimed as a great British victory and was certainly a miracle of fortitude and endurance, for the Rifle Brigade, as for every other infantry Regiment engaged, it was something also of a tragedy.

*　　　*　　　*

For those who remained that winter when the fighting was over in the devastated Somme valleys and uplands there was little comfort. "The whole sector," wrote an officer of the 1st Battalion, "was a dreary waste of mud and shell-holes overflowing with water . . . For sheer undiluted misery and discomfort it was impossible to beat . . . One lived and slept and moved in mud . . . It is difficult to say whether the front or back areas were the most damnable. The

* R.B.C. *1927*, 190.　　† *Berkeley*, 237-8; R.B.C. *1914-16*, 237-8.

weather was poisonous wherever we were: rain, frost and thaw with
their attendant miseries of soaked clothes and mud, frost-bite and
trench feet, collapsed trenches and more mud . . . The so-called
Camps behind the lines were . . . seas of mud, traversed by trench-
board pathways, draughty huts empty of everything, . . . and
intensely cold all the time."*

Yet, just as their courage had done in the battle-line, the cheerful
philosophy of the Riflemen triumphed over their surroundings. " The
men in spite of the ghastly time they had," Colonel Fellowes wrote
in his diary, " are as cheery as anything. They really are marvellous
people, and every time I am more than ever filled with admiration
at their spirit. The way they stuck it out, living in the open in mud
and shell-holes, in torrents of rain, in bitter cold and under fire all
the time was beyond praise. I am proud beyond words to serve with
such men."† Whatever the weather, whatever the state of the road,
Captain Berkeley recalled, " it was rarely that a Battalion marched
at ease, whether to or from the trenches, without a catch of song . . .
The relations of officers and men in the Battalions of the Rifle
Brigade, under the combined spell of regimental tradition and
esprit de corps, was something for which a parallel has to be sought
in the relationship of the members of a Highland clan."‡

Wherever a Battalion found itself in the rear areas away from the
line, the strong social instinct of the Regiment reasserted itself. It
was in keeping with and characteristic of Rifle Brigade tradition that
when in March 1917 the 1st Battalion was billeted in the village of
La Thieuloye near St. Pol for training for the spring offensive, it
should have won golden opinions from the inhabitants by helping
to put out a fire and improving the roads of the commune—services
for which it was warmly thanked in a letter from the Mayor.§ The
regimental passion for sport also came out at such times; for a short
while at the beginning of the year the 1st and 2nd Battalions were
stationed in adjoining camps and had " a great *entente* together"
with a series of football matches. The 3rd Battalion, in divisional
reserve for a week in the January after the Somme, at once organised
a football match between the officers and sergeants and an Inter-
Company Falling Plate Competition. Later in the year, while

---

* "It was no uncommon thing to find one's poached egg at breakfast frozen nearly solid
and with a lump of ice sitting in the middle of it." *R.B.C. 1927*, 192-3; *1919*, 18.
   † *R.B.C. 1927*, 196-7.   ‡ *Berkeley*, 240.   § *R.B.C. 1923*, 184-5; *1927*, 193.

training in rest billets, it engaged in athletic sports, shooting competitions and a cross-country race. The war diaries of all the Service battalions, as well as those of the Regular ones, are full of references to cricket, football, boxing and wrestling matches and other activities of a sporting kind whenever a respite from duty occurred.

There was little to choose between the morale of the Regular Battalions and the Service ones, though perhaps the former were rather better at overcoming the appalling material discomforts with which all of them were faced. In the trenches with the 10th Battalion, R. E. Vernède—the poet and novelist—who, though four years over military age, enlisted in 1914 and was subsequently given a commission in the Rifle Brigade and served with the 3rd Battalion before being wounded on the Somme, wrote in January 1917: "For discomfort this part of the Front takes the cake,... nor does a Service Batt. know how to look after itself as well as a Regular. Many of the things we do and don't do would make the hair of the 3rd Batt. stand on end."* In a poem which made him famous this quiet unmilitary man expressed the faith which kept him, a subaltern of 42, to the sticking point:

" *All that a man might ask thou hast given me, England,*
  Birthright and happy childhood's long heart's ease,
And love whose range is deep beyond all sounding
  And wider than all seas:
A heart to front the world and find God in it,
  Eyes blind enow but not too blind to see
The lovely things behind the dross and darkness,
  And lovelier things to be;
And friends whose loyalty time nor death shall weaken,
  And quenchless hope and laughter's golden store—
All that a man might ask thou hast given me, England,
  Yet grant thou one thing more:
That now when envious foes would spoil thy splendour,
  Unversed in arms, a dreamer such as I,
May in thy ranks be deemed not all unworthy,
  England, for thee to die."

Vernède's prayer was granted on May 8th when he was mortally wounded while on patrol in Havrincourt Wood. Before that hap-

* R. E. Vernède, *Letters to his Wife,* 184.

pened another major British offensive had been launched in front of
Arras, this time in conjunction with an all-out and, as it turned out,
disastrously unsuccessful attempt by the French—under a new
Commander-in-Chief, General Nivelle—to break through the German defences on the Aisne. Five Rifle Brigade Battalions were involved—the 1st, 7th, 8th, 9th and 11th. On April 9th in pouring rain
the 1st Battalion under Colonel Fellowes opened the assault, advancing behind a football which was drop-kicked into the Hyderabad
Redoubt, its objective. It was brilliantly successful, penetrating
6000 yards behind the German front line and reaching and, for a
time, holding, the furthest point of the whole British advance. "A
great day full of excitement and interest," the Battalion's War
Narrative noted, ". . . chiefly remarkable for the utter demoralisa-
tion of the Boche and more especially for the extraordinary way in
which the advances were made exactly up to time, according to the
timetable laid down. It seemed far more like another of the many
rehearsals than one of the greatest battles of the War." Of the
thirteen officers and 342 other ranks who took part in the first day's
attack, three officers were killed or died of wounds—including the
subaltern who kicked the football—three were wounded, and 123
other ranks were killed, missing or wounded. Unfortunately, as
always seemed to happen, "when the good show was done lives
began to be wasted on a series of minor operations which proved
hopeless. The weather conditions throughout were exceptionally
severe and cover and shelter in the trenches were practically non-
existent." By the end of the operation the Battalion's casualties had
risen to nine officers and 252 other ranks.* In the course of the battle,
which continued till the middle of May, the 7th, 8th, 9th and 13th
Battalions suffered proportionately, the 13th—as did also the 7th—
losing its Commanding Officer, Lt.-Colonel Charles Pretor-Pinney—
"a man of great personal courage and charm, a magnificent disciplinarian, a Rifleman in every thought and action," who had raised
his fine Service Battalion to a high pitch of morale and died of his
wounds on April 29th.†

In June 1917, in a meticulously prepared operation resulting in
the capture of the Messines-Wytschate Ridge, the 3rd Battalion
under Lt.-Colonel Pigot put up one of the most spectacular per-
formances of the War, advancing 4000 yards immediately behind

C. 1919, 21-6; Seymour, 27-34.   † Seymour, 55.

and under shelter of the creeping barrage and, at the cost of a single casualty, capturing 200 prisoners and a complete German field battery. "I remember signalling the Brigade," Bob Pigot recalled, "that we had gone right through the German defences, that there was nothing now between us and Berlin, and asking for the next objective. But, alas, no preparations had been made for such a break through and we just had to dig in and start trench-warfare all over again. All along the front the success had been equally great, but I never heard of another Regiment getting away with just one minor casualty as we did."*

During that summer the Army, while continuing to hold the line from Flanders to Picardy, made itself ready for an even more ambitious offensive than that of the Somme. Called the Third Battle of Ypres—or, more often, from its final phase—Passchendaele, it was undertaken as a matter of high urgency both to prevent the Germans attacking the French Army, part of which, after the failure of Nivelle's spring offensive, had broken into open mutiny, and to wrest the Belgian coast from the enemy whose submarines were operating from it with increasingly alarming results against British shipping.

In this tremendous offensive, whose geographical objective was the high ground dominating the Belgian coastal plain but which was also intended to achieve Haig's persistently pursued aim of breaking the back and heart of the German Army, every one of the eleven Rifle Brigade Battalions on the Western Front was engaged. The battle went on from July 31st till November 10th, and most of the time under persistently adverse climatic conditions. The autumn of 1917 turned out to be one of the wettest in living memory, and the terrain—the heavy clay soil of Flanders—was liable to flooding and had been turned into a pitted morass by three years of continual shelling. The 2nd, 3rd and 16th Battalions were in the opening assault on July 31st, the 2nd losing fourteen officers and 290 men, the 3rd seven officers and 227 men, and the 16th nine officers and 319 men, most of them in later stages of the operation which the Higher Command as usual persisted in prolonging far beyond the time when the results justified the cost. The 16th—the youngest of the Service Battalions—did particularly well, the operation orders of its

* Communicated by Brig.-Gen. Sir Robert Pigot to Field Marshal Sir Francis Festing.

commander, Lt.-Colonel the Hon. Edward Coke, being so precise and clear* that every movement during the day followed almost exactly on the lines and at the time ordained. But the weather was so appalling that the advantages at first won could not be exploited, and the second stage of the battle was delayed till the middle of August, when the weather gave some signs, though only temporarily, of letting up. In fact, during the fighting between August 14th and 17th, when the 2nd, 10th, 11th and 12th Battalions were all engaged, "weather conditions," as the war diary of the 10th Battalion recorded, "surpassed anything yet experienced, even in winter on the Somme." The 2nd Battalion lost six officers and 149 men, the 10th Battalion nine officers and 199 men, without counting those who, though wounded, remained on duty, the 11th Battalion seven officers and 312 men, and the 12th ten officers and 148 men. Two Companies of the 10th were left without any officers at all, and both the 11th and 12th lost all their Company commanders. In the last week of August the 7th, 8th and 9th Battalions were also thrown into the battle, losing between them fifteen officers and 515 men.

In the third stage of the long drawn-out battle in September, when after the middle of the month the weather again showed signs of improving—it could hardly have become worse—the 10th, 11th, 12th and 16th Battalions, sadly reduced in numbers, were again sent into the fight. The 16th lost thirteen officers and 195 men, the 10th three officers and 120 men, the 11th thirteen officers and 193 men, and the 12th ten officers and 200 men—losses which, in proportion to the smaller numbers engaged, were even heavier than before. A further loss sustained by the Regiment was that of the commander of the 112th Brigade, Brigadier-General Ronald Maclachlan, who was killed by a sniper. Adjutant of the 3rd Battalion in India and commander of the Oxford University O.T.C. in 1914, he had trained and taken to France the 8th Battalion, and his death at forty-six deprived the Rifle Brigade and the Army of a born leader of men. Of him it was written that "he was universally beloved, . . . a good sportsman and a charming companion and a master of his profession," with an "amazing personality which enabled him to get the best out of all with whom he came in contact. There was no height to which he

---

* Colonel Coke's first operation order, issued before the Battalion crossed the Yser Canal , laid it down that "every man will have cotton-wool in his nose." *Seymour*, 102.

could not have risen . . . It is unlikely that the Regiment will ever again see his equal in character; his superior never."*

In the closing stage of the battle in October the 1st Battalion returned to the attack, losing another nine officers and 263 men. "It is quite impossible," the author of the official narrative wrote, "to describe the state of the ground . . . It rained steadily the whole time, and the darkness at night was intense . . . The country was one mass of shell-holes, and it really came to having to search every shell-hole to see if there were any troops in them. In spite of it all, and in spite of the perfectly appalling conditions everyone lived in, the men were simply wonderful . . . The way everyone hung on and stuck it out was marvellous. When we came out . . . the Battalion had been in the trenches for eight days and nine and a half nights, and next morning they were as cheery as ever."†

The British Army and the Rifle Brigade had one more major battle in 1917. On November 20th a surprise attack was launched against the German lines near Cambrai with 300 tanks supported by infantry. Hitherto these new instruments of warfare—a British invention used for the first time on the Somme—had only been employed in driblets and had produced, therefore, small effect. But on this occasion they broke through the German lines and penetrated for several miles beyond. The 10th, 11th and 12th Battalions took part in the accompanying attack and, though much under strength, all achieved their objectives. Unfortunately, owing to the 400,000 casualties the Army had just suffered in the prolonged Passchendaele offensive and the enforced despatch after the Caporetto disaster, of five British and five French divisions to Italy to save the defeated forces of that country from total collapse, there were no reserves available to exploit the success, and when the German counter-attack came, all three Battalions suffered severely. The 10th, whose head-quarters was overrun, was virtually wiped out, while the 11th lost six officers and 132 men, and the 12th four officers and 129 men. In the same month in which the Battle of Cambrai was won and lost, Sergeant W. F. Burman of the 16th Battalion was awarded the Victoria Cross for gallantry during the Ypres offensive; earlier in the year a similar award had been given posthumously to 2nd Lieutenant G. E. Cates of the 2nd Battalion for saving the lives of

---

* *Seymour*, 154.
† *R.B.C. 1919*, 43-5.

his men at the cost of his own by placing his foot on a live bomb.

*   *   *

With the coming of 1918 the British Army was confronted by a
graver threat to its existence than any since 1914. For Russia, broken
by three years of war, had disintegrated in revolution, and during
the winter of 1917-18 her new Communist rulers made an abject
peace, enabling the whole military might of Germany to be concentrated in the West. More than a million troops, trained in a new
technique of advance by infiltration, and three thousand guns were
transferred from the Eastern to the Western front. To relieve the
strain on the over-extended and still badly shaken French, though
dangerously short of reserves himself Haig, at the beginning of the
year, took over an additional twenty-eight miles of front south of
the old Somme battlefield. It was here, on a front of forty miles, that
the Germans concentrated thirty-seven divisions, and almost as
many in reserve, supported by 6000 guns, against seventeen British
divisions and 2500 guns with only five divisions in support. The odds
against Gough's Fifth Army and the right wing of Byng's Third
Army were two and a half to one and, in parts of the Fifth Army
front, four to one. Striking on the morning of March 21st in a dense
mist, the enemy overran and penetrated the advanced defences after
subjecting them to four hours of the most intensive shelling that
anyone had ever experienced. Within two days the whole of the Fifth
Army, its defences broken, and half the Third Army, with its southern
flank exposed, were in full retreat across a wasted countryside and
the cratered wilderness of the Somme.

Yet, though many units were broken and others almost totally
destroyed, it was a fighting retreat in which the defenders inflicted
twice as many casualties as they suffered. For all their improved
assault techniques, this time it was the Germans who paid the price
for using men's bodies as battering-rams against storms of steel.
Eight Battalions of the Rifle Brigade—the 7th, 8th, 9th, 11th, 12th
and 3rd—with the 16th in reserve, which had spent the day before
the battle in musketry training, and the 2nd, which moved into the
battle area on March 23rd—were involved. The 1st Battalion, on
the extreme left of the Third Army to the north, was only lightly
engaged. The 7th, in the most exposed position of all, was all but

annihilated, losing on the first day twenty officers and 525 other ranks. The 8th and 9th managed to withdraw, comparatively unscathed, behind the Crozat Canal, and the 12th suffered only 33 casualties, including three officers. The 3rd Battalion, true to its record and traditions and with its habitual efficiency, put up a magnificent fight in what at first seemed a hopeless situation. "All telephone communication forward of Battalion H.Q.," reported Lt.-Colonel Kewley—a former Company commander who had taken over command in the previous summer at the age of 27 from Bob Pigot— "went in the first few minutes and, though the linemen worked unceasingly, it was never re-established: the fog prevented any use of visual . . . 'C' Company under Captain Fenner put up a great resistance and it was not till about 6.30 p.m., when nearly surrounded, that the Company was skilfully withdrawn, having inflicted very severe losses on the enemy and having entirely upset his time-table. On the left 'A' Company, reinforced by 'D' rallied on a line just west of Dean Copse: here, though there were no trenches, these Companies put up a great fight against immense odds and only fell back step by step, again entirely upsetting the enemy's timetable . . . It was now touch and go whether the reinforcements or the enemy would arrive first; fortunately the former did." "It became," the Official Battalion narrative recorded, "a race for time; if we could stick it till dark something might be done, and, by the mercy of Providence and the fine leadership of Fenner commanding 'C' Company and other Company officers, and by the gallantry of our Riflemen, stick it we did." Fenner was killed in the orderly withdrawal next day, and, in the initial day's fighting and the fortnight of the retreat and subsequent stand and counter-attack in front of Amiens, the Battalion lost twenty-three officers and 410 other ranks. But it made the enemy pay a heavy price for them, and even in the worst confusion of what someone described as "the biggest cross-country race the world has ever seen," its Riflemen, emulating the performance of their 95th predecessors on the retreat to Vigo, still marched in fours."*

The men of the Reserve Battalions, too, continued to fight back throughout the retreat, despite their dwindling numbers, already reduced by their losses of the previous autumn and the gradual drying up of new drafts from England. By March 26th the 7th Bat-

* *Seymour*, 234-6; *R.B.C. 1919*, 157; *1963*, 85-8.

talion was down to three officers and 80 men, the 9th to nine officers and 215 men, and the 10th to ten officers and 305 men. By the night of the 29th that of the 11th had fallen to six officers and 40 other ranks, compared with 170 at the start of the day's fighting, while the command of the 12th had devolved on its Adjutant, Captain Tait, every senior officer having been killed or wounded. In a letter written by an officer, Captain C. E. Squire, of the 8th Battalion there is an account of a typical day's fighting on the retreat, with remnants of different units all supporting one another.

"There were only one hundred and thirty all ranks, together with about eighty of the Seventh Battalion details on the left and some sixty of the 8th Battalion 60th between Flavy and Cugny; there did not appear to be any other troops at all. But this body, with no bombs or rifle-grenades, only two Lewis guns and a limited amount of S.A.A., held in check strong enemy forces from 8 a.m. until dark. No ammunition was wasted, fire was controlled; during the twelve hours' contact with the enemy three distinct positions were taken up within four hundred yards of each other, and no withdrawal was made until large numbers of the enemy were round both flanks. Fire was so steady and deadly that the enemy never more than once dared to attempt a frontal attack, and thus time was saved while he had to work round the flanks . . . Considering that the enemy consisted of fresh troops . . . plentifully supplied with ammunition and greatly outnumbering our forces, and . . . that they had the support of artillery, light mortars, rifle-grenades and machine-guns, it was no disgrace that such a handful of men had to withdraw. The most that we could hope to do was to delay the enemy's advance so as to give time for the supports to come up behind. This we did."*

Among the supports which came up to help were the 2nd Battalion and the 16th. Both sacrificed themselves nobly. The 2nd lost its 26-year-old Colonel, Henry Peyton, who was mortally wounded,

---

* *Seymour*, 242-4. There is a postscript to Captain Squire's letter, "Sergeant Boughton was killed—an immense grief to me. He was a fine fellow. Rifleman Greenwell, 'A' Company Lewis gunner, did splendid work—wounded while staying to the last to give covering fire while the rest got back to the rear position. He is probably a prisoner; his only thought was of other people. He said to me when all the rest had gone: 'Don't stay, sir, leave me and save yourself, I shall be alright'. His leg was broken and I thought it was my duty to go and rally the men in the next position."

eighteen other officers and 437 other ranks; the 16th twenty-four officers and 446 other ranks. The 9th Battalion in one day of the retreat lost fourteen officers and 270 men; the 11th, in all, twenty-three officers and 418 men, and the 12th twenty-one officers and 437 men. In the case of the 7th, 8th, 9th and 10th Service Battalions, these losses were never made good, and they now ceased to exist as fighting units, being disbanded or reduced to training cadres.* The 10th had already gone that way, having been "cannibalized" in February, before the German offensive, to bring up the strength of the other Battalions.

The battle, and the German advance, ended on April 4th 1918. Both sides were completely exhausted, but the attempts to encircle and destroy the southern half of the British Army had been defeated. So had the hope of separating the French and British. For, five days after the March offensive began, the second Rifleman to be appointed Chief of the Imperial General Staff, Sir Henry Wilson, achieved—six weeks after taking up his office and with Haig's whole-hearted and selfless support—his long-cherished ambition of a supreme military Authority to co-ordinate the activities of the Allied Armies, with his friend, Foch, as co-ordinator and, by April 10th, as Commander-in-Chief.

Five days earlier on April 5th, the Germans attacked again, this time against the British in the north with the idea of reaching the Channel ports. It was now the turn of the 1st Battalion, and, once again, of the 2nd Battalion, to help stand in the breach, which both did successfully, the 1st with the loss of seven officers and 144 other ranks, and the 2nd with that of fifteen officers and 380 other ranks. Before the German assault in the north was finally stemmed, with the British fighting with their "backs to the wall" in the spirit of Haig's famous Order, the 13th Battalion was engaged in a battle which cost it seven officers and approximately 100 other ranks, but gained it two Victoria Crosses, awarded to Rifleman W. Beesley and Sergeant W. Gregg, the latter having already won the D.C.M. and the Military Medal.

So far as their attempt to destroy the British was concerned, the

* *Seymour*, 222-3, 295-6. "The Battalion now definitely disbanded, which, to us who have been with it since its formation, . . . is little short of a tragedy. Ypres—Hooge—Arras—Delville Wood—Flers—Passchendaele—St. Quentin—Villers-Bretonneux. It has fought and suffered much and this is the end." *Semi-official Diary* kept by the 8th Battalion.

Germans had shot their bolt. They made one final attempt, this time, against the French on the Aisne, at the end of May. In this one Battalion of the Rifle Brigade, the 2nd, paid the final instalment of the sacrificial price demanded of the British for keeping the French Army in being after its terrible blood-letting at Verdun and on the Chemin des Dames. Sent south with the five divisions of the IX Corps to strengthen the French forces between Rheims and Noyon, its orders were that not a yard of ground was to be given up and that the outpost-line was to fight to the last. At dawn on May 27th, holding a frontage of over two miles, it was subjected to a bombardment so intense that by the time the Germans attacked, in smoke so dense as to make them completely invisible, half its personnel had been killed or wounded. The rest were overwhelmed, twenty-six officers and 680 other ranks being killed, wounded or taken prisoner.

*   *   *

Yet it is an attribute of a great Regiment that it rises, phoenix-like, from the ashes of its dead. By the end of the summer the much-enduring, battered British Army, recovered from its spring ordeal, was ready under its indomitable chief to embark on the final offensive— perhaps the most surprising come-back and counter-attack in military annals. It was to carry it in three months, between August 8th and the German capitulation on November 11th, from the old front line to the towns with the familiar names—Mons, Le Cateau, Valenciennes—where it had begun the war. The 2nd Battalion was able to play its part with its sister Battalions in that final triumphant advance. It was reconstituted under a 33-year-old former officer of the 4th Battalion, Lt.-Colonel Reginald Leyland, who had been invalided out of the Army in June 1914 as a result of a hunting accident which had left him with a broken thigh and a stomach injury necessitating an invalid diet of milk and champagne. Returning to the Service as a machine-gun instructor and, later, as a staff officer at G.H.Q. in charge of the Machine Gun Corps, he insisted on taking on the job of reforming the 2nd Battalion, though his friends were convinced that, with his ill health, he would not last a week in the forward areas. Half a century later the man who was his Adjutant wrote an account of what he achieved in the three and a half months between the formation of the reconstituted Battalion and his death in action at the end of September.

"Rex was tireless in his drive to resurrect the Battalion and by the first days of August, when we were ordered to entrain for the Vimy area, what had been a collection of officers and men, strangers to one another, was now a fairly well knit Battalion, reasonably trained and well turned out. We had to march 15 miles to the entraining station. Officers' chargers were to be sent on ahead and to spare the Colonel the strain on his leg, I tried to persuade him to keep his horse, but he wouldn't hear of it. Defying pain, he allowed the Battalion—Companies marching at 100 yards distance—to pass him as he stopped to watch the march discipline and then caught up the head of the column again. Twice he did this, and I began to realise what I was in for when we reached the forward area.

"I wasn't mistaken. All day and some of the night, Rex was up among the Companies, ensuring good trench routine, helping and encouraging everywhere. Two runners he wore out each day, and he would usually arrive back at Battalion H.Q. in the small hours to deal with the paper work which needed his decision. At last I would get him to his bunk, where, unseen by other eyes except mine, he would collapse, often groaning in agony from the pain in his leg. No one must be allowed to know about this, as he feared the Battalion would lose faith in him should they learn of it. We scoured the country for his champagne and did our best to provide him with food he could eat. He continued to drive himself in his task of building up morale and efficiency. The first two or three raids which the Battalion undertook, he accompanied until Brigade heard of it and ordered him to stop doing so. He could then only watch the raiding parties set out and welcome them when they returned. He was everywhere, pain or no pain. Needless to say, the Battalion worshipped him, and when at the end of September, when visiting a forward Company a shell broke his tired body, every officer and man was numbed by the tragedy."*

* * *

* From Colonel J. M. West, to Lt. Colonel Ulick Verney, 23rd November, 1970.

During those final weeks of victory all the remaining Battalions of the Rifle Brigade, except the 4th, which was training Americans, bore their part in the advancing line of battle—the 1st, 2nd, 3rd, 11th, 12th and 13th. When on the 11th November, 1918, the bugles sounded the "Cease Fire", of more than 50,000 Officers, Warrant Officers, N.C.O.s and Riflemen who had been in the Regiment during the War, 11,575 had given their lives. Of those who served, 64 had won the D.S.O., 271 the M.C., 258 the D.C.M., 943 the Military Medal and 95 the Meritorious Service Medal. Ten, of whom only five survived, had gained the highest distinction of all, the Victoria Cross.*

Like all those other lives given by the officers and men of the British Army between 1914 and 1918, they were lives that a future Britain could ill spare. For they spelt a cumulative loss of leadership in every sphere, and at every level, of national life. They were given by men whose love of country and sense of honour had prevented them from shirking what they felt to be their duty. Having chosen to offer their all, before their final sacrifice was taken their characters had received the impress of the corps they had chosen, and whose mission, as that of every great Regiment, was to make men, by discipline, comradeship and *esprit de corps*, more selfless and more self-perfecting than they were before. The loss of such men in such numbers—the flower of a great nation—was more, despite the magnitude of her victory, than Britain could well bear. So many of her troubles since have stemmed in part from that sacrificial loss.

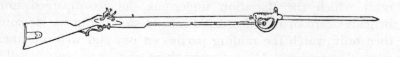

* *R.B.C. 1919, 266; 1925, 178.*

Chapter Eight

STARTING ALL OVER AGAIN

One has always known that there is no other Regiment quite
like ours, that is as efficient, has the same camaraderie between
all ranks, thus making a brotherhood which stands up to the
strains of war as well as the knocks of peacetime.
                                       Letter from Col. J. M. West,
                                              to Lt.-Col. Ulick Verney

HAVING finished the war on Armistice Day at Bavai on the road to
Mons and spent the winter in billets at Cheraing between Lille and
Tournai, on June 1st 1919 that great fighting corps and repository of
Rifle Brigade tradition, the 3rd Battalion, bade farewell to the village.
"Monsieur and Madame and Mademoiselle and the *petits*," the Battalion Letter recorded, "were all there to say goodbye as we marched
away to the tune of Ninety-five."* Of the original officers who had
sailed with it to France in August 1914 only the commanding officer,
Lt.-Colonel E. R. Kewley, D.S.O., M.C., and Captain L. E. K. Eastwood, M.C., the Quartermaster, were still with it. After crossing
from Antwerp to Tilbury, its remaining war-time personnel were
disbanded in June at the regimental home at Winchester, everyone
being struck off strength or proceeding on leave except the Adjutant
and Orderly Room Sergeant.

During the past six months the demobilisation of the vast khaki-
clad volunteer host which had broken the might of the *Wehrmacht*
had proceeded at ever accelerating speed as an unmilitary nation
returned as fast as possible to civilian life. Except for about half the
4th Battalion which, exiled in Salonica in 1915, was still on active
service on the shores of the Black Sea, trying to keep order in the
anarchical Russian-Turkish borderland, even the Regiment's Regular
battalions were all but denuded of officers and men. By February the
1st Battalion, before sailing in April from Dunkirk for home, was
down to two Companies, while the 2nd, quartered in Enghein in
Belgium until its return in the spring was so reduced in numbers

* *R.B.C. 1919*, 203.

that a fatigue party of sixteen left no men at all for church parade. As for the last surviving Service Battalions—the 11th, 12th, 13th and 16th—they melted away like snow.*

It was time to begin again. This involved teaching and learning. When at Christmas 1918 Vic Turner—just too young for the first World War and destined to become a V.C. in the second—was gazetted a 2nd Lieutenant in the Regiment, he received a printed letter marked "Private" from his commanding officer, Lt.-Colonel Alan Paley.

"Now that you have been gazetted to the Regiment, I should like to give you a few hints which may, I hope, be useful to you, and also to tell you something of our Regimental Customs.

"The Rifle Brigade is not a 'Line' regiment. In recognition of its services in the Peninsular War and at Waterloo, the 95th Rifles, by an Order in Council in 1816, was taken out of the Line and styled the Rifle Brigade. When brigaded with other regular Battalions on ceremonial parades, the Regiment stands on the left of the Line. Except in action and for special training purposes, such as musketry, arms drill, etc., we do not fix swords or slope arms. The order 'Attention' is not used in the Rifle Brigade. The order 'Party', 'Platoon', 'Company', 'Battalion', or 'Rifle Brigade' (if brigaded with other troops) is given, when any of the above units are to be called 'To Attention'. The above orders are preceded by the caution 'Stand to your front' if the troops are standing easy.

"The following expressions and titles are used in the Regiment:—

Rouse for Reveille.
Mess (or other) Horn for Mess (or other) Call.
Rifleman for Private.
Acting Corporal for Lance Corporal.
Acting Sergeant for Lance Sergeant.
Plain clothes for Mufti.
Swords for Bayonets.
Trousers for Slacks.

---

* *Seymour*, 371-5. On January 1st, 1920, even after refilling the ranks of the four Regular Battalions by young recruits, the Regimental State showed a decrease of 19,963 since January 1st, 1919. *R.B.C. 1919*, 242, 246.

"A roll is never called on parade. N.C.O.s are expected to know whether their men are present or otherwise without calling a roll.

"Except on parade, the only officer who is ever addressed as 'Sir' is the Commanding Officer. Never address a Field Officer in the Regiment as 'Major'.

"Never offer to stand a brother Rifleman a drink in a Rifle Brigade Mess.

"Rings are not worn.

"The Rifle Brigade does not carry colours.

"Foul and indecent language is punished very severely. It always entails a regimental entry.

"The band does not play returning from a funeral.

"Become a subscriber to the Rifleman's Aid Society as soon as possible.

"We *never* talk of a private soldier as a 'Tommy'. We Riflemen have far too much respect for the men in the ranks to give them such a common sounding name. We talk of our own men as Riflemen. Men in other regiments or branches of the service are spoken of as 'private soldiers'. *The interests of and care for his men and the very exact execution of all duties are the main considerations of an officer in the Rifle Brigade.*

"The comradeship which exists between Officers, N.C.O.s and Riflemen is a very marked characteristic of the Rifle Brigade. This comradeship must be fostered. It is one of the most important factors which help to maintain discipline of the right sort, i.e. a cheerful, ready and loyal obedience. An iron or Prussian system of discipline has never existed in the Regiment; we have never required it, because the traditions of the 95th Rifles, who helped to save Moore's Army in the retreat to Corunna, still remain with us.

"These traditions have also inspired a very great interest in the teaching of rifle shooting. The 95th Rifles was the first Regiment to be armed with the rifle, the Baker, a muzzle-loading, three-grooved rifle, which was issued to us in the Peninsula. The Rifle Brigade and our brother Riflemen of the King's Royal Rifle Corps are, and always have been, the best shooting regiments in the British Army.

"Your platoon should be to you what a pack of hounds is to its Master. The characteristics of each Rifleman in that platoon, his

good qualities and his weaknesses, should be known to you. His
training, his games, and his interests should be your continual
care. The welfare of your men must be your aim and object. If you
follow these principles, your men will love and respect you and
stand by you in battle. You will also play your part in maintaining
the glorious traditions of the Rifle Brigade.

"I hope that you will be very happy in the Rifle Brigade. You are
very fortunate indeed to be permitted by H.R.H. The Duke of
Connaught to belong to his Regiment. It is the finest Regiment in
the Army, and its record is second to none."

All this had to be imparted to the new entrant, whether officer or
private Rifleman. There is an account of the 2nd Battalion reforming
for the second time in a year—this time under peacetime conditions
—in the Battalion Letter to the Regimental Chronicle for 1919.

"It is no easy matter to describe the re-forming of the 2nd Battalion, such a series of pictures does it present, all different and yet
all succeeding one another in rapid succession and thus blending
into one continuous picture of progress from a disbanded cadre
and a pile of baggage at the Depot to a Battalion, far from complete it is true, but a Battalion all the same, with the spirit we all
hope and trust of the old 2nd Battalion. During the process of
evolution certain figures appear more prominently than others,
some for only part of the time, some for the whole time, and all
playing their particular role in the scene. There is Colonel
'Farmer'* with Anderson as Adjutant directing and supervising;
there is Alldridge, the veteran Quartermaster, performing not only
the herculean task of reproducing the order and exactitude of peace
from the chaos left by war, but also the even more valuable
function of bringing with him across the bridge with the past all
the spirit and traditions which are so near and dear to us."

For Major J. A. Alldridge, who had enlisted in 1885 and served with
the Battalion at Omdurman and Ladysmith, was an institution, to
whom the ways of behaviour, custom and speech of the Rifle Brigade
were the laws of the Medes and Persians. When, in the dark mid-
winter after the Somme, he rejoined the Battalion he had been received with joy. For with Alldridge about, noted the Regiment's
war historian, Brigadier-General William Seymour—himself an old

* Lt.-Col. (later Col.) W. E. Davies C.M.G., C.B.E.

2nd Battalion man—"the Battalion could be sure of getting at least its share of what was due. Also the never-failing joke could be begun again, the last-joined 2nd Lieutenant being always sent with the time-honoured request:—'Morning, Quarters, I want a Tommy's tunic and a pair of slacks, please.' The invariable answer was, 'I don't know who you mean by Quarters; my name's Alldridge; but if you want a Rifleman's jacket S.D. and a pair of trousers I daresay I've got some in my Stores!'"*

So "at the beginning," continued the 2nd Battalion Letter, "we see Lane creating interior economy, then Churcher bringing back the musketry spirit, Hanley the Regimental-Sergeant-Major, with an excellent team of W.O.s and N.C.O.s re-forming that absolutely invaluable stratum of N.C.O.s. Then appear Murray and Halloran re-establishing smartness and alertness by means of physical training and drill; and through it all we see the Company commanders and other older hands instructing and setting an example to the younger ones. . .

"The picture is always changing. At first we see a Battalion of New Army men gradually dwindling and finally going off, leaving a nucleus of very young, partly-trained recruits with everything to learn, yet taking in hand all the duties of a Battalion, and providing officers' servants, mess, police, sanitation, guards, etc. This lot of men is gradually replaced by others who meanwhile have been partly trained, in turn to be replaced by more, so that by degrees the whole advances in training and efficiency. . .

"The men, owing to their extreme youth, referred to one another as 'Boy'. 'Please, Sir, the other boy did it.' When the move to Aldershot took place, the W.O.s and N.C.O.s took off their coats and loaded the heavy baggage; for the men could not lift the heavy packages. On arrival, Alldridge and Lane swept out the Transport lines. Five days after our arrival it was found that the men were afraid to use the Recreation Room because with so much silver about (the Shields were out) they thought it could not be meant for them! At 2 p.m. (or 14.00 hours as we now call it) tomorrow's guard could be seen learning to present arms.

"Meanwhile recruits had been gradually arriving from the Depot, and what was of the greatest help, some older men. With the

* Seymour, 5-6; R.B.C. 1919, 193-4.

best of food, the recruits grew visibly; and with football, boxing, running and hockey, . . . combined with drill, physical training, etc., they improved out of all recognition . . .

"Now let us try and describe how this Phoenix emerged from the ashes of the old one which had flown from India to France and had been consumed in the furnace of war. After a brief spell at the Depot, we were ordered to Rugeley Camp on Cannock Chase. Now Rugeley has its bad points. In July it is as cold as it is in other places in March. It consists of condemned huts with no conveniences except to let the wind and rain into their interiors. It affords no accommodation for married people. But its drawbacks taken together constitute its one advantage, namely, it has no distracting influences. To this spot then, at the end of July, the embryo 2nd Battalion repaired and proceeded to re-form . . .

"The big event took place on 10th August when half the Reserve Battalion (some 500 strong) . . . picked up their packs, marched across the Square and became the 2nd Battalion, whilst the remaining half picked up their packs, sat down again and waited to become the 3rd Battalion . . . The 2nd Battalion was now a fairly solid affair, but it contained much demobilized personnel. While this slowly dwindled and finally disappeared altogether, recruits in small numbers, untrained and of small stature and age, came in from the Depot. However things went well, as Lane and Reeve and a small number of old hands of all ranks, such as the C.S.M.s of Companies, . . . got a very good move on, but we always had a serious shortage of old N.C.O.s and old Riflemen. On 25th August the Regimental Birthday came and went with customary honours. The Battalion was already beginning to catch the eye of the Brigade Staff."[*]

At this point, as had happened a century before when the Rifle Brigade returned from France after Waterloo, first industrial unrest at home and then political trouble in Ireland intervened. In the autumn of 1919 there was a railway strike, and the young Battalion, reinforced by two Companies from the 3rd, was despatched by lorry to Birmingham for its first "campaign". Here it took up its abode in a disused agricultural-show building whose bar—the officers' mess— was decorated by lists of vanished pre-war wines at pre-war prices

---

[*] *R.B.C. 1919*, 193-6. 2nd Bn. Record.

and notices of the sporting events of 1914. The young Riflemen settled down in their makeshift quarters like veterans, except that they left undrunk the cask of beer provided for them and went out instead on quarter-hour passes to buy buns and cakes. And, like their predecessors in strike-bound Glasgow a century before, they and their officers won the approval of the civic authorities and inhabitants who were "all very kind to them". The 4th Battalion—home at last that summer from far-away Tiflis for demobilisation, leave and new recruitment before embarking for India—provided its quota of volunteers for railway work. Captain Costobadie, M.C.—25-year-old veteran of Salonica and the Struma—"drove an engine over which he had a few minor troubles; such as overrunning Leicester Station a mile and then backing through it another mile too far. However, his passengers appear to have greatly appreciated his efforts, as one old lady presented him with half a crown."*

Back at Rugeley the pre-war officers of the 2nd Battalion resumed their task of instilling knowledge into the post-war ones, and its more experienced N.C.O.s that of teaching the young acting-corporals, N.C.O.s classes and Riflemen their duties. And the ex-schoolboy Riflemen began to grow in size and improve in discipline and turn-out. The Institutes, Sergeants' Mess and Corporals' Room resumed their former status; the pictures in the Officers' Mess, unearthed from war-time storage, were hung up, and the Mess plate put on display so that it became a place to which its members were not ashamed to invite friends and former officers of the Regiment. Yet just when musketry instruction had begun, and before there had been time to do any field-training, orders came to proceed at once to Ireland and everything had to be suspended. For there, with Sinn Fein waging guerilla war against the authorities, the Battalion found itself on "active service", and for the first month, with twenty-nine moves in thirty-one days, it was very active indeed. Its quarters in that time included schools, court-houses, a reformatory, a coast-guard station, a castle, a baker's shop, private houses, inns, bathing-machines, a workhouse, even a prison, where cells, specially designed to take one person unencumbered with kit, proved comfortless quarters for three Riflemen with all their belongings. The effect of all this and the campaigning against armed forays and ambushes which accompanied and followed it was curious. For while the young

* R.B.C. 1919, 209; 1922, 119.

soldiers rapidly gained experience of "moves" of all sorts and of detachment, patrol and sentry work, having had hardly any instruction in musketry and none in field work they found themselves applying principles to special conditions—the age-long function of Riflemen—without having been instructed in the principles themselves. They acquired experience of an advanced kind but had missed most of the elementary part of their education.*

However, they made do, and, in this, they proved themselves good Riflemen. Beating Irish gunmen at their own game, and doing so without injury or alienating the local community, was a kind of task for which the Rifle Brigade was particularly suited by its traditional expertise and its peculiar combination of social adaptibility, professional watchfulness and speed in action. Sent to western Donegal to support the outgunned and harassed Royal Irish Constabulary† and patrol approximately 2500 square miles of mountain and bog, it quickly established perfectly friendly relations with the inhabitants while keeping the local "baddies" so effectively under surveillance that, realising that they would get short shrift if they did, they gave very little trouble. This, the writer of the Battalion Letter to the 1920 Chronicle reported, "did not please the Sinn Fein leaders in the South.

"They sent for the local leader and, in response to his protest that nothing could be done with the troops in possession, they told him they would show him how to do it. They then sent up their expert 'Police Barracks Attacker' and a hundred men from the South. They mobilised the local contingents and put up innumerable road-blocks to prevent assistance being sent to Ardara, the barracks they proposed to reduce to ruins. In order to prevent any help being given by the platoon of 'C' Company at the other end of the village they posted two ambushes, one of twenty and one of ten men. (The platoon consisted of eighteen.) They then entered the Court-house, which was next to the police barracks, bored holes in the ceiling and roof and started on the roof of the barracks. The platoon then got suspicious and sent up a patrol (presumably the

---

* R.B.C. 1920, 151-2.

† Army Recruitment posters in Ireland at this time, with their invitation to "Join the Army and see the World", were often found in the morning to have been scrawled over with a further invitation to "Join the R.I.C. and see the Next!"

ambushers thought them too few to attack). The patrol reported and, as matters looked urgent, the acting-corporal in charge of the guard decided to act without waiting for the officer to get out of his pyjamas, and counter-attacked with nine men, which were all he had (apparently in this case the ambushers must have thought them too many to attack). Thereupon the whole 'expedition' fled. The nine Riflemen tried to surround the Court-House, but the attackers escaped by a ladder at the back. We fired twelve rounds and registered three hits, which was not bad considering we had done no musketry. We also captured some arms, ammunition, petrol and tools, and the Police barracks were saved! We had no more trouble after this incident."*

Having established peaceful conditions in West Donegal, the writer continued, " we were ordered to evacuate the western and occupy the eastern side of Donegal; this we did to the regret of most of its inhabitants. The behaviour of the men had been exemplary and had earned the genuine respect and admiration of the people. We left behind a good prestige and, if trouble is renewed, it will be due to the action of outside people coming in to stir it up." This, unfortunately, was what in the following year the British Government, under its mercurial Prime Minister, Lloyd George, did with its "Black and Tan" irregular gunmen.

The young Riflemen proved just as successful in East Donegal as in West. The early months of 1921, the writer of the Battalion Letter for that year recounted, " were spent in suppressing the activities of Sinn Fein ... with such good effect that, with a few exceptions, there were no attacks of any kind on our posts." In a rail ambush near Kincasslough,

"five Sinn Feiners were killed, but our casualties were nil ... In the Sinn Fein account they say they killed ten of our men and 'gallantly fought' their way out in spite of superior numbers. Company Sergeant-Major Bradley, who opened rapid fire with his rifle from the cab of the engine, was described as a Lewis gun! ... In March the Sinn Feiners burnt a bread-cart belonging to a loyalist in Strabane and were very surprised to find all the perpetrators arrested within 24 hours. They do not know to this day how it was done and so have not tried the experiment again . . . That our

* R.B.C. 1920, 156-7.

operations were successful there is no doubt, as all the 'bad' men either fled the country or went to the hills, and hence the neighbourhood was free of them except for flying visits when they came back and tried to stir up trouble, generally without success ... The local Company I.R.A. had announced that they would resist us to the last ditch, but cleared out on the approach of six men along the main road. Their women-folk were rather scathing about them."*

The 2nd was not the only Battalion of the Rifle Brigade sent to Ireland. The summons also came to the 3rd Battalion at the end of 1920 at Gosport. It was a mission most reluctantly undertaken, for it played havoc with the routine of training the young Riflemen, but, as the Battalion Letter put it, "though everyone relieved his feelings ... by a real good grouse, all ranks undertook their new and extremely unpleasant duty in a proper and cheery spirit as a good Rifleman should." Before they left for "the distressful country" they were visited by one of the oldest Riflemen of all, the 83-year-old Lord Ruthven, who had first joined the Battalion in India during the Mutiny and, before that, had served in the Crimea. During the 1914-18 war, though then in his seventies, he had visited France on several occasions as a King's Messenger and had contrived to get himself gazetted as a temporary major in his old Regiment. Spending with it what he expected to be—and was—his last Christmas on earth, "he accompanied Colonel Harrington round the Christmas dinners and attended church parade in his Rifle Brigade uniform, wearing his medals of the Crimea and the Great War, a rare and probably unique combination. His fine record and splendid appearance made a really valuable impression on a Battalion composed largely of young soldiers. He was extraordinarily active in his movements, and his appearance and bearing was that of a young man."†

Though the Irish Rebellion could scarcely be dignified by the name of war, it provided the young Riflemen with experience of bullets and explosives, "and so compensated in some ways for the dislocation in training and programmes it caused." There is an account in the Battalion's 1921 Letter describing how, while carrying out arms-searches in Dublin, these apprentices in the art of war gained some of this experience.

* *R.B.C. 1921*, 53-6.   † *R.B.C. 1920*, 216-17; *1921*, 118.

"Raids were not often attended with much success, though several important arrests were made. But on one occasion we were rewarded with the biggest haul yet made in Ireland. It consisted of 54 revolvers and automatic pistols, 54 swords, 14 rifles, 6 shot-guns, 10,739 rounds of rifle ammunition, 703 rounds of pistol ammunition, 127 shot-gun cartridges, 24 ordinance maps, 24 dirks with scabbards, an I.R.A. uniform and 10 green I.R.A. caps, 34 bombs, 8,993 detonators, 59 tubes of ammonite and 18 tins of other high explosives, as well as small items such as aluminium powder, Roman candles, rifles, bolts, tripods and gun-cases. The sight of the lorry returning with the swag was one to be remembered. The raiding party were all young soldiers immensely interested in the articles captured. Knee-deep in gelignite mixed with loose detonators, and shod in hob-nailed ammunition boots, they trampled about the lorry examining the different arms and throwing them down on the mass of high explosives rattling on the bottom of the lorry, which was driven at the usual break-neck speed, bumping over the cobbles of the Dublin streets. They were happy in their ignorance, for there were enough explosives there to blow up the whole of the Royal Dublin Show showgrounds."*

When after the Irish Treaty the Battalion, its work done—and wasted—"left the afflicted island", before it sailed in February 1922 for its new station at Gosport, the G.O.C. Dublin District described it, at a farewell inspection, as a Battalion with an excellent spirit and a fine body of officers, well-disciplined and exceptionally well turned out, the men very young and intelligent, keen in sport and exceptionally good at athletics. Though it still suffered from shortage of numbers, he said, it had all the makings of a first-rate Battalion."†

It was not to be. Even before it returned to England rumours were circulating that the Rifle Brigade's strength was to be reduced by half and its 3rd and 4th Battalions disbanded. "For a time," the Battalion Letter reported, "the prospect of disbandment was utterly discredited. It was thrust aside as a mere bugbear, and Buxton even suggested putting down a cellar of claret. But gradually the disturbing rumour rose like a moaning wind, causing widespread unrest and apprehension ... On Friday, March 10th, we heard in the evening that the warrant carrying it into effect had received the

* R.B.C. *1921*, 62-3, 70. † R.B.C. *1922*, 107.

royal signature ... The fate of every member of the Battalion hung in the balance, as the cadre was still to be maintained while the rest of the Battalion gradually drifted away. There was still room for the belief that the Government's commitments in various parts of the world and the possibility of future trouble might compel them to reconsider their act of vandalism ... On Sunday, 9th April, there was a ceremonial Church Parade, the whole Battalion attending, and the day afterwards Sir Henry Wilson"—the Field-Marshal and Colonel Commandant of the Battalion, who had just laid down his four years' task as Chief of the Imperial General Staff to represent the interests of his beloved Ulster in Parliament—"dined in Mess. During the course of a longish talk in the ante-room afterwards he reassured us by giving it as his opinion that the Battalion would some day, perhaps sooner than we expected, be re-embodied. It had been disbanded in 1818 after the Napoleonic wars to be re-embodied for the Crimean imbroglio, and history had a way of repeating itself."[*]

But, though, on the admission of almost every Brigade and Divisional Commander under whom the young Battalion had served, it was the best spirited and best disciplined unit in every place where it had been, on April 11th Colonel Harington, who had taken over command from Lt.-Colonel Kewley on the return to peace, took the final parade of the 3rd Battalion.[†] And two months later the brilliant Irish Field Marshal—the most famous Rifleman of his day—with his historic imagination and incurable optimism, was murdered by I.R.A. gunmen on the steps of his home in Eaton Place. The 4th Battalion, the other Rifle Brigade victim of the Geddes Axe and of a peace-loving nation's aversion to military expenditure, returned to England in May from Gibraltar to be disbanded at Gosport. Almost its last duty while on the Rock had been to parade at the funeral of that other great intellectual son of the Regiment, Willoughby Verner, who had died at his home at Algeçiras in January. "As soon as we arrived at Gosport disbandment began," ran the sad entry in the Battalion's Letter to the Chronicle he had founded and edited. "It was a dreary proceeding ... Officers and other ranks gradually

---

[*] *R.B.C. 1922*, 92. Because, when the Battalion had been re-formed in 1857, nothing had remained of the property and funds it had owned before being disbanded in 1818, its plate and other possessions were now vested under a trust deed in a committee of the Rifle Brigade Club, "in order to avoid coming to life again in such a way." *R.B.C. 1922*, 96.

[†] *R.B.C. 1922*, 91-3.

drifted away to leave, discharge and transfer to other Battalions or other Regiments, and the shutters were eventually put up on August 12th." "The disbandment of the 4th Battalion to me is like the loss of an old ship to a mariner," wrote Major, and former Quarter-master, Hone, now in his eightieth year, who had enlisted in it as a boy bugler on its formation in 1857. "Now that it has gone my thoughts must follow the 2nd Battalion in which my father served twenty-one years and in which I was born when the Battalion was stationed at Halifax, Nova Scotia, in November 1843."*

* * *

The Rifle Brigade was back where it had been in the long peace between its return from France after Waterloo and the Crimean War —a two now, instead of a four, Battalion Regiment. In a year its numbers had halved. Yet, though it no longer had to take its turn in the garrisoning of Ireland, the call for its services overseas had not grown less, but more; for the four years in which Europe had torn itself apart had left the rest of the world troubled and restless. Before it returned to England from India via Gibraltar for disbandment, the 4th Battalion had faced a war scare on the Afghan frontier and a sudden alarm—false as it turned out—that it was to go to Meso-potamia.† The 1st Battalion, re-formed after demobilisation, had already been hurried off in 1919 to that country where the Arabs, whom the British had liberated from the Turks, were in rebellion against both the British and one another. It was not a comfortable assignment, falling into the category into which Colonel—now General—Stephens had placed Kuldana in the Punjab as "of the many infernal spots chosen by Government for marooning troops hard to equal." The temperature in that desert land varied between dawn and midday by as much as 60 degrees, reaching a maximum of 125 degrees in the tents in August and falling to 20 degrees below

* R.B.C. *1923*, 128; *1922*, 111-12.
† "In July we received the somewhat staggering information that the Battalion was to proceed to Mesopotamia . . . Everyone felt rather downhearted at the prospect of such a change for the worse. However, in the middle of December a cable was received from Messrs. Simonds, the brewers, stating that the Battalion was going to Gibraltar and requesting that they should have the contract for supplying beer . . . A fortnight later the official information came that we really had escaped Mesopotamia . . . Life assumed a rosier aspect at once, as anyone who had ever been there said nothing but good about Gibraltar!" R.B.C. *1921*, 73.

freezing in November. It was a time for the Riflemen of endless marching through flat, barren country under most trying conditions, "with no excitements, no loot, continual load and unload," trying even to the most patient, "coupled," as the Battalion Letter put it, "with the feeling that, however justified or not the Arab may have been in his rising, he was getting off extremely lightly for all the trouble and damage he had caused."[*] The fact that, in their weary, dusty, fly-pestered foot-slogging, they were walking in biblical steps and doing what the Roman legions had once done was little consolation. Nor, with their bugles blowing, was the romance of marching—the first time a British Regiment had ever done so— into Kerbala, "the third holiest city in the Mahomedan world famed for its golden mosques."

Yet they would not have been Riflemen if they had not found compensations even in that barren land. Stationed in what the writer of the Sergeants' Letter described as "a little dump of a place called Jaiji," where the only view was a dreary foreground of mule lines and incinerators set against a desert,

"with the philosophy which characterizes the soldier all over the world we not only made the best of a bad business but so ordered things as to make our stay there enjoyable. Games were to be had in plenty; hockey, football and even cricket, not only amongst ourselves but with neighbouring native regiments who never failed to make us go 'all out'. What we liked most, however, was to meet a team of our own officers. These games usually contained a humorous element, and still fresh in the memory of most of us is the spectacle of Sergeant Bidlake crouching in fear and trembling (and a top hat!) in a vain endeavour to keep goal against the furious onslaughts of Captain H. M. R. Fairfax-Lucy, very ably supported by our gallant Quartermaster."[†]

As usual, too, the Regiment contrived to make human contacts with the more friendly of the remote peoples among whom they found themselves. "It would be unfair to leave the subject of Baghdad without mention of one of our most welcome visitors," the Sergeants' Letter for 1921 recalled, "a veritable Sinbad coming from goodness knows where and departing whither no one knew. Familiarly known as 'Baghdad', . . . he would blow into our mess,

[*] R.B.C. 1920, 144-7.   [†] R.B.C. 1922, 72, 1st Battalion Sergeants' Letter.

having walked presumably a distance of some thirty miles, and regale us with stories of his wonderful feats in every country of the world, bringing with him, as a sort of offering, numerous 'precious' stones which he had gathered from the river bed. Those of us who knew him will recall with pleasure the wonderful self-confidence and disarming audacity of this charming old scallywag."*

When, in January 1921, its mission accomplished, the Battalion was about to embark for its new station in India, at the last moment it was deflected—at 2 a.m. in the morning—to Zubait, ten miles from Basra, on account of an Arab raid on the town. "After this last episode, typical of so many others," it was reported, "we were all heartily glad to see the last of the Arabs."† A year later, when the 1st Battalion was at Cawnpore, the 2nd Battalion, having bidden farewell to Ireland, was packed off to Chanak in the Gallipoli Straits at a moment's notice for what turned out to be a confrontation with the Arabs' former oppressors, the Turks. With these the Prime Minister, Lloyd George, heedless of the now strongly pacific feelings of his countrymen, had become righteously embroiled over Kemal Pasha's non-observance of the peace treaties. "We arrived at Chanak about midday on October 7th," the Battalion Letter recounted, "after a most peaceful voyage during which we received no news of any sort. It was something of a shock when we were told that the Colonel and Company commanders were to go off at once and reconnoitre the front line on the Asiatic side, while the Battalion had to disembark at once at Kilia on the European side and be prepared to cross to Chanak at six that evening and give battle to the Turks. As we had only two old barges to do it in, it was somewhat of an undertaking, but luckily the Turks did not declare war that night!"

Having crossed to the Asian shore, where it was confronted by far superior forces, the Battalion was in a very tricky spot while the international crisis lasted.

"The 'local' situation at this time was extraordinary as our 'Front Line' consisted of a series of posts behind a so-called 'line' or wire which ran through the scrub. In some cases the wire did not exist at all or was only one strand thick and that strand probably lying on the ground. There appeared to be about four Turkish sentries to each one of ours, and in places where the wire was down, if our

* R.B.C. 1921, 74. 1st Battalion Sergeants' letter to the Editor.   † R.B.C. 1921, 43-4.

sentry moved away, the Turks' sentries would come forward and then refuse to go back, saying first that they had not crossed our wire and then, when the wire was pointed out, saying that that was merely a strand and did not count. As we had to avoid any 'incident' at all costs, we were not allowed to deal with them in a riflemanlike manner, which was more than annoying. As Follett once reported, 'according to latest instructions I have used tact rather than force.' As we were not able to work on our defences in case it might hinder the smooth working of the Mudania Conference, the situation became more and more exasperating, but any incident was avoided, and this reflected the greatest credit on all and was the subject of a Special Order of the day by the Commander-in-Chief.

"On 11th October news was received that the Conference had come to an agreement, and that no more work was to be done on our defences, and on the night of the 13th-14th the Turks withdrew from the Brigade Front. This was a great relief to us, as one was in exactly the same false position that we were in on many occasions in Ireland, in that we were not allowed to use force to stop the Turks from doing anything and always had to 'reason' with them."*

During all this time, the good sense and moral strength of the Battalion commander, Lt.-Colonel Harington—who seven years before had led the 4th Battalion in the inferno of Second Ypres—deeply impressed everyone. "Apart from our deep affection and respect for him as a friend and brother officer, his calm and unflurried outlook on the Turkish situation, when everybody else was in a constant state of nerves, made the whole difference to the efficiency and well-being of the Battalion."†

As usually happened with the Rifle Brigade, some comic relief was provided by a local Turkish fire-brigade, which, arriving on the scene of a fire four hours too late, "were deeply distressed to find no water available; their effect on the morale of the troops was incalculable." But when, after nearly a year guarding the historic frontier between Europe and Asia the Battalion left for England on August 25th, 1923—the Regimental Birthday—it was generally agreed that the best view of Chanak was "through the bottom of a glass on a boat heading due west."‡

* *R.B.C. 1922*, 82-4.　　† *R.B.C. 1923*, 68.　　‡ *R.B.C. 1923*, 68-70.

Gradually regimental and national life returned to normal, with half the Rifle Brigade serving abroad and half at home. For nearly a decade the much-travelled 2nd Battalion remained in England. Only once in that time did it look as if it might be called upon to face the ultimate test for which regiments and armies exist, and this happily, as at Chanak, proved a false alarm. In 1926 the industrial bitterness which had divided the nation ever since the War came to a head in a General Strike in support of the miners. The 2nd Battalion at Aldershot was then enjoying one of those periods of comparative ease and routine in comfortable quarters, with plenty of sport and games and reasonable periods of home leave, which every now and then came the way of the peacetime soldier. "The hunting and horse-racing were all safely over, company training had come and gone, . . . and at the beginning of May the stage was set for the annual musketry course, . . . and we were determined to engage the 2nd 60th in mortal combat for the shooting honours of the year. Everyone expected a ding-dong fight and every soul in the Battalion was out to win. After three days' shooting it became painfully clear that the miners were really going to carry out their threat to strike." On Saturday May 1st the T.U.C. decided to call a General Strike to begin at midnight on Monday. At that moment the country was faced with a head-on confrontation between the Government and organised labour, and violence and bloodshed and even civil war seemed inevitable.

Thanks to a Prime Minister who combined a capacity for standing firm on first principles with a genius for reconciling instead of exacerbating ideological and party differences, the nine days' strike ended in a bloodless acceptance by everyone of the rule of law. Yet this seemed far from likely on the afternoon of Saturday May 1st, when the Quartermaster and Adjutant sat down to frame some orders for an immediate move of the Battalion.

"It was not a moment too soon, for that evening orders came from the Brigade that we were almost certain to move on Monday. Next day brought orders to move by lorry to Catterick at 8 o'clock the day after, and during the afternoon a motley collection of charabancs rolled up together with some derelict-looking lorries for the baggage. Except for four R.A.S.C. lorries the vehicles and drivers were all civilians, and the position was not made . . . easier

by the fact that they were under the impression that they were
only engaged to bring the vehicles to Aldershot, whereas in reality
they were to drive off into the blue with the troops. They had no
kit whatever, and all things considered bore up amazingly well.

"The authorities did not take the great decision so early as 8
o'clock on Monday. And everyone hung about with nowhere to
go, with all the married families parading the Queen's Avenue and
evidently fearing the worst. At last we were ordered to move at
2.10 p.m. and the convoy started off . . . We careered along through
Reading, over the Thames at Shillingford . . . and fetched up for
the first night in a field close to Dorchester. No evening could be
more peaceful as we sat and shivered round our camp fire, and it
was not till long afterwards that we heard that pandemonium had
reigned that night in the married quarters, where rumours were
current that showers of missiles had struck the convoy in Reading,
where barbed wire was up in the street and forty casualties had
occurred. The next day we started at 7.30 in the morning and soon
were going through Oxford—'queer place this,' a Rifleman was
heard to say, 'all churches and no pubs'—then on through Banbury, . . . Rugby . . . and Leicester. At Leicester we skirted the town
by a by-pass road, as trouble was feared; however no signs of
hostility could be noticed. That night . . . we stopped in a field . . .
half way between Leicester and Newark. Next day we were faced
with a trip of over one hundred miles and again we rose with
the lark, paid for the field (not without a disagreement as to the
value of the field as a lodging) and set off again over the Trent at
Newark and through Retford and Doncaster. The towns were quiet
as if it were Sunday, shops opening in a half-hearted way, the
workless slouching about in their stiff Sunday suits, the rails rusty
and the chimneys smokeless. Presently the north wind began to
blow as we crossed into Yorkshire in the cold bitter rain. On and
on up the Great North Road we went till about half past six in the
evening we arrived at Catterick Bridge, where guides from the
Royal Signals met us and guided us to A Lines, an old war-time
camp which had not been touched since. And this was to be our
home for five months."

Apart from a room in the Garrison Club for the Commanding
Officer, the only officers' quarters available were two rooms in a hut,

christened by them the Senior and Junior Dormitories. "It would have needed an old Dutch master," wrote one of them, "to do justice to the nightly scene in the dorm. It took two hours to go to bed, and sleep was impossible till the last raconteur had come to the end of his story. The old 1st Battalion sweats compared it to Mesopotamia. The old 3rd Battalion sweats compared it to Ballsbridge. The old 4th Battalion sweats compared it to Chaman. But we think it will be agreed that Catterick may take a worthy place with Strabane, Stranorlar, Chaman, Cherat, Chanak and Chardakly." "The buildings we had been allotted," the Sergeants reported in their letter to the Regimental Chronicle, "certainly had been a mess at some period: windows out, not a door would shut and no fireplaces. However we fixed things up and got going."*

This capacity for making the best of things and extracting amusement from it was characteristic of the Rifle Brigade. Owing to the stubbornness of the miners, who remained on strike when abandoned by their Trades Unions comrades, the 2nd Battalion spent the whole summer in its comfortless quarters amid the northern cold and rain, without leave or entertainment and separated from its wives and families. "There we are," wrote the 1926 Chronicle's contributor, "all the time wondering how much longer we are to be here and purchasing stoves," which, like the panes of missing glass for its windswept huts, the War Office refused to supply. In September a detachment was posted to Strensall, which was a great improvement, as "there were some excursions to Leeds for the Test Match and also to Scarborough where the attractions were more varied. Your correspondents are, of course, discretion itself, but they believe that at least one reveller had to be reminded that Scarborough is not Constantinople."†

Relief came unexpectedly in the second week of October when orders were received to entrain at Richmond for Colchester. "The course of troop trains never runs smoothly, and our engine changed when we reached the main line. The new engine was taken ill at York, but a man in a bowler hat fetched another one which could only take us to Doncaster because it was busy. Our new engine at Doncaster took us to March where a very poor sort of herring-gutted engine took us in tow, but was in turn taken ill at Stowmarket with some obscure complaint which brought all sorts of people out to

* R.B.C. 1926, 66-9.   † R.B.C. 1926, 74.

shake their heads at it . . . Eventually the thing started again, but forty-five minutes late so that we were held up for half an hour more at Manningtree while boat-trains from Harwich and business-men's expresses from Clacton fizzed by. Then, as we crept into Colchester in the twilight it began to rain, with the result that under the arc lamps in the fog the General could have seen but little of the care with which we had creased our trousers and polished our boots. The Suffolks' band played us through the town, but the dreary wet evening drove away the young ladies of Colchester who should have been there in their best, looking out for prospective partners in the dance. Still it was Colchester, and there was hot supper and a good night's sleep."*

By now the young Riflemen of both Battalions had become ex-perienced, skilful and toughened soldiers, worthy of their famous predecessors. In India the corporals of the 1st Battalion in their newly-issued green walking-out dress prided themselves that they were "quite the smartest-dressed corporals in the sub-continent", and an inspecting General declared that the turn-out of all ranks, their steadiness on parade and general alertness and the precision with which ceremonial movements were carried out were "well up to the high standards of this distinguished corps."† When the Regiment's dedicated septuagenarian Colonel-in-Chief, that kindly royal perfectionist, the Duke of Connaught, visited the 2nd Battalion at Colchester, he was delighted to find that the marching and steadiness on parade were as good as ever and that "the general turn-out was excellent and showed that every man had taken real trouble to appear as smart and clean as a Rifleman should."‡

Already the Rifle Brigade had re-established its astonishing primacy in musketry; between 1923 and 1939 each of its Battalions won nine out of sixteen times, both in England and India, the Blue Riband of Army team shooting—the Queen Victoria Trophy. In 1926 Regimental Sergeant-Major Bill Apsey, D.C.M., won the King's Medal at Bisley for the best shot in the Army, and in 1931 Lieutenant Edward King-Salter did likewise, having in the previous year gained Third Place in the Army Revolver Championship, which Lieutenant des Graz had won before him in 1929. 1930 was for the 2nd Battalion an *annus mirabilis*, winning as it did the Queen Victoria Trophy for

---

* *R.B.C. 1926*, 82-3. 2nd Bn. Letter to the Editor.
† *R.B.C. 1923*, 44, 66.   ‡ *R.B.C. 1927*, 65-6.

the fourth consecutive year and the seventh time in eight years, the Royal Irish Cup for the second year running, the King George V Cup for the fourth consecutive year, and the new Company Shield for the first time. 1935 was equally remarkable, when the Regiment achieved the unique record of having the winners of all three classes in the Army Championship, and when Sergeant Pearce, like Bill Apsey before him, won both the Army Championship and the Roberts cup. So numerous and persistent were its successes at the Army Rifle Association's meetings that someone suggested that, having so often depleted the Association's funds for prize money, the least it could do was to make some contribution to them.*

The Regiment's record in intellectual achievement was almost as impressive. Though entry to the Staff College was now highly competitive and dependent on a very high level of attainment, in only one year between 1919 and 1937 was the Rifle Brigade without at least one student. Usually it had two; in 1921 it had three and in 1920 four. From 1930 to 1933 the Chief Instructor at the College was the future Field Marshal, Henry Maitland Wilson—"Jumbo" to the Regiment—who had previously commanded the 2nd Battalion. Another Rifleman, General Sir Reginald Stephens—the "Stiff'un"—who had been Wilson's first Company Commander when he joined the 2nd Battalion in South Africa, was Commandant of the Royal Military College, Sandhurst, from 1919 till 1923. Later, after commanding the 4th Division, he became Director General of the Territorial Army. Many of those who should have had high command in the 'twenties and 'thirties, like Johnny Gough and George Thesiger and, among younger soldiers, Billy Congreve, had fallen in battle, while that Bayard among soldiers and Riflemen, General Sir Walter Congreve— "Old Concrete" to the men who served under him—having won golden opinions by his handling of the VII Corps in the March retreat, was suffering from chronic ill-health as a result of excessive exposure during the War. Successively G.O.C. in Syria, Egypt and Southern Command, in 1924, in the hope of regaining his health, he accepted the appointment of Governor and Commander-in-Chief, Malta, where he died in February, 1928. But though both he and Henry Wilson were lost to the Army, their place in the 'thirties was taken by another brilliant Rifleman, "Jock" Burnett-Stuart, G.O.C. British Troops in Egypt from 1930 to 1934 and of

* R.B.C. 1929, 326-7; 1930, 66; 1932, 159-65; 1935, 145-9.

Southern Command from 1934 to 1938. His four years' spell at Southern Command, with Archibald Wavell as his Chief of Staff, was described as "one of the most formidable concentrations of lively, original and profound military thought that had ever been put into one peacetime Headquarters." In the opinion of many—including the future Field Marshal Montgomery of Alamein, who described him as "the most brilliant general in the Army"*—he should twice have been chosen as Chief of the Imperial General Staff. Unfortunately, like Henry Wilson before him, Burnett-Stuart had the kind of imaginative genius and impatience with rule-of-thumb, combined with a caustic wit, which aroused the distrust of more mediocre seniors, though his subordinates loved him for his humanity, charm and refreshing freedom from pomposity.†

There were other men of outstanding talent who had served in the Regiment in war but, not being Regulars, won distinction in non-military fields. Among them were Henry Williamson, the novelist and naturalist, author of *Tarka the Otter*, Eric Kennington, the painter and sculptor, whose portrait of Sergeant Edwards of the 3rd Battalion was one of the best known pictures of the First World War; Reginald Berkeley, author of the first volume of the Regimental War History whose play, *French Leave*, was one of the outstanding stage successes of the 'twenties, and C. A. Bennett, who had fought with the 16th Battalion in France and was the first Rifleman ever to become a High Court judge.‡ Another former Rifleman, Major the Hon. Lionel Tennyson, captained England at cricket in 1921; when he died it was written of him that "he boomed through life like a great gust of wind, and many, far more than he could know, will miss the sound."§

Perhaps the most remarkable, certainly the strangest, of the careers pursued by ex-Riflemen was that of A. L. de Mosley Mynn, who had been a sergeant in the Regiment in India in the 'eighties and

---

* "It has always been a mystery to me why this outstanding soldier, with a quick and clear brain, was not made C.I.G.S. in 1933 . . . The Army would have been better prepared for War in 1939 if he had been." *The Memoirs of Field Marshal Lord Montgomery of Alamein*, 39.

† *R.B.C. 1958*, 67-9. Sir Henry Wilson, too, though distrusted and resented by many of his slower-minded seniors and equals, made a strong appeal to youth. To Billy Congreve, he "was like a sort of delightful whirlwind; I do admire him more than anyone I know." *The Congreves*, 267.

‡ Another, Lord Hailsham, is, at the time of writing, Lord Chancellor.

§ *R.B.C. 1951*, 145-6.

who, when his time was finished, joined the Bombay police, subsequently prospecting for rubies in Burma, where he had fallen ill and been nursed and befriended by a Burmese priest or Poongi. Afterwards in gratitude he had donned the yellow robe and become his benefactor's disciple and, when the latter died, commuted his police pension and set up a dispensary in a cluster of small whitewashed mud-huts near the great bridge over the Ganges at Benares, where, with the herbs he grew in his compound, he ministered to the sick and needy. "No one," wrote Colonel Sir William Prescott-Westcar, who encountered him in India after the War, "would have thought that this simple little Buddhist dispensary would have aroused the hatred and envy of the rich Brahmin priests whose temples were covered with offerings brought from every part of India. Yet so it was, and, after their fiat had gone forth, none dared come for treatment . . . because the Poongi was one of the Ghora-log —the white people. Even the poor, who had been tended with a care and love that would never have been given them by one of their own countrymen, dared no longer show their gratitude by the few simple offerings they had been accustomed to give and which had kept the simple Poongi's body together." In the end, victim of racialist and priestly intolerance, he was forced to give up and seek the assistance of his old Regiment to enable him to return to his native land.*

To a greater or lesser degree, adventuring and going "all out to win", whether in matters great or small, was part of the true Rifleman's make-up. So Lieutenant Frankie Festing, the future Field Marshal, who had been gazetted to the 3rd Battalion at the end of 1921 and had served with the 2nd Battalion at Chanak, spent one leave in the remoter part of the Balkans, sitting up all night on cushionless wooden seats in the Mittel-Europa Express in order to get there on a subaltern's pay.† During another leave he sailed the Atlantic as one of the crew of the 44 ton yacht *Jolie Brise* in the Bermuda race from Plymouth to New York. Another officer, Captain F. O. Cave, M.C.—who, after a distinguished career in two world wars was to become a Monsignor of the Roman Catholic Church—

---

* *R.B.C. 1949*, 177-8.

† *R.B.C. 1929*, 226-37; *1932*, 176-95. On his Balkans journey he stayed at Kishinev, the capital of Bessarabia, "quite a large city, . . . unlike anything to be met with in Western Europe and consisting of miles and miles of thatched mud hovels with streets . . . which seemed to perform the treble duty of pigstye, sewer and children's playground."

helped to explore and map the Shaksgam valley, traversing, at altitudes of over 18,000 feet, a succession of mountain glaciers where no European had ever set foot before, and filling in one of the last blanks in the Ordnance Survey of India.*

Other Riflemen, in search of adventure in those peaceful years between the two world wars, volunteered for what was known as "scallywag soldiering", getting themselves seconded to such fine colonial units as the King's African Rifles and teaching the elements of their Rifleman's craft to tribal Africans or Somali Camel Corps.† Another field for such out of the run-of-the-mill soldiering was Mesopotamia where Captain Callum Renton, lately Adjutant of the 3rd Battalion, was D.A.A.G. to the Iraq Levies, training, among others, the Assyrians—"a cheery race and extraordinarily enthusiastic soldiers, far and away the finest fighting race in the country, . . . who will serve under no-one except British officers." "Such service brings responsibility one seldom gets in regimental soldiering," wrote Lt.-Col. Lord Lytton, who, as a subaltern, served with the King's African Rifles from 1922 to 1927; "an officer soon learns to make decisions for himself on every conceivable subject, instead of walking across the barrack square and consulting the C.O. or the Adjutant."‡

More usually adventuring for the Rifle Brigade officer took the form, at home, of hunting,§ horse-racing and steeple-chasing, and, overseas, of big game shooting. "The approach of the leave season," the 1st Battalion's 1929 letter from Jullundur reported, "saw various officers off on shooting trips: Wilbraham to Kashmir, Cave and Garmoyle to the Central Provinces, Renton to Kashmir on a trip to Ladak." "During May and June," it added next year, "Cave and Rogers betook themselves to the Central Provinces, their main object

---

* R.B.C. 1926, 195-8.

† "On the whole the Somali soldier is a lovable creature, though he wants knowing, and it is seldom that anything derogatory is heard or said about him by anyone who has experience of him . . . In temperament volatile and quarrelsome and often engaged in some interminable tribal blood feud, spurred on . . . by his womenfolk who are the root cause of half the crime and trouble in Somaliland, he makes a good soldier." R.B.C. 1933, 231-2.

‡ R.B.C. 1957, 124; 1926, 204-10; 1933, 231-2.

§ Never so exciting as in Ireland during the "Troubles". "At the tail end of the hunting season we had some great days with the Strabane Harriers. Everyone who could get a horse went, irrespective of whether they could ride or not or the horse could jump. The results were, needless to say, most amusing." R.B.C. 1922, 87. 2nd Battalion Letter.

being tigerland . . . When later Cave returned to England, many a tiger must have breathed a sigh of relief when the news of his departure filtered through the jungles of the Central Provinces."* Even the Sergeants' Mess, after a lecture on Shikar by one of the officers, formed a gun-club shoot and spent many a happy day after buck and boar in the jungle and duck on the neighbouring jheels. "A shooting holiday," one of them wrote, "is the finest holiday a soldier can have to break the monotony of cantonment life."†

When the 1st Battalion's turn came to leave India, its first station, the Sudan, offered a wonderful wealth of game for its young officers' guns—"lion, buffalo, elephant, hippopotamus, roan, reedbuck, giraffe, water-buck, gazelle, oribi, . . . tiang, duiker, serval cat, genet cat, crocodile, giant eland, harte beest, situtunga, warthog."‡ It was from this station that a few months earlier an officer of the Battalion, Captain R. D. Baird, during its brief stay there on its way back to England from India, contrived to find time for a quick expedition to Equatorial Africa. "Our camp here," he wrote of one night's halt, "was a delightful one, right down close beside the river, hidden in the deep shade of some real trees. Birds of many colours rioted amongst the branches and occasional gazelle would wander down from the far bank to drink, baboons barked their indignation at our presence, and from time to time a wary old crocodile would break the surface of the water with an inquisitive and inquiring eye." Nor was it only the animal world which unfolded its wonders. "As we reached the village and passed through it, suddenly from all sides burst out the ululations and cries of the women. They were invisible, hidden within the stockaded compounds of their houses, but from all sides came that high-pitched, liquid, long-drawn, primitive cry, to which our men gave full-throated answer, at the same time throwing their rifles up into the air and catching them again to show their strength."§ The same Riflemanlike interest and delight in the natural world around him animated Captain Vic Turner when, arriving with the Battalion a little later in the year, he made friends on a shooting trip up the White Nile with the Nuers of Nyong, "a most charming tribe of starknaked, smiling savages, who were most willing to help in any way they could."¶

* *R.B.C. 1929*, 52; *1930*, 52, 55.   † *R.B.C. 1925*, 273-81.   ‡ *R.B.C. 1933*, 221.
§ *R.B.C. 1933*, 191.   ¶ *R.B.C. 1933*, 214-17.
J.G.   x

It was this traditional, almost hereditary, talent of the Regiment for establishing an accord with all sorts and conditions of men—and doing so with humanity and humour—which made it in peace, wherever it happened to be, a calming and moderating influence. Before its eleven years' spell of duty in India ended, the 1st Battalion had several opportunities to show what it could do to calm inflamed passions. "We have passed yet another year in Peshawar in peaceful vigilance," its correspondent informed the Chronicle on New Year's Day, 1926, "there have been many alarums but no excursions. The Mohmands have kept quiet in their hills. The Maliks of the Khyber have taken their rewards for building the railway through their country with an ill grace but no violence. A successor to the old Mian Gull of Swat was, contrary to expectation peacefully installed, and the Mohammedans in the city have managed to hate the Hindus on all possible occasions without intervention by us."* Four years later, after the Peshawar riots had revealed to the civil and military authorities the strength and violence of the passions the Congress Movement could arouse, a platoon of the 1st Battalion, stationed at Jullundur, had to be sent to Amritsar to quell an expected riot which never happened, "All," it was reported, "passed off peaceably . . . The air at this time was full of wild rumours. On one occasion the Colonel" —Henry Maitland Wilson—"and Whiteley drove to Hoshiapur, armed to the teeth, on the receipt of a report of grave disorder in the town, only to find that a resident had tired of his wives and mistresses and had slain them all. As the number of these ladies was abnormally large, it was small wonder that the town was much stirred by this show of anti-feminism."†

In the following year, to counter Congress activities, the Government of India decided to send out during the cold weather small columns of troops on scattered marches throughout the country "to show that the British Lion was still alive. On one of these marches," Captain Baird, who took part in it, recalled, "the Rifle Brigade was ordered to proceed through a country where no British troops had ever been before . . . As soon as the date of our march and its direction was known, Renton as Mess President and Turner as Adjutant‡ rushed over to Amritsar by car to interview the legal authorities . . .

---

* R.B.C. 1925, 41.   † R.B.C. 1930, 51-2.

‡ Ten and twelve years later, these two officers were to command the Battalion, one at Beda Fomm and the other at Alamein—the two most important victories of the Desert War.

The first march was along the Grand Trunk Road to Kartapur, a distance of fourteen miles via Jullundur city. The city took not the slightest interest in us except for the Commissioner who came out to wish us good luck."

"*2 February*. If the previous day had proved to be a dull one, this more than made up for it. It was a warm, cloudy morning, and we marched to Batala, a distance of eight miles, turning off the road to pass through Masanian at Jaffa's request, as it was his village. At Masanian we received a magnificent reception. Bombs, rockets, guns and every conceivable form of noise-producing instruments were let off in our honour, while each man was given some oranges as he marched through. The Colonel, Baird and Turner had to dismount, be formally received and then led off to 'breakfast.' This meal consisted of oranges, very strong black tea, and a large slab each of the wettest, stickiest chocolate cream cake ever seen. Doubtless it was meant as a great kindness, but, as we had kippers for our real breakfast half an hour before, only being very fit and in good training enabled us to survive. This meal was given to us in a courtyard, in front of a mosque of singular beauty. It was very old, and the whole of the front wall was covered with blue and green tiles of exquisite colour and in a splendid state of repair, the tiles themselves being decorated with extracts from the Koran and very artistic patterns. This meal finished, the march to Batala continued without incident, though the road was very bad. Batala itself was the largest town that we visited . . . During the summer of 1930 it was a hot-bed of Congress agitation, and, though by February 1931, the general situation had greatly improved there, there was a distinct under-current of latent ill-will.

"At the outskirts of Batala the Battalion was halted before a triumphal arch while an address of welcome was read and every officer in turn was garlanded, and from there on to our camp, about a couple of miles, a succession of triumphal arches was passed through, more and more garlands were fastened round officers' necks, reception committees bobbed up at every conceivable spot, and no less than six native bands blasted their discordant, but doubtless loyal, music to high heaven.

". . . All the English inhabitants of Batala visited the camp during the afternoon to listen to the band, as did various Indian notables from the country round about. One of these latter bitterly denounced the Round Table Conference and roundly maintained that the English were mad, since they appeared to be bent on taking the government of the country away from the ruling classes and handing it over to petty lawyers and babus. That evening Tehesildar appeared and requested that the Colonel would write out for him the following two appreciations for his further use. They are given in full and exactly as written.

"*Sirdar Iqbal Singh Tehesildar of Batala comes of Punjab chief's family. He has got very splendid record at his back and has got wonderful influence in his Tehesil. We met with a very nice reception. If such like Tehesildar is in service there is every belief of good management and administration in the village. He was Recruiting Officer during the Great War and did excellent work in War Loans etc. He requires special distinction at the hands of Govt: for his loyalty and devotion for the Crown. There are very rare officers like him to whom we come in contact with.*"

And the second one:—

"One letter may be sent to E. M. Jenkins, Deputy Commissioner, Gurdaspur . . .

"*Dear Mr Jenkins, I am much grateful to you for deputing such nice and influential officer like Sirdar Iqbal Singh Tehesildar with my Battalion during the march in your district. We were afforded hearty receptions everywhere we passed during a week time sojourn, for the Battalion was entertained in each place. I would say that you would kindly recommend him for the distinction of Rai Sahib which he richly deserves.*

". . . and something more which Colonel Sahib may wish to write."

"*5 February.* It was again bitterly cold in the early morning and it remained chilly all day . . . We were followed all the way by every local notable for miles around, mounted on every sort of creature which possessed four legs and could possibly be called a horse. They were all in great heart, laughing and joking all the way, announcing that they were the 'Beas light cavalry,' and, at times, seriously getting mixed up with the troops who were trying to march."

"Such," ended Captain Baird, "was our 'Flag March'. Everybody who went on it was, on the whole, glad to have done it, though few would want to repeat it. It certainly showed everybody a side of Indian life and an outlook into Indian character such as normal barrack and cantonment life never gives a man a chance to see. There was much that was interesting in it, not a little that was distinctly entertaining and some that was very boring. As to whether it was a real success in so far as the local village people were concerned, we were not, of course, in a position to judge; but, from the friendly way in which we were received wherever we went, and the subsequent written appreciation sent us by the Punjab Government, we hope and have reason to feel that it may have been."[*]

Eighteen months later, at 3 p.m. on Monday, November 2nd, the Battalion, still at Jullundur, was suddenly given orders to entrain by 8.30 that evening for Jammu in Kashmir, where grave communal riots had broken out between the Hindu State authorities and the Moslem population, supported and incited by fellow Mohammedans from other parts of India who had invaded the country in armed bands or *jathas* wearing red shirts. The Battalion, after receiving further orders en route at Lahore, reached Jammu on the morning of November 4th and pitched camp in the Municipal Gardens, with the officers' mess in a cricket pavilion. "We were to restore order and confidence and generally take charge." A conference between the commanding officer, Lt.-Col. Moore-Gwyn, and the civic authorities revealed, according to the Battalion Letter, that "there was precious little authority being wielded by anyone."

"When we arrived the streets were deserted except for a few police patrols and State Force piquets, all shops were shut, and there were plentiful signs of looting, especially in the grain market where the street was littered with stones and the contents of many sacks. It soon appeared that the city was not going to be the only bit of trouble.

"The Red Shirts, as they appeared at the frontier, had been rounded up and collected in a poorly wired cage about five miles away known as Satwari jail. There were by now about five thousand of them, mostly old men and young boys, but quite capable of causing trouble owing to the fact that they had been given

[*] *R.B.C. 1931*, 60-83.

neither food nor blankets. Jenkins went down and talked to them. They expressed their great admiration for his honour's good self, but intimated that, if blankets and food were not forthcoming, they could not be held responsible for their actions . . .

"The first sight of the city was disappointing to anyone who had expected 'pure East'. We found . . . tarred motor roads, hospitals, a child-welfare centre, schools and colleges, electric light. Yet the sanitary system seemed to rely entirely on the hills on which Jammu stands and the flies were terrible . . . Our first impression of the city was that it was inhabited exclusively by flies, for only an occasional human, other than patrols or piquets, was to be seen.

"As yet we had no maps, and patrols wandered aimlessly, often finding themselves back where they started from when they were trying hard to get anywhere else. It was a weary business, this patrolling, . . . for there was little to distract the attention from feet which hourly became more tender on the badly set cobbles and the hot tarmac. Only one place caught our attention . . . Painted in large letters we found the inscriptions 'Hearty Welcome and Loyal Greetings to British Forces from Mahommedans' and 'Long Live the British Empire! God Save the King Emperor', and nailed to the wall was the following poem written on brown paper:

> '*1. Muslims of the State were helpless and dumb*
>   *Before the English, you have come.*
> *2. Partial, tyrant are the forces of State,*
>   *Justice and law they strictly hate.*
> *3. You would have seen with awe our fate*
>   *Had you, the English, come a bit late.*
> *4. They pierced, they shot, they killed to boot,*
>   *They robbed us freely, took part in loot.*
> *5. We rose from the graves, our spirits revived*
>   *When you, O English, here arrived.*
> *6. We thank H.E. The Lord Wallingdon,*
>   *For the noble and wise deed he has done.*
> *7. Up, up the Jack, the Queen and King,*
>   *May long they live, let us all sing.*
>   MUSLIMS OF JAMU.'

" 'I' Company had by this time been billeted in the city, two platoons in the Dak Bungalow and two in the High School. Their job was to patrol, night and day . . . The officers lived in the Head Master's study, a room annoyingly furnished with a bookcase full of books but locked up, a very enlarged photograph of Sir Hari Singh, a calendar which gave you three different dates for each day, and a clock which struck as it felt inclined. Its record was forty-four.

"Dinner that night was typical of that meal during our first three or four days, and the wise soon came in early and sat at the end of the table farthest from the telephone. First the Brigade-Major rang up to say that a cavalry patrol had rounded up a Red Shirt *Jatha*; the postmaster to say he must have a guard; the Brigade-Major to say that the *jatha* had been rounded up; the Head Jailer at Satwari jail to say he had received 1,500 blankets; the Brigade-Major to say that the *jatha* had turned nasty, were stoning the escort and had wounded two men; what was he to do about it? The Head Jailer to say that, as he had 5,123 prisoners, he did not see how he could equally divide 1,500 blankets. He was told to give them first to the old prisoners. 'The prisoners who have been in longest?' 'No, no, the greybeards.' 'And what shall I do with the rest—put them into store?' Followed several reports from the Brigade-Major that Satwari was burning fiercely, mixed with reports from the jail that the prisoners were settled down for the night and it seemed a pity to disturb them to issue blankets. Meanwhile a stream of wireless messages were coming in from the 2nd Cavalry Brigade at Sialkot and from Lahore District, both of whom were as yet undecided as to who should have the honour of telling us what to do. Actually we felt we were really doing the job quite well by ourselves.

" *Friday, 6 November*. It had been tactfully explained to the State Troops that, as they must have had a very trying time in the city, and, as they could deal with the collecting of the Red Shirts in the open country so much better than we, they should be withdrawn into their cantonments at Satwari. They were only too ready to fall in with this suggestion, and so on the morning of Friday they marched out and we were left in sole charge.

" . . . Several shops opened during the day, and a censor was appointed. At first Garmoyle was given the job, but before he had got further than appropriating a tent and putting his notice-board outside, it was taken over by Jardine, the First Assistant to the Resident. We were sorry about this for, what little we heard of the telegrams that originated from various Young Men's Associations and such like, they must have provided good reading. Wires which said that Mahommedans (or Hindus) were being massacred by thousands, their women raped and their children cut in pieces, were, we believe, fairly frequent...

"... After a good deal of sorting out it was decided which were the points most likely to be centres of disturbances, and there, since the shopkeepers particularly asked for it, piquets were established in place of some of the patrols. As the days went by we got to know these piquets only too well. The first was at 'Temple Corner' . . . Here four broad streets met and there was always plenty going on. The chief noise came from the vendor of water melons with his continual chant of 'Dudh-bubbly-ubbly' dudh-bubbly-ubbly' which seemed never to cease unless perhaps a sacred cow, carefully watching its opportunity, snaffled a juicy-looking melon from the edge of the pile. Then there would be much reviling, the cow shoo-ed away, and, as often as not, the half-eaten melon put back on the pile.

"Next came Ghas Mandi piquet, at the corner of Brick Street and the Urdu Bazaar. Here several drains met and the resultant smell and cloud of flies were worse than in most places. The third, Pir Mitha, and the fourth, Bazaar Barbaran, were up in the main native bazaar, now known as the 'Main Drain', a narrow, winding cobbled lane inhabited by sellers of cloth, shoes, brassware, sewing machines, saddlery, by bankers and silversmiths, carpenters, fruiterers and bakers. Later on these would open their shops soon after dawn, would sit or doze or chatter through the long day, and only shut up in time for curfew. Few of them ever seemed to be selling anything. At first they looked on us and the interest we took in their wares with the gravest suspicion, but when they realized that British troops did not take things without paying for them they became a deal more friendly.

"The fifth piquet was in another evil-smelling bazaar called Pukka Dangan, which was soon translated into English (possibly not quite correctly) as 'Proper Dunghill.' The sixth was in the open space at Purani Mandi, which was used for the vegetable market. British troops were at this time still a novelty, and one old man with a large bundle of turnips under his arm stood and gazed for some minutes till a gentle tug from behind brought to his notice the fact that a sacred cow was making a good meal off his bundle. These cows wander at will all over the city and get very much in the way in the narrow bazaars. They are not always so terribly holy either, as witness the episode when three bulls started fighting over a lady. That would not have been too bad, but unfortunately one of the bulls mistook Moore-Gwyn either for the lady or for one of his opponents. The proximity of an open doorway averted an accident, but we think it unlikely that Moore-Gwyn will readily be converted to Hinduism.

"By now it had been borne in upon us that Satwari was not the only jail under Jenkins' jurisdiction. There was another containing some eight hundred Red Shirts at Udhampur about forty miles away up the Srinagar road. The most alarming reports had been coming in from there, and it appeared that all the Hindus (with the possible exception of the one that sent the telegrams) had been killed, and that troops—British troops—must be sent at once . . . Jardine went over to see what the situation was like and where a camp could be pitched. His report came in on the evening of the 7th to say that the place was perfectly quiet, that there was no need of troops, and that anyhow there was no water for them.

". . . The continuous patrolling was a fairly severe strain . . . At the beginning it meant that every man did two hours on and four hours off, and later two hours on and six off throughout the twenty-four. After their five days' spell they came back looking as if they had a good deal of sleep to make up . . .

"Exaggeration and fear of what might happen, but never did, was the cause of many stories in Jammu. One fat old Sikh came up one day to say that he had been stabbed and generally set on by Mohammedans. No one could have looked in better health or shown less sign of bandages, but he was allowed to ramble on till he had forgotten half of what he had originally said. Then he was cross-questioned. 'Was the party that attacked you armed?' 'Oh, no. They were not armed.' 'Then they could not have stabbed you?' 'Well, they did not actually stab me, but they pulled my beard and they might have stabbed me if I had not run away' . . .

Incidentally Moore-Gwyn, on one of his nightly rounds, was appealed to by two Mohammedans in the police piquet of six to save them from four Hindus who, they said, had every intention of beating them up later on.

". . . On 1st December all our piquets were handed over to the police, our city duties being reduced to patrolling only by day and night, and we began to hope that we should get back to Jullundur in time for Christmas . . . Meanwhile the Battalion took the opportunity to do a little training for the annual test route march; the Weapon Training Officer borrowed a range and started practising his Young Soldiers, and the polo fanatics started hitting a ball about . . .

" . . . On Monday, 21 December, after being entertained at an excellent lunch provided by the local notables—the Prime Minister, the Governor of Jammu, the Commander-in-Chief, and several others—without further let or hindrance we got into our trains and moved quietly off . . . In conclusion, to show how our services were appreciated, we give an extract from a Mahommedan newspaper, the *Siyasat*, published in Lahore:—

" 'The British soldiers are seen sauntering along ("literary license" we hope) the streets and lanes of the Jammu City day and night in groups of ten and fifteen. In the evening and afterwards they are observed whistling and singing in low tones. But immediately they pass by a Mosque they become silent and remain so until they have gone 20 or 25 paces beyond the Mosque. It is due to this gentlemanly behaviour of these soldiers that the Moslems of Jammu consider them angels of mercy and the present Government of the State a blot on humanity and a veritable curse. The barbarous soldiers of the State, who without any rhyme or reason shower bullets on the mosques and shed blood in their compounds, and the judges of the State, who feel no hesitation in declaring the Id congregation as unlawful assemblies and who are afterwards eulogized by the Maharajah in his announcements, ought to feel ashamed in view of such instances of tolerance on the part of the British.'

"And so ends another episode. There are two morals to this tale, and we cannot point out the first without seriously upsetting the Disarmament Conference; nor the second without wrecking the Round Table Conference.

"In recognition of the services of the 1st Battalion, H.E. the Viceroy was pleased to send the following letter to H.E. the Commander-in-Chief in India:

'*My Dear Chetwode, Now that The Rifle Brigade have been withdrawn from Jammu, I wish to bring to your notice the reports which I have received as to their behaviour during the weeks which they spent there. I understand that their duties were frequently of a very difficult kind and included work such as escorts for funerals, identification of prisoners and so on, which they could not ordinarily be called upon to perform. All these duties were carried out with the greatest cheerfulness, tact and good temper, and there was not a single complaint at any time against any member of the Battalion. In fact, the almost complete absence of unpleasantness in Jammu City is stated to have been entirely due to the exemplary behaviour of the The Rifle Brigade. I should, therefore, be grateful if you would convey on my behalf and on that of the Government of India to the Commanding Officer and All Ranks of the Battalion our cordial appreciation and thanks for the excellent work performed by them in what must have been an unusual and sometimes unpleasant situation.*

Yours ever,

Willingdon.' "*

*   *   *

1933—the year in which Hitler came to power—was that long designated by Higher Authority for the two halves of the Regiment to exchange roles. "Early in December," the 1st Battalion's correspondent had written from Jullundur at the end of 1931, "a definite bombshell was hurled at us from the War Office to the effect that the Battalion would move during the trooping-season of 1932/33 to a station outside India to which no married families might proceed. We had hoped for a last year in India for the sake of polo and it is perhaps a bit hard on the wives, but, after all, that is the luck of the Army." "We are now wondering," the writer of the 2nd Battalion Letter speculated on New Year's Day, 1932, "where we shall be this time next year. Rumour is rife; the N.A.A.F.I., from whom an advance-copy of all trooping-season moves can usually be obtained

* *R.B.C. 1931 ,84-109.*

free, say Gibraltar; others think Malta, and again others think that
we may form some part of General Burnett-Stuart's Command in
Egypt; but, wherever it is, we are looking forward to the year 1933
with confidence."* In fact the 2nd Battalion was to spend the next
six years in Malta, India and Palestine.

The 1st Battalion, home in 1934 after its long sojourn abroad,
occupied itself with musketry courses, section, platoon and company
training, sporting engagements and shooting competitions, winning
the Queen Victoria Trophy in 1938 for the eighth consecutive time.
General Sir John Burnett-Stuart, its new Colonel Commandant, who
had now moved from Egypt to become G.O.C. Southern Command, came down to inspect it at Gosport, entertaining everyone by
his sympathetic but caustic comments on the accommodation provided in Fort Gomer, where "A" Company was undergoing its
annual musketry course. The 85-year-old Colonel-in-Chief, the Duke
of Connaught, also came over from Bagshot for his annual visit, and,
braving a singularly cold day, "strengthened the admiration and
affection" with which he was universally regarded by the Regiment.
"He inspected a guard-of-honour, . . . and the last squad of recruits, . . . listened to the Band and Buglers, visited the barrack
rooms, dining-hall and sergeants' mess, and had lunch with the
officers."†

The 1st Battalion also took part in the Tidworth Tattoo where it
gave a drill display in pre-war green uniform, winning universal
bouquets from high and low, including the Press. Two German
officers—one of whom, Major von Mellenthin, was to win fame as
an expert in armoured warfare—attended the event and the subsequent autumn manoeuvres, and were much amused at the long
harangue which the officer in charge of the parade delivered after a
very late tattoo rehearsal, remarking, "In the German Army also
the Captain likes to talk." And in Malta, during the same summer,
while Mussolini's legions overran an unarmed Abyssinia, the 2nd
Battalion took part with the Navy in repelling a mock invasion of
the island. "It will show the seriousness with which the rank and file
entered into these operations," the Battalion letter-writer reported,
"that a coast-watching post consisting of a small force, the size of
which (1 N.C.O. and 3 Riflemen) have served the Empire so well in
the past, arrested a full colonel complete with red hat and refused to

* *R.B.C. 1932*, 71.   † *R.B.C. 1936*, 48.

let him go on the grounds that he was a spy in disguise. The more powerful his language, the more alert and determined became the party of one N.C.O. and three Riflemen. Eventually a second lieutenant, having leisurely finished his supper, went to identify this highly-placed officer, and it is one of the author's deepest regrets that he was not present to witness the meeting. Late on the second night one of our posts, consisting of a young officer and his platoon, were put out of action and unable to take any further part in the battle. He, therefore, had all the doors of the building . . . locked and everybody turned in for the remainder of the night. The Commanding Officer was on his way to visit this post and, being half way there when the umpire had put this platoon out of action, had no knowledge of what had occurred. If one reflects on the incident quietly next day there is something definitely humorous in the fact of a Commanding Officer hammering with increasing violence on the doors and windows . . . The platoon commander is reported to have appeared eventually from an upper window, angrily demanding who required admittance . . . When asked to come downstairs and talk things over, they say he moved at Rifleman-like speed."*

It was all shadow-boxing, for after fifteen years of neglect by a parsimonious Parliament and Executive and the carefree, unrealist peace-loving nation they represented, the Army was almost completely without modern arms and with no prospect of receiving any. Its units for lack of recruits were dangerously under strength. During its training operations, non-existent tanks—a British invention of the first World War—were represented by flags, Battalions by sections, and Divisions by platoons.

Yet at the end of 1936 a rumour began to circulate in the Gosport canteen and orderly room that the 1st Battalion was to be mechanized and move to Salisbury Plain. "Not long afterwards," its excited chronicler wrote at the conclusion of his annual Letter, "official confirmation was received, and there seems no reason to doubt that the spring of 1937 will see us all in trucks or on motor-bicycles forming part of the 2nd Cavalry Brigade at Tidworth. The details of our proposed role are not yet known, nor have we yet been told what our organization or armament will be, or in what sort of vehicles we will ride. This does not worry us, as we are convinced that we will not have what we are supposed to have and that the

* R.B.C. 1936, 68-74.

game will still be played with dummy weapons, skeleton bodies and flags, to which the addition of 'token' trucks cannot be anything but an advantage. We are to be the last word in novelty, and with pleasure and satisfaction we see ourselves once more in the role of an 'Experimental Corps of Riflemen'."*

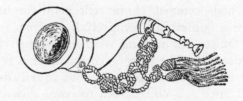

* R.B.C. 1936, 43-59.

Chapter Nine

"A HAWK UPON HIS WRIST"

From the sea,
From the sea,
He struck out from the sea,
And as heron falls to peregrine
They fell before his unforseen
And sudden blinding slaughter
From the sea.

Oh, he died,
Yes, he died,
As other brave men died,
But for valiant quenched vitality
Deeds spring to immortality:
A young man lingers lightly
Where he died.

PATRICK HORE-RUTHVEN,
Major, The Rifle Brigade.

Keep firing! Keep firing!
COL. VIC TURNER, V.C.
(During the "Snipe" action at Alamein)

THE decision taken by the War Office in 1936 to form an Experimental Mobile Division and turn the 1st Battalion Rifle Brigade into Motorised Infantry as part of it, was on a par with the decision taken in 1800 to form an Experimental Corps of Riflemen. The reason for the decision in each case was a new technique of war evolved by a powerful military and revolutionary neighbouring nation. When Coote Manningham and William Stewart formed their Experimental Rifle Corps, Britain was at war with Revolutionary France. But when, after the remilitarisation of the Rhineland in the spring of 1936, the Experimental Mobile Division was formed as an answer to the new mechanised armoured army of Hitler's revolutionary Germany, democratic and parliamentary Britain was not only not at war, but was lulled in a profound and apparently unwakable dream of peace. Until 1935 her Prime Minister for the past six years had been a pacifist deeply committed, as were so many of his countrymen, to the belief that unilateral disarmament was the key to international peace, whereas the all-powerful demagogue dictator of Germany had risen to power by advocating for his country unilateral and unlimited rearmament. Even a Conservative Government, at the insistence of the Treasury and of the then Chancellor of the Exchequer, Winston Churchill, had earlier, in 1929, based the country's defence expenditure on the assumption that no European War could happen for at least ten years. When later that summer the Socialists were returned to power, the Ten Years' Rule remained in force until it was abandoned by a Coalition Government in 1932, only seven years before a major European war occurred. Even in the early 'thirties rearmament was rendered politically impracticable by a trade depression and the almost impassioned reliance of the British public and electorate on the League of Nations and "collective security" as the only admissible form of defence. The official Opposition—led by another deeply sincere pacifist, George Lansbury—was totally committed to this creed, despite its increasing dislike of the militarist Fascist and Nazi dictators who had seized power in Italy and Germany.

When, therefore, after a General Election in 1935, Ramsay Macdonald's successor, Stanley Baldwin, secured a mandate for a limited measure of rearmament, ostensibly to strengthen the hands of the League of Nations, the amount both of money and popular support available was still very small. And, after fifteen years of progressive and cumulative disarmament, the state of Britain's defences was so deplorable and the rapid build-up of Nazi and Fascist air-power so alarming, that absolute priority had to be given to rearming the R.A.F. and Navy, and scarcely anything could be spared for the Army. The inception of the Hurricane and Spitfire programme and of Radar, the anti-aircraft defences of the Fleet, and the laying down of new battleships—*King George V, Prince of Wales, Duke of York*—date, as the latter's names suggest, from the two years of the Baldwin Administration of 1935-37. For the Army during this period little or nothing was done. Whereas in 1914 Britain had possessed a small but highly efficient, military striking-force of seven divisions ready for immediate despatch to the Continent, before 1939 her Army was only barely sufficient for garrisoning her vast, global Empire and—at a time of rapid new technical and scientific developments in weaponry—armed, so far as it was armed at all, for the 1914-18 war.

As that realist Rifleman, General Sir John Burnett-Stuart, put it after a War Game based on an imaginary European conflict, "It is suicide to send an army to France without air and without armour: the Germans won't halt for a blue and white flag! It is no use spending money on the Army if we are to be taught to fight the Battle of the Aisne again with the addition of a couple of Army Tank Battalions. If only our political leaders had learnt German at school as well as they have learnt French, perhaps they would be better able to appreciate the relative value of the German and French armies."* Such outspoken views did not commend the General to either Westminster or Whitehall.

None the less, under his and his Chief-of-Staff, Wavell's, watchful and germinating influence, the Experimental Mobile Division began its, at present, academic exercises on Salisbury Plain. And it did so on the basis that tanks could not, as some of their more extreme exponents argued, operate unsupported, and that they must be accompanied by mobile, and therefore motorised, infantry to take over from them and give them the necessary support whenever the lie and nature of the land fought over—woods, hills, rivers and cities, and other tank obstacles—impeded their advance. During the early nineteen thirties it had at last become realised that mounted cavalry could no longer hope to operate against modern mechanised forces and that the horse must give place to the tank. But cavalrymen in tanks could not dismount and continue the fight on foot as horsemen and mounted infantry had done in the past, and, when in 1935 the entire 2nd Cavalry Brigade at Tidworth was mechanised, a new role became available for the two classic Rifle Regiments of the British Army. A little earlier it had been suggested that they should be employed, in conjunction with the Brigade of Guards, as a Machine Gun Corps. But machine-guns are heavy weapons which cover the operations of infantry from the rear, whereas the traditional place of Riflemen, whether in an Army's advance or retreat, had been in front of the Army and in immediate contact with the enemy. When, therefore, the offer was made to the 1st Rifle Brigade to become a motor battalion brigaded with armoured cavalry and "Horse" Artillery, even though there were no up-to-date tanks as yet with which to operate, the proposal seemed a heaven-sent opportunity to return to the tactical role for which the Regiment had been

* *R.B.C. 1958*, 67-9.
J.G.   Y

founded. Except for a brief period in 1858, when they had worked
with cavalry in pursuit of the rebel Sepoys, not since the Peninsular
War had Riflemen had a real chance to do in battle that for which
they were originally intended and for which their forward-looking
philosophy and insistence on speed of thought and action so well
fitted them. Opportunities for fine marksmanship, for courage and
endurance, for cheerfulness and resilience in adversity, they had had
in plenty; but here was a challenge after their own hearts.

Brigaded at Tidworth with the Bays, 9th Lancers and 10th Hussars
as part of the 2nd Cavalry Brigade and as the first Motor Battalion in
the British Army, it was shortly afterwards joined in its novel role by
the 2nd Battalion of the King's Royal Rifle Corps, which became the
corresponding Motor Battalion of the 1st Cavalry Brigade. Together the two brigades formed what, in 1938, was renamed the 1st
Armoured Division—something of a misnomer at the time, for its
tanks were of the lightest kind and incapable of competing with the
armour of the Continental Powers. But its first Divisional Commander was Alan Brooke, the great soldier who was to share with
Winston Churchill the direction of Britain's strategy in the embattled
years ahead. And everything that was most forward-looking in the
pre-war British Army was concentrated in the experiments in
armoured warfare now being conducted on Salisbury Plain.

At the end of its initial year's training the Commanding Officer of
the 1st Battalion, Lt.-Col. Jack Reeve, wrote the first Motor Battalion
training manual, a work comparable to William Stewart's *Regulations for the Rifle Corps* of 1800. It set out the purposes for which a
motor battalion existed: to constitute a pivot from which armour
could operate; to overcome, with its rifles, bren-guns, mortars and
tactical expertise, any obstacles impeding an armoured advance; to
clear, when necessary, villages, woods and enclosed country; to force
the passage of rivers and deny them to the enemy; to protect the tank
leaguers at night; to hold captured positions and ground; to round
up and take charge of prisoners after a break-through; to carry out
patrols and reconnaissance, and to do for tanks whatever tanks could
not do for themselves. It was to be equipped with 15 cwt. trucks,
carriers, jeeps and scout-cars, so that the Riflemen could keep up with
the armour until the last moment before leaving their vehicles to
engage the enemy. They were to be highly mobile and independent
of day-by-day supply, and for this reason were to carry not only their

bedding but their ammunition, food and water, and were to be able to cook for themselves in vehicles or in the field. They were to act in self-contained units, not only Companies but platoons and even sections, operating whenever necessary at great distances both from one another and the main body. They were to be quick, adaptable, self-reliant and, above all, resourceful.

Though the Motor Battalion organisation was adapted and varied to meet the changing needs of War, it was basically made up of a Headquarters, Headquarters Company including its Administrative and Signal platoons, three or four Motor Companies, each with three Motor platoons and one Scout platoon, and a Support Company containing the Mortar, medium Machine-gun and Anti-Tank platoons. In addition, it contained a Light Aid Detachment manned by R.E.M.E. personnel for the repair of vehicles, and a Signals Troop manned by the Royal Corps of Signals for providing the rear link to Brigade Headquarters and doing the more highly specialised maintenance of signals equipment. Not only were the officers, N.C.O.s and Riflemen of a Motor Battalion to move quickly, but to be able to communicate quickly with one another, with their headquarters and with the armour. For proficiency in operating wireless and handling signals and messages was as essential to success in the conditions of mobile warfare as their traditional skill in weaponry. They were once more to be, as in the days of their Peninsular past under Wellington and Craufurd, "a light and beacon for the general".

So, under the guiding hand of Colonel Jack Reeve and of the great men—Alan Brooke at Divisional Headquarters, Burnett-Stuart and Wavell at Southern Command—who had overall responsibility for the experiment, the officers and men of the 1st Battalion learnt, pioneers once more, to master their new role—to drive, maintain and repair trucks, carriers and motor-bicycles; to operate them with speed and skilful care by day or night, often without lights and over the roughest ground; to carry blankets, sleeping kit, and their cookers with which to "brew-up" meals in the vehicle which became every Rifleman's moving home; to operate and service the complex technical mechanism of rapid, accurate wireless communication, with its phonetic alphabet and mysterious technician's code and vocabulary; and all at the highest possible speed—that is, at Riflemanlike pace. Though every man still carried his rifle or automatic weapon and learnt to shoot fast and straight as a Rifleman should—

in 1938 the Battalion won the Queen Victoria Trophy for the tenth year running and swept the board at Bisley*—the foot-slogging Greenjacket was transformed into a highly trained and expert mechanical fighting technician. Above all, from the highest to the lowest, he was taught to exercise the capacity for individual initiative which the first founders of the Regiment saw as the prerequisite of a rifle corps's success in the field. On this, and on the corporate *esprit de corps* which membership of the Rifle Brigade gave to all its members, victory in the swift-moving, swift-shooting, swift-communicating battles of armoured warfare would depend.

It was remarkable how quickly the Riflemen—most of them men with little more than elementary education—learnt their new craft: " the new-fangled soldiering", as some of the old hands called it. In the course of 1938 the eighty vehicles of the Battalion covered roughly 2000 miles per vehicle or about 160,000 miles in all, without a serious accident, much of it at night and without lights. And though most of the equipment needed for their future tasks in the field was still lacking—there were only Lewis guns as yet to use on the range in place of the prescribed Bren-guns, and the first Anti-Tank Rifles were only just starting to come in†—the Battalion made up in enthusiasm and application what it lacked in experience.

Like the rest of the Army in the mid-nineteen-thirties—with a total strength of under 150,000, or less than half what the Germans, before they encountered it, had called the "contemptible little Army" of 1914—the Battalion was sadly under-strength. The Regimental State on January 1st, 1939, was only 1436, of which the 1st Battalion at Tidworth accounted for 41 Officers and Warrant Officers and 476 other ranks, with 711 serving in the 2nd Battalion at Meerut in India, and 208 at the Depot at Winchester.‡ The nation's only other soldiers besides Regulars were Territorials—volunteers who, out of a sense of patriotic feeling, a desire for congenial company and a latent conviction, shared by few of their contemporaries, that one day their services might be required, had ignored the ridicule or indifference of the vast majority of their complacent countrymen and the cheese-paring neglect of the authorities, to put in a dozen drills a year at the local Territorial drill-hall and eight days attendance at a summer camp. There were three Territorial Regiments, all based in London, which formed part of the corpus

---

* *R.B.C. 1938*, 44-5, 139-47. † *R.B.C. 1938*, 43-51. * *R.B.C. 1938*, 112.

of the Rifle Brigade. They followed, in their part-time soldiering, the same type of drill and training as the Regular Battalions, and were staffed with a Regular Commanding Officer, Adjutant and a few N.C.O.s, either retired or seconded to them from the Regiment. These were the London Rifle Brigade, the Tower Hamlets Rifles, and the Artists' Rifles. In 1930, on the occasion of the Duke of Connaught's 80th birthday, all three had joined with the 2nd Battalion, then still in England, to march proudly past their Colonel-in-Chief in Hyde Park. Their numbers were absurdly low and, during the late 'twenties and early 'thirties, had been steadily declining; in 1933, when Lt.-Colonel E. R. Kewley, who had commanded the 3rd Battalion in France and Mesopotamia, took over the London Rifle Brigade from Colonel Paley,* its numbers were down to 289.

After 1936 the recruiting position improved, as a consciousness that war was a possibility started to dawn on the more thoughtful minority. In that year Mussolini absorbed Abyssinia despite the unavailing protests of the League of Nations; in 1937 Hitler swallowed Austria, all but encircling, in doing so, the defences of Czechoslovakia. By the summer of 1938 the London Rifle Brigade had reached and exceeded its modest peacetime establishment of 583. Then followed in quick succession the Munich crisis and, in the spring of 1939, Hitler's annexation, in flagrant breach of his word, of what was left of the Czech Republic, while his fellow dictator, Mussolini, seized Albania. When Neville Chamberlain and his Government responded by doubling the size of the Territorial Army the response was instantaneous; the London Rifle Brigade filled the ranks of its new 2nd Battalion in a matter of days. Unfortunately what the Government could not double or, for the moment, even begin to provide, were the arms and equipment needed by thousands of eager volunteers. Even after war broke out in September and compulsory national service was introduced, the supply position was no better; as late as January 1940 small-arms ammunition was so scarce that, to enable the new intake to the London Rifle Brigade to complete their

* Colonel Alan Paley, C.M.G., D.S.O., a most distinguished retired Rifle Brigade officer, assumed command of the London Rifle Brigade, with his cousin, Captain (afterwards Maj.-Gen. Sir Victor) Paley, a serving officer, as Adjutant. Among other officers of the Regiment who gave their services to the London Rifle Brigade in the years of national neglect before the war were Captain Vic Turner, the V.C. hero of Alamein, who was Adjutant from 1934 to 1938, and Lieutenant F. W. Festing, the future Field Marshal.

musketry courses, its 1st Battalion—then training on the Kentish coast—was forced to supply its own from stocks bought before the War for its own private Rifle Club.*

Neither of the Regular battalions of the Rifle Brigade nor any of the London Territorial Battalions attached to it—their purely voluntary character now changed by the imposition of National Service—formed part of the Expeditionary Force sent to France in the autumn of 1939. The 1st Battalion, like the rest of the 1st Armoured Division, was still awaiting its full complement of vehicles and equipment and continued to train with armour as a Motor Battalion. In April 1940 it and the 2nd Battalion of the 60th were hastily formed, together with the 1st Battalion of Queen Victoria's Rifles—a Territorial motor-bicycle Battalion attached to the latter—into an Infantry Brigade. Its purpose—never fulfilled owing to the German invasion of the Low Countries—was the capture of Trondheim in Norway. The 2nd Battalion was in Palestine, having been transferred there from India in June 1939 owing to civic disturbances caused by Arab resentment against the growing influx of Jews flying from Nazi persecution. It, too, was in process of mechanisation as a Motor Battalion, and, in January 1940, four months after the outbreak of war in Europe, was transferred to Egypt where, under General Wavell's Command, a second Mobile Division had been formed, shortly to become the 7th Armoured Division.

* * *

On May 10th the Germans, who had perfected their instruments for the new mobile armoured warfare, struck in the Ardennes, simultaneously invading the Low Countries. On May 20th, having overrun Holland and shattered and demoralised the French armies of the North, they reached the Channel coast at Abbeville, cutting the communications of the Expeditionary Force and the French northern armies with their main forces in the south and the British supply ports in Normandy and Brittany. The reaction of the new French Commander-in-chief, General Weygand, and of Britain's Prime Minister, Winston Churchill, who had taken office on the first day of the *Blitzkrieg*, was to order the Expeditionary Force to attack

---

* A. T. M. Durand and R. H. W. S. Hastings, *The London Rifle Brigade*, 58.

southwards across the line of the German armoured advance and rejoin its severed ally beyond. In pursuit of this desperate resolve—utterly unrealist in view of the almost complete breakdown of communications in northern France and of French military and civilian morale—orders were sent on the evening of May 21st to the 1st Battalion Rifle Brigade, then in Suffolk putting up road-blocks against an expected invasion, and the 2nd Battalion 60th, to proceed at once to Southampton for embarkation for France. Similar orders to repair to Dover for embarkation to Calais were sent to the 1st Battalion Queen Victoria's Rifles in Kent. The intention was that three Motorised Battalions and a hastily despatched Regiment of light tanks should operate from Calais on the right flank of the Expeditionary Force, still fighting around Lille, to help it break out across the corridor of defeat and confusion created by the German advance to the coast.

The order for the move reached the Rifle Brigade at 7 p.m. Though everyone was tired after a hard day's work, the entire Battalion was in its vehicles, with everything packed, by 11.15 p.m. Travelling through a night of torrential rain—almost the only one in that lovely summer—it reached Southampton before midday on the 22nd. Except for the men's rifles, a few Bren-guns and forty rounds of S.A.A. per man, its vehicles, weapons and ammunition were loaded on to a vehicle-ship, while the Riflemen, after a long hot afternoon march to the quayside, embarked in the S.S. *Archangel*, in which, packed like sardines, they sailed at dusk on a perfect summer's night for an unknown destination. It turned out at dawn to be Dover, but only until noon, when they sailed, with a destroyer escort, for Calais.

When on the afternoon of Wednesday May 23rd, the Battalion landed, after an unsuccessful attempt by the Luftwaffe to bomb the ship, the battle for the town had already begun. The all-but-deserted quays were full of broken glass and bomb-craters, sniping was going on in the streets, all telephone communication had been cut by fifth columnists, and German armour was reported to be advancing up the road from Boulogne, where two Battalions of the Guards, who had been defending the harbour, were being evacuated that night to England. To make matters worse, while the Rifles, digging trenches, waited in their dispersal areas among the sand dunes on either side of the harbour, their vehicle-ships were unable for several hours to reach the dockside for lack of tugs, and, when they at last did so, there was a dearth of working cranes and dock labour, all the French stevedores having fled. The 60th, whose ship berthed first, managed to get some of its equipment ashore by next day, but, through some misunderstanding, the Rifle Brigade's ship was sent back to England half unloaded, so that the Battalion had to fight with only half its vehicles, weapons and ammunition.

Yet for four days, as German armour and infantry closed round the doomed and burning town and the Luftwaffe attacked overhead, the force put up a magnificent fight. The original plan of advancing inland being plainly impracticable, the Rifle Brigade was ordered on the evening after it landed to co-operate with the Tank Battalion in clearing the road to Dunkirk—now the Expeditionary Force's sole remaining supply-base—for the passage of 355,000 rations which had been landed at Calais on the 22nd. To this end the Commanding Officer, Lt.-Colonel Chan Hoskyns, sent out a patrol to set up a protective road-block under a young officer named Tony Rolt, who was one day to become famous as the winner of the *Le Mans Grand Prix*. Rolt, who had never been in action before, was spoiling for a fight and pushed up the Dunkirk road for seven miles. The Tank Regiment, however, owing to the appalling conditions prevailing in the town, failed to start, and the column never got away. But Rolt, undeterred by his proximity to a column of the dreaded German armour, leaguered for the night with all-round defence and only with some difficulty, after he had queried the first verbal order to withdraw, was induced in the morning to abandon his perilously exposed position. It was characteristic of the way in which the whole Battalion accepted and transcended its forlorn and apparently hopeless fate. Desperate as its situation was, it seemed almost to welcome it.

For despite constant bombardment, repeated attacks by infantry and armour, sniping from concealed and infiltrating Germans and fifth columnists, shortage of equipment and ammunition, and exhaustion from lack of sleep and food, officers and Riflemen never lost their fighting spirit or their determination to inflict the maximum possible casualties on the enemy. On the morning of Friday 24th, fresh orders arrived from England: that the town and harbour should be held as long as possible, but that evacuation would probably be carried out that night. Later it was announced that it would be postponed till the following night. But in the course of Saturday the 25th—the day on which Lord Gort reached his momentous decision to retreat to Dunkirk and so save as much of his imperilled army as could be rescued by sea—a message from London reached the brigade commander, Brigadier Nicholson, that the defence of Calais was regarded by Downing Street as of the highest national importance, and that, by tying down a large part of the enemy's armoured forces, it was keeping open the Expeditionary Force's communications with the sea. "The eyes of the Empire," the message ended, "are upon the defence of Calais, and his Majesty's Government is confident that you and your gallant Regiments will perform an exploit worthy of the British name." Later a further message arrived, and this time from the Prime Minister himself:

> "Every hour you continue to exist is of the greatest help to the B.E.F. Have greatest possible admiration for your splendid stand. Evacuation will not (*repeat* not) take place, and craft required for above purpose are to return to Dover."

How worthy the defenders were of the trust bestowed on them is shown by an entry in an account of their four days' heroic, hopeless fight by Major J. A. Taylor, commanding "A" Company, who was dangerously wounded and evacuated to England in the last ship to leave.

> "During the morning Tony Rolt and Jerry Duncanson* arrived up at Coy. H.Q. in a couple of carriers. Each had a Bren gun carried like a Tommy-gun in or under his arms and each was prepared to take on anything on earth. Seldom can a couple of more welcome subalterns have reached any harassed Company commander. When joined by David Sladen the atmosphere was more like a point-to-point than a battle. It did everyone who saw them all the good in the world to see and hear these chaps. After a few minutes light-hearted conversation, Tony casually remarked that what he had really been sent up for was to remove all the carriers and tanks which could be spared, as 'C' and 'B' Coys. were about to do a counter attack right round on the left flank to relieve pressure. The fact that he was about to take part in it himself appeared to give him the greatest joy."

By the afternoon of Sunday the 26th the defenders were down to

---

* Lieutenant Duncanson was killed, but Tony Rolt survived and was taken prisoner, being awarded an M.C. for his gallantry at Calais, with a Bar later for his attempts to escape.

their last round of ammunition. Colonel Hoskyns had been mortally wounded, and Major Arthur Hamilton-Russell, his Second-in-Command, with many others, had been killed. In the evening all organised resistance ceased, for, with the Germans pouring into the town and infiltrating every position, no more was possible. Yet during the next ten days, protected from the west by the inundation of the Gravelines waterline, which the Rifles' stand had given time to be completed before the German armour could sweep into Dunkirk in the rear of the retreating Expeditionary Force, more than 300,000 British troops were evacuated from the Dunkirk beaches. "Calais," wrote Churchill in his history of the Second World War, "was the crux. Many other causes might have prevented the deliverance of Dunkirk, but it is certain that the three days gained by the defence of Calais enabled the Gravelines waterline to be held, and that without this, even in spite of Hitler's vacillations and Rundstedt's orders, all would have been cut off and lost."*

*   *   *

The price paid for that noble sacrifice was a heavy one—the loss of the only two Regular infantry Battalions who had been trained for the kind of lightning warfare which the German General Staff had launched on the world so successfully and which had already overwhelmed, in a matter of days, Poland, Norway, France, Holland and Belgium. And they had been sacrificed without any opportunity to use the new techniques which they had mastered and which they could have taught others. The British Army was still paying the price of that sacrifice two years later in the Western Desert, Malaya and Burma. For the Rifle Brigade it was a profound personal tragedy; as its war historian wrote, "At one blow we had been deprived of the whole of one of the two Regular Battalions ... In the 1st Battalion was collected almost one-half of the total resources of the Regiment. They were, too, our friends ... If the loss of one Battalion would shortly be forgotten by the public in the rush of events which were soon to deal in corps and armies and army groups, it was still to us an appalling calamity."†

* W. Churchill, *Second World War II*, 72-3; R. H. W. S. Hastings, *The Rifle Brigade in the Second World War*, 7-30; *R.B.C. 1940*, 45-6; *1945*, 50-3 (Major A. W. Allan, D.S.O., *Calais*); *1953*, 89-90; *MS. Narrative of Major now Lt.-Col J. A. Taylor*, M.C.
† *Hastings*, 28-9.

Yet it is the essence of a Regiment that nothing is irretrievable. The bugle sounds "Rouse"—or "Reveille"—and the living take over from the fallen. Scarcely had the nonagenarian Duke of Connaught expressed in a moving message his pride in the "magnificent action" and "superb conduct" of his Regiment* than a new 1st Battalion was formed under the command originally of Lt.-Colonel "Tim" Massy-Beresford and then of Jimmy Bosvile—both of whom had served with it in India—as part of the 1st Armoured Division from which its predecessor had been torn. And four former Territorial Battalions—soon to be re-named the 7th, 8th, 9th and 10th Rifle Brigade—were also training in England under officers of the Regiment and learning the technique of motorised war.

The fruits of that training lay in the future. For the moment, the Regiment's capacity to play a part in Britain's struggle for survival rested on the 2nd Battalion which, having returned from India to Palestine in the summer of 1939, had been training in Egypt to be a Motor Battalion as part of the Support Group of what was now the 7th Armoured Division. For here, as Churchill and the new Chief of the Imperial General Staff, Sir John Dill, saw, the future of Britain's single-handed struggle against the immense power of the Axis depended almost as much as on the impending battle for survival in the waters of the North Sea and Channel and the air over South-Eastern England. If the Battle of Britain could be won, by putting a ring of salt-water and desert round the enslaved continent which Germany and Italy had conquered and so prevent them from breaking out across the Eastern Mediterranean into Africa and Asia and so eventually joining up with the third Axis partner, Japan, in the Indian Ocean, Britain might still prevent her enemies from conquering and dominating the world. Yet unless that ring could be held by the tenuous and overstrained naval, air and military forces of Britain and her Commonwealth, even her defeat of the immediate threat to invade and bombard her into surrender from the air could not save her in the long run.

What made the chances of being able to hold that ring seem so frail was that the Axis already had a foothold in Africa, with nearly

---

* "I am prouder than I can say of the manner in which the Battalion I once commanded acquitted themselves in the defence of Calais." *R.B.C. 1951*, 31-4. Message of Colonel-in-Chief, 2nd June 1940.

half a million Italian troops—half of them in Eritrea and Abyssinia to the south of the Nile Valley and half in Libya and Tripolitania to the west. Seeing France broken and Britain apparently doomed to certain invasion and destruction from the air, Italy had entered the war on June 10th, ten days before the final French capitulation. With the collapse of her Mediterranean ally, Britain's land, sea and air forces in Egypt were now left without the aid of the French armies in Syria, Algeria, Tunisia and Morocco and of the French Toulon fleet on which, in the event of a war with Italy, they had counted.

Except for her inadequately armed Commonwealth partners and colonies Britain was now alone. It was this which made it so heroic, as well as far-seeing, a decision for Churchill and Dill in the lonely summer of 1940, before even the Battle of Britain had been fought, to entrust to the long 12,000 miles voyage round the Cape of Good Hope, the 7th Royal Tank Regiment with its fifty-seven "I" Matilda tanks, which, after the loss of the Expeditionary Force's entire equipment at Dunkirk, was virtually the only heavy armour Britain possessed. It was their arrival in Egypt that autumn which enabled one of the two great men who commanded Britain's hopelessly outnumbered military and naval forces in the Middle East to embark on a land offensive which would otherwise have been inconceivable and which, though conducted against immense odds, was to succeed beyond its projectors' wildest expectations. In the grim winter of 1940/41, when Britain stood single-handed against the Axis, when London and her industrial cities and ports were under nightly bombardment, and when her chances of survival, let alone of victory, seemed to everyone but her own people negligible, her triumphs on land in the Western Desert and at sea at Taranto and Matapan were, like the Battle of Britain which preceded them, a reminder to her enemies and the world that, hopeless though her position might seem, she was not finished yet and still had it in her to fight back and, ultimately, prevail.

In Britain's unexpected victories in the Western Desert and Libya the 2nd Battalion Rifle Brigade played a part and, at a crucial moment, a decisive one. At the time of Italy's entry into the War it was commanded by the 42-year-old Lt.-Col. Callum Renton, an outstanding trainer of officers and men, who had fought with it in the 1914-18 war and, for the past nine years, been one of its Company commanders. His immediate superior was Brigadier W. H. E. Gott, commanding the Support Group of the 7th Armoured Division of which the Battalion was part. "Straffer" Gott had until recently commanded the 1st Battalion of the 60th, the other motorised infantry unit of the 7th Armoured Division Support Group. The operational Commander of the Western Desert Force in which the 7th Armoured Division was to serve, was Lt.-General Dick O'Connor, a former officer of the Cameronians or Scottish Rifles, who, under an unassuming manner, combined the highest professional competence with an imaginative daring and unshakable resolve which few yet realised. Above him, and subject only to the overall Commander-in-Chief, General Wavell, was the G.O.C. British Troops, Egypt, Lt.-General Sir Henry Maitland Wilson, universally known as "Jumbo"—a monumental Rifleman of imperturbable calm and wisdom who had commanded the 1st Battalion in India and was trusted, loved and admired by the Regiment of which he was now the most famous member. Another leader, who was to play an outstanding part in the coming campaigns in the Desert and to be closely associated with the Battalion was Lt.-Col., later Brigadier, Jock Campbell of the Royal Horse Artillery, in charge of the anti-tank guns of the Support Group. A hunting man with tremendous drive and an unerring eye for country, he was to originate and lead the most famous of the far-ranging desert columns of all arms in which, bearing his name, many officers and Riflemen of the Regiment were to serve and which, operating far beyond the lines, harassed the enemy's communications and morale and gathered valuable information. All these officers had mastered the lesson that success in war depends on rapid correlation of diversified fire power and movement and believed that the best defence was to strike first.

Before Italy's declaration of war, the 2nd Battalion was stationed in the Citadel, Cairo. "None who were serving in the spring of 1940," wrote Captain C. Barclay, "will ever forget Wednesday, the 1st May. It was the Battalion holiday.* Everyone had made arrangements to go out for the afternoon and evening. General Wilson was coming to lunch in the Mess, and . . . on the following day there was to be a cocktail party . . . to which all Cairo had been invited. . . . After lunch we were all photographed outside the Mess and then

---

* To celebrate the Duke of Connaught's birthday and the 60th anniversary of his appointment as Colonel-in-Chief.

General Wilson spoke to Callum who then said, 'The Battalion will mobilize and be ready to move in eight hours.' We moved out of barracks at dawn on May 2nd, and, as we drove past the Pyramids—shell-pink in the light of the rising sun—I think most of us wondered how long it would be before we saw civilisation again. We drove into the desert for two hot, monotonous days, . . . halted to the west of Mersa Matruh and, after a few exhausting days of energetic preparation for the Italians, moved back to camp life at Mersa. The bathing here in the clear cold blue lagoon, surrounded by snow-white sand, was marvellous. While we were here we were subjected to two severe 'Khamseens' . . . We woke early in the morning to find a strong, hot dry south wind blowing and everything covered with a thick layer of fine dust. Soon there was a gale . . . and the whole camp resounded to the hollow metallic sounds of all the empty petrol-cans bumping across the rocks being blown towards the sea. Outside the tents it had become almost impossible to see or breathe. Visibility was about ten yards and we could hardly find our way from tent to tent. It was difficult to walk against the wind, and the fine, hard, driven particles of sand pricked our faces like a thousand needles. By midday, after a lot of tents had blown down, everyone was huddled up in some shelter waiting for the storm to stop. The only possible food was bully beef or beans straight out of the tin, and even this received its coating of sand before it reached our mouths. Our thirst was insatiable. Our tongues felt like blotting-paper, our bodies seemed to dry up with sand in every pore."*

On June 10th, the day Italy declared war, the 7th Armoured Division moved forward to the frontier a hundred and twenty miles to the west, and, crossing it before dawn next day, captured two small frontier posts, Fort Capuzzo and Fort Madalena, with 220 Italian prisoners, without suffering any casualties. Here the Battalion remained for the next three months, living on the ground of the brown, stony desert or in its vehicles and continually sending out night patrols to lay mines, recover a knocked-out tank or find out information about enemy dispositions or movements. "It was a case," wrote one who took part in them, "of bumping over the desert in a truck for some five to fifteen miles, then patrolling for the remaining three or four miles on foot, finding out the information, returning to the truck and driving home. One of the biggest prob-

* *R.B.C. 1941*, 101-2.

lems was . . . to find your way . . . Patrols were a great strain on everyone; few activities call for a higher standing of leadership."* "Companies," Captain Barclay recalled, "where often so far apart, that
friends in different companies were lucky if they met more than once
a month. One exciting incident during this time took place on the
morning of the Corps Commander's visit to Battalion H.Q. on the
shore near Sollum. Suddenly four Italian destroyers appeared, . . .
shelled Sollum and then steamed straight for the shore. It looked as
though they were going to try a landing, and General O'Connor
found himself in command of only three Bren guns, which he
promptly sited to defend the beach . . . At the last moment the
destroyers turned away."

In the middle of September, when the Battle of Britain was reaching its climax, the Italians started to move. A Rifleman on patrol
reported he had seen "a Wog beating a donkey," which Intelligence
interpreted as a proof that mule-borne mountain artillery were
being employed. Five Divisions, their supplies carried in hundreds of
huge black Diesel lorries, trundled slowly eastwards along the coastal
road on the first stage of what was intended to be a triumphal march
to Alexandria and Cairo, with another five Divisions leisurely following. The British Support Group fell back before them, one of its patrols, as it kept watch on the flanks of the advancing army in the vast
desert expanses to the south, capturing its first prisoner—forerunner
of many thousands to come. "A shape was seen wandering about in
the desert mirage," Captain Tom Bird reported in a letter, "and for
about ten minutes we shot at this shape until finally it stopped and
we went out to see what it was. It was a dear old Italian, quite bald,
who had got lost on his motor-bicycle. Eventually we had hit one of
the wheels and he had fallen off. I did feel sorry for him. But I think
he was far too old for fighting and much better off in a nice prisoner-
of-war camp, and I think he thought so too."†

During the eighty mile retreat across the desert, Colonel Jock
Campbell's 25-pounders were constantly in action, inflicting as much
damage on the invaders as their limited ammunition supply allowed.
"The weather was very hot, and this, combined with our natural
dislike of a withdrawal," Captain Barclay wrote, "made us all rather
short-tempered and depressed. We did not realize that we were the
bait which led forty thousand Italians into a trap from which they

* *Hastings*, 40.   † *Hastings*, 42.

were never to escape. By the end of September the Italians had established themselves in the line of six perimeter camps running south-west from Sidi Barrani for some sixty miles, and the period of comparative inactivity which had lasted throughout the summer was at an end."[*]

In the cooler autumn weather which followed the Battalion was continuously sending out patrols and raiding columns—each with its complement of armoured cars, 25-pounder guns and trucked infantry—to harass and reconnoitre the Italian perimeter camps until their every secret and weakness was known, including the precise position of their protective minefields and the ways through them. For, having by now been reinforced by the 57 heavy Matilda tanks so timely sent from England, Generals Wavell, Wilson and O'Connor decided to use them and the 4th Indian Division to surprise, overwhelm and, if possible, capture the vastly superior Italian army around Sidi Barrani before the still larger Italian forces concentrated behind them, at Bardia and Tobruk, could come to its rescue and resume the interrupted advance on Alexandria.

On the evening of December 8th, the 4th Indian Division arrived from its position a hundred miles in the rear. In the course of two night patrols, during which he and two Riflemen had crawled between Italian sentries and patrolling tanks, Lieutenant Charles Liddell[†] had pinpointed the gap in the minefield guarding the entrance to the Nibeiwa perimeter camp. During the night, while the 7th Armoured Division watched to see that no enemy interference from the west took place and to prevent the unsuspecting Italians from escaping, three young officers of the Rifle Brigade, who had reconnoitred every inch of the ground, led the attackers to their assault positions. Then, wrote General O'Connor, "shortly after first light the 'I' Tanks began to move from their area of assembly towards the north-west corner of Nibeiwa which was to be their point of entry . . . Before long the whole Regiment was operating within the perimeter . . . As soon as the tanks had effected an entry the 11th Indian Infantry Brigade was brought up to within a few

[*] R.B.C. 1941, 105.
[†] Afterwards Lt.-Col. C. H. Liddell, M.C., son of another distinguished Rifleman, Brigadier G. W. Liddell, D.S.O., who had been Adjutant of the 1st Battalion at the start of the 1914-18 War.

hundred yards of the perimeter ... and commenced their mopping up operations."* By 10.30 a.m. the capture of the first camp was complete, its commander killed and, despite some fierce resistance, 2000 of the garrison taken prisoner.

During the next three days every perimeter camp but one was similarly dealt with until almost the entire Italian advanced army had been rounded up or destroyed and 38,300 prisoners, 237 guns and 73 tanks captured. While the main part of the Rifle Brigade, with the rest of the motorised Support Group, took up the pursuit of the flying remnants towards Buq-Buq and the Libyan frontier, Captain Tony Palmer and "C" Company were left in charge of a whole Italian division of 15,000 prisoners. During the operation of shepherding them to the rear, Michael Cubitt, who spoke some Italian, adroitly extracted the divisional commander's cook, who as "Rifleman" Antonio, remained for the next month, unknown to the authorities, as cook to "C" Company officers' mess. The Company, Robin Hastings recalled, "received many congratulations on the standard of its mess and might long have continued to enjoy his services if he had not overdone the garlic, so that the officers of the Company had practically to live by themselves."†

The Italian advance on Egypt had been halted by a brilliant and well-planned operation, carried out by small forces superbly handled. It had been made possible, as a historian of the campaign has pointed out, "by the activities of the mobile forces who, for six months, had probed the enemy defences in search of information, and had so greatly lowered Italian morale before the offensive started."‡ But no one, except General O'Connor, expected such an offensive in the face of numerical odds to continue after the liquidation of the Italian advance-guard. Even in the middle of the battle he had been notified by Cairo that the 4th Indian Division, half his force, must be withdrawn at once for operations against the Italians in Abyssinia, transports having arrived at Suez which made its immediate transfer there possible. But, so complete and unexpected had been the victory that, despite a decision by the British Government to offer troops and supplies from Egypt to help the Greeks against an Italian invasion, O'Connor was now authorised by Generals Wavell and Wilson, to make a further assault on the strong Italian force in

* Brigadier C. N. Barclay, *Against Great Odds*, 32-3.   † *Hastings*, 46.
‡ Brigadier C. N. Barclay, *Against Great Odds*, 28.

the frontier town of Bardia which the Italian Commander-in-Chief, Marshal Graziani, had now ordered to be defended to the death. For so shattering had been the surprise and shock of the assault on Sidi Barrani that the Rome radio announced that the British were about to invade Libya with a quarter of a million men and a thousand aircraft.

In actual fact, even with the Indian Division, O'Connor had never had more than 30,000 troops under his command, while the R.A.F., with few and obsolete planes, was weaker than the Italian air force in everything except morale. To bring his numbers back even to that level a new Australian division, recently arrived in Egypt, was now allotted to him. With this and the 7th Armoured Division he at once invaded Libya, investing Bardia on Boxing Day. He had already sent the Rifle Brigade and the rest of the Support Group to cut the coastal road beyond Bardia and prevent the garrison from withdrawing along it to Tobruk, 80 miles to the west. On January 3rd, the Australians and the heavy Matildas stormed the town, employing the same tactics as before, while the 7th Armoured Division kept the ring to the west. By nightfall on the 4th a further 38,000 prisoners had been taken, with 120 tanks, 220 field guns, 146 anti-tank guns, and more than 700 motor vehicles.

So great was the haul of Italian transport and supplies that, though logistically it would have been otherwise impossible for the Western Desert Force—now renamed the XIII Corps—to have advanced further, this second victory made a third seem feasible. And as Tobruk possessed a good harbour which could simplify the problem of bringing up supplies from Alexandria 400 miles to the east, General Wavell gave his daring subordinate authority to proceed against it, with the rider that it should be taken as soon as possible. For it had become essential to relieve the strain on the Army's transport of bringing up supplies of petrol, oil, food and ammunition over such immense distances of desert, while at any moment orders from London might deflect forces from North Africa to Greece. Once again, therefore, the Rifle Brigade and the 60th moved westwards and took up a position beyond Tobruk to prevent the escape of its garrison. On January 21st, while it made a diversionary attack in which Captain Bird, commanding the "S" Company carriers, penetrated the defences and captured 2000 prisoners and 49 guns, the Australians and the remainder of the heavy Matilda tanks—now reduced by battle and wear-and-tear to a mere handful—again broke through the Italian lines and by the afternoon of the 22nd, ended all resistance. Another 25,000 troops, 87 tanks and 200 guns were taken for a loss of 400 Commonwealth casualties, most of them Australian.

Though even Churchill doubted if any further advance in the desert was feasible, O'Connor—set like a terrier to destroy the last of the Italian "Army of Egypt"—believed it possible. And, though London and G.H.Q. Cairo had agreed that Greece should have absolute priority over the African campaign, the Greek Prime Minister, General Metaxas, was reluctant to accept British help for fear it should bring a German, as well as an Italian, army into the Balkans. In the middle of January, therefore, after O'Connor had flown to Cairo for a conference with Wavell and after the latter had visited his Headquarters in the Desert, it was decided that for the present—acting directly under G.H.Q. Cairo, so that General Wilson's Headquarters could concentrate on the impending Greek campaign —the XIII Corps should proceed with its astonishing westward advance, using, as it had been doing, captured Italian transport and petrol to reach the capital of Cyrenaica, Benghazi. Here, 200 miles to the west, Italian airfields could greatly assist the R.A.F. and Navy in their struggle for mastery of the Greek seas and skies. Accordingly, advanced Field Supply dumps were established in the desert, and, while the Australian infantry moved along the coast round the Cyrenaican bulge towards Derna, the 7th Armoured Division struck west across the Desert to Mechili which was captured in the last week of January by the armour and "B" Company of the 2nd Battalion under its 33-year-old commander, Lord Garmoyle. Here the Battalion and the Support Group were to rest and re-service their vehicles while the Australian Division worked its way round the coast to Benghazi.

But on February 3rd, when everyone was settling down for a rest, two items of startling news arrived from Corps Headquarters. The Greek Prime Minister had died on January 29th, and the despatch of a British Expeditionary Force to that country from Egypt was now imminent, making an early capture of Benghazi imperative. Even more urgent was that large Italian convoys had been reported moving southwards from Barce and Benghazi as though to evacuate Cyrenaica and withdraw to Tripoli. There was, therefore, not a moment to be lost, and it was decided that what remained of the 7th Armoured Division—now reduced by wear and tear to a single Brigade—and its Support Group, should set off immediately south-westwards towards Msus and the coastal highway on the Gulf of Sirte, 150 miles away, to cut off the retreating Italians.

It was an astonishingly bold decision. Hitherto, daring as O'Connor's campaign had been, every phase of it had been meticulously planned. "The final operation which was to complete the destruction of the Tenth Italian Army was very different," the historian of the campaign has written. "The plan and initial moves were hastily arranged; the approach march was along an un-reconnoitred route; the plan was a fluid one and was indeed changed at short notice in the final stages of the movement. The battle itself was hardly planned at all, but was one of those in which success depends on the ability of comparatively junior commanders to make quick decisions to meet circumstances which could not be foreseen in advance."* And in that battle it was the 2nd Battalion Rifle Brigade which, perfectly fitted for the event by its training and character, played the final, decisive part.

As a result of General O'Connor's sudden decision to stake everything on cutting the coastal road before the Italian army could reach Agedabia and round the Gulf of Sirte, the 4th Armoured Brigade—all that now remained of the 7th Division's armour—set off on February 4th across unchartered desert in the direction of Msus. The going was very heavy and, operating so far ahead of the nearest desert dump, it was doubtful whether its petrol supply would enable the armour to reach the coast road in time. Because of this, a decision was reached to send the 2nd Battalion, with a battery of Royal Horse Artillery and a Territorial anti-tank battery, to join the 11th Hussars under Colonel John Coombe and, reaching the vital highway ahead of the rest of the Division, block it until the armour could arrive.

By the afternoon of February 4th this fast-moving force reached Msus, and then turned south-west along the desert track to Agedabia. After leaguering for the night near Antelat, it turned west again for the coastal road, striking it in the early afternoon of the 5th near Sidi Saleh, a little south of Beda Fomm. Here the 11th Hussars had arrived that morning to report that traffic was still moving in both

* Brigadier C. N. Barclay, *Against Great Odds*, 64.

directions and that the retreating Italian army had apparently still to arrive.

Scarcely had the advanced Company, "A", under Captain Tom Pearson,* reached the highway when several thousand Italian infantry appeared from the north, "the leading elements of the army which was making its way to Tripolitania, all unconscious that its way was blocked. These infantry never really knew what hit them," wrote the Regiment's war historian who was present. "It was a feature of this battle that the Italians never caught up with what was happening. They had imagined that the British were some hundred and fifty miles away. Now that their way of escape was closed, they simply piled up in a road block stretching for miles to the north and delivered a number of uncoordinated attacks straight down the road. Each attack was in itself of strength enough to envelop the Battalion; a flanking movement would have made its position impossible. But the Italians were caught on the wrong leg; the Riflemen had their tails up. The leading Italian formation set the example when their attack was repelled by 'A' Company and they sat down to think of a way out of the trap that had closed so unexpectedly. The vision of Tripoli faded."†

Colonel Renton now arrived on the scene with Chris Sinclair's "B" Company and the anti-tank guns in support. By the morning of the 6th the entire Battalion, except for half a Company guarding the prisoners, was drawn up on a 2½ mile front between the sea and the highway, with Tom Pearson's "A" Company still firmly straddling the latter, with "C" Company and Headquarters in support behind. In the meantime news had arrived that the main British armour was by now approaching Beda Fomm ten miles to the north, ready to assail the blocked and frustrated Italian army in flank. All that day and the following night the frontal attacks on the 2nd Battalion continued, most of them supported by artillery and tanks. Though "carried out with little originality, owing to the open country and the numbers of Italians involved, there was always a grave danger of their breaking through." At one moment on the sand dunes near the sea, Platoon Sergeant-Major Jarvis, commanding an isolated

---

* Now General Sir Thomas Pearson, K.C.B., C.B.E., D.S.O., Commander-in-Chief Allied Forces Northern Europe, and Colonel Commandant of the 1st Battalion Royal Green Jackets.

† *Hastings*, 56-7.

platoon of "S" Company, "saw in the moonlight two enemy medium tanks approaching along the beach. Accompanied by Rifleman O'Brien, he ran up to them, and both fired through the slits with their rifles, wounding the crews. One of the officers fired at the Platoon Sergeant-Major from the door of the tank. Jarvis hit him over the head with the butt of his rifle and so completed the capture of two medium tanks."*

On the morning of the 7th, the Italian Commander-in-Chief, General Bergonzoli—popularly known as "Electric Whiskers"—made a final attempt to break through to the south. Most of his armour was vainly trying to beat off the flank attack of the British armour at Beda Fomm, but, with some thirty medium tanks, he led an all-out attack on the thin line of Riflemen—he can hardly have guessed how thin—who for more than 36 hours had been holding up an entire army. At one moment, driving straight down the highway, some of the tanks did break through and reached Battalion headquarters; but the anti-tank gunners, firing at point-blank range, brought the attack to a halt. Shortly afterwards white flags began to appear, and General Bergonzoli himself surrendered to Captain Pearson. 25,000 officers and men, including six generals, with more than a hundred guns and a hundred tanks were taken, 15,000 of them surrendering to the 2nd Battalion, whose own casualties in the engagement were three killed and four wounded. Calais had been avenged.

Altogether in two months an Italian army of a quarter of a million men has been routed by a British force only an eighth of its size which had driven it back 500 miles, capturing 130,000 prisoners, nearly 850 guns, 400 tanks and many thousands of lorries. "One can search the annals of war," wrote the earliest historian of the campaign, "and not find a greater victory than this." As the Foreign Secretary, Anthony Eden—himself a former officer of the 60th—put it in a letter to the Prime Minister, never had "so much been surrendered by so many to so few."† And if those who suffered this spectacular defeat were of inferior military quality—though many of them fought, and died, most bravely—the discrepancy in the numbers and arms of the opposing forces was such that no one at the start of the campaign could have expected it to take the course it did. In the final battle it was a Battalion of the Rifle Brigade which, like the

---

* *Hastings*, 58.   † W. Churchill, *Second World War, III*, 13.

Dorsets at Plassey, had the honour both of making a vital contribution to a great commander's crowning victory and of being the only English infantry regiment present. That the victor was himself a Scottish Rifleman was only fitting in what was as much a Rifleman's battle as Barba del Puerco or the Bridge of Vera. Of him and his achievement, his chief of staff, Field Marshal Lord Harding, looking back fourteen years later when he himself was Chief of the Imperial General Staff, gave it as his opinion "Although he had the invaluable support and wise advice of Field Marshals Wavell and Wilson to aid him, the plan of battle was hatched in General O'Connor's brain, the tactical decisions on which success or failure depended were his, the grim determination that inspired all our troops stemmed from his heart; it was his skill in calculating the risks and his daring in accepting them that turned what might have been a limited success into a victorious campaign with far-reaching effects on the future course of the war. It was an honour and an education to serve with him."*

* * *

Less than two years later the same Battalion of the Rifle Brigade, fighting in the Desert, was to make a major contribution to a still more famous victory. In the intervening twenty months it and other Battalions of the Regiment were to suffer, learn and endure much before they passed, victors once more, to other scenes of conflict and triumph. For now a great change was coming to the desert war. Already German Air Force personnel were known to be in Libya, though the first German troops were not to reach Tripoli until nearly a week after the destruction of the Italian army they had been sent to reinforce. O'Connor and his staff were all set to follow up their victory by an immediate advance on Tripoli, more than 500 desert miles to the west along a first-class coastal military road. The logistical problems involved were immense but scarcely greater than those already overcome, and which, with maximum support from

* Brigadier C. N. Barclay, *Against Great Odds*, v-vi. "By his energy and aggression and his gift of leadership he kept the whole rickety, improvised campaign rolling forward on the heels of the demoralised Italians ... After the fall of Tobruk O'Connor's campaign entered its last phase, a finale of amazing brilliance in which great risks were daringly accepted and the allegedly impossible triumphantly overcome." Corelli Barnett, *The Desert Generals*, 47-8.

the Navy and Air Force, they were convinced they could surmount. For at that moment the remnant of the Italian forces in Libya were without either the physical or moral means to resist,* and the strategic prize to be won was beyond price. With the capture of Tripoli, despite its domination of Europe the Axis would have been left without a foothold in North Africa. Both Malta and the Nile Valley—the key to Britain's and her Commonwealth's survival in global war—would have been rendered secure, and the Mediterranean might have been opened in February 1941 instead of in November 1942, with an incalculable saving in human life, shipping-mileage and ships—shortage of which was the Achilles heel in a maritime nation's strategy.

It was not to be. Britain, which had won so much in the past two months from courage and planned daring, failed now to "put it to the touch to win or lose it all". Two days after the victory of Beda Fomm, almost the entire R.A.F. striking force in Cyrenaica, save for a single fighter-squadron, was withdrawn for impending operations over Greece, while the Navy, given the formidable task of conveying an army and its supplies across the Mediterranean in the teeth of numerically superior Italian naval power, was unable to spare the mine-sweepers and personnel to convert Benghazi into a base-port for the Western Desert Force. On February 12th the Prime Minister sent the Foreign Secretary and Chief of the Imperial General Staff to Cairo to ascertain "the minimum garrison that can hold the western frontier of Libya and Benghazi" and press for "the formation in the Delta of the strongest and best-equipped force . . . which can be dispatched to Greece at the earliest possible moment." "Your major effort," he wrote to Wavell on the same day, "must now be to aid Greece."† Accordingly the Australian Division which had captured Bardia, Tobruk and Benghazi was withdrawn from the desert preparatory to embarking for Greece, and its place was taken by an unfledged one, while what remained of the 7th Armoured Division was sent back to the Delta to rest and refit and be replaced

* Rommel, who arrived in Tripoli on February 12th, confirmed this. "If Wavell" (sic) "had continued his advance into Tripolitania, no resistance worthy of the name could be mounted against him." Corelli Barnett, *The Desert Generals*, 62.

† W. Churchill, *Second World War*, *III*, 58, 60. "You should, therefore, make yourselves secure in Benghazi and concentrate all available forces in the Delta in preparation for movement to Europe . . . We should try to get in a position to offer the Greeks the transfer to Greece of the fighting portion of the Army which has hitherto defended Egypt."

by the 1st Armoured Division, which had just arrived from England after the long two months' voyage round the Cape and was without either battle or desert experience. General O'Connor's highly experienced XIII Corps Headquarters was disbanded, O'Connor himself promoted G.O.C. British Troops in Egypt and relegated to administrative duties five hundred miles from the front, and a Commander new to the Desert, with a purely defensive role, appointed in his place.

It was all very natural, for apart from the daunting technical difficulties and risks involved in O'Connor's proposals, there were strong diplomatic and international—though not military—reasons for sending aid to Greece, while General Wavell in Cairo had already a major campaign on his hands against a quarter of a million Italians in Eritrea and Abyssinia, a threat from Vichy forces in Syria, and a potential rising, fomented by German intrigues, in Iraq. Yet decisive success was not followed up and exploited, the advantages won by courage and genius were thrown away, and a great opportunity wasted. Chivalry to a small nation in distress and an unrealist optimism in high places about the capacity of outnumbered and ill-equipped British troops to withstand the, as yet, untouched military might of Germany on her own ground caused the Government within nine months of Dunkirk to send British forces back to the European Continent from which they had so narrowly escaped with the loss of their entire equipment. Instead of continuing to hold the ring of salt-water and desert round the all-powerful enemy who had overrun Europe and so keep him imprisoned as in a cage until Britain's rising strength, and that of her potential allies, could enable her to enter the cage and destroy him, she thrust a finger through the bars and had it bitten off. Her unavailing military and naval losses in Greece and Crete and the seas around them—they included 25,000 British and Commonwealth troops—were the price paid for that error.

Nor did the price end there. The vital ring itself was dangerously weakened at its most vulnerable point. Having withdrawn half her land, air and sea forces from North Africa for Greece, Britain left herself inadequate strength to protect the Nile Delta, the Suez Canal, the Middle East oil-fields and the whole crucial strategic area between the Levant and India—the exposed flank not only of her own eastern dominions but of Russia's Caucasian oil-wells on which that vast enigmatic Power's ability to resist a German attack depended. For, with the withdrawal from the desert of the seasoned troops who had won O'Connor's victories, the size and fighting capacity of the British forces holding the desert defile between the marshes and the sea at Mersa Brega and Agheila on the Tripolitanian-Libyan border had been halved at the very moment when the strength and morale of those opposed to them had been immeasurably increased by the arrival at Tripoli of two German Armoured Divisions and a strong Luftwaffe contingent, sent by Hitler to put backbone into the demoralised forces of his ally and to strike again at Britain's under-garrisoned gateway to the East on the other side of the desert.

On March 31st they struck, and under a commander of genius— Lt.-General Erwin Rommel—a past-master of the *Blitzkrieg* who had led a Panzer Division in the victorious German campaigns in Poland and France. The weak British forces facing him were 500 miles from their base and dangerously off-balance. O'Connor, when his plans for going on to Tripoli had been rejected, had pointed out the danger of remaining in such an exposed position and had urged a withdrawal to a more defensible line nearer Egypt. But his advice had been ignored, apparently because the authorities there were deceived by the immense distance between them and the Tripolitanian frontier and forgot how quickly it had been traversed by their own forces. Nor did those in London and Cairo sufficiently appreciate the differences in fighting skill, training and equipment of German armoured units and Italian. "It is a great bit of luck," an officer of the 2nd Battalion had written during the winter's advance, "to have been able to have a practice over or two, so to speak, with the Italians—what more delightful people to fight could there be?"* The tough and battle-hardened men of Rommel's Afrika Korps were a different proposition.

Nor had the British troops who met the sudden shock of that first desert *Blitzkrieg* the advantage of a preliminary rehearsal enjoyed by the troops who had fought their way from Mersa Matruh to Beda Fomm. When on February 22nd the 2nd Battalion had been withdrawn to the Delta for a much-needed rest and refit for its worn-out vehicles, its place was taken by a former Territorial unit, the Tower Hamlets Rifles—now re-designated the 9th Rifle Brigade —which had reached Egypt from England on the last day of 1940

* *Hastings, 31; Barclay, 71-7.*

and which, with the other three Territorial Battalions affiliated to the Rifle Brigade, had now been officially embodied in the Regiment for the duration of the war. Its officers and men were as proud and keen to prove themselves as Riflemen can be, but of experience in desert fighting, or fighting of any kind, they had none. Their earliest role in Africa was to garrison and police the cultivated areas of the Djebel of Cyrenaica which the Australians had conquered in their coastal advance from Derna to Benghazi, and it was not till March 22nd, little more than a week before the Germans attacked, that they moved south into the desert to join the inexperienced and truncated Support Group—consisting of a Yeomanry regiment armed with 25-pounders and a battery of Royal Horse artillery—which, with two armoured regiments, one of them equipped with captured Italian tanks, was all there was to hold the front line and desert defile at Mersa Brega. The rest of the newly-arrived 2nd Armoured Division from England was on its way to Greece, while the nearest formation in the rear was the still raw Australian division garrisoning Benghazi 150 miles to the north.

It was a patrol of the 9th Battalion during the few days given it in the desert before the German attack which discovered that the Italians opposing it had already been joined by at least one Panzer division. On March 31st, after a preliminary bombardment by dive-bombers—the R.A.F., preoccupied with Greece, had only a single squadron of Gladiators to oppose the Luftwaffe—the luckless Battalion was subjected to the full *Blitzkrieg* treatment which had so successfully overwhelmed the Poles and the French, and which in a few days' time, as the Germans poured into Greece, was to be applied to the equally luckless British defenders of that country. Though resisting valiantly, one Company was cut off altogether, and in the eight days of confused withdrawal—as the slender British and Commonwealth garrison of Cyrenaica raced eastwards to avoid being cut off by Rommel's enveloping race across the desert to the south of them—the young Battalion lost sixteen officers and 350 men. For some days it was touch and go whether Rommel or the retreating British would reach Tobruk first. But a decision by Wavell to hold that port and supply and reinforce it from the sea meant that when, having outrun their supplies, the Germans and their Italian allies reached the Egyptian frontier, any further advance to seize the supreme prizes of Alexandria—base of Andrew Cunningham's

Mediterranean Fleet—the Suez Canal and Cairo, was for the moment countered by the presence of a British sally-port on their lines of communication.

The Nile Delta, and all that lay beyond it, was for the moment secure. Yet all the gains of O'Connor's desert victories had been lost,* and a German as well as an Italian army now stood at the gates of Egypt. To fling it back became to Churchill, indomitable and urgent for victory as ever, the supreme military objective for Britain and her Commonwealth. With her armies driven that spring out of Greece and Crete, as they had been driven in the previous year out of Norway and France, the Western Desert was now the only place in the globe where a British Army could challenge a German. Undeterred by the long sea route round the Cape through which it could alone be supplied, the great War Minister poured into the Middle East all the troops and equipment for which shipping could be found. With Wavell's liquidation that spring of the remaining quarter of a million Italians cut off by British sea-power in Eritrea and Abyssinia, and the return to Egypt of the survivors of the Grecian and Crete expeditions, British military man-power in Egypt was beginning to assume, even by the summer of 1941, quite respectable dimensions. When in June, after overrunning Greece and the Balkans, Hitler—to extend his conquests eastwards—struck at Russia, Britain, to aid her new ally, put everything into the desert she could muster.

Yet the results that Churchill and the High Command hoped to obtain from that war were at first strangely disappointing. When, urged on from Downing Street, Wavell twice tried to raise the siege of Tobruk by land, his armoured forces were on each occasion severely handled and driven back. On the grounds that he was tired—which he was—he was relieved of his command at the end of June and replaced by General Auchinleck from India. The desert victory which for more than a year both these fine commanders and their subordinates so bravely and persistently sought, and which Churchill so impatiently and imperiously demanded, proved, for all their hopes and efforts, an elusive mirage.

* One tragic by-product of the retreat was the capture by the enemy, through no fault of his own, of General O'Connor, who, hastily recalled from sick-leave, was sent by Wavell into the desert to advise his successor, Lt.-General Neame, only to be captured with the latter when the car in which they were travelling ran into a German column on the night of April 6th. Corelli Barnett, *The Desert Generals*, 63; *Barclay*, 77.

For at this time none but those actually engaged in it understood the nature of armoured war in the desert. Stretching for a thousand miles from east to west and two hundred miles south to the uninhabitable Sahara, it was like a vast, brown, grey and yellow sea of stony scrub, sand and, sometimes, rock, with scarcely any clearly recognisable features except for an occasional ridge, hummock or depression, and, at its Egyptian end, a few steep rocky escarpments running parallel to the sea and converging on the Egyptian-Libyan border. There were no trees or natural obstacles, and nothing except mirage or sandstorm between the eye and the horizon in every direction. There were scarcely any inhabitants except for a few nomad Arab tribes, no food and very little water.

For armoured warfare it was ideal—an illimitable plain without woods, valleys, rivers, hedges or natural tank-obstacles of any kind in which, so long as it could be supplied with fuel, spare parts and ammunition, armour could roam and destroy at will. In this ideal terrain a heavily-gunned tank, with a longer range and stronger protective armour, could always outshoot and destroy a weaker. Because for a decade, remembering the lessons of the first World War and eager for a second, the rulers of Nazi Germany had trained its soldiers and airmen for armoured warfare and the *Blitzkrieg* and set out to make the weapons with which to fight them, they possessed, when war came, effective armour in abundance. Britain did not. For, having resolved never to have another war and, even when one became inevitable, stubbornly refusing to contemplate its happening, her rulers and electors only started making tanks in earnest after it had started. Even when in 1941 these had begun to come off the assembly lines in large numbers, they were still far inferior in hitting-power to those of the Panzer Divisions they faced. "The Germans were possessed of tanks and guns capable of knocking out any armoured vehicle of ours at two thousand yards," wrote Robin Hastings, who fought through the Desert War with the Rifle Brigade. "The maximum effective range of any of our 2-pounder guns in tanks or out of them was six to eight hundred yards. There were no 6-pounders in the desert; we had no 75-mm tank guns. The only method of knocking out enemy tanks which proved effective was by the use of 25-pounder field guns firing over open sights. No-one could call this method satisfactory, since the crews were devoid of cover and, anyway, were intended to fire indirectly at targets more like ten thousand yards away. Two of our armoured brigades were armed with new cruiser tanks, pitifully undergunned and suffering from mechanical defects such as an imperfect cooling system, from which they were never to recover. The 4th Armoured Brigade had Honeys, American light tanks whose guns had no pretensions to compete with the Germans in a land battle."* And since armoured warfare in the desert was rather like naval warfare, the German tanks thus resembled battleships and ours only cruisers, incapable, when it came to ultimate battle, of standing up to those heavier gunned than themselves.

Nevertheless on November 18th, 1941, just under a year after the start of O'Connor's offensive, General Auckinleck and his desert commander, Lt.-General Sir Alan Cunningham—fresh from his triumphs in the Abyssinian campaign—launched a major offensive to relieve Tobruk and throw the Germans and Italians out of Cyrenaica. But "with tank armament"—as distinct from numbers—"incomparably weaker than the enemy's", the discrepancy in tank and gun power quickly became apparent. "In the early light, the autumn sun bright but not hot, the tanks moved forward into Libya," an eyewitness wrote of the start of the British offensive. "As the great columns of vehicles spread out into the desert our aircraft appeared punctually overhead . . . As far as the eye could see were tanks and vehicles streaming forward towards Tobruk, a sight to be remembered."† Yet, in the five days' ensuing battle of Sidi Resegh on the desert track to Tobruk, the British armour suffered what seemed at the time a shattering defeat, at the conclusion of which Rommel and his victorious tanks set out for the Egyptian frontier and Auchinleck's supply dumps, so that it seemed as though there was nothing capable of stopping him from reaching Alexandria.

He was thwarted and driven back by two factors. One was the performance of the R.A.F.—no longer handicapped by a Greek or Cretan campaign and during the summer strongly reinforced from England—which ceaselessly attacked the advancing German columns, inflicting such heavy losses on them that in the end they were forced to turn back. The other was the genius of "Strafer" Gott, now commanding the 7th Armoured Division, and the splendid resilience shown by its officers and men—the "Desert Rats" as they came to be called—and, in particular, of its Support Group, commanded

* *Hastings*, 81-2.   † *Hastings*, 82.

by Jock Campbell. For it was the fighting valour and skill of the motorised Support Groups of the Armoured Divisions which helped to redress the balance and make up for the inferior gun-power of the British tanks. The courage with which the Riflemen of both the 1st 60th and 2nd Rifle Brigade stood to their guns and fought back when the armour they supported was worsted was beyond all praise. Sometimes—as happened in the early morning of November 22nd at Sidi Resegh to the 1st Battalion of the 60th and " A " Company of the 2nd Rifle Brigade—they were overrun by the enemy's armour after the British Honeys and Crusaders had been shot out of the field by the enemy's heavy, long-range-gunned tanks. More often than not they played a part which was not merely defensive but, most skilfully in view of their own lack of armour, astonishingly offensive. At this time, under the leadership of " Strafer " Gott and Jock Campbell—both now generals—the one a Rifleman and the other, though a Gunner, always accompanied by one or other of his Rifle Brigade aides, Ian Whigham and Philip Flower—they increasingly acted in small self-contained columns on the flanks of the enemy. " They learnt to operate up to a hundred miles or more from the nearest supply dumps," Robin Hastings recalled, " to penetrate areas dominated by the enemy, to remain unconcerned for days and sometimes weeks, while the enemy were surrounding them in superior strength, and to make deadly and damaging thrusts, which he found it hard to parry, against his supply lines. Admittedly columns, as a method of fighting the Germans in Africa, had their limitations and considerable . . . drawbacks. But in the days of our weakness they provided an economical means of tying down superior enemy forces and of inflicting daily casualties on the Germans which in the aggregate constituted a running sore they could ill endure . . . All this time, while the fortunes of the battle were still in favour of the Germans, the columns continued to exact a heavy toll in prisoners taken and vehicles knocked out. It was a strenuous life, breaking leaguer as it got light, moving out to a gun position, changing position several times during the day, engaging the enemy, shelling and getting shelled, often attacked by aircraft, moving at dusk and not settling down in leaguer until eleven or later at night. The nights were short. There was little sleep, hard rations and few comforts. With all the various moves the Riflemen had little idea of what was going on. The enemy might be anywhere. There was no front and no safe rear. Occasionally there were good days when results spoke for themselves, as one when a liaison officer from Rommel's own staff was captured carrying a marked map. On the whole, all this activity did not seem to be achieving very much. But there gradually grew up a feeling that the enemy were being worn down, that their losses were mounting, that they were more and more on the defensive, until . . . in the first days of December the whole situation changed and it was suddenly clear that the enemy were on the run. The relief of Tobruk was complete."*

So once again, as a year before, the British armour and trucked infantry swept westwards across the Libyan desert. Benghazi was taken on Christmas Eve and Cyrenaica again conquered, though this time at a cost of 17,704 British and Commonwealth casualties compared with the minute price paid for General O'Connor's victories. And though the Support Group of the 7th Armoured Division, which included the 2nd Rifle Brigade and the 4th Armoured Brigade—to which the now also veteran 9th Battalion was attached—operated as before on the southern flank of the enemy, it failed to cut off the retreating Germans and Italians, who reached the defile between the sea and the salt marshes near the Tripolitanian frontier in safety. Here the discomfited enemy licked his wounds and prepared for a new attack on a once more distant Egypt, while the Eighth Army —as the former Western Desert Force was now called†—regrouped, sending back those who had borne the heat and brunt of the battle to the Delta to rest and refit and replacing them by untried troops fresh from England. Among these was the reconstituted 1st Battalion of the Rifle Brigade, a Motorised Battalion of the 1st Armoured Division, which, in the summer of 1941 had been sent by the Government—freed from the danger of invasion by Hitler's attack on Russia —round the Cape to the Middle East. Having reached Suez at the end of November, it took over from the 9th Battalion in January

---

* *Hastings*, 76, 96. "Columns were composite groups, and the friendships and loyalties which they evoked cut right across orthodox regimental ties. I think the 2nd Rifle Brigade had a genius for making friendships, and certainly the Battalion had unique opportunities for using this aptitude. Witness our deep personal pleasure and pride when the 11th Hussars were first into Benghazi, Tripoli and Tunis during the 1942-3 advance . . . The 11th Hussars were the oldest and most famous of the desert armoured-car regiments, but we also had many links with the Royals and the 4th South African Armoured Cars." Letter from Major Tim Marten, cit. *Hastings*, 76.

† The Riflemen in the desert, who were nothing if not realists, used to ask where the other Armies were.

1942 under its 44-year-old commander, Jimmy Bosvile, an M.C. of
the First World War, who had trained it since its formation after
Calais.

* * *

So it came about that for the second time in a year an untried
Battalion of the Regiment stood guard on the far desert frontier
while a highly experienced one, the 2nd Battalion, returned to Cairo
for a much-needed refit and, another, now almost equally experienced,
went to the rear to guard the supply-lines. When, strongly reinforced
by a convoy escorted across the Central Mediterranean by the Italian
Fleet, the Afrika Korps, moving even faster than before, broke
through the British lines at Mersa Brega, the 1st Battalion suffered
the same painful introduction to desert warfare as the 9th Battalion
a year earlier. With the Germans threatening it with encirclement as
they made for the soft-skinned units guarding the British supply
dumps, it found itself, with all the other units of the Cyrenaica
garrison, involved in a desperate race across the desert to avoid being
cut off. The Msus Stakes, the men of an incorrigibly sporting
Regiment called it. During it British, Commonwealth and German
units were sometimes inextricably mixed together. "People tacked
on to the enemy columns in the dark," wrote the Rifle Brigade's war
historian, "and drove off unscathed when the mistake was discovered." No one in the 1st Battalion—which thanks to its excellent
training escaped with the loss of only four officers and a hundred
other ranks—had a more exciting experience than Major Vic Turner,
whose vehicle had been knocked out in the early stages of the
operations.

"He, together with Geoffrey Fletcher and several Riflemen, set out
to walk back across that endless desert. To anyone who knows the
desert, the idea of walking across it is quite fantastic. But they set
out, lying up by day and walking at night. After six nights, during
each of which they walked for ten hours, torrential rain added to
their discomfort and they decided that they must somehow secure
a vehicle. They laid an ambush, featuring the apparently blood-
stained body of a Rifleman, and waited. For two days nothing
came. On the third day a German staff car appeared and stopped to
investigate. They set on the crew, seized the car and drove off

across the desert, leaving the astonished Germans still standing with their hands above their heads. Their troubles were not yet over, although the car was full of petrol and carried a reserve. When they were almost within our lines, the car broke down and the little party had to start off again on foot. They rejoined the Battalion after a memorable trek, avoiding capture chiefly by refusing to accept the apparently inevitable. They must have covered a hundred sandy miles on foot."*

After a four days' and nights' retreat the out-manoeuvred and out-gunned British and Commonwealth forces managed to form a defensive line running south from the sea at Gazala, fifty miles west of Tobruk. But they had lost almost the whole of Cyrenaica, including the vital airfields near Benghazi from which the R.A.F. could alone enable the Navy to succour beleaguered Malta, now under continuous bombardment from the air as the Germans and Italians tried to enforce its surrender and so free the short sea-crossing between Sicily and North Africa from the British submarines which were using the island as a base. For in the winter of 1941-2 the war had widened. The Americans, attacked at Pearl Harbour, were now allies, the Russians, though driven back to the gates of Moscow and Leningrad, were resisting strongly as they had done against Napoleon, and in the Far East the Japanese were advancing westwards in irresistible strength against Malaya, Singapore and Burma. Until the untapped military resources of the United States could be made ready and carried into battle across the Atlantic and Pacific, everything turned on Britain's sea communications and her defence of the Egyptian bastion, beyond which lay a defenceless Turkey and the oilfields of the Caucasus and Persian Gulf.

From February to May 1942 there was an uneasy calm in the desert. While the British, urged on by Churchill, made feverish preparations to recover the Benghazi airfields, the Germans and Italians built up their strength for a renewed advance on Egypt, as their victorious allies in South-East Asia moved remorselessly westwards towards the Indian Ocean and a restless India, and southwards towards Australia. Three Battalions of the Rifle Brigade were now in the desert, ready

---

* *Hastings*, 104-5. In his last letter to me, written on the day of his death, Vic Turner recalled an even more remarkable feat by another Rifleman, Victor Paley—then commanding a Battalion of Senussi—who, cut off by the German advance, walked with six of his men the whole way back from Antelat to the British lines.

either to help defend the Gazala Line or launch a new attack: the 1st in the north, the 9th in the centre, and the 2nd in the south. Almost every night Riflemen from one Battalion or other were on patrol, "creeping wretchedly across a bare desert, waiting for some Italian to shoot off or groping by compass with no landmark and perhaps no stars to help, or bumping over stony wastes on the return journey, the Riflemen asleep in the back of the truck, the driver fighting to keep his eyes open, the subaltern's eyes glued to his compass, expecting a volley of rounds to whistle at any moment past his ears, proclaiming either that the guard on his company leaguer were taking no chances or that he had navigated into the German lines."*

It was Rommel who was first off the mark. On May 25th, setting out in a wide sweeping movement to outflank the Gazala Line from the south, he caught the Eighth Army Commander, Lt.-General Neil Ritchie, off balance and achieved total surprise. Moving his columns by night and playing the ding-dong battle by ear in contrast to his slower and more rigid opponent, by June 13th he had inflicted on the British their greatest defeat since Dunkirk. In three days, Ritchie's armour, fighting round the defensive Knightsbridge "box" south-west of Tobruk, lost 260 tanks, while "the 1st Battalion, involved in all these battles, watched the tank strength gradually whittled down, as inferior armament and thinner armour told despite the skill and gallantry with which these cavalry Regiments fought."† In the precipitate retreat which followed across the Egyptian frontier to Mersa Matruh—Tobruk capitulated to a victorious Rommel on June 21st—each of the Rifle Brigade's three Battalions fought a rearguard action in the highest traditions of the Regiment. The 2nd Battalion, now commanded by Lord Garmoyle— a Rifleman akin to the paladins of the Peninsular War‡—formed part of the 7th Motor Brigade which, under Brigadier Callum Renton, its old Commanding Officer of Beda Fomm days, ranged far behind the German lines, alone and unsupported. "It was the sort of situation," wrote Robin Hastings, "in which Hugo Garmoyle excelled. He seemed to have an eye in every direction. We were always on the

---

* *Hastings*, 108.　　† *Hastings*, 118

‡ Both as a Company and Battalion commander he was adored by his men. He was very tall. In the battle of Sidi Rezegh, walking calmly from gun to gun to encourage the gun crews whose battery commander had been killed, he appeared to a watching Rifleman to have been hit by a shell. "Look, there's a shell fallen right on top of the Major," the latter cried. "What did he do?" said the other. "Took a longer stride," was the reply. *Hastings*, 90.

move, dodging an enemy thrust or creeping up to attack the track at another point. In the three days while the column was behind the enemy lines it destroyed over forty lorries, four tanks, six guns and one self-propelled gun . . . To say that the Battalion owed its survival to Hugo Garmoyle would be less than the truth; for it was the faith and confidence of every Rifleman in the judgment and leadership of the Colonel that had made it possible to operate continuously, offensively and successfully for so long and often at such great distances from the rest of the Army."[*]

The 1st Battalion, too, found itself during the retreat far behind the leading elements of the enemy. At one time it travelled for some distance as the centre of three columns, two of them German; at another a sergeant, "unconscious of the identity of his fellow travellers, is said to have stopped and calmly changed a wheel in the middle of the 'B' Echelon of the Italian Ariete Division".[†] In the latter stages of the withdrawal the 9th Battalion fought two successful actions, in one capturing an Italian tank and, in the other, one of its Companies ambushing and destroying German vehicles, taking twenty-five prisoners and dislocating all pursuing traffic for many hours. "This little affray," Major Paddy Boden reported, "was hugely enjoyed by the Company, coming, as it did, after a rather depressing month."[‡]

When at last on July 2nd, after the Army had lost 80,000 men, the withdrawal stopped, the three Battalions of the Rifle Brigade still had their tails up. "The Regiment," wrote its War Historian, "who had been among the first to meet the enemy on the 26th of May, had been the last to withdraw, the last through the wire, and, in a collection of vehicles which would have disgraced a circus, were among the last to reach Alamein."[§] Turning to fight under Auchinleck in that spiritual home of the British Army, the last ditch, the weary defenders held off every attempt by Rommel to reach Alexandria and the Delta. In this long drawn-out fight all three Battalions played a notable part, especially the 1st which, in the final action on Ruweisat Ridge, amid flies, heat, dust and unburied bodies, inflicted such losses on the Germans as to avenge all it had suffered since it first went into action at Mersa Brega six months before. The price paid by the Regiment in that desperate month's defensive fighting included the loss of Lord Garmoyle, who fell on July 4th, a few weeks

---

* *Hastings*, 124-5, 128.   † *Hastings*, 129.   ‡ *Hastings*, 132.   § *Idem*, 133.

before the death of his friend, "Strafer" Gott, and not long after that of Jock Campbell—the two great desert fighters who were his peers and who, like him, never lived to see the victory whose foundations they had done so much, with inadequate resources, to lay.

At one moment in the first Battle of Alamein there were no less than four Battalions of the Regiment engaged, for on July 21st, the 7th Battalion, fresh from England, entered the fight. Since the outbreak of war the 1st Battalion of the London Rifle Brigade (TA) had spent nearly three years training in a blacked-out, rationed, blitzed wartime island, moving from station to station and Exercise to Exercise, waiting for the summons that never seemed to come. "Then," wrote its historian, "at the beginning of April, 1942 came the orders for which all men of worth had been waiting, and this time there was confident expectation that there would be no cancellation. Additional embarkation leave was given, tropical kits were issued and on . . . May 1st, the Battalion, formed up on the playing fields of Brambletye, was inspected by the King.* . . . On the night of the 5/6th May two personnel trains left East Grinstead and arrived next afternoon in Glasgow where the Battalion embarked in H.M.T. *Mooltan* . . . So, after long and sometimes weary waiting the 1st London Rifle Brigade went to war."

"On the 7th of May the ship moved off slowly down the Clyde, past the shipbuilding yards and anchored opposite Gourock. . . . One could look north to the Highlands, to the heather-covered hills rising steeply behind Dunoon and all along the north bank of the river, the hills which hid Loch Lomond and stretched away to Loch Long and the north. Or one could look south to the Lowlands, to Ayrshire and the faint outline of low hills, to the east to the smoke-stacks and gantries of Glasgow and Greenock, or to the west to the river gradually widening past Toward Point with its White Lighthouse, the Island of Bute, and, in the distance, Arran, the Atlantic beyond. In the May sunshine it was a glorious setting for the start of an expedition . . .

"Early on the 11th of May the convoy set sail. By the time it was light they were heading for the open sea, the outline of the Sleeping Warrior on the Island of Arran gradually receding to the west. There were some fifteen ships in the convoy sailing in parallel

* The War Diary records that His Majesty expressed his interest in the word of command used to call the Battalion to attention.

rows of three. . . . There was an escort in sight of some ten or twelve destroyers, the light cruiser *Mauritius*, and an armed merchant cruiser. At first there was much interest taken in the escort and its tactics. People peered through field-glasses and wondered what plan the ships worked on. There was anti-aircraft practice for the guns at a target towed by an aircraft. But as the voyage went on we were apt to take for granted the protection of the Royal Navy and to forget that the ships to be seen in the distance or weaving about close in to the convoy or whose presence was represented by a trail of smoke on the horizon were ceaselessly listening and watching and probing for any enemy attack. We might be bored and cramped and uncomfortable: the Navy were cramped and uncomfortable but desperately on the alert.

" 'C' Company were, perhaps, less bored than the rest. They had been selected to be the anti-tank company immediately after leaving England. There was one 2-pounder gun on board and a Gunner officer who knew how it worked. Every day the company trained in the use of this gun and finally were allowed to shoot the weapon in the evenings, laying well off the stern of the last vessel in the convoy. Such training was to save much time and trouble when they arrived at the other end . . .

"The seas were calm . . . On the 27th Freetown was reached. In the sticky heat we gazed at the jumbled houses of the town on the south bank—as big, someone said, as Eastbourne—and the thick vegetation coming down to the shore to the north. The convoy did not stay long in Freetown, but sailed on, except for two choppy days, in calm weather, past St. Helena, a grey rock rising from the sea in the darkness. An albatross followed the ship, and on the 6th of June Table Mountain, with the sun just risen above it, came in sight straight ahead.

"As the convoy arrived in Capetown the *Queen Elizabeth* from Sydney and the *Queen Mary* from Glasgow made a fine sight as they sailed into the harbour from opposite directions. Much has been written of the hospitality of the South Africans to visiting convoys. The English element in the population surpassed themselves in providing entertainment for ship after ship . . . The Battalion moved for a day or two into a tented camp some fifteen miles outside Capetown. Not even rain could spoil those few days . . . But by the 10th of June they were back in the *Mooltan* and on the 11th they sailed. The Battle of Knightsbridge in the Western Desert was at its height. From the news bulletins it must still have seemed that we were winning.

"Those few days on land had done more than break the monotony of the voyage. The visit to Capetown remains a memory for everyone who went there, the more perfect because it was so short. For those four days enjoyment was not limited by considerations of expense or even by the capacity of the stomach. Sandwiched between the austerity of war-time England, the comfortless monotony of the voyage and the battles that lay ahead, it was an extraordinary experience, ephemeral though it was. . . .

"The convoy turned north in choppy seas and picked up its other half off Durban on the 24th of June . . . Although the *Mooltan* headed northwards, there was still no information about the ultimate destination of the Battalion. Before reaching Aden they could still turn left up the Red Sea to Suez, Port Sudan or Haifa, or right to India or the Persian Gulf or the Far East. . . . Anyone watching events in the Western Desert might by now have been excused for doubting if by the end of the month Suez would still be in our hands.

"On the last day of June the convoy reached the port of Aden, desolate, burnt-up harbour and colourless houses, surrounded by the hills of Hell, red-haired Somalis rowing in rickety boats, the headquarters of the Aden Field Force, . . . the Crescent Hotel . . . For a day the mystery of our destination remained unsolved . . . On the 1st of July, at nine in the morning, the *Mooltan* left Aden, turned to the right and set off independently up the Red Sea towards Suez.

"Although our destination was now known, there were still a few days, to read the last books in peace, . . . to squeeze the most out of the remaining rubbers of bridge, . . . to listen with a growing personal interest to the news of the war in the desert, where the Germans were being held on the so-called Alamein Line, held for no one knew how long. There was land in sight all the way: the Red Sea became the Gulf of Suez; there were burnt desert hills on either side. On the 5th of July the ship anchored off Suez in full view of the white houses, the neatly ordered Flamboyant trees, their flowering over, the dusty desert inland. It was two months since they had left East Grinstead."*

* Durand and Hastings. *The London Rifle Brigade, 1919-50*, 106-10.

Less than two weeks after the 7th Battalion landed at Suez, in the desperate emergency of the hour, it was moved to Burg el Arab in the desert and, three days later, into the front line with the rest of the 23rd Armoured Brigade. "To move armoured brigades after a long sea voyage straight from the boat into battle is to invite disaster. But in those critical days such risks had to be accepted. From the point of view of the Brigade the battle was a tragedy."* For when, on July 22nd, it went into action with the Australians near El Ruweisat, the inexperienced armour drove straight into a minefield and, though pressing home its attack with the utmost gallantry, few of its tanks returned, while the 7th Rifle Brigade, which was a helpless spectator of the disaster, lost many of its own vehicles. By the baffling logic of an administration which regarded figures as more important than battle experience or morale, the now veteran 9th Battalion, which had fought for 18 months in the desert, was disbanded at almost the same time on the grounds that, as there would not be sufficient reinforcements in the Middle East in future to maintain four Battalions of the Rifle Brigade and, as the number of the experienced 9th was higher than that of the 7th, it was dispensable.

*   *   *

At the beginning of August, soon after the first Battle of Alamein ended, the Prime Minister and Chief of Imperial General Staff, Sir Alan Brooke, arrived in Cairo. As a result of their visit General Alexander succeeded Auchinleck as Commander in Chief, Middle East Forces. Almost immediately afterwards, when the new commander elect of the Eighth Army, "Strafer" Gott, was shot down flying on August 7th, General Montgomery was summoned from England to succeed him. This was a guarantee that, when the British again took the offensive, they would only do so after everything possible had been done to ensure that they were adequately equipped for the task set them.

Before this happened, Rommel made one final attempt to defeat the Eighth Army and break into the Delta. But when on August 31st he did so Montgomery was ready for him, and in the Battle of Alam Halfa which followed all three Battalions of the Rifle Brigade, the 1st, 2nd and 7th, contributed to his defeat. The climax of the battle

* *Hastings*, 142.

came when three waves of German tanks, numbering nearly ninety, were halted—at the nearest point to the Nile Valley that the Afrika Korps was ever to reach—by the 6-pounder guns of "B" Company of the 1st Battalion and the machine-guns of "I" Company. Holding their fire till the enemy's armour was within three hundred yards, they knocked out no less than nineteen tanks. The Royal Air Force did the rest. By September 5th the battle was over.

Montgomery had taken command of the Eighth Army at a time when the nature of the desert war was again changing fast. Britain now possessed there, not only a two to one superiority in man-power and more than half again as much armour as the enemy, but, for the first time, with the new American Shermans, a tank which, if not equal to the Germans' best, was capable of giving almost as good as it took. Yet, with the rapid development of anti-tank guns and mine-fields, armour was no longer the queen of the battlefield as in the past two years. At the very time that Britain had built up a force which earlier would have been sufficient to drive the Germans and Italians back into Cyrenaica, the enemy, holding an unflankable front of less than 40 miles between the sea and the Quattara Depression, had established a fortified line in depth almost as formidable as that which had confronted the British Armies on the Somme and at Paschendaele a quarter of a century before. Its very narrowness at this point—unique in that vast desert—which had enabled Auchin-leck and Montgomery to defeat Rommel's attempts to reach Alexandria and the Canal, made it equally hard for the Eighth Army to dislodge the Germans and Italians from the threatening vantage-point they had gained. Facing Montgomery by October 1942, were more than a thousand anti-tank guns in prepared positions and nearly half a million mines. These last, laid in great depth in huge fields, stretching back for miles behind the front line, had to be neutralised under heavy artillery, mortar and machine-gun fire so that the British armour could cross them and deploy in the desert beyond, where German anti-tank guns and tanks were waiting to destroy it. Before Montgomery could, as he put it, "hit the Germans for six out of Africa", his Infantry and Sappers, in the face of inten-sive fire, had first to capture and occupy the enemies' minefields and then, working at high speed in the hours of darkness, clear corridors along which the armour could pass. Even when the latter emerged from these narrow and highly vulnerable lanes, it would have to survive and overcome the concentrated fire of the enemy's anti-tank guns and tanks firing hull down from well-prepared and concealed positions.

If the British offensive failed a stalemate would ensue in the Desert similar to that which existed on the Western Front in World War I. Its effects on Anglo-American strategy would be disastrous. For, unless an immediate break-through by the Army could give the R.A.F. possession of the Cyrenaican airfields, Malta would be starved into surrender and untramelled control of the central Mediterranean would pass into Axis hands. With the German armies in Russia hammering on the gates of Stalingrad and threatening the Caucasus oil-fields on which that country's war potential depended, Turkey's precarious neutrality, already menaced from the Balkans, would become impossible to maintain. A new German drive against Egypt could then be launched from the north through the Levant, while Rommel, massively reinforced from across the Mediterranean, continued to threaten it from the west. And this while the victorious armies and fleet of the Eastern Axis partner, Japan, were still moving inexorably westwards against India and across the Indian Ocean towards the vital British sea communications with Egypt along the East African coast.

Everything, therefore, depended on Montgomery's success. And as that most realist of battle commanders saw, because of the immense depth and strength of the German and Italian defences, despite his superiority of force, victory could only be won by a long, ding-dong battle in which the enemy's strength was gradually crumbled and worn down by attrition. Only if, in its course, Rommel could be induced to erode his own powerful, but numerically limited, armour in costly counter-attacks as he had done at Alma Halfa, could the British armour that survived the mutual hammering break clear into the open desert and destroy the German and Italian infantry from the rear.

In such a battle much was bound to depend, not only on the main body of Infantry who had first to gain possession of the positions from which the armour could operate, but on the Motor Battalions of Riflemen attached to the Armoured Divisions and, in particular, on those serving in Major-General Brigg's 1st Armoured Division and brigaded together under Brigadier Jimmy Bosvile—the 2nd and 7th Rifle Brigade, and the 2nd King's Royal Rifle Corps. Trained to operate with armour and to overcome the obstacles in its path, they could—and did—play a vital part, both in the initial task of clearing, and passing the cavalry through, the minefields, and then, with their anti-tank weapons and special expertise, in providing a pivot from which the armour could operate when it emerged from the lanes through the minefields and gave battle to the waiting defenders' tanks and guns beyond.

Montgomery's plan was meticulously prepared and rehearsed. It was based on his conviction that it would be a long battle which could only be won by taking, as well as giving, hard and continuous knocks. It consisted of three phases—the infantry break-in and capture of the minefields, the clearance of passages through them for the armour, and the destruction by the latter and its motorised supporters of the enemy's front-line infantry and tanks, what he called the "crumbling process", as an essential prelude to the final break-out. It depended on massive and continuous support from the Artillery and the Desert Air Force, both of which Montgomery received in full measure. Above all, it depended on his own will to victory and retention of the initiative, as he met and overcame, by ever-changing dispositions, each of the enemy's responses, and on his ability to inspire his troops with the same unshakable resolution and tenacity as his own.

Nor, for all their losses in the initial stages of the battle, did his troops for a moment fail him. Though the main break-in and breakthrough was planned for the northern half of the 38-mile front—where the 1st and 10th Armoured Divisions were concentrated—in order to deceive, hold and wear down the enemy a secondary attack was simultaneously launched in the south. Here the 1st Rifle Brigade, serving with the 7th Armoured Division under the shadow of Jebel Himeimat, helped to keep a German Armoured Division tied down for several vital days, though at a loss of nineteen of its officers and many of its best N.C.O.s and Riflemen. The opening stages of the battle, which, preceded by a massive barrage, began on the night of October 22/23rd, was attended by serious set-backs caused by the congestion and losses suffered in the narrow and heavily shelled and bombed corridors through which the armour had to pass and by the still greater losses inflicted on the latter as it tried to deploy in the teeth of the enemy's highly effective anti-tank guns and waiting armour. But the tide in favour of the attackers began to turn on the third day when, among other successes gained by the British and Commonwealth infantry, the 7th Rifle Brigade under Lt.-Colonel Geoffrey Hunt, advancing between the Australian and Highland Divisions and taking its stand in a highly exposed position, repelled an armoured attack with its 6-pounders, destroying 14 German and Italian tanks and damaging others.* But the Rifle Brigade's part in the battle took a still more dramatic turn on the night of October 26/27th and the day that followed, when its 2nd Battalion under Lt.-Colonel Vic Turner—who had joined it from the 1st Battalion during the earlier Battle of Alamein—inflicted such losses on the enemy's armour that it broke the back of what Rommel had planned as a major and decisive counter-attack.

This was the famous " Snipe" or Kidney Ridge action which, with the assaults on the breaches at Badajoz and Ciudad Rodrigo, was perhaps the most heroic single feat of arms in the Regiment's history. There are many accounts of the action. The most remarkable, though too long to quote in its entirety, is the chapter entitled " The Riflemen and the Gunners" from Brigadier C. E. Lucas Phillips's *Alamein*. It traces the story from the time when the 2nd Battalion, after two exhausting days of mine-clearance as Minefields Task Force, was ordered by Major-General Briggs, Commander of the 1st Armoured Division, to attack and capture a strong-point deep in the enemy lines to serve as a base from which the armour could subsequently pivot, but about whose precise position there turned out to be some confusion. Not only, as its author wrote, did the action which followed "show the British soldier in one of his finest hours, not only was it unexpectedly to deal one of the most telling blows against the German counter-attack that matured next afternoon, but also it was to illustrate in the most vivid fashion how the mischances, misunderstandings and dark uncertainties that beset the soldier in a vague and confused situation can be overcome by his own self-reliance and battle discipline."

 " The force allotted to Turner for this exploit consisted of his own Battalion of the Rifle Brigade, the residual part (after casualties) of a battery of 76th Anti-Tank Regiment, Royal Artillery, and

---

* "When they were some 250 yards away the tanks ceased to advance, and eventually firing more or less ceased. There were now fourteen smoking wrecks, some of them blazing infernos. They had halted in a beautiful straight line and might well have been dressed by the right." *Durand and Hastings*, 132.

sixteen sappers of 7th Field Squadron, Royal Engineers . . . The Riflemen and Sappers had been through a very trying time on the Minefield Task Force. After three days and two nights continuously on a mission that taxed their nerve and their stamina, they had been able to snatch only a few hours' sleep. Indeed, Tim Marten, the Rifle Brigade adjutant, had not slept for five days. The Riflemen had been operating in separate and dispersed Companies on different minefield lanes, and they had now to be hurriedly collected together and launched into an operation for which a Motor Battalion was not intended and for which it was not properly equipped. For . . . a Motor Battalion was very strong in fire power but very weak in numbers. It was trained as a highly mobile, semi-independent unit for ranging far and wide in the open desert. Its strength lay in the thirty-three bren-carriers of its Scout platoons, its anti-tank Company newly equipped with sixteen 6-pdrs, its machine-gun platoons equipped with the Vickers gun and its platoon of 3-inch mortars. Unlike the majority of conventional infantry units, it was highly efficient in radio telephony. In addition, 2nd RB quite unlawfully possessed a number of machine-guns which they had 'salvaged' from wrecked British aircraft and installed in their carriers and with which they had delighted during the desert war in sallying out at night like moss-troopers to 'beat-up' the enemy leaguers. Thus the only men armed with the rifle, bayonet and grenade of the assault soldier were the men in the three Motor Companies, who numbered only some ninety in all, unless the machine-gunners discarded their Vickers. Casualties in the mine-clearing had reduced this number to seventy-six and the bren-carriers were down to twenty-two. Indeed the whole combined force of Riflemen, Gunners and Sappers in the epic battle now to be fought numbered less than 300.

"Victor Turner himself was a Regular soldier . . . with many months' experience of desert warfare. Some of his officers and men had had more. In his Battalion there was a dash of Irish, but, otherwise, the rank and file were nearly all Londoners and very largely from the East End; the coming action, indeed, was to prove once more that in a tight corner there is no better fighter than your Cockney . . . Except for some recent reinforcements, they were young desert veterans who, like the other Rifle Regiments, had been accustomed to serving as handmaids to the armour, playing the less spectacular role on many a turbulent stage. They were not afraid of tanks, which they had faced many times, and were accustomed to living hard, to getting a move on and to fending for themselves in the most trying situations. Many of them were Regular soldiers and several had already been decorated...

"The Companies were commanded by David Bassett (A Company), Michael Mosley (B), Charles Liddell (C) and Tom Bird (Anti-Tank Company), who had already won the Military Cross and Bar; 'Tim' Marten, highly intelligent and fortunate in having a sense of humour, has been noted as Turner's Adjutant. The anti-tank platoons were commanded with a fire and spirit at times little short of the spectacular by Lieutenants J. E. B. Naumann, J. E. B. Toms, J. B. D. Irwin and A. B. Holt-Wilson; all but the last-named were to be hit and knocked out during the coming fight.

"Allotted to the Battalion for this exploit were eleven gun detachments and other details of 239th Anti-Tank Battery, from 76th Anti-Tank Regiment, Royal Artillery. Five of these guns, however, did not succeed in arriving at the rendezvous, and the remaining one and a half Troops were led by Lieutenant Alan Baer. . . . These gunners of 76th Anti-Tank Regiment were more experienced with the 6-pdr than the Riflemen, who had had little practice with it so far. As befitted those whose task was to await, while under close fire, the menacing onset of tanks, their great quality was their steadiness . . .

"What Turner was called upon to do with this force was to make a night dash through enemy-held country, to establish an island of resistance until the arrival of 24th Armoured Brigade next morning and to continue holding it while the tanks operated forward. . . . The advance was to be led by two bren-carrier platoons in the usual Motor Battalion method . . . All the guns, however, were to remain on the start-line under his second-in-command, Major Tom Pearson, together with the third Scout platoon, the wireless sets, the doctor (Captain Arthur Picton) and his ambulances and the Section trucks, carrying water, rations and ammunition, until the 'success signal' was given by the attacking Companies . . .

"The moon not yet being up, the night was very dark and cold, and the move forward of the sub-units out of the minefield lanes, now 18 in. deep in fine dust, had been made in conditions similar to those of a dense night fog . . . The start-line was under intermittent shellfire, but the force had just time to dispose itself in the order of attack before the barrage . . . It was not till ten past eleven, with the barrage already well ahead, that the carriers advanced, followed by the infantry and sappers. The moon was now up, its large face tinted yellow by the dust particles that filled the atmosphere . . .

"Some barbed wire was then encountered and the carriers were delayed for five minutes while Graham's sappers went in to test for mines. None was found and the advance continued. Parties of enemy were observed, running away, and the carriers opened fire on them. The going became exceedingly bad, with much soft sand. More scattered groups of the enemy were seen running away and twenty German prisoners were captured without resistance. . .

"The barrage however, went on and on. The 2,000 yards' advance that Turner had counted upon was passed and when some 3,000 yards had been traversed, Turner, his mind nagged all the time by the doubts about map locations, became anxious. He, therefore, asked Noyes, the Forward Observation Officer, to call for a round of smoke from 2nd RHA on the objective. As this landed within 300 yards of him, he thought it good enough and halted the advance. In fact, the force never reached the correct map reference of *Snipe* at all, and finished up 900 yards approximately SSE of it."

Pearson, with his anti-tank guns and vehicles, including the Medical Officer and his ambulance, was eagerly awaiting the order to advance. But when it came, artillery fire and enemy air action initially prevented movement despite repeated attempts. Eventually by moving individual vehicles, six Royal Artillery anti-tank guns were taken forward.

"Pearson, also making two or three trips, got forward thirteen of the Rifle Brigade guns, making, together with the RA guns, nineteen 6-pdrs in all. Water, rations and machine-gun ammunition arrived in sufficient quantities in trucks, but, as the unexpected events were to prove, there was far too little ammunition for the 6-pdrs. Off-loading was completed by 3.45 a.m.

"Meanwhile, the Motor Companies, very thin on the ground, had taken up their allotted sectors and had dug-in. The sand was excessively loose and would not hold to the shape of a trench or weapon pit, but slid back as it was dug. The place turned out to be

a German engineer-stores depot and it fortunately provided
Turner with a dug-out, which he took as his headquarters and in
which he posted Marten and the wireless set, manned by Signal-
man 'Busty' Francis and another. A few other small dug-outs were
also found in the area occupied. Telephone lines were run out from
Turner's command-post to each of the Companies. The ground was
foul with excreta and the bodies of some dead Germans lay
about . . .

" . . . While the Motor Companies were consolidating, the carriers
of the Scout platoons, as was their wont in Motor Battalions, drove
outwards to reconnoitre and cover the consolidation Those of
A Company went out north-westward without incident. Those of
C Company, under Dick Flower, however, had a spirited brush
with the enemy. Having gone 250 yards, they encountered barbed
wire, which suggested another minefield. Resolved to investigate,
Flower found a gap and went through it for fully a mile in the
moonlight. Some sixty enemy appeared and began to run away.
The carriers engaged them and took fourteen prisoners.

"About 200 yards away in the moonlight Flower then made out
the shapes of some thirty-five tanks together with a number of
soft-skinned vehicles. Most people would have been satisfied with
obtaining this useful information and would have withdrawn in
the presence of tanks, but Flower brazenly opened fire with his
bren-guns and set fire to three vehicles. At this contumacious behaviour, the enemy tanks moved out and opened fire. They hit an
old derelict vehicle a few yards from one of Flower's carriers. The
derelict burst into flames, the carriers were illuminated and one
of them was hit by a shot from the tanks. The prisoners made a
dash to escape but were mown down by both friend and enemy.
The tanks advanced menacingly against the carriers, firing both
their guns and machine-guns, and Flower, returning their fire, by
mere instinct, withdrew before them. Thus did Turner's small
force begin its exploit in the offensive spirit that was to inspire it
throughout.

"What Flower had stumbled upon was in fact a night leaguer of
a mixed force of tanks, self-propelled guns and vehicles, part
German and part Italian, under the command of the German,
Colonel Teege, and known as the Stiffelmayer Battle Group. It
was located on the long mound to the south-west which we have

called Hill 37 and beyond the brow of which Flower had pene-trated. It was soon evident to Turner, in fact, that the desert around him was, except to his rear, alive with enemy. All to the westward numerous camp fires were to be seen at no great distance. The moon and their lights enabled him to discover another tank leaguer about 1,000 yards to the northward, which was, in fact, a leaguer of 15th Panzer Division. Numbers of enemy vehicles could also be seen.

"By now the anti-tank guns had arrived and had been sited as well as was possible by night. The Vickers and bren-guns had been posted. Digging-in had been barely completed when, at about 3.45, the deep-throated rumble of tanks in motion was heard from the direction of Teege's leaguer. Very soon their sombre shapes could be seen advancing in two bodies. One was obviously shaping course to join the northern leaguer of 15th PZ Division, but the other made straight for Turner's position, moving in line-head.

"The guns were immediately manned and loaded. Fire was with-held until there was a certainty of a kill with the first shot, for the 6-pdr's poor sights made night-shooting very chancy. As the leading tank of the more southerly column drew near, it was seen to be a big Mark IV, with its menacing long gun. It was permitted to penetrate right into C Company's terrain and hit at a range of thirty yards by Sergeant Brown. The shot glowed red-hot as it sunk into the armour-plate and the tank burst into flames. At the same time a Russian 7.62 cm self-propelled gun was likewise knocked out and 'brewed up' on A Company's sector on the west by the broad-shouldered Sergeant Swann, who, determined that his position as platoon sergeant should not deny him a shoot, took control of Corporal Cope's gun.

"The remainder of the enemy force immediately altered course and made away, but a number, as was to appear at first light, halted and took cover in small, scrub-smudged folds in the ground only a few hundred yards to the west. Only one of the crew of the big Mark IV escaped. Leaping out, he ran to a trench a little way off, whence, with commendable aggression, he sniped at the British positions for the remainder of the night until a Rifleman, locat-ing him at first light, crept out and finished him off with a grenade.

"These two kills with the new guns caused immense jubilation.

The Riflemen had heard with delight of the exploit of the London Rifle Brigade two days before on the edge of the Australian front and were eager to emulate their brother Green Jackets. From this moment the garrison was fired to a most astonishing degree with an eager and offensive confidence. As events disclosed themselves, this spirit swelled into something even more impressive—the exultant spirit of the happy warrior . . .

"Shortly after this the garrison sustained a serious loss in the disappearance of 2nd RHA's Forward Observation Officer. He left Turner's dug-out at about 4 a.m. to reconnoitre, but had not gone far before he was seized by a German patrol. His signallers remained, but the lack of a FOO was to be sorely felt.

"At 5.45 a.m. Pearson returned to the Highland Division lines with the non-fighting transport, taking the prisoners with him. He also was never able to get back to the position, urgent though its needs became, for at the approach of daylight the pace of events began to quicken. Sergeant Swann and CSM Atkins should have gone back with him, but asked permission to stay.

"Half an hour later, as the sky began to change to the colour of pewter and the bitter pre-dawn wind whipped across the desert, Turner was able to assess more clearly the nature of his footing in the inhospitable landscape. The almost flat scene, stretching for a mile and a half all round, shadowed by the faint anonymous folds and ripples of the desert, was overlooked by the slight elevations that formed the horizon on all sides except the south. Patches of low, scrubby camel's thorn stippled and darkened the desert canvas here and there, affording some exiguous cover for those who knew how to use it. This scrub extended into the shallow oval in which the garrison had taken station and they had been quick to take advantage of it as they sited their weapon pits and trenches, knowing well, however, that full daylight would show the need to alter their dispositions. The excellence of their concealment and digging, indeed, saved them from a great many casualties in what Turner called the 'deluge of fire poured down on us for the rest of that day.' The gun-pits were never really pin-pointed by the enemy . . .

"It was in this grey dawn twilight that the enemy tank leaguers both to the north and to the south-west were to be seen starting into motion. For some such activity Turner had been watching, for he knew that at the approach of light all tanks would break leaguer and move out to whatever was their mission for the day. Contrary to his expectation, they moved westward. To the surprise of the garrison, a number of the German panzers which had halted in dead ground after their attempted move in the night suddenly broke cover at ranges of from 600 to 800 yards. They thus offered highly tempting rear and flank targets at killing ranges to the Riflemen's gun detachments as they peered out in the biting wind.

"In such circumstances, it was perhaps not in accord either with doctrine or with their mission for the garrison to disclose their positions and engage. But they did not feel in a calculating spirit that day and could not resist the temptation to attack. The dawn was shattered as eight or nine guns barked with the 6-pdr's sharp, high-velocity crack. The results were spectacular. Eight tanks and self-propelled guns were destroyed to the north (all being found derelict on the battlefield subsequently) and a further eight were claimed from Teege's battle group to the south-west, of which three were still derelict on the ground a month later. Upon the unfortunate crews who attempted to escape the machine-guns poured their streams of bullets. Bursts of unrestrained cheers ran through the garrison at the thrill of this dramatic success. A ripple of exaltation seized all ranks. From that moment they felt themselves to be on top of the enemy. Sixteen birds for breakfast was a very good start to the day's shooting.

"This display of aggression, however, was answered by the inevitable counter action. Their position disclosed, the garrison was heavily shelled. Sergeant Saunders was killed and his gun knocked out by a direct hit and two other guns were damaged beyond immediate use . . .

"To alter positions in daylight was a dangerous and difficult task. The bren-carriers had to be called upon to shift the guns, and the movement immediately attracted enemy fire. Captain Hugo Salmon, Bird's second-in-command, was gravely wounded and lingered for some six hours before he died, devotedly tended to the last by Rifleman Burnhope, the medical orderly. At about the same time a single German soldier, who had been lying concealed in the very centre of the position, was seen to leap up and run at full speed westward. He was unarmed. Quixotically, the

Riflemen let him go. Not a shot was fired. 'We all instinctively felt,' said Bird afterwards, 'that he was not fair game.'

" Full daylight revealed to Turner only too clearly the nakedness of his position ... To north, west and south enemy movement and activity of all sorts was to be seen. Marten, coming up from the dug-out, where he had been reporting events by wireless to 7th Motor Brigade, looked round the morning scene, where the shadows were beginning to sharpen under the rising sun, and asked:

" 'Have we come to the right place, Colonel?'

" Turner answered: 'God knows. But here we are and here we damned well stay.'

" He expected 24th Armoured Brigade to appear on the scene very soon but, meanwhile, long used to work in close association with gunners, he was fretting at the loss of his Forward Observation Officer. The picture around him was alive with targets and he would need gunner support if attacked by infantry. On his orders, Marten reported the loss ... to Brigade Headquarters and asked urgently for a replacement. One was promised, but never arrived, for from now onwards the British lines to the east and the approaches to them were so scourged by enemy shellfire that nothing could get forward.

" The anticipated appearance of 24th Armoured Brigade was not long delayed, but it was of a totally unexpected nature. At 7.30 a.m., as the huge crimson globe of the sun began to climb out of the British lines, great clouds of dust heralded their approach. The Shermans and Grants breasted the slight crest of the *Oxalic* line and halted to search the exposed ground ahead with their field-glasses. Two thousand yards ahead they saw a strongpoint of guns and weapon pits among the camel's thorn, with a sprinkling of burnt-out German tanks hard by. Not recognizing what was intended to be their own 'pivot of manoeuvre', they promptly opened fire on it with high explosive. Much of the fire fell on 239th Battery, who lay nearest to them. This was galling. In an attempt to stop it, Turner sent out his Intelligence Officer, Jack Wintour, on the dangerous mission of making his way to our tanks in a bren-carrier. This Wintour accomplished. He succeeded in abating the fire of the leading squadron, but the remainder of

the brigade continued to bombard their friends. The irrepressible
Wintour then calmly returned.

"At 8 o'clock, 24th Brigade began to move forward towards
Turner's position. Immediately they did so Turner observed about
twenty-five German tanks, nearly all of which were the latest and
most powerful long-gunned 'Specials', taking up hull-down
positions . . . to oppose them. In doing so, they presented themselves as targets to Turner's guns. In spite of the long range, the
6-pdrs at once engaged the big tanks and brewed up three of them
at 1,100 yards. As their crews baled out they were shot down by
machine-guns from the advancing Shermans. The armoured
brigade now knew who were their friends.

"Half-an-hour later the Shermans joined hands with the garrison. Instead of bringing the relief that it promised, however, their
arrival brought on a fight of violence and confusion. Drawn as by
a magnet, the enemy attacked our exposed and halted tanks with
every weapon that they could bring to bear—from their hull-down
tanks, from the anti-tank guns of 115th Panzer Grenadiers and
33rd Panzerjagers and from the heavy shells of their medium
artillery. In this onslaught our tanks got very much the worst of
things. Both sides laid down smoke screens and the whole area
became an inferno of smoke, bursting high explosive, dust and
darting tracers. The German armour employed the highly effective tactics of putting down a round of smoke accurately just in
front of one of our tanks and then firing into the smoke with
armour-piercing shot. Within fifteen minutes seven Shermans
were on fire within Turner's position.

"The worst of this fierce conflict took place in the sector occupied
by 239th Battery. Sergeant Bob Smith's gun, which was close to
one of our Shermans, was knocked out by a direct hit, and he was
blinded for several hours; Bombardier Barnes and Gunner Mercer
were killed and Gunner Kane shell-shocked. The stalwart sergeant,
in spite of his blindness, moved over to join his friend, Sergeant
Ronald Wood, taking Kane with him and nursing him until he
recovered. Sergeant Norry's gun, similarly placed close to a
Sherman, was also knocked out, but with no serious casualties. A
moment later the tank itself was hit and burst into flames with
great violence. . . .

"Quite clearly, it was out of the question for the armoured

brigade to stay in this death trap. It was certainly not the 'firm base' it was intended to be. Very rightly, they withdrew to hull-down positions on the *Oxalic* ridge, leaving a void of a mile and a quarter between themselves and the garrison, who were not sorry to see them go. As they withdrew, they were attacked by some German tanks and guns from the north in the Kidney area and this gave the gunners of 239th Battery an opportunity to have their first shoot. A Mark IV was clearly visible at about 1,800 yards. The range was extreme for a 6-pdr, and Sergeant Binks, when urged to shoot by Mike Mosley, the RB Company commander, rightly declined. This was completely against his training. A little later, when the Mark IV moved, Binks, to the mild annoyance of his own watching Troop commander, was persuaded by Mosley to 'have a go'. With his third shot Binks hit and halted the tank, which was immediately towed away by another.

"At about the same time (9 a.m.) considerable movement of Italian troops gave indications that they were about to attack the garrison on the south with infantry. Turner ordered the Scout platoon of C Company to 'see them off'. The carriers did so accordingly, engaging the enemy infantry with small arms so effectively that many were killed and wounded and the rest ran away westwards. Two captured British 6-pdrs were then seen being towed into position. These also the carriers engaged and put the towing vehicles out of action. 'During the next half-hour,' Flower recorded, 'many excellent sniping targets were offered by small groups of Italians as they tried to run away.' With their bren-gun ammunition running low, rifles only were used.

"Turner, 'hopping mad' at being shelled by his friends, as he continued to be for some time, and exasperated by the lack of a FOO, became seriously concerned also for the wounded. If the doctor could not come up, somehow an attempt must be made to get the more seriously wounded back to him, whatever the risk. Turner accordingly ordered Captain Peter Shepherd-Cross, accompanied by Sergeant Sampher, to make a dash in three bren-carriers. The loading of the wounded into the carriers was done under fire and the little convoy was shelled all the way back. Shepherd-Cross's carrier actually sustained a direct hit from a 75-mm but miraculously was not seriously damaged . . . It was Shepherd-Cross's intention to bring back Picton, together with

more ammunition, which was urgently needed. He found Tom
Pearson standing by with a convoy trying to get through, as he
continued to do most of the day, but whenever he attempted to
cross the ridge the convoy was immediately lashed with fire which
it could not hope to get through.

"The garrison was, therefore, now alone and cut-off, with
virtually no hope of relief. Turner and Bird went round the
position telling the men so and that they would have to stick it-out.
The officers were answered by little grins and Cockney jokes. The
men closed more firmly up to their weapons, bracing themselves,
entirely confident. What had happened so far had been a sharp
enough experience, but not a severe test. They had no doubt that
such a test would come.

"The continued resistance of the island outpost had become a
serious nuisance to the enemy, who now evidently decided that
they must wipe it out. Two further direct attacks upon it were
mounted at 10 o'clock. They were part of a two-pronged offensive
operation ordered by Colonel Teege from behind Hill 37. One
prong of this operation was directed against 24th Armoured
Brigade, who had just retired. This was to be carried out by some
twenty-five to thirty German tanks of the Stiffelmayer Group. To
make this attack, however, the German tanks would be exposed to
dangerous flanking fire from Turner's outpost, and Teege accordingly ordered the Italian element of this battle group to attack
the garrison and wipe it out. This attack was entrusted to Captain
Preve of 12th Battalion, 133rd Tank Regiment, Littorio Division.
He set out from Hill 37 with thirteen M13 tanks. On seeing them
advance, Turner ordered the guns of Sergeants Brown and Dolling
to be moved to the west sector at once. The detachments responded
without hesitation, but the soft sand caused the wheels to sink to
their axles. Carriers were then called in and, there being no proper
towing-hook, the trails of the guns were hitched up with tow
ropes. The awkward manoeuvre, naturally, drew enemy fire at
once, and Lieutenant R. M. Salt and three men were killed.

"The Italian attack was, however, easily beaten off. Four tanks
were hit quickly. The remainder did not attempt to press the attack
and withdrew. While this attempt was in progress, the German
tanks of the Stiffelmayer Group were seen to move out of their
hull-down positions behind Hill 37, driving eastwards across the

southern front of the garrison. Their intention to attack 24th Brigade was clear to Turner and his men.

"The Riflemen, having disposed of the Italians, at once engaged the Germans, who presented broadside-on targets at about 1,000 yards. Thereupon the German tank commander detached half his strength directly towards the garrison. Notwithstanding this threat, the Riflemen continued to engage the broadside-on tanks attacking 24th Brigade, and the latter were similarly presented with broadside-on targets by the tanks attacking the garrison. In this spirited 'cross ruff', as Turner described it, no fewer than eight German tanks were set on fire, several others were hit and the remainder withdrew behind Hill 37.

"By now it was nearly 11 o'clock in the forenoon and the position had become extremely hot in both senses of the word. The desert was quivering with heat. The gun detachments and the platoons squatted in their pits and trenches, the sweat running in rivers down their dust-caked faces. There was a terrible stench. The flies swarmed in black clouds upon the dead bodies and the excreta and tormented the wounded. The place was strewn with burning tanks and carriers, wrecked guns and vehicles, and over all drifted the smoke and the dust from bursting high explosive and from the blasts of guns. Six more carriers had been hit and set on fire. The 6-pdrs of Sergeants Hine and Dolling had been knocked out and only thirteen remained in action . . . Some of the detachments were down to two or three men, and officers were manning guns to replace casualties . . .

" . . . But the offensive spirit had firmly seized upon all ranks. The bursting shells that shook the ground and the heavy shot that smashed a gun or carrier, or that took the breath from one's lungs with the vacuum of its close passing, could not shake that spirit. Every kill was acclaimed. At last they had got a weapon that could knock out the panzers. Gone was any thought of 'lying doggo', any conception of mere defence of a 'pivot of manoeuvre'. They eagerly engaged every target within range. The gunners of 239th Battery, who so far had had only one target, buried their dead on the spot, manned their brens and rifles and occupied themselves with 'rabbit shooting'. On three sides of the island there were enemy movements of every sort—parties on foot, trucks, staff cars, motor-cycles. Turner, Bird and other officers moved about from gun to gun throughout the morning; so also did Rifleman Burnhope, giving to the wounded, including a few German wounded found in the position, such succour as his scanty medical stores allowed. The most serious concern, however, was the shortage of 6-pdr ammunition. Bird and the great-hearted Corporal Francis—the 'young old Bill', as Bird called him—set about transferring the heavy green boxes from one gun to another by jeep, unconcerned by the heavy burst of fire which this blatant movement invited. The shortage was particularly acute on the south-western sector, facing Hill 37, where Lieutenant Jack Toms's guns were sited.

"It was precisely from this direction that another attack was mounted at 1 o'clock, and again by Italian tanks. Believing, no doubt, that there could now be little left of the garrison after so long a drubbing, and having seen no gunfire for some time, eight tanks and one or more Semovente self-propelled field guns (of 105-mm calibre) advanced on the position, firing their machine-guns vigorously. Here there was now only one gun in action that could bear. It was that commanded by Sergeant Charles Calistan, the finely-built young athlete from the East End of London. He was alone, one of his detachment lying wounded and the others having, on his orders, crawled away to fetch more ammunition. Seeing his predicament, Turner himself and Jack Toms ran to join him. Calistan took post on the left of the gun as layer, Turner on the right as loader, and Toms behind as No. 1. Turner ordered fire to be held until the enemy tanks were within 600 yards. The sergeant and the two officers then opened a devastating fire. Five of the eight tanks and the Semovente were hit very quickly, one after the other, and burst into flames. The three remaining tanks still came on, however, with great spirit, machine-gunning hard, and there were only two rounds of ammunition left. Toms ran to his jeep, which was a hundred yards away, and quickly loaded several boxes of ammunition from a gun out of action. He drove back with the machine-gun bullets from the three tanks streaming down on him. It was an almost suicidal act. The jeep was riddled and burst into flames ten yards short of Calistan's gun. Turner ran to the jeep. So also did Corporal Francis, who had doubled over from Hine's gun to give a hand. Turner, Toms and Francis lugged

the ammunition from the burning vehicle and dragged it to the
gun.

"At this point a shell splinter penetrated Turner's steel helmet
and wounded him severely in the skull. He keeled over sideways
beside the gun, the blood streaming down over his eyes. Toms and
Calistan carried on, joined now by Corporal Barnett as loading
number. The three remaining Italian tanks, their machine guns
blazing, were now within 200 yards. The silent gun seemed to be
at their mercy. Their bullets were beating like rain upon the gunshield and kicking up spurts of sand in the shallow pit. Calistan,
who all this time had been keeping them in his sight with the
utmost unconcern, while he waited for the ammunition, laid with
coolness and deliberation. With three shots he killed all three
tanks, which added their conflagrations to those of the other six.
He then coolly turned round and said: 'We haven't had a chance of
a brew all morning, but the Eyeties have made us a fire, so let's
use it.' He thereupon poured some water into a billy-can, which he
set on the bonnet of the burning jeep, and brewed-up some tea.
To the wounded Turner, it was 'as good a cup as ever I've tasted.'*

"This must, without doubt, have been a disconcerting blow to
the enemy. An intercept of his wireless disclosed that he was
seriously concerned by this island of resistance just before he was
to launch his big counter-attack. No further tank activity, however, took place for another three hours, but in the meantime the
shelling continued.

"Turner, having lain down for a while under a camel's thorn
bush near Calistan's gun, insisted, against all persuasion, on visiting his guns once more, but the effort was too severe and he had
to be taken down into the small headquarters dug-out where
Marten and the wireless were. Even from here he occasionally
sallied out to give encouragement and example, but later in the
day he began to suffer from the hallucination that he was defending a harbour against hostile warships. On seeing a tank, he would
exclaim 'Open fire on that destroyer.' It was, indeed, a very good
simile and an hallucination of the sort that showed the spirit in
the man. At length his officers had to restrain him physically.

"The long, hot afternoon that followed under almost con-

---

* Calistan, with the DCM and the MM to his name, was later given a commission, but
was killed in Italy. He had been recommended for the Victoria Cross.

tinuous shell and mortar fire, with no chance of hitting back and with the desert floor dancing in the rays of the furnace overhead, was perhaps the hardest part of the day. After the fatigues of the long night, the strain of the gruelling hours under the sun became accentuated by hunger and thirst; there was no chance to eat anything and those who did not have full equipment 'on the man' had nothing to drink either. Before long Bird, Toms, Liddell, Flower, Irwin and Crowder had all been wounded. In the tiny command-post dug-out six wounded officers and men, two other officers and two signalmen were crowded together with a million flies. No officer was left on the western sector, and command fell to Sergeant Brown. It became impossible to move about in the position except at a crawl, but in A Company's sector Sergeant-Major Atkins crawled round from time to time to give cheer to the Riflemen of the motor platoons.

" Command and control thus became extremely difficult. Indeed, each sub-unit and even each gun was now acting mainly by instinct on its own initiative, an initiative that needed no spur. The Scout platoons, performing an equally valiant if less vital service, had been urged by the same spirit, engaging the enemy constantly with bren or rifle, but having their carriers hit one after another. By 4 p.m. the carriers of C Company, having fired 45,000 rounds, had no more ammunition.

"Meanwhile, at the headquarters of 1st Armoured Division, Raymond Briggs was following events, as disclosed by the radio, with mixed feelings. Naturally impelled to send help to the hard-pressed garrison, he had, on the other hand, to weigh carefully the new fact, of which he had become aware at 10.30 that morning, through wireless intercepts, that 21st Panzer Division had come up from the south overnight and that their headquarters had actually been located only a little west of Kidney. He must expect to have to face them very soon, as well as the remains of 15th Panzer and the Littorio. To do so he must conserve his armour. He had, therefore, to choose between the disagreeable alternatives of losing the Rifle Brigade or losing more tanks. He decided that he must leave the garrison to fight it out themselves. Never was a calculated risk more stoutly justified by those exposed to it.

" Greater trials, and with them greater triumphs, were still to come. Once more the garrison was attacked by its friends. This time it was 2nd Armoured Brigade, whose tanks breasted the eastern horizon at about 4 o'clock and whose gunners, 11th RHA, subjected the garrison to the most vicious shelling by the 105-mm guns of their Priests. As Turner said afterwards, during an 'unpleasant' day, this was the 'most unpleasant' thing of all.

"Though the garrison did not know it, this was the hour that Rommel had decided upon for his counter-attack and the area immediately to their north was one of the two principal points of thrust ordered by Rommel. Soon after this unpleasant shelling experience, the garrison could plainly see a powerful force of seventy German and Italian tanks, accompanied by self-propelled guns, forming up in the area west of Kidney Ridge, facing eastwards towards the British lines. They were in two groups, one behind the other. In the most forward group could be seen thirty Germans and ten Italians and in their rear were another thirty Germans. The Riflemen and the Gunners watched them mustering at about 1,200 yards and it was evident that a big action was about to begin. They sat tight in their pits and trenches speculating what might be their part in it. They had not long to wait for the answer.

"At 5 o'clock the first of these groups advanced south-eastward in clouds of dust to attack 2nd Armoured Brigade. The German tanks in this group were almost certainly from the newly arrived 21st Panzer Division, for the course of their advance took them within a few hundred yards of the watching garrison, broadside-on, and, as Turner was to say, 'it is inconceivable that the tanks which had been engaging us all day should have been so unwise.' Advancing in an open phalanx, the tanks shaped course to pass the north-east sector and it was now that the gunners of 239th Battery got their real shoot. They had four guns left in action—four small guns against forty tanks . . . Thrilled and fascinated, the Gunners watched the immensely impressive spectacle as the powerful force roared slowly athwart their front, the sand billowing from the tracks . . . All four guns were now scoring. Their shots struck home like hammers on an anvil, glowing red as they drilled through the steel walls. In two minutes a dozen tanks were crippled, half of them in flames. The nearest column then turned to face the guns with their frontal armour and attack them. As

they came on, they struck with every weapon in their armoury—
with machine-gun, high explosive and . . . armour-piercing shot.
The Gunners, filled with exaltation at their swift success, stuck to
their guns and gave shot for shot. A great long-gunned Mark IV
Special bore straight down upon Cullen, approaching to within
100 yards, 'hideously menacing', its machine-guns blazing and its
bullets penetrating the gunshield. Cullen stood fast and he and
Binks hit it together.

"A minute later Binks's gun, after having knocked out four
tanks, was smashed to pieces by a direct hit. Except for himself, all
his detachment were killed or mortally wounded, one of them
having his head severed from his body. Cullen, a model of steady
hand and heart, was also hit, together with his excited layer,
Gunner Evans. On the Gunners' left, some of Irwin's platoon also
engaged vigorously. Three tanks and a self-propelled gun fell to
Sergeant Pearson, but his own gun and Sergeant Brett's were, in
turn, knocked out. Meantime, bursts of fire from the Rifle Brigade
machine-gunners streamed out on the enemy tank crews as they
sought to escape.

"These few guns it was, therefore, that brought Rommel's
counter-attack to a standstill on this sector. Surprised and shaken,
with half his forty tanks halted in confusion and several of them
burning fiercely, and finding himself now attacked frontally by
2nd Armoured Brigade as well, the enemy commander called off
his attack, withdrew and took cover in low ground to the west of
Kidney Ridge, twenty-five minutes after he had begun his intended
attack.

"This, however, was only the first phase of the afternoon action.
On observing the reverse to his comrades ahead, the commander
of the enemy second wave, which was advancing in their rear,
detached 15 Mark III tanks in a direct assault upon the island outpost. They came in head-on, advancing cautiously on the northern
sector and making brilliant use of ground in their approach. It was
the most dangerous attack that had yet been made against the
garrison, and only two guns—those of Sergeant Hine and Sergeant
Miles—now remained that were in a position to oppose them. It
looked very much, indeed, like the end of things. Seeing the critical
situation, Lieutenant Barry Holt-Wilson, who . . . had been manning a gun in another sector with Sergeant Ayris and Rifleman

Chard, swung it right round from front to rear. The three guns had an average of only ten rounds of ammunition left.

"Sergeant-Major Atkins, from his slit trench at A Company's little command post, watched enthralled. He felt as though he were witnessing a Wild West film, with tanks for horses. He saw his machine-gunners with their weapons closely following the turrets of the panzers, ready to burst into fire the second that the tank crews leapt out. He saw the guns of Hine and Miles likewise following their targets in their sights and, as the panzers drew closer and closer, he asked himself: 'Why the hell don't they open fire?' Because of the enemy's shrewd use of small folds in the ground, effective fire could not be brought to bear until the range was very short indeed. As they came on, the panzers lashed the detachments with machine-gun fire, especially that of Sergeant Miles. Miles was hit and his detachment forced into their slit trench. It certainly looked like the end. The juggernauts were almost on top of them. Sergeant Swann, however, whose gun had been knocked-out earlier, seeing Miles's gun unmanned, crawled out from his position thirty yards away under the stream of bullets and manned it alone. The guns of Hine and Holt-Wilson stood their ground in the most determined fashion and at about 200 yards all three opened fire. Swann continued to load, lay and fire alone, until Miles's detachment, inspired by his leadership, jumped forward and joined him.

"As in all the previous encounters, the effect was shattering. All four of the leading tanks were knocked out. Two others in the rear of the leaders were also knocked out. All six went up in flames. Last to be destroyed was a Mark III that Swann hit at 100 yards and, as he did so, Wintour, watching from the battalion command post and giving physical expression to the exhilaration that filled every man who witnessed the spectacular action, leapt up and down with excitement, shouting:

" 'He's got him, he's got him, he's got him!'

"The remaining nine tanks of this assault force promptly backed and took up hull-down positions about 800 yards away, whence, immune from the fire of the 6-pdrs, they kept up a galling fire with their machine-guns. From the last tank that Swann had knocked out a man was heard screaming with agony and his screams were heard in all the remaining hours to come.

"The three guns that had repulsed this dangerous attack were now left with only three rounds each. Squatting in their gun-pits, the detachments, expecting the attack to be renewed, made ready to use them up to the very last. So certain had it appeared that the position was going to be overrun that Marten, on orders from Turner in the command post, had burnt all codes and maps.

"The enemy, however, Germans and Italians alike, had now had quite enough. The scene of desolation in and around the island outpost was staggering. Nearly seventy tanks and self-propelled guns, all but seven being of the enemy, lay wrecked or derelict, many still burning and the black smoke from their fuel trailing forlornly across the desert. To these were added the shattered remains of several tracked and wheeled vehicles. Hanging out of the open turrets of the tanks, or concealed within their bowels, were the charred corpses of their crews who had been unable to escape the flames. Around them sprawled the bodies of those caught by the Riflemen's machine guns. Within or immediately on the perimeter of the island were seven British tanks and one German, and the wreckages of sixteen bren-carriers, several jeeps and ten guns. Five other guns had been damaged; out of the original nineteen, not more than six remained that could be relied upon to engage.

"Within this panorama of desolation and death there still remained, however, some 200 gallant men, red-eyed, coated with dirt and sweat, hungry and thirsty, but their spirit even higher than when they had first set out. Within their desert keep, as the crimson sun began to damp down its fires and to tinge with blood the funeral plumes of smoke from the dead tanks, they waited calmly with their few remaining guns and their last rounds of ammunition for a final attack that never came. They waited also for night, which, whatever might be its fresh perils, they had been told would bring them relief. There had been good wireless communication all day with 7th Motor Brigade, and Marten had been talking freely to Charles Wood, but at 5.40 Bosvile himself spoke on the air and said:

" 'Friends will come and take your place at dinner time. You are to wait until they are happily settled in your place. Your carriages will then arrive and take you home.'

"Marten asked: 'Will it be an early dinner or a late one?' and was told:

" 'The fashionable time.'

" This typical radio cross-talk meant, though Turner and Marten did not know it, that one of the Sussex Battalions of 133rd Lorried Infantry Brigade had been ordered to relieve the garrison at about 9 o'clock that night. The codes having been destroyed, Bosvile could give them no more information.

" When last light came at 7.30 the enemy tanks to the north-west were seen to pull out from their hull-down positions and move farther back to go into night leaguer. Twenty minutes later they were seen nicely silhouetted against the pale evening sky, and such guns as could bear in that direction, in a spirit of jubilant defiance, shot off the last of their ammunition against them, scoring one hit at 1,200 yards.

" Some hours before this, Turner had been overcome by the heat and the effects of his head wound. The Company commanders and the adjutant therefore held a conference when darkness had fallen to determine the measures to be taken. Their chief anxiety now was that the enemy might mount an attack by infantry, which they had small chance of withstanding. However, they made such preparations as they could, contracting their perimeter, and decided meantime to evacuate the wounded as soon as it was fully dark, without waiting for their relief.

" No attack actually developed, but soon afterwards the enemy could be seen and plainly heard very close in on three sides collecting wounded and towing away the tank casualties considered repairable. The man wounded when the last tank was hit was still screaming. No offensive action was taken against these parties, however, as the garrison's own wounded were being collected for evacuation. For this purpose there remained three jeeps, six bren-carriers out of the twenty-two that had started, and one lorry, which had been unaccountably left in the position the night before and which, lying in a hollow to the east, had miraculously survived. So also had Baer's White scout car, riddled with bullets and shell splinters.

" It was now 9.30 and there was no sign of the relief. Holt-Wilson went round the whole position and removed the breech-blocks of every RB gun that still remained serviceable; Baer did the like for the RA guns. At 10.30 our artillery started shelling the German leaguer to the north-west. The enemy thereupon broke leaguer and his tanks began making straight for the garrison, forming a new leaguer very close to it. There was still no sign of relief, the Sussex Battalion having, in fact, been completely misdirected by the same sort of map-reading discrepancies which had led Turner's force itself astray. Bosvile accordingly gave Marten permission to withdraw.

"At 11.15, weary in body but not in spirit, the gallant company withdrew in good order, leaving behind them the bodies of their comrades who had won the soldier's highest honour. One 6-pdr was successfully towed out by the Gunners of 239th Battery . . .

"This heroic action illustrates not only the typical minor mischances and pitfalls of battle and of desert battles in particular; it illustrates not only the splendid fighting spirit and battle discipline of the two units that took part; it illustrates also the helplessness of tanks against good anti-tank guns, stoutly manned, even when sited on ground of no natural advantage. The immediate lesson that was read to the whole of the Army was that, when equipped with their own 6-pdrs, the infantry could themselves see off a tank attack and inflict severe losses upon the enemy. The Battalion and their Royal Artillery comrades, in resolutely holding ground that in itself was worthless, had that day struck one of the stoutest blows that helped to win the Alamein victory. They had destroyed or disabled more enemy tanks than had so far been destroyed or damaged in any single unit action and had shot one of the most crippling bolts in the destruction of Rommel's counter-attack of that day.

"The action gained such fame throughout the desert, becoming somewhat embroidered in the retailing, that a Committee of Investigation was appointed a month later to examine the ground, count the still remaining carcasses of the enemy tanks and sift all the evidence critically. Their inquiry was searching. They analysed the performance of every single gun. Taking into consideration the number of wrecks that had by then been removed by ourselves or by the enemy, the committee concluded that the minimum number of tanks burnt and totally destroyed was thirty-two— twenty-one German and eleven Italian—plus five self-propelled guns, and that certainly another fifteen, perhaps twenty—tanks had been knocked out and recovered, making a grand total of fifty-seven. A few tracked and wheeled vehicles had also been destroyed. Only a very few of the tanks recovered could have been repaired before the battle ended.

"This phenomenal success had not been won without its cost in flesh and blood, but, speaking relatively, the cost had not been grievously severe. Of the total force of less than 300 who had started out from the Highland lines, seventy-two Riflemen and Gunners had been killed or wounded, to which numbers were to be added some R.E. casualties, not ascertained. The figure would have been very much higher if they had not been well trained in the principle of 'dig or die' and in the craft of concealment.

"Montgomery was naturally delighted. This was just what he wanted. In due process of time there came the Victoria Cross for Victor Turner, the DSO for Bird, the DCM for Sergeants Calistan and Swann and Rifleman Chard, and the Military Cross and the Military Medal for those who were selected from the many more who earned them among that gallant company."*

The citation for Colonel Turner's Victoria Cross—the twenty-seventh won by the Regiment since the decoration was instituted, and the highest number won by any one infantry Regiment—read:

"Throughout the action Lieut.-Colonel Turner never ceased to go to each part of the front as it was threatened. Wherever the fire was heaviest there he was to be found. In one case, finding a solitary six-pounder gun in action (the others being casualties) and manned only by another officer and a sergeant, he acted as loader and with these two destroyed five enemy tanks. While doing this he was wounded in the head, but he refused all aid. His personal gallantry and complete disregard of danger as he moved about encouraging his Battalion to resist to the last, resulted in the infliction of a severe defeat on the enemy tanks. He set an example of leadership and bravery which inspired his whole Battalion."

* C. E. Lucas Phillips, *Alamein*, 267-97, "The Riflemen and the Gunners". "This account of the action," the author writes, "has been compiled mainly from the report of the Committee of Investigation, the official report after the action by Bird and Marten (incorporating a report by Flower), the accounts by Turner in the *British Army* and the *Rifle Brigade Chronicle*, the personal narratives to the author by Turner, Bird, Marten, Baer, Roper-Caldbeck, Atkins and Swann, and various other sources in matters of detail."

To this and Brigadier Lucas Phillips' magnificent narrative, there is a postscript in a letter written after the action by Sergeant Calistan, already the holder of the M.M., who was now awarded the D.C.M. and recommended for the V.C

"All our guns seemed to be firing at once. My target burst into flames but came on for another fifty yards before it was halted. Suddenly the night was bright with burning tanks. Over on my left one blew up at two hundred yards.

"We were giving them hell, but we weren't by any means getting away with it. Our position was rather exposed and they let us have everything they had got. They even attacked us with lorried infantry. It was our twelve guns against fifty tanks, and when they turned about and retired we knew that for the moment our guns had won. Some of the enemy tanks tried to hide by mixing up with knocked-out tanks and derelict vehicles—but we are used to most of Jerry's tricks. The crew of one German tank tried to repair it on the spot. We picked them off with a rifle. I heard an 88 mm banging away at us on a flank—then silence as one of our guns scored a direct hit.

"All this time the enemy never let up; nor did we. Time seemed to be lost in the battle. My gun had smashed up five tanks in that first attack—and I am only counting those that 'brewed up', that's our way of saying they burnt out. Some of our guns were out of action. Some had run out of ammo. I can't remember how many. The thing that sticks out is the Company commander saying that we were cut off and that there wasn't anything that could get through to us. We would fight it out. Keep on firing as long as we had a shell or bullet! Yes. We understood.

"And when you had time to listen, it was only then you realised that you had fewer and fewer guns firing. We were also short of water, but somehow you didn't think about that. Two of my gun crew crept out on their bellies—right into the open to get to some ammo. They were under enemy fire the whole time and their progress was terribly slow. Then our platoon officer decided to reach his Jeep, which had four boxes of ammo on board. God knows how he got to it—they were machine gunning the whole way. He started coming towards us and then they hit the Jeep and it caught fire, but he kept on coming. We got the ammo off, and then I had an idea. We hadn't had a thing to drink and we naturally hadn't been able to light a fire, but here was a perfectly good one. So I put a can of water on the Jeep and it brewed up well enough for three cups of tea!

"Our Colonel kept going from gun to gun. How he inspired us! The enemy tried to shift us with an infantry attack, but we soon sent them on their way with our Bren-carriers and our infantry, who were in position in front of us. When the next tank attack came in, the Colonel was acting as loader of my gun. He got wounded in the head—a nasty wound and we wanted to bind it up, but he wouldn't hear of it. 'Keep firing!'—that's what he wanted, and we didn't pause. When the gun ran short of ammo he got it from one of the others.

"When the Colonel was too weak to refuse attention we bound up his head and put him behind some scrub. He called out that he wanted to know what was happening and my officer kept up a running commentary. We hit three tanks with three successive shots and the Colonel yelled out; 'Good work—a hat trick!' Another gun got two tanks with one shell—they were one behind the other and it passed right through the nearest one into the other and knocked both of them out.

"The ground was littered with broken tanks. We had been fighting for nearly thirty-six hours. I've been talking most of the time about my own gun, but what I've said goes for all of them. There was a Rifleman and a sergeant who had fourteen tanks to their credit; and a sergeant who had four and so on. The officers were all of them working on the guns with us. Suddenly I realised that my gun was the only one firing and that we had only two rounds of ammunition left . . . We took a line on two tanks and got both of them.

"Then came the order to make our way back to our own lines as best we could. We had to go under fire the whole way for two and a half miles. We removed the breech-blocks and the sights of our guns. We had men with tommy-guns leading and we carried the wounded in the centre. Before we moved off I did something you may think rather stupid—I went back and kissed my gun.

"I carried one of our wounded on my back. Freddie—that was his name. He had volunteered to come out here. Been out only a few weeks. He had a wife and four children. He had been wounded trying to help someone else. They got him on the way back—shot him through the head. It took us four hours to do that two and a half miles and then we reached our own lines. We had about thirty-three casualties and we had had to destroy our guns—but there were at least thirty-seven enemy tanks smashed beyond hope of recovery and about twenty more knocked out.

"Today, I heard that some of our troops are back on our position. I hope they have our guns—we still have the breech-blocks you know!"*

Rommel and his army never recovered from the failure of what was to have been his decisive counter-attack, when he lost to the First Armoured Division, including the victors of the "Snipe" action, more than a hundred tanks, three quarters of them German. Though the battle continued with the utmost stubbornness for a further week, the "crumbling" process, on which Montgomery had counted, went on inexorably, while one after another of the German and Italian units suffered a cumulative erosion of men and weapons. The British, too, paid the inevitable price for their hard-won victory. On the night of November 2/3rd, little more than twenty-four hours before the final break-through, the survivors of the 2nd Battalion under Tom Pearson suffered almost as many casualties as at "Snipe" in an attack which they, with the 7th Battalion and the 2nd 60th, made on the Aqqaqir Ridge and Sidi Rahman Track. But on the morning of November 4th the triumphant British armour and its accompanying Motor Battalions drove, as Robin Hastings recalled, "clear out of the maze of minefields and set off at last across the open desert" with "a wonderful feeling of release from congestion. It was as if out hunting one had galloped round the deep rides of endless woodlands, never able to see far ahead, never able to get clear of the crowd and then suddenly, and after so long, unexpectedly, hounds had broken cover and sped off across the best of the vale."†

*   *   *

With the defeated Afrika Korps in full retreat, the rest of the German and Italian army lay at the mercy of Montgomery's armour. It had lost 55,000 men or just under half its total personnel. The British took

* *R.B.C. 1942*, 150-3.   † *Hastings*, 161.

30,000 prisoners, 350 tanks and 4000 guns at a cost of 13,500 casualties. The pursuit of Rommel's armour across the Western and Libyan deserts was left to what remained of the 7th Armoured Division under the command of O'Connor's former Chief of Staff, John Harding. At its head went those old allies and comrades in arms the 11th Hussars and the 1st Rifle Brigade, following, after the frontier was crossed at Sollum, the old desert tracks through Sidi Resegh and Msus towards the Gulf of Sirte. But this time there was little or no hope of cutting off the enemy's retreat along the fast coastal motor-road; exceptionally heavy and early November rains had turned part of the desert into a morass, while problems of supplies, especially of petrol, made any repetition of O'Connor's great achievement of two years before impossible. Yet when a month after Alamein the 11th Hussars and "A/B" Company of the 1st Battalion rode, victors, into Benghazi, the full strategic consequences of that saving victory became apparent. For with the capture of the Italian airfields on the Gulf of Sirte, the R.A.F. could once more operate over Malta where Lord Gort and a starving garrison were still defying the Luftwaffe and the waiting paratroop invaders. At the moment when it had seemed about to pass into Axis hands and when its retention had become vital to the Allies' victory, the key to sea-command of the central Mediterranean was saved.

On November 12th 1942, two days after the 1st Battalion crossed the Libyan-Egyptian frontier, men of another Battalion of the Rifle Brigade, the 10th, set foot on African soil nearly two thousand miles to the west at Algiers where, on November 6th, an American-British Army, sailing in the utmost secrecy under escort of a British battle-fleet, had landed to liberate Algeria, Morocco and French North-West Africa from Vichy control and place the re-treating Germans and Italians in Tripolitania between two fires. Formerly the 2nd Battalion of the Tower Hamlets Rifles and, as such, sister Battalion to the disbanded 9th, the 10th Battalion, like all the other territorial units affiliated to the Rifle Brigade, had been trained as a Motor Battalion and, at the beginning of 1941, had been officially embodied in the Regiment. A week before a Company of the 1st Battalion entered Benghazi, one of the 10th set off eastwards as part of a flying column called "Bladeforce" to cover the four hundred miles to the Tunisian border. Conducted in pouring rain, during the next forty-eight hours, it was a race against

time to capture Tunis, fifty miles further on, and the great French
naval base of Bizerta commanding the Sicilian Narrows.

But though the little force ultimately got to within ten miles from
Tunis, and though the French civilian population and, more
dubiously, part of the French army, rallied to its support, it failed to
reach its objective, and was forestalled and driven back at the eleventh
hour by the Luftwaffe and by German troops and armour, rushed
across the Sicilian Narrows with the connivance of Tunisia's Vichy
French rulers. When on December 7th the rest of the 10th Battalion,
under Lt.-Colonel Adrian Gore, landed at Bone in eastern Algeria it
found itself, like the First Army of which it was part, held up in the
mountains of western Tunisia by severe winter weather and German
land and air forces which, operating from much shorter communications, were for the moment better armed and equipped.

Meanwhile, leading units of the Eighth Army, including the
1st Battalion, continued their westward advance, crossing into
Tripolitania just before Christmas and moving steadily forward
along, and to the south of, the 470 miles of coastal road between
El Agheila and Tripoli. Ahead of them, as they did so, minute raiding
parties of picked volunteers from the Long Range Desert Force,
among them many Riflemen, operated in the interminable desert to
the south—wild desolate country which few men had ever crossed—
establishing secret dumps of food and petrol from which to sally
forth with bomb and explosive-charge to strike at the Italian and
German transport along the coastal highway. One such party of nine
men in three jeeps, led by Major Vivian Street, evading watching
Italian aircraft, armoured cars and patrols, reached the road about
fifty miles east of Tripoli and 250 miles behind the German front.
Creeping forward on foot in the moonlight, they surprised a sleeping
convoy of lorries parked beside the highway, planting incendiaries
against each in turn.

"We crept away and waited. A few minutes later the first in-
cendiary went off, enveloping the vehicle in a sheet of flame. Then
another, and another, and another. Soon all twenty lorries were
burning furiously, their Italian drivers scurrying round in panic
with no idea of what had happened. Meanwhile others from our
party had been busy mining the road and destroying the telegraph
poles. This accomplished they returned to join us, and for a

minute we stood and watched the great bonfire of vehicles which was lighting up the countryside. Then, jumping into our jeeps, we drove out into the desert and hurried away. As the first streaks of dawn appeared we reached our hide-out near Bir Dufan. It had been a night of great adventure, so easy that it seemed unreal, like some elaborate game of Red Indians. We felt there was nothing to prevent us repeating the performance on the main square of Tripoli. We were very tired, but before we crept under the bushes to snatch some sleep we pulled out our last bottle of rum and drank to further successes against 'the road'."*

Yet when, a few weeks later, Vivian Street, weary, half-starved and ragged, reached Tripoli, it was as a prisoner. For after further adventures he and his comrades had run out of petrol and when, after a long trek on foot without food, they reached their dump it was to find it occupied by a party of soldiers to whom, after an unavailing fight, they were forced to surrender.

Another young Rifle Brigade officer of the Long Range Desert Group, Major the Hon. Patrick Hore-Ruthven, who had accompanied Street in the attack on the lorries but subsequently separated from him to work on a sector of his own, was badly wounded in the course of a successful attack on an enemy force leaguered for the night. Two of his three jeeps were knocked out, and, not wishing to endanger the lives of his men by encumbering the third, he ordered his sergeant to leave him and take the party back. Then he remained with his gun behind a bush and, when the enemy approached, engaged them, killing several before being taken prisoner. Mortally wounded, he died on Christmas Day in an Italian field hospital. An inveterate individualist, the son of a V.C. and grandson of the Lord Ruthven who had fought with the Regiment in the Crimea and served with it again in the First World War, this gay, gallant young man wrote, a few months before his heroic death, a poem in memory of his friend, Geoffrey Keyes, who had been killed and given a posthumous V.C., in an unsuccessful raid a year earlier on Rommel's headquarters. Inscribing it to "A Young Man Who Died", in it he foretold and described the manner of his own death.†

---

* *R.B.C. 1946*, 87-101. Major V. W. Street, *Some Men have Nine Lives*. Reprinted from *Blackwood's*.

† Patrick Hore-Ruthven, *Desert Warrior*, 24-5.

On his wrist,
On his wrist,
With a hawk upon his wrist
As the dawn was breaking clearly,
A gentleman rode early,
With a hawk, a hooded hawk
Upon his wrist.

At a hern,
At a hern,
He flew her at a hern
And her strike was like the frightening
White wickedness of lightning;
With a cry of deadly anguish
Fell the hern.

From the sea,
From the sea,
He struck out from the sea
And as heron falls to peregrine
They fell before his unforeseen
And sudden blinding slaughter
From the sea.

Oh, he died,
Yes, he died,
As other brave men died,
But for valiant quenched vitality
Deeds spring to immortality:
A young man lingers lightly
Where he dies.

On his wrist,
On his wrist,
With a hawk upon his wrist
In a dawn that breaks more clearly
A young man still rides early
With a hawk, a hooded hawk
Upon his wrist.

Only a few weeks before Patrick Hore-Ruthven's death, another poet officer of the Regiment, Tony Naumann, had been blinded at the head of his platoon while taking part in Bladeforce's abortive advance on Tunis.

Four weeks after Pat Hore-Ruthven's death, on January 23rd, 1943, the 1st Battalion, which he had joined as a subaltern in 1934,* entered Tripoli in triumph, its commanding officer, Lt.-Colonel Freddie Stephens—son of the "Stiff'un"—riding immediately behind General Montgomery, rather as the Adjutant of the 2nd Battalion had, at Wellington's orders, headed the victory march into Paris after Waterloo. Three weeks later, with the rest of the Eighth Army's advanced guard, the Battalion crossed from the east the Tunisian border which the First Army had crossed from the west. But though barely a hundred miles now separated the two armies, the Germans and Italians, in strong hill positions and with the advantage of interior lines, lay between them, ready to strike back at either if a favourable opportunity offered. On February 20th the Americans, on the First Army's right, were attacked in the Kasserine Pass by Rommel's tanks, and were only saved from disaster by the timely intervention of a British armoured brigade in which part of the 10th Battalion was serving. Turning south, Rommel then threatened to drive Montgomery back into Tripolitania. But the latter was too quick for him. Instead, bringing up the rest of the Eighth Army from Libya, where since Alamein it had been resting and training, he prepared to assault the Mareth Line. When towards the end of March he did so, all three Battalions of the Rifle Brigade took part, the 1st distinguishing itself by the speed and fire of its frontal assault on the Djebel Saikhra, and the 2nd and 7th Battalions taking part in the famous 160 mile flanking march round the Matmata Hills which ultimately decided the battle. A few days later the 7th Battalion, under 28-year-old Lt.-Col. Douglas Darling, who had commanded a Company at Beda Fomm, carried out on the all but impregnable Akarit pass a brilliant assault which—had it been supported in time by artillery and armour—could have resulted in the 1st Armoured Division streaming through the pass into the Tunisian Plain in the rear of the enemy's main defences.

That spring, with the desert left behind and the Tunisian country-

* He had spent most of his time in the Regiment in the 2nd Battalion, where his Company commander had been Callum Renton. *Joy of Youth*, 164-85.

side a carpet of wild flowers, the entire armour of the Eighth Army, and with it the 1st, 2nd and 7th* Battalions, was transferred, for strategic reasons, to the First Army. All four Battalions of the Rifle Brigade serving in Africa thus came under a single command, that of General Alexander. The desert-hardened veterans of the Eighth Army at first treated the newcomers of the First with something approaching contempt; the 10th Battalion's pet pig, reared by the men of its anti-tank platoon, mysteriously disappeared without trace as soon as the "Desert Rats" arrived in the vicinity. That veteran of the desert war, Major Paddy Boden, wrote an amusing account of the impact of the two Armies on each other.

"First Army lorries were all painted dark green and brown, and when in harbour were parked in huddles, making the best use of any available cover. Eighth Army transport was painted the colour of sand and the drivers continued to rely on dispersal as the best protection against air attack . . . The officers and men of the First Army were readily distinguishable from those of the Desert Army by their dress. The former were more or less correctly dressed and, more often than not, wore steel helmets as a matter of routine. In the Eighth Army it was almost unheard of for an officer to wear battledress trousers, and steel helmets were worn only on very rare occasions . . . A large body of men sharing a common experience over a period of months and even years, isolated from all contact with their home country, developed a set of habits, customs and even a jargon of their own. We felt different from, and, by reason of our longer experience and of the flattering accounts of our exploits which appeared in the Press, superior to the men from England, sometimes mockingly referred to as 'those bloody Inglese' . . . These differences of outlook seem rather petty in retrospect, but they were real at the time. I like to think that our stupid conceit and our failure to appreciate the efforts of the First Army were short-lived and I hope that our friends in the First Army were not unduly offended by the 'blood and sand' we threw at them."†

* The 7th Battalion was joined at this time as Second-in-Command by Vivian Street, who, after his capture in Tripoli, had been shipped across the Mediterranean in an antiquated Italian submarine which was sunk on the way by a British destroyer. Providentially rescued, he was later parachuted into Jugoslavia during 1943-4.

Hastings, 223-5.

In the brief victorious campaign which followed, the men of both armies fought side by side. On April 23rd, St. George's Day, the 10th Battalion went into action with the armour on the Goubellat Plain in a partially successful offensive in which the 7th Battalion later joined. Yet it was not till the morning of May 6th that the 4th Indian Division, with its magnificent Gurkha Rifle Regiments, made a clear break through the enemy lines along the Medjez road, and the 7th Armoured Division, with the 1st Battalion, entered Tunis led by the 11th Hussars. At the same time the 6th Armoured Division, with the 10th Battalion, swept across the base of the Cape Bon peninsula to trap the Axis forces between it and the Eighth Army formations near Enfidaville. After a night advance and a brilliant surprise attack on the strongly gunned defile at Hammamet guarding the northern entrance to the Cape, the Division compelled the surrender of the Italian Ariete and Young Fascist Divisions and of the crack German 90th Light Division—veteran opponent of Riflemen in many a desert battle. In this operation the Motor Companies perfectly fulfilled their role, attacking pockets of enemy resistance and rounding up thousands of prisoners. On that day, May 12th, General von Brausch of the 10th Panzer Division surrendered to 28-year-old Lt.-Col. Tom Pearson of the 2nd Battalion, who, two and a quarter years earlier, as a Company commander, had received the surrender of General Bergonzoli at Sidi Saleh. Nearly a quarter of a million German and Italian troops, including six Italian and five German Divisions, three of them armoured, laid down their arms with a thousand guns and two hundred and fifty tanks and all their equipment, supplies and transport.

It was the greatest surrender made to a British commander after a single battle in the Army's history, and the end of the war in Africa. In that three years' campaign no Regiment had played a greater part than the Rifle Brigade, five of whose six Battalions had fought in it. Even the latest joined, the 10th, had been almost continuously engaged throughout its six months in Africa, paying the price for what it had so nobly endured and achieved with a casualty list of twelve officers and 231 other ranks.

* * *

With the elimination of Axis forces from Africa, the opening of the Mediterranean and the failure, after Stalingrad, of Germany's attempt to repeat her 1917 victory over a Russia whose resistance during the past two years had begun to wear down even the *Wehrmacht*'s seemingly invincible might, the ring of British and American sea and Russian land power began to close round the Axis from south and east. From the sandy desert and the rolling cornfields of the Tunisian plain the war in the south now passed, by way of Sicily— conquered by Montgomery's 8th Army and the Americans in July and August—to the toe of Italy. Because it was surrounded by, and vulnerable on both sides from sea which the Allies now commanded, and because the German communications were most strained and extended in the south of that long, narrow, mountainous peninsula, it was the one place on the circumference of Hitler's European fortress where the Western Allies could engage him until their land forces were strong enough to strike directly across the Channel ditch against the immensely formidable fortifications of his Western Wall and at the heart of German industry and power behind it. By doing so and forcing the stubborn Teuton to fight, and supply, a campaign in so, for him, strategically disadvantageous a field, they could relieve pressure on their Russian ally in the only way yet possible for them, and, at the same time, pin down enemy forces which would otherwise remain concentrated on the Channel coast ready to repel their coming attack on the enemy's heart. For both these ends a campaign in the Italian peninsula was doubly advantageous since, with their command of the Mediterranean and the mobility and surprise given by sea-power, they could simultaneously pose a threat of further landings at any point on the coastline of southern Europe. This compelled the Germans, as an insurance against such a contingency, to maintain large and otherwise useless forces in northern Italy, southern France and the Balkans, where they were also having to wage a harrassing guerilla campaign against two rival bodies of elusive and persistent Jugoslav partisans.

Yet if, by engaging the enemy in the south of Italy and, sustained from the sea, fighting their way slowly northwards up that narrow mountainous peninsula, the Western Allies tied down and drew to the Mediterranean littoral a disproportionate number of German divisions which would otherwise be available both in Russia and on the future invasion beaches of northern France, they set their armies there a tactical problem as difficult as their choice of terrain was strategically advantageous. They had to maintain continuous pressure on an enemy who, though unable to throw them back into the sea because of the narrow and restricted front they had chosen for their initial toe-hold, could repel their attempts to advance up the peninsula with the minimum difficulty to himself and the maximum hardship and loss to themselves. For it was a country which favoured the defenders, who could nearly always overlook the attackers, and who, in that jumble of rocky valleys and mountains, had an inexhaustible choice of new and seemingly all but impregnable positions to which to retire as soon as the British and Americans had exhausted themselves struggling under fire up one precipitous and exposed ridge after another. "If night patrols had been the bane of platoons in the desert, in Italy," recalled one who fought in both, "it was continually necessary 'to find out if the enemy had gone'. That generally meant finding out *how far* the enemy had gone, and ended inevitably in an encounter for the leading section or the leading carrier—an encounter in which the enemy, sitting waiting in ambush, had an initial advantage."*

It was a hard and wearing campaign, therefore, for the British and American attackers, very different to that of the desert. If the latter was ideal terrain for tanks and carriers, the mountains, steep hills and close cultivated valleys of the Appenines were the very opposite. A war in Italy had to be fought, too, under great extremes of heat and cold—particularly, in the winter, of cold—for by far the larger part of the peninsula was mountainous and subject to icy winds and blinding storms of snow and rain. The attackers had only two advantages: that, the Italian Government having surrendered and made peace, the civil population was friendly—despite its natural terror of the Germans who had proceeded to take over almost the entire country with their customary ruthlessness—and that, possessing command of the sea and, increasingly, of the air over it, they could ultimately force the defenders to retire by a threat to the sea-flanks behind the lines.

As there seemed so little scope for armour in the mountains of southern Italy, and as the Rifle Brigade was trained and equipped as motorised infantry to move and fight with armour, only one of its four Battalions in Africa was used at the start of the Italian invasion. This was the 1st, which since Alamein had been part of the 7th

* *Durand and Hastings*, 174.

Armoured Division—the one British cavalry division chosen for the campaign. The other three Battalions spent the rest of the summer of 1943 and the winter of 1943-44 in North Africa, the 2nd and 7th returning to Egypt to train and refit, and the 10th remaining in Tunisia where, on Adrian Gore's promotion to Brigadier, its second-in-command, 30-year-old Dick Fyffe, took over temporary command. The 1st Battalion proceeded to Homs on the Tripolitanian coast to prepare for its part in the coming invasion, under Victor Paley—nephew and son of two distinguished old Rifle Brigade officers—who had taken the place of Freddie Stephens.

Before the Tunisian victors dispersed to their several stations, a Rifle Brigade dinner was held on May 16th in Tunis, with Brigadier Jimmy Bosvile in the chair and 64 officers from all four Battalions attending. A similar dinner, attended by the officers of its then three Battalions, had been held after the storming of San Sebastian in 1813. Just four months later, on September 22nd, 1943, two weeks after the dramatic announcement of the Italian Government's capitulation to the Allies and the simultaneous landing of an Anglo-American force in Salerno Bay, the 1st Battalion disembarked there with the rest of the 7th Armoured Division, ready for a lightning dash to seize Naples, thirty miles to the north. But though the bridgehead established by the infantry was by then secure and it was soon afterwards relieved by Montgomery's 8th Army—which in three weeks advanced two hundred miles up the western coast of Calabria after crossing the Straits of Messina from Sicily on September 3rd—and though the capture of Naples followed a fortnight later, preceded by a brilliant operation by the 1st Battalion at Cardito on October 3rd, the Allies' hopes of a quick advance to Rome were disappointed. Their forces, instead, remained bogged down for the winter in the mountains above the Garigliano and the ancient hill monastery of Cassino.

But the 1st Battalion's stay in Italy was brief, for that autumn it was decided that the veteran 7th Armoured Division, like the victor of Alamein himself, should return to England to prepare for the invasion of France. On December 20th, the 1st Battalion sailed for home, just two years and three months after it had embarked for the Cape and Egypt. It was left to the other three Mediterranean Battalions of the Regiment to reinforce the Eighth and Fifth Armies in Italy. For in the spring a new attempt was to be made to break the deadlock on the Garigliano and anticipate, if possible, the now imminent landing in France by the capture of Rome.

The 10th Battalion, still part of the 6th Armoured Division, was the first to arrive, landing in Naples in the middle of March 1944 when Lt.-Col. Dick Southby took over its command. On April 7th it went into the line just south-west of Cassino for a fortnight or so of action which provided an invaluable introduction to its part in the final Battle of Cassino which began on 11th May. While the Polish Corps attacked the Monastery itself and the French Corps under Juin attacked the hills to the west, the British 13th Corps made the main attack over the Rapido into the Liri Valley. The 10th Battalion crossed into the bridgehead a few hours after the initial assault and, operating near the centre of the Valley, made a series of attacks which finally brought it to the heavily fortified edge of Aquino in the Hitler Line. The Battalion was far up the Liri Valley as the last successful attack of the Poles went in on the Monastery. After a short pause, while the Canadians broke through the Hitler Line defences, it resumed the advance, over the River Melfa. In helping, with its habitual efficiency, to clear the Liri Valley, repeatedly driving back first-class German troops from one formidable defensive position after another, it lost six officers and 86 other ranks, a sacrifice small, however, in relation to what it achieved.

Meanwhile the 2nd and 7th Battalions, sailing from Alexandria with the 9th Armoured Brigade on April 30th, landed at Taranto early in May and had at once moved up to the battle area in the mountains east of Monte Cassino. Here, owing to the crying need for infantry, they found themselves stripped of their mobile functions and of most of their vehicles. From a total divorce from the skilled specialist functions for which they had been trained and which they had discharged with such skill in the desert and Tunisia, they were rescued by their fellow Rifleman, General "Jumbo" Wilson— now Allied Supreme Commander in the Mediterranean. It was largely due to him that—as a part of the 6th Armoured Division— they were formed with the 10th Battalion into a Rifle brigade under Adrian Gore. The 10th retained its full Motor Battalion establishment, while the 2nd and 7th were given a mainly infantry one and were carried henceforward, not, as in the past, in their own trucks, but in Royal Army Service Corps transport driven by R.A.S.C. drivers. This was the first time in the Regiment's history that three of its Battalions had been brigaded together. It afforded, at least, a comradeship in battle of those trained in a single philosophy and mould and went some way to compensate for the substitution of mules for mechanical transport and foot-slogging and perpetual tramping up hill for travel in trucks. Platoons and Companies still kept some of the additional wireless sets with the help of which, fighting with fast-moving armour, Riflemen had learnt to place at the service of their commanders their traditional qualities of quick thinking and action. It seemed, though, a sad waste of the technical and mechanical skills they had mastered over the past few years, and of the swift tactical control of the battlefield which such mobile skills had given their Commanding and Company officers. Perhaps for the ordinary Rifleman what seemed the greatest loss of all was that of the moving home in which to "brew up" meals at pleasure and in which to carry his sleeping kit and personal belongings.

It was fortunate that the mobility of the new Infantry Brigade had not been entirely lost, for, at the end of May, the Germans, who since the fall of Cassino had been fighting a stubborn delaying action in the Liri Valley, were faced with a threat of encirclement by the Americans breaking out of the Anzio beachhead. Suddenly the position, which had been static all the winter, became fluid, and the enemy began to fall back towards the north. Pursuit now being both possible and necessary, the armoured cavalry once more needed mobile infantry to clear a path for it, protect it from counter-attacks and guard its leaguers at night. On June 4th the Germans pulled out of Rome, and on the 5th the Americans entered the city. Next day, as, headed by the 7th Battalion, the 6th Armoured Division began to move up the Tiber in pursuit, news came that British and American forces had landed that morning in Normandy and that the long heralded "Second Front" had opened at last.

*   *   *

From the second week in June, when the 1st and 8th Battalions, following the assault divisions, landed in Normandy, all five Battalions of the Rifle Brigade were more or less continually engaged until the end of the war, two in North-West Europe and three—later reduced by casualties to two—in Italy. The 1st Battalion, after its two and a half years' foreign service, had been training in the Norfolk

Breckland since January for the new task before it. In the middle of May, it had left for the marshalling area in Essex. Thence it sailed in the first days of June from the London Docks for Arromanches. For the 8th Battalion—the Second Battalion of the London Rifle Brigade (TA)—which had been training in England ever since the war began, the summons brought an end to an almost intolerable period of waiting. A year earlier, when it had been inspected by the King and the Regiment's royal Colonel-in-Chief—the Duke of Connaught's successor, the Duke of Gloucester—it had seemed certain that the Battalion was to join its four sister Battalions in North Africa. But at the last moment, after the convoys had left for the embarkation ports and the carriers had been loaded, the move had been cancelled, a decision having been taken at the highest level that no more armoured divisions were to be sent to North Africa. When in the spring of 1944 the King again inspected the Battalion, everyone felt that the test for which it had been preparing was at last at hand. On the 9th it embarked from Tilbury. Looking back from the years of peace and disillusionment which followed the War that moment of departure seemed, to those who had waited so long for it, the very epitome of romance.

"Many tides have ebbed and flowed in the Thames since the Battalion sailed down from Tilbury to join its convoy, and to some those days of high adventure may seem remote, unreal and profitless. Lesser men have stolen the political stage; the Welfare State has failed to arouse the best instincts of its beneficiaries; England's word counts for less than in the days of our forefathers . . . So for the returning Greeks the slaying of Agamemnon dimmed the glories of the Trojan War. But it is with that war and with the march of Alexander of Macedon that, as it recedes into the mists of legend, the liberation of Europe will take its place as long as courage and skill-at-arms are held in honour among men. And by the prophetic insight of England's greatest genius the opening phase of that liberation was described for all time four hundred years ago when an earlier watcher on the coasts of France reported to his King:

> England . . .
> . . . has put himself in arms, . . .
> His forces strong, his soldiers confident, . . .

To make a hazard of new fortunes here.
In brief, a braver choice of dauntless spirits,
Than now the English bottoms have waft o'er,
Did never float upon the swelling tide
To do offence and scathe in Christendom."

Both Battalions suffered much disappointment and loss during the first seven weeks in France. The 1st, which landed with the 7th Armoured Division, was to have made a quick thrust inland through Bayeux on the British right, while the 8th, operating with the 11th Armoured Division on the left towards Caen, was to take part in a great armoured break-through. Speed, it was hoped, would be the essence of both operations. But Normandy in the leafy summer was hardly more favourable to a quick armoured offensive than the Italian mountains. The countryside consisted of innumerable small fields, surrounded by high thick hedges and steep banks, interspersed with woods and orchards. With every tree and hedge in full leaf and the corn high in the fields, it was impossible to foresee what opposition from enemy armour or infantry was waiting in the next meadow, copse or village. It was a country which used up infantry and caused casualties at an even higher rate than the Appenines. From the start the Motor Battalions had to fight almost every yard of the way, protecting the armour from Spandau or anti-tank gun, lurking bazooka men or armoured counter-attack. Though for a short time the 7th Armoured Division's advance to Villers Bocage looked like being a spectacular success, its thrust was soon halted, and in its ceaseless day and night battle to protect the cavalry, as it vainly struggled to break through by day or leaguered by night, the 1st Battalion, in a fortnight's fighting, lost fourteen officers and 163 other ranks. The first engagement of the 8th Battalion was even more disappointing. Set to secure a bridgehead over the Odon and become the spearhead of the 11th Armoured Division's advance towards Caen, it captured a wooded hill which had been holding up the armour, but from which it was subsequently ordered to withdraw, after a prolonged and murderous bombardment. As the war historian of the London Rifle Brigade put it, " There had been many casualties in this first action for no apparent purpose and without coming to grips with the enemy. Hardly a German had been seen.

* *Durand and Hastings*, 93, 96-7, 100-1.

Hill 112 will be remembered as one of those places which neither side could hold, though both could mortar. The fighting had been carried on in an atmosphere in which the air was full of a fine grey powder, covering everyone with grey dust which made the wounded look more ghastly than ever, to the accompaniment of a smell of burning, the earth being covered with smouldering shell-holes and burning vehicles."* Even the Battalion's brilliant second engagement three weeks later was followed by disappointment and frustration, for though its capture of the villages of Bras and Hubert-Folie on July 18th and 19th was a classic example of the role of motor infantry in restoring the mobility of armour, the losses suffered by the latter, four of whose Regiments lost 115 tanks, were so heavy that the attempt to break out of the bridgehead had again to be abandoned.

Yet, just as in Italy that summer, stubborn German resistance in one Appenine stronghold after another ended in the capture, in the mountains west of Perugia, of Monte Malbe by the 7th Battalion and of Monte Rentella by the 10th, and later, despite cumulative and heartbreaking casualties,† in an advance to the Arno valley, so in Normandy the long and bloody British offensive in the Bocage and Plains of Caen so weakened the enemy that the Americans on their right were able to break out and, sweeping round the Germans' flank, threaten them with encirclement and destruction. And at the end of August, following the German debacle in the Falaise pocket, both the 8th and 1st Battalions were able to drive northward into the blue with their accompanying armour in the swiftest cavalry advance in British military history. In eight days, starting on August 28th and crossing the Seine that night, the 8th Battalion covered more than 250 miles through enemy territory, liberating Amiens on the 31st, Arras on September 1st and, after traversing the historic battlefields of Artois and Flanders, Tournai on the 3rd. On the 4th it reached Antwerp. Even Guderian's 1940 *Blitzkrieg* from the Ardennes to the Channel coast was surpassed in speed.

Owing to its relative position at the end of the Falaise battle, the advance of the 1st Battalion with the 7th Armoured Division was not quite so spectacular. Yet it, too, crossing the Seine on August 31st and

---

* *Durand and Hastings*, 224.

† They included one of the heroes of Snipe, the former Cockney boxer, Sergeant Charles Calistan, who had been given a commission in the 7th Battalion and was killed by a sniper's bullet on a reconnaissance patrol on July 29th, *Durand and Hastings*, 189.

the Somme on September 2nd, reached the La Bassée Canal near Bethune on the evening of the 3rd, and entered Belgium on the 8th. Following a precedent of the Peninsular War, when Spanish volunteers were recruited to fill the depleted ranks of the 95th and "made excellent Riflemen, distinguished for their bravery", the Battalion filled some of the gaps made by the fighting in Normandy by accepting volunteers from members of the French and Belgian Resistance Movements.

"They came at a time when the Battalion was under strength and so were particularly welcome, remaining with us for nearly ten months . . . The regular forces of France were expanding too suddenly to accept all volunteers immediately and the Belgians had to start practically from scratch. It was natural that there were young Frenchmen and Belgians who saw their best opportunity to strike a blow at the Germans in joining the first British unit which would take them . . .

"The first Frenchman to join was Yves Dumy . . . He was immediately nicknamed 'Ifs and Buts' by the Riflemen. Noel Paniez was, perhaps inevitably, called 'Christmas Basket', which gave pleasure to all. By the 7th of September the numbers had risen to seventeen, divided more or less evenly between 'C' and 'I' Companies, and scattered among the various platoons and sections, where their local knowledge of languages was found to be very useful. Practically none of them spoke English at all. A few days later we were joined by a Belgian, Dennis Vanoystaeyen, who spoke perfect English and whose brother also came in November.

"At first when they joined they wore rather nondescript uniform, composed mainly of a battledress blouse and civilian trousers with a pair of German jackboots to complete the picture. Alan Parker, the Adjutant, was rather taken aback—and the Regimental Sergeant-Major still farther—when inspecting some men one day to find one of the parade wearing check trousers. It was a very broad check and visible a good way off. Later, however, they were all issued with Army kit and went about looking extremely smart, most of them with a large 'France' written on their shoulders for all to see.

"Giving them leave to go home was quite easy, and they seemed never to have any trouble lorry-hopping to their destination or in getting back to us, even though we had moved, as on one occasion, seventy miles across the front. They spoke little or no English, and, in spite of their uncertain and erratic method of travelling, they always seemed to get back at about the right time, even when we were on the Dutch-German border, usually loaded with parcels of cakes and presents for their friends . . . Their brother Riflemen always kept them supplied with cigarettes."*

On the great "swan", as in mobile parlance it was called, many astonishing things happened. The fluid front had vanished; the countryside was swarming with surprised Germans in various states of bewilderment or indignant reaction; the streets of villages and towns delirious with welcoming crowds interspersed with snipers' bullets. There was the German general whom the 8th Battalion captured placidly breakfasting by the roadside, and another whose headquarters in a farmhouse near Bailleul was rudely surprised by the arrival of "G" Company and an accompanying squadron of the 23rd Hussars.

"As they drew near a German general was seen at a window. Soon an assortment of staff officers, signallers, clerks and orderlies came tumbling out to surrender. It was the complete divisional headquarters of the 276th Infantry Division. The old general, General Kurt Badinsky, had no idea what was happening around him and had no division left to command. He was none the less most anxious to observe the proprieties. He wished to surrender to an officer, but nothing would make him believe that Michael Anderson held commissioned rank . . . He could hardly be persuaded that British officers dressed like their men in action . . . Having eventually agreed to surrender, he was allowed to say goodbye to his staff and, with much heel-clicking and saluting, he was driven off to captivity." And there was the extraordinary episode of Sergeant Fruin of "F" Company, whose carrier ran out of petrol and who found himself in the middle of a German echelon, "and after various twists of fortune eventually returned to the Battalion with a score of twenty-five prisoners, five dead Germans and nine wounded to show for no loss of his own."†

*   *   *

* *Hastings*, 378-9.
† *Durand and Hastings*, 240, 242.

At the beginning of September, both on the Western Front and in Italy, it looked as though the war was ending. In the hills above the Arno, after what seemed an eternity of "always going uphill, providing endless targets for enemy guns and mortars and being held up continually by damage to roads and bridges,"* the three Battalions of the 61st Brigade celebrated the Regimental Birthday together on August 25th while resting at Faella, and then resumed their northward advance. By September 11th, having surmounted "miles of mountains", they were able to look down on the distant Lombardy plain and could even see in places the famous Route 9 from Milan to Rimini which enabled the enemy to switch his forces from one threatened point to another. But though the advancing armies had penetrated the enemy's Gothic Line and it seemed as though his last mountain defences would soon be breached, the expectant visitors had overlooked two facts. One was the severity of winter in the Appenines, and the other the astonishing resilience and tenacity of the Germans after the first shock of defeat. Torrential rain began to fall in the middle of September, turning every valley into a quagmire, and before the end of the month, so bitter were the nights, that a sentry died of exposure on Monte Fuso. And the paratroopers, Spandau gunners and mine-laying engineers of Kesselring's army, though without hope now of victory, fought back with everything they had.

It was so, too, in the Low Countries. After the astonishing rapidity of the armoured advance from Normandy to the Dutch-Belgian frontier it seemed inconceivable that the enemy could recover balance, reorganise and fight back. "No division," it was written of the 11th Armoured, "could have moved faster or completed more effectively the disorganisation of the enemy." Yet Montgomery's bold bid in September to seize the crossings of the Meuse and Rhine at Arnhem was defeated, and it took weeks of patient, costly fighting to clear the Scheldt and the indispensable port of Antwerp. By the end of the month it was clear that the Germans were going to hold out for another winter and that the expectations of an immediate surrender were not to be fulfilled. Both the Rifle Brigade's Battalions spent the months of early winter in a melancholy landscape of misty rivers and frozen water-meadows, squat houses and smelly byres where cattle and Riflemen sheltered together, and where the only

* *Durand and Hastings*, 188.

landmarks were church spires and windmills, over frequented by artillery observers and shelled impartially by both sides. It was a time of constant mortaring and sniping and small, hard paid-for gains, of "patrols and slow advances across bogs liberally strewn with mines, over canals, from one church tower or one windmill to another over the charred bodies of ruined villages."*

In mid December there was a release for the 8th Battalion from struggling with the mists and mud of the Maas and its tributary streams and paratrooper-haunted ditches. Ordered back to Poperinghe, with its ghosts of World War I, it joined the armoured Regiments of 29th Armoured Brigade to refit and train for the spring advance. But scarcely had the Riflemen unloaded their trucks and dismantled their vehicles and equipment when, having made themselves unoperational† with every expectation of a peaceful Christmas, at 8 a.m. on the morning of December 20th news arrived that the Germans had broken through the American lines in the Ardennes and that the panzers were advancing on Charleroi. As at that moment the Brigade was the only British reserve available it left four hours later for the front, driving all out for Brussels and thence, watched by anxious and apprehensive crowds, along the road to Charleroi, down which the 1st Battalion of the Regiment had marched to Quatre Bras a hundred and thirty years before. But though each of the Companies, with an accompanying Tank Battalion, took station at one or other of the historic Meuse crossings, the Germans never reached the river, and the Battalion saw the New Year in amid snow-covered hills of almost incredible coldness. Meanwhile the 1st Battalion spent an equally cold winter on the Dutch-German border near Roermond where, towards the end of January, they were engaged in heavy fighting to help capture the village of St. Joost and close up to the German frontier.

Winter in the Appenines was even colder. Before it set in with frozen intensity and a snow-covered panorama of cheerless mountain peaks, the 61st Brigade made a final attempt to break the deadlock by capturing the town of Borgo-Tossignano in the Santerno valley. On

---

* *Durand and Hastings*, 258.

† "By the 19th December practically everyone's belongings and all equipment lay spread upon the ground in an apparently inextricable muddle. The armoured Regiments had already handed in their Sherman tanks and were waiting to be issued with Comets." *Hastings*, 390.

the night of 12/13 December, after a feint attack by the 7th Battalion, the 2nd, under Owain Foster who had temporarily succeeded Chris Sinclair, advanced under heavy shell-fire and, despite the little hilltown's great strength, succeeded in establishing five platoons in it. But the defenders were troops of a quality comparable to that of the attackers, and, though an entry had been gained, it was impossible to reinforce the latter by daylight when a murderous fire and streams swollen by rain made any approach to the town—almost a miniature Cassino—impossible. Attempts by the 10th Battalion on the following night to bring up ammunition to the outnumbered and encircled platoons in the town proved unavailing. By the night of the 14th their position under repeated counter-attacks was desperate, and, as each section ran out of ammunition, resistance ceased. Described by the Divisional Commander as "a magnificent failure", the attack cost the Brigade thirteen officers and 207 Riflemen, of whom seven officers and 147 other ranks were missing. The Brigade was eager to renew the attack and made careful preparations, but was forbidden by higher authority to do so, and for the rest of the winter Tossignano, much to the annoyance of the Riflemen, remained in German hands.

That last winter of static war in the high central mountains of northern Italy was an experience none of those who endured it can ever forget. "Tunisia was a gentleman's war, and everybody packed up when the sun went down; not so in this infernal country," one of them wrote in the drenching autumn before the snow and frost came. "This business is just infantry slogging away in pretty foul conditions and in country ideal for the enemy. The only thing in favour of the war here is the fact that there are far more buildings than in Africa, so that one generally gets a roof (or part of one) over one's head at night, and somewhere to eat under cover." But for the outposts and patrols on the icy ridges and rocky crevices of that polar landscape in mid December and January there was little shelter or comfort. Opposed to them were some of the finest troops of the Reich under a general of the highest competence, confidence in whom, despite the growing hopelessness of their country's position, reinforced the professional German soldier's stoic philosophy of enduring, fighting and dying. For it was no easy adversary the men of the 5th and 8th Armies had to overcome with forces which, with the overriding demands of the war on Rhine and Maas, were little, if at all, numerically superior. And that adversary had all the advantages of ground in a mountain terrain which was easy to defend and very hard to attack and where the choice of ground lay always with the defender. It would have been easy, after hopes of an early victory had vanished with the autumn's rains and tempests, for the British in the central Appenines to have accepted a passive role and waited till their more numerous comrades in the North and the advancing Russian masses in the East could, with the spring, close in on the Reich and overwhelm it. Instead, even though there were times when they felt themselves forgotten, they continued to play their part in bringing pressure to bear on the enemy, wearing down his strength and making it impossible for him to reinforce those defending Germany elsewhere. Even in the depth of the winter patrolling continued incessantly.

> "There was first the problem of finding your way in the dark, of not making a noise, of not showing up against the moon or the skyline, and of distinguishing between bushes and enemy sentries. There was much creeping forward, much stopping to listen, many false alarms. And then, when something was found, there was the further reconnaissance, the little tactical plan, to gain more information or to try to nab a prisoner. On the return there was still a chance of being lost, of meeting an enemy patrol, of stepping on a mine, or of the coughers and stone-kickers giving away the path of the patrol, and then when our lines were reached there was always a chance that some trigger-happy sentry of our own might fire off in the darkness into the patrol. It was often after a hard day's fighting that an officer would be called on to take out a patrol to harass the enemy or destroy an abandoned tank or try (and this is the hardest of all) for a prisoner or just to find out how far the enemy have gone. Riflemen were sometimes so tired that they would fall asleep at each pause of the patrol, although they knew that the enemy might be anywhere in the dark around them."*

And, as often as not, patrolling cost lives, and, with few or no replacements available for Italy, casualties were cumulative and increasingly a wasting liability.

As, since the demands of North-west Europe were paramount, the

---

* *Hastings* 251; *Durand and Hastings* 142.

casualties sustained by the 2nd Battalion at Tossignano could not be made good by new drafts from the Depot, it was decided that its depleted ranks should be filled by a wholesale transfer from the 10th Battalion. Accordingly, in spite of its fine record of almost unbroken success in the two years since it landed in Algeria, the latter was broken up, in keeping with the military administrative principle that a higher, and therefore junior, numerically designated unit must always yield precedence to a lower and older one—in this case a historic Regular one with the proud Battalion call of "Fighting all over the World." Dick Fyffe, its commanding officer, who in the previous summer had temporarily commanded the 7th while its formidable chief, Douglas Darling, was recovering from wounds, now took over the combined Battalion, so happening to command in the course of a single year three Battalions of the Rifle Brigade, the 10th—twice—the 7th, and the 2nd, a unique record.

Though in the autumn of 1944 winter had come sooner than usual, the Italian spring of 1945 was exceptionally early. During March, in preparation for a new attempt to break into the Lombardy plain, the 61st Brigade was transferred from the mountain front to Cattolica on the Adriatic coastal strip, where, refurbished with new transport, it spent a month training for the coming mobile campaign. To bring it up to three battalion strength, the 1st Battalion of the 60th took the place of the disbanded 10th Battalion, so making it a Green-jacket Brigade in place of a Rifle Brigade one. Everyone was full of confidence, and determined, by breaking at last into the Lombardy plain, to deal the enemy a decisive blow and avenge the disappointments and frustrations of the past eighteen months.

Before they could do so the Allied Armies in north-western Europe were on the move again. In March the 1st and 8th Battalions had been withdrawn from the line to train with the cavalry in Belgium, while the latter were re-equipped with the new Comet tanks whose issue in place of the more vulnerable Shermans, the "Ronson Burners"—or "Tommy cookers" of the enemy's contemptuous phrase—had been interrupted in December by Rundstedt's Ardennes offensive. It was the first time since the war began that the British had possessed armour with hitting and protective*

---

* The American Shermans, which first reached the Desert just before Alamein, had been an immense improvement on their predecessors, but those fuelled with petrol burnt easily.

power fully equal to that of the German. On March 27th, following the establishment of bridgeheads beyond the Rhine three days earlier, the Motor Companies of the 1st Battalion joined their armoured Regiments and with them crossed the river. The 8th followed a day later on a parallel course a little to the south. Their sweep ahead of the armies across the North German plain and its river lines—Ems, Ems-Dortmund Canal, Hunte, Aller and Weser—was not quite as swift and spectacular as that of the previous autumn across northern France and Belgium. For, though the fear that the German civilian population would rise *en masse* in a final *Götterdämmerung* proved a chimera, strong resistance was encountered from German training and other units, particularly along the wooded ridge of the Teutoburger Wald. Before the Ems could be crossed it became necessary for the 8th Battalion and its old partner, the 23rd Hussars, to operate once more as a single armoured group—a well-practised example of perfect mobile co-operation under which, when the advance was swift, Colonel Perry Harding of the Hussars took command and, when the tanks became held up, Colonel Tony Hunter of the Motor Battalion.

On April 19th, having traversed the northern German plain as far as Lüneburg Heath, the British armour halted temporarily while the Russians, in accordance with arrangements made between them and the American High Command, continued to press westwards towards Berlin and the Elbe. On the same day in Italy the 2nd and 7th Battalions, now fully motorised again and operating with the cavalry of the 26th Armoured Brigade of the 6th Armoured Division, went into action in the Argenta gap on the Adriatic coast north of Ravenna where the infantry of the Eighth Army had broken through after a week's hard fighting. Though Kesselring's Army, unlike the broken, piecemeal formations still resisting in the dissolving Reich, was still a formidable and cohesive fighting force, little inferior in numbers to its British and American assailants, Field Marshal Alexander, relying on the superior mobility of his armour, was resolved to encircle and destroy it, leaving it no chance to retreat northwards into the mountain fastness of the Dolomites and Julian Alps. This, thanks to the speed with which the armour and Motor Battalions moved, he almost achieved in the course of four exciting days, though not completely as the 1st Parachute Corps—the finest remaining fighting unit in the German Army—just managed to get across the Po in time, though with the loss of most of its equipment and at the sacrifice of the 278th Division which covered its retreat. To this success, and the immense number of prisoners taken, the 2nd Battalion, operating with the Lothians and Border Horse, and the 7th Battalion with the 17th/21st Lancers, made a major contribution. It was the first time in the long, wearing Italian campaign that Companies of the Motorised Battalions and squadrons of the cavalry had been able to move relatively freely.*

After the Po had been reached on the 23rd there was a brief pause for regrouping before the advance was resumed on April 26th, when both Battalions crossed the river, determined by the pace of their advance to forestall any possibility of the Germans' recovery. By May 1st the 2nd Battalion and a squadron of the 27th Lancers had reached Trevisio, twenty miles north of Venice, and next day Belluno, nearly forty miles further on in the Venetian Alps, thus cutting off and enforcing the surrender of the German 65th Infantry Division. At Belluno, Lt.-Colonel Fyffe, in charge of a Battalion Group, moved with such speed that he succeeded in cutting off a German force over 5000 strong, fully armed and supported by tanks and S.P. guns. Twice this force tried to break out, but both attempts failed. Next day he went blindfolded through the German lines to negotiate the surrender of a further 6000 of the enemy, including the artillery of an entire division—an exercise in military diplomacy which he repeated three days later at Plezzo on the Isonzo, close to the Austrian frontier.† Meanwhile the fiery and indomitable colonel of the 7th, Douglas Darling—who, except for a brief absence through wounds, had commanded the Battalion continuously since the aftermath of Alamein—led his men and the 27th Lancers eastwards towards the Jugoslav frontier, which Tito's Communist guerillas had already crossed in an attempted invasion of Italy. Far outstripping the rest of the Eighth Army, on his own sole initiative—for, owing to the speed of his advance, wireless contact with both Brigade and Division had been lost—he pushed on at 40 miles an hour to Udine, entering it on the 1st of May. Here, in the last engagement of the war, he defeated a small force of German tanks and, by a combination of good sense, bluff and firmness, blocked the roads out of the town, so saving a retreating Chetnik army from its revengeful Communist countrymen.

* *Hastings*, 333.   † *R.B.C.1945*, 10-11; *Hastings*, 339.

On May 8th, V.E. Day, the 7th Battalion crossed the Austrian frontier, the first unit of the British Army to do so, and, again forestalling Tito's partisans by a few hours by the pace of its advance, occupied Klagenfurt—an action of far reaching political consequence. Four days earlier, renewing their advance to and beyond the Elbe, the 1st Battalion, accompanied by the 8th Hussars, crossed the river into the devastated city of Hamburg, while the 8th Battalion—sister Territorial Battalion to the 7th—and the 23rd Hussars, driving at full speed along the autobahn from Hamburg to Lübeck, entered the latter, so saving Schleswig-Holstein and Denmark from a Russo-Communist take-over. "The Battalion," wrote its War Historian, "passed through this ancient city, leaving behind its red buildings and curiously carved gateways, and hurried northwards along the banks of the ship canal, until, as they neared Travemünde, the roads began to be blocked by crowds of refugees, fugitives from the Russian armies to their east. Soon they could see in front of them the Baltic, ice-blue in the spring sunshine, and they knew that there was now nowhere for the German armies to retreat."* It was the furthest point of the British advance, and for the Battalion, as for its sister Battalions in Italy, the end of the war.

---

* Durand and Hastings, 286.

"SUCCESS TO THE RIFLES!"

DURING the War Riflemen did not only fight in their Battalions and Companies, living up to the motto of their predecessors of the old 95th, "the first in the field and the last out of it". There were others who, by reason of seniority, exercised high command or helped to direct the administration and supply of the Forces. As well as "Jumbo" Wilson—who became Field-Marshal Lord Wilson of Libya* and was successively G.O.C. British Troops in Egypt, Commander-in-Chief in Greece, Syria, Persia-Iraq and the Middle East, and ultimately Supreme Allied Commander in the Mediterranean—there were Lt.-General Sir Ronald Weeks who, having won a D.S.O. and M.C. with the Regiment in the First World War, returned to the Army on the outbreak of the Second to become Director-General of Army Equipment and, from 1942 to the end of the war, Deputy-Chief of the Imperial General Staff; Robert, Major-General Viscount Bridgeman, who had also won an M.C. with the 3rd Battalion in the First World War and a C.B. and D.S.O. with Bar in the Second, and who served as Director-General of the Territorial Army and Deputy Adjutant-General; Major-General Callum Renton, who after commanding the 7th Armoured Division in the Desert, became Head of the British Military Mission in Iraq; and Major-General Jack Reeve, who wrote the first handbook on Motor Battalion Training before the war and served during it as Deputy Adjutant General to both Home and Middle East Forces.

Among younger representatives of the Regiment was the Northumbrian, Francis Festing, who as a Brigadier led the Assault Brigade which landed in Madagascar in the perilous spring of 1942 where, it was stated in his citation for the D.S.O., he was "continually in the more forward areas, carrying out personal reconnaissances regardless of danger and cheering up the troops . . . His leadership

---

* Well-described by his old Company Commander of South African days, General Sir Reginald Stephens, as "undemonstrative in success and undismayed when trouble comes . . . Trusted and beloved by all his subordinates and by the entire Regiment." *R.B.C. 1945*, 3.

was always an inspiration, as on occasions when he applied his walking-stick to the backsides of the few recalcitrants who appeared to have an unnecessary interest in the rear areas."* He, too, like Jumbo Wilson, was to become a Field Marshal and, from 1958 to 1961, Chief of the Imperial General Staff. At that time the Regiment had no less than three holders of the Army's highest rank, the other being the Duke of Gloucester, its Colonel-in-Chief, who, like his predecessor and great-uncle, the Duke of Connaught, was in his heart a soldier before he was a Prince and proud to be the first of Riflemen.

Perhaps, after Jumbo Wilson, the most distinguished of the Regiment's wartime generals was "Monty"—General Sir Montagu—Stopford, also a D.S.O. and M.C. of the First World War who, in 1951 became its by then sole Colonel Commandant. GSOI at the Staff College when war broke out in 1939, he commanded, the 17th Infantry Brigade in 1940, fighting no less than three rearguard actions while covering the retreat to Dunkirk. Three years later, he took over the 33rd Indian Corps in Burma. In the spring and early summer of 1944, it played under his command a principal part in the four months' battle of Kohima, which ended in the relief of Imphal and the first major defeat of the Japanese Army. In the next six months Stopford led his corps in the 600 mile advance from the Indian frontier to the Irrawaddy and the Prome, fighting its way through mountain pass and jungle amid appalling climatic conditions, but never allowing the Japanese time to halt and recover. Later he succeeded Slim as Army Commander in the final stages of the Burma War and became successively G.O.C.-in-Chief Allied Forces in the Netherlands East Indies and Commander-in-Chief of Allied Land Forces South East Asia. Of him it was well said that "he inspired his troops by his energy and optimism and gained their loyalty and affection by his kindliness and sense of humour. He was the most delightful of companions; he had a quick wit, a gift for repartee and a fund of good stories. His zest for life and enjoyment of everyday affairs enabled him to get pleasure and laughter out of even the dullest day's work."†

---

* *R.B.C. 1942*, 49.
† *The Times*, 11th March, 1971. Another Rifleman who distinguished himself in both World Wars, commanding the 2nd and 12th Battalions while still under thirty in 1918-19, and a Division in France in 1939-40, was Lt.-General Sir Ralph Eastwood. He was unlucky in

*   *   *

In the two decades between the end of the War and the formation of the Royal Green Jackets on January 1st, 1966, when the Rifle Brigade finally ceased to exist as a separate Regiment, this famous corps, like so many of the nation's traditional institutions, suffered a decline in size and strength, though never, thanks to the unchanging spirit and devotion of its members, in quality of achievement and striving for perfection. In those years, as in the days of Shakespeare's King John and Richard II, England helped to wound herself. The last of the wartime Battalions, the 7th, was disbanded in May, 1946, after serving for a year in Egypt under Vivian Street—a future Major-General whose brilliant career was tragically cut short by enforced retirement and an early death. In 1948 the axe fell on the 2nd Regular Battalion, commanded by the V.C. hero of "Snipe", Vic Turner, who in 1946 had succeeded Robin Hastings. "We cannot but feel," the last contributor of the Battalion Letter to the Regimental Chronicle wrote of this breach with a great past, "that 31st July, 1948, is rather a dark day in the history of the British Army." Thereafter the 1st—now the sole survivor of the four Regular Battalions—continued for a further seventeen years, being commanded successively by Lt.-Colonels Dick Poole, Freddie Stephens, Mike Edwardes, Dick Fyffe—who ended his Army career as a Lieutenant-General and Deputy Chief of the Defence Staff (Intelligence)—Paddy Boden, Tony Mellor, Gris Davies-Scourfield formerly of the 60th, Hew Butler, and Mark Bond.

During these years the Regiment, as its surviving Battalion had now become, served almost continuously abroad—at Glückstadt, Osnabrück, Minden and Celle in Germany before 1952; then, after a brief spell at Bulford, from 1954 to 1956 in Kenya in operations against the Mau Mau, and from 1956 to 1957 in Malaya. In 1958, while enjoying at Tidworth a brief spell of home service, it suffered a change of name, becoming the 3rd Green Jackets, The Rifle Brigade, as one of the three single battalion Regiments of the newly-formed Green Jackets Brigade, the others being the Oxfordshire and Bucking-

---

that after Dunkirk, through no fault of his own, he never held command again in the field, being successively Director-General of the Home Guard, G.O.C. Northern Command and, in 1944 Governor-General and Commander-in-Chief Gibraltar. A year later he became Colonel Commandant of the 1st Battalion, a rank he held until 1951.

J.G.   2E hamshire Light Infantry and the King's Royal Rifle Corps. Then in 1959 it returned to Germany, remaining at Wuppertal till 1961, when it went to Cyprus, subsequently becoming part of the United Nations Peace-Keeping Force. Thereafter in 1965 it moved to Hong Kong and Sarawak, where it finished its separate career by a brilliantly conducted and successful jungle campaign against the Indonesians of Borneo.

Throughout all the changes and discouragements of this declining time the Regiment remained what it had always been, true to itself and its traditions. Its members showed the same virtues of courage, self-reliance, keenness, gaiety and good humoured acceptance of disappointment and adversity, with the resource and resolve to surmount them, which had distinguished their predecessors in more buoyant times. There was the same enthusiasm for every kind of corporate and individual enterprise, adventure and sport, and a capacity to organise the latter at the drop of a hat. In Germany, during the drab years of occupation, cricket, football, boxing, hockey, cross-country running, ski-ing and horse-racing all flourished and were pursued with inter-unit competitive avidity. After 1947, when the Army Rifle Association matches were restarted, the performance of the Regiment matched that of the years between the wars. Everything it did was done with zest, thoroughness and Riflemanlike celerity.

In the early days of policing and garrisoning a conquered and war-wrecked Germany, the occupying Army was well off compared with the civilian population, but the position became reversed during the second decade of the Occupation. "Training facilities have become very restricted in recent years," the Battalion Letter to the 1961 Chronicle reported, "and half our effort is spent in appeasing Germans. Indeed, the importance of not offending the Chief of Police of Sodersdorf village (pop. 250) seems to have taken the place of the defence of the Suez Canal as a cardinal point of British foreign policy."* Yet, in a time of imperial retreat and defeatism, whatever task the Regiment was given, however seemingly trivial, its officers and men put all they had into it. It was this and its tactical habitude of operating to a common purpose in the smallest units that made it so successful in forest and jungle warfare both against the Mau Mau in Kenya—where its section patrols stalked terrorists with infinite

* R.B.C. 1961, 25.

quietness and unrelenting patience—and later in Malaya. "Of all the security Forces who at different times have operated in the area," a member of the Malayan Administration in Johore reported in 1957, "the Rifle Brigade was far and away the best. Their operations were more carefully planned; they were better led; they shot straight; they patrolled more quietly and they hung on more tenaciously than anyone else."* Operating for 13 months at a time when the guerillas, because of earlier successes, were getting fewer and fewer on the ground, two Companies of the Regiment accounted for 21 terrorists killed and one captured, including the most important single kill of the entire emergency period. One small party from "S" Company remained out for nine days on a reduced scale of kit, covering 30,000 yards of mountainous jungle in the first four days, and continuing for two more days on short rations. Finally they lay in ambush for five more days at the end of their ordeal—"a notable feat," as the Regimental Chronicle recorded, "of jungle craft and endurance. They found one dead terrorist and killed another—a relatively light reward considering the effort. This was 'S' Company's first kill and the men celebrated the occasion by composing a song called 'Yonder Hill' which is printed below and was sung on every appropriate occasion and on some inappropriate ones as well.† . . . Later 'S' Company, after killing several more terrorists, captured three, whom the Riflemen immediately adopted as pets, but, as they could not manage their Chinese names, rechristened Mr. Wong, Chopper Gleasby and the Ponce."

* *R.B.C. 1957, 28-47.*

† "*One day twelve men and Mr. Peel*
Set forth to go up yonder hill,
They tramped and tramped until last light,
And then they made camp for the night.

"*They found the C.T. camp one morn*
Just as another day was born,
And from that camp there came a stench
Of one dead C.T. on a bench.

"*'Oh Smudger, Smudger,' said John Peel,*
'Go dig his grave on yonder hill.'
'Oh Sir, oh Sir, why pick on me
I'm no grave digger as you see.'

"*He dug his grave and dug it deep*
And buried him all but his feet;

R.B.C. 1957, 28-47.

He knew the boys would go through hell
Because there was a ghastly smell.

"*At ten o'clock in three days' time*
The hill a courier did climb,
With thumping heart we watched until
With lead his stomach we could fill.

"*As he came walking down the track*
Our sergeant hit him in the back,
The next shot spun him round and round,
We fired until he hit the ground.

"*Oh Shiny Shiny Shiny 'S'!*
At last we have achieved success,
Now we're as proud as you can see
'Cos we belong to 'S' Company."

"Looking back on the achievements of those fifteen months," the Battalion Letter writer concluded, " the chief memory is a feeling of frustration—the frustration experienced after countless hours of sweat and toil while patrolling in the jungle, always hoping that the next tree would disclose a C.T." (Communist terrorist) " ... Memory recalls the heat, the wet, the smell and—in the jungle—the gloom. Memory also recalls how the Riflemen, as usual, rose above this sense of frustration. One remembers their high morale, which remained constant in the face of many disappointments, their determination, their energy and their proverbial good humour. One remembers the great weight of responsibility placed on Subalterns, Sergeants and Corporals—it was largely their war, and they had to bear the brunt—and how cheerfully, willingly, and effectively they accepted their burden. One remembers those in administrative jobs who earned no headlines but who seven days a week ensured that nothing should be held up through any fault of theirs . . . Finally one remembers the families patiently sitting in their houses at Kuala Lumpur wondering when they would next see their husbands."

Before the Battalion left Malaya the Administrative Officer for the District wrote to the Colonel telling him that the chief single reason for the collapse of the terrorists' campaign was considered to be " the prolonged pressure applied by the Rifle Brigade . . . The people are free of both terrorism and restrictions for the first time in ten years (or sixteen counting the Japanese occupation) and are wandering about bemused but happy."*

Having in the 'fifties helped to rid one country from the plague of Communist terrorism and intimidation enforced by a ruthless minority on an unorganised and helpless majority—and having done so with a remarkable economy of life and force, use of individual skill, high morale and training—the Rifle Brigade, after a further spell of garrisoning a now thriving Germany, took a hand in relieving another land from a destructive menace of a different kind. In 1961 the Battalion was posted to Cyprus as part of the United Nations Peace Keeping Force in that island. Here it was confronted with the violence and misery loosed by the inflamed passions of two racial communities living within the confines of a single State. Two days before Christmas 1963, the Battalion Letter recorded, "the Cyprus which we had all come to regard as a dreamy haven from the world's

* R.B.C. 1957, 28-47.

trouble spots erupted overnight, engulfing its inhabitants in a torrent of violence . . . The Battalion . . . was spread along two miles of the border between the Greek and Turkish communities. With a few minor alterations this deployment held good for two months, and, while it did so, it put a premium on the ability of the platoon and section commanders. These people had to deal with many problems as they occurred. If they were effective the trouble blew over. If they were slow or unlucky a major crisis could develop before the Company Commander or Colonel could arrive on the scene . . . Better training could hardly be imagined. The aim was to stop either of the two communities from crossing the line which divided their respective areas and engaging in a major battle. The authority accorded to the Peace-Keeping Force was nil. It had no legal right to fire a single shot other than in self-defence, neither could it make an arrest."*

What the opening months of that year brought forth for the Riflemen at their ever-changing but constant business of restoring or maintaining the peace of the world was set out in an account of their doings by a Public Relations Officer of the Cyprus Peace-Keeping Force:

"Silent, deserted, empty; nothing is heard in the bare, narrow streets, the battle-scarred Turkish suburb of the hate-riven, strife-torn capital of Nicosia in the turbulent and immeasurably sad island of Cyprus. The inhabitants have fled from the terror that came upon them, leaving everything behind. Only the rustle of debris from burnt and looted homes, swept along the streets by the cold winter wind, disturbs the awful stillness—that, and the ringing clump of British Army boots, echoing through the hollow caverns between the blackened buildings, as an anti-looting patrol goes by; just the rustling debris and the occasional Cockney or Liverpool voice at the Union-Jack-draped, sand-bagged, roadblocks, manned by British soldiers, standing between the Greeks and Turks to prevent the fiery fanaticism of extremist elements on both sides erupting into new violence. These are men of the 3rd Green Jackets—The Rifle Brigade—men from London and Liverpool . . . Each soldier did 2 hours on duty and 4 hours off 24 hours a day . . . A pitched battle of great violence had resulted in some 25 people being killed. The Turkish population fled to safety, . . .

* *R.B.C. 1963*, 23-32; *1964*, 27-6.

leaving the area deserted with 50 burnt-out houses and over 70 looted and damaged. Some 200 hostages were seized and held for a week before being released. Here was where a 75-year-old man fell dead with a spray of seven bullets across his chest; in this house an eleven-year-old girl was shot in the back and died with wide-eyed open astonishment on her face; and in that house, in a small dark bunk at the back, a blind and completely paralysed boy of 17 had been lying for years—the blood-drenched pillow shows where a sub-machine-gun shattered his skull. Did they die by accident in the cross-fire of men fighting for a cause in which they believed, or were they butchered by psychopathic adolescents taking advantage of the situation to indulge in a 'kill-for-kicks' spree? Imagine only the feelings of British soldiers in these circumstances and marvel at their restraint, their patience, tact, and cool-headedness and their refusal to be provoked. Every soldier feels a sense of personal responsibility in his unenviable tasks. One false move, however insignificant, by any individual soldier could explode this electric atmosphere into fresh fury, but no such move has been made. Every soldier has stood firm and carried out his tasks with commendable patience and cheerfulness and with impartiality to both sides. London and Liverpool and indeed, all of Britain, can be proud of the 3rd Green Jackets."*

Inevitably, despite the restraint of the peace-keeping troops, both sides turned against them. "By the middle of February," the Regimental chronicler for 1964 noted, "the Turkish Cypriots were becoming disillusioned with us as a communal defence, at the same time the Greeks began to see us as the major obstacle to the achievement of their aims . . . The grounds of this feeling were readily measurable at Battalion Headquarters because of the presence of a huge girls' school . . . To start with the pupils waved and smiled at the sentries, but gradually became more and more reserved. In the end they staged demonstrations complete with the usual slogan, i.e. 'British Go Home!' This was too much for the soldiers, some of whom crowded round the boundary fence shouting, 'We want to go home!' or words to that effect† . . . It was only natural that under

* *R.B.C. 1963*, 33-5. Major Onslow Dent, Cyprus Public Relations. "Green Jackets stand between Greeks and Turks."
† *R.B.C. 1964*, 26-7.

these circumstances some of the wives should have become a bit upset and Col. Hew tried whenever possible to get every man home once a week to reassure his family . . . To their great credit . . . not one wife gave up or caused her husband to be sent back for compassionate reasons. Of all the people in the Regiment they suffered most, were in the greatest danger and deserved as much credit as anyone. At any rate the families were the happiest people in the Battalion when the men came home at Easter."*

They were soon separated again, for, its mission in Cyprus accomplished, the Battalion was sent, via Hong Kong, to help restore peace to another trouble-spot, this time in Borneo, where the Indonesians, having shaken off Dutch rule, were engaged in an expansionist and imperialistic adventure on their own account by invading the peaceful territory of what had been British North Borneo, Brunei and Sarawak, now part of the new Federation of Malaya. The forest war that followed—in which, with their well-practised jungle skills and the whole-hearted support of the Dyack population, the Riflemen, at minimal loss, drove the Indonesians back across the border—was the last of many campaigns, great and small, in which the Rifle Brigade was engaged during its hundred and sixty-five years of history. For by 1965, when the Battalion returned to England, with a Labour Government committed to further reduction in the Army's size following its Conservative predecessor's abandonment of National Service, the decision had been reached to amalgamate the three historic Regiments of the Green Jackets Brigade. Henceforward they were to be a single three-battalion Regiment known as the Royal Green Jackets with the Queen as Colonel-in-Chief and the Duke of Gloucester as Deputy Colonel-in-Chief, each Battalion keeping its own Colonel-Commandant.†

On January 1st, 1966, the Rifle Brigade as such, therefore, ceased to exist as a separate entity—except in the hearts and memories of its former members. Its serving Battalion, under the command of Peter Hudson,‡ became the 3rd Battalion (The Rifle Brigade) of the Royal Green Jackets. The way for the unity of the new Regiment had already been prepared by the far-sighted agreement in 1958 of the three Colonels Commandant of the Green Jackets Brigade to adopt a

* R.B.C. 1964, 26-8.

† That of the 3rd Battalion (The Rifle Brigade) at the time of the amalgamation was Field Marshal Sir Francis Festing who was succeeded in 1968 by Lt.-Gen. Sir Richard Fyffe.

‡ Succeeded by David Alexander-Sinclair and, in 1969, by Jimmy Glover.

common drill and cap-badge, incorporating the stringed bugle horn common to all its three Regiments which was also to be borne on all its members' black buttons. For the Rifle Brigade, as for the other two allied Regiments, it meant a few changes in time-hallowed customs, in uniform, and in those marks distinguishing it from others on which every military corps prides itself. But in the forward-looking spirit of the Riflemen, pride in their traditions and cheerful acceptance of every challenge and determination to overcome them, there was no change at all. They remained Greenjackets and they remained Riflemen.

*　　　*　　　*

"Never be dull," Jock Burnett-Stuart told Dick Fyffe when the latter asked for advice on how to command a Battalion. No three words could have better defined the spirit of the Rifle Brigade. From its earliest days there had always been something gay and contemptuous of dullness and pomposity in its outlook. "Cock it a bit," the Duke of Connaught told Quartermaster Hone of his busby, "it's how I think a Rifleman should wear it: there is a bit of dash about it. Not straight up, like those in 'red regiments'." Panache in dress was matched by a certain panache in speech and conduct amounting, for all the Riflemen's flawless discipline, at times almost to cheekiness. "It needs a better man than a Brigadier to catch a Rifleman," Bob Pigot's soldier servant remarked after one such had tried to stop him as he returned from a nocturnal visit during the winter of 1914-15 to the deserted Armentières trenches in search of abandoned chickens and ducks for the Company's Mess. In times of crisis such lightly borne insouciance could prove a dissolvent of dismay and despair. During the murderous inferno of the "Snipe" action at Alamein, one young officer was heard to say to another: "My dear, I *don't* think we will bring the children here next year!"* Adventuring in a spirit of gaiety and courage, whether as a corps or as an individual, and making light of wounds, death and misfortune, was always an attribute of the Regiment.

This capacity for transcending the vicissitudes of fate derived largely from the Rifleman's self-reliance—indoctrinated in him from

* Communicated to the writer by Lord Hailsham, who served in the 2nd Battalion in the Desert and who, though not at Alamein, heard it from a fellow Rifleman, who was present, shortly after the battle.

the moment he joined the Regiment—and, on what went with it, reliance on his fellow Riflemen. The comradeship of the Regiment was a kind of invisible armour which every Rifleman wore and to which, by joining the corps and accepting its disciplines and duties, he had become for ever entitled. "Having given me a nickname during the first few days," E. T. Aspinall—the "City Man"—wrote of his posting to the 2nd Battalion during the South A‛rican War, "everyone treated me as one of themselves from the start, and I was never allowed to feel that I was only an attached Militia subaltern in all the months I served in the Battalion."* The one calamity a Rifleman found it hard to face with equanimity was to be parted from the Regiment. Ned Pinnock, Quartermaster of the 2nd Battalion in the Desert, used to say that for him the only unendurable hardship would be separation from it for more than a week! The knowledge that one belonged to this proud, cheerful brotherhood made up for everything. When, during the "doodlebug" summer of 1944, more than a quarter of a century after they had fought together in France, the veterans of the 13th Service Battalion Old Comrades' Association gathered for their annual reunion at the Distillers' Arms in the Fulham Palace Road, Mr. Travers, the landlord, had just had his house wrecked by a bomb. But as a former member of the 13th Battalion, the Regimental Chronicle reported, enemy action made little difference to him, "and a most successful meeting was held."†

The unshakable self-sufficiency of the Rifleman rested partly on his reliance on his weapon and his superlative skill in using it. Bob Pigot, who commanded the 3rd Battalion in World War I, took a special delight in proving to visiting weapon experts, the immense superiority, in the hands of a Rifleman, of the bullet-firing rifle to that clumsy makeshift of trench warfare, the rifle grenade. "By 1917," he recalled, "the Army had largely given up the rifle in favour of the bomb, but in the 3rd Battalion we never allowed a bomb to be used; the rifle was our weapon and we had no use for bombs." On one occasion, while in command of a divisional school for teaching open warfare, with the help of a demonstration Company from his Battalion he proved his point to his Corps Commander—an enthusiastic champion of the rifle grenade.

"We started our attack demonstration from 200 yards with rifle

* R.B.C. 1936, 242.   † R.B.C. 1944, 187.

grenades, the range of which was a bare 100 yards, and when finished I asked the Corps Commander to come and count the hits. There were just a few. We then went back 1000 yards and repeated the attack with bullets, and I again asked him to come and count the shots. There were no targets left—we had shot them to pieces. He was not at all pleased and told me that I did not know how to use rifle grenades . . . My Divisional Commander, who was present, supported me nobly. 'We must remember, Sir,' he said, 'that Colonel Pigot is a Rifleman, and he has no use for bombs of any sort or even shells. He wants the rifle!' "

Shortly afterwards during the battle of Loos the 3rd Battalion attacked two large concrete pillboxes, known as Crook and Crazy, stuffed with Germans and machine-guns, and Major Tommy Boscawen, attacking with his Company and advancing by rushes under Lewis gun cover, took them both without a casualty. The captured Germans testified that the Riflemen's fire was so devastating that they had been unable to use their loopholes on account of the bullets streaming through. When next day a staff officer from the Corps Commander came to congratulate the Battalion and ask for any points of special interest, Pigot replied: "Tell him about Crook and Crazy and ask him if he could have done that with rifle grenades!"*

All this was part of a certain separateness—a proud awareness of being a little apart from their fellow Regiments and comrades of the "red" Army. If the latter called the Riflemen "Sweeps" from their dark uniforms, they took it as a compliment. "They do not slope arms," ran the caption to Eric Kennington's portrait, "Sergeant of the Rifle Brigade," in his war paintings. "They always march with arms trailed. They salute when carrying arms in a way of their own. In fact they are, like the man in Shakespeare, 'full of excellent differences'."† It was in wartime that these differences became, in the Rifleman's belief, most marked: when—as Danny Meighar-Lovett recalled of the 3rd Battalion in the 1914-18 War—its officers and men seemed cleaner, better shaved and had better-kept trenches than any-

* Communicated by Brigadier General Sir Robert Pigot to Field Marshal Sir Francis Festing.

† Cit. *R.B.C. 1931*, 320-1. Eric Kennington himself served with the 3rd Battalion in the First World War.

one else. Even if this were not true, in their hearts all Riflemen felt it was.

The greatest of the Rifle Brigade's assets, and the source from which its qualities sprang, was the responsibility which its founders laid on its officers for the well-being of their men. "Stewart," wrote Charles Napier of its pioneer days, "makes it a rule to strike at the heads. With him the field officers must first be steady, and then he goes downwards. Hence the privates say: 'We had better look sharp if he is so strict with the officers'."* From this arose the mutual trust between all ranks which distinguished the Regiment in every period of its history. In 1805, when the newly raised 2nd Battalion was temporarily brigaded with the 1st at Canterbury, some drunken newcomers fresh from the Irish Militia encountered on the Ashford road the wife, together with her child and nurse, of the Commanding Officer—Thomas Beckwith—and "most grossly insulted them."† "The culprits were discovered but not punished; for Beckwith next day on parade, forming the Battalion into square, addressed them, and, after relating the outrage, added; 'Although I know who the ruffians are, I will not proceed any further in the business because it was my own wife whom they attacked. But had it been the wife of the meanest soldier in the Regiment, I solemnly declare I would have given the offenders every lash to which a Court Martial might have sentenced them.'" It was no wonder, wrote the Rifle Brigade's first historian, that by such acts of generosity as well as by his leading them in the field, this man "won the heart of every soldier in the Battalion, as Surtees tells us, who served in the ranks under him."‡

In other words, from the start Riflemen came to respect their officers, and model themselves on their standards. Chivalry, forbearance, consideration for others and a refusal to put oneself forward before one's comrades and the Regiment, were the indispensable qualities of a good officer and had to be learnt by everyone who aspired to be one. When Sir John Kincaid—who, for all the light hearted badinage of his rambling reminiscences, was "a tall, stern-looking but most amiable man"—after being called on to return thanks for his health at a regimental dinner, got up, stammered and,

---

* *Life of Sir C. J. Napier*, I, 19.
† "Proceeding to such lengths as delicacy forbids to mention." *Surtees*, 53-5, cit. *Cope*, 11
‡ *Cope*, 11

finally exclaiming "I'd rather lead a forlorn hope than make a speech
—*I can't do it*", sat down defeated, he was greeted with uproarious
applause.* Kincaid's own model of a good Rifleman was his old
Commanding Officer, Sir Alexander Cameron, whom he described in
a letter, written after the latter's death in 1850, as "an undaunted
soldier, a skilful leader whom all soldiers love to follow, and . . . a
generous and devoted friend in all the relations of life."†

The influence during its history of the Rifle Brigade's philosophy,
training and example on the British Army is hard to over-estimate.
More, perhaps, than any other single factor it helped to wean
it from the ramrod, pipe-clay, "there's not to reason why" Prussian military ideal so dear to British military administrators in
the 18th and again in the mid-19th century, and to substitute for
it Moore's ideal of the "thinking, fighting soldier". It helped
to pave the way for the adoption of tactical operations capable
of overcoming the murderous effect of automatic weapons on
troops operating in close formation. In the years after the Boer War
every cadet and officers' training corps was trained in the extended
drill prescribed a century earlier for the Rifle Brigade, while the
latter's standards of individual marksmanship and company training
were adopted by every infantry Regiment. And Rifle Brigade ideals
and practice were carried into every corner of the British Empire;
into the magnificent Ghurka Rifle Regiments which became the
fine flower of the 19th and 20th century Indian Army; into the King's
African Rifles; and into the fine allied Rifle Regiments of the old
Commonwealth countries—Princess Patricia's Canadian Light Infantry, the Winnipeg Rifles, the 1st British Columbia Regiment or
Duke of Connaught's Own, the Melbourne University Rifles, who
produced in General Sir John Monash one of the ablest commanders
of the First World War, the Durban Light Infantry, and the Ceylon
Planters' Rifle Corps.

Above all, the Rifle Brigade always looked to the future, and for
this reason, even when it ceased to be a separate Regiment, its
former members, though now part of a new Regiment embodying its
traditions and virtues, continued to look forward, not back. Six years
after the latter's formation one of its Company Commanders,
formerly in the Rifle Brigade, wrote to General Fyffe, under whom

* *Diaries of Sir William White-Cooper*, cit. *R.B.C. 1894*, 125.
† *R.B.C. 1931*, 236-7.

he had once served, describing how superlatively the Riflemen of the 2nd Royal Green Jackets—formed from men of the three component Regiments—were behaving under their grim ordeal in Northern Ireland. "We Riflemen," he wrote, "have always been optimistic and, in particular when things look their blackest. Morale in the Battalion has never been better than it is at this moment when we are stretched to the limit, overworked and called upon to change tactics almost daily. The Riflemen seem to thrive in these conditions and accept everything as a personal challenge . . . It is nice to know that they never change. I have had letters from lots of friends whom I have not seen for years, and it is surprising how far they are spread, Green Jackets all over the world showing the flag."* There could hardly be a finer tribute to the validity of the Rifle Brigade's philosophy or better witness to its immortality.

* Letter from Captain F. R. Sainsbury, M.C., 2nd Bn. The Royal Green Jackets, to Lt.-Gen. Sir Richard Fyffe, 8th June, 1972.

APPENDICES

APPENDICES

APPENDIX A

The Rifle Brigade Chronicles are full of references to "the Families", that is to the wives and children of Riflemen of all ranks, whose care and welfare—particularly during those recurrent moves and separations which are part of a soldier's life—have always been a matter of major concern to its members. This early example of that concern is of historic as well as of romantic interest. The incident described in Appendix A occurred during the early months of 1814, when Wellington's victorious army was advancing into south-western France. The lady was Juana Smith, the young Spanish wife of Harry Smith, who appears in Chapter 2 of this book.

Juana Smith's Ride

"The night was showery, with sleet drifting, frosty and excessively cold. My poor wife was almost perished. We at last got her into a comfortable little house, where the poor Frenchwoman, a widow, lighted a fire, and in about half an hour produced some bouillon in a very handsome Sèvres slop-basin, saying this had been a present to her many years ago on the day of her marriage, and that it had never been used since her husband's death. She, therefore, wished my wife to know how happy she was to wait on the nation who was freeing France of an usurper. The widow was a true 'Royaliste', and we were both most grateful to the poor woman. The next day we were ordered back to St. Sever, on the high-road to Toulouse, and parted with our widow with all mutual concern and gratitude, our baggage being left to follow. We had a very showery, frosty, and miserable long march over an execrable road, after which we and Barnard got into a little cottage on the roadside. At daylight the following morning we were expecting to move, but, having received no order, we turned to to breakfast, my wife relating to Barnard the kindness she had received the previous night and the history of the basin. To our horror in came my servant, Joe Kitchen, with the identical slop-basin full of milk. The tears rolled down my wife's cheeks. Barnard got in a storming passion. I said, 'How dare you, sir, do anything of the sort?' (he was an excellent servant.) 'Lord, sir,' he says, 'why, the French soldiers would have carried off *the widow*, an' she had been young, and I thought it would be so nice for the goat's milk in the morning; she was very angry, though, 'cos I took it.'

"Barnard got on his horse, and rode to headquarters. About ten o'clock he came back and said the Duke told him the army would not march until to-morrow. My wife immediately sent for the trusty groom, old West, and said, 'Bring my horse and yours too, and a feed of corn in your haversack.' She said to me, 'I am going to see an officer who was wounded the day before yesterday, and if I am not back until late, do not be alarmed.' Young as she was, I never controlled her desire on such occasions, having perfect confidence in her superior sense and seeing her frequently visit our wounded or sick. I went to my Brigade, having various duties, just before she started. It became dark, she had not returned, but Barnard would wait dinner for her, saying, 'She will be in directly.' She did arrive soon, very cold and splashed from hard riding on a very dirty, deep, and wet road. She laughed and said, 'Well, why did you wait dinner? Order it; I shall soon have my habit off.' Barnard and I exclaimed with one voice, '*Where have you been?*' 'Oh,' she says, 'do not be angry, I am not taken prisoner, as you see. I have been to Mont de Marsan, to take back the poor widow's basin.' I never saw a warm-hearted fellow so delighted as Barnard. 'Well done, Juana, you are a heroine. The Maid of Saragossa is nothing to you.' She said the widow cried exceedingly with joy, but insisted on her now keeping the basin for the milk, which my wife would on no account do. She had ridden that day thirty miles and had every reason to expect to meet a French patrol. I said, 'Were you not afraid of being taken prisoner?' 'No, I and West kept a good look-out, and no French dragoon could catch me on my Spanish horse, Tiny.' She was tired from the excessive cold, but the merit of her act sustained her as much as it inspired us with admiration. The story soon got wind, and the next day every officer in the Division loaded her with praise. It was a kind and noble act which few men, much less a delicate girl of sixteen, would have done under

all the circumstances. Our worthy friend, Bob Digby, of the 52nd
Regiment, Barnard's A.D.C., overhearing my wife's orders to West,
after she had started, most kindly followed and joined my wife on
the road, for, as he said, he was alarmed lest she should fall in with a
patrol."*

* *Autobiography of Sir Harry Smith, I, 167-9.*

APPENDIX B

The Rifle Brigade was much addicted to pets. Appendix B is about an unusual one which joined it comparatively early in its history, in the eighteen forties. Its regimental life was recalled in the 1897 Chronicle by General W. H. Bradford, who had been a Captain in the 2nd Battalion at the time.

"*Doctor Dakins*"

Halifax, Nova Scotia, January 31st, 1844.—"Doctor Dakins" is dead—frozen 2,000 miles from his native land. It was only yesterday that I passed him in his accustomed place under the verandah of the North Barracks. There was a suspicious circle round the sun, and the air was hazy and cold. "Sharp weather, Doctor," I said, and the Doctor, turning to the right about—he had a particular dislike to sitting with his tail facing you—looked up at the sky, and seemed to nod his head indifferently, as much as to say that if *that* was all, it was not worth while disturbing him. The most furious snowstorm and lowest thermometer we have yet had in this place came on during the night, and in the morning the Doctor was found below scarcely alive. He was immediately taken to Sergeant Evans,* his greatest friend in the two Barracks, and all that was possible was done, but in vain—we could not revive him.

Doctor Dakins is not unknown to fame. He was born the summer of 1837, on the top of a tree in the Long Walk, Windsor, where his parents—ravens of very ancient lineage—had established themselves for the season. The place was a mistake; it was too much frequented. Accordingly we learn that a boy, whose papa was a trooper in the

* Sergeant Evans was, I believe, our last Waterloo man serving . . . He was a very fine-looking soldier and always wore his medal, which was what, perhaps, first attracted the Doctor's notice.

Blues, became possessed of our hero at an early age, and took him to the Cavalry Barracks. Here he soon became a favourite; but having taken to pecking saddles, also the horses' heels, the men had to get rid of him, and he was made over to the Foot Guards. From them he got his name of Doctor Dakins; for when the Chaplain-General came into the Square for Divine Service, using the big drum for his reading-desk, the bird would station himself by the side of that instrument and there remain. Advantage was taken of this one Sunday by a young drummer, who tied a pair of bands round his neck. But his appearance having had an effect on the congregation hardly in character with Church Parade, the Commanding Officer got angry and ordered Doctor Dakins, junior, out of Barracks. However, the men contrived to hide him until the *route* came, when, unable to take him to London they transferred him to our 2nd Battalion, who relieved them, in Ship Street Barracks. The Doctor by this time had acquired considerable military experience. He knew most of the bugle calls, especially those that related to rations. He knew all the ladies who kept hens. He was a personal friend of the contract butcher. He had quarters in the building that neither the Barrack Master, nor anybody else, knew of. One of them had been discovered; and in it were found some very incongruous articles—a razor, a cup, a prayer-book, a regimental button, a coin, and a surgical instrument. He robbed me of a sovereign once, but I must own it was all my fault. For, wishing one morning to see which metal he would show a preference for, I put a gold piece and a silver one before him, counting on the rapidity with which I should prevent him taking either; but in an instant he had the sovereign, and with it flew to the top of the guardhouse. I looked foolish enough while a ladder was fetched, for the men having got wind of it, turned out in numbers. The Doctor, evidently enjoying the joke, laid the sovereign on the very edge of the stone coping, and with his head on one side and a twinkle in his eye stood watching it. The bugler's fingers were only a few inches off when Dakins picked it up and disappeared over the roof. Those twenty shillings are somewhere in the neighbourhood now.

Of all the Barrack Square characters and there were many of them, none came up to the Doctor for regularity. He never missed a Parade. When Corporal Bates had done drilling his recruits, Dakins would fall his own squad in. It consisted of half a dozen or more puppy dogs with sore tails. The Doctor's great pleasure was to march these round the square himself, hopping in command behind them, and woe to the pup who tried to stray or appealed for a halt by lying on his back, with his thick legs in the air like an upset foot-stool A sharp prod at his stump soon brought him to a sense of discipline. The dogs at that time, I may mention, were a regular nuisance, the Colonel* never going anywhere, even to a field-day, without his Scotch terriers. A large sporting public followed the example. Quartermaster Trafford alone had his dozen curs, and to prevent their peaceful slumbers in the rays of the sun was one of the Doctor's favourite amusements. The dogs hated and dreaded him, and would sometimes pretend to sleep so as to get him at a disadvantage. The Doctor, perfectly aware of the sham, would cautiously approach like a skilful fencer, with his wings in his hand, as it were, and ready for a backward spring. Suddenly he lunges and is as instantly in the air. A savage howl proclaims that there is no button to that true weapon and the dog is two foot short of his return snap at his tormentor's tail.

These and other ways of the Doctor gave him some celebrity, and many strangers asked to see him. On April 6th he was presented at Court, or rather Prince Albert came by special appointment to be introduced to the Doctor on his own square. He was in great force that afternoon, for in the morning he had exposed and defeated what might have become a rival in the shape of a large horned owl. There was a rage in the Regiment at that time for animals. The Queen had presented us with a couple of red deer. Minerva's wise bird was proposed as a novel as well as an appropriate emblem for the 2nd Battalion, and Luther Watson† was selected as a fit person to go to Hungerford Market and try to secure the finest specimen there. He returned in triumph with a large basket, and the owl inside; it was turned out and given something to eat in the Barrack Square. It was remarked that he crouched down before his food in an unusual way. Dakins, who had been observing him thoughtfully, now came forward, and by a judicious poke caused the owl to rise. It was then seen that he had only one leg. Though Luther vowed it was all right, and that horned owls of that size never had more than one leg, the owl

* Lt.-Col. (later Col. Sir) George Brown.

† "Dear cheery Luther Watson, who remembers him? I believe the son of some bishop. He was the life of the mess."

committee declared that he had been cheated, and required him to take his purchase back.

Dakins afterwards went into Wales to put down the Chartists. At Dover, in the spring of 1840, he completely lost his heart, and would sit on the edge of the cliff talking to himself in the strangest tones and apparently spouting verses composed for the occasion. The lady to whose charms the Doctor had succumbed lived on the east side of Folkestone, where the gault beds are. Having had the advantage of frequent visits to France, there was a style of flying about her quite different to anybody else, especially a graceful way of scratching her head on the wing. On these occasions, rising high in the air, she would drop forty or fifty feet down in a perfectly straight line, then beautifully recover herself and continue her flight.

Watching from the cliff, Dakins became madly in love. As his own glossy pinions had never known scissors or knife, it is not unlikely it would have ended in the crime of desertion but for a lamentable incident which it pains me to relate. Certain red recruits were passing through Dover to reach their head-quarters, a scampish lot apparently, and a pity they had not taken some other route. Dakins was known to the whole of the Household Brigade, and half the British army besides, and, in the confidence of his large acquaintance, sat fearlessly at the edge of the Castle heights. Tufts of gilly-flower, wild mignonette and scented herbs of many kinds were springing from the clefts and un-come-at-able ledges of the steep, chalky wall, so white, it looked, against the blue sky, and from a long way down samphire and other plants sloped up until there was nothing for them to hold on to. A pleasant, fresh smell of seaweed and flowers stole from over the face of the cliff. In the distance, and hardly discernible from the smoke of some steamer, stretched the long diminishing coast of France

Dakins, as I have said, sat on a nodule of flint at the very edge, and looked fiercely over to the opposite land. He was composing a new ditty in which he had already called his rival from Boulogne by an uncourteous name, and dared him to come on and try his metal with a raven from Berkshire. "I'll pull your French beard," he said, and plucking from a stunted sprig of thyme a striped snail that clung to the stem, hurled it in defiance in the air.

Thirteen long seconds elapsed ere it struck the pebbly beach. Now, whether it was that St. Louis heard the threat, but unmerited vengeance was at hand. For that marauding band aforesaid armed with stones were stealing on our bold champion from behind. Suddenly they flung them, and one sharp flint, catching the Doctor on the side of the head, cut his right eye completely out. He would have been killed but that some Riflemen came and hunted the young ruffians off.

Dakins was never the same man after. On July 25th, 1842, he embarked for America in the good old sailing ship *Boyne* . . . The Doctor was in good company; there was . . . Elrington,* Stewart, John Cod Rooper, Newdigate, and I.

Careless always of life, Dakins had well-nigh lost it in mid-Atlantic. It was blowing fresh, and having rigged out a so-called fiddle to keep the plates on the table, we were eating our dinner with what appetite we might. A cry was raised, "The Doctor is overboard!" Startling cry this, but especially if anything of a sea is running. The Doctor! What Doctor? The captain and we all rushed on deck. Our human comrades we found to be safe; but with expanded, wet, and helpless wing, poor Dakins was soon discovered beaten down by the wind on the waves. Furrow after furrow was gathering between us and him, and white top after white top. But the Doctor did not struggle. We watched him—small as a bottle—as he rose, then sank in the distance, but always in the same position—his one bright eye fixed steadily on us as though in full confidence. The prestige of the Doctor still hung around him, and many sad and wistful looks turned towards our commander; but no one spoke. The kind sailor knew how to interpret them. He glanced at the sea and sky. " 'Bout ship!" he suddenly and cheerily cried; "who'll save the Doctor?" " 'Bout ship!" broke in chorus from the men, and a dozen volunteers sprang forward, the mate at their head. A boat was lowered, and I gazed with a rather choking sensation at these fine fellows pulling back to save the life of a bird. I don't know how the Doctor felt— sentiment had never, perhaps, been strong in his character—and the salt drops that fell so freely from his cheeks as once more he stood on deck were, I think, only fresh from the death he had so narrowly escaped.

W. H. BRADFORD.†

* Lieutenant, later General, F. R. Elrington, a future hero of the Crimean War and later Colonel Commandant of the 2nd Battalion.

† *R.B.C. 1895*, 111-18.

ABBREVIATIONS
List of Abbreviated Titles of Sources
given as references in the footnotes

A British Rifleman.—*A British Rifleman* (ed. Col. Willoughby Verner), 1899

Barnard Letters.—*The Barnard Letters* (ed. A. Powell), 1928

Berkeley.—Reginald Berkeley, *The History of the Rifle Brigade in the War of 1914-18, Vol. I, August 1914 to December 1916*, 1927

Callwell.—Major-General Sir C. E. Callwell, *Field Marshal Sir Henry Wilson*, 1927

Clifford.—*Henry Clifford, V.C., his Letters and Sketches from the Crimea*, 1956

The Congreves.—Lt.-Col. L. H. Thornton and Pamela Fraser, *The Congreves*, 1930

Cope.—Sir William H. Cope, *The History of the Rifle Brigade*, 1877

Costello.—Edward Costello, *Adventures of A Soldier*

D.N.B.—*Dictionary of National Biography*

Durand and Hastings.—Major A. T. M. Durand and Major R. H. W. S. Hastings, *The London Rifle Brigade 1919-50*, 1952

Harry Smith.—*The Autobiography of Lieutenant-General Sir Harry Smith* (ed. G. C. Moore-Smith), 1902

Hastings.—Major R. H. W. S. Hastings, *The Rifle Brigade in the Second World War 1939-1945*, 1950

Joy of Youth.—*Joy of Youth, Letters of Patrick Hore-Ruthven* (ed. Ethel Anderson), 1950

Kincaid, Adventures in the Rifle Brigade.—J. Kincaid, *Adventures in the Rifle Brigade*, 1830

Kincaid, Random Shots.—J. Kincaid, *Random Shots from a Rifleman*, 1835

Lucas Phillips.—Brigadier C. E. Lucas Phillips, *Alamein*, 1962

R.B.C.—*The Rifle Brigade Chronicle* (yearly from 1890 to 1965)

Rifleman Harris.—*Recollections of Rifleman Harris*, 1848

Seaton.—*Life of John Colborne, Field Marshal Lord Colborne* (ed. G. C. Moore-Smith), 1903

Seymour.—Brigadier William W. Seymour, *The History of the Rifle Brigade in the War of 1914-18, Vol. II, January 1917- June 1919*, 1936

Twelve Years' Military Adventures.—Major John Blakiston, *Twelve Years' Military Adventures in Three-Quarters of the Globe*, 1829

ACKNOWLEDGMENT

The author is grateful for permission to quote the poem "To A Young Man Who Died" from *Desert Warrior* by Patrick Hore-Ruthven. Published by John Murray, (1943).

INDEX

Abbeville, 342
Abu Klea, 163
Abyssinia, 332, 341, 348, 353, 361, 364, 366
Adam, Maj.-Gen. Sir Frederick, 96-7
Aden, 147, 205, 375
Aden Field Force, 375
Adriatic, the, 144, 427, 428
Afrika Korps, 362, 365, 369, 377, 405
Afghanistan, 14, 161, 173, 175-6, 221, 227, 309
Agedabia, 356
Agheila, 362, 407
Agueda, R., 54
Ailwyn, Lord, see Fellowes
Aisne, R., 286, 294
—, battle of the, 225, 232, 233, 337
Akarit Pass, battle of, 410
Alam Halfa, battle of, 376-7
Alamein, battles of, 12, 14, 18, 322, 335, 341, 359, 372-3, 375-6, 377-406, 410, 414, 415, 428, 429, 440
Alanbrooke, Lord, see Brooke, Sir Alan
Albania, 341
Albemarle Street, 123
Albert, H.R.H. The Prince Consort, 125, 130, 148, 156, 159, 165, 454
Albert, Lake, 214
Aldershot, 154, 159, 177, 181, 182, 184, 207, 210, 212, 228, 230, 278, 301, 313, 314
Alexander, Lieut. Boyd, 215-16
Alexander, Lt.-Col. B. F., 216
Alexander, Claud, 215
Alexander, General (later Field Marshal Earl) Sir Harold, 376, 411, 428
Alexander, Capt. (later Lt.-Col.) Reginald, 200, 201-3, 226
Alexander-Sinclair, Lt.-Col. (later Brigadier) David, 440
Alexandria, 351, 352, 354, 363-4, 366, 372, 377, 416
Algoa Bay, 114
Algeciras, 308
Algeria, 348, 406, 407, 427
Algiers, 406

Ali Musjid, 175
Aliwal, battle of, 119-22
Allahabad, 144
Alldridge, Major J. H., 300-1
Allen, Colonel, 72
Aller, R., 427
Alma, R., battle of, 5, 129-38, 141, 148, 149, 184, 378
Almack's, 79
Almeida, 57, 121
Alten, Maj.-Gen. Count Victor, 83
American Civil War, 148, 149-50
Amiens, 291, 420
—, Peace of, 30
Amritsar, 322
Ancre, R., 283
Andalusia, 64
Anderson, Captain G. H. G., 300
Anderson, Lieut. Michael, 422
Antelat, 356, 370
"Antonio, Rifleman", 353
Antwerp, 63, 89, 233, 297, 420, 423
Anzio, 417
Apennines, 14, 414, 419, 420, 423, 424-5, 426, 427
Apsey, Sgt.-Maj. (later Major) W. H., 316 317
Apsley House, 108
Aqquqit Ridge, 405
Aquino, 416
Arabs, the, 205, 216, 309-11, 342, 365
Archangel, S.S., 343
Ardara, 304
Ardennes, 342, 420, 424
Argenta Gap, 428
Ariete Division, 372, 412
Armentières, 229, 440
Armoured Divisions, British,
 1st, 335, 338, 342, 361, 368, 378, 379, 380, 382, 388, 389, 391, 395, 396, 397, 399, 405, 410, 411
 2nd, 363
 6th, 412, 416, 417, 428-9
 7th, 342, 347, 349, 350-1, 352 354, 35

Armoured Divisions, British [*contd.*]
356-8, 360, 366-7, 368, 379, 405, 406, 411, 414, 419, 420, 427-8, 430
10th, 379
11, 419, 420, 423, 424, 427-8, 430
Armstrong, Sgt. T., 174, 177
Army Revolver Championship, 316
Army Rifle Association, 156, 210-11, 317, 434
Army Temperance Association, 168
Arnhem, 423
Arno, R., 420, 423
Arran, 373
Arras, 420
—, battle of, 286, 293
Arromanches, 418
Arruda, 62
Artois, 233, 237 *et seq.*, 420
Ash, 210
Ashanti Wars, 174, 176, 177
Ashford, 443
Aspinall, Lieutenant (later Major) E. T., 191-200, 201-4, 207-8, 441
Assyrians, the, 320
Atherley, Captain (later Colonel) F. H., 145
Atkins, Sgt.-Maj., 386, 395, 398, 402
Aubers Ridge, battle of, 237-8, 239, 240, 244
Auchinleck, General (later Field Marshal) Sir Claude, 364, 366, 372, 376, 377
Australia, 157, 273, 280, 348, 354, 355, 360, 361, 363, 376, 380, 386
Austria, 14, 41, 63, 89, 341, 429, 430
Ayris, Sgt., 397-8
Ayrshire, 373

Badajoz, storming of, 69, 70-2, 98, 102, 270, 380
Badinsky, Gen. Kurt, 422
Baer, Lieut. Alan, 382, 400, 402
Baghdad, 310
Bagshot, 332
Bahuta, the, 215
Bailleul, 422
Baird, Major (later Lt.-Col.) R. D., 321, 322, 323, 324-5
Baker Rifle, the, 22, 28, 143, 299
Bakiga, the, 215
Balaclava, battle of, 138, 140
Baldwin, Rt. Hon. Stanley (later Earl), 336
Balkans, the, 303, 319, 355, 364, 378, 413
Ballsbridge, 315
Baltic, the, 14, 218, 430
—battle of the, 29-30, 42
Banbury, 314
Barba del Puerco, 57, 121, 359

Barce, 355
Barclay, Capt. C., 349-50, 351, 352
Barclay, Brig. C. N., 353, 356, 359
Barnard, Lt.-Col. (later Lt.-Gen. Sir) Andrew, 15, 64, 70, 71, 90, 93, 101, 103, 106, 123, 449, 450, 451
—, Anne Lady, 15, 101
Bardia, 352, 354
Baring, Lieut. (later Major) T. E., 210
Barnes, Bombardier, 389
Barnett, Corelli, 359, 364
Barnett, Corporal, 394
Barrosa, battle of, 64, 98, 101
Basra, 311
Bassett, Major (later Col.) R. T., 382
Bassett, Lieut. (later Lt.-Col.) W. F., 200
Basuto Campaign, 124-5
Batala, 323-4
Bates, Corporal, 453
Bath, 119
Bavai, 297
Bavarians, 236
Bayeux, 419
Bayuda Desert, 176
Beckett, Rifleman, 263
Beckwith, Capt. (later Maj.-Gen.) Charles, 72, 85, 122-3, 130
Beckwith, Lt.-Col. Sidney, 126, 129, 137
Beckwith, Lt.-Col. (later Lt.-Gen. Sir) Thomas Sydney, 42, 51-2, 53, 57, 59-60, 62, 63, 65, 110, 126, 443
—, Lady, 443
Beda Fomm, battle of, 322, 356-7, 358, 360, 362, 372, 410, 412
Bedford, Duke of, 149
Beesley, Rifleman W., 293
Belem, 61, 62, 120
Belfast (Transvaal), 191
Belgaum, 153
Belgium, 14, 89, 90-7, 215, 225, 230, *et seq.*, 287, 297, 342, 346, 421, 423, 427
Bell, John, 123
Bellerophon. H.M.S., 52
Belluno, 429
Belmont, battle of, 183
Benares, 319
Bengal, 144
Benghazi, 355, 360, 363, 368, 370, 406
Bennett, Mr. Justice C. A., 318
Bennett, Rifleman Peter, 263
Berea, battle of, 124-5
Bergendal, battle of, 191-200, 207, 225, 237
Bergen-op-Zoom, 89
Bergonzoli, Gen., 358, 412

Berkeley, Capt. (later Major) R. C., 17, 282-3, 284, 318
Berkeley Square, 103
Berkshire, 455
Berlin, 287, 428
Bermuda Race, the, 319
Berry, Rifleman William, 148
Bessarabia, 319
Bethune, 420
Bidassoa R., 82-3, 101
Bidlake, Sgt., 310
"Billy" the ram, 165-6
Binks, Sgt. R. W., 390, 397
Bird, Capt. (later Major) T. A., 351, 354-5, 382, 387, 388, 391, 392, 393, 395, 402
Bird, Maj.-Gen., 179
Bir Dufan, 407
Birmingham, 107, 302-3
Bisley, 316-17, 340
Bizerta, 407
Black Prince, H.M.S., 226
Black Sea, 126-7, 143, 294
"Black and Tans", 305
Blackwood's, 409
"Bladeforce", 406, 410
Blatchington, 22
Blishen, Rifleman Henry, 164-5
Blitzkreig, 342-3, 346, 362, 363, 365, 420, 421
Bloem, Capt., 230
Bloemfontein, 205
Blücher, Field Marshal Prince von, 90
Bocage, the, 420
Boden, Maj. (later Col.) P. A. D., 372, 411, 433
Boer Wars, 116-17, 123-4, 174, 182-206, 210, 211, 214, 441, 444
Boesinghe, 263, 265, 269
Boemplaats, battle of, 123-4, 139
Bombay, 151, 226, 319
Bond, Lt.-Col. (later Maj.-Gen.) H. M. G., 433
Bone, 407
Borneo, 434, 439
—, British North, 439
Boscawen, Capt. (later Lt.-Col.) Hon. M. T., 442
Bosvile, Lt.-Col. (later Brig.) T. J. B., 347, 369, 378, 399, 400, 401, 415
Botha, Gen. Louis, 191
Boulogne, 343, 455
Bourchier, Lieut. (later Col.) C. T., 141
Boughton, Sgt., 292
Boxer Rising, 219
Boyle, Lieut. the Hon. E. G., 180

Bradley, Sgt.-Maj., 305
Bradford, Maj. (later Gen.) W. H., 135, 165, 452-6
Bradshaw, Surgeon Maj.-Gen. A. F., 152, 171, 173
Bradshaw, Rifleman Joseph, 141
Brahmins, 319
Brambletye, 373
Bramshill, 137
Bras, 420
Brausch, Gen. von, 412
Breckland, the, 418
Bren guns, 338, 340, 343, 345, 351, 381, 382, 384, 385, 387, 392, 395, 399, 400
Brett, Sgt., 397
Bridgeman, Maj.-Gen. Robert, Viscount, 152, 229, 431
Briggs, Maj.-Gen. Raymond, 378, 380, 395
Britain, Battle of, 347, 348, 351
Brittany, 342
Brooke, Lt.-Gen. Sir Alan (later Field Marshal Lord Alanbrooke), 338, 339, 376
Brooke, Lieut., 197
Brown, Lt.-Gen. Sir George, 127, 128, 134, 136-7, 454
Brown, Sgt., G. H., 385, 391, 395
Brownrigg, Surgeon, 63
Brunei, 439
Brussels, 90, 91, 121, 424
Buckingham Palace, 157
Budumas, the, 215
Buenos Ayres, 44, 121
Bulford, 433
Bulganak, R., 129-30
Bull, Sgt.-Major, 172
Buller, Lt.-Col. (later Gen. Sir) George, 139, 140, 141
Buller, Gen. Sir Redvers, 184-5, 189, 190, 191, 193, 200, 214
Buq Buq, 353
Burg el Arab, 376
Burgos, 76
Burma, 14, 157, 176, 319, 346, 370, 432
Burman, Sgt. W. F., 289
Burnett-Stuart, Gen. Sir John, 317, 318, 332, 337, 339, 440
Burnhope, Rifleman, S. H., 387, 393
Bussaco, battle of, 63, 98
Busy-de-Long, 232
Bute, 373
Butler, Lt.-Col. (later Maj.-Gen.) H. M. G., 433, 439
Butler, Lieut. L. G., 281
Buxton, Lt.-Col. (later Col.) J. L., 307

Byng, Gen. (later Field Marshal Lord), 290
Byrne, Rifleman, 254

Cadiz, 30, 61, 64
Cadoux, Capt. Daniel, 15, 83-4
Caen, 419, 420
Caesar's Camp, battle of, 186-9
Cairo, 177, 205, 349, 351, 353, 355, 360, 361, 362, 364, 369, 376
Calabria, 415
Calais, 14, 104, 233, 242, 343-7, 369
Calcavellos, 53, 101
Calcutta, 121, 144, 145
Calistan, Sgt. (later Lieut.) Charles, 393, 394, 402, 403-5
Callwell, Maj.-Gen. Sir C. E., 232
Cambridge, 119
—, University O.T.C., 228
Cambridge, Field Marshal the Duke of, 129
Cameron, Lt.-Col. (later Maj.-Gen. Sir) Alexander, 69, 89, 93, 444
Cambrai, battle of, 289
Campbell, Gen. Sir Colin (later Lord Clyde), 145
Campbell, Capt., 112
Campbell, Capt. E. G., 200
Campbell, Lieut. (later Lt.-Col.) Hon. H. W., 134
Campbell, Lt.-Col. (later Brig.) Jock, 349, 351, 367, 373
Campbell, Capt. (later Maj.-Gen. Sir) Neil, 112-13
Campbell, Lieut. W. S., 161
Canada, 30, 107, 108, 109, 123, 124, 148-50, 172, 237, 242, 246, 247, 309, 416, 456
Canfor Rifleman, 250, 254, 257, 258, 261, 262
Cannock Chase, 302
Canterbury, 42, 43, 124, 443
Cape Bon, 412
Cape Colony, 109-17, 123-4, 125-6, 154, 182, 183-4, 374-5
Cape Mounted Rifles, 112, 123
Cape of Good Hope, 348, 361, 364, 368, 415
Cape Town, 109, 110, 111, 114, 205, 374-5
Caporetto, battle of, 289
Cardigan, Lt.-Gen. the Earl of, 129
Cardito, 415
Cardwell Reforms, 159
Carey, Lieut. (later Lt.-Col.) G. V., 278
Carlist Wars, 102
Cashel, 43
Cassel, 245
Cassino, battle of, 415, 416, 418, 425
Cates, Lieut. G. E., 289

Cathcart, Gen. Sir George, 125-6, 127
Catterick, 313, 314-15
Cattolica, 427
Caucasus, The, 361, 372, 378
Cave, Capt. (later Col. and Monsignor) F. O., 319, 320-1
Cawnpore, battle of, 144-5, 311
Cecil, Hotel, 208
Celle, 433
Central Provinces, 320-1
Chad, Lake, 215-16
Chaman, 315
Chamberlain, Rt. Hon. Neville, 341
Chanak, 311-12, 313, 315
Chard, Rifleman D., 397-8, 402
Chardakly, 315
Charleroi, 91, 424
Charles II, 209
Chartists, 108, 455
Chatham, 102
Chelsea, 102, 103
—, Royal Hospital, 5, 102-3, 104, 136, 147
Cheltenham, 212
Chemin des Dames, 294
Cheraing, 297
Cherat, 315
Chetniks, 429
Chetwode, Field Marshal Lord, 331
China, 218, 219-20, 435
Cholera March, 178-9
Churcher, Lieut. H. G., 301
Churchill, Rt. Hon. (later Sir) Winston, 234, 336, 338, 342-3, 345, 346, 347, 348, 355, 358, 360, 364, 370, 376
Ciudad Rodrigo, 53
—, storming of, 65, 69-70, 98, 102, 109, 121, 380
Clacton, 316
Clarence, Duke of, see William IV
Clarke, Lieut. (later Capt.) W. C., 168
Clifford, Capt. (later Maj.-Gen. Sir) the Hon. Henry, 16, 139-41
Clinton, Lt.-Col. (later Col.) Lord Edward, 173
Clive, Robert Lord, 118, 359
Clonmell, 43
Clyde, Lord, see Campbell,
Clyde, R., 373
Coa, R., 63
—, battle of, 57-9, 60, 270
Cochrane, Lieut. Tom, 81
Cockburn, Lieut. (later Col.) George, 160
Codrington, Gen. Sir William John, 133, 134, 135

Coke, Lt.-Col. Hon. Edward, 288
Coke, Lt.-Col. the Hon. Wenman, 161
Colborne, Col. (later Field Marshal Sir) John, Lord Seaton, 82, 83, 90, 96
Colchester, 162, 214, 225, 270, 315, 316
Cole, Capt. (later Lt.-Col.) J. J. B., 226
Coleman, Rifleman, 271
Colenso, battle of, 184, 185, 207, 281
"Collective Security", 336
Collins, Capt. (later Lt.-Col.) R. L. H., 236-7, 238, 241, 271
Colville, Capt. (later Col. Hon.) Sir William, 132-3, 135
Communist Terrorists, 429, 435-6
Congo, the, 214, 216
Congreve, Capt. (later Gen. Sir) Walter, 185, 207, 211, 212, 225, 228, 233, 234, 239, 240, 280, 281, 317
Congreve, Major William, 139, 233, 234-6, 239, 241, 271, 274, 281, 317, 318
Congress Movement, 322, 323
Connaught, Field Marshal Prince Arthur, Duke of, 148-9, 150, 159, 164, 166, 172, 209, 221, 300, 316, 332, 341, 347, 349, 418, 432, 440
Connaught, Duchess of, 221
Constantinople, 126, 315
Conway, Sir Martin, 281
Coomassie, 157, 175, 177
Coombe, Col. John, 356
Cope, Corporal, E., 385
Cope, Lieut. (later Sir) William, 5, 17, 108, 124, 137, 145, 163, 171, 443
Copenhagen, 29, 42, 43, 44, 98
Corfu, 108, 123
Cork, 107, 225
Cornhill, 104
Corunna, 16, 45, 50, 54, 168, 225, 299
—, battle of, 52-3, 98, 100, 101
Cossacks, 128-9, 130, 132, 218
Costobadie, Capt. (later Major) H. C., 303
Costello, Mrs. Augustine, 102-4, 106
Costello, Sgt. Edward, 16, 102-6
Cottesloe, Lord, 156
Cotton, Lt.-Col. A. E., 282
Couper, Col. (later Maj.-Gen. Sir) Victor, 207, 274
Cowans, Maj.Gen. (later Gen. Sir) John, 207
Cox, Major (later Maj.-Gen.) William 114
Craufurd, Maj.-Gen. Robert, 14, 16, 46-50, 54-8, 59, 64, 80, 339
Creswell, Capt., 129
Crete, 184, 189, 361, 364, 366

Crimea, 5, 16, 101, 117, 126-43, 144, 148, 149, 154, 159, 161-2, 164, 165, 166, 167, 168, 170, 175, 179, 306, 308, 309, 408, 456
Crompton, Lieut. (later Lt.-Col.) R. E., 151, 153, 154, 156-7
Crompton, Parkinson & Co., 157
Crosbie, Lieut. (later Col.) J. P. G., 153
Crowder, Lieut., 395
Crozat Canal, 291
Cubitt, Lieut. Michael, 353
Cugny, 292
Cullen, Sgt., 397
Cunningham, Lt.-Gen. Sir Alan, 366
Cunningham, Adm. (later Adm. of the Fleet Lord) Sir Andrew, 348, 363-4
Cunningham, Lieut. (later Col. Sir) William, 141
Curragh Challenge Cup, 211
Curtis, Col. W. P. S., 17
Curzon, Lieut. (later Gen. Sir) the Hon. Leicester, 125
Curzon, Maj. (later Col.) the Hon. Montagu, 156
Cyprus, 220, 434, 436-9
Cyrenaica, 355, 356, 360, 363, 366, 368, 370, 377, 378
Czechoslovakia, 341

Dacoits, 176
Dagshai, 226
Dalhousie, Lt.-Gen. Lord, 80-1
"Dakins, Doctor", 165, 452-6
Daniels, Sgt.Maj. H., 238
Danton, Sgt. W. E., 186, 189-90
Darling, Lt.-Col. (later Maj.-Gen.) Douglas, 410, 427, 429
Davies, Lt. (later Col.) W. E., 182-3, 186-9, 190, 200, 300
Davies, Maj. W. H., 240
Davies-Scourfield, Lt.-Col. (later Brig.) E. G. B., 433
Deal, 124
Dean Copse, 291
Delhi, 152, 153, 174, 220
Delville Wood, 292
Denmark, 29, 44, 430
Derejat, 177
Dent, Maj. Onslow, 438
Derna, 355, 363
des Graz, Lieut. (later Lt.-Col.) E. P. A., 316-17
Devonport, 226
Dhala, 205, 220
Digby, Capt. Robert, 451

Dill, Gen. (later Field Marshal) Sir John, 347, 348, 360
Dimsdale, Lieut. T. F., 153
Dinapore, 153
Dinkas, the, 215
Disarmament Conference, 330
"Distillers Arms", Fulham, 441
Djebel Saikhra, 410
Dolling, Sgt., 391, 392
Dolomites, the, 428
Doncaster, 314, 315
Donegal, 304-6
Dorchester (Oxon.), 314
Dorset, 16, 43, 45
Dortmund, 428
Douro, R., 54, 57, 79
—, passage of, 54
Dover, 79, 85, 102, 104-6, 124, 151, 343, 345, 455
Downing Street, 345
Downpatrick, 109
Drake, Corp. A., 278
Drake, Major (later Col.) Thomas, 80-1
Drummond, Capt. Algernon, 151, 155
Dublin, 43, 167, 174, 306-7
Dugdale, Lieut. (later Col.) H. C. G., 152
Duke of York, H.M.S., 336
Dumy, Rifleman Yves, 421
Duncanson, Lieut. J., 345
Dundas, Gen. Sir David, 98, 103
Dunkirk, 297, 344, 345, 346, 348, 361, 371, 432, 433
Dunoon, 373
Durand, Major A. T. M., 17, 380, 418-19, 424, 430
Durban, 184, 189, 204, 205, 375
Durrant, Rifleman A. E., 191
Dyacks, 439

Earle, Maj.-Gen. William, 137
East Africa, 162, 214-15, 321, 378, 434-5
Eastbourne, 374
—, College, 278
East Grinstead, 373, 375
East India Company, 106, 144
East Indies, 432
Eastmead, Capt. (later Major) L. E. K., 297
Eastwood, Lt.-Gen. Sir Ralph, 433
Eaton Place, 308
Eden, Rt. Hon. Anthony, 358, 360
Edinburgh, 149
Edward VII, King, 148, 164, 166, 208
Edwards, Sgt., 318
Edwardes, Lt.-Col. Hon. M. G., 433

Eeles, Lieut. (later Capt.) Charles, 61, 85-6
Eeles, Lt.-Col. William, 143
Egerton, T., 34
Egypt, 14, 31, 150, 163, 177, 179, 221, 222, 317, 318, 332, 342, 347, 348-73, 375, 378, 406, 415, 431, 433
Elandsgate, battle of, 184
Elba, 90
Elbe, R., 428, 430
Elephant, H.M.S., 29
El Gabut, 163
Elizabeth II, Queen, 439
Ellis, Sgt., 199
Elrington, Lt.-Col. (later Gen.) Frederick, R., 144, 150-1, 172-3, 456
El Ruweisat, 376
Elverdinghe, 263, 264
Ems, R., 428
Ems-Dortmund Canal, 428
Enfidaville, 412
Enfield rifle, 143, 179
Enghein, 297
Eritrea, 348, 361, 364
Erroll, Capt. (later Major) W. H. H., Earl of, 132
Esher Committee, 206
Essex, 397
—, Volunteers, 174
Estrella, Serra de, 57
Eton Boating Song, 151, 155
Evans, Bombardier D., 397
Evans, Sgt., 452
Experimental Corps of Riflemen, 22 seq., 89, 335
Experimental Mobile Division, 335, 337-40
Eyre, Lieut. (later Col.) Henry, 126

Faella, 423
Fairfax-Lucy, Capt. H. M. R., 310
Falaise, battle of, 420
Fearn, Rifleman "Beaky", 141
Fellowes, Lt.-Col. Hon. R. T. F. (later Lord Ailwyn), 272-3, 282, 283-4, 285
Felgate, Corporal, 239
Fenians, 148, 149
Fenner, Capt. T., 291
Ferguson, Capt. (later Lt.-Col. Sir) A. G., 217
Ferguson, Rifleman, 172
Ferrol, 22, 31, 43, 171
Festing, Lieut. (later Field Marshal Sir) Francis, 281, 287, 319, 341, 431, 439, 442
"Figure of Fame", the, 98
Fiji, 273

Fingoes, the, 115
Firozshah, battle of, 118
Fish, R., 114
Fisher, Colour-Sgt. J., 126, 136, 138-9, 140, 141
Fitzgerald, Colour-Sgt., 210
Flag March, the, 322-5
Flanders, 211, 234, 237 et seq., 280, 286 et seq., 420
Flavy, 292
Flers, 293
Fletcher, Lieut. (later Major) Geoffrey, 369
Flower, Lieut. (later Lt.-Col.) P. T., 367
Flower, Lieut. (later Lt.-Col.) R. A., 384-5, 390, 395, 402
Flushing, 64
Foch, Marshal, 293
Folkestone, 455
Follett, Lt.-Col., R. S., 312
Forbes, Rifleman, W. K., 271
Ford, Col., 103-6
Forman, Capt. E. R., 132
Forster, Rt. Hon. W. E., 169
Fort Beaufort, 125
Fort Capuzzo, 350
Fort Gomer, 332
Fort Madalena, 350
Fort Willshire, 113
Fortescue, Lt.-Col. The Hon. C. G., 162-3, 171-2
Fortuin, 247
Foster, Major O. H. J., 260, 425
Foster, Rifleman, 261
France, 13, 21, 29, 30, 31, 40, 43-8, 50-3, 57-60, 62, 64, 66, 69-71, 76-9, 80-5, 88-98, 102, 104, 106, 117, 118, 127, 128, 139, 140, 141, 144, 182, 209, 211, 220, 221, 225, 226, 230-94, 279, 280, 296, 302, 309, 335, 337, 341, 342-6, 348, 362, 363, 364, 406, 407, 413, 415, 416, 417, 418, 419-22, 423, 428, 431, 432, 449-51, 455
Francis, Corporal A., "Busty", 384, 393
Franco-Prussian War, 182, 225
Fraser, Mrs. Pamela, 185, 211
Frederick the Great, 13
Freer, Lieut. R. B., 71
Freetown, 374
French, Gen. Sir John (later Field Marshal Earl), 230, 231, 237, 272, 279
Frere, Major Sir Bartle, 161
Fromelles, battle of, 239-40
Fruin, Sgt., 422
Fuentes d'Onoro, battle of, 64, 98
Fulham Palace Road, 441
Futtehpore, 144

Fyers, Capt. (later Maj.) H. A. N., 151
Fyers, Capt. (later Lt.-Gen. Sir) William Augustus, 132, 144
Fyffe, Lt.-Col. (later Lt.-Gen. Sir) Richard, 18, 415, 427, 429, 433, 439, 440, 444-5

Galicia, 46, 237
Gallipoli, 126, 220, 245, 310-11
Ganges, R., 144, 319
Garigliano, R., 415, 416
Garmoyle, Capt. (later Brig.) Viscount H. G., 320, 327-8, 355, 371-2, 373
Gascony, 84
Gazala, 371
Geddes Axe, 308
General Strike, the, 313-15
George IV, 30, 98
George V, 326
George VI, 373, 418
George Inn (Portsmouth), 53
George Street, 102
German General Staff, 14, 206, 346
Germany, 30, 184, 211, 215, 225-95, 297, 332, 335-7, 340-7, 355, 359-73, 376-430, 433-4, 436, 442
Gibbons, Rifleman, 264, 268
Gibbs, Lieut., 259
Gibraltar, 150-1, 160, 177, 308, 309, 332, 433
Gilbert, Colour-Sgt., 172
Gilbert, W. S., 16
Glasgow, 107, 109, 119, 303, 373, 374
Globe, the, 170
Gloucester, 212
Gloucester, H.R.H. Field Marshal the Duke of, 418, 432, 439
Glover, Lt.-Col. (later Col.) J. M., 439
Gluckstadt, 433
Glyn, Lt.-Col. (later Gen. Sir) Julius, 145
Gold Coast, 174
Golden Square (Soho), 102
Goodall, Rifleman, 153
Gordon, Gen. Charles, 176, 179
Gore, Lt.-Col. (later Brig.) A. C., 407, 415, 416
Gore, Lieut. Charles, 79, 406
Gort, Field Marshal Lord, 345
Gosling, Capt. G. B., 215
Gosport, 99-100, 209, 306, 307, 308, 332, 333
Gothic Line, 423
Gott, Brig. (later Lt.-Gen.) W. H. E., 349, 366, 367, 373, 376
Gough, Col. (later Gen. Sir) Hubert, 191, 290
Gough, Gen. Sir Hugh (later Lord), 117, 118

Gough, Capt. (later Brig.-Gen. Sir) John Edmund, 185, 191, 207, 228, 237, 239, 317
Goubellat Plain, battle of, 412
Gourock, 373
Graaf Reinet, 113
Graham, Lieut. N., 383
Graham, Gen. Sir Thomas (later Lord Lynedoch), 89
Grahamstown, 111-14
Graspan, battle of, 163, 183-4
Gravelines, 346
Gravenstafel, battle of, 243, 252, 257 et seq., 267
Gravesend, 208
Gray, Capt. (later Lt.-Col.) Loftus, 85-6
Grayson, Gunner, 172
Graziani, Marshal, 354
Great Fish River, 111, 115
Great Wall of China, 219
Greece, 348, 353-4, 355, 359-61, 363, 364, 366, 373, 431, 437, 438
Green, Lieut. (later Col.) Andrew, 147
Green, Bugler William, 16, 43, 49-52
Greenock, 373
Greenwell, Rifleman, 292
Gregg, Sgt. W., 293
Grenfell, Field Marshal Lord, 214
Guadarramas, the, 46
Guderian, Gen., 420
Guernsey, 123
Guerville, A. B. De, 222
Guillemont, 281, 282, 283
Guizot, F.-P.-G., 220
Gurdaspur, 324
Gurkhas, 220-1, 412, 444

Habarovsk, 218-19
Haifa, 375
Haig, Gen. Sir Douglas (later Field Marshal Earl), 207, 237, 279, 281, 287, 290, 293
Hailsham, Lord, 318, 440
Hanley, Regt. Sgt-Major, 301
Halifax (Canada), 108, 309, 452
Halloran, Capt. W., 301
Hamburg, 430
Hamilton (Canada), 149
Hamilton-Russell, Major A. G. L., 346
Hammamet, 412
Hampton, Colour-Sgt. Mark, 173
Hanley, Regt. Sgt.-Major, 301
Hannan, Rifleman Hughie, 134
Hanoverians, 53, 57, 94
Harding, Brig. (later Field Marshal Lord) John, 359, 406

Harding, Lt.-Col. (later Maj.Gen.) R. P., 428
Hardinge of Penshurst, Lord, 221
Hardinge, Gen. Sir Henry (later Lord), 122
Hardy, Capt. (later Vice-Admiral Sir) Thomas, 31
Hargreaves, Lieut. (later Capt.) R. C., 236, 239
Harrington, Lt.-Col. (later Brig.-Gen.) J., 306, 308, 312
Harris, Rifleman Benjamin, 16, 43, 44-5, 45-50, 102
Harwich, 315
Hasler, Brig.-Gen., 246, 263
Hastings, Capt. (later Lt.-Col.) R. H. W. S., 17, 346-7, 351-3, 357, 365, 366, 367, 368, 369, 371, 372, 380, 405, 418-19, 424, 430, 433
Havelock, Lieut. (later Maj.-Gen. Sir) Henry, 99, 107
Havrincourt Wood, 285
Hawkes, Rifleman David, 146
Hazebrouck, 245
Helder, the, 22, 218
Hell Fire Corner, 242
Hell, Hills of, 375
Heriot-Maitland, Capt. J. D., 200
Henderson, Col. G. F. R., 66
Higgins, Surgeon, 62
Hill 37, 248, 384-5, 391, 392
Hill 112, battle of, 419-20
Himalayas, 122, 152
Himeimat, 379
Hindu Rao's House (Delhi), 221
Hine, Sgt., J., 392, 397, 398
Hintza, Chieftain, 115
Hitler, Adolf, 331, 335, 336, 341, 346, 362, 364, 368, 413, 416
Hitler, Line, 416
Holland, 89, 90, 342, 346, 422, 423-4
Holt-Wilson, Lieut. A. B., 382, 397, 398, 400
Home Guard, 433
Homs, 415
Hone, Major H., 129, 159, 160, 168, 173, 175, 309, 440
Hong Kong, 169-70, 172, 215-16, 273, 434, 439
Hood, Capt. Arthur, 177
Hooge, battle of, 277, 293
Hore-Ruthven, Maj. the Hon. A. H. Patrick, 335, 408-10
Horse Guards, the, 102, 124
Horsford, Lt.-Col. (later Gen. Sir) A. H., 145
Horsham, 22
Hoshiapur, 321
Hoskyns, Lt.-Col. C. B. A., 344, 346

Hottentots, 111, 114
Howans, Rifleman Daniels, 48
Howard, Lt.-Col. (later Maj.-Gen. Sir) Francis, 172-3, 179-80, 206-7, 214
Hubert-Folie, 112
Hudson, Lt.-Col. (later Maj.-Gen.) Peter, 439
Hughes, Rifleman, 187
Humbley, Lieut. (later Lt.-Col.) William, 101
Humpston, Rifleman R., 141
Hungerford Market, 454
Hunt, Lt.-Col. (later Col.) G. H., 380
Hunte, R., 428
Hunter, Lt.-Col. (later Brig.) J. A., 428
Hursley, 226
Hyde Park, 108, 142, 165, 341
Hyderabad Redoubt, 286
Hythe, 121, 211

Imperial General Staff, 206, 209, 293, 308, 318, 347, 359, 360, 376, 431, 432
Imphal, 432
India, 14, 117, 126, 144-7, 150, 151, 152, 153-4, 156-7, 158, 166, 173, 174-5, 176, 177-8, 205, 210, 214, 218, 225-6, 288, 302, 303, 306, 309, 311, 312, 316, 319, 320, 321, 322-32, 342, 347, 349, 364, 370, 375, 378
Indian Army, 13, 117-18, 119, 158, 220-1, 352, 353, 354, 370, 380, 412, 432
Indian Mutiny, 143-7, 148, 152, 154, 155, 158, 175, 179, 221, 307, 337
Indian Ocean, 347, 378
Indonesia, 434, 439
Inkerman, battle of, 137-9, 144, 149
Institute of Electrical Engineers, 157
Inter-Regimental Indian Polo Tournament, 152
Ionian Islands, 108
Iraq, 361, 431
—, Levies, 320
Ireland, 43, 65, 77, 98, 100, 107, 108, 109, 148, 149, 153, 167, 168, 205, 210, 213, 230, 302, 303-7, 308, 312, 320-1, 381, 445
Irish Militia, 22, 43, 443
I.R.A., 151, 306, 307, 308
Ironmonger, Major, 61
Irrawaddy, R., 432
Irwin, Lieut. J. B. D., 382, 395, 397
Isis, H.M.S., 29
Isonzo, R., 429
Italy, 14, 279, 289, 336, 341, 347-60, 362, 363, 364, 368, 369, 370, 371, 372, 377, 378, 380, 384, 390-4, 395, 396, 399, 401, 405, 406,
407-8, 410, 411, 412, 413-17, 419, 420, 422, 423-7, 428-9, 430

Jackman, Rifleman, 64
Jaiji, 310
Jamaica, 101, 109
Jammu, 325-31
Japan, 217, 219, 347, 370, 378, 432
Jardine, L. W., 328, 329
Jarvis, Sgt.-Major, 357-8
Jellalabad, 221
Jenkins, E. M., 324, 326, 329
Jersey, 120
Jews, 342
Johannesburg, 199
Johnston, Lieut. (later Major) William, 59, 85-6
Johore, 435
Jolie Brise, 319
Jones, Frank, 149
Jordan, Rifleman, 154
Jones, Major, 203-4
Joseph Bonaparte, King of Spain, 79
Jowakis, the, 175
Jubilee, Diamond, 214
—, Golden, 177
Jugoslavia, 411, 413, 429-30
Juin, Gen. (later Marshal) A. P., 416
Jullundur, 177, 320, 322, 323, 330, 332
Julian Alps, 428
Junot, Gen. Androche, Duc d'Abrantes, 44

Kaffir Land, 113, 114-16, 123, 124, 125
Kaffirs, 111-12, 113-17, 124, 167
Kagera Plains, 215
Kalamita Bay, 126-7
Kalka, 226
Kamisly, 128, 129
Kandahar, 176
Kane, Gunner, 389
Karen Expedition, 176
Kartapur, 322-3
Kashmir, 320, 325-31
Kasserine Pass, battle of, 410
Keiskamma, R., 114
Kei, R., 115, 124, 125
Kemel Pasha, 311
Kempt, Maj.-Gen. Sir John, 92, 117
Kennard, Capt. (later Lt.-Col.) A. C. H., 197
Kennington, Eric, 318, 442
Kensan, 217
Kent, 31, 34, 44, 342, 343
Kenya, 433, 434
Kesselring, Field Marshal A., 423, 425, 428

Kerbala, 310
Keyes, Lt.-Col. Geoffrey, 408-9
Kewley, Capt. (later Brig.) Edward Rigby, 229, 291, 297, 308, 341
"Khamseens", 349
Khartoum, 176, 205, 221-2
Khyber Pass, 161, 175, 322
Kidney Ridge, 380, 390, 395, 396, 397
Kilia, 311
Kincasslough, 305
Kincaid, Capt. (later Sir John), 15, 16, 41, 55, 56, 58, 64-70, 72-4, 76, 78-9, 85-6, 90-5, 97-8, 101, 119, 123, 443-4
King, Major A. M., 239
King George V, H.M.S., 336
King George V Cup, 317
King, Major A. M., 239
King's African Rifles, 207, 320
Kingham, 213
Kinglake, Alexander William, 128-9
King-Salter, Lieut. (later Lt.-Col. and Rev.) Edward, 316-17
Kingston (Canada), 108
Kiöge, battle of, 44, 101
Kipling, Rudyard, 181
Kirwan, Company Sgt.-Major, 249
Kishinev, 319
Kitchen, Rifleman Joe, 450
Kitchener, Lt.-Col. (later Field Marshal Earl) Herbert, 163, 206, 221, 227
Klagenfurt, 430
Knight, Col. Sir J., 109
Knightsbridge, battle of, 371, 374
Knox, Lieut. (later Major) John, 141-2
Kofi-Kari-Kari, King, 175
Kohima, battle of, 432
Korea, 217
Kowloon, 169-70
Krüger, President, 182
Kuala Lumpur, 436
Kuldana, 309

La Bassée, 421
La Belle Alliance, 97
La Brique, 265, 269
Ladysmith, 184-91, 192, 205, 207, 225, 237, 254, 300
La Haye Sainte, 91, 94, 97
Ladak, 320
Lahore, 325, 327, 330
Lambert, Maj.-Gen. Sir John, 93, 95
Lane, Major (later Lt.-Col.) G. E. W., 301, 302
Lansbury, Rt. Hon. George, 336

La Thieuloye, 284
Lawrence, Col. (later Gen. Sir) Arthur Johnstone, 130, 135, 160
Lawrence, Capt. F. E., 162
Leach, Lieut. (later Lt.-Col.) Jonathan, 42, 63, 102, 123, 152
League of Nations, 336, 341
Le Cateau, battle of, 225, 230-1, 234, 294
Lee-Metford Rifle, 179
Leeds, 315
Leicester, 43, 303, 314
Lendu, the, 215
Leningrad, 370
Leslie, Capt. N. J. B., 234
Levant, the, 378
Lewis gun, 292, 293, 305, 337, 340
Leyland, Lt.-Col. R. H., 294-5
Libya, 348-9, 353, 354, 359, 360, 362, 365, 366, 368, 406, 410, 431
Liddell, Lieut. (later Lt.-Col.) C. H., 352, 382, 395
Liddell, Brig. G. W., 352
Light Brigade and Division, 31-4, 39-40, 41, 46-53, 54-60, 64-5, 65-8, 69, 70-2, 75, 76, 80-1, 85, 119, 120, 123, 127, 135, 136, 139, 159
Ligny, battle of, 90
Lille, 297, 343
Lincolnshire, 59
Lindsay, Maj.-Gen. G. M., 167
Lindsay, Lieut. (later Lt.-Col.) H. G., 125, 167, 168
Liri, R., 416, 417
Lisbon, 44, 45, 46, 60, 62-3
Littorio Division, 391, 395
Liverpool, 198, 226, 437, 438
Lloyd George, Rt. Hon. David, 305, 311
Lloyd-Verney Lieut. (later Col.) G. H., 152
Logan, Capt. Charles, 96, 97
Lombardy, 14, 423, 427
Loch Lomond, 373
Loch Long, 373
London "blitz", 348, 373
London, City of, 119
London Docks, 418
Long, Major (later Lt.-Col.) S. C., 207
Longchamps, 221
Long Range Desert Force, 404, 405, 407, 408
Loodiana, 120
Loos, battle of, 239, 278, 442
Lowe, Sgt. John, 65
Lübeck, 430
Lucknow, 99, 144, 145-6, 149, 166
Luftwaffe, 336, 343, 344, 362, 363, 406, 407

Lüneburg Heath, 428
Lutterworth, 43
Lydenburg, 198, 201, 204
Lysley, Capt. G. L., 200
Lyttelton Maj.-Gen. (later Gen.) Hon. Sir Neville, 179, 184-5, 191, 193, 200, 206, 209-10, 214
Lytton, Lt.-Col. Lord, 320

Maas, R., 424, 425
Mabin, Rifleman G. W., 165
Macaulay, Lord, 111
McCarthy, Rifleman F. J., 17, 225, 243-70, 273-4
McDermot, Dr., 203
Macdonald, Rt. Hon. Ramsay, 335-6
MacGregor, Col., 199
MacGregor, Rifleman Roderic, 141
Maclachlan, Capt. (later Brig.-Gen.) R. C., 193, 196, 288
Macleod, Col., 71
Madagascar, 431-2
Magdalen Hill Camp, 226
Madrid, 46, 53, 76, 77
Maggersfontein, battle of, 184
Maharajpur, 117
Mahrattaland, 153
Mahrattas, 113
Mahdi, the, 179, 180
Maidan, the, 153
Maitland, Maj.-Gen. (later Gen. Sir) Peregrine, 96
Maiwand, battle of, 176
Malaya, 346, 370, 433, 435-6, 439
Maliks, the, 322
Malta, 107, 108, 126, 150-1, 154, 164, 166, 205, 214, 317, 332-3, 360, 370, 378, 406
Manchuria, 217-18
Manningham, Col. (later Maj.-Gen.) Coote, 13, 21, 22, 23, 27, 31, 32, 34-9, 42, 53, 103, 117, 335
Manningtree, 316
March, 315
Mareth Line, battle of, 410
Marks, D., 162
Marlborough School, 275
Marines, Royal, 163, 183-4
Marne, R., battle of, 232, 233
Marsh, Rifleman J., 179, 180
Marten, Capt. (later Lt.-Col.) F. W., 368 381, 382, 384, 388, 394, 399-400, 401, 402
Martini-Henry Rifle, 179, 197
Masanian, 323

Masséna, Marshal André, Prince of Essling, 63-4
Massy-Beresford, Lt.-Col. (later Brig.) T. H., 347
Matapan, battle of, 348
Matmata Hills, 410
Matterhorn, 157
Matthews, Acting Corporal, 172
Mau Mau, 433, 434
Mauritius, H.M.S., 374
Maxim gun, 179, 182, 184, 193
Maxwell, Lieut. J., 153
May, Rifleman D., 176, 187
Mechili, 355
Meddemen, Acting-Corporal, 172
Mediterranean, command of, 347, 360, 369, 378, 406, 411, 413, 416
Medjez, 412
Meerut, 340
Meighar-Lovett, Capt. P. G., 16, 228-30, 442
Melfa, R., 416
Mellenthin, Major (later Gen.) von, 332
Mellor, Lt.-Col. (later Brig.) A. H. S., 433
Menin Gate, the, 241
Menshikoff, Prince, 129
Mercer, Gunner, 389
Mersa Brega, 363, 369, 373
Mersa Matruh, 350, 362, 371
Merthyr Tydfil, 108
Merxem, battle of, 89-90
Mesopotamia, 309, 315, 320, 341
Messina, Straits of, 415
Messines-Wytschate Ridge, battle of, 286
Metaxas, General, 365
Metcalfe, Lt.-Col. (later Maj.-Gen.) C. T. E., 185-6, 200
Metrie, Vicomte de la, 242
Meuse, R., 233, 423, 424
Mian Gull of Swat, 322
Middelburg (S. Africa), 204
Middle East Oilfields, 360-1, 370
Milan, 423
Mildmay, Lt.-Col. Herbert St. John, 165
Miles, Sgt., 397, 398
Mills, Capt. Sydney, 187
Miller, Bandmaster William, 125, 154, 163
Minden, 433
Minié Rifle, 143, 179
Mitchell, Sir Thomas, 157
Mitchell-Innes, Lieut. T. L., 154
Mittel Europa Express, 319
Modder River, battle of, 184
Mohmund Campaign, 147, 177

Mohmaunds, the, 321
Monash, Gen. Sir John, 444
Mondego Bay, 44
Mondego, R., 60-1
Mons, battle of, 225, 230, 232, 294, 297
Mont Blanc, 157
Mont de Marsan, 450
Monte Fuso, 423
Monte Malbe, 420
Monte Rentella, 420
Monte Video, 44, 98
Montreal, 108, 149
Montgomery, Lt.-Gen. Sir Bernard (later Field Marshal Lord), 318, 376, 377, 378, 379, 402, 405, 410, 413, 415, 423
Montgomery, Col. A. H. S., 161
Montreuil, 279
"Monymusk" march, 155
Mooltan, H.M.T., 373-5
Moore, Lt.-Gen. Sir John, 14, 31-4, 46, 54, 56, 110, 117, 270, 299, 444
Moore-Gwyn, Lt.-Col. (later Col.) H. G., 323, 324, 325, 329, 330
Morell, Staff Surgeon, 62
Morocco, 347, 406
Morrish, Quartermaster W., 168-9, 172
Moscow, 370
Mosley, Capt. M., 382, 390
Mosley Mynn, Sgt. A. L. de, 318-19
Msus, 356, 369, 406
Mudania, Conference, 312
Mukdi, battle of, 118
Munich Crisis, 341
Muree, 153-4, 158
Murray, Lt.-Gen. Sir Archibald, 231
Murray, Major S. W., 301
Mussolini, Benito, 332, 336, 341

N.A.A.F.I., 331
Nana Sahib, 144
Napier, Charles, 443
Napier, Col. (later Gen. Sir) William, 39-40, 60, 64, 110, 123, 243
Naples, 415, 416
Napoleon I, Emperor, 13, 21, 31, 32, 39, 40, 41, 44, 46, 53, 54, 59, 63, 84, 89, 90, 92, 96, 124, 164, 370
Napoleon III, Emperor, 153-4
Nash, Corporal W., 146
Natal, 182, 183, 184-91, 205
National Education, 27, 169
National Rifle Association, 156
National Service, 342, 439

Naumann, Lieut. A., 410
Naumann, Lieut. (later Major) J. E. B., 382
Navy, Royal, 13, 22, 28-30, 52, 184, 218, 287, 332, 336, 347, 348, 355, 360, 364, 370, 374, 378, 406, 411, 413, 414
Neame, Lt.-Gen. Sir P., 364
Nelson, Vice-Admiral Horatio, Lord, 28-31, 42, 208
Nepal, 220, 221
Netherlands, Kingdom of, 89
—, East Indies, 432
Neuve Chapelle, battle of, 233, 237, 239, 244
Neville, Col. Sir James, 91
Newark, 314
New Brunswick, 149
Newdegate-Newdigate, Lieut. (later Lt.-Gen. Sir) Edward, 456
New Orleans, 89, 90, 107
Newport (Mon.), 108
New South Wales, 157
New York, 149, 319
New Zealand, 347, 361, 370, 380
Ney, Marshal, Duc d'Elchingen, 90
Nicholson, Brig. Claude, 345
Nibeiwa, 352
Nicosia, 437
Niger, R., 215
Nile, battle of the, 29
Nile Valley, 163, 214, 215, 321, 348, 360, 361-2, 364, 376, 377
"Ninety-five" march, 125, 154, 159, 160, 175, 244, 297
Nive, battle of the, 98, 101
Nivelle, battle of, 85, 98, 101
Nivelle, Gen., 286, 287
Noble, Corporal C. R., 238
Noel, Lieut. (later Lt.-Col.) The Hon. Edward, 157
Norcott, Col. (later Maj.-Gen. Sir) Amos G. R., 62-5, 90, 96, 99, 127, 161-2
Norcott, Lieut. Col. (later Col.) C. H. B., 160, 161-2, 170-1
Norcott, Lt.-Col. H. B., 162
Norcott, Maj. (later Gen. Sir) William, 127-136, 137-8, 161-2, 171
Norfolk, 417-18
Normandy, 342, 417, 419-20, 421, **423**
Norry, Sgt., 389
North West Frontier, 14, 147, 175, 176, 177
Norway, 342, 346
Nowshera, 151
Nova Scotia, 108, 160, 309, 452
Noyes, Capt., 383, 386, 388, 390
Noyon, 294

Nuers, the, 321
Nuffield Nursing Home Trust, 228
Nyong, 321

Obidos, 44
O'Brien, Rifleman, 358
O'Connor, Lt.-Gen. (later Gen. Sir) Richard, 349, 351, 352-9, 361, 362, 364, 366, 368, 406
Odon, R., 419
O'Hare, Capt. (later Major) Peter, 59, 71, 77
O'Hea, Rifleman Timothy, 148
Oliver, Rifleman, 164
Oman, Sir Charles, 57
Omdurman, battle of, 179, 180, 181, 206, 300
Oporto, 54
Orange Free State, 182
Orange River, 123
Orthez, battle of, 98, 101
Osnabrück, 433
Ossulston, Lieut. Lord, 175
Oudh, 145-6
Ovens, the (Crimea), 141
Oxalic Line, 388, 390
Oxford, 314
—, University Officers' Training Corps, 228, 289

Paget, Gen. Sir Bernard, 272
Paget, Maj.-Gen. The Hon. Sir Edward, 53
Paget, Lt.-Col., 208
Palestine, 332, 342, 347
Paley, Lt.-Col. (later Brig.-Gen.) Alan, 298-300, 341, 415
Paley, Lt.-Col. (later Maj.-Gen. Sir) Victor, 341, 370, 415
Palmer, Capt. (later Lt.-Col.) A. G. D., 353
Paniez, Rifleman Noel, 421
Panzer Divisions,
    10th, 412
    15th, 385, 395
    21st, 379, 395, 396
    (90th Light), 412
Paris, 98, 101, 410
Parachute Corps, 1st German, 428
Parker, Capt. Alan, 421
Parker, A. W., 198
Parkyn, Major H. G., 17, 179
Passchendaele, battle of, 287-9, 293, 377
Pathans, 158
Patriotic Fund, 104
Peachey, Rifleman David, 162
Peachey, Rifleman William, 162
Pearce, Sgt. G., 317
Pearl Harbour, 370

Pearson, Capt. (later Gen. Sir) Thomas, 357, 382, 383, 386, 390-1, 405, 412
Pearson, Sgt. T., 397
Peel, Lieut. (later Capt.) J. S., 435
Peking, 219
Pemberton, Major (later Col.) A. R., 172
Pemberton, Lieut. (later Capt.) A. W., 85
Percival, Capt. (later Lt.-Col.) William, 86
Persia, 431
Persian Gulf, 370, 375
Perugia, 420
Peshawar, 158, 176, 322
Petite Rhone, 84
Peyton, Lt.-Col. H. S. C., 292
Phillips, Brig. C. E. Lucas, 17, 380 et seq., 402, 403
Picardy, 278-83, 386-7
Piccadilly, 108, 177
Picton, Capt. Arthur, 382, 383, 390-1
Picton, Lt.-Gen. Sir Thomas, 90, 92
Piedmont, 122
Pigot, Lt.-Col. (later Brig.-Gen. Sir) Robert, 281, 286-7, 291, 440, 441-2
Pilckem, 242, 243, 265
Pinhel, 60, 61
Pinnock, Lieut. (later Lt.-Col.) E. T., 441
Plassey, battle of, 359
Plumer, Field Marshal Lord, 281
Plezzo, 429
Ploegsteert, 243, 274
Plymouth, 89, 319
Po, R., 428, 429
Poland, 346, 362, 363
Polish Corps, 416
Pompa, Colour-Sgt., 271
Pontifex, Brig. David, 18
Poole, Lt.-Col. R. D., 433
Poongi, the White, 319
Poperinghe, 242, 245, 269, 424
Porter, Corporal, 198
Portobello Barracks, 167, 174
Portsmouth, 53, 147, 175, 205
Port Sudan, 375
Portugal, 44-6, 53, 54, 56, 57, 64, 71, 75, 76, 79, 117
Portuguese Caçadores, 54
Potijze Wood, 242
Powell, Major (later Lt.-Col.) Thomas, 109-10
Pratt, Lieut. Mathias, 59, 61
Prempeh, King, 177
Pretor-Pinney, Lt.-Col. C. F., 275, 286
Pretoria, 191, 204
Preve, Capt., 391

472 INDEX

Prescott-Westcar, Lt.-Col. Sir William, 319
Prideaux-Brune, Lt.-Col. D. E., 283
Prince of Wales, H.M.S., 336
Prittie, Lieut. (later Capt.) The Hon. F. R.
 D., 214, 215
Prome, R., 432
Prowse, Col., 263
Prussia, 32, 41, 90, 93, 97, 182, 237, 299,
 444
Puerto de Olivença, 72
Punjab, 118-19, 122, 158, 309, 324, 325
Pyramids, the, 350
Pyrenees, 100, 272

Quatre Bras, battle of, 90-1, 101, 102, 424
Quattara Depression, 377
Quebec, 108, 148, 149, 169
Queen Adelaide's Land, 125
Queenborough, 243
Queen Elizabeth, 374
Queen Mary, 374
Queen's Medal, 156, 175, 316
Queen Victoria Trophy, 316, 332, 340

Radar, 336
Raglan, Field Marshal Lord, *see* Somerset,
 Lord Fitzroy
Railston, Lieut. (later Capt.) H. G. M., 153,
 249, 258, 268
Rainbow Trench, 283
Rajputana, 214
Rampore, 153
Rapido, R., 416
Ravenna, 428
Rawalpindi, 225
Reading, 314
Redan, the, 142
Redhina, 68, 75
Red Sea, 375
Reeve, Lt.-Col. (later Maj.-Gen.) J. T. W.,
 338, 339, 431
REGIMENTS, BRITISH
 Artillery, Royal Regiment of, 142, 239,
  351, 352, 379
  Royal Horse, 54, 159, 209, 337, 349, 356,
   363, 383, 396
  Chestnut Troop, 54, 159, 208
  76th Anti-Tank Regiment, 380-1, 382,
   383-402
  239th Anti-Tank Battery, 380-1, 382,
   383-402
 Cavalry Regiments,
  Life Guards, 93
  Horse Guards, Royal, 453, 455
  Queen's Bays, 338

7th Hussars, 146
8th Hussars, 430
9th Lancers, 338
10th Hussars, 338
11th Hussars, 57, 129, 159, 356, 368, 388,
 406, 412
17/21st Lancers, 429
23rd Hussars, 422, 428, 430
27th Lancers, 429
Lothians & Border Horse, 429
Engineers, Corps of Royal
 7th Field Squadron, 381, *et seq*.
Infantry
 Guards, Brigade of, 12, 53, 62, 96, 129,
  134-5, 165, 213, 337, 343, 453, 455
 Grenadier Guards, 81-5
 Scots Guards, 141
 5th (Northumberland Fusiliers), 262
 12th (Suffolk), 316
 13th (Someset Light Infantry), 232, 248
 19th (Yorkshire), 136
 23rd (Royal Welsh Fusiliers), 136
 Cameronians (Scottish Rifles), 159, 349,
  359
 27th (Royal Inniskilling Fusiliers), 95,
  190-1, 198, 199
 29th (Worcestershire), 61
 30th (East Lancashire), 267
 35th (Royal Sussex), 400-1
 39th (Dorset), 359
 43rd (Oxfordshire and Buckinghamshire Light Infantry), 31, 39, 50, 54,
  58-60, 65, 71, 79, 159, 208, 433-4, 439-40
 45th (Sherwood Foresters), 123
 52nd (Oxfordshire and Buckinghamshire Light Infantry), 31, 39, 50, 54,
  58-9, 65, 79, 80, 82-3, 90, 96-7, 159,
  208-9, 433-4, 439-40, 451
 60th (Royal Americans), 30
 60th (King's Royal Rifle Corps), 30, 44,
  153, 155, 156, 159, 181, 182, 210, 220,
  221, 223 228, 229, 274, 275, 291, 299,
  313, 337-8, 342-6, 349, 354, 358, 367,
  378-9, 405, 427, 433, 434, 439-40, 445
 (T.A. Bn. Queen Victoria's Rifles), 342-3
 The Manchester Regiment, 186, 189,
  192, 193
 68th (Durham Light Infantry), 152
 71st (Highland Light Infantry), 96
 72nd (Seaforth Highlanders), 113, 114
 75th (Gordon Highlanders), 114-15
 84th (York and Lancashire), 164
 86th (Royal Irish Rifles), 159, 243
 88th (Connaught Rangers), 62, 65, 198

91st (Argyll and Sutherland Highlanders), 123

92nd (Gordon Highlanders), 42, 192, 199

Rifle Brigade, *see under*

Machine Gun Corps, 294

Royal Army Service Corps, 313

Royal Corps of Signals, 314, 339

Royal Electrical and Mechanical Engineers, 339

Royal Tank Regiment, 337, 344, 348, 351-2, 354

Militia, 43

Territorials, 207, 211, 218, 227, 237, 317, 340-3, 347, 356, 362-3, 373, 374, 375, 376, 380, 406, 410, 412, 415, 416-17, 418-20, 422, 427, 429, 430, 431 (*see also under* Rifle Brigade)

Volunteers, 156, 207, 211

Renton, Lt.-Col. (later Maj.-Gen.) J. M. L., 320, 322, 348, 350, 372, 410, 431

Repington, Col. Charles 'A Court-, 14, 272

Retford, 314

Rheims, 294

Rhine, R., 423, 425, 428

Rhineland, remilitarisation of, 335

Rhune, Petite, 85

Richmond (Yorks.), 315

Rickman, Capt. (later Major) S. H., 205

Rietfontein, battle of, 184

RIFLE BRIGADE, THE

General, 11-16, 21-2, 149-74, 179, 181, 205, 207, 214, 216, 219, 228, 230, 265, 273-4, 282-4, 295-7, 298-300, 304, 307, 317, 321, 331, 340, 346, 359, 440-5

Originally (1800-2): An Experimental Rifle Corps, 21-32, 39, 41, 335

From 1803 to 1816: 95th (Rifle) Regiment, 5, 31-4, 39, 41-50, 298-9

1st Bn., 39, 44, 46, 54, 58-60, 63, 69-72, 76, 85, 89-93, 98, 99, 415, 421, 424, 443, 449-56

2nd Bn., 42-4, 46, 50, 51-4, 63-5, 69-72, 76, 81, 82-5, 89-90, 96-99, 101, 415, 444

3rd Bn., 61, 64, 70-2, 76-7, 85, 89-90, 96-9, 101, 415

After Feb. 16th, 1816: The Rifle Brigade: Regular Bns.

1st Bn., 107-8, 123-9, 137-9, 141-2, 148-49, 155-6, 160-2, 164-6, 169-70, 172, 176-7, 184, 186, 191, 205-6, 214, 225, 230-2, 234, 243, 244-69, 280, 282-6, 288-90, 293, 295, 297, 309-11, 315-16, 322-33, 335, 337-40, 343-6, 268-9, 371-2, 377, 376-7, 379, 380, 406, 407,

410, 411, 412, 414, 415, 417-18, 419-20, 420-2, 423, 424, 428, 430, 433-9

2nd Bn., 107-9, 123-36, 141-7, 151-2, 161-2, 173-4, 177, 179, 184-206, 210, 214, 221, 225-6, 237-40, 278, 282, 284, 287, 290, 292-5, 298, 300-1, 303-6, 309, 311, 313-17, 319, 321, 331-3, 340, 342, 347-54, 356-9, 362, 367-72, 372, 376-7, 380-405, 410, 411, 412, 415, 416, 417, 423, 424-7, 428-9, 431, 433, 441-2, 452-6

3rd Bn., 143, 145-7, 150, 152, 154, 158, 160, 165, 173, 177-9, 205, 210-14, 220, 225-6, 229-30, 233-6, 280-1, 283-88, 290-1, 295, 297, 301, 306-8, 319-20, 341, 441, 442

4th Bn., 144, 150, 154-5, 160-1, 167, 172, 174-7, 205, 207, 214, 220-1, 225-26, 236, 238-43, 270-2, 274, 294-5, 297, 302, 307-9, 312

Special Reserve Bns.

5th, Bn., 227

6th Bn., 226, 243

Service Bns. (1914-19)

7th Bn., 227, 274, 278, 282, 285-6, 288, 290-2

8th Bn., 227, 274-8, 282, 285-6, 288, 290-2

9th Bn., 227, 274, 277, 282, 285-6, 288, 290-2

10th Bn., 228, 274, 282-4, 287-9, 291-2, 295

11th Bn., 228, 274, 282-3, 285, 287-92, 298

12th Bn., 227, 274, 282-3, 287-92, 295, 298, 433

13th Bn., 227, 280, 282, 286, 293, 295, 298, 441

16th Bn., 227, 272, 282, 287-90, 292, 295, 298, 318

Territorial Battalions embodied in Regiment (1939-46)

London Rifle Brigade, 17, 341, 342

1st Bn. (7th R.B. in '39-'45 War), 341-2, 372, 373-7, 380, 386, 410, 411, 412, 415, 416, 417, 420, 421, 423, 428-9, 430, 433

2nd Bn. (8th R.B. in '39-'45 War), 341-2, 417, 418-19, 420, 422, 423, 424-7, 428, 430

Tower Hamlets Rifles, 156, 341

1st Bn. (9th R.B. in '39-'45 War), 156, 341, 362-3, 368-9, 372, 376, 406, 412

2nd Bn. (10th R.B. in '39-'45 War),

RIFLE BRIGADE, THE [contd.]
    406-7, 410, 411, 412, 415, 416, 417,
    420, 423, 424-7
  Volunteer Battalions (affiliated to R.B. in
    1860s and 1870s)
    Artists Rifles, 156, 227, 341
    City of London Volunteer Rifle
      Corps, 156
    Inns of Court Rifles, 156
    London Irish Rifles, 156, 227
    London Scottish, 156
  Gazetted back to the R.B. by 1916
    Hackney Rifles, 227
    St. Pancras Rifles, 227
    Stepney Rifles, 227
    Post Office Rifles, 227
    Artists Rifles, 156, 227
    Cyclists Rifles, 227
    London Irish Rifles, 227
  The Rifle Depot (Winchester), 150, 168,
    209, 227, 229, 297, 301, 302, 340, 427
  Allied Regiments
    Princess Patricia's Canadian Light
      Infantry, 271, 444
    The Winnipeg Rifles, 444
    1st British Columbia Regiment, 444
    Melbourne University Rifles, 444
    Durham Light Infantry, 444
    Ceylon Planters Rifle Corps, 444
  See also Royal Green Jackets
Rifle Brigade Association, 17, 166, 209-10,
    228, 299, 441
Rifle Brigade Regimental Birthday, 22, 100-
    101, 172, 302, 312, 423
Rifle Brigade Club, 166, 209
Rifle Brigade Chronicle, 17, 151, 160-1, 163,
    168, 170, 172, 184, 189, 191, 200, 208, 209,
    214, 216-17, 220, 243, 300, 308, 315, 321,
    322, 333, 402, 433, 435, 438, 441, 449
Rifle Brigade Dinners, 100-1, 164, 166, 171,
    209-10, 415
Rifle Brigade Museum, 161, 168, 234
Rifle Brigade uniform, 22, 26-7, 108, 125, 127,
    129, 137, 146, 149, 159 168, 316, 332, 439-
    40
Riflemen's Aid Association, 209-10, 441
Rifle Corps, King's Royal, see under Regi-
    ments
Rimini, 423
Ritchie, Lt.-Gen. (later Gen. Sir) Neil, 371
Ritchie, Lieut. T. P. A., 239
Ritchie, Corporal, 242
Roberts, Field Marshal Earl, 176, 185, 191,
    200

Roberts, Lieut. Hon. F., 185
Roberts Cup, the, 317
Robins, Sgt., 197
Roermond, 424
Rogers, Lieut. (later Lt.-Col.) W. E., 320
Rohilkand, 146
Rolica, battle of, 44, 98, 101
Rolt, Lieut. (later Major) A. R. P., 344, 345
Rome, 354, 415, 416, 417
Rommel, Lt.-Gen. (later Field Marshal)
    Erwin, 360, 362, 363, 366, 368, 371, 372,
    376, 377, 378, 396, 397, 401, 405, 406, 408,
    410
Roper-Caldbeck, Brig. W. N., 402
Rooper, Capt. John, 456
Rorke's Drift, 165
Round Table Conference, 324, 330
Rowan, Charles, 123
Royal Air Force, 336, 347-8, 354, 355, 360,
    363, 366-7, 370, 376, 377, 378, 379, 406, 414
Royal Geographical Association, 216
Royal Green Jackets, 11, 15, 17, 357, 433,
    439-40, 444-5
Royal Irish Constabulary, 304
Royal Irish Cup, 317
Royal Oak (Cashel), 44
Royal United Service Institution, 161
Ruanda, 215
Rugby, 314
Rugeley, 302-3
Rundstedt, Field Marshal von, 346, 427
Russell, Lt.-Col. (later Gen.) Lord Alex-
    ander, 149, 164
Russell, Lord John (later Earl), 149
Russell, Sir William Howard, 146
Russia, 41, 126-44, 149, 166, 218-19, 225, 237,
    279, 290, 297, 364, 368-9, 370, 378, 380, 385,
    413, 426, 428, 430
Ruthven, Lt.-Col. Lord, 306, 408
Ruweisat Ridge, 372, 376
Rye, 32
Ryneveld, Commissioner, 113

Sabugal, battle of, 65
Sainsbury, Capt. F. R., 444-5
St. Cross, 153
St. Eloi, battle of, 238-9, 240
St. Germain-en-Laye, 101
St. Helena, 374
St. James's Street, 108
St. Jean, 245, 247
St. Julien, 243, 252, 265
St. Joost, 424

St. Leonard's on Sea, 170
St. John's, 149
St. Nazaire, 225
St. Omer, 104, 240
St. Paul's Cathedral, 124, 125
St. Pol, 284
St. Quentin, 293
St. Sever, 449
St. Vincent, Admiral Lord, 30
St. Yves, 243
Salerno, 415
Sahara, the, 365
Salamanca, 53
—, battle of, 75-6, 77, 98, 101
Salisbury Plain, 211, 333, 337, 338
Salmon, Capt. Hugo, 387
Salonica, 273, 297, 303
Salt, Lieut. R. M., 391
Salter, Rifleman William, 5, 136-7, 166
Sampher, Sgt., 390
Sanctuary Wood, 271
Sandhurst, Royal Military College, 163, 317
Sanguessa, 79
San Sebastian, 415
Santarem, 62
Santerno, R., 424-5
Saragossa, Maid of, 450
Sarawak, 434, 439
Satwari, 325, 327, 329
Saunders, Sgt. J., 387
Saunders, Col. Chester R., 133, 135
Savile, Capt. J. H. D., 211
Scarborough, 315
Scheldt, R., 423
Schleswig-Holstein, 430
Schlieffen Plan, 225
Schoeman, David, 201, 202, 203, 204
School of Musketry, 207, 211
Scotland, 42, 77, 128, 166, 278, 284, 373-4
—, Highlanders, 22, 135, 158, 192, 380, 386, 402
Scott, Rev. Dr. A. J., 30
Scott-Moncrieff, Charles, 224
Seaton, Lord, see Colbourne, Sir John
Scutari, 126
Sebastopol, 126-7, 129, 137-43, 149, 166
Sedan, battle of, 230
Seine, R., 420
Semliki Forest, 214
Semliki R., 214-15
Senussi, 370
Sepoys, 118, 144-7, 221, 338
Seymour, Brig.-Gen. W. W., 17, 286, 288, 292-3, 300

Shakespeare, William, 418-19, 433, 442
Shaksgam Valley, 320
Shanghai, 219
Shaw, Corporal Samuel, 146
Shaw-Stewart, Lieut. N., 262
Shepherd-Cross, Capt. Peter, 390
Shell-trap Farm, 270
Sheppey, Isle of, 229
Shillingford, 314
Shorncliffe, 31-2, 34, 42, 80, 98, 102, 163, 165, 225
Shute, Brig.-Gen. (later Gen. Sir) Cameron, 275, 282
Sialkot, 327
Siberia, 217, 218
Sicilian Narrows, the, 407
Sicily, 370, 413
Sidi Barrani, battle of, 352-3, 354,
Sidi Rahman, 405
Sidi Resegh, 366-7, 371, 406
Sidi Saleh, 356-9, 412
Signalling, School of, 207
Sikhs, 118-19, 122-3
Simla, 226
Simonds, Messrs. (Brewers), 309
Simmons, Lieut. (later Major) George, 16, 46, 58-61, 61-2, 63, 77, 85, 119
Sinclair, Capt. (later Lt.-Col.) T. C., 357, 425
Singapore, 370
Singh, Sir Harry, Maharajah of Kashmir, 327, 330
Sinn Fein, 303-7
Skerret, Maj.-Gen., 80-4
Sirte, Gulf of, 356, 406
Sladen, Lieut. D. R., 345
Slaymaker, Rifleman, 271
Slim, Field Marshal Lord, 432, 433
Smith, Lieut. (later Lt.-Col.) Charles, 75
Smith, Capt. (later Lt.-Gen. Sir) Harry, 15, 16, 41, 42, 52-3, 59-63, 65, 70-6, 77, 79, 80-5, 89, 98, 99, 100, 101, 107, 109-24, 137-8, 139, 148, 184, 208, 449-51
Smith, Juana, Lady, 16, 73-6, 99, 100, 110, 111, 120, 121, 122-3, 138, 184, 449-51
Smith, Sgt. R. D., 389
Smith, Lieut. (later Col.) Thomas, 59, 60, 83, 98, 410
Smith-Dorrien, Gen. Sir Horace, 210, 232
Snider-Enfield Rifle, 179
"Snipe" Action, 15, 17, 335, 379-405, 421, 433, 440
Sobraon, battle of, 118

Sodersdorf, 434
Sollum, 351, 406
Solly-Flood, Capt. (later Brig.-Gen.) R. E., 220
Somali Camel Corps, 320
Somaliland, 207, 214, 320, 375
Somerset, Capt. The Hon. Arthur, 155, 169
Somerset, Lt.-Col. (later Gen.) Edward, 149, 155
Somerset, Col. Lord Fitzroy (later Field Marshal Lord Raglan), 72, 128, 135, 136
Somerset, Col. (later Maj.-Gen.) Henry, 112
Somme, battle of the, 280-83, 285, 287, 289, 263, 290, 377
Somme, R., 421
Soult, Marshal, Duc de Dalmatia, 52, 64, 84, 99, 108
South Africa, 109-17, 123-4, 125-6, 127, 164, 177, 182-206, 210, 214, 273, 279, 368, 370, 374-5, 431, 441
South America, 44
Southampton, 184, 205, 225, 343
Southby, Lt.-Col. A. R. C., 416
Southern Command, 317, 318, 332, 339
Spain, 22, 44, 46-81, 89, 91, 102, 117, 121, 123, 421
Spion Kop, battle of, 184
Squire, Capt. C. E., 292
Srinagar, 329
Staff College, the, 163, 206, 231, 317, 432
Stalingrad, 378
Steenkampsburg Mountains, 201
Steenwerck, 243, 244
Stephens, Lt.-Col. (later Brig.) Frederick, 410, 415, 433
Stephens, Capt. (later Gen. Sir) Reginald, 191, 193, 194, 195, 196, 197, 198, 199, 204-5, 207-8, 225-6, 228, 237-8, 239-40, 309, 317, 410, 431
Steward, Capt. W. H. W., 200
Stewart, Capt. (later Lt.-Col.) Hon. J. H. K., 51, 62
Stewart, Lt.-Col. (later Lt.-Gen. Sir) the Hon. William Stewart, 22-32, 41-2, 117, 335, 443
Stifflemayer Group, 384-5, 391
Stock Exchange, 196
Stonesfield, 164
Stopford, Maj.-Gen. (later Gen. Sir) Montagu, 432
Stopford-Sackville, Col. L. R., 238
Stopford-Sackville, Lieut. (later Major) L. C., 238
Stormberg, battle of, 184

Stowmarket, 315-16
Stow on the Wold, 212
Strabane, 305, 315, 320
Stranorlar, 315
Street, Lt.-Col. (later Maj.-Gen.) V. W., 407-408, 411, 433
Strenshall, 315
Struma, R., 303
Sudan, 14, 177, 179-80, 214, 221-2, 320
Suez, 205, 353, 368, 375-6
Suez Canal, 226, 361-2, 375-6, 434
Suffolk, 343
Summer Palace, 219
Surprise Hill, battle of, 185-6
Surtees, Quartermaster W., 443
Sussex, 22, 44
Sutlej, R., 122
Swann, Sgt., J. E., 385, 386, 398, 402
Swansea, 108
Sydney, 374
Syria, 317, 348, 431

Table Mountain, 374
Talana Hill, battle of, 184
Tait, Capt., 292
Talavera, battle of, 54, 55, 85, 145, 270
Talbot, Capt. (later Lt.-Col.) F. G., 216-20
Taranto, 348, 416
Tarbes, battle of, 84, 101, 270
Tarifa, 64
Taylor, Major (later Lt.-Col.) J. A., 345
Teege, Col., 384-5, 387, 391
Tel-el-Kebir, 150
Ten Years' Rule, 336
Tennyson, Alfred Lord, 156
Tennyson, Major The Hon. Lionel (later Lord), 318
Tehesildar, Sirdar Iqbal Singh, 324
Teutoburger Wald, 428
Thames, R., 314, 418
Thesiger Major (later Maj.-Gen.) G. H., 185-6, 191, 207, 225, 226, 238-9, 278, 317
Thompson, Rifleman "Long", 149-50
Thornton, Lt.-Col. L. H., 185, 211
Tiber, R., 417
Tidworth, 332, 333, 337, 340, 433
Tiflis, 303
Tilbury, 297, 418
Times, The, 127, 146, 156, 272
Tito, Marshal, 429, 430
Tobruk, 352, 354-5, 359, 363, 364, 366, 368, 370, 371
Tochi Valley, 177-9
Todleben, Gen. F. E. I., 143

Toms, Lieut. (later Major) J. E. B., 382, 393, 395, 397
Tormes, R., 75
Toronto, 108
Torres Vedras, Lines of, 61, 63
Tossignano, Borgo-, 424-5, 427
Toulon, 348
Toulouse, 449
—, battle of, 75, 84, 98, 101, 111
Tournai, 297, 420
Tower of London, 16, 102, 177
Trades Union Congress, 313
Trafalgar, battle of, 29-30, 42, 102
Trafford, Quartermaster, 454
Transvaal, 182, 191, 202, 204, 205
Travemunde, 430
Travers, Mr., 441
Trent, R., 314
Trevelyan, G. M., 11
Trevisio, 429
Trinity College, Cambridge, 11
Tripoli, 355, 357, 359, 360, 362, 370, 407, 408, 410, 411
Tripolitania, 348, 357, 360, 362, 368, 406, 407, 410, 415
Trondheim, 342
Trotter, Lieut. K. S., 245, 249
Tryon, Lieut. Henry, 141
T'slambie tribe, 115
Tubus, the, 215-16
Tucker, Col., 61
Tugela, R., 185
Tunis, 14, 348, 370, 407, 410, 412, 415
—, battle of, 412
Tunisia, 406, 407, 410, 411-12, 413, 415, 416, 418, 425, 427
Turcos, 242
Turin, 122
Turkey, 126, 220, 297, 309, 312, 370, 378, 437-8
Turner, Major (later Lt.-Col.) Vic, 15, 18, 298, 320, 322, 323, 335, 341, 369-70, 380, 381-94, 396, 399, 400, 401, 402, 403, 404, 433
Turner, Rifleman, 245, 247, 248, 250

Udhampur, 329
Udine, 429
Uganda, 214, 215
Uitenhage, 111
Umballa, 179
Ulster, 308
Umhala, Chief, 115
United Nations Peace-Keeping Force, 434, 436-8

United States of America, 14, 89, 90, 107, 109, 148, 149, 150, 295, 366, 370, 377, 378, 406, 410, 413, 414, 415, 417, 420, 424, 428

Valenciennes, 294
Vallé, 63
Vandeleur, Maj.-Gen. (later Gen. Sir) John, 80-1
"Vanity Fair", 180-1
Vanoystaeyn, Rifleman Dennis, 421
Varna, 126
Venetia, 14
Venetian Alps, 429
Venice, 429
Vera, Bridge of, 15, 80-4, 209, 359
—, Heights of, 101
Verdun, battle of, 280, 294
Vernede, Lieut. R. E., 285
Verner, Col. Willoughby, 17, 34, 75, 136-7, 151, 163, 164, 208, 308
Verney, Lt.-Col. U. O. V. L., 17, 18, 295, 297
Vichy, 361, 406, 407
Vickers gun, 381, 385
Victor, Marshal, Duc de Belluno, 64
Victoria Cross, 15, 91, 135, 137, 140, 141-2, 145-6, 153, 166, 185, 191, 238, 277, 278, 281, 289-90, 293, 296, 298, 394, 402, 408
Victoria, Queen, 108, 122, 142, 148, 154, 157, 164, 165, 177, 454
Victory, H.M.S., 30-1
Vienna, Congress of, 89
Vigo, 50, 291
Viljoen, 188
Villers-Bretonneux, 293
Villers Bocage, 419
Vimiero, battle of, 44-6, 98, 100, 101
Vimy, 294
Virgil, 21
Vittoria, battle of, 79-81, 98, 101
Vladivostock, 217-18
Vlamertinghe, 246, 264, 269

Wadham, Major W., 173
Wagon Hill, battle of, 186
Waight, Colour-Sgt., 172
Wainwright, Henry, 169
Walcheren Expedition, 63, 101, 102
Waldenses, the, 122
Wales, 108, 455
Walmer, 124
Walsford, Mr., 104
Warley, 177
Waterloo, battle of, 12, 39, 90-8, 99, 100, 101, 102, 106, 109, 117, 121, 124, 125, 127, 148, 149, 161, 165, 279, 298, 302, 309, 410

Watson, Lieut. Luther, 454
Wavell, Lt.-Gen. Sir Archibald (later Field Marshal Earl), 12, 318, 337, 339, 342, 348, 349, 352, 353-4, 355, 359, 360, 363, 364
Waziris, the, 176
Weeks, Brig. (later Lt.-Gen. Sir) Ronald, 431
Wellesley, the Rev. Gerald Valerian, 103
Wellington, Field Marshal Duke of, 12, 15, 39, 44, 54, 57, 58, 61, 62, 64, 65, 69, 76, 78, 79, 82-3, 84, 85, 90-1, 93, 95-8, 103, 108, 117, 119, 120, 124, 125, 143-4, 157, 272, 279, 339, 410, 450
Wells, Capt., 59
Weser, R., 427
West, Col. J. M., 295, 297
West, Rifleman, 75, 100, 450
Western Desert, 14, 346, 348, 350 et seq., 364, 365 et seq., 375, 376, 411, 416, 442
"Western Wall", 413
Weygand, Gen., 342
Wheatley, Rifleman Francis, 141
Whigham, Capt. (later Lt.-Col.) I. H. D., 367
White, Gen. Sir George, 184, 186, 205
Whitehall, 34, 337
Whiteley, Capt., 322
Whittlesea, 109
Wieltz, 247
Wight, Isle of, 151
Wilbraham, Lieut. (later Major) T. R., 320
William II, Kaiser, 233
William IV, 124
Williams, Colour-Sgt., 175, 210
Williamson, Henry, 318
Williamstown, 123
Willingdon, Rt. Hon. Lord, 326, 331
Wilmot, Capt. (later Col.) Henry, 146
Wilson, Brig.-Gen. (later Field Marshal Sir) Henry, 163, 206, 210, 228, 231-2, 237, 281, 293, 308, 317, 318
Wilson, Lieut. (later Lt.-Gen. Sir) H. F. M., 175-6, 228

Wilson, Lt.-Gen. (later Field Marshal Lord), Sir Henry Maitland, 317, 322, 349, 350, 352, 353, 355, 359, 416, 431, 432
Wimberley, Maj.-Gen. (later Lt.-Gen.) Douglas, 11
Wimbledon, 156
Winchester, 144, 153, 161, 168, 209, 226, 227, 228, 229, 234, 297, 340
Windsor Forest, 22
Windsor, 452
Wintour, Lieut. H. J. F., 388-9, 398
Wolseley, Maj.-Gen. Sir Garnet (later Lord), 142, 163, 174
Wood, Lieut. (later Lt.-Col.) Donald, 153
Wood, Charles, 399
Wood, Sgt. Ronald, 389
Woodford, Lt.-Col. C. J., 144-5
Woodroffe, Lieut. K. H. C., 277
Woodroffe, Capt. Leslie, 277
Woodroffe, Lieut. Sidney, 275-7
Woolwich, 214
Woronzoff, 142
Wuppertal, 434
Wynberg, 177

Ymen, the, 220
Yo, the, 215-16
Yokohama, 217
York, 315
Yorkshire, 16, 57, 91, 314, 315
Young Soldiers' Cup, 156, 211
Ypres, 233, 240-1, 243, 244, 245, 246, 247, 262, 263, 270, 272, 275, 282
—, 1st battle of, 233-4
—, 2nd battle of, 16, 241-71, 293, 312
—, 3rd battle of, 287-9
Yser Canal, 241, 263, 288

Zouaves, 128, 242
Zubait, 311
Zulus, 116-17